If you are frequently puzzled by the complexities of English spelling and pronunciation, then this handy reference work is what you have been waiting for. It contains more than 23,000 entries with special emphasis on:

MAJOR PRONUNCIATION ERRORS

☐ Improper enunciation
☐ Wrong accent
☐ Accent shifts

MAJOR SPELLING ERRORS

☐ When to drop the final "e"
☐ When to double final letters
☐ When to use a hyphen
☐ When to use a compound word
☐ Correct abbreviations
☐ Proper nouns and foreign phrases

If you can spell the word but cannot pronounce it correctly, or if you can pronounce it but cannot spell it correctly, or if you're puzzled by both points, this new unique reference work will enable you to master both problems at once and for all time.

WORDS MOST OFTEN MISSPELLED AND MISPRONOUNCED

Ruth Gleeson Gallagher and James Colvin

A KANGAROO BOOK

PUBLISHED BY POCKET BOOKS NEW YORK

WORDS MOST OFTEN MISSPELLED
AND MISPRONOUNCED

POCKET BOOK edition published August, 1963

14th printing.......................June, 1977

The system of indicating pronunciation is used
by permission. From THE NEW MERRIAM-
WEBSTER DICTIONARY, copyright, ©, 1964,
by G. & C. Merriam Company, publishers of the
Merriam-Webster Dictionaries.

Words Most Often Misspelled and Mispronounced
was originally published under the imprint of
Washington Square Press, a Simon & Schuster division of Gulf & Western Corporation.

This original POCKET BOOK edition is printed from brand-new
plates made from newly set, clear, easy-to-read type.
POCKET BOOK editions are published by
POCKET BOOKS,
a Simon & Schuster Division of
GULF & WESTERN CORPORATION
1230 Avenue of the Americas,
New York, N.Y. 10020.
Trademarks registered in the United States
and other countries.

PREFACE

Words Most Often Misspelled and Mispronounced is a quick reference guide to the trickiest words in the English language. Ours being a problem-laden language, the list is long—over 23,000 words. These are the words likeliest to be looked up by the student, secretary, businessman, and writer—in fact, anyone to whom correct spelling and pronunciation are vital in social and business life.

Keep this book handy. A quick reference guide will do little good on a high shelf. *Words Most Often Misspelled and Mispronounced* is compact enough to keep in your desk drawer. Use it every time you have a word question, until "looking it up" is an engrained habit. Never let yourself get away with a sloppy guess. The most important single aid in improving your word skills is the habit of looking up words *as you use them, as questions arise.*

You might find it helpful to circle words you have to look up. Unless your memory is better than most, you will probably be looking up the same word again. When you write the word, look at it for a second or two. You might even jot it down a couple of times on a scratch pad. Next time you have to refer to this word it will come more easily; soon it will be a confident part of your vocabulary.

For pronunciations the same general idea applies. Say the word a time or two; get the sound of it in your ear. This will lead you into the habit of correct usage, so that in future conversation the right pronunciation comes naturally, without doubts or fumbling.

USING THIS BOOK

This book has been designed to clear up everyday problems in spelling and pronunciation and to make it quick and easy to find words.

Problems in Spelling and Pronunciation

Endings. Misspellings commonly result from changes in the root word with the addition of suffixes. For example, *cause* loses its final *e* when the final *-ing* is added; thus:

cause, causing

A word like *block* does not alter the spelling of its root when *-ing* is added:

block, blocking

Obviously, this isn't a problem. But a few endings cause questions even though the root remains the same:

canoe, canoeing

Words like this are considered problems; consequently, the suffixes have been included in the book. The concern here is to leave no question in the user's mind.

Other examples in this category are words in which the final consonant is doubled with the addition of suffixes:

essential, essentially
occur, occurring

. . . or changes that occur in the plural of nouns:

ability, abilities

As in many traditional dictionaries, the simplest endings (*-ed*, *-ing*, and *-ies*) are picked up at the last unchanged syllable and immediately follow the main entry. Other derivatives follow:

> accumulate
>   -lating
>   accumulable
>   accumulation
>   accumulative
>   accumulator

But even the simplest endings are never broken between double letters. Thus, instead of *accede, -ceding,* the word *acceding* is written out in full. This is done to avoid careless omission of the second *c.*

Pronunciations. The major pronunciation errors of English speakers are the result of improper enunciation or accent. This work uses the standard phonetic symbols of the Merriam-Webster Dictionaries. See page x for the list of these symbols.

Both primary and secondary accents are shown:

> primary: ′
> secondary: ′
> Example: **aberration** (ab′er · a′shun)

When the accent shifts as a result of a change in the word's form, the editors have included this face in the sub-entry:

> **apocalypse** (a · pok′a · lips)
> **apocalyptic** (a · pok′a · lip′tik)

When the accent has been omitted from one of the sub-entries (for example, *abnormally*), the user should assume the accent is that of the original entry (ab · nor′mal).

Hyphen problems. "Is it one word, two words, or hyphenated?"

In an attempt to answer this question, extended lists of word compounds and combinations are included. Such lists show the preferred form of compounds in commonest usage. Very often these words are so simple there is no other reason for including them. For example:

> good-bye
> goodhearted
> good-humored
> good will

Confusing similarities. Brief definitions and cross references are included for words often mistaken for each other, like *disperse-disburse, serge-surge* and *bouillon-bullion.* For example:

> **bouillon** (soup; see *bullion*)

These definitions are intended as quick reference hints. For your knottier word problems, consult a dictionary.

Places, people, brands, and foreign phrases. State names are listed, along with the preferred abbreviations and correct terms for state residents. For example, a native of Michigan may correctly be called a *Michiganite* or a *Michigander.* Town, city, or river names are included if they are sources of spelling or pronunciation difficulties. Also provided are a selected list of world figures like *Khrushchev, Macmillan,* and *Mao Tse-tung;* brand names that are a part of the language like *Kodachrome;* and common foreign phrases like *coup d'état.*

Choice of words to be included in this book. The editors didn't include words so simple you'd never look them up—words like *man, fan,* and *ran;* nor the blockbusters used to stump the experts, like *cuproiodargyrite.* This left room for words that people do look up and for endings that cause questions.

Some of the words may seem much too simple for a "problem list," but consider the following hardy perennials among the most commonly misspelled words in the language:

> there, their
> receive
> exist, existence, existent
> separate, separation
> occur, occurred, occurring, occurrence
> occasion
> definite, definitely
> definition
> believe, belief

Ease of Finding Words

Have you ever hunted up and down a dictionary page for a word you weren't quite sure of? Sometimes a word and its derivatives are widely separated alphabetically. Many reference works put the derivatives with the main entry; others list them alphabetically. For example, *drier* is a long way from *dry,* and it is a derivative that has considerable importance of its own. In this book, the word *drier* is listed both in straight alphabetical order, and under *dry.* This way, you'll find it whichever place you look first.

Ease of finding main entries is further enhanced by the modern system of syllabifying by centered dots, omitting accent marks. Words are less "broken up" this way and more quickly spotted on the page. If you wish to know the correct accent or a word, it is included in the pronunciation that follows the word.

Fast identification is aided by including the context of certain specialized words. Thus, rather than *sleight*, the entry is *sleight of hand.*

The dominating editorial principle of this book has been the ease with which it could be used, still maintaining a maximum of information. Where the user desires further information on the meanings and uses of words he is referred to the Merriam-Webster series of dictionaries.

The concept of this book originated with James Colvin and the late Frederick Gleeson. They saw the need for a convenient reference work that would clarify two of the greatest irregularities in the English language: *spelling* and *pronunciation.* Both Mr. Colvin and Mr. Gleeson were closely associated with the National Spelling Bee, which is administered by the Scripps-Howard Newspapers. When Mr. Gleeson died, his widow completed the book. She had been his research teammate and has since become a faculty member of St. John College of Cleveland.

—The Publisher

KEY TO THE SYMBOLS
USED IN THE RESPELLING
FOR PRONUNCIATION

The system of indication pronunciation used throughout this book is taken from the 1964 *Merriam-Webster Dictionary*.

ā, *as in* āle, fāte, lā'bor, chā'os.

å, *as in* chå·ot'ic, få·tal'i·ty, in·an'·i·måte.

â, *as in* câre, pâr'ent, com·pâre', beâr, âir.

ă, *as in* ădd, ăm, făt, ăc·cept'.

ȧ, *as in* ȧc·count'. in'fȧnt, guid'ȧnce.

ä, *as in* ärm, fär, fä'ther, pälm.

à, *as in* àsk, gràss, dànce, stàff, påth.

à, *as in* so'fȧ, i·de'ȧ, ȧ·bound', di'ȧ·dem.

b, *as in* ba'by, be, bit, bob, but.

ch, *as in* chair, much; *also for* tch *as in* match; *for* ti *as in* ques'tion; *for* te *as in* right'eous.

d, *as in* day, add'ed; *also for* ed *as in* robbed.

dũ: *for* du *as in* ver'dure; *for* deu *as in* gran'deur.

ē, *as in* ēve, mēte, se·rēne'.

ẽ, *as in* hẽre, fẽar, wẽird, dẽer (dẽr).

ê, *as in* ê·vent', dê·pend', crê·ate'.

ĕ, *as in* ĕnd, ĕx·cuse', ĕf·face'.

ẽ, *as in* si'lĕnt, pru'dĕnce, nov'ĕl.

ẽ, *as in* mak'ẽr, pẽr·vert', in'fẽr·ence.

f, *as in* fill, feel; *for* ph *as in* tri'umph; *for* gh *as in* laugh.

g, (*always* "*hard*"), *as in* go, be·gin'; *also for* gu *as in* guard; *for* gue *as in* plague; *for* gh *as in* ghost.

gz: *for* x *as in* ex·ist', ex·am'ple.

h, *as in* hat, hot, hurt, a·head'.

hw: *for* wh *as in* what, why, where.

ī, *as in* īce, sīght, in·spīre', ī·de'a.

ĭ, *as in* ĭll, ad·mĭt', hab'ĭt, pit'y (pĭt'ĭ).

ĭ, *as in* char'ĭ·ty, pos'sĭ·ble, dĭ·rect', A'prĭl.

j, *as in* joke, jol'ly; *also for* "*soft*" g, *as in* gem, gi'ant; *for* gi *and* ge *as in* re·li'gion, pi'geon; *for* di *as in* sol'dier; *for* dg(e) *as in* edge, judg'ment.

k, *as in* keep; *also for* "*hard*" ch, *as in* cho'rus; *for* "*hard*" c, *as in* cube; *for* ck, *as in* pack; *for* qu *as in* con'quer; *for* que *as in* pique.

ᴋ, (*small capital*): *for* ch *as in* German ich, ach, *etc.*

ks: *for* x *as in* vex, ex'e·cute, per·plex'.

kw: *for* qu *as in* queen, quit, qual'i·ty.

l, *as in* late, leg, lip, hol'ly.

m, *as in* man, mine, hum, ham'mer.

n, *as in* no, man, man'ner; *also for* gn *as in* sign.

ɴ, (*small capital*): *without sound of its own indicates the nasal tone* (*as in French or Portuguese*) *of the preceding vowel, as in* bon (bôɴ)

ng, *as in* sing, long, sing'er; *also for* ngue, *as in* tongue; *for* n *before the sound of* k *or* "*hard*" g, *as in* bank, junc'tion, lin'ger.

ō, *as in* ōld, nōte, cal'i·cō.

ŏ, *as in* ŏ·bey', a·nat'ŏ·my, prŏ·pose'.

ô, *as in* ôrb, lôrd, ôr·dain'; law (lô), bought (bôt), caught (kôt). all (ôl)

ŏ, *as in* ŏdd, nŏt, tŏr'rid, fŏr'est.

ô, *as in* sôft, dôg, clôth, lôss, côst.

ȯ, *as in* cȯn·nect', ȯc·cur', co'lȯn, cȯm·bine'.

oi, *as in* oil, nois'y, a·void', goi'ter.

x

ōō, *as in* fōōd, fōōl, nōōn; rude (rōōd), ru'mor (rōō'mẽr).

ŏŏ, *as in* fŏŏt, wŏŏl; put (pŏŏt), pull (pŏŏl).

ou, *as in* out, thou, de·vour'.

p, *as in* pa'pa, pen, pin, put.

r, *as in* rap, red, rip, hor'rid; *also for* rh *as in* rho'do·den'dron.

s (*always voiceless, or "sharp"*), *as in* so, this, haste; *also for* "*soft*" c, *as in* cell, vice; *for* sc *as in* scene, sci'ence; *for* ss *as in* hiss.

sh, *as in* she, ship, shop; *also for* ch *as in* ma·chine'; *for* ce *as in* o'cean; *for* ci *as in* so'cial; *for* sci *as in* con'scious; *for* s *as in* sure; *for* se *as in* nau'seous; *for* si *as in* pen'sion; *for* ss *as in* is'sue; *for* ssi *as in* pas'sion; *for* ti *as in* na'tion.

t, *as in* time, talk; *also for* ed *as in* baked; *for* th *as in* Thom'as.

th (*voiced*): *for* th *as in* then, though, this, smooth, breathe.

th (*voiceless*), *as in* thin, through, wealth, worth, width.

tū̇: *for* tu *as in* na'ture, cul'ture, pic'ture.

ū, *as in* cūbe, pūre, tūne, lūte, dū'ty.

ů, *as in* ů·nite', for'mů·late, hů·mane'.

û, *as in* ûrn, fûrl, con·cûr'; her (hûr), fern (fûrn), fir (fûr); *for German* ö, oe, *as in* schön (shûn), Goe'the (gû'tĕ); *for French* eu, *as in* jeu (zhû), seul (sûl).

ŭ, *as in* ŭp, tŭb, stŭd'y, ŭn'der.

ŭ, *as in* cir'cŭs, dā'tŭm, cir'cŭmstance, de'mon (-mŭn), na'tion (-shŭn).

ü: *for German* ü, *as in* grün; *for French* u, *as in* me·nu' (mĕnü').

v, *as in* van, vote, re·vise'; *also for* f *as in* of.

w, *as in* want, win; *also for* u *as in* per·suade' (-swād') *or* o *as in* choir (kwīr).

y, *as in* yet, be·yond'; *also for* i *as in* un'ion (-yŭn).

z, *as in* zone, haze; *also for voiced* ("*soft*") s, *as in* is, lives, wise, mu'sic, ears; *for* x *as in* xy'lophone.

zh: *for* z *as in* az'ure; *for* zi *as in* bra'zier; *for* s *as in* pleas'ure, u'su·al; *for* si *as in* vi'sion; *for* ssi *as in* re·scis'sion; *for* g *as in* rouge, mi·rage'.

' *as in* par'don (pär'd'n), eat'en (ēt''n), e'vil (ē'v'l), *indicates that the following consonant is syllabic.*

SYMBOLS FOR PHONETIC RESPELLING USED IN *WEBSTER'S THIRD INTERNATIONAL DICTIONARY*

Webster's Third International Dictionary, published in 1967, uses a new system of symbols for indicating pronunciation. That system is reproduced on the following page for your convenience in using any dictionary in conjunction with WORDS MOST COMMONLY MISSPELLED AND MISPRONOUNCED.

MERRIAM-WEBSTER
PRONUNCIATION SYMBOLS

ə .....alone, silent, capital, collect, suppose

ˈə, ˌə..humdrum, abut

ə .....(in ᵊl, ᵊn) battle, cotton; (in lᵊ, mᵊ, rᵊ) French table, prisme, titre

ər ....operation, further

a ....map, patch

ā ....day, fate

ä ....bother, cot, father

à ....a sound between \a\ and \ä\, as in an Eastern New England pronunciation of aunt, ask

aù ...now, out

b ....baby, rib

ch ...chin, catch

d ....did, adder

e .....set, red

ē .....beat, nosebleed, easy

f ....fifty, cuff

g ....go, big

h ....hat, ahead

hw ...whale

i .....tip, banish

ī .....site, buy

j .....job, edge

k ....kin, cook

ḳ ....loch as commonly pronounced in Scotland (it is \k\ without actual contact between tongue and palate)

l .....lily, cool

m ....murmur, dim

n ....nine, own

ⁿ ....indicates that a preceding vowel or diphthong is pronounced through both nose and mouth, as in French bon \bōⁿ\

ŋ ....sing, singer, finger, ink

ō ....bone, hollow

ȯ ....saw, cork

œ ....\e\ with lip rounding, as in French bœuf, German Hölle

œ̄ ....\ā\ with lip rounding, as in French feu, German Höhle

ȯi ....toy, sawing

p ....pepper, lip

r .....raxity

s .....source, less

sh ...shy, mission

t .....tie, attack

th ...thin, ether

t͟h ...then, either

ü ....boot, few \ˈfyü\

u̇ ....put, pure \ˈpyu̇r\

ᵫ ...\i\ with lip rounding, as in German füllen

ᵫ̄ ....\ē\ with lip rounding, as in French rue, German fühlen

v ....vivid, give

w ....we, away

y ....yard, cue \ˈkyü\

ʸ ....indicates that a preceding \l\, \n\, or \w\ is modified by the placing of the tongue tip against the lower front teeth, as in French digne \dēnʸ\

z .....zone, raise

zh ...vision, pleasure

\.....slant line used in pairs to mark the beginning and end of a transcription: \ˈpen\

ˈ ....mark at the beginning of a syllable that has primary (strongest) stress: \ˈpen-mən-ˌship\

ˌ ....mark at the beginning of a syllable that has secondary (next-strongest) stress: \ˈpen-mən-ˌship\

- ....mark of syllable division in pronunciations (the mark of syllable division in entries is a centered dot ·)

( ) ....indicate that what is symbolized between sometimes occurs and sometimes does not occur in the pronunciation of the word: factory \ˈfakt(ə-)rē\ = \ˈfak-tə-rē, ˈfak-trē\

WORDS MOST OFTEN MISSPELLED AND MISPRONOUNCED

ABBREVIATIONS USED IN THIS BOOK

abbr.	abbreviated, abbreviation	n.	noun
adj.	adjective	N.C.	North Carolina
&	and	N. Dak.	North Dakota
Afr.	Africa	N. Mex.	New Mexico
Calif.	California	N.Y.	New York
Can.	Canada	O.	Ohio
Cen. Am.	Central America	Pa.	Pennsylvania
coll.	college	pl.	plural
fem.	feminine	riv.	river
Fla.	Florida	S. Afr.	South Africa
Ga.	Georgia	S. Amer.	South America
Ia.	Iowa	sing.	singular
Ill.	Illinois	St.	Saint
Ind.	Indiana	Tenn.	Tennessee
is.	island, islands	Tex.	Texas
Kans.	Kansas	Turk.	Turkey
masc.	masculine	univ. or U.	university
Md.	Maryland	v.	verb
Me.	Maine	Va.	Virginia
Mex.	Mexico	Wash.	Washington
Minn.	Minnesota	Wyo.	Wyoming
mt(s)	mount(s), mountain(s)		

A

ab·a·cus   (ăb′ a̍·kŭs)
   pl. ab·a·ci   (-sī)
a·ban·don   (a̍·băn′ dŭn)
   a·ban·don·ment
a·base   (a̍·bās′)
   -bas·ing   a·base·ment
a·bate   (a̍·bāt′)
   -bat·ing   a·bat·a·ble
   a·bate·ment
ab·bey   (ăb′ ĭ)
ab·bre·vi·ate   (a̍·brē′ vĭ·āt)
   -at·ing
   ab·bre·vi·a·tion
         (a̍·brē′ vĭ·ā′ shŭn)
ab·di·cate   (ăb′ dĭ·kāt)
   -cat·ing
   ab·di·ca·tion   (ăb′ dĭ·kā′ shŭn)
ab·do·men   (ăb·dō′ měn)
   ab·dom·i·nal   (ăb·dŏm′ ĭ·năl)
   -nal·ly
ab·duct   (ăb·dŭkt′)
   ab·duc·tion   ab·duc·tor
ab·er·rant   (ăb·ěr′ ănt)
   ab·er·rance
   ab·er·ra·tion   (ăb′ ěr·ā′ shŭn)
a·bet   (a̍·bět′)
   -bet·ted   -bet·ting
   a·bet·tor
a·bey·ance   (a̍·bā′ ăns)
ab·hor   (ăb·hôr′)
   -horred   -hor·ring
   ab·hor·rence   ab·hor·rent
a·bide   (a̍·bīd′)
   -bid·ing
a·bil·i·ty   (a̍·bĭl′ ĭ·tĭ)
   -ties
ab·ject   (ăb′ jěkt)
a·ble   (ā′ b'l)
   a·ble-bod·ied   a·bly

ab·nor·mal   (ăb·nôr′ măl)
   ab·nor·mal·i·ty
         (ăb′ nôr·măl′ ĭ·tĭ)
   -ties   ab·nor·mal·ly
a·board   (a̍·bōrd′)
a·bode   (a̍·bōd′)
a·bol·ish   (a̍·bŏl′ ĭsh)
   a·bol·ish·a·ble
   a·bol·ish·ment
ab·o·li·tion   (ăb′ ō·lĭsh′ ŭn)
   ab·o·li·tion·ist
A-bomb   (ā′ bŏm′)
a·bom·i·na·ble   (a̍·bŏm′ ĭ·na̍·b'l)
   a·bom·i·na·bly
   a·bom·i·na·tion
         (a̍·bŏm′ ĭ·nā′ shŭn)
ab·o·rig·i·nes   (ăb′ ō·rĭj′ ĭ·nēz)
a·bor·tion   (a̍·bôr′ shŭn)
   a·bor·tive
a·bout-face   (a̍·bout′ fās′)
a·bove   (a̍·bŭv′)
   a·bove·board   a·bove-cit·ed
   a·bove·ground
   a·bove-men·tioned
   a·bove-named   a·bove-said
ab·ra·sion   (ăb·rā′ zhŭn)
a·breast   (a̍·brěst′)
a·bridge   (a̍·brĭj′)
   -bridg·ing   a·bridg·ment
a·broad   (a̍·brôd′)
ab·ro·gate   (ăb′ rō·gāt)
   -gat·ing
   ab·ro·ga·tion   (ăb′ rō·gā′ shŭn)
   ab·ro·ga·tor
ab·rupt   (ăb·rŭpt′)
ab·scess   (ăb′ sěs)
ab·scond   (ăb·skŏnd′)
ab·sent   (ăb′ sěnt)
   ab·sence
   ab·sen·tee   (ăb′ sěn·tē′)
   ab·sent-mind·ed

1

ab·so·lute (ăb′ sŏ·lūt)
  ab·so·lute·ly
  ab·so·lut·ism (ăb′ sŏ·lūt·ĭz′m)
ab·solve (ăb·sŏlv′)
  -solv·ing
  ab·so·lu·tion (ăb′ sŏ·lū′ shŭn)
ab·sorb (ăb·sôrb′)
  ab·sorb·a·bil·i·ty
      (ăb·sôrb′ ȧ·bĭl′ ĭ·tĭ)
  ab·sorb·a·ble
  ab·sorb·en·cy -ent
  ab·sorp·tion (ăb·sôrp′ shŭn)
ab·stain (ăb·stān′)
ab·ste·mi·ous (ăb·stē′ mĭ·ŭs)
ab·sten·tion (ăb·stĕn′ shŭn)
ab·sti·nence (ăb′ stĭ·nĕns)
  -nent
ab·stract (ăb′ străkt)
      adj., n.
      (ăb·străkt′) v.
  ab·strac·tion (ăb·străk′ shŭn)
ab·struse (ăb·strōōs′)
ab·surd (ăb·sûrd′)
  ab·surd·i·ty (ăb·sûr′ dĭ·tĭ)
a·bun·dance (ȧ·bŭn′ dȧns)
  -dant
a·buse (ȧ·būz′) v.
      (ȧ·būs′) n.
  -bus·ing
  a·bu·sive (ȧ·bū′ sĭv)
a·but (ȧ·bŭt′)
  -but·ted -but·ting
  a·but·ment
a·bys·mal (ȧ·bĭz′ mȧl)
  a·bys·mal·ly
a·byss (ȧ·bĭs′)
ac·a·dem·ic (ăk′ ȧ·dĕm′ ĭk)
  ac·a·dem·i·cal·ly
  a·cad·e·mi·cian
      (ȧ·kăd′ ĕ·mĭsh′ ȧn)
  a·cad·e·my (ȧ·kăd′ ĕ·mĭ)
  -mies
ac·cede (ăk·sēd′)
  (to agree; see exceed)
  ac·ced·ing
ac·cel·er·ate (ăk·sĕl′ ēr·āt)
  -at·ing
  ac·cel·er·a·tion
      (ăk·sĕl′ ēr·ā′ shŭn)
  ac·cel·er·a·tor
ac·cent (ăk′ sĕnt)
ac·cen·tu·ate (ăk·sĕn′ tů·āt)
  -at·ing
  ac·cen·tu·a·tion
      (ăk·sĕn′ tů·ā′ shŭn)

ac·cept (ăk·sĕpt′)
  ac·cept·a·bil·i·ty
      (ăk·sĕp′ tȧ·bĭl′ ĭ·tĭ)
  ac·cept·a·ble ac·cept·ance
ac·cess (ăk′ sĕs)
  ac·ces·si·bil·i·ty
      (ăk·sĕs′ ĭ·bĭl′ ĭ·tĭ)
  ac·ces·si·ble (ăk·sĕs′ ĭ·b′l)
ac·ces·sion (ăk·sĕsh′ ŭn)
ac·ces·so·ry (ăk·sĕs′ ŏ·rĭ)
  -ries
ac·ci·dent (ăk′ sĭ·dĕnt)
  ac·ci·den·tal (ăk′ sĭ·dĕn′ tȧl)
  -tal·ly
ac·claim (ȧ·klām′)
  ac·cla·ma·tion
      (ăk′ lȧ·mā′ shŭn)
  (applause; see acclimation)
ac·cli·mate (ȧ·klī′ mĭt)
  -mat·ing
  ac·cli·ma·tion (ăk′ lĭ·mā′ shŭn)
  (of climate; see acclamation)
  ac·cli·ma·tize -tiz·ing
ac·co·lade (ăk′ ŏ·lād′)
ac·com·mo·date
      (ȧ·kŏm′ ŏ·dāt)
  -dat·ing
  ac·com·mo·da·tion
      (ȧ·kŏm′ ŏ·dā′ shŭn)
ac·com·pa·ny (ȧ·kŭm′ pȧ·nĭ)
  -nied -ny·ing
  ac·com·pa·ni·ment
  ac·com·pa·nist
ac·com·plice (ȧ·kŏm′ plĭs)
ac·com·plish (ȧ·kŏm′ plĭsh)
  ac·com·plish·a·ble
  ac·com·plish·ment
ac·cord (ȧ·kôrd′)
  ac·cord·ance ac·cord·ing·ly
ac·cor·di·on (ȧ·kôr′ dĭ·ŭn)
ac·cost (ȧ·kôst′)
ac·count (ȧ·kount′)
  ac·count·a·bil·i·ty
      (ȧ·koun′ tȧ·bĭl′ ĭ·tĭ)
  ac·count·a·ble ac·count·ing
  ac·count·ant (ȧ·koun′ tȧnt)
  -an·cy
ac·cred·it (ȧ·krĕd′ ĭt)
  -it·ed -it·ing
ac·crete (ȧ·krēt′)
  ac·cret·ing
  ac·cre·tion (ȧ·krē′ shŭn)
ac·crue (ȧ·krōō′)
  ac·cru·ing ac·cru·al

ac·cu·mu·late   (å·kū́′ mů·lāt)
 -lat·ing
 ac·cu·mu·la·ble
 ac·cu·mu·la·tion
       (å·kū́′ mů·lā́′ shŭn)
 ac·cu·mu·la·tive
       (å·kū́′ mů·lā́′ tĭv)
 ac·cu·mu·la·tor
ac·cu·rate   (ăk′ ů·rĭt)
 ac·cu·ra·cy   ac·cu·rate·ly
ac·cuse   (å·kūz′)
 ac·cus·ing   ac·cus·al
 ac·cu·sa·tion   (ăk′ ů·zā́′ shŭn)
 ac·cu·sa·to·ry   (å·kū́′ zå·tō′ rĭ)
ac·cus·tom   (å·kŭs′ tŭm)
 -tomed
ac·e·tate   (ăs′ ĕ·tāt)
a·ce·tic   (å·sē′ tĭk)
ac·e·tone   (ăs′ ĕ·tōn)
a·cet·y·lene   (å·sĕt′ ĭ·lēn)
ache   (āk)
 ach·ing
a·chieve   (å·chēv′)
 -chiev·ing   a·chiev·a·ble
 a·chieve·ment   a·chiev·er
A·chil·les′ ten·don
       (å·kĭl′ ēz)
ac·id   (ăs′ ĭd)
 ac·id-form·ing
 a·cid·ic   (å·sĭd′ ĭk)
 a·cid·i·fy   (å·sĭd′ ĭ·fī)
 a·cid·i·ty   (å·sĭd′ ĭ·tĭ)
 ac·i·do·sis   (ăs′ ĭ·dō′ sĭs)
 a·cid·u·lous   (å·sĭd′ ů·lŭs)
ac·knowl·edge   (ăk·nŏl′ ĕj)
 -edg·ing   ac·knowl·edge·a·ble
 ac·knowl·edg·ment
ac·me   (ăk′ mĕ)
ac·ne   (ăk′ nĕ)
ac·o·lyte   (ăk′ ŏ·līt)
a·cous·tics   (å·kōōs′ tĭks)
 a·cous·ti·cal   -cal·ly
ac·quaint   (å·kwānt′)
 ac·quaint·ance
ac·qui·esce   (ăk′ wĭ·ĕs′)
 -esc·ing   ac·qui·es·cence
ac·quire   (å·kwīr′)
 -quir·ing   ac·quir·a·ble
 ac·quire·ment
ac·qui·si·tion   (ăk′ wĭ·zĭsh′ ŭn)
ac·quis·i·tive   (å·kwĭz′ ĭ·tĭv)
 ac·quis·i·tive·ness
ac·quit   (å·kwĭt′)
 -quit·ted   -quit·ting
 ac·quit·tal   ac·quit·tance

a·cre   (ā′ kĕr)
 a·cre·age   (ā′ kĕr·ĭj)
ac·rid   (ăk′ rĭd)
ac·ri·mo·ni·ous
       (ăk′ rĭ·mō′ nĭ·ŭs)
 ac·ri·mo·ny   (ăk′ rĭ·mō′ nĭ)
ac·ro·bat   (ăk′ rŏ·băt)
 ac·ro·bat·ic   (ăk′ rŏ·băt′ ĭk)
a·cross   (å·krôs′)
ac·tion   (ăk′ shŭn)
 ac·tion·a·ble
ac·ti·vate   (ăk′ tĭ·vāt)
 -vat·ing
 ac·ti·va·tion   (ăk′ tĭ·vā′ shŭn)
ac·tive   (ăk′ tĭv)
 ac·tive·ly
 ac·tiv·i·ty   (ăk·tĭv′ ĭ·tĭ)
ac·tor   (ăk′ tĕr)
 ac·tress
ac·tu·al   (ăk′ tů·ăl)
 ac·tu·al·ly
 ac·tu·al·i·ty   (ăk′ tů·ăl′ ĭ·tĭ)
 -ties
ac·tu·ar·y   (ăk′ tů·ĕr′ ĭ)
 -ar·ies
 ac·tu·ar·i·al   (ăk′ tů·âr′ ĭ·ăl)
ac·tu·ate   (ăk′ tů·āt)
 -at·ing
a·cu·i·ty   (å·kū́′ ĭ·tĭ)
 -ties
a·cu·men   (å·kū́′ mĕn)
a·cute   (å·kūt′)
 a·cute·ly
ad·age   (ăd′ ĭj)
a·da·gio   (å·dä′ jō)
ad·a·mant   (ăd′ å·mănt)
a·dapt   (å·dăpt′)
 (adjust; see *adept, adopt*)
 a·dapt·a·bil·i·ty
       (å·dăp′ tå·bĭl′ ĭ·tĭ)
 a·dapt·a·ble
 ad·ap·ta·tion   (ăd′ ăp·tā′ shŭn)
 a·dapt·er   a·dap·tive
ad·den·dum   (å·dĕn′ dŭm)
 pl. ad·den·da
ad·der   (ăd′ ĕr)
ad·dict   (ăd′ ĭkt) *n.*
       (å·dĭkt′) *v.*
 ad·dict·ed   (å·dĭk′ tĕd)
 ad·dic·tion   (å·dĭk′ shŭn)
ad·di·tion   (å·dĭsh′ ŭn)
 ad·di·tion·al   -al·ly
ad·di·tive   (ăd′ ĭ·tĭv)
ad·dle·brained   (ăd′′l·brānd′)

ad·dress (*ă·*drĕs′)
  ad·dress·ee   ad·dress·er
  Ad·dres·so·graph
ad·duce (*ă·*dūs′)
  ad·duc·ing   ad·duc·i·ble
ad·e·noid (ăd′ ĕ·noid)
a·dept (*ă·*dĕpt′)
  (expert; see *adapt, adopt*)
ad·e·quate (ăd′ ĕ·kwĭt)
  ad·e·qua·cy (-kwȧ·sĭ)
  ad·e·quate·ly
ad·here (ăd·hēr′)
  -her·ing
  ad·her·ence   -ent
ad·he·sion (ăd·hē′ zhŭn)
  ad·he·sive (ăd·hē′ sĭv)
ad hoc (ăd hŏk′)
a·dieu (*ȧ·*dū′)
Ad·i·ron·dack (ăd′ ĭ·rŏn′ dăk)
  (mts.)
ad·ja·cent (*ă·*jā′ sĕnt)
  -cen·cy
ad·jec·tive (ăj′ ĕk·tĭv)
  ad·jec·ti·val (ăj′ ĕk·tī′ văl)
ad·join·ing (*ă·*join′ ĭng)
ad·journ (*ă·*jûrn′)
  ad·journ·ment
ad·judge (*ă·*jŭj′)
  -judg·ing
ad·ju·di·cate (*ă·*jōō′ dĭ·kāt)
  -cat·ing
  ad·ju·di·ca·tion
           (*ă·*jōō′ dĭ·kā′ shŭn)
  ad·ju·di·ca·tor
ad·junct (ăj′ ŭngkt)
ad·jure (*ă·*jōōr′)
  -jur·ing
ad·just (*ă·*jŭst′)
  ad·just·a·ble   ad·just·er
  ad·just·ment
ad·ju·tant (ăj′ ŏō·tănt)
ad-lib (ăd′ lĭb′)
  -libbed   -lib·bing
ad·min·is·ter (ăd·mĭn′ ĭs·tẽr)
  ad·min·is·tra·ble
ad·min·is·trate (ăd·mĭn′ ĭs·trāt)
  -trat·ing
  ad·min·is·tra·tion
         (ăd·mĭn′ ĭs·trā′ shŭn)
  ad·min·is·tra·tive (-trā′ tĭv)
  ad·min·is·tra·tor (-trā′ tẽr)
ad·mi·ra·ble (ăd′ mĭ·rȧ· b'l)
ad·mi·ral (ăd′ mĭ·răl)
  ad·mi·ral·ty

ad·mire (ăd·mīr′)
  -mir·ing
  ad·mi·ra·tion (ăd′ mĭ·rā′ shŭn)
  ad·mir·er
ad·mis·si·ble (ăd·mĭs′ ĭ·b'l)
ad·mis·sion (ăd·mĭsh′ ŭn)
ad·mit (ăd·mĭt′)
  -mit·ted   -mit·ting
  ad·mit·tance   ad·mit·ted·ly
ad·mix·ture (ăd·mĭks′ tŭr)
ad·mon·ish (ăd·mŏn′ ĭsh)
  ad·mo·ni·tion (ăd′ mŏ·nĭsh′ŭn)
  ad·mon·i·to·ry
         (ăd·mŏn′ ĭ·tō′ rĭ)
ad nau·se·am (ăd nô′ shē·ăm)
a·do (*ȧ·*dōō′)
a·do·be (*ȧ·*dō′ bĭ)
ad·o·les·cent (ăd′ ŏ·lĕs′ ĕnt)
  -cence
a·dopt (*ȧ·*dŏpt′)
  (to choose; see *adapt, adept*)
  a·dopt·a·ble   a·dop·tion
  a·dop·tive
a·dore (*ȧ·*dōr′)
  -dor·ing   a·dor·a·ble
  ad·o·ra·tion (ăd′ ŏ·rā′ shŭn)
a·dorn·ment (*ȧ·*dôrn′ mĕnt)
ad·re·nal (ăd·rē′ năl)
ad·ren·al·ine (ăd·rĕn′ ăl·ĭn)
A·dri·at·ic (ā′ drĭ·ăt′ ĭk)
a·droit (*ȧ·*droit′)
ad·u·la·tion (ăd′ û·lā′ shŭn)
a·dult (*ȧ·*dŭlt′)
a·dul·ter·ant (*ȧ·*dŭl′ tẽr·ănt)
a·dul·ter·ate (*ȧ·*dŭl′ tẽr·āt)
  -at·ing
  a·dul·ter·a·tion
         (*ȧ·*dŭl′ tẽr·ā′ shŭn)
a·dul·ter·y (*ȧ·*dŭl′ tẽr·ĭ)
  a·dul·ter·ess *n.*
  a·dul·ter·er
  a·dul·ter·ous *adj.*
ad va·lo·rem (ăd·vȧ·lō′ rĕm)
ad·vance (ăd·văns′)
  -vanc·ing   ad·vance·ment
ad·van·tage (ăd·văn′ tĭj)
  ad·van·ta·geous
         (ăd′ văn·tā′ jŭs)
ad·ven·ture (ăd·vĕn′ tŭr)
  ad·ven·ture·some
  ad·ven·tur·ess *n.*
  ad·ven·tur·ous *adj.*
ad·verb (ăd′ vûrb)
  ad·ver·bi·al (ăd·vûr′ bĭ·ăl)

ad·ver·sar·y   (ăd′ vẽr·sẽr′ ĭ)
  -sar·ies
ad·verse   (ăd·vûrs′)
  ad·verse·ly
ad·ver·si·ty   (ăd·vûr′ sĭ·tĭ)
  -ties
ad·ver·tise   (ăd′ vẽr·tīz)
  -tis·ing
  ad·ver·tise·ment
          (ăd·vûr′ tĭz·mĕnt)
  ad·ver·tis·er
ad·vice   (ăd·vīs′) n.
  (recommendation)
ad·vise   (ăd·vīz′) v.
  (give advice to)
  -vis·ing
  ad·vis·a·bil·i·ty
          (ăd·vīz′ ȧ·bĭl′ ĭ·tĭ)
  ad·vis·a·ble   ad·vis·ed·ly
  ad·vise·ment   ad·vis·er
  ad·vi·so·ry
ad·vo·cate   (ăd′ vō·kăt) n.
          (-kāt) v.
  -cat·ing
  ad·vo·ca·cy   (ăd′ vō·kȧ·sĭ)
Ae·ge·an   (ē·jē′ ăn)
ae·gis   (ē′ jĭs)
a·er·ate   (ā′ ẽr·āt)
  -at·ing
  a·er·a·tion   (ā′ ẽr·ā′ shŭn)
  a·er·a·tor
a·e·ri·al   (ȧ·ẽr′ ĭ·ăl)
a·er·i·fy   (ā′ ẽr·ĭ·fĭ)
  -fied   -fy·ing
a·er·o·dy·nam·ics
          (ā′ ẽr·ō·dī·năm′ ĭks)
a·er·o·nau·tics   (ā′ ẽr·ō·nô′ tĭks)
a·er·o·sol   (ā′ ẽr·ō·sŏl′)
Aes·chy·lus   (ĕs′ kĭ·lŭs)
Ae·sop   (ē′ sŏp)
aes·thete   (ĕs′ thēt)
  aes·thet·ic   (ĕs·thĕt′ ĭk)
  (of beauty; see *ascetic*)
  aes·thet·i·cism
          (ĕs·thĕt′ ĭ·sĭz′m)
af·fa·ble   (ăf′ ȧ·b′l)
  af·fa·bil·i·ty   (ăf′ ȧ·bĭl′ ĭ·tĭ)
af·fair   (ȧ·fâr′)
af·fect   (ȧ·fĕkt′) v.
  (assume; see *effect*)
  af·fec·ta·tion   (ăf′ ĕk·tā′ shŭn)
  af·fect·ed·ly
af·fec·tion   (ȧ·fĕk′ shŭn)
  af·fec·tion·ate (-ĭt)
  -ate·ly

af·fi·da·vit   (ăf′ ĭ·dā′ vĭt)
af·fil·i·ate   (ȧ·fĭl′ ĭ·āt) v.
  -at·ing   (-ăt) n.
  af·fil·i·a·tion   (ȧ·fĭl′ ĭ·ā′ shŭn)
af·fin·i·ty   (ȧ·fĭn′ ĭ·tĭ)
  -ties
af·firm   (ȧ·fûrm′)
  af·firm·a·ble
  af·fir·ma·tion   (ăf′ ẽr·mā′ shŭn)
af·firm·a·tive   (ȧ·fûr′ mȧ·tĭv)
  -tive·ly
af·fix   (ȧ·fĭks′)
af·flict   (ȧ·flĭkt′)
  af·flic·tion   (ȧ·flĭk′ shŭn)
af·flu·ence   (ăf′ lū·ĕns)
  -ent
af·ford   (ȧ·fōrd′)
af·fray   (ȧ·frā′)
af·front   (ȧ·frŭnt′)
Af·ghan·i·stan   (ăf·găn′ ĭ·stăn)
a·field   (ȧ·fēld′)
a·float   (ȧ·flōt′)
a·fore·said   (ȧ·fōr′ sĕd′)
a·fore·thought   (ȧ·fōr′ thôt′)
  (malice aforethought)
a·fraid   (ȧ·frād′)
Af·ri·can   (ăf′ rĭ·kăn)
aft·er   (ăf′ tẽr)
  aft·er·burn·er
  aft·er-din·ner speech
  aft·er·ef·fect   aft·er·math
  aft·er·noon   aft·er·taste
  aft·er·thought   aft·er·ward
a·gain   (ȧ·gĕn′)
a·gainst   (ȧ·gĕnst′)
ag·ate   (ăg′ ĭt)
age   (āj)
  ag·ing   age·less
  age·long
a·gen·da   (ȧ·jĕn′ dȧ)
a·gent   (ā′ jĕnt)
  a·gen·cy   -cies
ag·glom·er·ate   (ȧ·glŏm′ ẽr·āt)
  -at·ing
  ag·glom·er·a·tion
          (ȧ·glŏm′ ẽr·ā′ shŭn)
ag·gran·dize·ment
          (ȧ·grăn′ dĭz·mĕnt)
ag·gra·vate   (ăg′ rȧ·vāt)
  -vat·ing
  ag·gra·va·tion   (ăg′ rȧ·vā′ shŭn)
ag·gre·gate   (ăg′ rĕ·gĭt) adj.
          (-gāt) v.
  -gat·ing
  ag·gre·ga·tion   (ăg′ rĕ·gā′ shŭn)

ag·gres·sive (ă·grĕs′ ĭv)
ag·gres·sion ag·gres·sor
ag·grieved (ă·grēvd′)
a·ghast (ă·găst′)
ag·ile (ăj′ ĭl)
ag·ile·ly
a·gil·i·ty (ă·jĭl′ ĭ·tĭ)
ag·i·tate (ăj′ ĭ·tāt)
-tat·ing
ag·i·ta·tion (ăj′ ĭ·tā′ shŭn)
ag·i·ta·tor
ag·nos·tic (ăg·nŏs′ tĭk)
ag·nos·ti·cism (-tĭ·sĭz′m)
ag·o·nize (ăg′ ŏ·nīz)
-niz·ing
ag·o·ny (ăg′ ŏ·nĭ)
-nies
a·grar·i·an (ă·grâr′ ĭ·ăn)
a·gree (ă·grē′)
a·gree·a·bil·i·ty
(ă·grē′ ă·bĭl′ ĭ·tĭ)
a·gree·a·ble a·gree·ment
ag·ri·cul·ture (ăg′ rĭ·kŭl′ tûr)
ag·ri·cul·tur·al
(ăg′ rĭ·kŭl′ tûr·ăl)
ag·ri·cul·tur·ist
(ăg′ rĭ·kŭl′ tûr·ĭst)
a·gron·o·my (ă·grŏn′ ŏ·mĭ)
a·gron·o·mist
a·hoy (ă·hoi′)
aid (ād) v.
(to help)
aide (ād) n.
(assistant)
aide-de-camp (ād′ dĕ·kămp′)
ail·ment (āl′ mĕnt)
air (âr)
air base air-borne
air-con·di·tion
air-con·di·tioned
air-con·di·tion·er
air-con·di·tion·ing
air-cooled air·craft
air-dried air drill
air-driv·en air·field
air-filled air fil·ter
air force air·lift
air·line air·mail
air·man air-mind·ed
air·plane air·port
air·proof air raid
air·strip air·tight
Aire·dale (âr′ dāl′)
aisle (īl)
(of a church; see isle)

a·jar (ă·jär′)
a·kim·bo (ă·kĭm′ bō)
a·kin (ă·kĭn′)
Al·a·bam·a (ăl′ ă·băm′ ă)
abbr. Ala.
Al·a·bam·i·an (ăl′ ă·băm′ ĭ·ăn)
al·a·bas·ter (ăl′ ă·bás′ tĕr)
à la carte (ä lä kärt′)
a·lac·ri·ty (ă·lăk′ rĭ·tĭ)
A·lad·din (ă·lăd′ ĭn)
a·la·mode (ä′ lă·mōd′)
a·larm·ist (ă·lär′ mĭst)
A·las·ka (ă·lăs′ kă)
A·las·kan
al·ba·tross (ăl′ bă·trŏs)
al·be·it (ôl·bē′ ĭt)
al·bi·no (ăl·bī′ nō)
-nos
al·bum (ăl′ băm)
al·bu·men (ăl·bū′ mĕn)
Al·bu·quer·que, (ăl′ bŭ·kûr′ kĕ)
N. Mex.
al·che·my (ăl′ kĕ·mĭ)
al·che·mist (-mĭst)
al·co·hol (ăl′ kŏ·hŏl)
al·co·hol·ic (ăl′ kŏ·hŏl′ ĭk)
al·co·hol·ism (ăl′ kŏ·hŏl·ĭz′m)
al·cove (ăl′ kōv)
al·der·man (ôl′ dĕr·măn)
A·leu·tian (ă·lū′ shăn)
al·fal·fa (ăl·făl′ fă)
al·ga (ăl′ gă)
pl. al·gae (-jē)
al·ge·bra (ăl′ jĕ·bră)
al·ge·bra·ic (ăl′ jĕ·brā′ ĭk)
a·li·as (ā′ lĭ·ăs)
al·i·bi (ăl′ ĭ·bī)
-bis
al·ien (āl′ yĕn)
al·ien·a·ble al·ien·ate
al·ien·a·tion (āl′ yĕn·ā′ shŭn)
a·lign (ă·līn′)
a·lign·ment
al·i·men·ta·ry (ăl′ ĭ·mĕn′ tă·rĭ)
al·i·mo·ny (ăl′ ĭ·mō′ nĭ)
al·ka·li (ăl′ kă·lĭ)
-lies
al·ka·line (ăl′ kă·līn)
al·ka·lin·i·ty (ăl′ kă·lĭn′ ĭ·tĭ)
al·ka·loid (ăl′ kă·loid)
all (ôl)
all-A·mer·i·can
all-out ef·fort
all·o·ver pat·tern
all right (not alright)

al·lay (ă·lā′)
al·le·ga·tion (ăl′ ĕ·gā′ shŭn)
al·lege (ă·lĕj′)
   al·leg·ing
   al·leg·ed·ly (ă·lĕj′ ĕd·lĭ)
Al·le·ghe·ny (ăl′ ĕ·gā′ nĭ)
   (mts.) -nies
al·le·giance (ă·lē′ jăns)
al·le·go·ry (ăl′ ĕ·gō′ rĭ)
   -ries
   al·le·gor·i·cal (ăl′ ĕ·gŏr′ ĭ·kăl)
al·ler·gy (ăl′ ĕr·jĭ)
   -gies
   al·ler·gic (ă·lûr′ jĭk)
al·le·vi·ate (ă·lē′ vĭ·āt)
   -at·ing
   al·le·vi·a·tion (ă·lē′ vĭ·ā′ shŭn)
al·ley (ăl′ ĭ)
   al·leys   al·ley·way
al·li·ance (ă·lī′ ăns)
al·lied (ă·līd′)
al·li·ga·tor (ăl′ ĭ·gā′ tēr)
al·lit·er·a·tion (ă·lĭt′ ēr·ā′ shŭn)
al·lo·cate (ăl′ ŏ·kāt)
   -cat·ing
   al·lo·ca·tion (ăl′ ŏ·kā′ shŭn)
al·lot (ă·lŏt′)
   al·lot·ted   al·lot·ting
   al·lot·ment
al·low (ă·lou′)
   al·low·a·ble   al·low·ance
al·loy (ă·loi′)
all right (ôl rīt)
all·spice (ôl′ spīs′)
al·lude (ă·lūd′)
   (to refer; see *elude*)
   al·lud·ing
al·lure (ă·lūr′)
   al·lur·ing   al·lure·ment
al·lu·sion (ă·lū′ zhŭn)
   (indirect reference; see *illusion*)
   al·lu·sive
al·lu·vi·al (ă·lū′ vĭ·ăl)
al·ly (ă·lī′)
   al·lied   al·ly·ing
Al·ma Ma·ter (ăl′ mă mā′ tēr)
al·ma·nac (ôl′ mă·năk)
al·might·y (ôl·mīt′ ĭ)
   al·might·i·ly
al·mond (ä′ mŭnd)
al·most (ôl′ mōst)
alms·house (ämz′ hous′)
a·lo·ha (ä·lō′ hä)
a·long·side (ă·lŏng′ sīd′)
a·loof (ă·lōōf′)

a·loud (ă·loud′)
al·pac·a (ăl·păk′ ă)
al·pha·bet (ăl′ fă·bĕt)
   al·pha·bet·ic (ăl′ fă·bĕt′ ĭk)
   al·pha·bet·ize -iz·ing
al·read·y (ôl·rĕd′ ĭ)
   (*Already* means previously: "He had *already* arrived"; all ready means prepared.)
Al·sace-Lor·raine (ăl′ săs lŏ·rān′)
   Al·sa·tian (ăl·sā′ shăn)
al·tar (ôl′ tēr)
   (in church)
   al·tar·piece
al·ter (ôl′ tēr)
   (to modify)
   al·ter·a·tion (ôl′ tēr·ā′ shŭn)
   al·ter·a·ble
al·ter·ca·tion (ôl′ tēr·kā′ shŭn)
   (quarrel)
al·ter e·go (ăl′ tēr ē′ gō)
al·ter·nate (ôl′ tēr·nĭt) *adj.*
   (-nāt) *v.*
   -nat·ing
   al·ter·nate·ly (ôl′ tēr·nĭt·lĭ)
   al·ter·na·tion (ôl′ tēr·nā′ shŭn)
al·ter·na·tive (ôl·tûr′ nă·tĭv)
   al·ter·na·tive·ly
al·though (ôl·thō′)
al·tim·e·ter (ăl·tĭm′ ĕ·tēr)
al·ti·tude (ăl′ tĭ·tūd)
al·to·geth·er (ôl′ tŏŏ·gĕth′ ēr)
al·tru·ism (ăl′ trōō·ĭz′m)
   al·tru·ist
   al·tru·is·tic (ăl′ trōō·ĭs′ tĭk)
al·um (ăl′ ŭm)
a·lu·mi·num (ă·lū′ mĭ·nŭm)
a·lum·na (ă·lŭm′ nă) ; *fem. pl.* a·lum·nae (-nē)
a·lum·nus (ă·lŭm′ nŭs)
   masc.; *pl.* a·lum·ni (-nī)
al·ways (ôl′ wâz)
a·mal·gam·ate (ă·măl′ gă·māt)
   -at·ing
   a·mal·gam·a·tion (ă·măl′ gă·mā′ shŭn)
a·mass (ă·măs′)
am·a·teur (ăm′ ă·tûr′)
   am·a·teur·ish
am·a·to·ry (ăm′ ă·tō′ rĭ)
a·maze (ă·māz′)
   -maz·ing   a·maz·ed·ly
   a·maze·ment

Am·a·zon (ăm′ a·zŏn)
Am·a·zo·ni·an
(ăm′ a·zō′ nĭ·ăn)
am·bas·sa·dor (ăm·băs′ a·dĕr)
am·bas·sa·do·ri·al
(ăm·băs′ a·dō′ rĭ·ăl)
am·ber (ăm′ bĕr)
am·bi·dex·trous
(ăm′ bĭ·dĕk′ strŭs)
am·bi·gu·i·ty (ăm′ bĭ·gū′ ĭ·tĭ)
-ties
am·big·u·ous (ăm·bĭg′ û·ŭs)
am·bi·tion (ăm·bĭsh′ ŭn)
am·bi·tious
am·biv·a·lence (ăm·bĭv′ a·lĕns)
-lent
am·ble (ăm′ b′l)
-bling
am·bro·si·a (ăm·brō′ zhĭ·a)
am·bro·si·al
am·bu·lance (ăm·bû·lăns)
am·bu·la·tory (ăm′ bû·la·tō′ rĭ)
am·bush (ăm′ bŏŏsh)
a·mel·io·rate (a·mēl′ yŏ·rāt)
-rat·ing
a·mel·io·ra·tion
(a·mēl′ yŏ·rā′ shŭn)
a·men (ā′ mĕn′)
a·me·na·ble (a·mē′ na·b′l)
a·mend (a·mĕnd′)
a·mend·ment
a·men·i·ty (a·mĕn′ ĭ·tĭ)
-ties
A·mer·i·ca·na (a·mĕr′ ĭ·kā′ na)
A·mer·i·can·ism
(a·mĕr′ ĭ·kăn·ĭz′m)
am·e·thyst (ăm′ ê·thĭst)
Am·herst (coll.) (ăm′ ĕrst)
a·mi·a·ble (ā′ mĭ·a·b′l)
-bly
a·mi·a·bil·i·ty
(ā′ mĭ·a·bĭl′ ĭ·tĭ)
am·i·ca·ble (ăm′ ĭ·ka·b′l)
-bly
a·mid (a·mĭd′)
a·midst (a·mĭdst′)
a·miss (a·mĭs′)
am·i·ty (ăm′ ĭ·tĭ)
(friendship; see *enmity*)
-ties
am·mo·ni·a (a·mō′ nĭ·a)
am·mu·ni·tion (ăm′ û·nĭsh′ ŭn)
am·ne·si·a (ăm·nē′ zhĭ·a)
am·nes·ty (ăm′ nĕs·tĭ)

a·moe·ba (a·mē′ ba)
pl. a·moe·bae (-bē)
a·moe·bic
a·mong (a·mŭng′)
a·mongst
a·mor·al (ā·mŏr′ ăl)
a·mo·ral·i·ty (ā′ mŏ·răl′ ĭ·tĭ)
am·o·rous (ăm′ ŏ·rŭs)
a·mor·phous (a·môr′ fŭs)
am·or·tize (ăm′ ĕr·tīz)
-tiz·ing
am·or·ti·za·tion
(ăm′ ĕr·tĭ·zā′ shŭn)
a·mount (a·mount′)
am·phib·ian (ăm·fĭb′ ĭ·ăn)
am·phib·i·ous
am·phi·the·a·ter
(ăm′ fĭ·thē′ a·tĕr)
am·ple (ăm′ p′l)
-ply
am·pli·fy (ăm′ plĭ·fī)
-fied -fy·ing
am·pli·fi·ca·tion
(ăm′ plĭ·fĭ·kā′ shŭn)
am·pli·fi·er
am·pu·tate (ăm′ pû·tāt)
-tat·ing
am·pu·ta·tion (ăm′ pû·tā′ shŭn)
am·pu·tee (ăm′ pû·tē′)
a·muck (a·mŭk′)
am·u·let (ăm′ û·lĕt)
a·muse (a·mūz′)
-mus·ing a·mus·a·ble
a·muse·ment
a·nach·ro·nism
(a·năk′ rŏ·nĭz′m)
a·nach·ro·nis·tic
(a·năk′ rŏ·nĭs′ tĭk)
an·a·con·da (ăn′ a·kŏn′ da)
an·al·ge·si·a (ăn′ ăl·jē′ zĭ·a)
an·al·ge·sic (-jē′ sĭk)
an·a·logue (ăn′ a·lŏg)
com·put·er
a·nal·o·gy (a·năl′ ŏ·jĭ)
-gies
an·a·log·i·cal (ăn′ a·lŏj′ ĭ·kăl)
a·nal·o·gous (a·năl′ ŏ·gŭs)
a·nal·y·sis (a·năl′ ĭ·sĭs)
pl. a·nal·y·ses (-sēz)
an·a·lyst (ăn′ a·lĭst)
an·a·lyt·ic (ăn′ a·lĭt′ ĭk)
an·a·lyze (ăn′ a·līz)
-lyz·ing
an·a·lyz·a·ble (ăn′ a·līz·a·b′l)

an·arch·y (ăn′ ár·kĭ)
  -arch·ies   an·arch·ism
  an·arch·ist
a·nath·e·ma (á·năth′ ĕ·má)
a·nat·o·my (á·năt′ ŏ·mĭ)
  -mies
  an·a·tom·i·cal
             (ăn′ á·tŏm′ ĭ·kăl)
an·ces·tor (ăn′ sĕs′ tẽr)
  an·ces·tral (ăn·sĕs′ trăl)
  an·ces·try (ăn′ sĕs′ trĭ)
an·chor (ăng′ kẽr)
  an·chor·age (-ĭj)
an·cho·vy (ăn·chō′ vĭ)
  -vies
an·cient (ān′ shĕnt)
an·cil·lar·y (ăn′ sĭ·lĕr′ ĭ)
an·ec·dote (ăn′ ĕk·dōt)
  (story; see *antidote*)
  an·ec·do·tal (-dō′ tăl)
a·nem·o·ne (á·něm′ ŏ·nĕ)
an·es·the·si·a (ăn′ ĕs·thē′ zhĭ·á)
  an·es·thet·ic (-thĕt′ ĭk)
  an·es·the·tist (ăn·ĕs′ thĕ·tĭst)
  an·es·thet·i·za·tion
      (ăn′ ĕs·thĕt′ ĭ·zā′ shŭn)
  an·es·the·tize (ăn·ĕs′ thĕ·tīz)
  -tiz·ing
an·gel (ān′ jĕl)
  an·gel·ic (ăn·jĕl′ ĭk)
an·ger (ăng′ gẽr)
an·gle (ăng′ g′l)
  -gling   an·gler
  an·gle·worm
An·gli·can (ăng′ glĭ·kăn)
An·glo-Sax·on (ăng′ glŏ·săk′ s′n)
An·go·la, Afr. (ăng·gō′ lá)
An·go·ra (ăng·gō′ rá)
an·gry (ăng′ grĭ)
  an·gri·er   -gri·est
  -gri·ly   -gri·ness
an·guish (ăng′ gwĭsh)
an·gu·lar (ăng′ gû·lẽr)
  an·gu·lar·i·ty (ăng′gŭ·lăr′ĭ·tĭ)
an·i·mal (ăn′ ĭ·măl)
  an·i·mal·i·ty (ăn′ ĭ·măl′ ĭ·tĭ)
an·i·mate (ăn′ ĭ·māt) *v.*
      (-măt) *adj.*
  -mat·ing
  an·i·ma·tion (ăn′ ĭ·mā′ shŭn)
an·i·mos·i·ty (ăn′ ĭ·mŏs′ ĭ·tĭ)
  -ties
an·ise (ăn′ ĭs)
  an·i·seed
An·ka·ra, Turk. (ăng′ ká·rá)

an·kle (ăng′ k′l)
  an·kle·bone   an·klet
an·nals (ăn′ ălz)
An·nap·o·lis, (ă·năp′ ŏ·lĭs)
  Md.
an·neal (ă·nēl′)
  an·neal·ing
an·nex (ă·nĕks′) *v.*
      (ăn′ ĕks) *n.*
  an·nex·a·tion (ăn′ ĕk·sā′ shŭn)
an·ni·hi·late (ă·nī′ ĭ·lāt)
  -lat·ing
  an·ni·hi·la·tion
      (ă·nī′ ĭ·lā′ shŭn)
  an·ni·hi·la·tor
an·ni·ver·sa·ry (ăn′ ĭ·vûr′ sá·rĭ)
  -sar·ies
an·no·tate (ăn′ ŏ·tāt)
  -tat·ing
  an·no·ta·tion (ăn′ ŏ·tā′ shŭn)
an·nounce (ă·nouns′)
  an·nounc·ing
  an·nounce·ment
  an·nounc·er
an·noy (ă·noi′)
  an·noy·ance
an·nu·al (ăn′ û·ăl)
  an·nu·al·ly
an·nu·i·ty (ă·nū′ ĭ·tĭ)
  -ties
an·nul (ă·nŭl′)
  an·nulled   an·nul·ling
  an·nul·la·ble   an·nul·ment
an·nun·ci·a·tion
      (ă·nŭn′ sĭ·ā′ shŭn)
an·ode (ăn′ ōd)
a·noint (á·noint′)
  a·noint·ment
a·nom·a·ly (á·nŏm′ á·lĭ)
  -lies
  a·nom·a·lous (-lŭs)
a·non (á·nŏn′)
a·non·y·mous (á·nŏn′ ĭ·mŭs)
  an·o·nym·i·ty (ăn′ ŏ·nĭm′ ĭ·tĭ)
an·oth·er (ă·nŭth′ ẽr)
an·swer (án′ sẽr)
  an·swer·a·ble
an·tag·o·nize (ăn·tăg′ ŏ·nīz)
  -niz·ing
  an·tag·o·nism an·tag·o·nist
  an·tag·o·nis·tic
      (ăn·tăg′ ŏ·nĭs′ tĭk)
Ant·arc·ti·ca (ănt·ärk′ tĭ·ká)
an·te- (ăn′ tĕ)
  (prefix meaning *before*)

an·te-bel·lum   an·te·cham·ber
an·te·date
an·te·di·lu·vi·an (-dĭ·lū′ vĭ·ăn)
an·te me·rid·i·em (*abbr.* a.m.)
                    (-mĕ·rĭd′ ĭ·ĕm)
an·te·room
an·te·ced·ence (ăn′ tĕ·sēd′ ĕns)
  -ent
an·te·lope   (ăn′ tĕ·lōp)
an·ten·na   (ăn·tĕn′ à)
an·te·ri·or   (ăn·tẽr′ ĭ·ēr)
an·them   (ăn′ thĕm)
an·thol·o·gy   (ăn·thŏl′ ŏ·jĭ)
  -gies
an·thra·cite   (ăn′ thrà·sīt)
an·thro·poid   (ăn′ thrŏ·poid)
an·thro·pol·o·gy
               (ăn′ thrŏ·pŏl′ ŏ·jĭ)
  an·thro·pol·o·gist
an·thro·po·mor·phize
          (ăn′ thrŏ·pŏ·môr′ fīz)
  -phiz·ing
an·ti·air·craft (ăn′ tĭ·âr′ kráft′)
an·ti·bi·ot·ic (ăn′ tĭ·bī·ŏt′ ĭk)
an·ti·bod·y   (ăn′ tĭ·bŏd′ ĭ)
  -bod·ies
an·tic   (ăn′ tĭk)
an·tic·i·pate   (ăn·tĭs′ ĭ·pāt)
  -pat·ing
  an·tic·i·pa·tion
          (ăn·tĭs′ ĭ·pā′ shŭn)
  an·tic·i·pa·to·ry
          (ăn·tĭs′ ĭ·pà·tō′ rĭ)
an·ti·cli·max (ăn′ tĭ·klī′ măks)
  an·ti·cli·mac·tic
          (-klĭ·măk′ tĭk)
an·ti·dote   (ăn′ tĭ·dōt)
  (remedy; see *anecdote*)
an·ti·freeze   (ăn′ tĭ·frēz′)
an·ti·his·ta·mine
          (ăn′ tĭ·hĭs′ tà·mēn)
an·ti·ma·cas·sar
          (ăn′ tĭ·mà·kăs′ ēr)
an·ti·pa·sto   (ăn′ tĕ·päs′ tŏ)
an·tip·a·thy   (ăn·tĭp′ à·thĭ)
  -thies
an·ti·quar·i·an
          (ăn′ tĭ·kwâr′ ĭ·ăn)
an·ti·quat·ed (ăn′ tĭ·kwāt′ ĕd)
an·tique   (ăn·tēk′)
an·tiq·ui·ty   (ăn·tĭk′ wĭ·tĭ)
  -ties
an·ti-Sem·i·tism
          (ăn′ tĭ·sĕm′ ĭ·tĭz′m)

an·ti-Se·mit·ic
              (ăn′ tĭ·sĕ·mĭt′ ĭk)
an·ti·sep·tic (ăn′ tĭ·sĕp′ tĭk)
  an·ti·sep·ti·cize (-tĭ·sīz)
  -ciz·ing
an·tith·e·sis (ăn·tĭth′ ĕ·sĭs)
an·ti·tox·in   (ăn′ tĭ·tŏk′ sĭn)
an·ti·trust   (ăn′ tĭ·trŭst′)
an·vil   (ăn′ vĭl)
anx·i·e·ty   (ăng·zī′ ĕ·tĭ)
  -ties
anx·ious   (ăngk′ shŭs)
  anx·ious·ly
an·y   (ĕn′ ĭ)
  an·y·bod·y   an·y·how
  an·y·more
  an·y·thing   an·y·way
  an·y·where
a·or·ta   (â·ôr′ tà)
a·part·heid   (à·pärt′ hāt)
a·part·ment   (à·pärt′ mĕnt)
ap·a·thy   (ăp′ à·thĭ)
  ap·a·thet·ic (ăp′ à·thĕt′ ĭk)
a·pé·ri·tif   (à′ pā′ rē′ tēf′)
ap·er·ture   (ăp′ ẽr·tûr)
a·pex   (ā′ pĕks)
aph·o·rism   (ăf′ ŏ·rĭz′m)
aph·ro·dis·i·ac (ăf′ rŏ·dĭz′ ĭ·ăk)
a·pi·ar·y   (ā′ pĭ·ĕr′ ĭ)
  -ar·ies
a·piece   (à·pēs′)
ap·ish   (āp′ ĭsh)
a·plomb   (à·plŏm′)
a·poc·a·lypse (à·pŏk′ à·lĭps)
  a·poc·a·lyp·tic
              (à·pŏk′ à·lĭp′ tĭk)
a·poc·ry·phal (à·pŏk′ rĭ·fàl)
a·pol·o·gy   (à·pŏl′ ŏ·jĭ)
  -gies
  a·pol·o·get·ic (à·pŏl′ ŏ·jĕt′ ĭk)
  -i·cal·ly   a·pol·o·gist
  a·pol·o·gize -giz·ing
ap·o·plex·y   (ăp′ ŏ·plĕk′ sĭ)
  ap·o·plec·tic (ăp′ ŏ·plĕk′ tĭk)
a·pos·tle   (à·pŏs′ 'l)
  ap·os·tol·ic (ăp′ ŏs·tŏl′ ĭk)
a·pos·tro·phe (à·pŏs′ trŏ·fē)
a·poth·e·car·y (à·pŏth′ ĕ·kĕr′ ĭ)
  a·poth·e·car·ies′ meas·ure
ap·o·thegm   (ăp′ ŏ·thĕm)
a·poth·e·o·sis (à·pŏth′ ĕ·ŏ′ sĭs)
  pl. a·poth·e·o·ses (-sēz)
Ap·pa·la·chian (ăp′ à·lā′ chàn)
  (mts.)
ap·pall   (à·pôl′)

ap·pa·ra·tus   (ăp′ à·rā′ tŭs)
  n. sing. & pl.
ap·par·el   (à·păr′ ĕl)
  -eled.   -el·ing
ap·par·ent   (à·păr′ ĕnt)
ap·pa·ri·tion   (ăp′ à·rĭsh′ ŭn)
ap·peal   (à·pēl′)
  ap·peal·ing
ap·pear   (à·pēr′)
  ap·pear·ance
ap·pease   (à·pēz′)
  ap·peas·ing   ap·pease·ment
  ap·peas·er
ap·pel·late   (à·pĕl′ ăt)
ap·pel·la·tion   (ăp′ ĕ·lā′ shŭn)
ap·pend   (à·pĕnd′)
  ap·pend·age   (à·pĕn′ dĭj)
ap·pen·dec·to·my
                (ăp′ ĕn·dĕk′ tô·mĭ)
  ap·pen·di·ci·tis
               (à·pĕn′ dĭ·sī′ tĭs)
ap·pen·dix   (à·pĕn′ dĭks)
  -dix·es
ap·per·tain   (ăp′ ĕr·tān′)
ap·pe·tite   (ăp′ ĕ·tīt)
  ap·pe·tiz·er   ap·pe·tiz·ing
Ap·pi·an Way   (ăp′ ĭ·ản)
ap·plaud   (à·plôd′)
ap·plause   (à·plôz′)
ap·ple   (ăp′ ′l)
  ap·ple·sauce
ap·pli·ance   (à·plī′ ản s)
ap·pli·ca·ble   (ăp′ lĭ·kà·b′l)
  ap·pli·ca·bil·i·ty
             (ăp′ lĭ·kà·bĭl′ ĭ·tĭ)
ap·pli·cant   (ăp′ lĭ·kănt)
ap·pli·ca·tion   (ăp′ lĭ·kā′ shŭn)
ap·pli·ca·tor   (ăp′ lĭ·kā′ tĕr)
ap·pli·ca·to·ry   (ăp′ lĭ·kà·tō′ rĭ)
ap·pli·qué   (ăp′ lĭ·kā′)
ap·ply   (à·plī′)
  ap·plied   ap·ply·ing
  ap·pli·er
ap·point   (à·point′)
  ap·point·ee   (à·poin′ tē′)
  ap·poin·tive   ap·point·ment
Ap·po·mat·tox,   (ăp′ ô·măt′ ŭks)
  Va.
ap·por·tion   (à·pōr′ shŭn)
  ap·por·tion·ment
ap·praise   (à·prāz′)
  (to judge; see *apprise*)
  ap·prais·ing   ap·prais·al
  ap·praise·ment   ap·prais·er

ap·pre·ci·a·ble   (à·prē′shĭ·à·b′l)
  -bly
ap·pre·ci·ate   (à·prē′ shĭ·āt)
  -at·ing
ap·pre·ci·a·tion
             (à·prē′ shĭ·ā′ shŭn)
ap·pre·ci·a·tive
             (à·prē′ shĭ·ā′ tĭv)
ap·pre·ci·a·to·ry
              (-à·tō′ rĭ)
ap·pre·hend   (ăp′ rĕ·hĕnd′)
  ap·pre·hen·si·ble   (-hĕn′ sĭ·b′l)
  ap·pre·hen·sion   (-hĕn′ shŭn)
  ap·pre·hen·sive   (-hĕn′ sĭv)
ap·pren·tice   (à·prĕn′ tĭs)
  -tic·ing   ap·pren·tice·ship
ap·prise   (à·prīz′)
  (to inform; see *appraise*)
  ap·pris·ing
ap·proach   (à·prōch′)
  ap·proach·a·ble
ap·pro·ba·tion   (ăp′ rô·bā′ shŭn)
ap·pro·pri·ate   (à·prō′ prĭ·ĭt)
             adj.
             (-āt) *v.*
  -at·ing
  ap·pro·pri·a·tion
             (à·prō′ prĭ·ā′ shŭn)
ap·prove   (à·prōōv′)
  ap·prov·ing   ap·prov·a·ble
  ap·prov·al
ap·prox·i·mate   (à·prŏk′ sĭ·mĭt)
             adj.
             (-māt) *v.*
  -mat·ing
  ap·prox·i·mate·ly
             (à·prŏk′ sĭ·mĭt·lĭ)
  ap·prox·i·ma·tion
             (à·prŏk′ sĭ·mā′ shŭn)
ap·pur·te·nance
             (à·pûr′ tĕ·nản s)
a·pri·cot   (ā′ prĭ·kŏt)
a·pri·o·ri   (ā′ prī·ō′ rĭ)
a·pron   (ā′ prŭn)
ap·ro·pos   (ăp′ rô·pō′)
ap·ti·tude   (ăp′ tĭ·tūd)
apt·ly   (ăpt′ lĭ)
aq·ua   (ăk′ wà)
  aq·ua·cade   aq·ua·lung
  aq·ua·ma·rine   *But:* aq·ue·duct
a·quar·i·um   (à·kwâr′ ĭ·ŭm)
a·quat·ic   (à·kwăt′ ĭk)
aq·ue·duct   (ăk′ wĕ·dŭkt)
a·que·ous   (ā′ kwĕ·ŭs)
aq·ui·line   (ăk′ wĭ·lĭn)

A·qui·nas,   (a·kwī′ nås)
  St. Thom·as
ar·a·besque   (är′ a·bĕsk′)
A·ra·bi·an   (a·rā′ bĭ·ån)
  Ar·a·bic   (ăr′ a·bĭk)
ar·a·ble   (ăr′ a·b'l)
  ar·a·bil·i·ty   (ăr′ a·bĭl′ ĭ·tĭ)
ar·bi·ter   (är′ bĭ·tēr)
  ar·bi·tral
  ar·bit·ra·ment   (är·bĭt′ rå·mĕnt)
ar·bi·trar·y   (är′ bĭ·trĕr′ Ĭ)
  ar·bi·trar·i·ly   -i·ness
ar·bi·trate   (är′ bĭ·trāt)
  -trat·ing
  ar·bi·tra·tion   (är′ bĭ·trā′ shŭn)
  ar·bi·tra·tor
ar·bor   (är′ bēr)
  ar·bo·re·al   (är·bō′ rĕ·ål)
  ar·bo·re·tum   (är′ bō·rē′ tŭm)
  ar·bor·vi·tae   (är′ bŏr·vī′ tē)
ar·bu·tus   (är·bū′ tŭs)
arc   (ärk)
  (bowlike curve; see ark)
  arced
ar·cade   (är·kād′)
arch   (ärch)
  arch·bish·op   arch·dea·con
  arch·di·o·cese   arch·duke
  arch·duch·ess   arch·en·e·my
  But: ar·che·type
ar·chae·ol·o·gy
                      (är′ kĕ·ŏl′ ō·jĭ)
  -gist
ar·cha·ic   (är·kā′ ĭk)
arch·an·gel   (ärk′ ān′ jĕl)
arch·er·y   (är′ chēr·Ĭ)
ar·che·type   (är′ kĕ·tĭp)
Ar·chi·me·des   (är′ kĭ·mē′ dēz)
  Ar·chi·me·de·an
                      (är′ kĭ·mē′ dĕ·ån)
ar·chi·pel·a·go   (är′ kĭ·pĕl′ a·gō)
  -goes
ar·chi·tect   (är′ kĭ·tĕkt)
  ar·chi·tec·tur·al
                      (är′ kĭ·tĕk′ tûr·ål)
  ar·chi·tec·ture   (är′ kĭ·tĕk′ tûr)
ar·chives   (är′ kīvz)
arc·tic   (ärk′ tĭk)
  (frigid)
Arc·tic   (ärk′ tĭk)
  (Ocean, Circle, zone)
ar·dent   (är′ dĕnt)
  -den·cy
ar·dor   (är′ dēr)
ar·du·ous   (är′ dū̵·ŭs)

a·re·a   (ā′ rē·a)
  (flat surface; see aria)
  a·re·a·way
a·re·na   (a·rē′ na)
aren't   (ärnt)
ar·go·sy   (är′ gŏ·sĭ)
  -sies
ar·gue   (är′ gū)
  -gu·ing   ar·gu·a·ble
  ar·gu·er
ar·gu·ment   (är′ gū·mĕnt)
  ar·gu·men·ta·tion
                      (är′ gū·mĕn·tā′ shŭn)
  ar·gu·men·ta·tive
                      (är′ gū·mĕn′ ta·tĭv)
a·ri·a   (ä′ rĭ·a)
  (melody; see area)
ar·id   (är′ ĭd)
  a·rid·i·ty   (a·rĭd′ ĭ·tĭ)
a·ris·to·crat   (a·rĭs′ tō·krăt)
  ar·is·toc·ra·cy   (ăr′ ĭs·tŏk′ rå·sĭ)
  -cies
  a·ris·to·crat·ic
                      (a·rĭs′ tō·krăt′ ĭk)
Ar·is·toph·a·nes
                      (ăr′ ĭs·tŏf′ a·nēz)
Ar·is·tot·le   (ăr′ ĭs·tŏt′ 'l)
  Ar·is·to·te·li·an
                      (ăr′ ĭs·tō·tē′ lĭ·ån)
a·rith·me·tic   (a·rĭth′ mĕ·tĭk)
  ar·ith·met·i·cal
                      (är′ ĭth·mĕt′ ĭ·kål)
  a·rith·me·ti·cian
                      (a·rĭth′ mĕ·tĭsh′ ån)
Ar·i·zo·na   (ăr′ ĭ·zō′ na)
  abbr. Ariz.
  Ar·i·zo·nan or Ar·i·zo·ni·an
                      (-nĭ·ăn)
ark   (ärk)
  (ship; see arc)
Ar·kan·sas   (är′ kăn·sô)
  abbr. Ark.
  Ar·kan·san   (är·kăn′ zån)
ar·ma·da   (är·mä′ då)
ar·ma·dil·lo   (är′ må·dĭl′ ō)
ar·ma·ment   (är′ må·mĕnt)
ar·ma·ture   (är′ må·tûr)
arm·ful   (ärm′ fŏŏl)
ar·mi·stice   (är′ mĭ·stĭs)
ar·mor   (är′ mēr)
ar·mor·y   (är′ mēr·Ĭ)
  -mor·ies
ar·my   (är′ mĭ)
  -mies
a·ro·ma   (a·rō′ må)

ar·o·mat·ic   (ăr′ ŏ·măt′ ĭk)
-i·cal·ly
a·round   (á·round′)
a·rouse   (á·rouz′)
-rous·ing
ar·peg·gio   (är·pĕj′ ō)
ar·raign   (ă·rān′)
ar·raign·ment
ar·range   (ă·rānj′)
ar·rang·ing
ar·range·ment   ar·rang·er
ar·rant   (ăr′ ănt)
(notorious; see *errant*)
ar·ray   (ă·rā′)
ar·rears   (ă·rērz′)
ar·rest   (ă·rĕst′)
ar·rive   (ă·rīv′)
ar·riv·ing   ar·riv·al
ar·ro·gance   (ăr′ ŏ·gă̆ns)
-gant
ar·ro·gate   (ăr′ ŏ·gāt)
-gat·ing
ar·ro·ga·tion   (ăr′ ŏ·gā′ shŭn)
ar·row   (ăr′ ō)
ar·row·head
ar·se·nal   (är′ sĕ·nă̆l)
ar·se·nic   (är′ sĕ·nĭk)
ar·son   (är′ s'n)
ar·son·ist
ar·te·ri·al   (är·tēr′ ĭ·ă̆l)
ar·te·ri·o·scle·ro·sis
         (är·tē′ rĭ·ŏ·sklĕ·rō′ sĭs)
ar·ter·y   (är′ tēr·ĭ)
-ter·ies
ar·te·sian well   (är·tē′ zhă̆n)
art·ful   (ärt′ fŏŏl)
-ful·ly   -ful·ness
ar·thri·tis   (är·thrī′ tĭs)
ar·thrit·ic   (-thrĭt′ ĭk)
ar·ti·choke   (är′ tĭ·chōk)
ar·ti·cle   (är′ tĭ·k'l)
ar·tic·u·late   (är·tĭk′ ŭ·lăt)
         adj.
         (-lāt) *v.*
-lat·ing
ar·tic·u·late·ly   (-lăt·lĭ)
ar·tic·u·la·tion
         (är·tĭk′ ŭ·lā′ shŭn)
ar·tic·u·la·tive   (-lā′ tĭv)
ar·tic·u·la·tor   (-lā′ tēr)
ar·ti·fact   (är′ tĭ·făkt)
ar·ti·fice   (är′ tĭ·fĭs)
ar·ti·fi·cial   (är′ tĭ·fĭsh′ ă̆l)
ar·ti·fi·ci·al·i·ty
         (är′ tĭ·fĭsh′ ĭ·ăl′ ĭ·tĭ)

ar·ti·fi·cial·ly
ar·til·ler·y   (är·tĭl′ ēr·ĭ)
ar·til·ler·y·man
ar·ti·san   (är′ tĭ·ză̆n)
art·ist   (är′ tĭst)
ar·tis·tic   (är·tĭs′ tĭk)
art·ist·ry
art·less   (ärt′ lĕs)
Ār·y·an   (âr′ ĭ·ă̆n)
as·bes·tos   (ăs·bĕs′ tŏs)
as·cend   (ă·sĕnd′)
as·cend·ance   (ă·sĕn′ dă̆ns)
-an·cy   -ant
as·cen·sion   (ă·sĕn′ shŭn)
as·cent   (ă·sĕnt′)
(rise; see *assent*)
as·cer·tain   (ăs′ ēr·tān′)
as·cer·tain·a·ble
as·cer·tain·ment
as·cet·ic   (ă·sĕt′ ĭk)
(self-denying; see *aesthetic*)
as·cet·i·cism   (-ĭ·sĭz′m)
as·cot tie   (ăs′ kŏt)
as·cribe   (ăs·krīb′)
-crib·ing   as·crib·a·ble
as·crip·tion   (ăs·krĭp′ shŭn)
a·sep·tic   (á·sĕp′ tĭk)
ash   (ăsh)
ash·en   ash·es
a·shamed   (á·shāmd′)
a·sham·ed·ly   (á·shăm′ ĕd·lĭ)
Ā·sian   (ā·zhă̆n)
A·si·at·ic   (ā′ zhĭ·ăt′ ĭk)
a·side   (á·sīd′)
as·i·nine   (ăs′ ĭ·nīn)
as·i·nin·i·ty   (ăs′ ĭ·nĭn′ ĭ·tĭ)
a·skance   (á·skăns′)
a·skew   (á·skū′)
a·sleep   (á·slēp′)
as·par·a·gus   (ăs·păr′ á·gŭs)
as·pect   (ăs′ pĕkt)
as·pen   (ăs′ pĕn)
as·per·i·ty   (ăs·pĕr′ ĭ·tĭ)
-ties
as·per·sion   (ăs·pûr′ shŭn)
as·phalt   (ăs′ fôlt)
as·phyx·i·ate   (ăs·fĭk′ sĭ·āt)
-at·ing   as·phyx·i·a
as·phyx·i·a·tion
         (ăs·fĭk′ sĭ·ā′ shŭn)
as·pic   (ăs′ pĭk)
as·pir·ant   (ăs·pīr′ ă̆nt)
as·pi·rate   (ăs′ pĭ·rĭt) *n.*
-rat·ing   (-rāt) *v.*
as·pi·ra·tion   (ăs′ pĭ·rā′ shŭn)

as·pire (ăs·pīr′)
  -pir·ing
as·pi·rin (ăs′ pĭ·rĭn)
as·sail (ă·sāl′)
  as·sail·a·ble as·sail·ant
as·sas·sin (ă·săs′ ĭn)
  as·sas·si·nate
as·sault (ă·sôlt′)
  as·sault·er
as·say (ă·sā′)
  as·say·er
as·sem·ble (ă·sĕm′ b'l)
  -bling
  as·sem·blage (-blĭj)
as·sem·bly (ă·sĕm′ blĭ)
  -blies as·sem·bly line
  as·sem·bly·man
as·sent (ă·sĕnt′)
  (agree; see *ascent*)
  as·sent·or
as·sert (ă·sûrt′)
  as·ser·tion as·ser·tive·ness
as·sess (ă·sĕs′)
  as·sess·a·ble as·sess·ment
  as·ses·sor
as·set (ăs′ ĕt)
as·sid·u·ous (ă·sĭd′ û·ŭs)
  as·si·du·i·ty (ăs′ ĭ·dū′ ĭ·tĭ)
as·sign (ă·sīn′)
  as·sign·a·ble
  as·sign·ee (ăs′ ĭ·nē′)
  as·sign·er as·sign·ment
as·sig·na·tion (ăs′ ĭg·nā′ shŭn)
as·sim·i·late (ă·sĭm′ ĭ·lāt)
  -lat·ing
  as·sim·i·la·ble (-lă· b'l)
  as·sim·i·la·tion
      (ă·sĭm′ ĭ·lā′ shŭn)
  as·sim·i·la·tive (-lā′ tĭv)
  as·sim·i·la·to·ry (-lă·tō′ rĭ)
as·sist (ă·sĭst′)
  as·sist·ance as·sist·ant
as·so·ci·ate (ă·sō′ shĭ·āt) *v.*
  -at·ing (-ăt) *n., adj.*
  as·so·ci·a·ble (-shĭ·ă· b'l)
  as·so·ci·a·tion (ă·sō′ sĭ·ā′ shŭn)
  -tion·al
  as·so·ci·a·tive (-shĭ·ā′ tĭv)
as·so·nance (ăs′ ŏ·năns)
as·sort (ă·sôrt′)
  as·sort·ment
as·suage (ă·swāj′)
  as·suag·ing as·suage·ment
  as·sua·sive

as·sume (ă·sūm′)
  as·sum·ing
as·sump·tion (ă·sŭmp′ shŭn)
as·sure (ă·shoor′)
  as·sur·ing as·sur·ance
  as·sur·ed·ly as·sur·ed·ness
as·ter (ăs′ tēr)
as·ter·isk (ăs′ tēr·ĭsk)
as·ter·oid (ăs′ tēr·oid)
asth·ma (ăz′ mà)
  asth·mat·ic (ăz·măt′ ĭk)
a·stig·ma·tism (à·stĭg′ mà·tĭz'm)
  as·tig·mat·ic (ăs′ tĭg·măt′ ĭk)
as·ton·ish (ăs·tŏn′ ĭsh)
  as·ton·ish·ment
as·tound·ing (ăs·tound′ ĭng)
as·tral (ăs′ trăl)
a·stride (à·strīd′)
as·trin·gent (ăs·trĭn′ jĕnt)
  as·trin·gen·cy
as·trol·o·gy (ăs·trŏl′ ŏ·jĭ)
  as·tro·log·i·cal
      (ăs′ trŏ·lŏj′ ĭ·kăl)
as·tro·naut (ăs′ trŏ·nôt)
as·tron·o·my (ăs·trŏn′ ŏ·mĭ)
  as·tron·o·mer
  as·tro·nom·i·cal
      (ăs′ trŏ·nŏm′ ĭ·kăl)
as·tro·phys·ics (ăs′ trŏ·fĭz′ ĭks)
as·tute (ăs·tūt′)
  as·tute·ness
a·sun·der (à·sŭn′ dēr)
a·sy·lum (à·sī′ lŭm)
a·sym·me·try (à·sĭm′ ĕ·trĭ)
  -tries
at·a·vism (ăt′ à·vĭz'm)
a·the·ist (ā′ thē·ĭst)
  a·the·is·tic (ā′ thē·ĭs′ tĭk)
ath·lete (ăth′ lĕt)
  ath·let·ic (ăth·lĕt′ ĭk)
At·lan·tic (ăt·lăn′ tĭk)
at·las (ăt′ lăs)
at·mos·phere (ăt′ mŏs·fēr)
  at·mos·pher·ic (ăt′ mŏs·fĕr′ ĭk)
at·oll (ăt′ ŏl)
at·om (ăt′ ŭm)
  a·tom·ic (ă·tŏm′ ĭk)
at·om·ize (ăt′ ŭm·īz)
  -iz·ing
a·tone (à·tōn′)
  -ton·ing a·tone·ment
a·tro·cious (à·trō′ shŭs)
  a·troc·i·ty (à·trŏs′ ĭ·tĭ)
at·ro·phy (ăt′ rŏ·fĭ)
  -phied -phy·ing

at·tach (ă·tăch′)
  at·tach·a·ble at·tach·ment
at·ta·ché (ăt′ á·shā′)
at·tack (ă·tăk′)
at·tain (ă·tān′)
  at·tain·a·ble at·tain·ment
at·tain·der (ă·tān′ dĕr)
  (bill of)
at·tar (ăt′ ĕr)
at·tempt (ă·tĕmpt′)
  at·tempt·a·ble
at·tend (ă·tĕnd′)
  at·tend·ance -ant
at·ten·tion (ă·tĕn′ shŭn)
at·ten·tive (ă·tĕn′ tĭv)
  at·ten·tive·ness
at·ten·u·ate (ă·tĕn′ û·āt)
  -at·ing
  at·ten·u·a·tion
    (ă·tĕn′ û·ā′ shŭn)
at·test (ă·tĕst′)
  at·tes·ta·tion (ăt′ ĕs·tā′ shŭn)
at·tic (ăt′ ĭk)
at·tire (ă·tīr′)
  at·tir·ing at·tire·ment
at·ti·tude (ăt′ ĭ·tūd)
at·tor·ney (ă·tûr′ nĭ)
  -neys
at·tract (ă·trăkt′)
  at·tract·a·ble
  at·trac·tion (ă·trăk′ shŭn)
  at·trac·tive (ă·trăk′ tĭv)
  at·trac·tor
at·trib·ute (ă·trĭb′ ût) v.
  -ut·ing
at·tri·bute (ăt′ rĭ·būt) n.
  at·trib·ut·a·ble
    (ă·trĭb′ ût·á·b′l)
  at·tri·bu·tion (ăt′ rĭ·bū′ shŭn)
  at·trib·u·tive (ă·trĭb′ û·tĭv)
at·tri·tion (ă·trĭsh′ ŭn)
at·tune (ă·tūn′)
  at·tun·ing
au·burn (ô′ bĕrn)
Auck·land, (ôk′ lănd)
  New Zea·land
auc·tion (ôk′ shŭn)
  auc·tion·eer (ôk′ shŭn·ĕr′)
au·da·cious (ô·dā′ shŭs)
  au·dac·i·ty (ô·dăs′ ĭ·tĭ)
au·di·ble (ô′ dĭ·b′l)
  au·di·bil·i·ty (ô′ dĭ·bĭl′ ĭ·tĭ)
au·di·ence (ô′ dĭ·ĕns)
au·di·o-vis·u·al
    (ô′ dĭ·ō·vĭzh′ û·ăl)

au·dit (ô′ dĭt)
  -dit·ed -dit·ing
  au·dit·or
au·di·tion (ô·dĭsh′ ŭn)
au·di·to·ri·um (ô′ dĭ·tō′ rĭ·ŭm)
au·di·to·ry (ô′ dĭ·tō′ rĭ)
au·ger (ô′ gĕr)
  (tool; see augur)
aught (ôt)
  (cipher; see ought)
aug·ment (ôg·mĕnt′)
  aug·ment·a·ble
  aug·men·ta·tion
    (ôg′ mĕn·tā′ shŭn)
au gra·tin (ō′ gră′ tăN′)
au·gur (ô′ gĕr)
  (foretell; see auger)
  au·gu·ry
au·gust (ô·gŭst′)
  (stately; see August)
Au·gust (ô′ gŭst)
  (month; see august)
auld lang syne (ôld lăng sīn)
aunt (ănt)
au·ral (ô′ răl)
  (of the ear; see oral)
au·re·o·my·cin (ô′ rē·ō·mī′ sĭn)
au re·voir (ō′ rĕ·vwár′)
au·ro·ra bo·re·a·lis
    (ô·rō′ rá bō′ rē·ā′ lĭs)
aus·pi·ces (ôs′ pĭ·sĕz)
aus·pi·cious (ôs·pĭsh′ ŭs)
aus·tere (ôs·tēr′)
  aus·tere·ly
  aus·ter·i·ty (ôs·tĕr′ ĭ·tĭ)
Aus·tra·lia (ôs·trāl′ yá)
au·then·tic (ô·thĕn′ tĭk)
  au·then·ti·cal·ly
  au·then·ti·cate -cat·ing
  au·then·tic·i·ty
    (ô′ thĕn·tĭs′ ĭ·tĭ)
au·thor (ô′ thĕr)
  au·thor·ess
au·thor·i·tar·i·an
    (ô·thŏr′ ĭ·târ′ ĭ·ăn)
au·thor·i·ty (ô·thŏr′ ĭ·tĭ)
  -ties
  au·thor·i·ta·tive
au·thor·ize (ô′ thĕr·īz)
  -iz·ing
  au·thor·i·za·tion
    (ô′ thĕr·ĭ·zā′ shŭn)
au·to·bi·og·ra·phy
    (ô′ tô·bĭ·ŏg′ rá·fĭ)
  -phies

au·to·bi·o·graph·i·cal
    (ô′ tô·bī′ ô·grăf′ ĭ·kăl)
au·to·crat   (ô′ tô·krăt)
  au·toc·ra·cy   (ô·tŏk′ rá·sĭ)
  au·to·crat·ic   (ô′ tô·krăt′ ĭk)
au·to·graph   (ô′ tô·gráf)
au·to·mat   (ô′ tô·măt)
au·to·mat·ic   (ô′ tô·măt′ ĭk)
  au·to·mat·i·cal·ly
au·to·ma·tion   (ô′ tô·mā′ shŭn)
au·tom·a·ton   (ô·tŏm′ á·tŏn)
au·to·mo·bile   (ô′ tô·mô·bēl′)
  au·to·mo·tive   (ô′ tô·mō′ tĭv)
au·ton·o·my   (ô·tŏn′ ô·mĭ)
  au·ton·o·mous
au·top·sy   (ô′ tŏp·sĭ)
  -sies
au·to·sug·ges·tion
    (ô′ tô·sŭg·jĕs′ chŭn)
au·tumn   (ô′ tŭm)
  au·tum·nal   (ô·tŭm′ nál)
aux·il·ia·ry   (ôg·zĭl′ yá·rĭ)
  -ries
a·vail·a·ble   (á·vāl′ á·b′l)
a·vail·a·bil·i·ty
    (á·vāl′ á·bĭl′ ĭ·tĭ)
av·a·lanche   (ăv′ á·lánch)
a·vant-garde   (ā·vänt′ gärd′)
av·a·rice   (ăv′ á·rĭs)
  av·a·ri·cious   (ăv′ á·rĭsh′ ŭs)
a·venge   (á·vĕnj′)
  -veng·ing   a·veng·er
av·e·nue   (ăv′ ĕ·nū)
a·ver   (á·vûr′)
  -verred   -ver·ring
av·er·age   (ăv′ ēr·ĭj)
a·verse   (á·vûrs′)
  a·verse·ly
a·ver·sion   (á·vûr′ zhŭn)
a·vert   (á·vûrt′)
  a·vert·i·ble
a·vi·ar·y   (ā′ vĭ·ĕr′ ĭ)
  -ar·ies
a·vi·a·tion   (ā′ vĭ·ā′ shŭn)
a·vi·a·tor   (ā′ vĭ·ā′ tēr)
a·vi·a·trix   (ā′ vĭ·ā′ trĭks)
av·id   (ăv′ ĭd)
  a·vid·i·ty   (á·vĭd′ ĭ·tĭ)
av·o·ca·do   (ăv′ ô·kä′ dō)
  -dos
av·o·ca·tion   (ăv′ ô·kā′ shŭn)
a·void   (á·void′)
  a·void·a·ble   a·void·ance
av·oir·du·pois   (ăv′ ēr·dŭ·poiz′)

a·vow   (á·vou′)
  a·vow·al
a·wak·en   (á·wāk′ ĕn)
a·ware·ness   (á·wâr′ nĕs)
awe   (ô)
  awe·some   awe-strick·en
  aw·ing
a·weigh   (á·wā′)
aw·ful   (ô′ fŏŏl)
  -ful·ly   -ful·ness
awk·ward   (ôk′ wĕrd)
awl   (ôl)
awn·ing   (ôn′ ĭng)
a·wry   (á·rī′)
ax   (ăks)
  ax·es
ax·i·al   (ăk′ sĭ·ăl)
ax·i·om   (ăk′ sĭ·ŭm)
  ax·i·o·mat·ic   (ăk′ sĭ·ô·măt′ ĭk)
ax·is   (ăk′ sĭs)
  pl. ax·es   (-sēz)
ax·le   (ăk′ s′l)
a·zal·ea   (á·zāl′ yá)
az·ure   (ăzh′ ēr)

B

bab·ble   (băb′ ′l)
  bab·bling
ba·boon   (bă·bōōn′)
ba·bush·ka   (bá·bŏŏsh′ ká)
ba·by   (bā′ bĭ)
  -bies   ba·bies′-breath
  ba·by·hood   ba·by·ish
  ba·by-sit   ba·by sit·ter
Bab·y·lon   (băb′ ĭ·lŏn)
  Bab·y·lo·ni·an
    (băb′ ĭ·lō′ nĭ·ăn)
bac·ca·lau·re·ate
    (băk′ á·lô′ rē·ăt)
bach·e·lor   (băch′ ĕ·lēr)
ba·cil·lus   (bá·sĭl′ ŭs)
  pl. ba·cil·li   (-ī)
back   (băk)
  back·bite   back·bone
  back·gam·mon back·ground
  back·hand·ed   back·log
  back·stairs   back·stop
  back·stroke   back·talk
  back·ward   back·wa·ter
  back·woods
  back·woods·man
ba·con   (bā′ kŭn)

bac·te·ri·a (băk·tẽr′ ĭ·á)
  sing. bac·te·ri·um
  bac·te·ri·al
bac·te·ri·ol·o·gy
    (băk·tẽr′ ĭ·ŏl′ ŏ·jĭ)
  bac·te·ri·ol·o·gist
badg·er (băj′ ẽr)
bad·i·nage (băd′ ĭ·năzh′)
bad·min·ton (băd′ mĭn′ t′n)
baf·fle (băf′ ′l)
  baf·fling baf·fle·ment
bag·a·telle (băg′ á·tĕl′)
bag·gage (băg′ ĭj)
bag·gy (băg′ĭ)
Bagh·dad, I·raq (băg′ dăd)
ba·guette (bá·gĕt′)
Ba·ha·ma is. (bá·hä′ má)
  Ba·ha·mi·an (-mĭ·ắn)
bail (bāl)
  (set free; see *bale*)
bail·iff (bāl′ ĭf)
bail·i·wick (bāl′ ĭ·wĭk)
bait (bāt)
  (a lure; see *bate*)
bak·er·y (bāk′ ẽr·ĭ)
  -er·ies
bal·ance (băl′ ắns)
  -anc·ing
bal·co·ny (băl′ kŏ·nĭ)
  -nies
bald-head·ed (bôld′ hĕd′ ĕd)
bale (bāl)
  (bundle; see *bail*)
  bal·ing
bale·ful (bāl′ fŏŏl)
Bal·e·ar·ic (is.) (băl′ ê·ăr′ ĭk)
Ba·li (bä′ lĕ)
  Ba·li·nese (bä′ lĕ·nēz′)
balk·y (bôk′ ĭ)
ball (bôl)
  ball-and-sock·et joint
  ball bear·ing ball-point pen
  ball·room
bal·lad (băl′ ắd)
bal·last (băl′ ắst)
bal·le·ri·na (băl′ ĕ·rē′ ná)
bal·let (băl′ ắ)
bal·lis·tic (bắ·lĭs′ tĭk)
bal·loon (bắ lŏŏn′)
bal·lot (băl′ ŭt)
bal·ly·hoo (băl′ ĭ·hŏŏ)
balm (bäm)
  balm·i·ness
bal·sa (bôl′ sá)
bal·sam (bôl′ săm)

bal·us·trade (băl′ ŭs·trād′)
bam·boo (băm·bŏŏ′)
bam·boo·zle (băm·bŏŏ′ z′l)
  -zling
ba·nal (bā′ nắl)
  ba·nal·i·ty (bá·năl′ ĭ·tĭ)
  ba·nal·ly
ba·nan·a (bá·năn′ á)
band·age (băn′ dĭj)
  -ag·ing
ban·dan·na (băn·dăn′ á)
ban·deau (băn·dō′)
ban·dit (băn′ dĭt)
  ban·dit·ry
band·stand (bănd′ stănd′)
ban·dy (băn′ dĭ)
  -died -dy·ing
  ban·dy-leg·ged
bane·ful (bān′ fŏŏl)
Banff, Can. (bămf)
Bang·kok, (băng′ kŏk)
  Thai·land
ban·ish (băn′ ĭsh)
ban·is·ter (băn′ ĭs·tẽr)
ban·jo (băn′ jō)
  -jos
bank·rupt (băngk′ rŭpt)
  bank·rupt·cy (-rŭpt·sĭ)
ban·ner (băn′ ẽr)
ban·quet (băng′ kwĕt)
  -quet·ed
ban·shee (băn′ shē)
ban·tam (băn′ tăm)
  ban·tam·weight
ban·ter·ing (băn′ tẽr·ĭng)
bap·tism (băp′ tĭz′m)
  bap·tis·mal (băp·tĭz′ măl)
  Bap·tist bap·tize
Bar·ba·dos (is.) (bär·bā′ dōz)
bar·bar·i·an (bär·bâr′ ĭ·đa)
  bar·bar·ic (bär·bâr′ ĭk)
  bar·ba·rism (bär′ bá·rĭz′m)
  bar·bar·i·ty (bär·bâr′ ĭ·tĭ)
  -ties
  bar·ba·rous (bär′ bá·rŭs)
bar·be·cue (bär′ bĕ·kū)
  -cu·ing
bar·ber (bär′ bĕr)
bar·bi·tu·rate (bär′ bĭ·tū′ rāt)
bar·ca·role (bär′ ká·rōl)
bare (bâr)
  bar·ing bare·ly
  bare·back bare·head·eđ
bar·gain (bär′ gĭn)
  bar·gain·er

barge (bärj)
  barg·ing
bar·i·tone (băr′ ĭ·tōn)
bar·keep·er (bär′ kēp′ ẽr)
bar·ley (bär′ lĭ)
bar·na·cle (bär′ nȧ·k'l)
ba·rom·e·ter (bȧ·rŏm′ ē·tẽr)
  bar·o·met·ric (băr′ ō·mĕt′ rĭk)
bar·on (băr′ ŭn)
  (nobleman; see *barren*)
  bar·on·age (-ĭj)
  bar·on·ess
  ba·ro·ni·al (bȧ·rō′ nĭ·ȧl)
ba·roque (bȧ·rōk′)
bar·racks (băr′ ȧks)
bar·ra·cu·da (băr′ ȧ·kōō′ dȧ)
  n. sing. & pl.
bar·rage (bȧ·räzh′)
bar·rel (băr′ ĕl)
  bar·reled bar·rel chair
  bar·rel house bar·rel or·gan
bar·ren (băr′ ĕn)
  (sterile; see *baron*)
  bar·ren·ness
bar·ri·cade (băr′ ĭ·kād′)
  -cad·ing
bar·ri·er (băr′ ĭ·ẽr)
bar·ris·ter (băr′ ĭs·tẽr)
bar·room (băr′ rōōm′)
bar·tend·er (băr′ tĕn′ dẽr)
bar·ter (băr′ tẽr)
bas·al me·tab·o·lism
    (bās′dl mē·tăb′ō·lĭz'm)
ba·salt (bȧ·sôlt′)
  ba·sal·tic (bȧ·sôl′ tĭk)
base (bās)
  bas·ing base·ball
  base·board base·less
  base·ly base·ment
  base·mind·ed
bash·ful (băsh′ fŏŏl)
  bash·ful·ly -ful·ness
bas·ic (bās′ ĭk)
  bas·i·cal·ly
bas·il (băz′ ĭl)
ba·sil·i·ca (bȧ·sĭl′ ĭ·kȧ)
ba·sin (bā′ s'n)
ba·sis (bā′ sĭs)
  pl. ba·ses (-sēz)
bas·ket (bás′ kĕt)
  bas·ket·ball bas·ket·ful
  bas·ket·ry
bas-re·lief (bä′ rē·lēf′)
bass (bās)
  bass clef bass drum

bass vi·ol
bas·set hound (băs′ ĕt)
bas·si·net (băs′ ĭ·nĕt′)
bas·so (bás′ ō)
bas·soon (bȧ·sōōn′)
bas·tard (băs′ tẽrd)
baste (bāst)
  bast·ing
bas·tille (băs·tēl′)
bas·tion (băs′ chŭn)
batch (băch)
bate (bāt)
  (to reduce; see *bait*)
  bat·ing
bathe (bāth) *v.*
  bath·ing
ba·tiste (bȧ·tēst′)
ba·ton (bȧ·tŏn′)
Bat·on Rouge, (băt′ 'n rōōzh′)
  La.
bat·tal·ion (bȧ·tăl′ yŭn)
bat·ten (băt′ 'n)
bat·ter·y (băt′ ẽr·ĭ)
  bat·ter·ies
bat·tle (băt′ 'l)
  bat·tling bat·tle-ax
  bat·tle cruis·er bat·tle cry
  bat·tle·field bat·tle·ground
  bat·tle·ship
bau·ble (bô′ b'l)
baux·ite (bôks′ ĭt)
bawd (bôd)
  bawd·i·ness bawd·y
bawl·ing (bôl′ ĭng)
bay·o·net (bā′ ō·nĕt)
bay·ou (bī′ ōō)
ba·zaar (bȧ·zär′)
  (market; see *bizarre*)
ba·zoo·ka (bȧ·zōō′ kȧ)
beach (bēch)
  (seashore; see *beech*)
  beach·comb·er beach·head
  beach wag·on
bea·con (bē′ kŭn)
bead·y (bēd′ ĭ)
bea·gle (bē′ g'l)
bear·a·ble (bâr′ ȧ·b'l)
beard (bērd)
beast·ly (bēst′ lĭ)
  bes·tial (bĕst′ yȧl)
be·at·i·fy (bē·ăt′ ĭ·fĭ)
  (canonize)
  -fied -fy·ing
be·at·i·fi·ca·tion
    (bē·ăt′ ĭ·fĭ·kā′ shŭn)

beau (bō)
   pl. beaux (bōz)
beau·ty (bū′ tĭ)
  -ties
  beau·te·ous (bū′ tĕ·ŭs)
  beau·ti·cian (bū·tĭsh′ ăn)
  beau·ti·ful -ful·ly
  beau·ti·fy -fied, -fy·ing
beaux-arts (bō′ zár′)
bea·ver (bĕ′ vĕr)
be·calm (bĕ·käm)
be·cause (bĕ·kôz′)
Bech·u·a·na·land
    (bĕch′ ŏŏ·ä′ nä·länd′)
beck·on·ing (bĕk′ ŭn·ĭng)
be·come (bĕ·kŭm′)
  -com·ing
bed (bĕd)
  bed·ded bed·ding
  bed·bug bed·clothes
  bed·fel·low bed lamp
  bed lin·en bed pad
  bed·post bed·rid·den
  bed·roll bed·room
  bed sheet bed·side
  bed·spread bed·stead
  bed·time bed warm·er
be·daub (bĕ·dôb′)
bed·lam (bĕd′ lăm)
Bed·ou·in (bĕd′ ŏŏ·ĭn)
be·drag·gled (bĕ·drăg′ ′ld)
beech (bēch)
  (tree; see *beach*)
beef·steak (bēf′ stāk′)
bee·hive (bē′ hīv′)
bee·keep·ing (bē′ kēp′ ĭng)
Be·el·ze·bub (bĕ·ĕl′ zĕ·bŭb′)
beet (bēt)
  (vegetable)
Bee·tho·ven, (vän bā′ tŏ′ vĕn)
  Lud·wig van
bee·tle (bē′ t′l)
  bee·tle-browed
be·fit (bĕ·fĭt′)
  -fit·ted -fit·ting
be·fore·hand (bĕ·fôr′ hănd′)
be·fud·dle (bĕ·fŭd′ ′l)
  -fud·dling be·fud·dle·ment
beg·gar (bĕg′ ĕr)
be·gin (bĕ·gĭn′)
  -gan -gin·ning
  be·gin·ner
be·go·ni·a (bĕ·gō′ nĭ·à)
be·grudge (bĕ·grŭj′)
  -grudg·ing

be·guile (bĕ·gīl′)
  -guil·ing be·guile·ment
be·half (bĕ·häf′)
be·have (bĕ·hāv′)
  -hav·ing
  be·hav·ior (bĕ·hāv′ yĕr)
be·hest (bĕ·hĕst′)
be·hind (bĕ·hīnd′)
be·hold·en (bĕ·hōl′ d′n)
be·hoove (bĕ·hōōv′)
  -hoov·ing
beige (bāzh)
be·ing (bē′ ĭng)
Bei·rut, (bā·rōōt′)
  Leb·a·non
be·la·bor (bĕ·lā′ bĕr)
be·lat·ed·ly (bĕ·lāt′ ĕd·lĭ)
belch (bĕlch)
be·lea·guer (bĕ·lē′ gĕr)
bel·fry (bĕl′ frĭ)
  -fries
Bel·gium (bĕl′ jŭm)
  Bel·gian (bĕl′ jăn)
be·lie (bĕ·lī′)
  -lied -ly·ing
be·lief (bĕ·lēf′)
be·lieve (bĕ·lēv′)
  -liev·ing be·liev·a·ble
  be·liev·er
be·lit·tle (bĕ·lĭt′′ l)
  -lit·tling be·lit·tle·ment
bel·la·don·na (bĕl′ à·dŏn′ à)
belles-let·tres (bĕl′ lĕt′ r′)
bell·hop (bĕl′ hŏp′)
bel·li·cose (bĕl′ ĭ·kōs)
bel·lig·er·ence (bĕ·lĭj′ ĕr·ĕns)
  -en·cy -ent
bel·lows (bĕl′ ōz)
bell·weth·er (bĕl′ wĕth′ ĕr)
be·long·ing (bĕ·lông′ ĭng)
be·lov·ed (bĕ·lŭv′ ĕd)
be·low (bĕ·lō′)
be·muse (bĕ·mūz′)
  -mus·ing
be·neath (bĕ·nēth′)
Ben·e·dic·tine (bĕn′ ĕ·dĭk′ tĭn)
  (pron. -tĕn when referring to the
  drink of this name.)
ben·e·dic·tion (bĕn′ ĕ·dĭk′ shŭn)
  ben·e·dic·to·ry
ben·e·fac·tor (bĕn′ ĕ·făk′ tĕr)
  ben·e·fac·tress
be·nef·i·cence (bĕ·nĕf′ ĭ·sĕns)
  -cent

ben·e·fi·cial (bĕn′ ĕ·fĭsh′ ăl)
  -cial·ly
ben·e·fi·ci·ar·y
      (bĕn′ ĕ·fĭsh′ ĭ·ĕr′ ĭ)
  -ar·ies
ben·e·fit (bĕn′ ĕ·fĭt)
  -fit·ed -fit·ing
be·nev·o·lence (bĕ·nĕv′ ŏ·lĕns)
  -lent
Ben-Gur·ion, (bĕn′ gŏŏr·yôn′)
  Da·vid
be·nign (bĕ·nīn′)
  be·nig·nant (bĕ·nĭg′ nănt)
  -nan·cy
  be·nig·ni·ty (bĕ·nĭg′ nĭ·tĭ)
  -ties
be·numb (bĕ·nŭm′)
  -numbed
Ben·zed·rine (bĕn·zĕd′ rēn)
ben·zine (bĕn′ zēn)
  (cleaning fluid)
be·queath (bĕ·kwēth′)
be·quest (bĕ·kwĕst′)
be·rate (bĕ·rāt′)
  -rat·ing
be·reave (bĕ·rēv′)
  -reav·ing be·reave·ment
be·ret (bĕ·rā′)
ber·i·ber·i (bĕr′ ĭ·bĕr′ ĭ)
Be·ring (strait) (bĕr′ ĭng)
Berke·ley, Calif. (bûrk′ lĭ)
ber·ry (bĕr′ ĭ)
  ber·ries
ber·serk (bûr′ sûrk)
berth (bûrth)
  (a bunk; see *birth*)
be·seech·ing (bĕ·sēch′ ing)
be·set (bĕ·sĕt′)
  -set·ting
be·side (bĕ·sīd′)
be·siege (bĕ·sēj′)
  -sieg·ing
be·smear (bĕ·smēr′)
be·smirch (bĕ·smûrch′)
be·speak (bĕ·spēk′)
best (bĕst)
  best-known best-liked
  best man best sel·ler
  best-sell·ing
bes·tial (bĕst′ yăl)
  bes·ti·al·i·ty (bĕs′ tĭ·ăl′ ĭ·tĭ)
be·stow (bĕ·stō′)
be·ta ray (bē′ tá)
Be·thes·da, Md. (bĕ·thĕz′ dá)
Beth·le·hem, Pa. (bĕth′ lĕ·ĕm′)

be·tide (bĕ·tīd′)
be·tray (bĕ·trā′)
  -trayed -tray·ing
  be·tray·al be·tray·er
be·troth (bĕ·trŏth′)
  be·troth·al
bet·ter·ment (bĕt′ ēr·mĕnt)
be·tween (bĕ·twēn′)
be·twixt (bĕ·twĭkst′)
bev·el (bĕv′ ĕl)
  -eled -el·ing
bev·er·age (bĕv′ ēr·ĭj)
Bev·er·ly Hills, (bĕv′ ēr·lĭ)
  Calif.
bev·y (bĕv′ ĭ)
  bev·ies
be·wail (bĕ·wāl′)
  -wailed -wail·ing
be·ware (bĕ·wâr′)
be·wil·der·ing (bĕ·wĭl′ dēr·ĭng)
be·witch·ing (bĕ·wĭch′ ĭng)
be·yond (bĕ·yŏnd′)
bi·an·nu·al (bī·ăn′ û·ăl)
  (occurring twice a year; see
  biennial)
  bi·an·nu·al·ly
bi·as (bī′ ăs)
  bi·ased
Bi·ble (bī′ b'l)
  Bib·li·cal (bĭb′ lĭ·kăl)
bib·li·og·ra·phy
     (bĭb′ lĭ·ŏg′ rá·fĭ)
  -phies
  bib·li·o·graph·i·cal
     (bĭb′ lĭ·ŏ·grăf′ ĭ·kăl)
bib·u·lous (bĭb′ û·lŭs)
  (tippling; see *bilious*)
bi·cam·er·al (bī·kăm′ ēr·ăl)
bi·car·bon·ate (bī·kär′ bŏn·āt)
bi·cen·ten·ni·al (bī′ sĕn·tĕn′ ĭ·ăl)
bi·ceps (bī′ sĕps)
bick·er·ing (bĭk′ ēr·ĭng)
bi·cy·cle (bī′ sĭk'l)
  bi·cy·cling bi·cy·clist
bid (bĭd)
  bid·ding bid·da·ble
  bid·den
bide (bīd)
  bid·ing
bi·en·ni·al (bī·ĕn′ ĭ·ăl)
  (once in two years; see *biannual*)
  bi·en·ni·al·ly bi·en·ni·um
bier (bēr)
  (coffin)
bi·fo·cal (bī·fō′ kăl)

big·a·my (bĭg′ ȧ·mĭ)
  big·a·mist big·a·mous
big·ot (bĭg′ ŭt)
  -ot·ed big·ot·ry
big·wig (bĭg′ wĭg′)
bi·ki·ni (bĭ·kē′ nĭ)
bi·lat·er·al (bĭ·lăt′ ēr·ȧl)
  -al·ly
bilge wa·ter (bĭlj)
bi·lin·e·ar (bĭ·lĭn′ ê·ēr)
bi·lin·gual (bĭ·lĭng′ gwȧl)
  bi·lin·guist
bil·ious (bĭl′ yŭs)
  (ill-tempered; see bibulous)
bilk (bĭlk)
bill·board (bĭl′ bōrd′)
bil·let (bĭl′ ĕt)
  bil·let·ed
bil·let-doux (bĭl′ ȧ·dōō′)
bill·fold (bĭl′ fōld′)
bil·liards (bĭl′ yērdz)
bil·lion (bĭl′ yŭn)
bill of: (bĭl ŏv)
  bill of fare bill of lad·ing
  bill of rights bill of sale
bil·low (bĭl′ ō)
bi·me·tal·lic (bī′ mė·tăl′ ĭk)
bi·month·ly (bī·mŭnth′ lĭ)
  (once in two months)
bi·na·ry (bī′ nȧ·rĭ)
bin·au·ral (bĭn·ô′ rȧl)
bind·er·y (bīn′ dēr·ĭ)
  -er·ies
bin·oc·u·lars (bĭn·ŏk′ û·lērz)
bi·o·chem·is·try
    (bī′ ô·kĕm′ ĭs·trĭ)
  bi·o·chem·ist
bi·og·ra·phy (bī·ŏg′ rȧ·fĭ)
  -phies
  bi·o·graph·i·cal
    (bī′ ô·grăf′ ĭ·kȧl)
bi·ol·o·gy (bī·ŏl′ ô·jĭ)
  bi·o·log·i·cal (bī′ ô·lŏj′ ĭ·kȧl)
  -cal·ly
bi·o·syn·the·sis
    (bī′ ô·sĭn′ thê·sĭs)
bi·par·ti·san·ship
    (bī·pär′ tĭ·zȧn·shĭp′)
bi·par·tite (bī·pär′ tīt)
bi·po·lar (bī·pō′ lēr)
  bi·po·lar·i·ty (bī′ pō·lăr′ ĭ·tĭ)
birch (bûrch)
bird (bûrd)
  bird dog bird·house

bird of par·a·dise
bird of prey bird's-eye view
bird watch·er
bird·ie (bûr′ dĭ)
  (golf term)
birth (bûrth)
  (origin; see berth)
  birth·day birth·mark
  birth·place birth rate
  birth·right birth·stone
Bis·cayne Bay, (bĭs′kān)
  Fla.
bis·cuit (bĭs′ kĭt)
bi·sect (bī′ sĕkt′)
  bi·sec·tion·al (bī·sĕk′ shŭn·ȧl)
bi·sex·u·al (bī·sĕk′ shōō·ȧl)
bish·op (bĭsh′ ŭp)
  bish·op·ric
Bis·marck, (bĭz′ märk)
  N. Dak.
bi·son (bī′ s'n)
bisque (bĭsk)
bite (bīt)
  bit·ing
  bit·ten (bĭt′ 'n)
bit·ter (bĭt′ ēr)
  bit·ter·ness bit·ter·sweet
bi·tu·mi·nous (bī·tū′ mĭ·nŭs)
  coal
biv·ouac (bĭv′ wăk)
  -ouacked -ouack·ing
bi·week·ly (bī·wēk′ lĭ)
bi·zarre (bĭ·zär′)
  (odd; see bazaar)
  bi·zarre·ly
black (blăk)
  black·ball black·ber·ry
  black·board Black Death
  black·ened
  black-eyed Su·san
  black·head black-list v.
  black mag·ic black·mail
  black mar·ket·eer
  black·out black sheep
  black·smith
blad·der (blăd′ ēr)
blame (blām)
  blam·ing blam·a·ble
  blame·less
  blame·wor·thi·ness
blan·dish·ment (blăn′ dĭsh·mĕnt)
blan·ket (blăng′ kĕt)
  -ket·ed -ket·ing
blar·ney (blär′ nĭ)
bla·sé (blä·zā′)

blas·phe·my   (blăs′ fĕ·mĭ)
  -mies
blas·phem·er   (blăs·fĕm′ ĕr)
blas·phe·mous   (blăs′ fĕ·mŭs)
bla·tant   (blā′ tănt)
  -tan·cy
blaz·er   (blāz′ ĕr)
bla·zon   (blā′ z'n)
  bla·zon·ry
bleach   (blēch)
bleach·ers   (blēch′ ĕrz)
bleak   (blēk)
blear·y   (blēr′ ĭ)
bleat   (blēt)
bleed   (blēd)
blem·ish   (blĕm′ ĭsh)
bless   (blĕs)
  bless·ed·ness
blight   (blīt)
blind   (blīnd)
  blind·fold
  blind·man's buff
blink·er   (blĭngk′ ĕr)
bliss   (blĭs)
blis·ter   (blĭs′ tĕr)
blithe   (blīth)
  blithe·ly
blitz·krieg   (blĭts′ krēg′)
bliz·zard   (blĭz′ ĕrd)
bloat   (blōt)
bloc   (blŏk)
  (political group)
block   (blŏk)
  block·bust·er   block·head
  block·house
block·ade   (blŏk·ād′)
  block·ade-run·ner
blond   (blŏnd)
  adj. & n. masc.
blonde   (blŏnd) *n. fem.*
blood   (blŭd)
  blood·cur·dling
  blood·hound   blood·ied
  blood·i·est   blood pres·sure
  blood·shed
  blood·thirst·i·ness
  blood ves·sel
bloom·er   (bloom′ ĕr)
blos·som   (blŏs′ ŭm)
blot   (blŏt)
  blot·ting   blot·ter
blotch   (blŏch)
  blotch·es   blotch·y
blow   (blō)

blow·gun   blow·out
blow·pipe   blow·up
blown   (blōn)
blowz·y   (blouz′ ĭ)
blub·ber   (blŭb′ ĕr)
bludg·eon   (blŭj′ ŭn)
blue   (bloō)
  blue·ber·ry   blue·bird
  blue blood   blue·bon·net
  blue book   blue chip
  blue-eyed   blue·grass
  blue jay   blue laws
  blue-pen·cil *v.*   blue·print
bluff   (blŭf)
blu·ing   (bloō′ ĭng)
blun·der·buss   (blŭn′ dĕr·bŭs)
blur   (blûr)
  blurred   blur·ry
blurb   (blûrb)
blurt   (blûrt)
boa con·stric·tor   (bō′ à)
boar   (bōr)
  (hog; see *bore*)
board·er   (bōr′ dĕr)
  (one who boards; see *border*)
  board·ing·house
  board·ing school
boast   (bōst)
  boast·ful   -ful·ly
boat·swain   (bō′ s'n)
bob·bin   (bŏb′ ĭn)
bob·by-sox   (bŏb′ ĭ·sŏks′)
  bobby-sox·er
bob·o·link   (bŏb′ ô·lĭngk)
bob·sled   (bŏb′ slĕd′)
bob·tail   (bŏb′ tāl′)
Bo·ca Ra·ton,   (bō′ kà rà·tōn′)
  Fla.
bock beer   (bŏk)
bode   (bōd)
  bod·ing
bod·ice   (bŏd′ ĭs)
bod·y   (bŏd′ ĭ)
  bod·ies   bod·ied
  bod·i·less
  bod·i·ly   (bŏd′ ĭ·lĭ)
  bod·y·guard
Boer   (boōr)
bo·gey   (bō′ gĭ)
  (golf term)   -geys
bog·gle   (bŏg′ 'l)
  bog·gling
bo·gus   (bō′ gŭs)
bo·gy   (bō′ gĭ)
  (goblin)   -gies

Bo·he·mi·an   (bǒ·hē′ mǐ·ɑ̇n)
boil·er   (boil′ ēr)
bois·ter·ous   (bois′ tēr·ŭs)
bold-faced   (bōld′ fāst′)
bo·le·ro   (bǒ·lâr′ ō)
Bo·liv·i·a   (bǒ·lǐv′ ǐ·ȧ)
boll wee·vil   (bōl)
bo·lo·ney   (bǒ·lō′ nǐ)
  (also baloney)
Bol·she·vik   (bŏl′ shě·vǐk)
bol·ster   (bōl′ stēr)
bomb   (bŏm)
  bomb·proof   bomb·shell
  bomb shel·ter   bomb·sight
bom·bard   (bŏm·bärd′)
bom·bard·ier   (bŏm′bēr·dēr′)
bom·bast   (bŏm′ băst)
  bom·bas·tic   (bŏm·băs′ tǐk)
bo·na fi·de   (bō′ nȧ fī′ dè)
bo·nan·za   (bǒ·năn′ zȧ)
Bo·na·parte, Na·po·le·on
       (bō′ nȧ·pärt, nȧ·pō′ lě·ŭn)
bond   (bŏnd)
  bond·hold·er   bond·man
  bond ser·vant
bond·age   (bŏn′ dǐj)
bon·fire   (bŏn′ fīr′)
bon·net   (bŏn′ ĕt)
  bon·net·ed
bon·ny   (bŏn′ ǐ)
bo·nus   (bō′ nŭs)
  -nus·es
bon voy·age   (bôɴ′ vwȧ′ yȧzh′)
bon·y   (bŏn′ ǐ)
  bon·i·ness
boob·y trap   (boo′ bǐ)
book   (book)
  book·bind·er   book·case
  book end   book·keep·er
  book·keep·ing   book·let
  book·lov·er
  book·mak·er   (bookie)
  book·mark   book·mo·bile
  book re·view   book·shelf
  book·store   book val·ue
  book·worm
boom·er·ang   (boom′ ēr·ăng)
boon·dog·gle   (boon′ dŏg′′ l)
  -dog·gling
boor·ish   (boor′ ǐsh)
boost·er   (boos′ tēr)
boot   (boot)
  boot·black   boot·leg
  boot·leg·ger   boot·lick·er

boot·ee   (boo′ tě′)
  (baby's boot)
boo·ty   (boo′ tǐ)
  (plunder)
booze   (booz)
bo·rax   (bō′ răks)
Bor·deaux   (bôr′ dō′)
bor·del·lo   (bôr·děl′ ō)
bor·der   (bôr′ dēr)
  (edge: see boarder)
  bor·der·line adj.
bore   (bōr)
  (dull person; see boar)
  bor·ing   bore·dom
bo·ric acid   (bō′ rǐk)
born   (bôrn)
  (given birth)
borne   (bōrn)
  (carried)
bo·ron   (bō′ rǒn)
bor·ough   (bûr′ ō)
  (town)
bor·row   (bŏr′ ō)
borsch   (bôrsh)
bos·om   (booz′ ŭm)
boss·y   (bŏs′ ǐ)
  boss·i·ness
bot·a·ny   (bŏt′ ȧ·nǐ)
  bo·tan·i·cal   (bǒ·tăn′ ǐ·kȧl)
  bot·a·nist   (bŏt′ ȧ·nǐst)
botch   (bŏch)
  botch·er·y
both·er·some   (bŏth′ ēr·sŭm)
bot·tle   (bŏt′ ′l)
  bot·tling   bot·tle-fed
  bot·tle·neck   bot·tle wash·er
bot·tom   (bŏt′ ŭm)
bot·u·lism   (bŏt′ ū·lǐz′m)
bou·clé   (boo′ klā′)
bou·doir   (boo′ dwär)
bough   (bou)
bought   (bôt)
bouil·la·baise   (boo(l)′ yȧ·bās′)
bouil·lon   (boo′ yôɴ′)
  (soup; see bullion)
boul·der   (bōl′ dēr)
bou·le·vard   (boo′ lě·värd)
bounce   (bouns)
  bounc·ing   bounc·er
bound·a·ry   (boun′ dȧ·rǐ)
  -ries
bound·less   (bound′ lěs)
boun·te·ous   (boun′ tě·ŭs)
boun·ty   (boun′ tǐ)
  -ties

boun·ti·ful   -ful·ly
bou·quet   (boo·kā′)
bour·bon   (boor′ bŭn)
bour·geois   (boor′ zhwä′)
  bour·geoi·sie   (boor′ zhwà′ zē′)
bou·ton·niere   (boo′ tŏ·nyâr′)
bo·vine   (bō′ vīn)
bowd·ler·ize   (boud′ lĕr·īz)
  -iz·ing
Bow·doin (coll.)   (bō′ d′n)
bow·el   (bou′ ĕl)
bow·er   (bou′ ĕr)
bow·er·y   (bou′ ĕr·ĭ)
  -er·ies
bow·ie knife   (bō′ ĭ)
bow·knot   (bō′ nŏt′)
bow·leg·ged   (bō′ lĕg′ ĕd)
bowl·ing al·ley   (bōl′ ĭng)
bow·string   (bō′ strĭng′)
box   (bŏks)
  box·car   box eld·er
  box·ing glove   box kite
  box of·fice   box spring
boy·cott   (boi′ kŏt)
boy·sen·ber·ry   (boi′ s′n·bĕr′ ĭ)
  -ber·ries
brace·let   (brās′ lĕt)
brac·ing   (brās′ ĭng)
brack·et   (brăk′ ĕt)
  -et·ed   -et·ing
brack·ish   (brăk′ ĭsh)
brag   (brăg)
  brag·ging
  brag·ga·do·ci·o
     (brăg′ à·dō′ shĭ·ō)
  brag·gart
Brahms, Jo·han·nes
     (brämz, yŏ·hän′ ĕs)
braid   (brād)
Braille   (brāl)
brain   (brān)
  brain·i·ness   brain·less
  brain storm   brain·wash·ing
  brain·y
brake   (brāk)
  (to slow down; see *break*)
  brak·ing   brake·man
bram·ble   (brăm′ b′l)
bran·dish   (brăn′ dĭsh)
brand-new   (brănd′ nū′)
bran·dy   (brăn′ dĭ)
  -died
Bra·si·lia,   (brà·zēl′ yà)
  Bra·zil
bras·sière   (brà·zẹr′)

brass·y   (brás′ ĭ)
  brass·i·ness
bra·va·do   (brá·vä′ dō)
brav·er·y   (brāv′ ĕr·ĭ)
bra·vo   (brä′ vō)
  -voes
bra·vu·ra   (brà·vū′ rà)
brawl   (brôl)
  brawl·er
brawn·y   (brôn′ ĭ)
  brawn·i·ness
bra·zen   (brā′ z′n)
  bra·zen·ness
Bra·zil·ian   (brà·zĭl′ yăn)
breach   (brēch)
  (violation; see *breech*)
bread·bas·ket   (brĕd′ bás′ kĕt)
breadth   (brĕdth)
  (width)
break   (brāk)
  (burst; see *brake*)
  break·a·ble   break·age (-ĭj)
  break·down   break·through
  break·up   break·wa·ter
break·fast   (brĕk′ fást)
breast·bone   (brĕst′ bōn′)
breath   (brĕth)
  breath·less   breath-tak·ing
breathe   (brēth) *v.*
  breath·ing
breech   (brēch)
  (rear; see *breach*)
breech·es   (brĭch′ ĕz)
breed·ing   (brĕd′ ĭng)
breeze   (brēz)
  breeze·way   breez·y
  breez·i·er   -i·est
  -i·ly   -i·ness
breth·ren   (brĕth′ rĕn)
bre·vet   (brĕ·vĕt′)
  -vet·ted   -vet·ting
bre·vi·ar·y   (brē′ vĭ·ĕr′ ĭ)
  -ar·ies
brev·i·ty   (brĕv′ ĭ·tĭ)
brew·er·y   (broo′ ĕr·ĭ)
  -er·ies
bribe   (brīb)
  brib·ing   brib·a·ble
  brib·er·y   -er·ies
bric-a-brac   (brĭk′ à·brăk′)
brick   (brĭk)
  brick·bat   brick·lay·er
  brick-red *adj.*   brick·yard
bride   (brīd)
  brid·al (of a wedding; see *bridle*)

bride·groom   brides·maid
bridge   (brĭj)
  bridg·ing   bridge·a·ble
  bridge·work
bri·dle   (brī' d'l)
  (harness; see *bridal*)
  -dling   bri·dle path
brief   (brēf)
  brief case   brief·ly
bri·er   (brī' ẽr)
brig   (brĭg)
bri·gade   (brĭ·gād')
brig·a·dier   (brĭg' à·dẽr')
  gen·er·al
brig·and   (brĭg' ånd)
bright   (brīt)
  bright·en   bright-eyed
Brigh·ton,   (brī' t'n)
  Eng·land
bril·liance   (brĭl' yǎns)
brim   (brĭm)
  brimmed   brim·ming
  brim·ful   brim·stone
brine   (brīn)
  brin·ish   brin·y
bri·quet   (brĭ·kĕt')
bris·ket   (brĭs' kĕt)
bris·tle   (brĭs' 'l)
  -tling
Bris·tol,   (brĭs' t'l)
  Eng·land
Brit·ain   (brĭt' 'n)
Brit·ish   (brĭt' ĭsh)
Brit·on   (brĭt' ŭn)
  (native of Britain)
Brit·ta·ny   (brĭt' 'n·ĭ)
  (region of France)
brit·tle   (brĭt' 'l)
  brit·tle·ness
broach   (brōch)
  (to utter first; see *brooch*)
broad   (brôd)
  broad·ax   broad·cast
  broad·cloth   broad·en·ing
  broad-gauge   broad jump
  broad-mind·ed   broad·side
  broad·sword   broad·tail
bro·cade   (brô·kād')
broc·co·li   (brŏk' ô·lĭ)
bro·chure   (brô·shŏŏr')
brogue   (brōg)
broil   (broil)
  broil·er
bro·ken   (brō' kĕn)
  bro·ken·heart·ed

bro·ker·age   (brō' kẽr·ĭj)
bro·mide   (brō' mĭd)
bron·chi·al   (brŏng' kĭ·ðl)
  bron·chi·tis   (brŏn·kī' tĭs)
  bron·chit·ic   (brŏn·kĭt' ĭk)
bron·co·bust·er
        (brŏng' kō·bŭs' tẽr)
bron·to·sau·rus
        (brŏn' tô·sô' rŭs)
bronze   (brŏnz)
brooch   (brōch)
  (jewelry; see *broach*)
brood   (brōōd)
brook·let   (brŏŏk' lĕt)
Brook·line,   (brŏŏk' lĭn)
  Mass.
Brook·lyn,   (brŏŏk' lĭn)
  N.Y.
broom·stick   (brōōm' stĭk')
broth   (brŏth)
broth·el   (brŏth' ĕl)
broth·er   (brŭth' ẽr)
  broth·er·hood   broth·er-in-law
  broth·ers-in-law
  broth·er·ly
brought   (brôt)
brow·beat   (brou' bēt')
brown   (broun)
  brown Bet·ty   brown·ie
  brown·stone   brown sug·ar
browse   (brouz)
  brows·ing
bruise   (brōōz)
  bruis·ing
bru·nette   (brōō·nĕt')
brush-off   (brŭsh' ôf')
brusque   (brŭsk)
  brusque·ly
Brus·sels,   (brŭs' 'lz)
  Bel·gium
  Brus·sels lace
  Brus·sels sprouts
bru·tal   (brōō' tðl)
  bru·tal·i·ty   (brōō·tǎl' ǐ tǐ)
  bru·tal·ize   -iz·ing
  bru·tal·ly
brute   (brōōt)
  brut·ish
Bryn Mawr   (brĭn' mär')
  (coll.)
bub·ble   (bŭb' 'l)
  bub·bling   bub·ble gum
  bub·bly
bu·bon·ic   (bû·bŏn' ĭk)
  plague

buc·ca·neer (bŭk′ á·nēr′)
Bu·cha·rest, (bōō′ ká·rĕst)
  Ro·ma·nia
buck (bŭk)
  buck·board   buck pri·vate
  buck·saw   buck·shot
  buck·skin   buck·tail
  buck·tooth   buck·wheat
buck·a·roo (bŭk′á·rōō′)
buck·et (bŭk′ ĕt)
  buck·et·ful   buck·et seat
buck·le (bŭk′ ′l)
  -ling
buck·ram (bŭk′ rǎm)
bu·col·ic (bū·kŏl′ ĭk)
Bud·dha (bōōd′ á)
  Bud·dhism   Bud·dhist
budge (bŭj)
  budg·ing
budg·et (bŭj′ ĕt)
  -et·ed   -et·ing
  budg·et·ar·y
Bue·nos Ai·res, (bwā′ nŭs âr′ ēz)
  Ar·gen·ti·na
buf·fa·lo (bŭf′ á·lō)
  -loes   buf·fa·lo fish
buff·er state (bŭf′ ēr)
buf·fet (bŭf′ ĕt)
  (slap)
buf·fet (bōō·fā′)
  (sideboard)
buf·foon·er·y (bŭ fōōn′ ēr·ĭ)
  -er·ies
bug·a·boo (bŭg′ á·bōō′)
bug·gy (bŭg′ ĭ)
  bug·gies
bu·gle (bū′ g′l)
  -gling   bu·gler
build (bĭld)
  build·ing   build-up
  built
bulb (bŭlb)
  bulb·ar (bŭl′ bĕr)
  bulb·ous
bulge (bŭlj)
  bulg·ing
bulk·head (bŭlk′ hĕd′)
bulk·y (bŭl′ kĭ)
  bulk·i·ness
bull (bōōl)
  bull·dog   bull·doz·er
  bull·fight   bull·finch
  bull·frog   bull·head·ed
  bull pen   bull's-eye
  bull ter·ri·er bull·whip

bul·let (bōōl′ ĕt)
  bul·let·proof
bul·le·tin (bōōl′ ĕ·tĭn)
bul·lion (bōōl′ yŭn)
  (gold or silver; see *bouillon*)
bul·rush (bōōl′ rŭsh′)
bul·wark (bōōl′ wērk)
bum·ble·bee (bŭm′ b'l·bē′)
bump·kin (bŭmp′ kĭn)
bump·tious (bŭmp′ shŭs)
bun·dle (bŭn′ d'l)
  -dling
bun·ga·low (bŭng′ gá·lō)
bun·gle (bŭng′ g'l)
  -gling   bun·gler
bun·ion (bŭn′ yŭn)
bunk·house (bŭngk′ hous′)
Bun·sen burn·er
          (bŭn′ s'n)
bun·ting (bŭn′ tĭng)
buoy (bōō′ ĭ)
  buoy·ant (bōō′ yǎnt)
  -an·cy
bur (bŭr)
  (weed; see *burr*)
bur·den (bŭr′ d'n)
  bur·den·some
bu·reau (bū′ rō)
bu·reauc·ra·cy (bū·rŏk′ rá·sĭ)
  -cies
  bu·reau·crat·ic
          (bū′ rŏ·krăt′ ĭk)
bu·rette (bū·rĕt′)
bur·geon·ing (bûr′ jŭn·ĭng)
burgh·er (bûr′ gēr)
bur·glar (bûr′ glēr)
  bur·glar·ize -iz·ing
  bur·gla·ry   -ries
bur·i·al (bĕr′ ĭ·ăl)
bur·lap (bûr′ lăp)
bur·lesque (bûr·lĕsk′)
bur·ley (bûr′ lĭ)
  (tobacco)
bur·ly (bûr′ lĭ)
  (brawny)
  bur·li·ness
Bur·mese (bûr′ mēz′)
bur·nish (bûr′ nĭsh)
burnt (bûrnt)
burp (bûrp)
burr (bûr)
  (roughness or accent; see *bur*)
bur·ro (bûr′ ō)
  (donkey)
  bur·ros

bur·row   (bûr′ ō)
  (to dig)
bur·sar   (bûr′ sĕr)
burst   (bûrst)
bur·y   (bĕr′ ĭ)
  bur·ied   bur·y·ing
  bur·i·al
bus   (bŭs)
  bus·es   bus boy
bush·el   (bŏŏsh′ ĕl)
  -eled   -el·ing
bush·y   (bŏŏsh′ ĭ)
  bush·i·ness
busi·ness   (bĭz′ nĕs)
  busi·ness·like   busi·ness·man
bus·tle   (bŭs′ 'l)
  -tling
bus·y   (bĭz′ ĭ)
  bus·ied   bus·y·ing
  bus·i·er, -i·est, -i·ly, -i·ness
  bus·y·bod·y
butch·er   (bŏŏch′ ĕr)
  butch·er·y
but   (bŭt)
  (*prep.*, *conj.*; see *butt*)
butt   (bŭt)
  (end)
butte   (būt)
  (hill)
but·ter   (bŭt′ ĕr)
  but·ter·cup   but·ter·fat
  but·ter·fin·gered
  but·ter·fly   -flies
  but·ter·milk   but·ter·scotch
but·tock   (bŭt′ ŭk)
but·ton   (bŭt′ 'n)
  but·ton·hole
but·tress   (bŭt′ rĕs)
buy·er   (bī′ ĕr)
buz·zard   (bŭz′ ĕrd)
by   (bī)
  by-and-**by**   by·gone
  by·law   by-line
  by·name   by·pass
  by·path   by-prod·uct
  by·stand·er   by·street
  by·way   by·word
By·zan·tine   (bĭ·zăn′ tĭn)

C

ca·bal   (kȧ·băl′)
  cab·a·lis·tic   (kăb′ ȧ·lĭs′ tĭc)
cab·a·ret   (kăb′ ȧ·rā′)

cab·bage   (kăb′ ĭj)
cab·in   (kăb′ ĭn)
  cab·in class   cab·in cruis·er
cab·i·net   (kăb′ ĭ·nĕt)
  cab·i·net·mak·er
ca·ble   (kā′ b'l)
  -bling   ca·ble car
ca·ble·gram
ca·boose   (kȧ·bōōs′)
cache   (kăsh)
ca·chet   (kă·shā′)
cack·le   (kăk′ 'l)
  -ling
ca·coph·o·ny   (kȧ·kŏf′ ō·nĭ)
cac·tus   (kăk′ tŭs)
  pl. cac·ti   (-tī)
ca·dav·er   (kȧ·dăv′ ĕr)
  ca·dav·er·ous
cad·die   (kăd′ ĭ)
  cad·died   cad·dy·ing
cad·dish   (kăd′ ĭsh)
ca·dence   (kā′ dĕns)
  -dent
ca·det   (kȧ·dĕt′)
Cad·il·lac   (kăd′ 'l·ăk)
Cae·sar·e·an   (sē·zâr′ ē·ȧn)
  (also spelled *Cesarean*)
ca·fé   (kȧ′ fā′)
caf·e·te·ri·a   (kăf′ ĕ·tẽr′ ĭ·ȧ)
caf·fe·ine   (kăf′ ē·ĭn)
cage·y   (kāj′ ĭ)
  cag·i·ness
Cai·ro, E·gypt   (kī′ rō)
Cai·ro, Ill.   (kâr′ ō)
cais·son   (kā′ sŭn)
ca·jole   (kȧ·jōl′)
  -jol·ing   ca·jole·ment
  ca·jol·er·y
cake   (kāk)
  cake·box   cake pan
  cake·walk
cal·a·boose   (kăl′ ȧ·bōōs)
cal·a·mine   (kăl′ ȧ·mīn)
ca·lam·i·ty   (kȧ·lăm′ ĭ·tĭ)
  -ties   ca·lam·i·tous
cal·ci·fy   (kăl′ sĭ·fī)
  -fied   -fy·ing
  cal·ci·fi·ca·tion
           (kăl′ sĭ·fĭ·kā′ shŭn)
cal·ci·mine   (kăl′ sĭ·mīn)
cal·ci·um   (kăl′ sĭ·ŭm)
cal·cu·late   (kăl′ kŭ·lāt)
  -lat·ing   cal·cu·la·ble
  cal·cu·la·tion   (kăl′kŭ·lā′ shŭn)
  cal·cu·la·tor

cal·cu·lus (kăl′ kū lŭs)
  pl. cal·cu·li (-lī)
Cal·cut·ta, (kăl·kŭt′ à)
  In·di·a
cal·dron (kôl′ drŭn)
cal·en·dar (kăl′ ĕn·dẽr)
calf (kăf)
  calves   calf·skin
Cal·ga·ry, (kăl′ gà·rĭ)
  Can.
cal·i·ber (kăl′ ĭ·bẽr)
cal·i·co (kăl′ ĭ·kō)
  -coes
Cal·i·for·nia (kăl′ ĭ·fôrn′ yà)
  abbr. Calif. *or* Cal.
  Cal·i·for·nian
ca·liph (kā′ lĭf)
cal·is·then·ics (kăl′ ĭs·thĕn′ ĭks)
calk (kôk)
cal·lig·ra·phy (kă·lĭg′ rá·fĭ)
cal·lous (kăl′ ŭs) *adj.*
  (unfeeling)
cal·low (kăl′ ō)
cal·lus (kăl′ ŭs) *n.*
  (thickened skin)
calm (käm)
  calm·ly
cal·o·rie (kăl′ ô·rĭ)
  ca·lor·ic (kà·lŏr′ ĭk)
cal·um·ny (kăl′ ŭm·nĭ)
  -nies
Cal·va·ry (kăl′ và·rĭ)
Cal·vin·ist (kăl′ vĭn·ĭst)
ca·lyp·so (kà·lĭp′ sō)
ca·ma·ra·de·rie
    (kä′ mà·rä′ dĕ·rē)
cam·el (kăm′ ĕl)
ca·mel·li·a (kà·mĕl′ ĭ·à)
cam·e·o (kăm′ ĕ·ō)
cam·er·a (kăm′ ẽr·à)
cam·i·sole (kăm′ ĭ·sōl)
cam·o·mile tea (kăm′ ô·mīl)
cam·ou·flage (kăm′ ŏŏ·fläzh)
  -flag·ing
cam·paign (kăm·pān′)
camp·fire (kămp′ fīr′)
cam·phor (kăm′ fẽr)
  cam·phor·at·ed
cam·pus (kăm′ pŭs)
Can·a·da (kăn′ à·dà)
  Ca·na·di·an (kà·nā′ dĭ·ăn)
ca·nal (kà·năl′)
  -nalled   -nal·ling
  ca·nal·boat

can·a·pé (kăn′ à·pā)
ca·nard (kà·närd′)
ca·nar·y (kà·nâr′ ĭ)
  -nar·ies
ca·nas·ta (kà·năs′ tà)
Ca·nav·er·al, (kà·năv′ ẽr·ál)
  Cape
Can·ber·ra, (kăn′ bẽr·à)
  Aus·tra·lia
can·can (kăn′ kăn)
can·cel (kăn′ sĕl)
  -celed   -cel·ing
  can·cel·er
  can·cel·la·tion (kăn′ sĕ·lā′ shŭn)
can·cer (kăn′ sẽr)
  can·cer·ous
can·de·la·brum (kăn′ dĕ·lä′ brŭm)
  pl. can·de·la·bra
can·des·cence (kăn·dĕs′ ĕns)
  -cent
can·did (kăn′ dĭd)
can·di·date (kăn′ dĭ·dāt)
  can·di·da·cy (kăn′ dĭ·dà·sĭ)
  can·di·da·ture (kăn′ dĭ·dà·tụ̈r)
can·died (kăn′ dĭd)
can·dle (kăn′ d′l)
  can·dle·light   can·dle·pow·er
  can·dle·stick
  can·dle·wick bed·spread
can·dor (kăn′ dẽr)
can·dy (kăn′ dĭ)
  -dies, -died, -dy·ing
ca·nine (kā′ nīn)
can·is·ter (kăn′ ĭs·tẽr)
can·ker (kăng′ kẽr)
  can·ker·ous   can·ker sore
  can·ker·worm
can·ner·y (kăn′ ẽr·ĭ)
  can·ner·ies
Cannes, France (kăn)
can·ni·bal (kăn′ ĭ·bǎl)
  can·ni·bal·ism
  can·ni·bal·is·tic
    (kăn′ ĭ·bǎl·ĭs′ tĭk)
can·ning (kăn′ ĭng)
can·non (kăn′ ŭn)
  (gun; see *canon*)
  can·non·ade (kăn′ ŭn·ād′)
  can·non ball
  can·non·eer (kăn′ ŭn·ẽr′)
can·not (kăn′ nŏt)
can·ny (kăn′ ĭ)
  can·ni·ness

ca·noe (ká·nōō′)
  -noed   -noe·ing
  ca·noe·ist
can·on (kăn′ ŭn)
  (decree; see *cannon*)
  ca·non·i·cal (ká·nŏn′ ĭ·kál)
  ca·non·ize   -iz·ing
  can·on law
can·o·py (kăn′ ŏ·pĭ)
  -pies
can't (kănt)
can·ta·loupe (kăn′ tá·lōp)
can·tan·ker·ous
          (kăn·tăng′ kĕr·ŭs)
can·ta·ta (kăn·tä′ tá)
can·teen (kăn·tēn′)
can·ter (kăn′ tĕr)
  (light gallop; see *cantor*)
Can·ter·bur·y (kăn′ tĕr·bĕr·ĭ)
can·ti·cle (kăn′ tĭ·k'l)
can·ti·le·ver (kăn′ tĭ·lĕ′ vĕr)
can·to (kăn′ tō)
  -tos
can·ton (kăn′ tŏn)
Can·ton·ese (kăn′ tŏn·ēz′)
can·tor (kăn′ tôr)
  (singer; see *canter*)
can·vas (kăn′ vás)
  (cloth)
  can·vas·back duck
can·vass (kăn′ vás)
  (to solicit)   can·vass·er
can·yon (kăn′ yŭn)
ca·pa·ble (kā′ pá·b'l)
  -bly
  ca·pa·bil·i·ty (kā′ pá·bĭl′ ĭ·tĭ)
ca·pa·cious (ká·pā′ shŭs)
ca·pac·i·ty (ká·păs′ ĭ·tĭ)
  -ties
ca·per (kā′ pĕr)
cape·skin (kāp′ skĭn′)
cap·il·lar·y (kăp′ ĭ·lĕr′ ĭ)
  -il·lar·ies
cap·i·tal (kăp′ ĭ·tál)
  (property)
  cap·i·tal cit·y
  cap·i·tal goods
  cap·i·tal·ism   -ist
  cap·i·tal·i·za·tion
        (kăp′ ĭ·tál·ĭ·zā′ shŭn)
  cap·i·tal·ize   -iz·ing
  cap·i·tal lev·y
  cap·i·tal stock
cap·i·tol (kăp′ ĭ·tŏl)
  (statehouse)

ca·pit·u·late (ká·pĭt′ û·lāt)
  -lat·ing
  ca·pit·u·la·tion
        (ká·pĭt′ û·lā′ shŭn)
ca·pon (kā′ pŏn)
ca·price (ká·prēs′)
ca·pri·cious (ká·prĭsh′ ŭs)
cap·size (kăp·sīz′)
  -siz·ing
cap·sule (kăp′ sūl)
cap·tain (kăp′ tĭn)
  cap·tain·cy
cap·tion (kăp′ shŭn)
cap·tious (kăp′ shŭs)
cap·ti·vate (kăp′ tĭ·vāt)
  -vat·ing
  cap·ti·va·tion
        (kăp′ tĭ·vā′ shŭn)
  cap·ti·va·tor
cap·tive (kăp′ tĭv)
  cap·tiv·i·ty (kăp′ tĭv′ ĭ·tĭ)
cap·tor (kăp′ tĕr)
cap·ture (kăp′ tûr)
  -tur·ing
car·a·mel (kăr′ á·mĕl)
car·at (kăr′ ăt)
  (unit of weight; see *caret, carrot*)
car·a·van (kăr′ á·văn)
car·a·way seeds (kăr′ á·wā)
car·bide (kär′ bĭd)
car·bine (kär′ bĭn)
car·bo·hy·drate (kär′ bŏ·hī′ drāt)
car·bol·ic ac·id (kär·bŏl′ ĭk)
car·bon (kär′ bŏn)
  car·bo·na·ceous
        (kär′ bŏ·nā′ shŭs)
  car·bo·nat·ed
  car·bon·a·tion
        (kär′ bŏn·ā′ shŭn)
  car·bon bi·sul·fide
  car·bon black
  car·bon cop·y
  car·bon di·ox·ide
  car·bon di·sul·fide
  car·bon·ic (kär·bŏn′ ĭk)
  car·bon·if·er·ous
        (kär′ bŏn·ĭf′ ĕr·ŭs)
  car·bon mon·ox·ide
  car·bon pa·per
  car·bon proc·ess
  car·bon tet·ra·chlo·ride
car·bun·cle (kär′ bŭng·k'l)
car·bu·ret·or (kär′ bû·rā′ tĕr)
car·cass (kär′ kás)
  -cass·es

car·ci·no·ma (kär′ sĭ·nō′ mȧ)
  pl. car·ci·no·ma·ta (-mȧ·tȧ)
car·da·mom (kär′ dȧ·mŭm)
card·board (kärd′ bôrd′)
car·di·ac (kär′ dĭ·ăk)
car·di·gan (kär′ dĭ·gȧn)
car·di·nal (kär′ dĭ·nȧl)
car·di·o·gram (kär′ dĭ·ȯ·grăm′)
  car·di·o·graph
  car·di·ol·o·gy (kär′ dĭ·ŏl′ ȯ·jĭ)
card·sharp (kärd′ shärp′)
care (kâr)
  car·ing   care·free
  care·ful, -ful·ly, -ful·ness
  care·less   -less·ly
  care·tak·er   care·worn
ca·reen (kȧ·rēn′)
  -reen·ing
ca·reer (kȧ·rêr′)
ca·ress (kȧ·rĕs′)
  ca·ress·ing·ly
car·et (kär′ ĕt)
  (proofreaders' mark; see *carat*,
  carrot)
car·go (kär′ gō)
  -goes
Car·ib·be·an (kär′ ĭ·bē′ ȧn)
  (sea)
car·i·bou (kär′ ĭ·bōō)
  n. sing. & pl.
car·i·ca·ture (kär′ ĭ·kȧ·tụ̄r)
car·i·es (kâr′ ĭ·ēz)
  (tooth decay)
car·il·lon (kär′ ĭ·lŏn)
car·mine (kär′ mĭn)
car·nage (kär′ nĭj)
car·nal (kär′ nȧl)
  car·nal·i·ty (kär·năl′ ĭ·tĭ)
  car·nal·ly
car·na·tion (kär·nā′ shŭn)
car·ni·val (kär′ nĭ·vȧl)
car·ni·vore (kär′ nĭ·vōr)
  car·niv·o·rous (kär·nĭv′ ȯ·rŭs)
car·ol (kär′ ŭl)
  -oled   -ol·ing
car·om shot (kär′ ŭm)
ca·rous·al (kȧ·rouz′ ȧl)
  (drunken revel; see *carrousel*)
  ca·rouse   -rous·ing
car·pen·ter (kär′ pĕn·tẽr)
  car·pen·try
car·pet (kär′ pĕt)
  -pet·ed   -pet·ing
  car·pet·bag·ger
  car·pet bee·tle

carp·ing (kär′ pĭng)
car·port (kär′ pôrt′)
car·riage (kär′ ĭj)
car·ri·er pi·geon
               (kär′ ĭ·ẽr)
car·ri·on (kär′ ĭ·ŭn)
car·rot (kär′ ŭt)
  (vegetable; see *carat*, *caret*)
car·rou·sel (kär′ ŏŏ·zĕl′)
  (merry-go-round; see *carousal*)
car·ry (kär′ ĭ)
  car·ried   car·ry·ing
  car·ri·er   car·ry·all
  car·ry-o·ver
cart·age (kär′ tĭj)
carte blanche (kärt′ blänsh′)
car·tel (kär·tĕl′)
Car·te·sian (kär·tē′ zhȧn)
car·ti·lage (kär′ tĭ·lĭj)
  car·ti·lag·i·nous
          (kär′ tĭ·lăj′ ĭ·nŭs)
car·tog·ra·phy (kär·tŏg′ rȧ·fĭ)
  car·to·graph·i·cal
         (kär′ tȯ·grăf′ ĭ·kȧl)
car·ton (kär′ tŏn)
  (box)
car·toon (kär·tōōn′)
  (drawing)   car·toon·ist
car·tridge (kär′ trĭj)
ca·sa·ba mel·on
           (kȧ·sä′ bȧ)
Cas·a·blan·ca, (kăs′ ȧ·blăng′ kȧ)
  Mo·roc·co
cas·cade (kăs·kād′)
  -cad·ing
cas·car·a (kăs·kâr′ ȧ)
ca·se·in (kā′ sē·ĭn)
case·ment (kās′ mĕnt)
case·work·er (kās′ wûrk′ ẽr)
cash (kăsh)
  n. sing. & pl.
  cash·book
  cash reg·is·ter
ca·shew nut (kȧ·shōō′)
cash·ier (kăsh·ẽr′)
  cash·ier's check
cash·mere (kăsh′ mẽr)
ca·si·no (kȧ·sē′ nō)
  (gambling place; see *cassino*)
  -nos
cas·ket (kás′ kĕt)
Cas·san·dra (kȧ·săn′ drȧ)
cas·se·role (kăs′ ĕ·rōl)
cas·si·a (kăsh′ ĭ·ȧ)

cas·si·no (kā·sē′ nō)
  (card game; see *casino*)

Cas·si·o·pe·ia′s Chair
  (kās′ ĭ·ō·pē′ yāz)

cas·sock (kās′ ŭk)

cast (kāst)
  (throw; see *caste*)

cas·ta·net (kās′ tā·nĕt′)

cast·a·way (kāst′ à·wā′)

caste (kāst)
  (social class; see *cast*)

cast·er (kās′ tēr)
  (wheel; see *castor*)

cas·ti·gate (kās′ tĭ·gāt)
  -gat·ing
  cas·ti·ga·tion (kās′ tĭ·gā′ shŭn)
  cas·ti·ga·tor

cas·tile soap (kās′ tēl)

cas·tle (kás′ 'l)

cast·off (kást′ ôf′)

cas·tor (kás′ tēr)
  (oil; see *caster*)

cas·trate (kās′ trāt)
  -trat·ing
  cas·tra·tion (kās·trā′ shŭn)

Cas·tro, Fi·del (kās′ trô)

cas·u·al (kāzh′ ū·ǎl)
  cas·u·al·ly cas·u·al·ness

cas·u·al·ty (kāzh′ ū·ǎl·tĭ)
  -ties

cas·u·ist (kāzh′ ū·ĭst)
  cas·u·ist·ry (kāzh′ ū·ĭs·trĭ)

cat (kāt)
  cat·bird cat·boat
  cat·call cat·fish
  cat·gut cat·nap
  cat·nip cat-o′-nine-tails
  cat′s-eye cat′s-paw
  cat·tail cat·walk

cat·a·clysm (kāt′ à·klĭz′m)
  cat·a·clys·mal (kāt′ à·klĭz′ mǎl)
  cat·a·clys·mic (kāt′ à·klĭz′ mĭk)

cat·a·comb (kāt′ à·kōm)

cat·a·lep·sy (kāt′ à·lĕp′ sĭ)
  cat·a·lep·tic (kāt′ à·lĕp′ tĭk)

cat·a·log (kāt′ à·lôg)
  -loged -log·ing
  cat·a·log·er cat·a·log·ist

ca·tal·pa (kà·tǎl′ pá)

cat·a·lyst (kāt′ à·lĭst)

cat·a·ma·ran (kāt′ à·mà·rǎn′)

cat·a·pult (kāt′ à·pŭlt)

cat·a·ract (kāt′ à·rǎkt)
  (waterfall, eye defect)

ca·tarrh (kà·tär′)

ca·tas·tro·phe (kà·tǎs′ trô·fē)
  cat·a·stroph·ic (kāt′ à·strôf′ ĭk)

cat·a·ton·ic (kāt′ à·tŏn′ ĭk)

Ca·taw·ba (kà·tô′ bà)

catch (kāch)
  catch·all catch·er
  catch·ment catch·word
  catch·y

cat·e·chism (kāt′ ē·kĭz′m)
  cat·e·chize (kāt′ ē·kĭz)
  -chiz·ing

cat·e·chu·men (kāt′ ē·kū′ mĕn)

cat·e·go·ry (kāt′ ē·gō′ rĭ)
  -ries
  cat·e·go·ri·cal
     (kāt·ē·gŏr′ ĭ·kǎl)
  -cal·ly

ca·ter (kā′ tēr)
  -tered -ter·ing
  ca·ter·er ca·ter·ess

cat·er-cor·nered
     (kāt′ ēr·kôr′ nērd)

cat·er·pil·lar (kāt′ ēr·pĭl′ ēr)

ca·thar·sis (kà·thär′ sĭs)
  ca·thar·tic

ca·the·dral (kà·thē′ drǎl)

cath·e·ter (kāth′ ē·tēr)
  cath·e·ter·ize -iz·ing

ca·thex·is (kà·thĕk′ sĭs)
  ca·thec·tic (kà·thĕk′ tĭk)

cath·ode (kāthĭ′ ōd)

cath·o·lic (kāth′ ō·lĭk)
  (universal)
  ca·tho·lic·i·ty (kāth′ ō·lĭs′ ĭ·tĭ)

Cath·o·lic (kāth′ ō·lĭk)
  (church)
  Ca·thol·i·cism
     (kà·thŏl′ ĭ·sĭz′m)

cat·sup (kāt′ sŭp)

cat·tle (kāt′ 'l)
  cat·tle·man

cat·ty (kāt′ ĭ)
  cat·ti·ly cat·ti·ness

Cau·ca·sian (kô·kā′ zhǎn)

cau·cus (kô′ kŭs)
  -cused -cus·ing

cau·dal (kô′ dǎl)

caught (kôt)

cau·li·flow·er (kô′ lĭ·flou′ ēr)

caus·al (kôz′ ǎl)
  cau·sal·i·ty (kô·zǎl′ ĭ·tĭ)
  caus·al·ly

cause (kôz)
  caus·ing caus·a·ble
  cau·sa·tion (kô·zā′ shŭn)

caus·a·tive (kôz′ à·tǐv)
cause·less cause·way
caus·tic (kôs′ tǐk)
cau·ter·ize (kô′ tĕr·īz)
-iz·ing
cau·tion (kô′ shŭn)
cau·tion·ar·y (kô′ shŭn·ĕr′ ǐ)
cau·tious (kô′ shŭs)
cav·al·cade (kăv′ ál·kād′)
cav·a·lier (kăv′ à·lẽr′)
cav·al·ry·man (kăv′ ál·rǐ·mǎn)
cave (kāv)
cav·ing cave-in
cave man
cav·ern (kăv′ ẽrn)
cav·ern·ous
cav·i·ar (kăv′ ǐ·är)
cav·il (kăv′ ǐl)
-iled -il·ing
cav·i·ty (kăv′ ǐ·tǐ)
-ties
ca·vort (ká·vôrt′)
cay·enne pep·per
(kī·ĕn′)
cease (sēs)
ceas·ing cease·less
ce·dar (sē′ dẽr)
cede (sēd)
(yield)
ced·ing
ces·sion (sĕsh′ ŭn)
ceil·ing (sēl′ ĭng)
Cel·a·nese (sĕl′ à·nēs)
cel·e·brate (sĕl′ ĕ·brāt)
-brat·ing cel·e·brant
cel·e·bra·tion (sĕl′ ĕ·brā′ shŭn)
cel·e·bra·tor
ce·leb·ri·ty (sĕ·lĕb′ rǐ·tǐ)
-ties
ce·ler·i·ty (sĕ·lĕr′ ǐ·tǐ)
cel·er·y (sĕl′ ẽr·ǐ)
ce·les·tial (sĕ·lĕs′ chál)
cel·i·bate (sĕl′ ǐ·bát)
cel·i·ba·cy (sĕl′ ǐ·bà·sǐ)
cel·lar (sĕl′ ẽr)
cel·lo (chĕl′ ō)
cel·list
cel·lo·phane (sĕl′ ō·fān)
cel·lu·lar (sĕl′ û·lẽr)
cel·lu·loid (sĕl′ û·loid)
cel·lu·lose (sĕl′ û·lōs)
ce·ment (sĕ·mĕnt′)
ce·ment·er
cem·e·ter·y (sĕm′ ĕ·tĕr′ ǐ)
-ter·ies

cen·sor (sĕn′ sẽr)
(examiner)
cen·so·ri·al (sĕn·sõ′ rǐ·ál)
cen·so·ri·ous (sĕn·sõ′ rǐ·ŭs)
cen·sor·ship
cen·sure (sĕn′ shẽr)
(criticize)
-sur·ing
cen·sur·a·bil·i·ty
(sĕn′ shẽr·à·bǐl′ ĭ·tǐ)
cen·sur·a·ble
cen·sus (sĕn′ sŭs)
cen·taur (sĕn′ tôr)
cen·te·nar·y (sĕn′ tĕ·nẽr′ ǐ)
cen·te·nar·i·an
(sĕn′ tĕ·nâr′ ǐ·án)
cen·ten·ni·al (sĕn·tĕn′ ǐ·ál)
cen·ter (sĕn′ tẽr)
cen·ter·piece
cen·ti- (sĕn′ tǐ-)
cen·ti·grade cen·ti·gram
cen·ti·me·ter cen·ti·pede
cen·tral (sĕn′ trál)
cen·tral·i·za·tion
(sĕn′ trál·ǐ·zā′ shŭn)
cen·tral·ize -iz·ing
cen·tral·ly
cen·trif·u·gal (sĕn·trǐf′ û·gál)
(going away from center)
cen·trip·e·tal (sĕn·trǐp′ ĕ·tál)
(going toward center)
cen·tu·ri·on (sĕn·tū′ rǐ·ŭn)
cen·tu·ry (sĕn′ tû·rǐ)
-ries
ce·phal·ic (sĕ·fǎl′ ǐk)
ce·ram·ics (sĕ·rǎm′ ǐks)
ce·re·al (sẽr′ ĕ·ál)
(grain; see serial)
cer·e·bel·lum (sẽr′ ĕ·bĕl′ ŭm)
cer·e·bral pal·sy
(sẽr′ ĕ·brál)
cer·e·brum (sẽr′ ĕ·brŭm)
cer·e·mo·ny (sĕr′ ĕ·mõ′ nǐ)
-nies
cer·e·mo·ni·al (sẽr′ ĕ·mõ′ nǐ·ál)
cer·e·mo·ni·ous
(sẽr′ ĕ·mõ′ nǐ·ŭs)
ce·rise (sĕ·rēz′)
cer·tain (sûr′ tǐn)
cer·tain·ly cer·tain·ty, -ties
cer·tif·i·cate (sẽr·tǐf′ ǐ·kǐt)
cer·ti·fy (sûr′ tǐ·fī)
-fied -fy·ing
cer·ti·fi·a·ble (sûr′ tǐ·fī′ à·b′l)

cer·ti·fi·ca·tion
         (sûr′ tĭ·fĭ·kā′ shŭn)
  cer·ti·fi·er
cer·ti·o·ra·ri   (sûr′ shĭ·ô·rā′ rĭ)
cer·ti·tude   (sûr′ tĭ·tūd)
ce·ru·le·an   (sĕ·rōō′ lĕ·ɑ̆n)
cer·vix   (sûr′ vĭks)
  pl. cer·vi·ces (sûr·vī′ sēz)
  cer·vi·cal
Ce·sar·e·an   (sĕ·zâr′ ĕ·ɑ̆n)
ces·sa·tion   (sĕ·sā′ shŭn)
  (a stop)
ces·sion   (sĕsh′ ŭn)
  (yielding; see *session*)
cess·pool   (sĕs′ pōōl′)
Cey·lon   (sĕ·lŏn′)
Cé·zanne, Paul (sā′ zán′)
Cha·blis wine (shä′ blē′)
chafe   (chāf)
  chaf·ing
chaff   (chăf)
cha·grin   (shá·grĭn′)
  -grined   -grin·ing
chain   (chān)
  chain gang   chain let·ter
  chain mail
  chain-re·act·ing pile
  chain re·ac·tion
  chain re·ac·tor
  chain stitch   chain store
chair·man   (châr′ mɑ̆n)
  chair·man·ship
  chair·wom·an
chaise longue (shāz′ lôɴg′)
chal·ced·o·ny (kăl·sĕd′ ô·nĭ)
cha·let   (shă·lā′)
chal·ice   (chăl′ ĭs)
chalk   (chôk)
  chalk·stone   chalk·y
chal·lenge   (chăl′ ĕnj)
  chal·leng·ing chal·lenge·a·ble
  chal·leng·er
chal·lis   (shăl′ ĭ)
cham·ber   (chăm′ bĕr)
  cham·ber con·cert
  cham·ber·maid
  cham·ber mu·sic
  cham·ber of com·merce
cham·ber·lain (chăm′ bĕr·lĭn)
cham·bray   (shăm′ brā)
cha·me·le·on (ká·mē′ lĕ·ŭn)
cham·fer   (chăm′ fĕr)
cham·ois   (shăm′ ĭ)
  n. sing. & pl.
cham·pagne   (shăm·pān′)

Cham·paign, Ill. (shăm·pān′)
cham·pi·on   (chăm′ pĭ·ŭn)
  cham·pi·on·ship
Cham·plain,   (shăm·plān′)
  Lake, N.Y.
Champs É·ly·sées
         (shäɴ′ -zā′ lĕ′ zā′)
chance   (cháns)
  chanc·ing   chance·ful
  chanc·y   chanc·i·ness
chan·cel   (chán′ sĕl)
chan·cel·lor   (chán′ sĕ·lĕr)
  chan·cel·ler·y -cel·ler·ies
  chan·cel·lor of the ex·cheq·uer
chan·cer·y   (chán′ sĕr·ĭ)
  -cer·ies
chan·de·lier   (shăn′ dĕ·lĕr′)
change   (chānj)
  chang·ing
  change·a·bil·i·ty
  change·a·ble   change·ful
  change·less   change·ling
chan·nel   (chăn′ ĕl)
  chan·neled   chan·nel·ing
chan·teuse   (shäɴ′ tûz′)
chant·ey   (shán′ tĭ)
  -eys
chan·ti·cleer (chăn′ tĭ·klęr)
cha·os   (kā′ ŏs)
  cha·ot·ic   (kā·ŏt′ ĭk)
chap·ar·ral   (shăp′ ɑ̆·răl′)
cha·peau   (shá′ pō′)
  pl. cha·peaux (-pōz′)
chap·el   (chăp′ ĕl)
chap·er·on   (shăp′ ĕr·ōn)
  chap·er·on·age
chap·lain   (chăp′ lĭn)
  chap·lain·cy
chap·ter   (chăp′ tĕr)
char·ac·ter   (kăr′ ɑ̆k·tĕr)
  char·ac·ter·is·tic
         (kăr′ ɑ̆k·tĕr·ĭs′ tĭk)
  -ti·cal·ly
  char·ac·ter·i·za·tion
         (kăr′ ɑ̆k·tĕr·ĭ·zā′ shŭn)
  char·ac·ter·ize -iz·ing
cha·rade   (shá·rād′)
char·coal   (chär′ kōl′)
charge   (chärj)
  charg·ing   charge·a·ble
char·gé d′af·faires
         (shär′ zhā′ dɑ̆·fâr′)
char·i·ot   (chăr′ ĭ·ŭt)
  char·i·ot·eer (chăr′ ĭ·ŭt·ęr′)
cha·ris·ma   (ká·rĭz′ má)

char·is·mat·ic (kăr′ ĭz·măt′ ĭk)
char·i·ty (chăr′ ĭ·tĭ)
  -ties   char·i·ta·ble
  char·i·ta·ble·ness
cha·ri·va·ri (shä′ rĕ·vä′ rĕ or
           shĭv′ á·rē)
char·la·tan (shär′ lá·tăn)
  char·la·tan·ry
Char·le·magne (shär′ lĕ·mān)
Char·ley horse (chär′ lĭ)
char·lotte russe (shär′ lŏt rōōs′)
charm·ing (chärm′ ĭng)
char·nel (chär′ nĕl)
char·ter (chär′ tēr)
char·treuse (shär·trōōz′)
char·wom·an (chär′ wŏŏm′ ăn)
char·y (chăr′ ĭ)
  char·i·ly
chasm (kăz′m)
chas·sis (shăs′ ĭ)
  pl. chas·sis (shăs′ ĭz)
chaste (chāst)
  chaste·ly
  chas·ten (chās′ ′n)
chas·tise (chăs·tĭz′)
  -tis·ing
  chas·tise·ment (chăs′ tĭz·mĕnt)
chas·ti·ty (chăs′ tĭ·tĭ)
châ·teau (shă·tō′)
  pl. châ·teaux (-tōz′)
chat·e·laine (shăt′ ĕ·lān)
Chat·ta·noo·ga, (chăt′ á·nōō′ gá)
  Tenn.
chat·tel mort·gage
           (chăt′ ′l)
chat·ter·box (chăt′ ēr·bŏks′)
chat·ty (chăt′ĭ)
  chat·ti·ness
chauf·feur (shō·fûr′)
chau·vin·ism (shō′ vĭn·ĭz′m)
  chau·vin·is·tic (shō′ vĭn·ĭs′ tĭk)
cheap (chēp)
  cheap·en   cheap·skate
cheat·er (chēt′ ēr)
check (chĕk)
  check·book   check·mate
  check·room
check·er (chĕk′ ēr)
  check·er·board
  check·ered
Ched·dar cheese
           (chĕd′ ēr)
cheek (chēk)
cheer (chĕr)
  cheer·ful, -ful·ly, -ful·ness

cheer·y   cheer·i·er
  -i·est, -i·ly, -i·ness
cheese (chēz)
  cheese·cake   cheese·cloth
  chees·y
chee·tah (chē′ tá)
chef (shĕf)
chef·-d′oeu·vre (shĕ′ dû′ vr′)
Che·khov, An·ton
           (chĕ′ ᴋŭf)
chem·i·cal (kĕm′ ĭ·kál)
  chem·i·cal·ly
che·mise (shĕ·mēz′)
chem·ist (kĕm′ ĭst)
  chem·is·try
che·nille (shĕ·nēl′)
cher·chez la femme
        (shĕr′ shā′ lá fám′)
cher·ish (chĕr′ ĭsh)
Cher·o·kee (chĕr′ ō·kē′)
che·root (shĕ·rōōt′)
cher·ry (chĕr′ ĭ)
  cher·ries
cher·ub (chĕr′ ŭb)
  che·ru·bic (chĕ·rōō′ bĭk)
  pl. cher·u·bim or cher·ubs
cher·vil (chûr′ vĭl)
Ches·a·peake (bay)
        (chĕs′ á·pēk)
Chesh·ire cat (chĕsh′ ēr)
chess·board (chĕs′ bōrd′)
ches·ter·field coat
        (chĕs′ tēr·fēld)
chest·nut (chĕs′ nŭt)
chev·a·lier (shĕv′ á·lēr′)
chev·ron (shĕv′ rŭn)
Chey·enne, Wyo.
        (shī·ĕn′)
Chi·an·ti wine (kĭ·än′ tĭ)
chic (shēk)
  chic·quer   -quest
chi·can·er·y (shĭ·kăn′ ēr·ĭ)
chick·a·dee (chĭk′ á·dē)
chick·en (chĭk′ ĕn)
  chick·en·heart·ed
  chick·en pox
chick-pea (chĭk′ pē′)
chic·le (chĭk′ ′l)
chic·o·ry (chĭk′ ō·rĭ)
chide (chīd)
  chid·ing
chief (chēf)
  chief·ly
  chief·tain (chēf′ tĭn)
  chief·tain·cy

chif·fon   (shǐ·fŏn′)
chif·fo·nier   (shǐf′ ŏ·nēr′)
chig·ger   (chǐg′ ēr)
chi·gnon   (shēn′ yŏn)
Chi·hua·hua   (chĕ·wä′ wä)
chil·blain   (chǐl′ blān′)
child   (chǐld)
  child·bear·ing   child·birth
  child·hood   child·like
chil·dren   (chǐl′ drĕn)
Chil·e   (chǐl′ ĕ)
  Chil·e·an   (chǐl′ ĕ·ǎn)
chil·i   (chǐl′ ǐ)
  chil·i con car·ne
                     (chǐl′ ǐ kŏn kär′ nĕ)
  chil·i sauce
chill·y   (chǐl′ ǐ)
  chill·i·ness
chime   (chīm)
  chim·ing
chi·me·ra   (kǐ·mēr′ ȧ)
chi·mer·i·cal   (kǐ·mĕr′ ǐ·kȧl)
chim·ney   (chǐm′ nǐ)
  -neys
chim·pan·zee   (chǐm′ păn·zē′)
chi·na   (chī′ nȧ)
  chi·na·ber·ry   Chi·na·town
  chi·na·ware
chinch bug   (chǐnch)
chin·chil·la   (chǐn·chǐl′ ȧ)
Chi·nese   (chī′ nēz′)
Chi·nook   (shǐ·nŏok′)
chintz   (chǐnts)
chip·munk   (chǐp′ mŭngk)
Chip·pen·dale   (chǐp′ ĕn·dāl)
Chip·pe·wa   (chǐp′ ĕ·wä)
chi·rop·o·dy   (kǐ·rŏp′ ŏ·dǐ)
  chi·rop·o·dist
chi·ro·prac·tor   (kǐ′ rŏ·prăk′ tēr)
  chi·ro·prac·tic   (kǐ′ rŏ·prăk′ tǐk)
chis·el   (chǐz′ ′l)
  -eled   -el·ing
  chis·el·er
chi-square   (kī′ skwâr′)
chit·chat   (chǐt′ chăt′)
  chat·ted   chat·ting
chit·ter·lings   (chǐt′ ēr·lǐngz)
chiv·al·ry   (shǐv′ ǎl·rǐ)
  chiv·al·rie   chiv·al·rous
chlo·rine   (klō′ rēn)
  chlo·rin·ate   (klō′ rǐ·nāt)
  -nat·ing
  chlo·rate   (klō′ rāt)
  chlo·ride   (klō′ rǐd)
  chlo·rite   (klō′ rīt)

chlo·ro·form   (klō′ rŏ·fôrm)
chlo·ro·phyll   (klō′ rŏ·fǐl)
chock-full   (chŏk′ fŏol′)
choc·o·late   (chŏk′ ŏ·lǐt)
choice   (chois)
choir   (kwīr)
  choir·boy   choir loft
  choir·mas·ter
choke   (chōk)
  chok·ing   choke·cher·ry
  chok·er
chol·er·a   (kŏl′ ēr·ȧ)
chol·er·ic   (kŏl′ ēr·ǐk)
cho·les·ter·ol   (kŏ·lĕs′ tēr·ōl)
choose   (chōōz)
  choos·ing   choos·i·ness
  choos·y
chop   (chŏp)
  chopped   chop·ping
  chop·house   chop·py
  chop·stick   chop su·ey
cho·ral   (kō′ rǎl)
  cho·ral·ly
chord   (kôrd)
  (music; see cord)
chore   (chōr)
cho·re·og·ra·phy
                     (kō′ rĕ·ŏg′ rȧ·fǐ)
  cho·re·og·ra·pher
chor·tle   (chôr′ t′l)
  -tling
cho·rus   (kō′ rǔs)
chose   (chōz)
  cho·sen
Chou En-lai   (jō′ ĕn′ lī′)
chow·der   (chou′ dēr)
chow mein   (chou′ mān′)
chris·ten   (krǐs′ ′n)
  -ten·ing
Chris·ten·dom   (krǐs′ ′n·dǔm)
Chris·tian   (krǐs′ chǎn)
  Chris·ti·an·i·ty
                     (krǐs′ chǐ·ǎn′ ǐ·tǐ)
  Chris·tian·ize   -iz·ing
Christ·like   (krīst′ līk′)
Christ·mas   (krǐs′ mȧs)
chro·mat·ic   (krŏ·măt′ ǐk)
chrome   (krōm)
chro·mi·um   (krō′ mǐ·ŭm)
chron·ic   (krŏn′ ǐk)
  chron·i·cal·ly
chron·i·cle   (krŏn′ ǐ·k′l)
  -cling

chron·o·log·i·cal
    (krŏn′ ô·lŏj′ ĭ·kăl)
  -cal·ly
chro·nol·o·gy (krô·nŏl′ ô·ji)
 -gies
chrys·a·lis (krĭs′ à·lĭs)
chrys·an·the·mum
    (krĭs·ăn′ thê·mŭm)
chub·by (chŭb′ ĭ)
  chub·bi·ness
chuck·le (chŭk′ ′l)
 -ling
chum·my (chŭm′ ĭ)
  chum·mi·ness
Chung·king, Chi·na
    (chŏŏng′ kĭng′)
chunk·y (chŭngk′ ĭ)
church (chûrch)
  church·go·er church·ly
  church·yard
Church·ill, Win·ston
    (chûrch′ ĭl)
churl·ish (chûr′ lĭsh)
churn (chûrn)
chute (shōōt)
chut·ney (chŭt′ nĭ)
ci·ca·da (sĭ·kā′ dà)
ci·der (sī′ dēr)
ci·gar (sĭ·gär′)
cig·a·rette (sĭg′ à·rĕt′)
cinch (sĭnch)
Cin·cin·nat·i, O.
    (sĭn′ sĭ·năt′ ĭ)
cin·der (sĭn′ dēr)
Cin·der·el·la (sĭn′ dēr·ĕl′ à)
cin·e·ma (sĭn′ ê·mà)
  cin·e·mat·ic (sĭn′ ê·măt′ ĭk)
  cin·e·ma·tog·ra·phy
    (sĭn′ ê·mà·tŏg′ rà·fĭ)
cin·na·bar (sĭn′ à·bär)
cin·na·mon (sĭn′ à·mŭn)
ci·pher (sī′ fēr)
cir·ca (sûr′ kà)
  abbr. c.
cir·cle (sûr′ k′l)
 -cling cir·clet
cir·cuit (sûr′ kĭt)
 -cuit·ed ·cuit·ing
cir·cu·i·tous (sēr·kū′ ĭ·tŭs)
cir·cu·lar (sûr′ kû·lēr)
  cir·cu·lar·i·ty (sûr′ kû·lăr′ ĭ·tĭ)
  cir·cu·lar·ly
  cir·cu·lar·ize -iz·ing
cir·cu·late (sûr′ kû·lāt)
 -lat·ing

cir·cu·la·tion (sûr′ kû·lā·shŭn)
cir·cu·la·to·ry (sûr′ kû·là·tō′rĭ)
cir·cum·cise (sûr′ kŭm·sīz)
 -cis·ing
cir·cum·ci·sion
    (sûr′ kŭm·sĭzh′ ŭn)
cir·cum·fer·ence
    (sēr·kŭm′ fēr·ĕns)
cir·cum·flex (sûr′ kŭm·flĕks)
cir·cum·lo·cu·tion
    (sûr′ kŭm·lô·kū′ shŭn)
cir·cum·scribe (sûr′ kŭm·skrīb′)
 -scrib·ing
cir·cum·scrip·tion
    (sûr′ kŭm·skrĭp′ shŭn)
cir·cum·spect (sûr′ kŭm·spĕkt)
cir·cum·stance (sûr′ kŭm·stăns)
cir·cum·stan·tial
    (sûr′ kŭm·stăn′ shăl)
cir·cum·stan·ti·ate
    (sûr′ kŭm·stăn′ shĭ·āt)
 -at·ing
cir·cum·vent (sûr′ kŭm·vĕnt′)
cir·cum·ven·tion
    (-vĕn′ shŭn)
cir·cus (sûr′ kŭs)
cir·rho·sis (sĭ·rō′ sĭs)
cir·ro-cu·mu·lus
    (sĭr′ ô·kū′ mû·lŭs)
cir·ro-stra·tus (sĭr′ ô·strā′ tŭs)
cir·rus (sĭr′ ŭs)
cis·tern (sĭs′ tērn)
cit·a·del (sĭt′ à·dĕl)
ci·ta·tion (sĭ·tā′ shŭn)
cite (sīt)
  (quote; see *site, sight*)
  cit·ing cit·a·ble
cit·i·zen (sĭt′ ĭ·zĕn)
  cit·i·zen·ry
cit·ric ac·id (sĭt′ rĭk)
cit·ron (sĭt′ rŭn)
cit·ron·el·la (sĭt′ rŭn·ĕl′ à)
cit·rus fruit (sĭt′ rŭs)
cit·y (sĭt′ ĭ)
  cit·ies
  cit·i·fied (sĭt′ ĭ·fīd)
  cit·y-born cit·y·folk
civ·et (sĭv′ ĕt)
civ·ic (sĭv′ ĭk)
civ·il (sĭv′ ĭl)
  civ·il en·gi·neer
  civ·il law civ·il·ly
  civ·il rights civ·il serv·ice
ci·vil·ian (sĭ·vĭl′ yăn)

ci·vil·i·ty   (sĭ·vĭl′ ĭ·tĭ)
  -ties
civ·i·lize   (sĭv′ ĭ·līz)
  -liz·ing   civ·i·liz·a·ble
  civ·i·li·za·tion
          (sĭv′ ĭ·lĭ·zā′ shŭn)
claim·ant   (klām′ ănt)
clair·voy·ance   (klâr·voi′ ăns)
  -ant
clam·bake   (klăm′ bāk′)
clam·ber   (klăm′ bẽr)
clam·my   (klăm′ ĭ)
  clam·mi·ness
clam·or   (klăm′ ẽr)
  clam·or·ous
clan   (klăn)
  clan·nish   clans·man
clan·des·tine   (klăn·dĕs′ tĭn)
  -tine·ly
clang·or   (klăng′ ẽr)
  clang·or·ous
clap·board   (klăb′ ẽrd)
clap·per   (klăp′ ẽr)
claque   (klăk)
  (paid applauders)
clar·et   (klăr′ ĕt)
clar·i·fy   (klăr′ ĭ·fī)
  -fied,   -fy·ing
  clar·i·fi·ca·tion
         (klăr′ ĭ·fĭ·kā′ shŭn)
  clar·i·fi·er   (-fī′ ẽr)
clar·i·net   (klăr′ ĭ·nĕt′)
  clar·i·net·ist
clar·i·on   (klăr′ ĭ·ŭn)
clar·i·ty   (klăr′ ĭ·tĭ)
class   (klás)
  class·a·ble   class-con·scious
  class·mate   class·room
clas·sic   (klăs′ ĭk)
  clas·si·cal   -cal·ly
  clas·si·cism   (klăs′ ĭ·sĭz′m)
clas·si·fy   (klăs′ ĭ·fī)
  -fied,   -fy·ing
  clas·si·fi·a·ble   (-fī′ à·b′l)
  clas·si·fi·ca·tion
         (klăs′ ĭ·fĭ·kā′ shŭn)
clat·ter   (klăt′ ẽr)
clause   (klôz)
claus·tro·pho·bi·a
      (klôs′ trŏ·fō′ bĭ·à)
clav·i·chord   (klăv′ ĭ·kôrd)
clav·i·cle   (klăv′ ĭ·k′l)
clay   (klā)
  clay·ey   clay pi·geon

clean   (klēn)
  clean·a·ble   clean-cut
  clean·er
  clean·li·ness   (klĕn′ lĭ·nĕs)
  clean·ly   (klĕn′ lĭ)
  clean·ness
cleanse   (klĕnz)
  cleans·ing   cleans·er
clear   (klçr)
  clear-cut   clear-eyed
  clear·head·ed   clear·ing·house
  clear-sight·ed
  clear·ance   (klçr′ăns)
cleat   (klēt)
cleave   (klēv)
  cleav·ing
  cleav·age   (-ĭj)
  cleav·ers
clef   (klĕf)
  (musical notation; see *cliff*)
cleft pal·ate   (klĕft)
clem·en·cy   (klĕm′ ĕn·sĭ)
  -ent
clench   (klĕnch)
Cle·o·pat·ra   (klē′ ŏ·păt′ rà)
cler·gy·man   (klûr′ jĭ·măn)
cler·ic   (klĕr′ ĭk)
  cler·i·cal
clev·er   (klĕv′ ẽr)
cli·ché   (klē·shā′)
cli·ent   (klī′ ĕnt)
  cli·en·tele   (klī′ ĕn·tĕl′)
cliff   (klĭf)
  (rock; see *clef*)
cli·mate   (klī′ mĭt)
  cli·mat·ic   (klī·măt′ ĭk)
cli·max   (klī′ măks)
  cli·mac·tic   (klī·măk′ tĭk)
climb   (klīm)
cling·stone   (klĭng′ stōn′)
clin·ic   (klĭn′ ĭk)
  clin·i·cal   -cal·ly
  cli·ni·cian   (klĭ·nĭsh′ ăn)
clip·per   (klĭp′ ẽr)
clique   (klēk)
  cli·quish
clob·ber   (klŏb′ ẽr)
cloche   (klōsh)
clock·wise   (klŏk′ wīz′)
clod·dish   (klŏd′ ĭsh)
cloi·son·né   (kloi′ zŏ·nā′)
clois·ter   (klois′ tẽr)
close   (klōs) *adj*
  close·fist·ed   close·ly
  close-up

close (klōz) *v.*
  clos·ing
clos·et (klŏz′ ĕt)
  -et·ed -et·ing
clo·sure (klō′ zhẽr)
cloth (klôth) *n.*
clothe (klōth) *v.*
  cloth·ing
clothes (klōthz)
  clothes·bas·ket
  clothes·brush clothes·line
cloth·ier (klôth′ yẽr)
cloud·burst (kloud′ bûrst′)
cloud·y (kloud′ ĭ)
  cloud·i·est -i·ness
clout (klout)
clo·ver-leaf (klō′ vẽr·lēf′)
  adj.
clown·ish (kloun′ ĭsh)
cloy·ing (kloi′ ĭng)
club (klŭb)
  clubbed club·bing
  club car club chair
  club·foot·ed club·room
  club steak
clue (klōō)
  clu·ing
clum·sy (klŭm′ zĭ)
  clum·si·er -si·est
  -si·ly -si·ness
clus·ter (klŭs′ tẽr)
clutch (klŭch)
clut·ter (klŭt′ ẽr)
coach·man (kōch′ mǎn)
co·ag·u·late (kō·ăg′ ū·lāt)
  -lat·ing co·ag·u·lant
  co·ag·u·la·tion
    (kō·ăg′ ū·lā′ shŭn)
  co·ag·u·la·tor
coal (kōl)
  coal·bin coal gas
  coal mine coal tar
  coal·yard
co·a·lesce (kō′ à·lĕs′)
  -lesc·ing co·a·les·cence,
  -cent
co·a·li·tion (kō′ à·lĭsh′ ŭn)
coarse (kōrs)
  (rough; see *course*)
  coars·en coarse·ness
coast (kōst)
  coast·al coast ar·til·ler·y
  coast·er coast guard
  coast·ward
co·au·thor (kō·ô′ thẽr)

coax (kōks)
co·ax·i·al ca·ble
    (kō·ăk′ sĭ·ǎl)
cob·bler (kŏb′ lẽr)
cob·ble·stone (kŏb′ ′l·stōn′)
co·bra (kō′ brà)
cob·web (kŏb′ wĕb′)
  cob·web·by
co·caine (kō·kān′)
coc·cyx (kŏk′ sĭks)
  pl. coc·cy·ges (kŏk·sī′ jēz)
  coc·cyg·e·al (kŏk·sĭj′ ê·ǎl)
cock·a·too (kŏk′ à·tōō′)
cock·er span·iel
    (kŏk′ ẽr)
cock·eyed (kŏk′ īd′)
cock·le·shell (kŏk′ ′l·shĕl′)
cock·ney (kŏk′ nĭ)
cock·pit (kŏk′ pĭt′)
cock·roach (kŏk′ rōch′)
cock·sure (kŏk′ shōōr′)
cock·tail (kŏk′ tāl′)
cock·y (kŏk′ ĭ)
  cock·i·er -i·est
  -i·ly -i·ness
co·co mat·ting (kō′ kō)
co·coa (kō′ kō)
co·co·nut (kō′ kō·nŭt′)
co·coon (kō·kōōn′)
cod·dle (kŏd′ ′l)
  cod·dling
co·de·fend·ant (kō′ dĕ·fĕn′ dǎnt)
co·de·ine (kō′ dĕ·ēn)
cod·fish (kŏd′ fĭsh′)
codg·er (kŏj′ ẽr)
cod·i·cil (kŏd′ ĭ·sĭl)
cod·i·fy (kŏd′ ĭ·fī)
  -fied -fy·ing
  cod·i·fi·ca·tion
    (kŏd′ ĭ·fī·kā′ shŭn)
cod-liv·er oil (kŏd′ lĭv′ ẽr)
co·ed (kō′ ĕd′)
  co·ed·u·ca·tion·al
    (kō′ ĕd′ ū·kā′ shŭn·ǎl)
co·ef·fi·cient (kō′ ĕ·fĭsh′ ĕnt)
co·e·qual (kō·ē′ kwǎl)
co·erce (kō·ûrs′)
  -erc·ing
  co·er·ci·ble (kō·ûr′ sĭ·b′l)
  co·er·cion (-shŭn)
  co·er·cive (-sĭv)
co·es·sen·tial (kō′ ĕ·sĕn′ shǎl)
co·ex·ec·u·tor
  n. masc. (kō′ ĕg·zĕk′ ū·tẽr)
  co·ex·ec·u·trix (-trĭks) *n. fem.*

co·ex·ist (kō′ ĕg·zĭst′)
  co·ex·ist·ence
cof·fee (kôf′ ĭ)
  cof·fee·house   cof·fee·pot
  cof·fee shop   cof·fee ta·ble
cof·fers (kôf′ ērz)
cof·fin (kôf′ ĭn)
co·gent (kō′ jĕnt)
  co·gen·cy
cog·i·tate (kŏj′ ĭ·tāt)
  -tat·ing
  cog·i·ta·tion (kŏj′ ĭ·tā′ shŭn)
  cog·i·ta·tive (kŏj′ ĭ·tā′ tĭv)
  cog·i·ta·tor (kŏj′ ĭ·tā′ tēr)
co·gnac (kō′ nyăk)
cog·nate (kŏg′ nāt)
cog·ni·tion (kŏg·nĭsh′ ŭn)
cog·ni·zant (kŏg′ nĭ·zănt)
  -zance
cog·no·men (kŏg·nō′ mĕn)
cog·wheel (kŏg′ hwēl′)
co·hab·it (kō·hăb′ ĭt)
  co·hab·i·ta·tion
      (kō·hăb′ ĭ·tā′ shŭn)
co·here (kō·hēr′)
  -her·ing   co·her·ence,
  -ent
co·he·sion (kō·hē′ zhŭn)
  co·he·sive   -sive·ly
co·hort (kō′ hôrt)
coif (koif)
  coif·fure (kwä·fūr′)
coin (koin)
  coin·age (-ĭj)
co·in·cide (kō·ĭn·sīd′)
  -cid·ing
  co·in·ci·dence (kō·ĭn′ sĭ·dĕns)
  co·in·ci·dent·al
      (kō·ĭn′ sĭ·dĕn′ tăl)
co·in·her·it·ance
      (kō′ ĭn·hĕr′ ĭ·tăns)
co·in·sure (kō′ ĭn shōōr′)
co·i·tion (kō·ĭsh′ ŭn)
  co·i·tus (kō′ ĭ·tŭs)
col·an·der (kŭl′ ăn·dēr)
·ld (kōld)
  cold-blood·ed   cold cream
  cold sore   cold war
cole·slaw (kōl′ slô′)
col·ic (kŏl′ ĭk)
col·i·se·um (kŏl′ ĭ·sē′ ŭm)
  (any stadium; see *Colosseum*)
co·li·tis (kō·lī′ tĭs)
col·lab·o·rate (kō·lăb′ ō·rāt)
  -rat·ing

col·lab·o·ra·tion
      (kō·lăb′ ō·rā′ shŭn)
col·lab·o·ra·tive
      (kō·lăb′ ō·rā′ tĭv)
col·lab·o·ra·tor
      (kō·lăb′ ō·rā′ tēr)
col·lapse (kō′ lăps′)
  col·laps·ing   col·laps·i·ble
col·lar (kŏl′ ēr)
  col·lar·band   col·lar·bone
  col·lar but·ton
col·late (kō·lāt′)
  col·lat·ing
  col·la·tion (-lā′ shŭn)
col·lat·er·al (kō·lăt′ ēr·ăl)
  -al·ly
col·league (kŏl′ ēg)
col·lect (kō·lĕkt′)
  col·lect·i·ble   col·lec·tion
  col·lec·tive   -tive·ly
  col·lec·tiv·ism
  col·lec·tiv·i·ty
      (kŏl′ ĕk·tĭv′ ĭ·tĭ)
  col·lec·tiv·ize   -iz·ing
  col·lec·tor
col·lege (kŏl′ ĕj)
  col·le·gi·an (kō·lē′ jĭ·ăn)
  col·le·gi·ate (kō·lē′ jĭ·ĭt)
col·lide (kō·līd′)
  col·lid·ing
  col·li·sion (kō·lĭzh′ ŭn)
col·lie (kŏl′ ĭ)
col·lier·y (kŏl′ yēr·ĭ)
  col·lier·ies
col·li·sion (kō·lĭzh′ ŭn)
col·lo·di·on (kō·lō′ dĭ·ŭn)
col·loid (kŏl′ oid)
  col·loi·dal (kō·loi′ dăl)
col·lo·qui·al (kō·lō′ kwĭ·ăl)
  -al·ly
  col·lo·qui·al·ism
col·lo·quy (kŏl′ ō·kwĭ)
  -quies
col·lude (kō·lūd′)
  col·lud·ing   col·lu·sion
co·logne (kō·lōn′)
Co·lom·bi·a, (kō·lŭm′ bĭ·à)
  S. Amer.
  (see *Columbia*)
co·lon (kō′ lŏn)
colo·nel (kûr′ nĕl)
  colo·nel·cy
col·on·nade (kŏl′ ō·nād′)
col·o·ny (kŏl′ ō·nĭ)
  -nies

co·lo·ni·al (kŏ·lō′ nĭ·ᶑl)
col·o·nist
col·o·ni·za·tion
 (kŏl′ ŏ·nĭ·zā′ shŭn)
col·o·nize -niz·ing
col·o·phon (kŏl′ ŏ·fŏn)
col·or (kŭl′ ẽr)
col·or·a·tion (kŭl′ ẽr·ā′ shŭn)
col·or-blind col·or·ful,
-ful·ly -ful·ness
col·or·less -less·ness
Col·o·ra·do (kŏl′ ŏ·rä′ dō)
abbr. Colo.
Col·o·ra·dan (-rä′ d′n)
col·o·ra·tu·ra so·pran·o
 (kŭl′ ẽr·ᶑ·tū′ rᶑ)
co·los·sal (kŏ·lŏs′ ᶑl)
co·los·sal·ly
Col·os·se·um (kŏl′ ŏ·sē′ ŭm)
(Roman amphitheater; see
coliseum)
co·los·sus (kŏ·lŏs′ ŭs)
Co·lum·bi·a (kŏ·lŭm′ bĭ·ᶑ)
(University, River, District of;
see Colombia)
col·um·bine (kŏl′ ŭm·bīn)
Co·lum·bus (kŏ·lŭm′ bŭs)
col·umn (kŏl′ ŭm)
co·lum·nar (kŏ·lŭm′ nẽr)
col·um·nist
co·ma (kō′ mᶑ)
(trance; see comma)
com·bat (kŏm′ băt) n.
com·bat (kŏm′ băt′) v.
-bat·ing com·bat·a·ble
com·bat·ant (kŏm′ bᶑ·tᶑnt)
com·bat·ive
com·bine (kŏm′ bīn) n.
com·bine (kŏm·bīn′) v.
-bin·ing com·bin·a·ble
com·bi·na·tion
 (kŏm′ bĭ·nā′ shŭn)
com·bus·tion (kŏm′ bŭs′ chŭn)
com·bus·ti·ble
com·bus·tive com·bus·tor
come·back (kŭm′ băk′)
co·me·di·an (kŏ·mē′ dĭ·ᶑn)
co·me·di·enne (kŏ·mē′ dĭ·ĕn′)
n. fem.
come·down (kŭm′ doun′)
com·e·dy (kŏm′ ĕ·dĭ)
-dies
come·ly (kŭm′ lĭ)
come·li·er -li·est
-li·ness

com·et (kŏm′ ĕt)
come·up·pance
 (kŭm·ŭp′ ᶑns)
com·fort (kŭm′ fẽrt)
com·fort·a·ble
com·ic (kŏm′ ĭk)
com·i·cal -cal·ly
com·ing (kŭm′ ĭng)
com·ma (kŏm′ ᶑ)
(punctuation; see coma)
com·mand (kŏ·mánd′)
com·mand·er com·mand·ment
com·man·dant (kŏm′ ᶑn·dănt′)
com·man·deer (kŏm′ ᶑn·dẹr′)
com·man·do (kŏ·mán′ dō)
-dos
com·mem·o·rate
 (kŏ·mĕm′ ŏ·rāt)
-rat·ing
com·mem·o·ra·tion
 (kŏ·mĕm′ ŏ·rā′ shŭn)
com·mem·o·ra·tive
 (kŏ·mĕm′ ŏ·rā′ tĭv)
com·mence (kŏ·mĕns′)
com·menc·ing
com·mence·ment
com·mend (kŏ·mĕnd′)
com·mend·a·ble
com·mend·a·tion
 (kŏm′ ĕn·dā′ shŭn)
com·mend·a·tory
com·men·su·rate
 (kŏ·mĕn′ shŏŏ·rĭt)
com·men·su·ra·ble
com·men·su·rate·ly
com·men·su·ra·tion
 (kŏ·mĕn′ shŏŏ·rā′ shŭn)
com·ment (kŏm′ ĕnt)
com·men·tar·y
 (kŏm′ ĕn·tẽr′ ĭ)
-tar·ies
com·men·ta·tor (-tā′ tẽr)
com·merce (kŏm′ ûrs)
com·mer·cial (kŏ·mûr′ shᶑl)
com·mer·cial·ism
com·mer·cial·i·za·tion
 (kŏ·mûr′ shᶑl·ĭ·zā′ shŭn)
com·mer·cial·ize
-iz·ing com·merc·ial·ly
com·min·gle (kŏ·mĭng′ g′l)
-gling
com·mis·er·ate
 (kŏ·mĭz′ ẽr·āt)
-at·ing

com·mis·er·a·tion
    (kŏ·mĭz′ ẽr·ā′ shŭn)
com·mis·sar (kŏm′ ĭ·sär′)
  com·mis·sar·i·at
    (kŏm′ ĭ·sâr′ ĭ·ăt)
com·mis·sar·y (kŏm′ ĭ·sĕr′ ĭ)
  com·mis·sar·ies
com·mis·sion (kŏ·mĭsh′ ŭn)
  com·mis·sioned of·fi·cer
com·mit (kŏ·mĭt′)
  com·mit·ted com·mit·ting
  com·mit·ment com·mit·tal
com·mit·tee (kŏ·mĭt′ ĭ)
  com·mit·tee·man
com·mode (kŏ·mōd′)
com·mod·i·ous
    (kŏ·mō′ dĭ·ŭs)
com·mod·i·ty (kŏ·mŏd′ ĭ·tĭ)
  -ties
com·mo·dore (kŏm′ ŏ·dōr′)
com·mon (kŏm′ ŭn)
  com·mon de·nom·i·na·tor
  com·mon·er
  com·mon-law mar·riage
  com·mon·ly com·mon·ness
  com·mon·place
  com·mon sense *n.*
  com·mon-sense *adj.*
  com·mon stock
  com·mon weal
  com·mon·wealth
com·mo·tion (kŏ·mō′ shŭn)
com·mu·nal (kŏm′ û·nǎl)
  com·mu·nal·ly
com·mune (kŏ·mūn′) *v.*
  com·mun·ing (kŏm′ ûn) *n.*
com·mu·ni·cate
    (kŏ·mū′ nĭ·kāt)
  -cat·ing
  com·mu·ni·ca·ble
    (-kȧ·b'l)
  com·mu·ni·cant
    (-kȧnt)
  com·mu·ni·ca·tion
    (kŏ·mū′ nĭ·kā′ shŭn)
  com·mu·ni·ca·tive
    (-kā′ tĭv)
  com·mu·ni·ca·tor
    (-kā′ tẽr)
com·mun·ion (kŏ·mūn′ yŭn)
com·mu·ni·qué (kŏ·mū′ nĭ·kā′)
com·mu·nist (kŏm′ û·nĭst)
  com·mu·nism
  com·mu·nis·tic
    (kŏm′ û·nĭs′ tĭk)

com·mu·nize -niz·ing
Com·mu·nist kŏm′ û·nĭst)
  (specific political party)
com·mu·ni·ty (kŏ·mū′ nĭ·tĭ)
  -ties
com·mute (kŏ·mūt′)
  com·mut·ing
  com·mu·ta·tion
    (kŏm′ û·tā′ shŭn)
  com·mut·er
com·pact (kŏm·păkt′) *adj.*
    (kŏm′ păkt) *n.*
com·pan·ion (kŏm·păn′ yŭn)
  com·pan·ion·a·bil·i·ty
    (kŏm·păn′ yŭn·ȧ·bĭl′ ĭ·tĭ)
  com·pan·ion·a·ble
  com·pan·ion·ate
    (-ăt)
  com·pan·ion·ship
com·pa·ny (kŭm′ pȧ·nĭ)
  -nies
com·pare (kŏm·pâr′)
  -par·ing
  com·pa·ra·bil·i·ty
    (kŏm′ pȧ·rȧ·bĭl′ ĭ·tĭ)
  com·pa·ra·ble (kŏm′ pȧ·rȧ·b'l)
  com·par·a·tive
    (kŏm·păr′ ȧ·tĭv)
  -tive·ly
  com·pa·ri·son (kŏm·păr′ ĭ·sŭn)
com·part·ment (kŏm·pärt′ mĕnt)
com·pass (kŭm′ pȧs)
com·pas·sion (kŏm·păsh′ ŭn)
  com·pas·sion·ate (-ĭt)
com·pat·i·ble (kŏm·păt′ ĭ·b'l)
  com·pat·i·bil·i·ty
    (kŏm·păt′ ĭ·bĭl′ ĭ·tĭ)
com·pa·tri·ot (kŏm·pā′ trĭ·ŭt)
com·pel (kŏm·pĕl′)
  -pelled -pel·ling
com·pen·di·ous
    (kŏm·pĕn′ dĭ·ŭs)
com·pen·di·um
    (kŏm·pĕn′ dĭ·ŭm)
com·pen·sate (kŏm′ pĕn·sāt)
  -sat·ing
  com·pen·sa·tion
    (kŏm′ pĕn·sā′ shŭn)
  com·pen·sa·tive
    (kŏm′ pĕn·sā′ tĭv)
  com·pen·sa·to·ry
    (kŏm·pĕn′ sȧ·tō′ rĭ)
com·pete (kŏm·pēt′)
  -pet·ing

com·pe·tence (kŏm′ pĕ·tĕns)
  -ten·cy,   -tent
com·pe·ti·tion
     (kŏm′ pĕ·tĭsh′ ŭn)
  com·pet·i·tive
     (kŏm·pĕt′ ĭ·tĭv)
  -tive·ly
  com·pet·i·tor (kŏm·pĕt′ ĭ·tĕr)
com·pile (kŏm·pīl′)
  -pil·ing
  com·pi·la·tion
     (kŏm′ pĭ·lā′ shŭn)
com·pla·cent (kŏm·plā′ sĕnt)
  (self-satisfied; see *complaisant*)
  com·pla·cence
com·plain (kŏm·plān′)
  com·plain·ant com·plaint
com·plai·sant (kŏm·plā′ zănt)
  (obliging; see *complacent*)
  com·plai·sance
com·plect·ed (kŏm·plĕk′ tĕd)
com·ple·ment (kŏm′ plĕ·mĕnt)
  (that which completes; see
  compliment)
  com·ple·men·tal
  com·ple·men·ta·ry
     (kŏm′ plĕ·mĕn′ tå·rĭ)
com·plete (kŏm·plēt′)
  -plet·ing   com·plete·ly
  -plete·ness
  com·ple·tion (-plē′ shŭn)
com·plex (kŏm·plĕks′) *adj*
     (kŏm′ plĕks) *n.*
  com·plex·i·ty (kŏm·plĕk′ sĭ·tĭ)
com·plex·ion (kŏm·plĕk′ shŭn)
  com·plex·ioned
com·pli·ant (kŏm·plī′ ănt)
  -ance
com·pli·cate (kŏm′ plĭ·kāt)
  -cat·ing
  com·pli·ca·tion
     (kŏm′ plĭ·kā′ shŭn)
com·plic·i·ty (kŏm·plĭs′ ĭ·tĭ)
com·pli·ment (kŏm′ plĭ·mĕnt)
  (flattery; see *complement*)
  com·pli·men·ta·ry
     (kŏm′ plĭ·mĕn′ tå·rĭ)
com·ply (kŏm·plī′)
  -plied   -ply·ing
  com·pli·a·ble (kŏm·plī′ å·b'l)
com·po·nent (kŏm·pō′ nĕnt)
com·port (kŏm·pōrt′)
com·pose (kŏm·pōz′)
  -pos·ing   com·posedly
  com·pos·er

com·pos·ite (kŏm·pŏz′ ĭt)
com·po·si·tion
     (kŏm′ pŏ·zĭsh′ ŭn)
comp·os·i·tor (kŏm·pŏz′ ĭ·tĕr)
com·pos·ure (kŏm·pō′ zhĕr)
com·pote (kŏm′ pōt)
com·pound (kŏm·pound′) *v.*
     (kŏm′ pound) *n.,*
     adj.
  com·pound·a·ble
     (kŏm·pound′ å·b'l)
  com·pound in·ter·est
     (kŏm′ pound)
com·pre·hend (kŏm′ prĕ·hĕnd′)
  com·pre·hen·si·ble
     (-hĕn′ sĭ·b'l)
  com·pre·hen·sion
     (-hĕn′ shŭn)
  com·pre·hen·sive
     (hĕn′ sĭv)
com·press (kŏm·prĕs′) *v.*
     (kŏm′ prĕs) *n.*
  com·press·i·ble
     (kŏm·prĕs′ ĭ·b'l)
  com·pres·sion (kŏm·prĕsh′ ŭn)
  com·pres·sor (kŏm·prĕs′ ĕr)
com·prise (kŏm·prīz′)
  -pris·ing
com·pro·mise (kŏm′ prŏ·mīz)
  -mis·ing   com·pro·mis·er
Comp·tom·e·ter
     (kŏmp·tŏm′ ĕ·tĕr)
comp·trol·ler (kŏn·trōl′ ĕr)
com·pul·sion (kŏm·pŭl′ shŭn)
  com·pul·sive (-sĭv)
  com·pul·so·ry (-sŏ·rĭ)
  com·pul·so·ri·ly
com·punc·tion
     (kŏm·pŭngk′ shŭn)
com·pute (kŏm·pūt′)
  -put·ing   com·put·a·ble
  com·pu·ta·tion
     (kŏm′ pû·tā′ shŭn)
  com·put·er
com·rade (kŏm′ răd)
  com·rade·ship
con·cave (kŏn′ kāv)
  con·cav·i·ty (kŏn·kăv′ ĭ·tĭ)
con·ceal (kŏn·sēl′)
  -cealed   -ceal·ing
  con·ceal·a·ble con·ceal·ment
con·cede (kŏn·sēd′)
  -ced·ing
con·ceit (kŏn·sēt′)
  -ceit·ed

con·ceive (kŏn·sēv′)
  -ceiv·ing   con·ceiv·able,
  -bly
con·cen·trate (kŏn′ sĕn·trāt)
  -trat·ing
  con·cen·tra·tion
        (kŏn′ sĕn·trā′ shŭn)
  con·cen·tra·tor
con·cen·tric (kŏn·sĕn′ trĭk)
con·cept (kŏn′ sĕpt)
  con·cep·tion (kŏn·sĕp′ shŭn)
  con·cep·tu·al (kŏn·sĕp′ tû·ăl)
con·cern (kŏn·sûrn′)
  -cern·ing
con·cert (kŏn·sûrt′) v.
     (kŏn·sûrt′) n.
con·cer·ti·na (kŏn′ sĕr·tē′ nà)
con·cer·to (kŏn·chĕr′ tō)
  -tos
con·ces·sion (kŏn·sĕsh′ ŭn)
  con·ces·sion·aire
     (kŏn·sĕsh′ ŭn·âr′)
  con·ces·sion·ar·y
     (kŏn·sĕsh′ ŭn·ĕr′ ĭ)
conch shell (kŏngk)
con·cil·i·ate (kŏn·sĭl′ ĭ·āt)
  -at·ing
  con·cil·i·a·tion
     (kŏn·sĭl′ ĭ·ā′ shŭn)
  con·cil·i·a·tor (kŏn·sĭl′ ĭ·ā′ tĕr)
  con·cil·i·a·to·ry
     (kŏn·sĭl′ ĭ·à·tō′ rĭ)
con·cise (kŏn·sīs′)
  -cise·ly
con·clave (kŏn′ klāv)
con·clude (kŏn·klōōd′)
  -clud·ing
  con·clu·sion (-klōō′ zhŭn)
  con·clu·sive   -sive·ly
con·coct (kŏn·kŏkt′)
  con·coc·tion (kŏn·kŏk′ shŭn)
con·com·i·tant
     (kŏn·kŏm′ ĭ·tănt)
  -tance
con·cord (kŏn′ kôrd)
  con·cord·ance (kŏn·kôr′ dăns)
con·course (kŏn′ kōrs)
con·crete (kŏn′ krēt)
  -crete·ness
con·cu·bine (kŏng′ kû·bīn)
  con·cu·bi·nage
     (kŏn·kū′ bĭ·nĭj)
con·cu·pis·cent
     (kŏn·kū′ pĭ·sĕnt)
  -cence

con·cur (kŏn·kûr′)
  -curred   -cur·ring
  con·cur·rence   -cur·rent
con·cus·sion (kŏn·kŭsh′ ŭn)
con·demn (kŏn·dĕm′)
  con·dem·na·ble
  con·dem·na·tion
     (kŏn′ dĕm·nā′ shŭn)
  con·dem·na·to·ry
     (kŏn′ dĕm′ nà·tō′ rĭ)
  con·demn·er (-dĕm′ ēr)
con·dense (kŏn·dĕns′)
  -dens·ing   con·den·sa·ble
  con·den·sa·tion
     (kŏn′ dĕn·sā′ shŭn)
  con·dens·er
con·de·scend (kŏn′ dè·sĕnd′)
  con·de·scend·ing·ly
  con·de·scen·sion
     (-sĕn′ shŭn)
con·di·ment (kŏn′ dĭ·mĕnt)
con·di·tion (kŏn·dĭsh′ ŭn)
  con·di·tion·al -al·ly
con·dole (kŏn·dōl′)
  -dol·ing
  con·do·lence (-dō′ lĕns)
con·done (kŏn·dōn′)
  -don·ing
con·dor (kŏn′ dĕr)
con·duce (kŏn·dūs′)
  -duc·ing
  con·du·cive (-dū′ sĭv)
con·duct (kŏn′ dŭkt) n.
con·duct (kŏn·dŭkt′) v.
  con·duct·i·ble con·duc·tion
  con·duc·tive con·duc·tor
con·duit (kŏn′ dwĭt)
Co·ney Is. (kō′ nĭ)
con·fec·tion (kŏn·fĕk′ shŭn)
  con·fec·tion·er, -er·y
con·fed·er·a·cy
     (kŏn·fĕd′ ĕr·à·sĭ)
  -cies
  con·fed·er·ate (-ĭt)
  con·fed·er·a·tion
     (kŏn·fĕd′ ĕr·ā′ shŭn)
con·fer (kŏn·fûr′)
  -ferred   -fer·ring
  con·fer·ee (kŏn′ fĕr·ē′)
  con·fer·ence (kŏn′ fĕr·ĕns)
  con·fer·ra·ble
con·fess (kŏn·fĕs′)
  con·fess·ed·ly
  con·fes·sion (kŏn·fĕsh′ ŭn)
  -fes·sion·al con·fes·sor

con·fet·ti (kŏn·fĕt′ ĭ)
con·fi·dant (kŏn′ fĭ·dănt′)
  n. masc., (friend)
  con·fi·dante (kŏn′ fĭ·dănt′)
  n. fem.
con·fide (kŏn·fīd′)
  -fid·ing
con·fi·dent (kŏn′ fĭ·dĕnt)
  (sure)
  con·fi·dence con·fi·dent·ly
con·fi·den·tial (kŏn′ fĭ·dĕn′ shăl)
  -tial·ly
con·fig·u·ra·tion
     (kŏn′ fĭg′ û·rā′ shŭn)
con·fine (kŏn′ fīn′) v.
  -fin·ing con·fin·a·ble
  con·fine·ment
con·fines (kŏn′ fīnz) n.
con·firm (kŏn′ fûrm′)
  con·firm·a·ble
  con·fir·ma·tion
     (kŏn′ fĕr·mā′ shŭn)
  con·firm·a·to·ry
     (kŏn′ fûr′ mȧ·tō′ rĭ)
con·fis·cate (kŏn′ fĭs·kāt)
  -cat·ing
  con·fis·ca·tion
     (kŏn′ fĭs·kā′ shŭn)
  con·fis·ca·to·ry
     (kŏn·fĭs′ kȧ·tō′ rĭ)
con·fla·gra·tion
     (kŏn′ flȧ·grā′ shŭn)
con·flict (kŏn·flĭkt′) v.
     (kŏn′ flĭkt) n.
con·flu·ence (kŏn·flōō′ ĕns)
con·form (kŏn·fôrm′)
  con·form·able
  con·for·ma·tion
     (kŏn′ fôr·mā′ shŭn)
  con·form·ist con·form·ity
con·found (kŏn·found′)
  con·found·ed·ly
con·frere (kŏn′ frâr)
con·front (kŏn·frŭnt′)
  con·fron·ta·tion
     (kŏn′ frŭn·tā′ shŭn)
Con·fu·cius (kŏn·fū′ shŭs)
  Con·fu·cian·ism
     (kŏn·fū′ shŭn·ĭz′m)
con·fuse (kŏn·fūz′)
  -fus·ing con·fus·ed·ly
  con·fu·sion (-fū′ zhŭn)
con·fute (kŏn·fūt′)
  -fut·ing

con·fu·ta·tion
     (kŏn′ fû·tā′ shŭn)
con·ga (kŏng′ gȧ)
con·geal (kŏn·jēl′)
  -gealed -geal·ing
  con·geal·a·ble con·geal·ment
con·gen·ial (kŏn·jēn′ yăl)
  (compatible)
  con·ge·ni·al·i·ty
     (kŏn·jē′ nĭ·ăl′ ĭ·tĭ)
  con·gen·ial·ly
con·gen·i·tal (kŏn·jĕn′ ĭ·tăl)
  (inborn) con·gen·i·tal·ly
  con·gen·i·tal id·i·ot
con·gest (kŏn·jĕst′)
  con·ges·tion (-jĕs′ chŭn)
con·glom·er·ate
     (kŏn·glŏm′ ĕr·ĭt) adj.
  -at·ing (-āt) v.
  con·glom·er·a·tion
     (kŏn·glŏm′ ĕr·ā′ shŭn)
con·grat·u·late
     (kŏn·grăt′ û·lāt)
  -lat·ing
  con·grat·u·la·tion
     (kŏn·grăt′ û·lā′ shŭn)
  con·grat·u·la·tor (-lā′ tĕr)
  con·grat·u·la·to·ry (-lȧ·tō′ rĭ)
con·gre·gate (kŏng′ grĕ·gāt)
  -gat·ing
  con·gre·ga·tion
     (kŏng′ grĕ·gā′ shŭn)
Con·gre·ga·tion·al·ist
  (kŏng′ grĕ·gā′ shŭn·ăl·ĭst)
con·gress (kŏng′ grĕs)
  con·gres·sion·al
     (kŏn·grĕsh′ ŭn·ăl)
  con·gress·man
con·gru·ent (kŏng′ grōō·ĕnt)
  -ence
  con·gru·ity (kŏn·grōō′ ĭ·tĭ)
  con·gru·ous (kŏng′ grōō·ŭs)
con·ic (kŏn′ ĭk)
  con·i·cal
co·ni·fer (kō′ nĭ·fĕr)
  co·nif·er·ous (kō·nĭf′ ĕr·ŭs)
con·jec·ture (kŏn·jĕk′ tûr)
  con·jec·tur·al
con·ju·gal (kŏn′ jŏŏ·găl)
con·ju·gate (kŏn′ jŏŏ·gāt)
  -gat·ing
  con·ju·ga·tion
     (kŏn′ jŏŏ·gā′ shŭn)
con·junc·tion (kŏn·jŭngk′ shŭn)
  con·junc·tive con·junc·ture

con·jure   (kŭn′ jẽr)
  -jur·ing
  con·ju·ra·tion
           (kŏn′ jŏŏ·rā′ shŭn)
  con·jur·er   (kŭn′ jẽr·ẽr)
con·nect   (kŏ·nĕkt′)
  con·nect·ed·ly con·nec·tion
  con·nec·tive   con·nec·tor
Con·nect·i·cut (kŏ·nĕt′ ĭ·kŭt)
  abbr. Conn.
con·nip·tion fit (kŏ·nĭp′ shŭn)
con·nive   (kŏ·nīv′)
  con·niv·ing   con·niv·ance
  con·niv·er
con·nois·seur (kŏn′ ĭ·sûr′)
con·note   (kŏ·nōt′)
  con·not·ing
  con·no·ta·tion (kŏn′ ŏ·tā′ shŭn)
  con·not·a·tive (kŏ·nōt′ ȧ·tĭv)
con·nu·bi·al   (kŏ·nū′ bĭ·ȧl)
con·quer   (kŏng′ kẽr)
  con·quer·a·ble con·quer·or
con·quest   (kŏng′ kwĕst)
con·quis·ta·dor
         (kŏn·kwĭs′ tȧ·dôr)
con·san·guin·i·ty
       (kŏn′ săng·gwĭn′ ĭ·tĭ)
  con·san·guin·e·ous (-ê·ŭs)
con·science   (kŏn′ shĕns)
  con·science·less
con·sci·en·tious
       (kŏn′ shĭ·ĕn′ shŭs)
con·scious   (kŏn′ shŭs)
  con·scious·ness
con·script   (kŏn′ skrĭpt)
      adj., n.
      (kŏn·skrĭpt′) *v.*
  con·scrip·tion (kŏn·skrĭp′ shŭn)
con·se·crate   (kŏn′ sê·krāt)
  -crat·ing
  con·se·cra·tion
        (kŏn′ sê·krā′ shŭn)
  con·se·cra·tor
con·sec·u·tive (kŏn·sĕk′ û·tĭv)
  -tive·ly
con·sen·sus   (kŏn·sĕn′ sŭs)
  con·sen·su·al (-shû·ȧl)
con·sent   (kŏn·sĕnt′)
con·se·quence (kŏn′ sê·kwĕns)
  con·se·quent, -quent·ly
  con·se·quen·tial
       (kŏn′ sê·kwĕn′ shȧl)
  -tial·ly

con·serv·a·to·ry
       (kŏn·sûr′ vȧ·tō′ rĭ)
  -ries
con·serve   (kŏn·sûrv′)
  -serv·ing
  con·ser·va·tion
       (kŏn′ sẽr·vā′ shŭn)
  -tion·al
  con·serv·a·tism
       (kŏn·sûr′ vȧ·tĭz′m)
  con·serv·a·tive   (-tĭv)
  -tive·ly
con·sid·er   (kŏn·sĭd′ ẽr)
  con·sid·er·a·ble, -bly
  con·sid·er·ate (-ĭt)
  -ate·ly
  con·sid·er·a·tion
       (kŏn·sĭd′ ẽr·ā′ shŭn)
con·sign   (kŏn·sīn′)
  con·sign·ee (kŏn′ sĭ·nē′)
  con·sign·ment con·sign·or
con·sist   (kŏn·sĭst′)
  con·sist·ent (kŏn·sĭs′ tĕnt)
  con·sist·en·cy con·sist·ent·ly
con·sole   (kŏn·sōl′) *v.*
  -sol·ing
  con·so·la·tion
       (kŏn′ sŏ·lā′ shŭn)
  con·so·ler
con·sole ta·ble (kŏn′ sōl)
con·sol·i·date (kŏn·sŏl′ ĭ·dāt)
  -dat·ing
  con·sol·i·da·tion
       (kŏn·sŏl′ ĭ·dā′ shŭn)
con·som·mé   (kŏn′ sŏ·mā′)
con·so·nance (kŏn′ sŏ·nȧns)
  -nant
con·sort   (kŏn′ sôrt) *n.*
      (kŏn·sôrt′) *v.*
con·spic·u·ous (kŏn·spĭk′ û·ŭs)
con·spir·a·cy (kŏn·spĭr′ ȧ·sĭ)
  -cies
con·spir·a·tor (kŏn·spĭr′ ȧ·tẽr)
  con·spir·a·to·ri·al
       (kŏn·spĭr′ ȧ·tō′ rĭ·ȧl)
con·spire   (kŏn·spīr′)
  -spir·ing
con·sta·ble   (kŭn′ stȧ·b′l)
con·stab·u·lar·y
       (kŏn·stăb′ û·lẽr′ ĭ)
  -lar·ies
con·stant   (kŏn′ stȧnt)
  -stan·cy
con·stel·la·tion
       (kŏn′ stĕ·lā′ shŭn)

con·ster·na·tion
      (kŏn′ stĕr·nā′ shŭn)
con·sti·pat·ed (kŏn′ stĭ·pāt′ ĕd)
  con·sti·pa·tion
      (kŏn′ stĭ·pā′ shŭn)
con·stit·u·en·cy
      (kŏn·stĭt′ û·ĕn·sĭ)
  -ent
con·sti·tute (kŏn′ stĭ·tūt′)
  -tut·ing
con·sti·tu·tion (kŏn′ stĭ·tū′ shŭn)
  con·sti·tu·tion·al, -al·ism,
  -al·ly
  con·sti·tu·tion·al·i·ty
    (kŏn′ stĭ·tū′ shŭn·ăl′ ĭ·tĭ)
con·strain (kŏn·strān′)
  con·strain·ed·ly
     (-strān′ ĕd·lĭ)
  con·straint
con·strict (kŏn·strĭkt′)
  con·stric·tion (-strĭk′ shŭn)
  con·stric·tive con·stric·tor
con·struct (kŏn·strŭkt′)
  con·struc·ter
  con·struc·tion (-strŭk′ shŭn)
  con·struc·tive -tive·ly
con·strue (kŏn·strōō′)
  -stru·ing
con·sul (kŏn′ sŭl)
  (diplomat; see *council, counsel*)
  con·su·lar (kŏn′ sû·lĕr)
  con·su·late (kŏn′ sû·lăt)
con·sult (kŏn·sŭlt′)
  con·sult·ant (-tănt)
  con·sul·ta·tion
      (kŏn′ sŭl·tā′ shŭn)
  con·sul·tive (-tĭv)
con·sume (kŏn·sūm′)
  -sum·ing con·sum·a·ble
  con·sum·ers′ goods
con·sum·mate (kŏn·sŭm′ ĭt)
  adj. (perfect)
con·sum·mate (kŏn′ sŭ·māt) *v.*
  (to complete)
  -sum·mat·ing
  con·sum·ma·tion
      (kŏn′ sŭ·mā′ shŭn)
con·sump·tion (kŏn·sŭmp′ shŭn)
con·sump·tive (kŏn·sŭmp′ tĭv)
con·tact (kŏn′ tăkt)
  con·tact lens con·tact print
con·ta·gion (kŏn·tā′ jŭn)
  con·ta·gious (-jŭs)
con·tain (kŏn·tān′)
  con·tain·a·ble con·tain·er

con·tam·i·nate (kŏn·tăm′ ĭ·nāt)
  -nat·ing
  con·tam·i·na·tion
      (kŏn·tăm′ ĭ·nā′ shŭn)
  con·tam·i·na·tor
con·tem·plate (kŏn′ tĕm·plāt)
  -plat·ing
  con·tem·pla·tion
      (kŏn′ tĕm·plā′ shŭn)
  con·tem·pla·tive
      (kŏn·tĕm′ plă·tĭv)
con·tem·po·rar·y
      (kŏn·tĕm′ pŏ·rĕr′ ĭ)
  -rar·ies
  con·tem·po·ra·ne·ous
      (-tĕm′ pŏ·rā′ nē·ŭs)
con·tempt (kŏn·tĕmpt′)
  con·tempt·i·ble
  con·temp·tu·ous
      (-tĕmp′ tû·ŭs)
con·tend (kŏn·tĕnd′)
  con·tend·er
con·tent (kŏn′ tĕnt) *n.*
con·tent (kŏn·tĕnt′) *adj.*
  con·tent·ed con·tent·ment
con·ten·tion (kŏn·tĕn′ shŭn)
con·ten·tious (kŏn·tĕn′ shŭs)
con·ter·mi·nous
      (kŏn·tûr′ mĭ·nŭs)
con·test (kŏn′ tĕst) *n.*
con·test (kŏn·tĕst′) *v.*
  con·test·a·ble con·test·ant
con·text (kŏn′ tĕkst)
con·tig·u·ous (kŏn·tĭg′ û·ŭs)
  con·ti·gu·i·ty (kŏn′ tĭ·gū′ ĭ·tĭ)
con·ti·nence (kŏn′ tĭ·nĕns)
  -nen·cy
con·ti·nent (kŏn′ tĭ·nĕnt)
  con·ti·nen·tal (kŏn′ tĭ·nĕn′ tăl)
con·tin·gent (kŏn·tĭn′ jĕnt)
  -gen·cy
con·tin·ue (kŏn·tĭn′ û)
  -u·ing
  con·tin·u·al -al·ly
  con·tin·u·ance
  con·tin·u·a·tion
      (kŏn·tĭn′ û·ā′ shŭn)
  con·tin·u·ous
con·ti·nu·i·ty (kŏn′ tĭ·nū′ ĭ·tĭ)
  -ties
con·tort (kŏn·tôrt′)
  con·tor·tion·ist
      (-tôr′ shŭn·ĭst)
con·tour (kŏn′ tōōr)
con·tra·band (kŏn′ trá·bănd)

con·tra·cep·tion
   (kŏn′ trȧ·sĕp′ shŭn)
 con·tra·cep·tive
con·tract (kŏn′ trăkt) n.
 con·trac·tor
con·tract (kŏn·trăkt′) v.
 con·tract·i·ble
 con·trac·tion (-trăk′ shŭn)
 con·trac·tu·al (-trăk′ tū̇·ȧl)
con·tra·dict (kŏn′ trȧ·dĭkt′)
 con·tra·dic·tion (-dĭk′ shŭn)
 con·tra·dic·to·ry (-dĭk′ tō̇·rĭ)
con·tra·dis·tinc·tion
   (kŏn′ trȧ·dĭs·tĭngk′ shŭn)
con·tral·to (kŏn·trăl′ tō)
 -tos
con·tra·ry (kŏn′ trĕr·ĭ)
 con·tra·ri·ly (-trĕr·ĭ·lĭ)
 con·tra·ri·ness (-ĭ·nĕs)
 con·tra·ri·wise (ĭ·wīs′)
con·trast (kŏn·trăst′) v.
 con·trast·a·ble
con·trast (kŏn′ trăst) n.
con·tra·vene (kŏn′ trȧ·vēn′)
 -ven·ing
 con·tra·ven·tion
   (kŏn′ trȧ·vĕn′ shŭn)
con·trib·ute (kŏn·trĭb′ ūt)
 -but·ing
 con·trib·ut·a·ble
 con·tri·bu·tion
   (kŏn′ trĭ·bū′ shŭn)
 con·trib·u·tor
 con·trib·u·to·ry
   (-trĭb′ ū·tō̇′ rĭ)
con·trite (kŏn′ trīt)
 -trite·ly
 con·tri·tion (kŏn·trĭsh′ ŭn)
con·trive (kŏn·trīv′)
 -triv·ing
 con·triv·ance (kŏn·trīv′ ȧns)
con·trol (kŏn·trōl′)
 -trolled -trol·ling
 con·trol·la·ble con·trol·ler
con·tro·ver·sy (kŏn′ trō̇·vûr′ sĭ)
 -sies
 con·tro·ver·sial
   (kŏn′ trō̇·vûr′ shȧl)
 -sial·ly
con·tro·vert (kŏn′ trō̇·vûrt)
con·tu·ma·cious
   (kŏn′ tū̇·mā′ shŭs)
 con·tu·ma·cy (kŏn′ tū̇·mȧ·sĭ)
con·tu·sion (kŏn·tū′ zhŭn)
co·nun·drum (kō̇·nŭn′ drŭm)

con·va·lesce (kŏn′ vȧ·lĕs′)
 -lesc·ing
 con·va·les·cent, -cence
con·vec·tion (kŏn·vĕk′ shŭn)
 con·vec·tive (-vĕk′ tĭv)
con·vene (kŏn·vēn′)
 -ven·ing
con·ven·ience (kŏn·vēn′ yĕns)
 -ient
con·vent (kŏn′ vĕnt)
con·ven·tion (kŏn·vĕn′ shŭn)
 con·ven·tion·al, -al·ly
 con·ven·tion·al·i·ty
   (kŏn·vĕn′ shŭn·ăl′ ĭ·tĭ)
con·verge (kŏn·vûrj′)
 -verg·ing
 con·ver·gence (-vûr′ jĕns)
 -gent
con·verse (kŏn·vûrs′) v.
 -vers·ing
 con·ver·sance (kŏn′ vĕr·sȧns)
 -sant
 con·ver·sa·tion
   (kŏn′ vĕr·sā′ shŭn)
 -tion·al
con·verse (kŏn′ vûrs)
 adj., n.
con·ver·sion (kŏn·vûr′ shŭn)
con·vert (kŏn·vûrt′) v.
 con·vert·i·ble (-vûr′ tĭ·b′l)
con·vert (kŏn′ vûrt) n.
con·vex (kŏn′ vĕks)
 con·vex·i·ty (kŏn·vĕk′ sĭ·tĭ)
con·vey (kŏn·vā′)
 con·vey·ance (kŏn·vā′ ȧns)
 con·vey·er
con·vict (kŏn′ vĭkt) n.
con·vict (kŏn·vĭkt′) v.
 con·vic·tion (-vĭk′ shŭn)
con·vince (kŏn·vĭns′)
 -vinc·ing con·vin·ci·ble
 con·vinc·ing·ly
con·viv·i·al (kŏn·vĭv′ ĭ·ȧl)
 con·viv·i·al·i·ty
   (kŏn·vĭv′ ĭ·ăl′ ĭ·tĭ)
 con·viv·i·al·ly
con·vo·ca·tion
   (kŏn′ vō̇·kā′ shŭn)
con·voke (kŏn·vōk′)
 -vok·ing
con·vo·lu·tion (kŏn′ vō̇·lū′ shŭn)
con·voy (kŏn·voi′) v.
   (kŏn′ voi) n.
con·vulse (kŏn·vŭls′)
 -vuls·ing

con·vul·sion (-vŭl′ shŭn)
con·vul·sive (-vŭl′ sĭv)
cook·book (kŏŏk′ bŏŏk′)
cook·er·y (kŏŏk′ ẽr·ĭ)
cook·y (kŏŏk′ ĭ)
  cook·ies
cool (kōōl)
  cool·ant (kōōl′ ănt)
  cool·er   cool·ly
  cool·ness
coo·lie (kōō′ lĭ)
  (laborer; see *coulee*)
coop·er·age (kōōp′ ẽr·ĭj)
co·op·er·ate (kō·ŏp′ ẽr·āt)
  -at·ing
  co·op·er·a·tion
        (kŏ·ŏp′ ẽr·ā′ shŭn)
  co·op·er·a·tive
        (kŏ·ŏp′ ẽr·ā′ tĭv)
  -tive·ness
co·opt (kō·ŏpt′)
  co·op·ta·tion (cō′ ŏp·tā′ shŭn)
co·or·di·nate (kō·ôr′ dĭ·nāt) *v.*
  -nat·ing (-ăt) *n., adj.*
  co·or·di·na·tion
        (kō·ôr′ dĭ·nā′ shŭn)
co·part·ner (kō·pärt′ nẽr)
Co·pen·ha·gen, (kō′ pĕn·hā′ gĕn)
  Den·mark
Co·per·ni·cus (kō·pûr′ nĭ·kŭs)
  Co·per·ni·can (kō·pûr′ nĭ·kăn)
cop·ing saw (kōp′ ĭng)
co·pi·ous (kō′ pĭ·ŭs)
cop·per (kŏp′ ẽr)
  cop·per·head   cop·per·plate
  cop·per·smith
cop·u·late (kŏp′ û·lāt)
  -lat·ing
  cop·u·la·tion (kŏp′ û·lā′ shŭn)
cop·y (kŏp′ ĭ)
  cop·ies   cop·y·book
  cop·y·cat   cop·y·hol·der
  cop·y·ist   cop·y·right
co·quette (kō·kĕt′)
  co·quet·ry (kō′ kĕ·trĭ)
  co·quet·tish
cor·al (kŏr′ ăl)
  (as in *coral* reef; see *corral*)
cord (kôrd)
  (string; see *chord*)
  cord·age (kôr′ dĭj)
cor·dial (kôr′ jăl)
  cor·dial·i·ty (kôr·jăl′ ĭ·tĭ)
  cor·dial·ly
cor·don (kôr′ dŏn)

cor·do·van (kôr′ dŏ·văn)
cor·du·roy (kôr′ dŭ·roi)
co·re·spond·ent
        (kŏ′ rĕ·spŏn′ dĕnt)
  (legal term; see *correspondent*)
co·ri·an·der (kō′ rĭ·ăn′ dẽr)
cork·screw (kôrk′ skrōō′)
cor·mo·rant (kôr′ mŏ·rănt)
corn (kôrn)
  corn bor·er   corn bread
  corn·cake   corn·cob
  corn·flow·er   corn pone
  corn sir·up   corn starch
  corn sug·ar
cor·ne·a (kôr′ nê·ȧ)
  cor·ne·al
cor·ner (kôr′ nẽr)
  cor·ner·stone
cor·net (kôr′ nĕt)
  (horn; see *coronet*)
  cor·net·tist (kôr′ nĕt′ ĭst)
cor·nice (kôr′ nĭs)
cor·nu·co·pi·a (kôr′ nŭ·kō′ pĭ·ȧ)
cor·ol·lar·y (kôr′ ŏ·lẽr′ ĭ)
  -ol·lar·ies
co·ro·na (kō·rō′ nȧ)
cor·o·nar·y throm·bo·sis
        (kôr′ ŏ·nẽr′ ĭ)
cor·o·na·tion (kôr′ ŏ·nā′ shŭn)
cor·o·ner (kôr′ ŏ·nẽr)
cor·o·net (kôr′ ŏ·nĕt)
  (crown; see *cornet*)
cor·po·ral (kôr′ pŏ·răl)
cor·po·rate (kôr′ pŏ·rĭt)
  cor·po·ra·te·ly
cor·po·ra·tion (kôr′ pŏ·rā′ shŭn)
  cor·po·ra·tive (kôr′ pŏ·rā′ tĭv)
cor·po·re·al (kôr·pŏ′ rĕ·ăl)
corps (kōr)
  corps·man (kōr′ măn)
cor·pu·lent (kôr′ pû·lĕnt)
  -lence
Cor·pus Chris·ti,
  Tex. (kôr′ pŭs krĭs′ tĭ)
cor·pus·cle (kôr′ pŭs·′l)
cor·ral (kŏ·răl′)
  (stockade; see *coral*)
  cor·ralled
cor·rect (kŏ·rĕkt′)
  cor·rec·tion·al (-rĕk′ shŭn·ăl)
  cor·rec·tive   cor·rec·tor
cor·re·late (kôr′ ĕ·lāt)
  -lat·ing
  cor·re·la·tion (kôr′ ĕ·lā′ shŭn)
  cor·rel·a·tive (kŏ·rĕl′ ȧ·tĭv)

cor·re·spond   (kŏr′ ĕ·spŏnd′)
cor·re·spond·ent
               (kŏr′ ĕ·spŏn′ dĕnt)
  (letter writer; see *corespondent*)
  cor·re·spond·ence
cor·ri·dor   (kŏr′ ĭ·dôr)
cor·rob·o·rate   (kŏ·rŏb′ ô·rāt)
  -rat·ing
  cor·rob·o·ra·tion
           (kŏ·rŏb′ ô·rā′ shŭn)
  cor·rob·o·ra·tive (-rā′ tĭv)
cor·rode   (kŏ·rōd′)
  cor·rod·ing
cor·ro·sion   (kŏ·rō′ zhŭn)
  cor·ro·sive   (-sĭv)
cor·ru·gat·ed i·ron
         (kŏr′ û·gāt′ ĕd)
  cor·ru·ga·tion (kŏr′ û·gā′ shŭn)
cor·rupt   (kŏ·rŭpt′)
  cor·rupt·er cor·rupt·i·ble
  cor·rup·tion cor·rup·tive
cor·sage   (kŏr·säzh′)
cor·sair   (kŏr′ sâr)
cor·set   (kŏr′ sĕt)
cor·tege   (kŏr·tĕzh′)
cor·tex   (kŏr′ tĕks)
  pl. cor·ti·ces (-tĭ·sēz)
  cor·ti·cal (-tĭ·kăl)
cor·ti·sone   (kŏr′ tĭ·sōn)
Cor·vette   (kŏr·vĕt′)
cos·met·ic   (kŏz·mĕt′ ĭk)
  cos·met·i·cal·ly
cos·mic   (kŏz′ mĭk)
  cos·mi·cal·ly cos·mic dust
  cos·mic ray
cos·mol·o·gy   (kŏz·mŏl′ ô·jĭ)
  -gies
  cos·mo·log·i·cal
        (kŏz′ mŏ·lŏj′ ĭ·kăl)
cos·mo·pol·i·tan
        (kŏz′ mŏ·pŏl′ ĭ·tăn)
  cos·mop·o·lite (kŏz·mŏp′ ô·līt)
cos·mos   (kŏz′ mŏs)
Cos·sack   (kŏs′ ăk)
Cos·ta Ri·ca   (kŏs′ tà rē′ kà)
cost·ly   (kŏst′ lĭ)
  cost·li·ness
cos·tume   (kŏs′ tūm)
co·te·rie   (kō′ tĕ·rĭ)
co·til·lion   (kŏ·tĭl′ yŭn)
cot·tage   (kŏt′ ĭj)
cot·ter pin   (kŏt′ ēr)
cot·ton   (kŏt′ ′n)
  cot·ton belt cot·ton flan·nel
  cot·ton gin cot·ton·mouth

  cot·ton·seed cot·ton·tail
  cot·ton·wood
couch   (kouch)
cou·gar   (kōō′ gēr)
cough   (kŏf)
could   (kŏŏd)
cou·lee   (kōō′ lĭ)
  (deep valley; see *coolie*)
coun·cil   (koun′ sĭl)
  (assembly; see *consul, counsel*)
  coun·cil·man
coun·sel   (koun′ sĕl)
  (advice; see *council, consul*)
  -seled   -sel·ing
  coun·se·lor
count   (kount)
  count·a·ble count·less
coun·te·nance (koun′ tĕ·nǎns)
coun·ter-   (koun′ tēr-)
  coun·ter·act
  coun·ter·bal·ance
  coun·ter·charge, -charg·ing
  coun·ter·claim
  coun·ter·clock·wise
  coun·ter·cur·rent
  coun·ter·es·pi·o·nage
  coun·ter·feit, -feit·er
  coun·ter·in·tel·li·gence
  coun·ter·ir·ri·tant
  coun·ter·mand
  coun·ter·of·fen·sive
  coun·ter·part
  coun·ter·prop·a·gan·da
  coun·ter·rev·o·lu·tion
  coun·ter·sign
  coun·ter·vail·ing
count·ess   (koun′ tĕs)
coun·try   (kŭn′ trĭ)
  -tries
  coun·tri·fied (kŭn′ trĭ·fīd)
  coun·try-bred coun·try·man
  coun·try·side coun·try-style
coun·ty   (koun′ tĭ)
  -ties
coup d′é·tat   (kōō dā′ tá′)
cou·pé   (kōō′ pā′)
cou·ple   (kŭp′ ′l)
  -pling
  cou·plet (kŭp′ lĕt)
cou·pon   (kōō′ pŏn)
cour·age   (kûr′ ĭj)
  cou·ra·geous (kǔ·rā′ jǔs)
cour·i·er   (kŏŏr′ ĭ·ēr)
course   (kōrs)
  (path; see *coarse*)

court (kōrt)
  court·house   court-mar·tial
  court·room   court·ship
  court·yard
cour·te·ous (kûr′ tē·ŭs)
cour·te·san (kōr′ tē·zǎn)
cour·te·sy (kûr′ tē·sǐ)
  -sies
court·ly (kōrt′ lǐ)
  court·li·ness
cous·in (kŭz′ 'n)
cou·tu·rier (kōō′ tū·ryā′)
  n. masc.
  cou·tu·rière (kōō′ tū·ryâr′)
  n. fem.
cov·e·nant (kŭv′ ě·nǎnt)
cov·er·age (kŭv′ ēr·ǐj)
cov·er·let (kŭv′ ēr·lět)
cov·ert (kŭv′ ērt)
cov·et (kŭv′ ět)
  -et·ed   -et·ing
  cov·et·ous (kŭv′ ě·tŭs)
cov·ey (kŭv′ ǐ)
  (flock)
cow (kou)
  cow·bell   cow·bird
  cow·boy   cow·hide
  cow·man
cow·ard (kou′ ērd)
  cow·ard·ice (kou′ ēr·dǐs)
  cow·ard·li·ness
cow·lick (kou′ lǐk′)
co-work·er (kō·wûr′ kēr)
cox·swain (kŏk′ s'n)
coy·ness (koi·něs)
coy·ote (kī′ ōt)
co·zy (kō′ zǐ)
  co·zi·er   -zi·est
  -zi·ly   -zi·ness
crab (krǎb)
  crab ap·ple   crab·by
  crab grass
crack (krǎk)
  crack·down   crack·pot
  crack-up
crack·er (krǎk′ ēr)
crack·le (krǎk′ 'l)
  -ling   crack·ly
cra·dle (krā′ d'l)
  -dling
craft (kráft)
  crafts·man·ship
  craft·y   craft·i·er
  -i·est, -i·ly, -i·ness

crag (krǎg)
  crag·gi·ness   crag·gy
cram·pon (krǎm′ pǒn)
cran·ber·ry (krǎn′ běr′ ǐ)
  -ber·ries
cra·ni·al (krā′ nǐ·ǎl)
  -al·ly
cra·ni·um (krā′ nǐ·ǔm)
crank (krǎngk)
  crank·case   crank·pin
  crank·shaft   crank·y
cran·ny (krǎn′ ǐ)
  cran·nied
crap·pie (krǎp′ ǐ)
crass (krǎs)
crate (krāt)
  crat·ing
cra·ter (krā′ tēr)
cra·vat (krà·vǎt′)
crave (krāv)
  crav·ing
cra·ven (krā′ věn)
  cra·ven·ly   cra·ven·ness
crawl (krôl)
cray·fish (krā′ fǐsh)
cray·on (krā′ ǒn)
cra·zy (krā′ zǐ)
  cra·zi·er, -zi·est, -zi·ly, -zi·ness
  cra·zy bone   cra·zy quilt
creak (krēk)
  (sound; see creek)
  creak·i·ness   creak·y
cream·er·y (krēm′ ēr·ǐ)
  -er·ies
crease (krēs)
  creas·ing
cre·ate (krē·āt′)
  -at·ing   cre·a·tion
  cre·a·tive   cre·a·tor
crea·ture (krē′ tůr)
crèche (krāsh)
cre·dence (krē′ děns)
cre·den·tial (krē·děn′ shǎl)
cred·i·ble (krěd′ ǐ·b'l)
  cred·i·bil·i·ty (krěd′ ǐ·bǐl′ ǐ·tǐ)
cred·it (krěd′ ǐt)
  -it·ed   -it·ing
  cred·it·a·ble   cred·i·tor
cre·do (krē′ dō)
  -dos
cre·du·li·ty (krē·dū′ lǐ·tǐ)
cred·u·lous (krěd′ û·lŭs)
creek (krēk)
  (stream; see creak)

creep (krēp)
  crept (krĕpt)
cre·mate (krē' māt)
  -mat·ing
  cre·ma·tion (krĕ·mā' shŭn)
  crem·a·to·ri·um
       (krĕm' à·tō' rĭ·ŭm)
cre·ole (krē' ōl)
cre·o·sol (krē' ô·sōl)
cre·o·sote (krē' ô·sōt)
crepe (krāp)
  crepe pa·per *n.*
  crepe-pa·per *adj.*
  crepe rub·ber
  crepe su·zette (krāp' sōō·zĕt')
cre·scen·do (krĕ·shĕn' dō)
  -dos
cres·cent (krĕs' ĕnt)
crest·fall·en (krĕst' fôl' ĕn)
cre·tin (krē' tĭn)
cre·tonne (krĕ·tŏn')
cre·vasse (krĕ·văs')
crev·ice (krĕv' ĭs)
crib·bage (krĭb' ĭj)
crick·et (krĭk' ĕt)
cried (krīd)
  cri·er (krī' ĕr)
crim·i·nal (krĭm' ĭ·nãl)
  -nal·ly
  crim·i·nal·i·ty
       (krĭm' ĭ·nãl' ĭ·tĭ)
  crim·i·nol·o·gy
       (krĭm' ĭ·nŏl' ô·jĭ)
crim·son (krĭm' z'n)
cringe (krĭnj)
  cring·ing
crin·kle (krĭng' k'l)
  -kling
crin·o·line (krĭn' ô·lĭn)
crip·ple (krĭp' 'l)
  crip·pling crip·pler
cri·sis (crī' sĭs)
  pl. cri·ses (-sēz)
crisp·y (krĭs' pĭ)
criss·cross (krĭs' krŏs')
cri·te·ri·on (krī·tẽr' ĭ·ŭn)
  pl. cri·te·ri·a
crit·ic (krĭt' ĭk)
  crit·i·cal -cal·ly
  crit·i·cism (krĭt' ĭ·sĭz'm)
  crit·i·cize (-sīz)
  -ciz·ing
cri·tique (krĭ·tēk')
croak (krōk)

cro·chet (krô·shā')
  -chet·ing
crock·er·y (krŏk' ẽr·ĭ)
croc·o·dile (krŏk' ô·dĭl)
cro·cus (krō' kŭs)
  -cus·es
Croe·sus (krē' sŭs)
Cro-Ma·gnon (krō·mănʹ yŏn)
cro·ny (krō' nĭ)
  -nies
crook·ed (krŏŏk' ĕd)
cro·quet (krô·kā')
  (game)
cro·quette (krô·kĕt')
  (food)
cross (krŏs)
  cross·bar cross·bow
  cross·bred cross-coun·try
  cross·cut cross-ex·am·ine
  cross-eyed
  cross-fer·ti·li·za·tion
  cross fire cross-grained
  cross in·dex *n.* cross-in·dex *v.*
  cross·o·ver
  cross-pol·li·na·tion
  cross-ques·tion
  cross ref·er·ence
  cross·road cross·ruff
  cross sec·tion cross-stitch
  cross·walk cross·wise
  cross·word puz·zle
crotch·et·y (krŏch' ĕ·tĭ)
  crotch·et·i·ness
crouch (krouch)
croup (krōōp)
crou·pi·er (krōō' pĭ·ẽr)
crou·ton (krōō·tŏɴ')
crow·bar (krō' băr')
crowd (kroud)
cru·cial (krōō' shãl)
  -cial·ly
cru·ci·ble (krōō' sĭ·b'l)
cru·ci·fix (krōō' sĭ·fĭks)
  cru·ci·fix·ion
       (krōō' sĭ·fĭk' shŭn)
cru·ci·fy (krōō' sĭ·fī)
  -fied -fy·ing
crude (krōōd)
  crude·ly
  cru·di·ty (krōō' dĭ·tĭ)
cru·el (krōō' ĕl)
  cru·el·ly cru·el·ty
cru·et (krōō' ĕt)
cruise (krōōz)
  cruis·ing cruis·er

crul·ler (krŭl′ ẽr)
crum·ble (krŭm′ b'l)
  -bling
crum·ple (krŭm′ p'l)
  -pling
cru·sade (krōō·sād′)
  -sad·ing   cru·sad·er
crus·ta·cean (krŭs·tā′ shăn)
  crus·ta·ceous (-shŭs)
crust·y (krŭs′ tĭ)
  crust·i·ness
crutch (krŭch)
crux (krŭks)
cry (krī)
  cried   cry·ing
  cri·er   cries
crypt (krĭpt)
  cryp·tic (krĭp′ tĭk)
  cryp·tog·ra·phy
      (krĭp·tŏg′ ră·fĭ)
crys·tal (krĭs′ tăl)
  crys·tal·line (krĭs′ tăl·ĭn)
  crys·tal·li·za·tion
      (krĭs′ tăl·ĭ·zā′ shŭn)
  crys·tal·lize (krĭs′ tăl·īz)
  -tal·liz·ing
cu·bic (kū′ bĭk)
cu·bi·cal (kū′ bĭ·kăl)
  (cube-shaped)
cu·bi·cle (kū′ bĭ·k'l)
  (compartment)
cuck·old (kŭk′ ŭld)
cuck·oo (kŏŏk′ ōō)
cu·cum·ber (kū′ kŭm·bẽr)
cud·dle (kŭd′ 'l)
  cud·dling   cud·dle·some
  cud·dly
cudg·el (kŭj′ ĕl)
  -geled   -gel·ing
cue (kū)
  (hint; see queue)
cue ball (kū)
cuff (kŭf)
cui·rass (kwĕ·răs′)
cui·sine (kwĕ·zēn′)
cul-de-sac (kŏŏl′ dĕ·săk′)
cu·li·nar·y (kū′ lĭ·nẽr′ ĭ)
cul·mi·nate (kŭl′ mĭ·nāt)
  -nat·ing
  cul·mi·na·tion
      (kŭl′ mĭ·nā′ shŭn)
cu·lottes (kū·lŏts′)
cul·pa·ble (kŭl′ pá·b'l)
  cul·pa·bil·i·ty (kŭl′ pá·bĭl′ ĭ·tĭ)
cul·prit (kŭl′ prĭt)

cult·ist (kŭl′ tĭst)
cul·ti·vate (kŭl′ tĭ·vāt)
  -vat·ing
  cul·ti·va·ble (kŭl′ tĭ·vá·b'l)
  cul·ti·va·tion (kŭl′ tĭ·vā′ shŭn)
  cul·ti·va·tor
cul·ture (kŭl′ tŭr)
  cul·tur·al
cum·ber·some (kŭm′ bẽr·sŭm)
cum·brous (kŭm′ brŭs)
cum·in (kŭm′ ĭn)
cum laude (kŭm lô′ dē)
cum·mer·bund (kŭm′ ẽr·bŭnd)
cu·mu·la·tive (kū′ mū·lā′ tĭv)
cu·mu·lus (kū′ mū·lŭs)
cu·ne·i·form (kū·nē′ ĭ·fôrm)
cun·ning (kŭn′ ĭng)
cup·board (kŭb′ ẽrd)
cup·ful (kŭp′ fŏŏl)
  -fuls
cu·pid·i·ty (kū·pĭd′ ĭ·tĭ)
cu·po·la (kū′ pŏ·lá)
cu·ra·çao (kū′ rá·sō′)
cu·rate (kū′ răt)
  cu·ra·cy (kū′ rá·sĭ)
cu·ra·tor (kū·rā′ tẽr)
curb·stone (kûrb′ stōn′)
cur·dle (kûr′ d'l)
  -dling
cure (kūr)
  cur·ing   cur·a·ble
  cure-all
cu·rette (kū·rĕt′)
cur·few (kûr′ fū)
cu·ri·ous (kū′ rĭ·ŭs)
  cu·ri·os·i·ty (kū′ rĭ·ŏs′ ĭ·tĭ)
  -ties
curl·i·cue (kûr′ lĭ·kū)
curl·y (kûr′ lĭ)
  curl·i·ness
cur·mudg·eon (kẽr·mŭj′ ŭn)
cur·rant (kûr′ ănt)
  (fruit)
cur·rent (kûr′ ĕnt)
  (timely)   cur·ren·cy
cur·ric·u·lum (kŭ·rĭk′ ū·lŭm)
cur·ry (kûr′ ĭ)
  cur·ried   cur·ry·ing
curse (kûrs)
  curs·ing
cur·so·ry (kûr′ sŏ·rĭ)
curt (kûrt)
cur·tail·ment (kûr·tāl′ mĕnt)
cur·tain (kûr′ tĭn)

curt·sy   (kûrt′ sĭ)
  -sied   -sy·ing
curve   (kûrv)
  curv·ing
  cur·va·ceous   (kûr·vā′ shŭs)
  cur·va·ture   (kûr′ và·t̯ûr)
cush·ion   (kŏŏsh′ ŭn)
cus·pi·dor   (kŭs′ pĭ·dôr)
cuss·ed·ness   (kŭs′ ĕd·nĕs)
cus·tard   (kŭs′ tērd)
cus·to·dy   (kŭs′ tô·dĭ)
  -dies
  cus·to·di·al   (kŭs·tō′ dĭ·ăl)
  cus·to·di·an   (kŭs·tō′ dĭ·ăn)
cus·tom   (kŭs′ tŭm)
  cus·tom·ar·i·ly   (-ĕr′ ĭ·lĭ)
  cus·tom·ar·y   (-ĕr′ ĭ)
  cus·tom·house
cus·tom·er   (kŭs′ tŭm·ēr)
cut   (kŭt)
  cut·ting   cut·a·way
  cut·back   cut·off
  cut·out   cut·o·ver
  cut-rate   cut·throat
cu·ta·ne·ous   (kŭ·tā′ nē·ŭs)
cute   (kŭt)
  cute·ness
cu·ti·cle   (kū′ tĭ·k'l)
cut·lass   (kŭt′ làs)
cut·ler·y   (kŭt′ lēr·ĭ)
cut·let   (kŭt′ lĕt)
cy·an·am·ide   (sī′ ăn·ăm′ ĭd)
cy·a·nide   (sī′ à·nīd)
cy·cle   (sī′ k'l)
  cy·cli·cal   (sī′ klĭ·kăl)
  cy·clist   (sī′ klĭst)
cy·cloid   (sī′ kloid)
cy·clom·e·ter   (sī·klŏm′ ê·tēr)
cy·clone   (sī′ klōn)
cy·clo·pe·di·a   (sī′ klô·pē′ dĭ·à)
cy·clo·tron   (sī′ klô·trŏn)
cyg·net   (sĭg′ nĕt)
cyl·in·der   (sĭl′ ĭn·dēr)
  cy·lin·dri·cal   (sĭ·lĭn′ drĭ·kăl)
cym·bal   (sĭm′ băl)
  (musical instrument; see *symbol*)
  cym·bal·ist
cyn·ic   (sĭn′ ĭk)
  cyn·i·cal   -cal·ly
  cyn·i·cism   (sĭn′ ĭ·sĭz′m)
cy·press   (sī′ prĕs)
Cy·prus (is.)   (sī′ prŭs)
cyst   (sĭst)
  cyst·ic
cy·tol·o·gy   (sī·tŏl′ ô·jĭ)

czar   (zär)
Czech·o·slo·va·ki·a
                    (chĕk′ ô·slô·vä′ kĭ·à)

D

dab·ble   (dăb′ 'l)
  dab·bling
Dachs·hund   (däks′ hŏŏnt′)
Da·cron   (dā′ krŏn)
daf·fo·dil   (dăf′ ô·dĭl)
dag·ger   (dăg′ ēr)
da·guerre·o·type
                    (dà·gĕr′ ô·tīp)
dahl·ia   (dăl′ yà)
Da·ho·mey,   (dà·hō′ mĭ)
  Re·pub·lic of
dai·ly   (dā′ lĭ)
  -lies
dain·ty   (dān′ tĭ)
  dain·ti·ly
dair·y   (dâr′ ĭ)
  dair·ies   dair·y cat·tle
  dair·y·ing   dair·y·man
da·is   (dā′ ĭs)
dai·sy   (dā′ zĭ)
  -sies
Da·lai La·ma   (dä·lī′ lä′ mà)
dal·ly   (dăl′ ĭ)
  dal·lied   dal·ly·ing
  dal·li·ance   (dăl′ ĭ·ăns)
Dal·ma·tian dog   (dăl·mā′ shăn)
dam   (dăm)
  (water barrier see *damn*)
  dammed
dam·age   (dăm′ ĭj)
  -ag·ing   dam·age·able
dam·ask   (dăm′ àsk)
damn   (dăm)
  (to condemn; see *dam*)
  dam·na·ble   (dăm′ nà·b'l)
  dam·na·tion   (dăm·nā′ shŭn)
dam·sel   (dăm′ zĕl)
dan·de·li·on   (dăn′ dĕ·lī′ ŭn)
dan·druff   (dăn′ drŭf)
dan·ger·ous   (dān′ jēr·ŭs)
dan·gle   (dăng′ g'l)
  -gling
Dan·ish   (dān′ ĭsh)
dap·per   (dăp′ ēr)
dap·pled   (dăp′ 'ld)
Dar·da·nelles   (där′ d'n·ĕlz′)
dare·dev·il   (dâr′ dĕv′ 'l)
dar·ing   (dâr′ ĭng)

dar·ling (där′ lĭng)
Dar·win·i·an (där wĭn′ ĭ·ɑn)
dash·board (dăsh′ bōrd′)
das·tard·ly (dăs′ tērd·lĭ)
da·ta (dā′ tȧ) n. pl.
  sing. da·tum
da·tive (dā′ tĭv)
daub (dôb)
daugh·ter-in-law (dô′ tēr·ĭn·lô′)
  pl. daugh·ters-in-law
daunt·less (dônt′ lĕs)
dau·phin (dô′ fĭn)
dav·en·port (dăv′ ĕn·pōrt)
Da·vy Jones's lock·er
      (dā′ vĭ jōn′ zĭz)
daw·dle (dô′ d'l)
  -dling
dawn (dôn)
day (dā)
  day·bed   day·break
  day·dream   day let·ter
  day·light sav·ing
  day·time
daze (dāz)
  daz·ing   daz·ed·ly
daz·zle (dăz′ 'l)
  daz·zling
DDT (dē′ dē′ tē′)
dea·con (dē′ kŭn)
  dea·con·ess
dead (dĕd)
  dead·en·ing   dead·line
  dead·lock
  dead·ly, -li·er, -li·est, -li·ness
  dead weight   dead·wood
deaf (dĕf)
  deaf-and-dumb al·pha·bet
  deaf·en   deaf-mute
deal·er (dē′ lēr)
dearth (dûrth)
death (dĕth)
  death·bed   death war·rant
de·ba·cle (dĕ·bä′ k'l)
de·bar (dĕ·bär′)
  -barred   -bar·ring
  de·bar·ment
de·bar·ka·tion (dē′ bär·kā′ shŭn)
de·base·ment (dĕ·bās′ mĕnt)
de·bate (dĕ·bāt′)
  -bat·ing   de·bat·a·ble
  de·bat·er
de·bauch (dĕ·bôch′)
  de·bauch·er·y
de·ben·ture (dĕ·bĕn′ tу̇r)

de·bil·i·tate (dĕ·bĭl′ ĭ·tāt)
  -tat·ing
  de·bil·i·ta·tion
        (dĕ·bĭl′ ĭ·tā′ shŭn)
  de·bil·i·ty   -ties
deb·it (dĕb′ ĭt)
deb·o·nair (dĕb′ ȯ·nâr′)
de·bris (dĕ·brē′)
debt·or (dĕt′ ēr)
de·bunk (dē·bŭngk′)
de·but (dā′ bū)
  deb·u·tante (dĕb′ û·tänt′)
dec·ade (dĕk′ ād)
de·ca·dence (dĕ·kā′ dĕns)
  -dent
de·cal (dē′ kăl)
de·cant·er (dĕ·kăn′ tēr)
de·cap·i·tate (dĕ·kăp′ ĭ·tāt)
  -tat·ing
  de·cap·i·ta·tion
        (dĕ·kăp′ ĭ·tā′ shŭn)
de·cath·lon (dĕ·kăth′ lŏn)
de·cay (dĕ·kā′)
  -cayed
de·ceased (dĕ·sēst′)
  de·ce·dent (dĕ·sē′ dĕnt)
de·ceit (dĕ·sēt′)
  de·ceit·ful, -ful·ly, -ful·ness
de·ceive (dĕ·sēv′)
  -ceiv·ing   de·ceiv·a·ble
  de·ceiv·er
de·cel·er·ate (dē·sĕl′ ēr·āt)
  -at·ing
De·cem·ber (dĕ·sĕm′ bēr)
de·cent (dē′ sĕnt)
  de·cen·cy
de·cen·tral·ize (dē·sĕn′ trȧl·īz)
  -iz·ing
de·cep·tion (dĕ·sĕp′ shŭn)
  de·cep·tive   -tive·ly
dec·i·bel (dĕs′ ĭ·bĕl)
de·cide (dĕ·sīd′)
  -cid·ing   de·cid·ed·ly
de·cid·u·ous (dĕ·sĭd′ û·ŭs)
dec·i·mal (dĕs′ ĭ·mȧl)
dec·i·mate (dĕs′ ĭ·māt)
  -mat·ing
de·ci·pher (dĕ·sī′ fēr)
  de·ci·pher·a·ble
de·ci·sion (dĕ·sĭzh′ ŭn)
de·ci·sive (dĕ·sī′ sĭv)
  -sive·ness
dec·la·ma·tion
        (dĕk′ lȧ·mā′ shŭn)

de·clare   (dĕ·klâr′)
  -clar·ing
  de·clar·a·tion   (dĕk′ lȧ·rā′ shŭn)
  de·clar·a·tive   (dĕ·klăr′ ȧ·tĭv)
  -to·ry
de·clen·sion   (dĕ·klĕn′ shŭn)
de·cline   (dĕ·klīn′)
  -clin·ing
de·cliv·i·ty   (dĕ·klĭv′ ĭ·tĭ)
  -ties
de·code   (dē·kōd′)
  -cod·ing
dé·col·le·té   (dā′ kŏl′ ĕ·tā′)
  dé·col·le·tage   (dā′ kŏl′ ĕ·täzh′)
de·com·pose   (dē′ kŏm·pōz′)
  -pos·ing
  de·com·po·si·tion
                    (dē′ kŏm·pȯ·zĭsh′ ŭn)
de·com·press   (dē′ kŏm·prĕs′)
  de·com·pres·sion (-prĕsh′ ŭn)
de·con·tam·i·nate
                    (dē′ kŏn·tăm′ ĭ·nāt)
  -nat·ing
  de·con·tam·i·na·tion
                    (dē′ kŏn·tăm′ ĭ·nā′ shŭn)
dé·cor   (dā′ kôr′)
dec·o·rate   (dĕk′ ȯ·rāt)
  -rat·ing
  dec·o·ra·tion   (dĕk′ ȯ·rā′ shŭn)
  dec·o·ra·tive   (-rā′ tĭv)
  dec·o·ra·tor
dec·o·rous   (dĕk′ ȯ·rŭs)
de·co·rum   (dĕ·kō′ rŭm)
de·coy   (dĕ·koi′)
de·crease   (dĕ·krēs′) v.
  -creas·ing   (dē′ krēs) n.
de·cree   (dĕ·krē′)
de·crep·it   (dĕ·krĕp′ ĭt)
  de·crep·i·tude   (dĕ·krĕp′ ĭ·tūd)
de·cry   (dĕ·krī′)
  -cried   -cry·ing
ded·i·cate   (dĕd′ ĭ·kăt)
  -cat·ing
  ded·i·ca·tion   (dĕd′ ĭ·kā′ shŭn)
  ded·i·ca·to·ry   (dĕd′ ĭ·kȧ·tō′ rĭ)
de·duce   (dĕ·dūs′)
  -duc·ing   de·duc·i·ble
de·duct   (dĕ·dŭkt′)
  de·duct·i·ble   de·duc·tion
  de·duc·tive
deem   (dēm)
deep   (dēp)
  deep·en   Deep·freeze
  deep-root·ed   deep-sea div·er
  deep-seat·ed

deer·skin   (dēr′ skĭn′)
de·face   (dĕ·fās′)
  -fac·ing   de·face·ment
de·fame   (dĕ·fām′)
  -fam·ing
  def·a·ma·tion   (dĕf′ ȧ·mā′ shŭn)
  de·fam·a·to·ry (dĕ·făm′ ȧ·tō′ rĭ)
de·fault   (dĕ·fôlt′)
de·feat   (dĕ·fēt′)
  de·feat·ism   -ist
def·e·cate   (dĕf′ ĕ·kāt)
  -cat·ing
  def·e·ca·tion   (dĕf′ ĕ·kā′ shŭn)
de·fect   (dĕ·fĕkt′)
  de·fec·tion   de·fec·tive
de·fend   (dĕ·fĕnd′)
  de·fend·ant
de·fense   (dĕ·fĕns′)
  de·fense·less   de·fen·si·ble
  de·fen·sive   -sive·ly
de·fer   (dĕ·fûr′)
  -ferred   -fer·ring
  de·fer·ment   de·fer·ra·ble
def·er·ence   (dĕf′ ēr·ĕns)
def·er·en·tial   (dĕf′ ēr·ĕn′ shȧl)
de·fi·ance   (dĕ·fī′ ȧns)
  -ant
de·fi·cien·cy   (dĕ·fĭsh′ ĕn·sĭ)
  -cies   de·fi·cient
def·i·cit   (dĕf′ ĭ·sĭt)
de·file   (dĕ·fīl′)
  -fil·ing   de·file·ment
de·fine   (dĕ·fīn′)
  -fin·ing   de·fin·a·ble
def·i·nite   (dĕf′ ĭ·nĭt)
  def·i·nite·ly   -nite·ness
  def·i·ni·tion   (dĕf′ ĭ·nĭsh′ ŭn)
  de·fin·i·tive   (dĕ·fĭn′ ĭ·tĭv)
de·flate   (dĕ·flāt′)
  -flat·ing
  de·fla·tion   (dĕ·flā′ shŭn)
  de·fla·tion·ary
de·flect   (dĕ·flĕkt′)
  de·flec·tion
de·flow·er   (dĕ·flou′ ēr)
de·form   (dĕ·fôrm′)
  de·for·ma·tion
                    (dē′ fôr·mā′ shŭn)
  de·formed
  de·form·i·ty   (dĕ·fôr′ mĭ·tĭ)
  -ties
de·fraud   (dĕ·frôd′)
de·fray   (dĕ·frā′)
  de·fray·ment

de·frost (dē·frôst′)
deft (dĕft)
de·funct (dē·fŭngkt′)
de·fy (dē·fī′)
 -fied -fy·ing
de Gaulle, Charles (dē·gōl′)
de·gen·er·ate (dē·jĕn′ ĕr·ĭt)
 adj., n.
 (-āt) v.
 -at·ing
 de·gén·er·a·cy (-á·sĭ)
 de·gen·er·a·tion (dē′ jĕn·ĕr·ā′ shŭn)
de·grade (dē·grād′)
 -grad·ing
 deg·ra·da·tion (dĕg′ rá·dā′ shŭn)
de·gree (dē·grē′)
de·hu·man·ize (dē·hū′ mǎn·īz)
 -iz·ing
 de·hu·man·i·za·tion (dē·hū′ mǎn·ĭ·zā′ shŭn)
de·hu·mid·i·fy (dē′ hú·mĭd′ ĭ·fī)
 -fied -fy·ing
 de·hu·mid·i·fi·er
de·hy·drate (dē·hī′ drāt)
 -drat·ing
de·i·fy (dē′ ĭ·fī)
 -fied -fy·ing
deign (dān)
de·i·ty (dē′ ĭ·tĭ)
 -ties
 de·is·tic (dē·ĭs′ tĭk)
de·ject (dē·jĕkt′)
 de·jec·tion (-jĕk′ shŭn)
Del·a·ware (dĕl′ á·wâr)
 abbr. Del.
 Del·a·war·e·an (dĕl′ á·wâr′ ĕ·ǎn)
de·lay (dē·lā′)
de·lec·ta·ble (dē·lĕk′ tá·b′l)
 de·lec·ta·tion (dē′ lĕk·tā′ shŭn)
del·e·gate (dĕl′ ê·gât)
 -gat·ing
 del·e·ga·tion (dĕl′ ê·gā′ shŭn)
de·lete (dē·lēt′)
 -let·ing
 de·le·tion (dē·lē′ shŭn)
del·e·te·ri·ous (dĕl′ ê·tēr′ ĭ·ŭs)
delft·ware (dĕlft′ wâr′)
de·lib·er·ate (dē·lĭb′ ĕr·ĭt)
 adj.
 -at·ing (-āt) v.

de·lib·er·a·tion (dē·lĭb′ ĕr·ā′ shŭn)
del·i·cate (dĕl′ ĭ·kĭt)
 -cate·ly
 del·i·ca·cy (-ká·sĭ)
de·li·cious (dē·lĭsh′ ŭs)
de·light (dē·līt′)
 de·light·ed·ly de·light·ful
 -ful·ly -ful·ness
de·lim·it (dē·lĭm′ ĭt)
 -it·ed -it·ing
 de·lim·i·ta·tion (dē·lĭm′ ĭ·tā′ shŭn)
de·lin·e·ate (dē·lĭn′ ê·āt)
 -at·ing de·lin·e·a·tor
de·lin·quen·cy (dē·lĭng′ kwĕn·sĭ)
 de·lin·quent
de·lir·i·ous (dē·lĭr′ ĭ·ŭs)
de·lir·i·um (dē·lĭr′ ĭ·ŭm)
 de·lir·i·um tre·mens (trē′ mĕnz)
de·liv·er (dē·lĭv′ ĕr)
 de·liv·er·a·ble de·liv·er·ance
 de·liv·er·y
del·phin·i·um (dĕl·fĭn′ ĭ·ŭm)
de·lude (dē·lūd′)
 -lud·ing
 de·lu·sion (-lū′ zhŭn)
del·uge (dĕl′ ûj)
 -ug·ing
de luxe (dē·lŏŏks′)
delve (dĕlv)
 delv·ing
de·mag·net·ize (dē·măg′ nĕ·tīz)
 -iz·ing
dem·a·gogue (dĕm′ á·gŏg)
 dem·a·gog·uer·y (-gŏg′ ĕr·ĭ)
 dem·a·gog·ic (dĕm′ á·gŏj′ ĭk)
de·mand (dē·mǎnd′)
 de·mand·a·ble
de·mar·cate (dē·mär′ kāt)
 -cat·ing
 de·mar·ca·tion (dē′ mär·kā′ shŭn)
de·mean (dē·mēn′)
de·mean·or (dē·mēn′ ĕr)
de·ment·ed (dē·mĕn′ tĕd)
de·men·ti·a prae·cox (dē·mĕn′ shĭ·á prē′ kŏks)
de·mer·it (dē·mĕr′ ĭt)
de·mesne (dē·mān′)
de·mil·i·ta·rize (dē·mĭl′ ĭ·tá·rīz)
 -riz·ing
 de·mil·i·ta·ri·za·tion (dē·mĭl′ ĭ·tá·rĭ·zā′ shŭn)

de·mise (dĕ·mīz′)
dem·i·tasse (dĕm′ ĭ·tăs)
dem·i·urge (dĕm′ ĭ·ûrj)
de·mo·bi·lize (dē·mō′ bĭ·līz)
  -liz·ing
  đe·mo·bi·li·za·tion
        (dē·mō′ bĭ·lĭ·zā′ shŭn)
de·moc·ra·cy (dē·mŏk′ rả·sĭ)
  -cies
  đem·o·crat (dĕm′ ỏ·krăt)
  đem·o·crat·ic (dĕm′ ỏ·krăt′ ĭk)
  đe·moc·ra·tize (dē·mŏk′ rả·tīz)
  -tiz·ing
de·mol·ish (dē·mŏl′ ĭsh)
  đem·o·li·tion (dĕm′ ỏ·lĭsh′ ŭn)
de·mon (dē′ mŭn)
  đe·mo·ni·a·cal
        (dē′ mỏ·nī′ ả·kả̆l)
  đe·mon·ic (dē·mŏn′ ĭk)
de·mon·e·tize (dē·mŏn′ ĕ·tīz)
  -tiz·ing
dem·on·strate (dĕm′ ŭn·strāt)
  -strat·ing
  đe·mon·stra·ble
        (dē·mŏn′ strả·b′l)
  đem·on·stra·tion
        (dĕm′ ŭn·strā′ shŭn)
  đe·mon·stra·tive
        (dē·mŏn′ strả·tĭv)
  đem·on·stra·tor
de·mor·al·ize (dē·mŏr′ ǎl·īz)
  -iz·ing
  đe·mor·al·i·za·tion
        (dē·mŏr′ ǎl·ĭ·zā′ shŭn)
de·mote (dē·mōt′)
  -mot·ing
  đe·mo·tion (dē·mō′ shŭn)
de·mur (dē·mûr′)
  (đelay)
  -murređ
  -mur·ring   đe·mur·rer
de·mure (dē·mūr′)
  (mođest)   đe·mure·ly
de·aa·tion·al·ize
        (dē·năah′ ŭn·ǎl·īz)
  -iz·ing
de·nat·u·ral·ize
        (dē·năt′ û·rǎl·īz)
  -iz·ing
de·na·ture (dē·nā′ tûr)
  -tur·ing
den·drite (dĕn′ drīt)
de·ni·al (dē·nī′ ǎl)
den·i·grate (dĕn′ ĭ·grāt)
  -grat·ing

den·im (dĕn′ ĭm)
den·i·zen (dĕn′ ĭ·zĕn)
de·nom·i·na·tion·al
de·nom·i·na·tor
        (dē·nŏm′ ĭ·nā′ tĕr)
de·note (dē·nōt′)
  -not·ing
de·noue·ment (dā·nōō′ mⱯn)
de·nounce (dē·nouns′)
  -nounc·ing   đe·nounce·ment
dense (dĕns)
  dense·ly
den·si·ty (dĕn′ sĭ·tĭ)
den·tal (dĕn′ tǎl)
  den·ti·frice (dĕn′ tĭ·frĭs)
  đen·tist (dĕn′ tĭst)
  đen·ture (dĕn′ tûr)
de·nude (dē·nūd′)
  -nuđ·ing
de·nun·ci·ate (dē·nŭn′ shĭ·āt)
  -at·ing
  đe·nun·ci·a·tion
        (dē·nŭn′ sĭ·ā′ shŭn)
  đe·nun·ci·a·to·ry
        (-nŭn′ shĭ·ả·tō′ rĭ)
de·ny (dē·nī′)
  -nieđ   -ny·ing
de·ni·al   de·ni·er
đe·o·đor·ant (dē·ō′ dēr·đnt)
  de·o·đor·ize   -iz·ing
de·ox·i·dize (dē·ŏk′ sĭ·dīz)
  -điz·ing
de·part (dē·pärt′)
  đe·par·ture (dē·pär′ tûr)
de·part·ment (dē·pärt′ mĕnt)
  đe·part·men·tal
        (dē′ pärt·mĕn′ tǎl)
De Paul (univ.) (dē̆ pôl′)
De·Pauw (univ.) (dē̆·pô′)
de·pend (dē·pĕnd′)
  đe·pend·a·bil·i·ty
        (dē·pĕn′ đả·bĭl′ ĭ·tĭ)
  đe·pend·a·ble (dē·pĕn′ đả·b′l)
  đe·pend·ence (dē·pĕn′ đĕns)
  -en·cy   -ent
de·pict (dē·pĭkt′)
  de·pic·tion (dē·pĭk′ shŭn)
de·pil·a·to·ry (dē·pĭl′ ả·tō′ rĭ)
  -tor·ies
de·plete (dē·plēt′)
  -plet·ing
  đe·ple·tion (dē·plē′ shŭn)
de·plore (dē·plōr′)
  -plor·ing   đe·plor·a·ble

de·ploy·ment (dē·ploi′ mĕnt)
de·po·lar·ize (dē·pō′ lēr·īz)
  -iz·ing
de·pop·u·late (dē·pŏp′ ū·lāt)
  -lat·ing
de·port (dē·pōrt′)
  de·por·ta·tion
      (dē′ pŏr·tā′ shŭn)
  de·por·tee (dē′ pōr·tē′)
  de·port·ment
de·pose (dē·pōz′)
  -pos·ing   de·pos·al
de·pos·it (dē·pŏz′ ĭt)
  -it·ed   -it·ing
  de·pos·i·tor (dē·pŏz′ ĭ·tēr)
  de·pos·i·to·ry (dē·pŏz′ ĭ·tō′ rĭ)
dep·o·si·tion (dĕp′ ŏ·zĭsh′ ŭn)
de·pot (dē′ pō)
dep·ra·va·tion (dĕp′ rȧ·vā′ shŭn)
  (corruption; see *deprivation*)
de·praved (dē·prāvd′)
  de·prav·i·ty (dē·prăv′ ĭ·tĭ)
  -ties
dep·re·cate (dĕp′ rē·kāt)
  -cat·ing
  dep·re·ca·tion
      (dĕp′ rē·kā′ shŭn)
de·pre·ci·ate (dē·prē′ shĭ·āt)
  -at·ing
  de·pre·ci·a·ble
      (-ȧ·b′l)
  de·pre·ci·a·tion
      (dē·prē′ shĭ·ā′ shŭn)
dep·re·da·tion (dĕp′ rē·dā′ shŭn)
de·press (dē·prĕs′)
  de·pres·sant   de·pres·sive
  de·pres·sor
de·pres·sion (dē·prĕsh′ ŭn)
dep·ri·va·tion (dĕp′ rĭ·vā′ shŭn)
  (loss; see *depravation*)
depth (dĕpth)
dep·u·ta·tion (dĕp′ û·tā′ shŭn)
dep·u·ty (dĕp′ û·tĭ)
  -ties
  dep·u·tize (dĕp′ û·tīz)
de·ranged (dē·rānjd′)
  de·range·ment
der·e·lict (dĕr′ ĕ·lĭkt)
  der·e·lic·tion (dĕr′ ĕ·lĭk′ shŭn)
de·ride (dē·rīd′)
  -rid·ing
  de·ri·sion (dē·rĭzh′ ŭn)
  de·ri·sive (dē·rī′ sĭv)
de·rive (dē·rīv′)
  -riv·ing

der·i·va·tion (dĕr′ ĭ·vā′ shŭn)
de·riv·a·tive (dē·rĭv′ ȧ·tĭv)
der·ma·ti·tis (dûr′ mȧ·tī′ tĭs)
  der·ma·tol·o·gy
      (dûr′ mȧ·tŏl′ ŏ·jĭ)
der·o·gate (dĕr′ ŏ·gāt)
  -gat·ing
  der·o·ga·tion (dĕr′ ŏ·gā′ shŭn)
  de·rog·a·tive (dē·rŏg′ ȧ·tĭv)
  de·rog·a·to·ry
      (dē·rŏg′ ȧ·tō′ rĭ)
der·rick (dĕr′ ĭk)
der·ring-do (dĕr′ ĭng·dōō′)
der·vish (dûr′ vĭsh)
des·cant (dĕs·kănt′)
de·scend (dē·sĕnd′)
  de·scend·ant (dē·sĕn′ dȧnt)
  de·scent (dē·sĕnt′)
  (ancestry; see *dissent*)
de·scribe (dē·skrīb′)
  -scrib·ing   de·scrib·a·ble
  de·scrip·tion (dē·skrĭp′ shŭn)
  de·scrip·tive (dē·skrĭp′ tĭv)
des·e·crate (dĕs′ ē·krāt)
  -crat·ing
  des·e·cra·tion (dĕs′ ē·krā′ shŭn)
de·seg·re·gate (dē·sĕg′ rē·gāt)
  -gat·ing
  de·seg·re·ga·tion
      (dē·sĕg′ rē·gā′ shŭn)
de·sen·si·tize (dē·sĕn′ sĭ·tīz)
  -tiz·ing
des·ert (dĕz′ ērt)
  (arid region)
de·sert (dē·zûrt′)
  (to abandon; see *dessert*)
  de·sert·er
  de·ser·tion (dē·zûr′ shŭn)
de·serve (dē·zûrv′)
  -serv·ing
  de·serv·ed·ly (-zûr′ vĕd·lĭ)
des·ic·cate (dĕs′ ĭ·kāt)
  -ic·cat·ing
de·sid·er·a·tum
      (dē·sĭd′ ēr·ā′ tŭm)
  pl. de·sid·er·a·ta
de·sign (dē·zīn′)
  de·sign·er
des·ig·nate (dĕz′ ĭg·nāt)
  -nat·ing
  des·ig·na·tion (dĕz′ ĭg·nā′ shŭn)
de·sire (dē·zīr′)
  -sir·ing
  de·sir·a·bil·i·ty
      (dē·zīr′ ȧ·bĭl′ ĭ·tĭ)

de·sir·a·ble de·sir·ous
de·sist (dĕ·zĭst′)
Des Moines, Ia. (dĕ moin′)
des·o·late (dĕs′ ŏ·lĭt) *adj.*
 -lat·ing (-lāt) *v.*
 des·o·late·ly (-lĭt·lĭ)
 des·o·la·tion (dĕs′ ŏ·lā′ shŭn)
de·spair (dĕ·spâr′)
 de·spair·ing·ly
des·per·a·do (dĕs′ pĕr·ä′ dō)
 -does
des·per·ate (dĕs′ pĕr·ĭt)
 (without hope; see *disparate*)
 des·per·ate·ly
 des·per·a·tion
  (dĕs′ pĕr·ā′ shŭn)
des·pi·ca·ble (dĕs′ pĭ·ká·b'l)
de·spise (dĕ·spīz′)
 -spis·ing
de·spite (dĕ·spīt′)
de·spoil (dĕ·spoil′)
 de·spoil·er
de·spond·ence (dĕ·spŏn′ dĕns)
 -enc·y -ent
des·pot (dĕs′ pŏt)
 des·pot·ic (dĕs·pŏt′ ĭk)
 -i·cal·ly
 des·pot·ism (dĕs′ pŏt·ĭz'm)
des·sert (dĭ·zûrt′)
 (sweets; see *desert*)
des·ti·ny (dĕs′ tĭ·nĭ)
 -nies
 des·ti·na·tion (dĕs′ tĭ·nā′ shŭn)
 des·tined
des·ti·tute (dĕs′ tĭ·tūt)
 des·ti·tu·tion (dĕs′ tĭ·tū′ shŭn)
de·stroy (dĕ·stroi′)
 de·stroy·er
de·struc·tion (dĕ·strŭk′ shŭn)
 de·struct·i·ble
 de·struc·tive -tive·ness
des·ue·tude (dĕs′ wē·tūd)
des·ul·to·ry (dĕs′ ŭl·tō′ rĭ)
 des·ul·to·ri·ness
de·tach (dĕ·tăch′)
 de·tach·a·ble de·tach·ment
de·tail (dĕ·tāl′)
 de·tailed
de·tain (dĕ·tān′)
 de·tain·ment
de·tect (dĕ·tĕkt′)
 de·tect·a·ble
 de·tec·tion (dĕ·tĕk′ shŭn)
 de·tec·tor
de·tec·tive (dĕ·tĕk′ tĭv)

de·ten·tion (dĕ·tĕn′ shŭn)
de·ter (dĕ·tûr′)
 -terred -ter·ring
 de·ter·ment de·ter·rent
de·ter·gent (dĕ·tûr′ jĕnt)
de·te·ri·o·rate (dĕ·tẽr′ ĭ·ō·rāt)
 -rat·ing
 de·te·ri·o·ra·tion
  (dĕ·tẽr′ ĭ·ō·rā′ shŭn)
de·ter·mine (dĕ·tûr′ mĭn)
 -min·ing
 de·ter·mi·nant
  (-mĭ′ nănt)
 de·ter·mi·na·tion
  (dĕ·tûr′ mĭ·nā′ shŭn)
 de·ter·mined·ly
  (-mĭnd·lĭ)
 de·ter·min·ism
  (-mĭn·ĭz'm)
de·ter·rent (dĕ·tûr′ ĕnt)
 -ter·rence
de·test (dĕ·tĕst′)
 de·test·a·ble
de·throne (dĕ·thrōn′)
 -thron·ing de·throne·ment
det·o·nate (dĕt′ ŏ·nāt)
 -nat·ing
 det·o·na·tion (dĕt·ŏ·nā′ shŭn)
de·tour (dē′ tōōr)
de·tract (dĕ·trăkt′)
 de·trac·tion (dĕ·trăk′ shŭn)
 de·trac·tor
det·ri·ment (dĕt′ rĭ·mĕnt)
 det·ri·men·tal (dĕt′ rĭ·mĕn′ tăl)
deuce (dūs)
de·val·u·ate (dĕ·văl′ û·āt)
 -at·ing
 de·val·u·a·tion
  (dĕ·văl′ û·ā′ shŭn)
dev·as·tate (dĕv′ ás·tāt)
 -tat·ing
 dev·as·ta·tion
  (dĕv′ ás·tā′ shŭn)
 dev·as·ta·tor
de·vel·op (dĕ·vĕl′ ŭp)
 -oped, -op·ing
 de·vel·op·er de·vel·op·ment
 de·vel·op·men·tal
  (dĕ·vĕl′ ŭp·mĕn′ tăl)
de·vi·ate (dē′ vĭ·āt)
 -at·ing
 de·vi·ant (dē′ vĭ·ănt)
 de·vi·a·tion (dē′ vĭ·ā′ shŭn)
de·vice (dĕ·vīs′) *n.*
 (a scheme)

dev·il (děv' 'l)
  dev·il·ish   dev·il·ment
  dev·il·try
de·vi·ous (dē' vǐ·ŭs)
de·vise (dĕ·vīz') v
  (to invent) -vis·ing
de·vi·tal·ize (dē·vī' tǎl·īz)
  -iz·ing
de·void (dĕ·void')
de·volve (dĕ·vŏlv')
  -volv·ing
de·vote (dĕ·vōt')
  -vot·ing   de·vot·ed·ly
  dev·o·tee (děv' ō·tē')
  de·vo·tion (dĕ·vō' shŭn)
  -tion·al
de·vour (dĕ·vour')
de·vout (dĕ·vout')
dew·drop (dū' drŏp')
dew·y (dū' ǐ)
  dew·i·ness
dex·ter·i·ty (děks·těr' ǐ·tǐ)
  dex·ter·ous (děk' stēr·ŭs)
dex·trose (děks' trōs)
di·a·be·tes (dī' ȧ·bē' tēz)
  di·a·bet·ic (-bět' ǐk)
di·a·bol·ic (dī' ȧ·bŏl' ǐk)
  di·a·bol·i·cal (-ǐ·kǎl)
di·a·crit·i·cal mark
    (dī' ȧ·krǐt' ǐ·kǎl)
di·a·dem (dī' ȧ·děm)
di·ag·nose (dī' ǎg·nōs')
  -nos·ing
  di·ag·no·sis (dī' ǎg·nō' sǐs)
  pl. -no·ses (-sēz)
  di·ag·nos·tic (dī' ǎg·nŏs' tǐk)
  di·ag·nos·ti·cian
    (dī' ǎg·nŏs·tǐsh' ȧn)
di·ag·o·nal (dī·ǎg' ō·nȧl)
  di·ag·o·nal·ly
di·a·gram (dī' ȧ·grǎm)
  -gramed   -gram·ing
  di·a·gram·mat·ic
    (dī' ȧ·grȧ·mǎt' ǐk)
di·al (dī' ȧl)
  di·aled   di·al·ing
di·a·lect (dī' ȧ·lěkt)
di·a·lec·tic (dī' ȧ·lěk' tǐk)
  di·a·lec·ti·cal ma·te·ri·al·ism
di·a·logue (dī' ȧ·lŏg)
di·am·e·ter (dī·ǎm' ě·tēr)
di·a·met·ric (dī' ȧ·mět' rǐk)
  di·a·met·ri·cal·ly
di·a·mond (dī' ȧ·mŭnd)
di·a·per (dī' ȧ·pēr)

di·aph·a·nous (dī·ǎf' ȧ·nŭs)
di·a·phragm (dī' ȧ·frǎm)
di·ar·rhe·a (dī' ȧ·rē' ȧ)
  di·ar·rhet·ic (-rět' ǐk)
di·a·ry (dī' ȧ·rǐ)
  -ries
di·a·ther·my (dī' ȧ·thûr' mǐ)
di·a·tribe (dī' ȧ·trīb)
dice (dīs) n pl
  sing. die
di·chot·o·my (dī·kŏt' ō·mǐ)
  -mies   di·chot·o·mize
  -miz·ing
dick·ey (dǐk' ǐ)
  -eys
Dic·ta·phone (dǐk' tȧ·fōn)
dic·tate (dǐk' tāt)
  -tat·ing
  dic·ta·tion (dǐk·tā' shŭn)
  dic·ta·tor
  dic·ta·to·ri·al (dǐk' tȧ·tō' rǐ·ȧl)
dic·tion (dǐk' shŭn)
dic·tion·ar·y (dǐk' shŭn·ěr' ǐ)
  -ar·ies
dic·tum (dǐk' tŭm)
  pl. dic·ta
di·dac·tic (dī·dǎk' tǐk)
  di·dac·ti·cal
die (dī)
  died   dy·ing
die·sel en·gine (dē' zěl)
di·et (dī' ět)
  di·e·tar·y (dī' ě·těr' ǐ)
  di·e·tet·ic (dī' ě·tět' ǐk)
  di·e·ti·tian (dī' ě·tǐsh' ȧn)
dif·fer (dǐf' ēr)
dif·fer·ence (dǐf' ēr·ěns)
  -ent
dif·fer·en·tial (dǐf' ēr·ěn' shȧl)
dif·fer·en·ti·ate
    (dǐf' ēr·ěn' shǐ·āt)
  -at·ing
  dif·fer·en·ti·a·tion
    (dǐf' ēr·ěn' shǐ·ā' shŭn)
dif·fi·cult (dǐf' ǐ·kŭlt)
  dif·fi·cul·ty
dif·fi·dence (dǐf' ǐ·děns)
  -dent
dif·fract (dī·frǎkt')
  dif·frac·tion (dī·frǎk' shŭn)
dif·fuse (dī·fūs') adj.
  (-fūz') v.
  dif·fus·ing
  dif·fu·sion (dī·fū' zhŭn)
di·gest (dī' jěst) n.

di·gest (dĭ·jĕst′) v.
  di·gest·ant (-jĕs′ tănt)
  di·gest·i·bil·i·ty
    (dĭ·jĕst′ ĭ·bĭl′ ĭ·tĭ)
  di·gest·i·ble   di·ges·tive
dig·it (dĭj′ ĭt)
  dig·it·al com·pu·ter
    (dĭj′ ĭ·tăl)
dig·i·tal·is (dĭj′ ĭ·tăl′ ĭs)
dig·ni·fy (dĭg′ nĭ·fī)
  -fied,   -fy·ing
dig·ni·tar·y (dĭg′ nĭ·tĕr′ ĭ)
  -tar·ies
dig·ni·ty (dĭg′ nĭ·tĭ)
  -ties
di·gress (dĭ·grĕs′)
  di·gres·sion (dĭ·grĕsh′ ŭn)
dike (dīk)
di·lap·i·dat·ed
    (dĭ·lăp′ ĭ·dāt′ ĕd)
  di·lap·i·da·tion
    (dĭ·lăp′ ĭ·dā′ shŭn)
di·late (dī·lāt′)
  -lat·ing
  di·la·tion (dī·lā′ shŭn)
dil·a·to·ry (dĭl′ ȧ·tō′ rĭ)
  dil·a·to·ri·ness
di·lem·ma (dĭ·lĕm′ ȧ)
dil·et·tan·te (dĭl′ ĕ·tän′ tĕ)
  dil·et·tant·ism
    (-tän′ tĭz′m)
dil·i·gence (dĭl′ ĭ·jĕns)
  -gent
dil·ly·dal·ly (dĭl′ ĭ·dăl′ ĭ)
  -dal·lied   -dal·ly·ing
di·lute (dĭ·lūt′)
  -lut·ing
  di·lu·tion (dĭ·lū′ shŭn)
di·men·sion (dĭ·mĕn′ shŭn)
  di·men·sion·al
di·min·ish (dĭ·mĭn′ ĭsh)
dim·i·nu·tion (dĭm′ ĭ·nū′ shŭn)
di·min·u·tive (dĭ·mĭn′ û·tĭv)
dim·i·ty (dĭm′ ĭ·tĭ)
dim·ple (dĭm′ p'l)
din·er (dīn′ ĕr)
din·ette (dī·nĕt′)
din·ghy (dĭng′ gĭ)
  (rowboat)   -ghies
din·gy (dĭn′ jĭ)
  (grimy)
  din·gi·ness
din·ing room (dīn′ ĭng)
din·ner (dĭn′ ĕr)
di·no·saur (dī′ nŏ·sôr)

di·o·cese (dī′ ô·sēs)
  di·oc·e·san (dī·ŏs′ ê·sȧn)
Di·og·e·nes (dī·ŏj′ ê·nēz)
di·o·ra·ma (dī′ ô·rä′ mȧ)
di·ox·ide (dī·ŏk′ sīd)
diph·the·ri·a (dĭf·thĕr′ ĭ·ȧ)
diph·thong (dĭf′ thŏng)
di·plo·ma (dĭ·plō′ mȧ)
di·plo·ma·cy (dĭ·plō′ mȧ·sĭ)
  dip·lo·mat (dĭp′ lô·măt)
  dip·lo·mat·ic (dĭp′ lô·măt′ ĭk)
dip·per (dĭp′ ĕr)
dip·so·ma·ni·a
    (dĭp′ sô·mā′ nĭ·ȧ)
  dip·so·ma·ni·ac
    (-ăk)
dire (dīr)
  dire·ness   dir·est
di·rect (dĭ·rĕkt′)
  di·rec·tion (dĭ·rĕk′ shŭn)
  -tion·al   di·rec·tive
  di·rec·tor
  di·rec·to·rate (dĭ·rĕk′ tô·rĭt)
  di·rec·to·ry (dĭ·rĕk′ tô·rĭ)
  -ries
dirge (dûrj)
dir·i·gi·ble (dĭr′ ĭ·jĭ·b′l)
dirn·dl (dûrn′ d'l)
dirt·y (dûr′ tĭ)
  dirt·ied   dirt·y·ing
dis·a·bil·i·ty (dĭs′ ȧ·bĭl′ ĭ·tĭ)
  -ties
dis·a·ble (dĭs·ā′ b′l)
  -bling   dis·a·ble·ment
dis·ad·van·tage
    (dĭs′ ăd·văn′ tĭj)
dis·af·fec·tion (dĭs′ ȧ·fĕk′ shŭn)
dis·a·gree (dĭs′ ȧ·grē′)
  dis·a·gree·a·ble
  dis·a·gree·ment
dis·al·low (dĭs′ ȧ·lou′)
dis·ap·pear (dĭs′ ȧ·pēr′)
  dis·ap·pear·ance
dis·ap·point (dĭs′ ȧ·point′)
  dis·ap·point·ed
  dis·ap·point·ment
dis·ap·pro·ba·tion
    (dĭs′ ăp·rô·bā′ shŭn)
dis·ap·prove (dĭs′ ȧ·prōōv′)
  -ap·prov·ing   dis·ap·prov·al
dis·ar·ma·ment
    (dĭs·är′ mȧ·mĕnt)
dis·arm·ing (dĭs·ärm′ ĭng)
dis·ar·range (dĭs′ ȧ·rānj′)
  -ar·rang·ing

dis·ar·ray (dĭs′ ä·rā′)
dis·as·sem·ble (dĭs′ ä·sĕm′ b'l)
  -bling
dis·as·so·ci·ate (dĭs′ ä·sō′ shĭ·āt)
  -at·ing
dis·as·ter (dĭ·zás′ tẽr)
  dis·as·trous (-trŭs)
dis·a·vow (dĭs′ ä·vou′)
  dis·a·vowal
dis·band (dĭs·bănd′)
dis·bar (dĭs·bär′)
  -barred   -bar·ring
  dis·bar·ment
dis·be·lief (dĭs′ bĕ·lēf′)
  dis·be·lieve   -liev·ing
dis·burse (dĭs·bûrs′)
  (to pay out; see *disperse*)
  -burs·ing   dis·burs·a·ble
  dis·burse·ment
disc (dĭsk)
  disc jock·ey
dis·card (dĭs·kärd′) v.
  (dĭs′ kärd) n.
dis·cern (dĭ·zûrn′)
  dis·cern·i·ble   dis·cern·ment
dis·charge (dĭs·chärj′)
  -charg·ing
dis·ci·ple (dĭ·sī′ p'l)
dis·ci·pline (dĭs′ ĭ·plĭn)
  dis·ci·pli·nar·i·an
    (dĭs′ ĭ·plĭ·nâr′ ĭ·ăn)
  dis·ci·pli·nar·y
    (dĭs′ ĭ·plĭ·nĕr′ ĭ)
dis·claim·er (dĭs·klām′ ẽr)
dis·close (dĭs·klōz′)
  -clos·ing
  dis·clo·sure (-klō′ zhẽr)
dis·col·or (dĭs·kŭl′ ẽr)
  dis·col·or·a·tion
    (dĭs·kŭl′ ẽr·ā′ shŭn)
dis·com·fit (dĭs·kŭm′ fĭt)
  (embarrass)
  dis·com·fi·ture (-fĭ·tụr)
dis·com·fort (dĭs·kŭm′ fẽrt)
dis·com·po·sure
  (dĭs′ kŏm·pō′ zhẽr)
dis·con·cert·ing
  (dĭs′ kŏn·sûrt′ ĭng)
dis·con·nect (dĭs′ kŏ·nĕkt′)
  dis·con·nect·ed·ly
dis·con·so·late (dĭs·kŏn′ sŏ·lĭt)
  -late·ly
dis·con·tent·ed
  (dĭs′ kŏn·tĕn′ tĕd)

dis·con·tin·ue (dĭs′ kŏn·tĭn′ ū)
  -u·ing
  dis·con·tin·u·a·tion
    (-tĭn′ ū·ā′ shŭn)
  dis·con·ti·nu·i·ty
    (-tĭ·nū′ ĭ·tĭ)
  dis·con·tin·u·ous
    (-tĭn′ ū·ŭs)
dis·cor·dant (dĭs·kôr′ dănt)
  -dance
dis·count (dĭs′ kount)
dis·cour·age (dĭs·kûr′ ĭj)
  -ag·ing
  dis·cour·age·ment
dis·course (dĭs·kōrs′)
dis·cour·te·ous (dĭs·kûr′ tĕ·ŭs)
  dis·cour·te·sy (dĭs·kûr′ tĕ·sĭ)
  -sies
dis·cov·er·a·ble
  (dĭs·kŭv′ ẽr·á·b'l)
dis·cov·er·y (dĭs·kŭv′ ẽr·ĭ)
  -er·ies
dis·cred·it (dĭs·krĕd′ ĭt)
  -it·ed   -it·ing
  dis·cred·it·a·ble
dis·creet (dĭs·krēt′)
  (prudent)
  dis·cre·tion (dĭs·krĕsh′ ŭn)
dis·crep·an·cy (dĭs·krĕp′ ăn·sĭ)
dis·crete (dĭs·krēt′)
  (separate)
dis·cre·tion (dĭs·krĕsh′ ŭn)
dis·crim·i·nate
  (dĭs·krĭm′ ĭ·nāt) v.
  -nat·ing
  dis·crim·i·na·tion
    (dĭs·krĭm′ ĭ·nā′ shŭn)
  dis·crim·i·na·to·ry
    (dĭs·krĭm′ ĭ·ná·tō′ rĭ)
dis·cur·sive (dĭs·kûr′ sĭv)
dis·cus (dĭs′ kŭs)
  (athletic device)
dis·cuss (dĭs·kŭs′)
  (to debate)
  dis·cus·sion (-kŭsh′ ŭn)
dis·dain·ful (dĭs·dān′ fŏŏl)
  -ful·ly   -ful·ness
dis·ease (dĭ·zēz′)
dis·em·bark (dĭs′ ĕm·bärk′)
  dis·em·bar·ka·tion
    (dĭs·ĕm′ bär·kā′ shŭn)
dis·em·bod·y (dĭs′ ĕm·bŏd′ ĭ)
  -bodied   -bodying
dis·em·bow·el (dĭs′ ĕm·bou′ ĕl)
  -eled   -eling

dis·en·chant·ment
    (dĭs′ ĕn·chánt′ mĕnt)
dis·en·cum·ber
    (dĭs′ ĕn·kŭm′ bēr)
dis·en·fran·chise
    (dĭs′ ĕn·frăn′ chīz)
 -chis·ing
 dis·en·fran·chise·ment
dis·en·gage   (dĭs′ ĕn·gāj′)
 -gag·ing
 dis·en·gage·ment
dis·en·tan·gle·ment
    (dĭs′ ĕn·tăng′ g'l·mĕnt)
dis·es·teem   (dĭs′ ĕs·tēm′)
dis·fa·vor   (dĭs·fā′ vēr)
dis·fig·ure·ment
    (dĭs·fĭg′ ûr·mĕnt)
dis·fran·chise (dĭs·frăn′ chĭz)
 chis·ing
dis·gorge   (dĭs·gôrj′)
 -gorg·ing
dis·grace·ful (dĭs·grās′ fŏŏl)
 -ful·ly   -ful·ness
dis·grun·tled (dĭs·grŭn′ t'ld)
dis·guise   (dĭs·gīz′)
 -guis·ing
dis·gust·ing (dĭs·gŭs′ tĭng)
dis·ha·bille (dĭs′ ā·bēl′)
dis·har·mo·ni·ous
    (dĭs′ här·mō′ nĭ·ŭs)
dis·heart·en (dĭs·härt′ t'n)
di·shev·eled (dĭ·shĕv′ ĕld)
 di·shev·el·ment
dis·hon·es·ty (dĭs·ŏn′ ĕs·tĭ)
 -ties
dis·hon·or·a·ble
    (dĭs·ŏn′ ēr·à·b'l)
dis·il·lu·sion (dĭs′ ĭ·lū′ zhŭn)
 (to free from illusion; see *dis-solution*)
dis·in·clined (dĭs′ ĭn·klīnd′)
 dis·in·cli·na·tion
    (dĭs·ĭn′ klĭ·nā′ shŭn)
dis·in·fect (dĭs′ ĭn·fĕkt′)
 dis·in·fect·ant dis·in·fec·tion
dis·in·gen·u·ous
    (dĭs′ ĭn·jĕn′ ū·ŭs)
dis·in·her·it (dĭs·ĭn·hĕr′ ĭt)
 -it·ed   -it·ing
 dis·in·her·it·ance
dis·in·te·grate (dĭs·ĭn′ tĕ·grāt)
 -grat·ing
 dis·in·te·gra·tion
    (dĭs·ĭn′ tĕ·grā′ shŭn)

dis·in·ter·est·ed
    (dĭs′ ĭn′ tēr·ĕs·tĕd)
dis·joint·ed (dĭs·join′ tĕd)
dis·junc·tion (dĭs·jŭngk′ shŭn)
disk   (dĭsk)
 (platelike object; also *disc*)
dis·like   (dĭs·līk′)
 -lik·ing
dis·lo·ca·tion (dĭs′ lō·kā′ shŭn)
dis·loy·al (dĭs·loi′ ăl)
 dis·loy·al·ty
dis·mal (dĭz′ măl)
 dis·mal·ly
dis·man·tle (dĭs·măn′ t'l)
 -tling
dis·may (dĭs·mā′)
dis·mem·ber·ment
    (dĭs·mĕm′ bēr·mĕnt)
dis·miss (dĭs·mĭs′)
 dis·mis·sal
dis·mount (dĭs·mount′)
dis·o·be·di·ence
    (dĭs′ ō·bē′ dĭ·ĕns)
dis·o·bey (dĭs′ ō·bā′)
dis·o·blig·ing (dĭs′ ō·blī′ ĭng)
dis·or·dered (dĭs·ôr′ dērd)
 dis·or·der·ly   -li·ness
dis·or·gan·ized
    (dĭs·ôr′ găn·ĭzd)
dis·o·ri·ent·ed (dĭs·ō′ rĭ·ĕnt·ĕd)
dis·own (dĭs·ōn′)
dis·par·age (dĭs·păr′ ĭj)
 -ag·ing
 dis·par·age·ment
dis·pa·rate (dĭs′ pà·răt)
 (dissimilar; see *desperate*)
 dis·par·i·ty (dĭs·păr′ ĭ·tĭ)
dis·pas·sion·ate
    (dĭs·păsh′ ŭn·ĭt)
dis·patch (dĭs·păch′)
dis·pel (dĭs·pĕl′)
 -pelled   -pel·ling
dis·pen·sa·ble (dĭs·pĕn′ sà·b'l)
 dis·pen·sa·bil·i·ty
    (dĭs·pĕn′ sà·bĭl′ ĭ·tĭ)
dis·pen·sa·ry (dĭs·pĕn′ sà·rĭ)
 -ries
dis·pen·sa·tion
    (dĭs′ pĕn·sā′ shŭn)
dis·pens·er (dĭs·pĕn′ sēr)
dis·perse (dĭs·pûrs′)
 (to scatter; see *disburse*)
 -pers·ing
 dis·per·sal (-pûr′ săl)
 dis·per·sion (-pûr′ shŭn)

dis·pir·it·ed   (dĭs·pĭr′ ĭt·ĕd)
dis·place   (dĭs·plās′)
   -plac·ing
   dis·placed per·son
   dis·place·ment
dis·play   (dĭs·plā′)
dis·please   (dĭs·plēz′)
   -pleas·ing
   dis·pleas·ure   (dĭs·plĕzh′ ēr)
dis·pose   (dĭs·pōz′)
   -pos·ing   dis·pos·al
   dis·po·si·tion   (dĭs′ pŏ·zĭsh′ ŭn)
dis·pos·sess   (dĭs′ pŏ·zĕs′)
dis·pro·por·tion
       (dĭs′ prŏ·pôr′ shŭn)
   dis·pro·por·tion·ate
       (-ĭt)
dis·prove   (dĭs·prōōv′)
   -prov·ing
dis·pute   (dĭs·pūt′)
   -put·ing   dis·pu·ta·ble
   dis·pu·tant   (dĭs′ pū·tănt)
   dis·pu·ta·tion   (dĭs′ pū·tā′ shŭn)
   dis·pu·ta·tious
       (dĭs′ pū·tā′ shŭs)
dis·qual·i·fy   (dĭs·kwŏl′ ĭ·fī)
   -fied   -fy·ing
   dis·qual·i·fi·ca·tion
       (dĭs·kwŏl′ ĭ·fĭ·kā′ shŭn)
dis·qui·et·ing   (dĭs·kwī′ ĕt·ĭng)
dis·re·gard   (dĭs′ rĕ·gärd′)
dis·re·pair   (dĭs′ rĕ·pâr′)
dis·re·pute   (dĭs′ rĕ·pūt′)
   dis·rep·u·ta·ble
       (dĭs·rĕp′ û·tá·b'l)
dis·re·spect   (dĭs′ rĕ·spĕkt′)
dis·rupt   (dĭs·rŭpt′)
   dis·rup·tion   (dĭs·rŭp′ shŭn)
   dis·rup·tive   (-tĭv)
dis·sat·is·fy   (dĭs·săt′ ĭs·fī)
   -fied,   -fy·ing
   dis·sat·is·fac·tion
       (dĭs′ săt·ĭs·făk′ shŭn)
dis·sect   (dĭ·sĕkt′)
   dis·sec·tion   (dĭ·sĕk′ shŭn)
dis·sem·ble   (dĭ·sĕm′ b'l)
   -bling
dis·sem·i·nate   (dĭ·sĕm′ ĭ·nāt)
   -nat·ing
   dis·sem·i·na·tion
       (dĭ·sĕm′ ĭ·nā′ shŭn)
dis·sen·sion   (dĭ·sĕn′ shŭn)
dis·sent   (dĭ·sĕnt′)
   (disagree; see *descent*)
   dis·sen·ter

dis·sen·tient   (dĭ·sĕn′ shĕnt)
dis·ser·ta·tion   (dĭs′ ēr·tā′ shŭn)
dis·serv·ice   (dĭs·sûr′ vĭs)
dis·si·dence   (dĭs′ ĭ·dĕns)
   -dent
dis·sim·i·lar   (dĭ·sĭm′ ĭ·lēr)
   dis·sim·i·lar·i·ty
       (dĭ·sĭm′ ĭ·lăr′ ĭ·tĭ)
dis·sim·u·late   (dĭ·sĭm′ û·lāt)
   -lat·ing
dis·si·pate   (dĭs′ ĭ·pāt)
   -pat·ing
   dis·si·pa·tion   (dĭs′ ĭ·pā′ shŭn)
   dis·si·pa·tor
dis·so·ci·ate   (dĭ·sō′ shĭ·āt)
   -at·ing
   dis·so·ci·a·tion
       (dĭ·sō′ sĭ·ā′ shŭn)
dis·so·lute   (dĭs′ ō·lūt)
   dis·so·lute·ness
dis·so·lu·tion   (dĭs′ ō·lū′ shŭn)
   (disintegration; see *disillusion*)
dis·solve   (dĭ·zŏlv′)
   dis·solv·ing   dis·sol·vent
dis·so·nance   (dĭs′ ō·năns)
   -nant
dis·suade   (dĭ·swād′)
   dis·suad·ing
   dis·sua·sion   (dĭ·swā′ zhŭn)
   dis·sua·sive   (-sĭv)
dis·sym·me·try
       (dĭs·sĭm′ ĕ·trĭ)
dis·taff   (dĭs′ tăf)
dis·tance   (dĭs′ tăns)
dis·taste   (dĭs·tāst′)
   dis·taste·ful   -ful·ly
   -ful·ness
dis·tem·per   (dĭs·tĕm′ pēr)
dis·tend   (dĭs·tĕnd′)
dis·till   (dĭs·tĭl′)
   dis·til·la·tion   (dĭs′ tĭ·lā′ shŭn)
   dis·til·ler·y   (dĭs·tĭl′ ēr·ĭ)
   -til·ler·ies
dis·tinct   (dĭs·tĭngkt′)
   dis·tinc·tion   (dĭs·tĭngk′ shŭn)
   dis·tinc·tive   (-tĭngk′ tĭv)
dis·tin·guished   (dĭs·tĭng′ gwĭsht)
   dis·tin·guish·a·ble
dis·tort   (dĭs·tôrt′)
   dis·tor·tion   (-tôr′ shŭn)
dis·tract   (dĭs·trăkt′)
   dis·tract·ed·ly   dis·tract·i·ble
   dis·trac·tion   (-trăk′ shŭn)
dis·traught   (dĭs·trôt′)

dis·tress   (dĭs·trĕs′)
  dis·tress·ful   dis·tress·ing·ly
dis·trib·ute   (dĭs·trĭb′ ût)
  -ut·ing   dis·trib·ut·a·ble
  dis·tri·bu·tion
                     (dĭs′·trĭ·bū′ shŭn)
  dis·trib·u·tor
dis·trict at·tor·ney
                     (dĭs′ trĭkt)
dis·trust·ful   (dĭs·trŭst′ fo͝ol)
dis·turb·ance   (dĭs·tûr′ băns)
dis·un·ion   (dĭs·ūn′ yŭn)
dis·use   (dĭs·ūs′) n.
ditch   (dĭch)
dit·to   (dĭt′ ō)
dit·ty   (dĭt′ ĭ)
  dit·ties
di·ur·nal   (dī·ûr′ năl)
  -nal·ly
di·van   (dī′ văn)
dive bomb·er   (dīv)
di·verge   (dī·vûrj′)
  -verg·ing   di·ver·gence,
  -gent
di·vers   (dī′ vĕrz)
  (several)
di·verse   (dī·vûrs′)
  (different)
  di·verse·ly
  di·ver·si·fy   (dĭ·vûr′ sĭ·fī)
  -fied,   -fy·ing
  di·ver·si·ty   (dĭ·vûr′ sĭ·tĭ)
  -ties
di·ver·sion   (dĭ·vûr′ shŭn)
  di·ver·sion·ar·y
di·vert·ing   (dĭ·vûrt′ ĭng)
di·vest   (dĭ·vĕst′)
di·vide   (dĭ·vīd′)
  -vid·ing   di·vid·a·ble
  div·i·dend   (dĭv′ ĭ·dĕnd)
div·i·na·tion   (dĭv′ ĭ·nā′ shŭn)
di·vine   (dĭ·vīn′)
di·vin·i·ty   (dĭ·vĭn′ ĭ·tĭ)
  -ties
di·vis·i·ble   (dĭ·vĭz′ ĭ·b′l)
di·vi·sion   (dĭ·vĭzh′ ŭn)
  di·vi·sion·al
di·vi·sive   (dĭ·vī′ sĭv)
di·vi·sor   (dĭ·vī′ zĕr)
di·vorce   (dĭ·vōrs′)
  -vorc·ing
  di·vor·cee   (dĭ·vōr′ sē′)
div·ot   (dĭv′ ŭt)
di·vulge   (dĭ·vŭlj′)
  -vulg·ing   di·vul·gence

Dix·ie   (dĭk′ sĭ)
diz·zy   (dĭz′ ĭ)
  diz·zi·ness
Do·ber·man pin·scher
                     (dō′ bĕr·măn pĭn′ shĕr)
doc·ile   (dŏs′ ĭl)
  doc·ile·ly
  do·cil·i·ty   (dŏ·sĭl′ ĭ·tĭ)
dock·et   (dŏk′ ĕt)
  -et·ed,   -et·ing
dock·yard   (dŏk′ yärd′)
doc·tor   (dŏk′ tĕr)
  doc·tor·al   (dŏk′ tĕr·ăl)
  doc·tor·ate   (dŏk′ tĕr·ĭt)
doc·trine   (dŏk′ trĭn)
  doc·tri·naire   (dŏk′ trĭ·nâr′)
  doc·tri·nal   (dŏk′ trĭ·năl)
doc·u·ment   (dŏk′ û·mĕnt)
  doc·u·men·ta·ry
                     (dŏk′ û·mĕn′ tá·rĭ)
  -ries
  doc·u·men·ta·tion
                     (dŏk′ û·mĕn·tā′ shŭn)
dod·der·ing   (dŏd′ ĕr·ĭng)
dodge   (dŏj)
  dodg·ing
do·er   (do͞o′ ĕr)
doe·skin   (dō′ skĭn′)
does·n't   (dŭz′ ĕnt)
dog   (dŏg)
  dog days   dog-eared
  dog·fight   dog·ged·ly
  dog·house   dog-tired
  dog·watch   dog·wood
dog·ger·el   (dŏg′ ĕr·ĕl)
dog·ma   (dŏg′ mȧ)
  dog·mat·ic   (dŏg·măt′ ĭk)
  dog·ma·tism   (dŏg′ mȧ·tĭz′m)
do-good·er   (do͞o′ go͝od′ ĕr)
doi·ly   (doi′ lĭ)
  -lies
dol·drums   (dŏl′ drŭmz)
dole·ful   (dōl′ fo͝ol)
  -ful·ly   -ful·ness
dol·lar   (dŏl′ ĕr)
dol·lop   (dŏl′ ŭp)
dol·man sleeve   (dŏl′ măn)
dol·or·ous   (dŏl′ ĕr·ŭs)
dol·phin   (dŏl′ fĭn)
dolt·ish   (dōlt′ ĭsh)
do·main   (dō·mān′)
do·mes·tic   (dō·mĕs′ tĭk)
  do·mes·ti·cate   (dō·mĕs′ tĭ·kāt)
  -cat·ing

do·mes·tic·i·ty
    (dō′ měs·tĭs′ ĭ·tĭ)
dom·i·cile   (dŏm′ ĭ·sĭl)
dom·i·nant   (dŏm′ ĭ·nănt)
  -nance
dom·i·nate   (dŏm′ ĭ·nāt)
  -nat·ing
  dom·i·na·tion
    (dŏm′ ĭ·nā′ shŭn)
dom·i·neer·ing
    (dŏm′ ĭ·nēr′ ĭng)
Do·min·i·can   (dô·mĭn′ ĭ·kăn)
  Re·pub·lic
do·min·ion   (dô·mĭn′ yŭn)
dom·i·no   (dŏm′ ĭ·nō)
  -noes
do·nate   (dō′ nāt)
  -nat·ing
  do·na·tion   (dô·nā′ shŭn)
Don Juan   (dŏn hwän′)
don·key   (dŏng′ kĭ)
  -keys
do·nor   (dō′ nĕr)
Don Quix·ote   (dŏn kĕ·hō′ tå)
don't   (dōnt)
doo·dle   (dōō′ d'l)
  -dling
dooms·day   (dōōmz′ dā′)
door   (dōr)
  door·keep·er   door·nail
  door·step   door·way
dope fiend   (dōp)
dope·y   (dōp′ ĭ)
dor·mant   (dôr′ mănt)
  -man·cy
dor·mer win·dow
    (dôr′ mĕr)
dor·mi·to·ry   (dôr′ mĭ·tō′ rĭ)
  -ries
dor·sal   (dôr′ săl)
do·ry   (dō′ rĭ)
  -ries
dos·age   (dōs′ ĭj)
dos·si·er   (dŏs′ ĭ·ā)
Do·sto·ev·ski, Fyo·dor
    (dŏs′ tŭ·yĕv′ skĭ, fyô′ dĕr)
dote   (dōt)
  dot·ing
  dot·age   (dōt′ ĭj)
  do·tard   (dō′ tĕrd)
dot·ted swiss   (dŏt′ ĕd)
dou·ble   (dŭb′ 'l)
  -bly
  dou·ble-breast·ed
  dou·ble-deal·ing

dou·ble-deck·er
dou·ble-en·ten·dre
dou·ble-head·er
dou·ble-take   dou·ble talk
dou·ble time
doubt   (dout)
  doubt·er   doubt·ful
  -ful·ly   -ful·ness
  doubt·less
douche   (dōōsh)
dough·boy   (dō′ boi′)
dough·nut   (dō′ nŭt′)
dour   (dōōr)
douse   (dous)
  dous·ing
dove·tail   (dŭv′ tāl′)
  -tailed   -tail·ing
dow·a·ger   (dou′ å·jĕr)
dow·dy   (dou′ dĭ)
  dow·di·ness
dow·el   (dou′ ĕl)
  dow·el·ing
down   (doun)
  down·beat   down·cast
  down·fall   down·heart·ed
  down·pour   down·stairs
  down·town   down·trod·den
  down·ward   down·y
dow·ry   (dou′ rĭ)
  -ries
dox·ol·o·gy   (dŏks·ŏl′ ô·jĭ)
  -gies
doze   (dōz)
  doz·ing
doz·en   (dŭz′ 'n)
drach·ma   (drăk′ må)
draft   (dráft)
  drafts·man
drag·net   (drăg′ nĕt′)
drag·on·fly   (drăg′ ŭn·flī′)
  -flies
drain   (drān)
  drain·age   (drān′ ĭj)
  drain·pipe
dra·ma   (drä′ må)
  dra·ma·tic   (drá·măt′ ĭk)
  -i·cal·ly
  dram·a·tist   (drăm′ á·tĭst)
  dram·a·ti·za·tion
    (drăm′ á·tĭ·zā′ shŭn)
dra·per·y   (drā′ pĕr·ĭ)
  -per·ies
dras·tic   (drăs′ tĭk)
  -ti·cal·ly
draw·back   (drô′ băk′)

draw·bridge   (drô′ brĭj′)
draw·er   (drô′ ẽr)
drawl   (drôl)
drawn   (drôn)
dray·age   (drā′ ĭj)
dread·ful   (drĕd′ fŏŏl)
   -ful·ly   -ful·ness
dread·nought   (drĕd′ nôt′)
dream·land   (drēm′ lănd′)
dream·y   (drēm′ ĭ)
   dream·i·ness
drear·y   (drẽr′ ĭ)
   drear·i·ly   drear·i·some
dredge   (drĕj)
   dredg·ing
dregs   (drĕgz)
drench   (drĕnch)
dress·mak·er   (drĕs′ māk′ ẽr)
dres·sy   (drĕs′ ĭ)
drib·ble   (drĭb′ l)
   drib·bling
dri·er   (drī′ ẽr)
drift·wood   (drĭft′ wŏŏd′)
drill·mas·ter   (drĭl′ más′ tẽr)
drink·a·ble   (drĭngk′ á·b′l)
drive   (drĭv)
   driv·ing   drive-in
   drive·way
driv·el   (drĭv′ 'l)
   -eled   -el·ing
driz·zle   (drĭz′ 'l)
   driz·zling
droll   (drōl)
   droll·er·y   (drōl′ ẽr·ĭ)
drom·e·dar·y   (drŏm′ ĕ·dĕr′ ĭ)
drone   (drōn)
   dron·ing
droop·y   (drŏŏp′ ĭ)
   droop·i·ness
drop   (drŏp)
   dropped   drop·ping
   drop-forge   drop leaf *n.*
   drop-leaf *adj.*   drop·let
drop·sy   (drŏp′ sĭ)
   drop·si·cal
drought   (drout)
   (dryness; also *drouth*)
drown   (droun)
   drowned   (dround)
drow·sy   (drou′ zĭ)
   drow·si·er   -si·est
   -si·ly   -si·ness
drudge   (drŭj)
   drudg·er·y

drug   (drŭg)
   drugged   drug·ging
   drug·gist   drug·less
   drug·store
dru·id   (drŏŏ′ ĭd)
drum   (drŭm)
   drum·head
   drum ma·jor·ette
   drum·mer   drum·ming
   drum·stick
drunk·ard   (drŭngk′ ẽrd)
drunk·en   (drŭngk′ ĕn)
   drunk·en·ly   drunk·en·ness
dry   (drī)
   dried   dry·ing
   dri·er   dri·est
   dry-clean   dry clean·ing
   dry goods   dry·ly
   dry·ness   dry rot
du·al   (dū′ ăl)
   (double; see *duel*)
   du·al·ism
   du·al·i·ty   (dū·ăl′ ĭ·tĭ)
   du·al·ly   du·al-pur·pose
du·bi·ous   (dū′ bĭ·ŭs)
du·cal   (dū′ kăl)
duc·at   (dŭk′ ăt)
duch·ess   (dŭch′ ĕs)
duch·y   (dŭch′ ĭ)
   duch·ies
duck·ling   (dŭk′ lĭng)
duc·tile   (dŭk′ tĭl)
   duc·til·i·ty   (dŭk·tĭl′ ĭ·tĭ)
duct·less gland
       (dŭkt′ lĕs)
dude ranch   (dūd)
dudg·eon   (dŭj′ ŭn)
du·el   (dū′ ĕl)
   (fight; see *dual*)
   du·eled   du·el·ing
   du·el·ist
du·en·na   (dū·ĕn′ á)
du·et   (dū·ĕt′)
duf·fel bag   (dŭf′ ĕl)
duf·fer   (dŭf′ ẽr)
dug·out   (dŭg′ out′)
duke·dom   (dūk′ dŭm)
dul·cet   (dŭl′ sĕt)
dul·ci·mer   (dŭl′ sĭ·mẽr)
dull   (dŭl)
   dull·ard   (dŭl′ ẽrd)
   dull·ness
   dul·ly   (dŭl′ lĭ)
du·ly   (dū′ lĭ)
   (in due manner)

dumb·bell (dŭm′ bĕl′)
dum·found (dŭm′ found′)
dum·my (dŭm′ ĭ)
 dum·mies
dump·ling (dŭmp′ lĭng)
Dun·can Phyfe (dŭng′ kăn fīf′)
dun·ga·rees (dŭng′ gȧ·rēz′)
dun·geon (dŭn′ jŭn)
du·o·de·num (dū′ ŏ·dē′ nŭm)
dupe (dūp)
 dup·ing
du·plex (dū′ plĕks)
du·pli·cate (dū′ plĭ·kȧt)
 adj., n.
 (-kāt) v.
 -cat·ing
 du·pli·ca·tion
 (dū′ plĭ·kā′ shŭn)
 du·pli·ca·tor (-kā′ tēr)
du·plic·i·ty (dû·plĭs′ ĭ·tĭ)
 -ties
du·ra·ble (dū′ rȧ·b′l)
 du·ra·bil·i·ty (dū′ rȧ·bĭl′ ĭ·tĭ)
du·ra·tion (dû·rā′ shŭn)
du·ress (dū′ rĕs)
dur·ing (dūr′ ĭng)
dusk·y (dŭs′ kĭ)
dust (dŭst)
 dust·bin dust bowl
 dust·pan
Dutch ov·en (dŭch)
du·ty (dū′ tĭ)
 -ties
 du·te·ous (dū′ tĕ·ŭs)
 du·ti·ful, -ful·ly, -ful·ness
dwarf (dwôrf)
dwell·ing (dwĕl′ ĭng)
dwin·dle (dwĭn′ d′l)
 -dling
dye (dī)
 dyed dye·ing
 dye·stuff
dy·ing (dī′ ĭng)
 (expiring)
dy·nam·ic (dī·năm′ ĭk)
 dy·nam·i·cal·ly
 dy·na·mism (dī′ nȧ·mĭz′m)
dy·na·mite (dī′ nȧ·mīt)
dy·na·mo (dī′ nȧ·mō)
 -mos
dy·nas·ty (dī′ nȧs·tĭ)
 -ties
 dy·nas·tic (dī·năs′ tĭk)
dys·en·ter·y (dĭs′ ĕn·tĕr′ ĭ)
dys·func·tion (dĭs·fŭngk′ shŭn)

dys·pep·sia (dĭs·pĕp′ shȧ)
 dys·pep·tic (dĭs·pĕp′ tĭk)
dys·tro·phy (dĭs′ trŏ·fĭ)

E

ea·ger (ē′ gēr)
ea·gle (ē′ g′l)
 ea·glet (ē′ glĕt)
ear (ēr)
 ear·ache ear·drum
 ear·phone ear·ring
 ear·shot
earl·dom (ûrl′ dŭm)
ear·ly (ûr′ lĭ)
 ear·li·er, -li·est, -li·ness
ear·nest (ûr′ nĕst)
earn·ing (ûr′ nĭng)
earth (ûrth)
 earth·en·ware earth·ling
 earth·ly -li·ness
 earth·quake earth·y
ease (ēz)
 eas·ing
ea·sel (ē′ z′l)
East·er (ēs′ tēr)
east·ern·er (ēs′ tēr·nēr)
east·ward (ēst′ wērd)
eas·y (ēz′ ĭ)
 eas·i·er eas·i·est
 eas·i·ly eas·i·ness
 eas·y·go·ing
Eau de Co·logne
 (ō dē kȯ·lōn′)
eaves·drop·per (ēvz′ drŏp′ ēr)
ebb tide (ĕb tīd)
eb·on·y (ĕb′ ŭn·ĭ)
e·bul·li·ence (ė·bŭl′ ĭ·ĕns)
 e·bul·li·ent
ec·cen·tric (ĕk·sĕn′ trĭk)
 ec·cen·tric·i·ty
 (ĕk′ sĕn·trĭs′ ĭ·tĭ)
Ec·cle·si·as·tes (ė·klē′ zĭ·ăs′ tēz)
ec·cle·si·as·ti·cal
 (ė·klē′ zĭ·ăs′ tĭ·kȧl)
ech·e·lon (ĕsh′ ė·lŏn)
ech·o (ĕk′ o)
 -oed -o·ing
 ech·oes
é·clair (ȧ·klâr′)
ec·lec·tic (ĕk·lĕk′ tĭk)
 ec·lec·ti·cism (-tĭ·sĭz′m)
e·clipse (ė·klĭps′)
 -clips·ing

ec·logue (ĕk′ lŏg)
e·col·o·gy (ĕ·kŏl′ ô·jĭ)
  e·col·o·gist (ĕ·kŏl′ ô·jĭst)
e·con·o·my (ĕ·kŏn′ ô·mĭ)
  -mies
  e·co·nom·ic (ē′ kô·nŏm′ ĭk)
  e·co·nom·i·cal
     (ē′ kô·nŏm′ ĭ·kăl)
  e·con·o·mist (ê·kŏn′ ô·mĭst)
  e·con·o·mize (ê·kŏn′ ô·mĭz)
  -miz·ing
ec·ru (ĕk′ rōō)
ec·sta·sy (ĕk′ stȧ·sĭ)
  -sies
  ec·stat·ic (ĕk·stăt′ ĭk)
  -i·cal·ly
ec·to·plasm (ĕk′ tô·plăz′m)
  ec·to·plas·mic
     (ĕk′ tô·plăz′ mĭk)
Ec·ua·dor (ĕk′ wȧ·dôr)
ec·u·men·i·cal
     (ĕk′ ů·mĕn′ ĭ·kăl)
ec·ze·ma (ĕk′ sĕ·mȧ)
E·dam cheese (ē′ dăm)
ed·dy (ĕd′ ĭ)
  ed·died   ed·dy·ing
  ed·dies
e·del·weiss (ā′ dĕl·vīs)
E·den (ē′ d′n)
edge (ĕj)
  edg·ing   edge·wise
  edg·y
ed·i·ble (ĕd′ ĭ·b′l)
  ed·i·bil·i·ty (ĕd′ ĭ·bĭl′ ĭ·tĭ)
e·dict (ē′ dĭkt)
ed·i·fice (ĕd′ ĭ·fĭs)
ed·i·fy (ĕd′ ĭ·fī)
  -fied   -fy·ing
  ed·i·fi·ca·tion
     (ĕd′ ĭ·fĭ·kā′ shŭn)
ed·it (ĕd′ ĭt)
  -it·ed   -it·ing
  e·di·tion (ê·dĭsh′ ŭn)
  ed·i·tor
  ed·i·to·ri·al (ĕd′ ĭ·tō′ rĭ·ăl)
  -al·ly
ed·u·cate (ĕd′ ů·kāt)
  -cat·ing
  ed·u·ca·ble (ĕd′ ů·kȧ·b′l)
  ed·u·ca·tion (ĕd′ ů·kā′ shŭn)
  -tion·al
  ed·u·ca·tive (ĕd′ ů·kā′ tĭv)
  ed·u·ca·tor (ĕd′ ů·kā′ tẽr)
e·duce (ê·dūs′)
  -duc·ing   e·duc·i·ble

ee·rie (ē′ rĭ)
  ee·ri·ly   -i·ness
ef·face (ĕ·fās′)
  ef·fac·ing   ef·face·ment
ef·fect (ĕ·fĕkt′)
  (result; see *affect*)
  ef·fec·tive
ef·fec·tu·al (ĕ·fĕk′ tů·ăl)
  ef·fec·tu·ate (-āt)
  -at·ing
ef·fem·i·nate (ĕ·fĕm′ ĭ·nĭt)
  ef·fem·i·na·cy (-nȧ·sĭ)
ef·fer·vesce (ĕf′ ẽr·vĕs′)
  -vesc·ing   ef·fer·ves·cence
ef·fete (ĕ·fēt′)
ef·fi·ca·cy (ĕf′ ĭ·kȧ·sĭ)
  ef·fi·ca·cious (ĕf′ ĭ·kā′ shŭs)
ef·fi·cient (ĕ·fĭsh′ ĕnt)
  ef·fi·cien·cy
ef·fi·gy (ĕf′ ĭ·jĭ)
  -gies
ef·fort (ĕf′ ẽrt)
  ef·fort·less·ly
ef·fron·ter·y (ĕ·frŭn′ tẽr·ĭ)
  -ter·ies
ef·fu·sion (ĕ·fū′ zhŭn)
ef·fu·sive (ĕ·fū′ sĭv)
e·gal·i·tar·i·an
     (ê·găl′ ĭ·târ′ ĭ·ȧn)
egg·head (ĕg′ hĕd′)
egg·nog (ĕg′ nŏg′)
e·go (ē′ gō)
  e·go·cen·tric (ē′ gô·sĕn′ trĭk)
  e·go·ism (ē′ gô·ĭz′m)
  -ist
  e·go·tism (ē′ gô·tĭz′m)
  -tist
  e·go·tis·ti·cal (ē′ gô·tĭs′ tĭ·kăl)
e·gre·gious (ê·grē′ jŭs)
e·gress (ē′ grĕs)
e·gret (ē′ grĕt)
E·gypt (ē′ jĭpt)
  E·gyp·tian (ê·jĭp′ shăn)
ei·der down (ī′ dẽr)
eight·een (ā′ tēn′)
eight·y (ā′ tĭ)
  eight·ies   eight·i·eth
Ein·stein the·o·ry (īn′ stīn)
Ei·sen·how·er, Dwight D.
     (ī′ z′n·hou′ ẽr)
ei·ther (ē′ thẽr)
e·jac·u·late (ê·jăk′ ů·lāt)
  -lat·ing

e·jac·u·la·tion
          (ê·jăk′ û·lā′ shŭn)
e·jac·u·la·tor
e·ject   (ê·jĕkt′)
  e·jec·tion   (-jĕk′ shŭn)
  e·jec·tor
eke   (ēk)
  ek·ing
e·lab·o·rate   (ê·lăb′ ô·rĭt)
    adj.
    (-rāt) *v.*
  -rat·ing
  e·lab·o·rate·ly   (-rĭt·lĭ)
  e·lab·o·ra·tion
        (ê·lăb′ ô·rā′ shŭn)
é· *lan*   (ā′ läɴ′)
e·lapse   (ê·lăps′)
  -laps·ing
e·las·tic   (ê·lăs′ tĭk)
  e·las·tic·i·ty (ê·lăs′ tĭs′ ĭ·tĭ)
e·late   (ê·lāt′)
  -lat·ing   e·lat·ed·ly
  e·la·tion
el·bow   (ĕl′ bō)
  el·bow·room
el·der·ber·ry (ĕl′ dĕr·bĕr′ ĭ)
  -ber·ries
eld·er·ly   (ĕl′ dĕr·lĭ)
El Do·ra·do (ĕl dô·rä′ dō)
e·lect   (ê·lĕkt′)
  e·lec·tion   (ê·lĕk′ shŭn)
  e·lec·tive   e·lec·tor
  e·lec·tor·al col·lege
      (ê·lĕk′ tēr·ăl)
  e·lec·tor·ate (ê·lĕk′ tēr·ĭt)
e·lec·tric   (ê·lĕk′ trĭk)
  e·lec·tri·cal
  e·lec·tri·cian (ê·lĕk′ trĭsh′ ăn)
  e·lec·tric·i·ty (ê·lĕk′ trĭs′ ĭ·tĭ)
e·lec·tri·fy   (ê·lĕk′ trĭ·fĭ)
  -fied   -fy·ing
  e·lec·tri·fi·ca·tion
    (ê·lĕk′ trĭ·fĭ·kā′ shŭn)
e·lec·tro·car·di·o·gram
    (ê·lĕk′ trô·kär′ dĭ·ô·grăm′)
e·lec·tro·cute (ê·lĕk′ trô·kūt)
  -cut·ing
  e·lec·tro·cu·tion
    (ê·lĕk′ trô·kū′ shŭn)
e·lec·trode   (ê·lĕk′ trōd)
e·lec·tro·dy·nam·ics
    (ê·lĕk′ trô·dī·năm′ ĭks)
e·lec·trol·y·sis (ê·lĕk′ trŏl′ ĭ·sĭs)
e·lec·tro·lyt·ic (ê·lĕk′ trô·lĭt′ ĭk)

e·lec·tro·mag·net·ic
    (ê·lĕk′ trô·măg·nĕt′ ĭk)
e·lec·tron   (ê·lĕk′ trŏn)
  e·lec·tron·ic (ê·lĕk′ trŏn′ ĭk)
e·lec·tro·plate (ê·lĕk′ trô·plāt′)
  -plat·ing
e·lec·tro·ther·a·py
    (ê·lĕk′ trô·thĕr′ á·pĭ)
el·ee·mos·y·nar·y
    (ĕl′ ê·mŏs′ ĭ·nĕr′ ĭ)
el·e·gance   (ĕl′ ê·gáns)
  -gant
el·e·gy   (ĕl′ ê·jĭ)
  -gies
  el·e·gi·ac   (ĕl′ ê·jĭ′ ăk)
  el·e·gize   (ĕl′ ê·jīz)
  -giz·ing
el·e·ment   (ĕl′ ê·mĕnt)
  el·e·men·tal (ĕl′ ê·mĕn′ tăl)
  el·e·men·ta·ry (ĕl′ ê·mĕn′ tá·rĭ)
el·e·phant   (ĕl′ ê·fănt)
  el·e·phan·tine (ĕl′ ê·făn′ tĭn)
el·e·vate   (ĕl′ ê·vāt)
  -vat·ing
  el·e·va·tion (ĕl′ ê·vā′ shŭn)
  el·e·va·tor (ĕl′ ê·vā′ tēr)
e·lev·en   (ê·lĕv′ ĕn)
elf·in   (ĕl′ fĭn)
e·lic·it   (ê·lĭs′ ĭt)
  (to draw forth; see *illicit*)
  -it·ed   -it·ing
e·lide   (ê·līd′)
  -lid·ing
  e·li·sion   (ê·lĭzh′ ŭn)
el·i·gi·ble   (ĕl′ ĭ·jĭ·b′l)
  el·i·gi·bil·i·ty (ĕl′ ĭ·jĭ·bĭl′ ĭ·tĭ)
e·lim·i·nate (ê·lĭm′ ĭ·nāt)
  -nat·ing
  e·lim·i·na·tion
    (ê·lĭm′ ĭ·nā′ shŭn)
e·li·sion   (ê·lĭzh′ ŭn)
e·lite   (á·lēt′)
e·lix·ir   (ê·lĭk′ sēr)
E·liz·a·be·than
    (ê·lĭz′ á·bē′ thăn)
el·lipse   (ê·lĭps′)
  el·lip·sis   el·lip·tic
  -ti·cal
el·o·cu·tion (ĕl′ ô·kū′ shŭn)
e·lon·gate   (ê·lŏng′ gāt)
  -gat·ing
  e·lon·ga·tion
    (ê·lŏng′ gā′ shŭn)
e·lope   (ê·lōp′)
  -lop·ing   e·lope·ment

el·o·quence (ĕl′ ŏ·kwĕns)
-quent

else·where (ĕls′ hwâr)

e·lu·ci·date (ē·lū′ sǐ·dāt)
-dat·ing
e·lu·ci·da·tion
(ē·lū′ sǐ·dā′ shǔn)

e·lude (ē·lūd′)
(evade; see *allude*)
-lud·ing
e·lu·sion (ē·lū′ zhǔn)
e·lu·sive (ē·lū′ sǐv)
(baffling; see *illusive*)

e·ma·ci·ate (ē·mā′ shǐ·āt)
(to make thin)
-at·ing
e·ma·ci·a·tion
(ē·mā′ sǐ·ā′ shǔn)

em·a·nate (ĕm′ ȧ·nāt)
(to flow)
-nat·ing
em·a·na·tion (ĕm′ ȧ·nā′ shǔn)

e·man·ci·pate (ē·măn′ sǐ·pāt)
(to free)
-pat·ing
e·man·ci·pa·tion
(ē·măn′ sǐ·pā′ shǔn)

e·mas·cu·late (ē·măs′ kū·lāt)
-lat·ing
e·mas·cu·la·tion
(ē·măs′ kū·lā′ shǔn)

em·balm (ĕm·bäm′)

em·bank·ment (ĕm·băngk′ mĕnt)

em·bar·go (ĕm·bär′ gō)
-goes

em·bark (ĕm·bärk′)
em·bar·ka·tion
(ĕm′ bär·kā′ shǔn)
em·bark·ment

em·bar·rass (ĕm·băr′ ȧs)
em·bar·rass·ment

em·bas·sy (ĕm′ bȧ·sǐ)
-bas·sies

em·bat·tle (ĕm·băt′ ′l)
-bat·tling

em·bed (ĕm·bĕd′)
-bed·ded -bed·ding

em·bel·lish (ĕm·bĕl′ ǐsh)

em·ber (ĕm′ bēr)

em·bez·zle (ĕm·bĕz′ ′l)
-bez·zling
em·bez·zle·ment
em·bez·zler

em·bit·ter (ĕm·bǐt′ ēr)

em·bla·zon (ĕm·blā′ z′n)

em·blem (ĕm′ blĕm)
em·blem·at·ic (ĕm′ blĕ·măt′ ǐk)

em·bod·y (ĕm·bŏd′ ǐ)
-bod·ied -bod·y·ing
em·bod·i·ment
(ĕm·bŏd′ ǐ·mĕnt)

em·bold·en (ĕm·bōl′ dĕn)

em·boss (ĕm·bôs′)

em·brace (ĕm·brās′)
-brac·ing

em·broi·der (ĕm·broi′ dēr)
em·broi·der·y

em·broil (ĕm·broil′)

em·bry·o (ĕm′ brǐ·ō)
-os
em·bry·o·log·i·cal
(ĕm′ brǐ·ō·lŏj′ ǐ·kȧl)
em·bry·ol·o·gy
(ĕm′ brǐ·ŏl′ ō·jǐ)
em·bry·on·ic (ĕm′ brǐ·ŏn′ ǐk)

em·cee (ĕm′ sē′)

e·mend (ē·mĕnd′)
e·men·da·tion
(ē′ mĕn·dā′ shǔn)

em·er·ald (ĕm′ ēr·ȧld)
Em·er·ald Isle

e·merge (ē·mûrj′)
-merg·ing e·mer·gent,
-gence

e·mer·gen·cy (ē·mûr′ jĕn·sǐ)
-cies

e·mer·i·tus (ē·mĕr′ ǐ·tǔs)

e·merse (ē·mûrs′)
-mers·ing
e·mer·sion (ē·mûr′ shǔn)

em·er·y (ĕm′ ēr·ǐ)

e·met·ic (ē·mĕt′ ǐk)

em·i·grate (ĕm′ ǐ·grāt)
(to leave one's homeland; see
immigrate) -grat·ing
em·i·grant (-grănt)
em·i·gra·tion (ĕm′ ǐ·grā′ shǔn)
é·mi·gré (ā′ mē′ grā′)

em·i·nence (ĕm′ ǐ·nĕns)
em·i·nent do·main

em·is·sar·y (ĕm′ ǐ·sĕr′ ǐ)
em·is·sar·ies

e·mis·sion (ē·mǐsh′ ǔn)

e·mit (ē·mǐt′)
-mit·ted -mit·ting

e·mol·li·ent (ē·mŏl′ ǐ·ĕnt)
(lotion)

e·mol·u·ment (ē·mŏl′ ū·mĕnt)
(wages)

e·mo·tion (ė·mō′ shŭn)
  e·mo·tion·al -al·ly
e·mo·tive (ė·mō′ tĭv)
em·pa·thy (ĕm′ pȧ·thĭ)
em·per·or (ĕm′ pĕr·ēr)
em·pha·sis (ĕm′ fȧ·sĭs)
  pl. em·pha·ses (-sēz)
  em·pha·size -siz·ing
  em·phat·ic (ĕm·făt′ ĭk)
  -i·cal·ly
em·pire (ĕm′ pīr)
em·pir·ic (ĕm·pĭr′ ĭk)
  em·pir·i·cal
  em·pir·i·cism (-ĭ·sĭz′m)
em·place·ment (ĕm·plās′ mĕnt)
em·ploy (ĕm·ploi′)
  em·ploy·a·ble em·ploy·ee
  em·ploy·er em·ploy·ment
em·po·ri·um (ĕm·pō′ rĭ·ŭm)
em·pow·er (ĕm·pou′ ēr)
emp·ty (ĕmp′ tĭ)
  -tied -ty·ing
  emp·ti·ly -ti·ness
em·py·re·an (ĕm′ pĭ·rē′ ȧn)
em·u·late (ĕm′ û·lȧt)
  -lat·ing
  em·u·la·tion (ĕm′ û·lā′ shŭn)
  em·u·la·tive (ĕm′ û·lā′ tĭv)
  em·u·la·tor (ĕm′ û·lā′ tēr)
e·mul·si·fy (ė·mŭl′ sĭ·fĭ)
  -fied -fy·ing
  e·mul·si·fi·ca·tion
    (ė·mŭl′ sĭ·fĭ·kā′ shŭn)
e·mul·sion (ė·mŭl′ shŭn)
en·a·ble (ĕn·ā′ b′l)
  -bling
en·act·ment (ĕn·ăkt′ mĕnt)
en·am·el (ĕn·ăm′ ĕl)
  -eled -el·ing
en·am·ored (ĕn·ăm′ ērd)
en·camp·ment (ĕn·kămp′ mĕnt)
en·ceph·a·lo·gram
    (ĕn·sĕf′ ȧ·lō·grăm′)
en·chant (ĕn·chȧnt′)
  en·chant·ress
en·cir·cle (ĕn·sûr′ k′l)
  -cling en·cir·cle·ment
en·clasp (ĕn·klȧsp′)
en·clave (ĕn′ klāv)
en·close (ĕn·klōz′)
  -clos·ing
  en·clo·sure (ĕn·klō′ zhēr)
en·co·mi·um (ĕn·kō′ mĭ·ŭm)
en·com·pass (ĕn·kŭm′ pȧs)
en·core (äng′ kōr)

en·coun·ter (ĕn·koun′ tēr)
en·cour·age (ĕn·kûr′ ĭj)
  -ag·ing
  en·cour·age·ment
en·croach (ĕn·krōch′)
en·crust (ĕn·krŭst′)
en·cum·ber (ĕn·kŭm′ bēr)
  en·cum·brance
en·cyc·li·cal (ĕn·sĭk′ lĭ·kȧl)
en·cy·clo·pe·di·a
  en·cy·clo·pe·dic
en·dan·ger (ĕn·dān′ jēr)
en·dear·ing (ĕn·dēr′ ĭng)
en·deav·or (ĕn·dĕv′ ēr)
en·dem·ic (ĕn·dĕm′ ĭk)
  en·dem·i·cal·ly
en·dive (ĕn′ dĭv)
end·less·ly (ĕnd′ lĕs·lĭ)
en·do·crine (ĕn′ dō·krĭn)
  en·do·cri·nol·o·gy
    (ĕn′ dō·krĭ·nŏl′ ō·jĭ)
en·dorse (ĕn·dôrs′)
  -dors·ing en·dors·a·ble
  en·dor·see (ĕn′ dôr·sē′)
  en·dorse·ment
en·dow·ment (ĕn·dou′ mĕnt)
en·due (ĕn·dū′)
  -du·ing
en·dure (ĕn·dūr′)
  -dur·ing en·dur·a·ble
  en·dur·ance
en·e·ma (ĕn′ ė·mȧ)
en·e·my (ĕn′ ė·mĭ)
  -mies
en·er·gy (ĕn′ ēr·jĭ)
  -gies
  en·er·get·ic (ĕn′ ēr·jĕt′ ĭk)
  -i·cal·ly
  en·er·gize (ĕn′ ēr·jīz)
  -giz·ing
en·er·vate (ĕn′ ēr·vāt)
  (to deprive of nerve; see *innervate*)
  -vat·ing
  en·er·va·tion (ĕn′ ēr·vā′ shŭn)
en·fee·ble (ĕn·fē′ b′l)
  -fee·bling
en·force (ĕn·fōrs′)
  -forc·ing en·force·a·ble
  en·force·ment
en·fran·chise (ĕn·frăn′ chīz)
  -chis·ing
  en·fran·chise·ment
en·gage (ĕn·gāj′)
  -gag·ing en·gage·ment

en·gen·der   (ĕn·jĕn′ dẽr)
en·gine   (ĕn′ jĭn)
en·gi·neer   (ĕn′ jĭ·nẽr′)
  en·gi·neer·ing
Eng·lish·man   (ĭng′ glĭsh·mǎn)
en·grave   (ĕn·grāv′)
  -grav·ing   en·grav·er
en·gross   (ĕn·grōs′)
en·gulf   (ĕn·gŭlf′)
en·hance   (ĕn·hǎns′)
  -hanc·ing   en·hance·ment
e·nig·ma   (ē·nĭg′ mȧ)
  e·nig·mat·ic   (ē′ nĭg·mǎt′ ĭk)
  -i·cal·ly
en·join   (ĕn·join′)
en·joy   (ĕn·joi′)
  en·joy·a·ble   en·joy·ment
en·large   (ĕn·lärj′)
  -larg·ing   en·large·ment
en·light·en·ment
                  (ĕn·līt′ 'n·mĕnt)
en·list   (ĕn·lĭst′)
  en·list·ment
en·liv·en   (ĕn·lĭv′ ĕn)
en masse   (ĕn mǎs′)
en·mesh   (ĕn·mĕsh′)
en·mi·ty   (ĕn′ mĭ·tĭ)
  (ill will; see amity)
  -ties
en·no·ble   (ĕ·nō′ b'l)
  -bling
en·nui   (än′ wē)
e·nor·mous   (ē·nôr′ mŭs)
  e·nor·mi·ty   (ē·nôr′ mĭ·tĭ)
e·nough   (ē·nŭf′)
en·plane   (ĕn·plān′)
  -plan·ing
en·rage   (ĕn·rāj′)
  -rag·ing
en·rap·ture   (ĕn·rǎp′ tửr)
  -tur·ing
en·rich   (ĕn·rĭch′)
en·roll   (ĕn·rōl′)
  en·roll·ment
en route   (än rōōt′)
en·sconce   (ĕn·skŏns′)
  -sconc·ing
en·sem·ble   (än·sŏm′ b'l)
en·shrine   (ĕn·shrīn′)
  -shrin·ing
en·shroud   (ĕn·shroud′)
en·sign   (ĕn′ sīn)
en·slave·ment   (ĕn·slāv′ mĕnt)
en·sue   (ĕn·sū′)
  -su·ing

en·tail   (ĕn·tāl′)
en·tan·gle   (ĕn·tǎng′ g'l)
  -gling   en·tan·gle·ment
en·tenté cor·diale
                  (än′ tänt′ kôr′ dyál′)
en·ter   (ĕn′ tẽr)
  en·trant
en·ter·prise   (ĕn′ tẽr·prīz)
  -pris·ing
en·ter·tain   (ĕn′ tẽr·tān′)
  en·ter·tain·ing·ly
  en·ter·tain·ment
en·thrall   (ĕn·thrôl′)
en·throne   (ĕn·thrōn′)
  -thron·ing   en·throne·ment
en·thu·si·asm   (ĕn·thū′ zĭ·ǎz'm)
  en·thu·si·ast   (ĕn·thū′ zĭ·ǎst)
  en·thu·si·as·tic
                  (ĕn·thū′ zĭ·ǎs′ tĭk)
  -ti·cal·ly
en·tice   (ĕn·tīs′)
  -tic·ing   en·tice·ment
en·tire·ty   (ĕn·tīr′ tĭ)
en·ti·tle   (ĕn·tī′ t'l)
  -ti·tling
en·ti·ty   (ĕn′ tĭ·tĭ)
  -ties
en·to·mol·o·gy   (ĕn′ tô·mŏl′ ô·jĭ)
en·tou·rage   (än·tōō′ räzh′)
en·trails   (ĕn′ trālz)
en·trance   (ĕn′ trȧns) n.
en·trance   (ĕn·trȧns′) v.
  -tranc·ing
en·trant   (ĕn′ trǎnt)
en·treat   (ĕn·trēt′)
  en·treat·ing·ly
  en·treat·y   -treat·ies
en·tree   (än′ trā)
en·trench·ment
                  (ĕn·trĕnch·mĕnt)
en·tre·pre·neur
                  (än′ trĕ·prĕ·nûr′)
en·trust   (ĕn·trŭst′)
en·try   (ĕn′ trĭ)
  -tries   en·try·way
en·twine   (ĕn·twīn′)
  -twin·ing
e·nu·mer·ate   (ē·nū′ mẽr·āt)
  -at·ing
  e·num·er·a·tion
                  (ē·nū′ mẽr·ā′ shŭn)
e·nun·ci·ate   (ē·nŭn′ shĭ·āt)
  -at·ing
  e·nun·ci·a·tion
                  (ē·nŭn′ sĭ·ā′ shŭn)

en·vel·op (ĕn·vĕl′ ŭp) *v.*
  (to wrap up)
  -oped   -op·ing
  en·vel·op·ment
en·ve·lope (ĕn′ vĕ·lōp) *n.*
  (letter container)
en·ven·om (ĕn·vĕn′ ŭm)
en·vi·a·ble (ĕn′ vĭ·à·b′l)
en·vi·ous (ĕn′ vĭ·ŭs)
en·vi·ron·ment
        (ĕn·vī′ rŭn·mĕnt)
  en·vi·ron·men·tal
     (ĕn·vī′ rŭn·mĕn′ tăl)
en·vi·rons (ĕn·vī′ rŭnz)
en·vis·age (ĕn·vĭz′ ĭj)
  -ag·ing
en·vi·sion (ĕn·vĭzh′ ŭn)
en·voy (ĕn′ voi)
en·vy (ĕn′ vĭ)
  -vied   -vy·ing
en·wrap (ĕn·răp′)
  -wrapped   -wrap·ping
en·zyme (ĕn′ zīm)
e·on (ē′ ŏn)
ep·au·let (ĕp′ ô·lĕt)
e·phem·er·al (ĕ·fĕm′ ēr·ăl)
ep·ic (ĕp′ ĭk)
ep·i·cure (ĕp′ ĭ·kūr)
  ep·i·cu·re·an (ĕp′ ĭ·kû·rē′ ăn)
ep·i·dem·ic (ĕp′ ĭ·dĕm′ ĭk)
ep·i·der·mis (ĕp′ ĭ·dûr′ mĭs)
ep·i·gram (ĕp′ ĭ·grăm)
  ep·i·gram·mat·ic
     (ĕp′ ĭ·grà·măt′ ĭk)
ep·i·lep·sy (ĕp′ ĭ·lĕp′ sĭ)
ep·i·lep·tic (ĕp′ ĭ·lĕp′ tĭk)
ep·i·logue (ĕp′ ĭ·lôg)
E·piph·a·ny (ĕ·pĭf′ à·nĭ)
E·pis·co·pa·li·an
    (ĕ·pĭs′ kô·pā′ lĭ·ăn)
ep·i·sode (ĕp′ ĭ·sōd)
e·pis·tle (ĕ·pĭs′ ′l)
ep·i·taph (ĕp′ ĭ·tăf)
  (tomb inscription)
ep·i·thet (ĕp′ ĭ·thĕt)
  (nickname)
e·pit·o·me (ĕ·pĭt′ ô·mē)
e·pit·o·mize (ĕ·pĭt′ ô·mīz)
  -miz·ing
ep·och (ĕp′ ŏk)
  ep·och·al
eq·ua·ble (ĕk′ wà·b′l)
e·qual (ē′ kwăl)
  -qualed   -qual·ing
e·qual·i·ty (ê·kwŏl′ ĭ·tĭ)

e·qual·ize   -iz·ing
e·qual·ly
e·qua·nim·i·ty (ē′ kwà·nĭm′ ĭ·t)
e·quate (ê·kwāt′)
  -quat·ing
e·qua·tion (ê·kwā′ zhŭn)
e·qua·tor (ê·kwā′ tēr)
  e·qua·to·ri·al (ē′ kwà·tō′ rĭ·ăl)
e·ques·tri·an (ê·kwĕs′ trĭ·ăn)
e·qui·dis·tant (ē′ kwĭ·dĭs′ tănt)
e·qui·lat·er·al (ē′ kwĭ·lăt′ ēr·ăl)
  -al·ly
e·qui·li·bra·tion
    (ē′ kwĭ·lĭ·brā′ shŭn)
e·qui·lib·ri·um
    (ē′ kwĭ·lĭb′ rĭ·ŭm)
e·quine (ē′ kwīn)
e·qui·nox (ē′ kwĭ·nŏks)
  e·qui·noc·tial
    (ē′ kwĭ·nŏk′ shăl)
e·quip (ê·kwĭp′)
  -quipped   -quip·ping
eq·ui·page (ĕk′ wĭ·pĭj)
e·quip·ment
eq·ui·ta·ble (ĕk′ wĭ·tà·b′l)
eq·ui·ty (ĕk′ wĭ·tĭ)
  -ties
e·quiv·a·lent (ê·kwĭv′ à·lĕnt)
  -lence
e·quiv·o·cal (ê·kwĭv′ ô·kăl)
  -cal·ly
e·quiv·o·cate (ê·kwĭv′ ô·kāt)
  -cat·ing
e·quiv·o·ca·tion
    (ê·kwĭv′ ô·kā′ shŭn)
e·ra (ē′ rà)
e·rad·i·cate (ê·răd′ ĭ·kāt)
  -cat·ing
  e·rad·i·ca·ble (ê·răd′ ĭ·kà·b′l)
  e·rad·i·ca·tion
    (ê·răd′ ĭ·kā′ shŭn)
  e·rad·i·ca·tor (ê·răd′ ĭ·kā′ tēr)
e·rase (ê·rās′)
  -ras·ing   e·ras·a·ble
  e·ras·er
  e·ra·sure (ê·rā′ zhēr)
e·rect (ê·rĕkt′)
  e·rect·er
  e·rec·tile (ê·rĕk′ tĭl)
  e·rec·tion
er·go (ûr′ gō)
er·mine (ûr′ mĭn)
e·rode (ê·rōd′)
  -rod·ing
  e·ro·sion (ê·rō′ zhŭn)

e·rot·ic (ĕ·rŏt′ ĭk)
err (ûr)
er·rand (ĕr′ ănd)
er·rant (ĕr′ ănt)
  (wandering; see *arrant*)
er·rat·ic (ĕ·răt′ ĭk)
  -i·cal·ly
er·ra·tum (ĕ·rā′ tŭm)
  pl. er·ra·ta
er·ro·ne·ous (ĕ·rō′ nĕ·ŭs)
er·ror (ĕr′ ĕr)
er·satz (ĕr·zäts′)
erst·while (ûrst′ hwīl′)
er·u·dite (ĕr′ ŏŏ·dīt)
  er·u·di·tion (ĕr′ ŏŏ·dĭsh′ ŭn)
e·rupt (ĕ·rŭpt′)
  e·rup·tion   e·rup·tive
es·ca·la·tor (ĕs′ ka·lā′ tēr)
es·ca·pade (ĕs′ ka·pād′)
es·cape (ĕs·kāp′)
  -cap·ing   es·cap·a·ble
  es·cape·ment   es·cap·ism, -ist
es·ca·role (ĕs′ ka·rōl)
es·carp·ment (ĕs·kärp′ mĕnt)
es·chew (ĕs·chōō′)
es·cort (ĕs′ kôrt) *n.*
   (ĕs·kôrt′) *v.*
es·crow (ĕs′ krō′)
es·cutch·eon (ĕs·kŭch′ ŭn)
Es·ki·mo (ĕs′ kĭ·mō)
  -mos
es·o·ter·ic (ĕs′ ō·tĕr′ ĭk)
es·pe·cial (ĕs·pĕsh′ ăl)
  es·pe·cial·ly
Es·pe·ran·to (ĕs′ pĕ·rän′ tō)
es·pi·o·nage (ĕs′ pĭ·ō·nĭj)
es·pla·nade (ĕs′ pla·nād′)
es·pouse (ĕs·pouz′)
  -pous·ing   es·pous·al
es·prit de corps
   (ĕs′ prē′ dĕ kôr′)
es·py (ĕs·pī′)
  -py·ing
es·quire (ĕs·kwīr′)
es·say (ĕ·sā′) *v.*
   (ĕs′ ā) *n.*
es·sence (ĕs′ ĕns)
es·sen·tial (ĕ·sĕn′ shăl)
  -tial·ly
es·tab·lish (ĕs·tăb′ lĭsh)
es·tate (ĕs·tāt′)
es·teem (ĕs·tēm′)
es·ti·ma·ble (ĕs′ tĭ·ma·b′l)
es·ti·mate (ĕs′ tĭ·māt) *n.*
  -mat·ing (-māt) *v.*

es·ti·ma·tion (ĕs′ tĭ·mā′ shŭn)
es·top (ĕs·tŏp′)
  -topped   -top·ping
  es·top·page
es·trange (ĕs·trānj′)
  -trang·ing   es·trange·ment
es·tro·gen (ĕs′ trō·jĕn)
  es·tro·gen·ic (ĕs′ trō·jĕn′ ĭk)
es·tu·ar·y (ĕs′ tū·ĕr′ ĭ)
  -ar·ies
et cet·er·a (ĕt sĕt′ ēr·ʻ)
etch·ing (ĕch′ ĭng)
e·ter·nal (ĕ·tûr′ năl)
  -nal·ly
e·ter·ni·ty (ĕ·tûr′ nĭ·tĭ)
e·ther (ē′ thēr)
e·the·re·al (ĕ·thĕr′ ĕ·ăl)
eth·ics (ĕth′ ĭks)
  eth·i·cal
eth·nic (ĕth′ nĭk)
e·thos (ē′ thŏs)
eth·yl (ĕth′ ĭl)
e·ti·ol·o·gy (ē′ tĭ·ŏl′ ō·jĭ)
et·i·quette (ĕt′ ĭ·kĕt)
E·ton jack·et (ē′ t'n)
E·trus·can (ĕ·trŭs′ kăn)
é·tude (ā′ tūd)
et·y·mol·o·gy (ĕt′ ĭ·mŏl′ ō·jĭ)
  et·y·mol·o·gist
eu·ca·lyp·tus (ū′ ka·lĭp′ tŭs)
Eu·cha·rist (ū′ ka·rĭst)
eu·chre (ū′ kēr)
Eu·clid (ū′ klĭd)
  Eu·clid·e·an (ū·klĭd′ ĕ·ăn)
eu·gen·ic (ū·jĕn′ ĭk)
eu·lo·gy (ū′ lō·jĭ)
  -gies
  eu·lo·gis·tic (ū′ lō·jĭs′ tĭk)
  eu·lo·gize (ū′ lō·jīz)
  -giz·ing
eu·nuch (ū′ nŭk)
eu·phe·mism (ū′ fĕ·mĭz′m)
  eu·phe·mis·tic (ū′ fĕ·mĭs′ tĭk)
  -ti·cal·ly
eu·phon·ic (ū·fŏn′ ĭk)
eu·pho·ri·a (ū·fō′ rĭ·à)
eu·re·ka (ū·rē′ ká)
Eu·ro·pe·an (ū′ rŏ·pē′ ăn)
Eu·sta·chi·an tube
   (ū·stā′ kĭ·ăn)
eu·tha·na·si·a (ū′ thá·nā′ zhĭ·à)
e·vac·u·ate (ĕ·văk′ û·āt)
  -at·ing
  e·vac·u·a·tion
   (ĕ·văk′ û·ā′ shŭn)

e·vac·u·ee (ĕ·văk′ û·ē′)
e·vade (ĕ·vād′)
-vad·ing
e·val·u·ate (ĕ·văl′ û·āt)
-at·ing
e·val·u·a·tion
    (ĕ·văl′ û·ā′ shŭn)
ev·a·nes·cent (ĕv′ ȧ·nĕs′ ĕnt)
-cence
e·van·gel·i·cal
    (ē′ văn·jĕl′ ĭ·kȧl)
e·van·ge·list (ĕ·văn′ jĕ·lĭst)
e·vap·o·rate (ĕ·văp′ ō·rāt)
-rat·ing
e·vap·o·ra·tion
    (ĕ·văp′ ō·rā′ shŭn)
e·va·sion (ĕ·vā′ zhŭn)
e·va·sive -sive·ly
e·ven (ē′ vĕn)
e·ven·ly e·ven·ness
eve·ning (ēv′ nĭng)
e·vent (ĕ·vĕnt′)
e·vent·ful, -ful·ly, -ful·ness
e·ven·tide (ē′ vĕn·tīd′)
e·ven·tu·al (ĕ·vĕn′ tû·ȧl)
e·ven·tu·al·i·ty
    (ĕ·vĕn′ tû·ăl′ ĭ·tĭ)
e·ven·tu·al·ly
ev·er (ĕv′ ēr)
the Ev·er·glades
ev·er·green ev·er·last·ing
ev·er·more
ev·er·y (ĕv′ ēr·ĭ)
ev·er·y·bod·y
ev·er·y·day adj.
ev·er·y·one pron.
ev·er·y·thing ev·er·y·where
e·vict (ĕ·vĭkt′)
e·vic·tion (ĕ·vĭk′ shŭn)
ev·i·dence (ĕv′ ĭ·dĕns)
ev·i·dent·ly
e·vil (ē′ v'l)
e·vil·do·er -do·ing
e·vil·ly e·vil-mind·ed
e·vince (ĕ·vĭns′)
-vinc·ing e·vin·ci·ble
e·vis·cer·ate (ĕ·vĭs′ ēr·āt)
-at·ing
e·vis·cer·a·tion
    (ĕ·vĭs′ ēr·ā′ shŭn)
e·voke (ĕ·vōk′)
-vok·ing
ev·o·ca·tion (ĕv′ ō·kā′ shŭn)
e·voc·a·tive (ĕ·vŏk′ ȧ·tĭv)

ev·o·lu·tion (ĕv′ ō·lū′ shŭn)
ev·o·lu·tion·ar·y
e·volve (ĕ·vŏlv′)
-volv·ing
ex·ac·er·bate (ĕg·zăs′ ēr·bāt)
-bat·ing
ex·ac·er·ba·tion
    (ĕg·zăs′ ēr·bā′ shŭn)
ex·act (ĕg·zăkt′)
ex·act·ing ex·ac·tion
ex·ag·ger·ate (ĕg·zăj′ ēr·āt)
-at·ing ex·ag·ger·a·tor
ex·ag·ger·a·tion
    (ĕg·zăj′ ēr·ā′ shŭn)
ex·alt (ĕg·zôlt′)
ex·al·ta·tion (ĕg′ zôl·tā′ shŭn)
ex·am·ine (ĕg·zăm′ ĭn)
-in·ing
ex·am·i·na·tion
    (ĕg·zăm′ ĭ·nā′ shŭn)
ex·am·ple (ĕg·zăm′ p'l)
ex·as·per·ate (ĕg·zăs′ pēr·āt)
-at·ing
ex·as·per·a·tion
    (ĕg·zăs′ pēr·ā′ shŭn)
Ex·cal·i·bur (ĕks·kăl′ ĭ·bēr)
ex·ca·vate (ĕks′ kȧ·vāt)
-vat·ing
ex·ca·va·tion
    (ĕks′ kȧ·vā′ shŭn)
ex·ca·va·tor
ex·ceed (ĕk·sēd′)
(to surpass; see accede)
ex·ceed·ing·ly
ex·cel (ĕk·sĕl′)
-celled -cel·ling
ex·cel·lent (ĕk′ sĕ·lĕnt)
-cel·lence
ex·cel·si·or (ĕk·sĕl′ sĭ·ôr)
ex·cept (ĕk·sĕpt′)
ex·cep·tion
ex·cep·tion·a·ble
ex·cep·tion·al, -al·ly
ex·cerpt (ĕk·sûrpt′) v.
(ĕk′ sûrpt) n.
ex·cess (ĕk·sĕs′)
ex·ces·sive
ex·change (ĕks·chānj′)
ex·change·a·ble
ex·cheq·uer (ĕks·chĕk′ ēr)
ex·cise (ĕk′ sīz) n.
-cis·ing (ĕk·sīz′) v.
ex·ci·sion (ĕk·sĭzh′ ŭn)
ex·cite (ĕk·sīt′)
-cit·ing

ex·cit·a·bil·i·ty
    (ĕk·sīt′ á·bĭl′ ĭ·tĭ)
ex·cit·a·ble
ex·ci·ta·tion   (ĕk′ sĭ·tā′ shŭn)
ex·cit·ed·ly   ex·cite′ ment
ex·claim   (ĕks·klām′)
ex·cla·ma·tion
    (ĕks′ klá·mā′ shŭn)
ex·clam·a·tor·y
    (ĕks·klăm′ á·tō′ rĭ)
ex·clude   (ĕks·kloōd′)
-clud·ing   ex·clu·sion
ex·clu·sive   -sive·ly
ex·com·mu·ni·cate
    (ĕks′ kŏ·mū′ nĭ·kåt)
-cat·ing
ex·co·ri·ate   (ĕks·kō′ rĭ·āt)
-at·ing
ex·ore·ment   (ĕks′ krĕ·mĕnt)
ex·cres·cence   (ĕks·krĕs′ ĕns)
ex·crete   (ĕks·krēt′)
-cret·ing   ex·cre·tion
ex·cre·to·ry   (ĕks′ krĕ·tō′ rĭ)
ex·cru·ci·at·ing
    (ĕks·kroō′ shĭ·āt′ ĭng)
ex·cru·ci·a·tion
    (ĕks·kroō′ shĭ·ā′ shŭn)
ex·cur·sion   (ĕks·kûr′ zhŭn)
ex·cuse   (ĕks·kūz′) v.
-cus·ing   (ĕks·kūs′) n.
ex·cus·a·ble   (ĕks·kūz′ á·b'l)
ex·e·cra·ble   (ĕk′ sĕ·krá·b'l)
ex·e·cute   (ĕk′ sĕ·kūt)
-cut·ing
ex·e·cu·tion   (ĕk′ sĕ·kū′ shŭn)
ex·ec·u·tive   (ĕg·zĕk′ û·tĭv)
ex·ec·u·tor   (ĕg·zĕk′ û·tĕr)
n. masc.
ex·ec·u·trix   (-trĭks) n. fem.
ex·e·ge·sis   (ĕk′ sĕ·jē′ sĭs)
pl. -ses   (sēz)
ex·em·pla·ry   (ĕg·zĕm′ plá·rĭ)
ex·em·pli·fy   (ĕg·zĕm′ plĭ·fī)
-fied   -fy·ing
ex·em·pli·fi·ca·tion
    (ĕg·zĕm′ plĭ·fĭ·kā′ shŭn)
ex·empt   (ĕg·zĕmpt′)
ex·empt·i·ble   ex·emp·tion
ex·er·cise   (ĕk′ sĕr·sĭz)
-cis·ing
ex·ert   (ĕg·zûrt′)
ex·er·tion
ex·hale   (ĕks·hāl′)
-hal·ing   ex·hal·ant
ex·ha·la·tion   (ĕks′ há·lā′ shŭn)

ex·haust   (ĕg·zôst′)
ex·haust·i·ble ex·haus·tion
ex·haus·tive
ex·hib·it   (ĕg·zĭb′ ĭt)
-it·ed   -it·ing
ex·hib·i·tor
ex·hi·bi·tion   (ĕk′ sĭ·bĭsh′ ŭn)
-tion·ist
ex·hil·a·rate   (ĕg·zĭl′ á·rāt)
-rat·ing
ex·hil·a·ra·tion
    (ĕg·zĭl′ á·rā′ shŭn)
ex·hort   (ĕg·zôrt′)
ex·hor·ta·tion (ĕg·zôr·tā′ shŭn)
ex·hume   (ĕks·hūm′)
-hum·ing
ex·i·gen·cy   (ĕk′ sĭ·jĕn·sĭ)
ex·ig·u·ous   (ĕg·zĭg′ û·ŭs)
ex·ile   (ĕk′ sīl)
ex·ist   (ĕg·zĭst′)
ex·ist·ence   -ent
ex·is·ten·tial·ism
    (ĕg′ zĭs·tĕn′ shăl·iz′m)
ex·it   (ĕg′ sĭt)
ex·o·dus   (ĕk′ sŏ·dŭs)
ex·on·er·ate   (ĕg·zŏn′ ĕr·āt)
-at·ing
ex·on·er·a·tion
    (ĕg·zŏn′ ĕr·ā′ shŭn)
ex·o·ra·ble   (ĕk′ sŏ·rá·b'l)
ex·or·bi·tant   (ĕg·zôr′ bĭ·tănt)
-tance
ex·or·cise   (ĕk′ sôr·sĭz)
(to expel)   -cis·ing
ex·ot·ic   (ĕks·ŏt′ ĭk)
ex·pand   (ĕks·pănd′)
ex·pand·a·ble
ex·panse   (ĕks·păns′)
ex·pan·sion ex·pan·sive
ex·pa·tri·ate   (ĕks·pā′ trĭ·åt)
ex·pect·ant   (ĕks·pĕk′ tănt)
ex·pect·an·cy
ex·pec·ta·tion
    (ĕks′ pĕk·tā′ shŭn)
ex·pec·to·rate (ĕks·pĕk′ tŏ·rāt)
-rat·ing   ex·pec·to·rant
ex·pec·to·ra·tion
    (ĕks·pĕk′ tŏ·rā′ shŭn)
ex·pe·di·ent   (ĕks·pē′ dĭ·ĕnt)
ex·pe·di·en·cy
ex·pe·dite   (ĕks′ pĕ·dīt)
-dit·ing   ex·pe·dit·er
ex·pe·di·tion   (ĕks′ pĕ·dĭsh′ ŭn)
ex·pe·di·tion·ar·y
ex·pe·di·tious   (ĕks′ pĕ·dĭsh′ ŭs)

ex·pel (ĕks·pĕl′)
-pelled -pel·ling
ex·pend·a·ble (ĕks·pĕn′ dȧ·b'l)
ex·pend·i·ture (ĕks·pĕn′ dĭ·tûr)
ex·pense (ĕks·pĕns′)
ex·pen·sive -sive·ly
ex·pe·ri·ence (ĕks·pēr′ ĭ·ĕns)
ex·per·i·ment (ĕks·pĕr′ ĭ·mĕnt)
ex·per·i·men·tal
(ĕks·pĕr′ ĭ·mĕn′ tȧl)
ex·per·i·men·ta·tion
(ĕks·pĕr′ ĭ·mĕn·tā′ shŭn)
ex·pert (ĕks·pûrt′) adj.
(ĕks′ pûrt) n.
ex·pi·ate (ĕks′ pĭ·āt)
-at·ing
ex·pi·a·tion (ĕks′ pĭ·ā′ shŭn)
ex·pi·ra·tion (ĕk′ spĭ·rā′ shŭn)
ex·plain (ĕks·plān′)
ex·plain·a·ble
ex·pla·na·tion
(ĕks′ plȧ·nā′ shŭn)
ex·plan·a·to·ry
(ĕks·plăn′ ȧ·tō′ rĭ)
ex·ple·tive (ĕks·plĕ′ tĭv)
ex·pli·ca·to·ry (ĕks′ plĭ·kȧ·tō′ rĭ)
ex·plic·it (ĕks·plĭs′ ĭt)
ex·ploit (ĕks′ ploit) n.
(ĕks′ ploit′) v.
ex·ploi·ta·tion
(ĕks′ ploi·tā′ shŭn)
ex·plore (ĕks·plōr′)
-plor·ing
ex·plo·ra·tion
(ĕks′ plŏ·rā′ shŭn)
ex·plor·a·to·ry
(ĕks·plōr′ ȧ·tō′ rĭ)
ex·plor·er
ex·plo·sion (ĕks·plō′ zhŭn)
ex·plo·sive
ex·po·nent (ĕks·pō′ nĕnt)
ex·port (ĕks·pōrt′) v.
(ĕks′ pōrt) n.
ex·por·ta·tion
(ĕks′ pŏr·tā′ shŭn)
ex·pose (ĕks′ pōz′) v.
-pos·ing
ex·po·sé (ĕks′ pŏ·zā′) n.
ex·po·si·tion (ĕks′ pŏ·zĭsh′ ŭn)
ex post fac·to (ĕks pōst făk′ tō)
ex·pos·tu·late (ĕks·pŏs′ tū·lāt)
-lat·ing
ex·pos·tu·la·tion
(ĕks′ pŏs′ tū·lā′ shŭn)
ex·po·sure (ĕks·pō′ zhēr)

ex·pound (ĕks·pound′)
ex·press (ĕks·prĕs′)
ex·press·i·ble ex·pres·sion
ex·pres·sive
ex·press·way
ex·pro·pri·ate (ĕks·prō′ prĭ·āt)
-at·ing
ex·pro·pri·a·tion
(ĕks·prō′ prĭ·ā′ shŭn)
ex·pul·sion (ĕks·pŭl′ shŭn)
ex·punge (ĕks·pŭnj′)
-pung·ing
ex·pur·gate (ĕks′ pĕr·gāt)
-gat·ing
ex·pur·ga·tion
(ĕks′ pĕr·gā′ shŭn)
ex·qui·site (ĕks′ kwĭ·zĭt)
ex·qui·site·ly
ex·tant (ĕks′ tănt)
(in existence; see extent)
ex·tem·po·ra·ne·ous
(ĕks·tĕm′ pŏ·rā′ nĕ·ŭs)
ex·tem·po·rize (ĕks·tĕm′ pŏ·rīz)
-riz·ing
ex·ten·sion (ĕks·tĕn′ shŭn)
ex·ten·sive (ĕks·tĕn′ sĭv)
-sive·ly
ex·tent (ĕks·tĕnt′)
(degree; see extant)
ex·ten·u·ate (ĕks·tĕn′ ū·āt)
-at·ing
ex·te·ri·or (ĕks·tēr′ ĭ·ēr)
ex·ter·mi·nate (ĕks·tûr′ mĭ·nāt)
-nat·ing -na·tor
ex·ter·mi·na·tion
(ĕks·tûr′ mĭ·nā′ shŭn)
ex·ter·nal (ĕks·tûr′ nȧl)
ex·ter·nal·ly
ex·tinct (ĕks·tĭngkt′)
ex·tinc·tion
ex·tin·guish (ĕks·tĭng′ gwĭsh)
ex·tin·guish·a·ble
ex·tin·guish·er
ex·tir·pate (ĕk′ stēr·pāt)
-pat·ing
ex·tol (ĕks·tŏl′)
-tolled -tol·ling
ex·tort (ĕks·tôrt′)
ex·tor·tion -tion·ist
ex·tract (ĕks′ trăkt) n.
ex·tract (ĕks·trăkt′) v.
ex·trac·tion ex·trac·tive
ex·trac·tor
ex·tra·cur·ric·u·lar
(ĕks′ trȧ·kŭ·rĭk′ ū·lēr)

ex·tra·dite (ĕks′ trȧ·dĭt)
  -dit·ing
  ex·tra·di·tion
    (ĕks′ trȧ·dĭsh′ ŭn)
ex·tra·mar·i·tal
    (ĕks′ trȧ·măr′ ĭ·tȧl)
ex·tra·ne·ous (ĕks·trā′ nĕ·ŭs)
ex·traor·di·nar·y
    (ĕks·trôr′ dĭ·nĕr′ ĭ)
  ex·traor·di·nar·i·ly
    (ĕks·trôr′ dĭ·nĕr′ ĭ·lĭ)
ex·trap·o·late (ĕks·trăp′ ō·lāt)
  -lat·ing
ex·tra·sen·so·ry perception
    (ĕks′ trȧ·sĕn′ sō·rĭ)
ex·tra·ter·ri·to·ri·al
    (ĕks′ trȧ·tĕr′ ĭ·tō′ rĭ·ȧl)
ex·trav·a·gance
    (ĕks·trăv′ ȧ·gȧns)
ex·treme (ĕks·trēm′)
  ex·treme·ly ex·trem·ism
  ex·trem·ist
  ex·trem·i·ty (ĕks·trĕm′ ĭ·tĭ)
ex·tri·cate (ĕks′ trĭ·kāt)
  -cat·ing
  ex·tri·ca·ble (ĕks′ trĭ·kȧ·b'l)
ex·trin·sic (ĕks·trĭn′ sĭk)
ex·tro·vert (ĕks′ trō·vûrt)
  ex·tro·ver·sion
    (ĕks′ trō·vûr′ shŭn)
ex·tru·sion (ĕks·trōō′ zhŭn)
ex·u·ber·ant (ĕg·zū′ bĕr·ȧnt)
  -ance
ex·ude (ĕks·ūd′)
  -ud·ing
ex·ult (ĕg·zŭlt′)
  ex·ult·an·cy ex·ult·ant
  ex·ul·ta·tion (ĕk′ sŭl·tā′ shŭn)
eye (ī)
  eye·brow eye·cup
  eye·let eye·lid
  eye·shot eye·strain
  eye·tooth eye·wit·ness

F

fa·ble (fā′ b'l)
fab·ric (făb′ rĭk)
fab·ri·cate (făb′ rĭ·kāt)
  -cat·ing
  fab·ri·ca·tion (făb′ rĭ·kā′shŭn)
  fab·ri·ca·tor
fab·u·lous (făb′ û·lŭs)
fa·çade (fȧ·säd′)

face (fās)
  fac·ing face card
  face val·ue fa·cial
fac·et (făs′ ĕt)
  -et·ed
fa·ce·tious (fȧ·sē′ shŭs)
  (joking; see *factious*)
fa·cial (fā′ shȧl)
fac·ile (făs′ ĭl)
fa·cil·i·tate (fȧ·sĭl′ ĭ·tāt)
  (help; see *felicitate*)
  -tat·ing
fa·cil·i·ty (fȧ·sĭl′ ĭ·tĭ)
  -ties
fac·sim·i·le (făk·sĭm′ ĭ·lē)
fac·tion (făk′ shŭn)
  fac·tion·al
fac·tious (făk′ shŭs)
  (dissenting; see *facetious*)
fac·tor (făk′ tēr)
fac·to·ry (făk′ tō·rĭ)
  -ries
fac·to·tum (făk·tō′ tŭm)
fac·tu·al (făk′ tû·ȧl)
  -al·ly
fac·ul·ty (făk′ ŭl·tĭ)
  -ties
fad·dist (făd′ ĭst)
fag·ot (făg′ ŭt)
  fag·ot·ing
Fahr·en·heit (făr′ ĕn·hīt)
fail·ure (fāl′ ûr)
faint (fānt)
  (lose consciousness; see *feint*)
  faint·heart·ed
fair (fâr)
  fair and square
  fair-mind·ed fair-sized
  fair-trade a·gree·ment
  fair·way
fair·y (fâr′ ĭ)
  fair·ies fair·y·land
  fair·y tale
fait ac·com·pli (fĕ′ tȧ′ kôn′ plē′)
faith (fāth)
  faith·ful, -ful·ly, -ful·ness
  faith·less
fak·er (fāk′ ēr)
  (fraud)
fa·kir (fȧ·kēr′)
  (yogi)
fal·con (fôl′ kŭn)
fal·la·cy (făl′ ȧ·sĭ)
  -cies
  fal·la·cious (fȧ·lā′ shŭs)

fall·en (fôl′ ĕn)
fal·li·ble (făl′ ĭ·b'l)
  fal·li·bil·i·ty (făl′ ĭ·bĭl′ ĭ·tĭ)
Fal·lo·pi·an tube
           (fă·lō′ pĭ·ăn)
fall-out (fôl′ out′)
fal·low (făl′ ō)
false (fôls)
  false·heart·ed   false·hood
  false·ly
fal·set·to (fôl·sĕt′ ō)
fal·si·fy (fôl′ sĭ·fī)
  -fied   -fy·ing
fal·si·ty (fôl′ sĭ·tĭ)
  -ties
Fal·staff·i·an (fôl·stăf′ ĭ·ăn)
fal·ter·ing (fôl′ tēr·ĭng)
fa·mil·iar (fà·mĭl′ yēr)
  fa·mil·i·ar·i·ty
           (fà·mĭl′ ĭ·ăr′ ĭ·tĭ)
  fa·mil·iar·ize, -iz·ing
fam·i·ly (făm′ ĭ·lĭ)
  -lies
  fa·mil·ial (fà·mĭl′ yăl)
  fam·i·ly cir·cle
  fam·i·ly name
fam·ine (făm′ ĭn)
fam·ish (făm′ ĭsh)
fa·mous (fā′ mŭs)
fa·nat·ic (fà·năt′ ĭk)
  fa·nat·i·cal   -cal·ly
  fa·nat·i·cism
fan·cy (făn′ sĭ)
  -cied   -cy·ing
  fan·cier
  fan·ci·ful, -ful·ly, -ful·ness
  fan·cy dress   fan·cy-free
  fan·cy·work
fan·dan·go (făn·dăng′ gō)
fan·fare (făn′ fâr)
fan·tas·tic (făn·tăs′ tĭk)
  -ti·cal·ly
fan·ta·sy (făn′ tà·sĭ)
  -sies
far (fär)
  far·a·way   Far East
  far·fetched   far-flung
  far-off *adj.*   far-reach·ing
  far·see·ing   far·sight·ed
farce (färs)
  far·ci·cal (fär′ sĭ·kăl)
fare·well (fâr′ wĕl′)
fa·ri·na (fà·rē′ nà)
farm (färm)
  farm hand   farm·house

farm·yard
far·ther (fär′ thēr)
  (refers only to spatial distance;
  see *further*)   far·thest
fas·ci·nate (făs′ ĭ·nāt)
  -nat·ing
  fas·ci·na·tion (făs′ ĭ·nā′ shŭn)
fas·cism (făsh′ ĭz'm)
  fas·cist
fash·ion (făsh′ ŭn)
  fash·ion·a·ble   fash·ion plate
fas·ten·ing (făs′ 'n·ĭng)
fas·tid·i·ous (făs·tĭd′ ĭ·ŭs)
fa·tal (fā′ tăl)
  fa·tal·i·ty (fà·tăl′ ĭ·tĭ)
  -ties   fa·tal·is·tic
  fa·tal·ly
fate (fāt)
  fate·ful   -ful·ly
fa·ther (fä′ thēr)
  fa·ther-in-law   fa·thers-in-law
  fa·ther·land   fa·ther·less
  Fa·ther's Day
fath·om (făth′ ŭm)
  fath·om·a·ble   fath·om·less
fa·tigue (fà·tēg′)
  -tigued   -ti·guing
  fa·ti·ga·ble
fat·ten (făt′ 'n)
fat·u·ous (făt′ û·ŭs)
  fa·tu·i·ty (fà·tū′ ĭ·tĭ)
fau·cet (fô′ sĕt)
fault (fôlt)
  fault·find·ing   fault·y
faun (fôn)
  (wood sprite; see *fawn*)
faux pas (fō′ pä′)
fa·vor (fā′ vēr)
  fa·vor·a·ble
fa·vor·ite (fā′ vēr·ĭt)
  fa·vor·it·ism
fawn (fôn)
  (young deer; see *faun*)
faze (fāz)
  (disconcert; see *phase*)
  faz·ing
fear (fẽr)
  fear·ful, -ful·ly, -ful·ness
  fear·some
fea·si·ble (fē′ zĭ·b'l)
  fea·si·bil·i·ty (fē′ zĭ·bĭl′ ĭ·tĭ)
feat (fēt)
  (deed; see *fete*)
feath·er (fĕth′ ēr)
  feath·er·bed   -bed·ding

feath·er·weight
fea·ture (fē' tūr)
  -tur·ing   fea·ture·less
Feb·ru·ar·y (fĕb' rōō·ĕr'ĭ)
feck·less (fĕk' lĕs)
fe·cund (fē' kŭnd)
  fe·cun·di·ty (fē·kŭn' dĭ·tĭ)
fed·er·al (fĕd' ĕr·ăl)
  fed·er·al·ist   fed·er·al·ly
fed·er·ate (fĕd' ĕr·āt)
  -at·ing
  fed·er·a·tion (fĕd' ĕr·ā' shŭn)
fee·ble (fē' b'l)
  fee·ble-mind·ed
  fee·ble·ness
  fee·bler, -blest, -bly
feed·back (fĕd' băk')
feign (fān)
feint (fānt)
  (trick; see *faint*)
fe·lic·i·tate (fē·lĭs' ĭ·tāt)
  (make happy; see *facilitate*)
  -tat·ing
  fe·lic·i·ta·tion
              (fē·lĭs' ĭ·tā' shŭn)
fe·lic·i·ty (fē·lĭs' ĭ·tĭ)
  -ties   fe·lic·i·tous
fe·line (fē' līn)
fel·low (fĕl' ō)
  fel·low·ship
  fel·low trav·el·er
fel·on (fĕl' ŭn)
  fe·lo·ni·ous (fē·lō' nĭ·ŭs)
  fel·o·ny   -nies
fe·male (fē' māl)
fem·i·nine (fĕm' ĭ·nĭn)
  fem·i·nin·i·ty (fĕm' ĭ·nĭn' ĭ·tĭ)
fence (fĕns)
  fenc·ing   fence·less
fend·er (fĕn' dĕr)
fen·nel (fĕn' ĕl)
fe·ral (fēr' ăl)
fer-de-lance (fâr' dĕ·läns')
fer·ment (fûr' mĕnt) n.
fer·ment (fĕr·mĕnt') v.
  fer·men·ta·tion
              (fûr' mĕn·tā' shŭn)
fe·ro·cious (fē·rō' shŭs)
  fe·roc·i·ty (fē·rŏs' ĭ·tĭ)
fer·ret (fĕr' ĕt)
Fer·ris wheel (fĕr' ĭs)
fer·rous (fĕr' ŭs)
fer·ry (fĕr' ĭ)
  fer·ried   fer·ry·ing
  fer·ry·boat

fer·tile (fûr' tĭl)
  fer·tile·ly
  fer·til·i·ty (fĕr·tĭl' ĭ·tĭ)
fer·ti·lize (fûr' tĭ·līz)
  -liz·ing
  fer·ti·li·za·tion
         (fûr' tĭ·lĭ·zā' shŭn)
  fer·ti·liz·er
fer·vent (fûr' vĕnt)
  -ven·cy
fer·vid (fûr' vĭd)
fer·vor (fûr' vēr)
fes·ti·val (fĕs' tĭ·văl)
fes·tive (fĕs' tĭv)
  fes·tiv·i·ty (fĕs·tĭv' ĭ·tĭ)
  -ties
fes·toon (fĕs·tōōn')
fetch (fĕch)
fete (fāt)
  (festival; see *feat*)
fet·id (fĕt' ĭd)
fe·tish (fē' tĭsh)
fet·ter (fĕt' ēr)
fe·tus (fē' tŭs)
  -tus·es
feud (fūd)
feu·dal (fū' dăl)
fe·ver (fē' vēr)
  fe·ver·ish   fe·ver·rid·den
fi·an·cé (fē' än·sā')
  n. masc.
  fi·an·cée (fē' än·sā') n. fem.
fi·as·co (fē·ăs' kō)
fi·at (fī' ăt)
fi·ber (fī' bēr)
  fi·ber·board   Fi·ber·glas
  fi·brous
fick·le (fĭk' 'l)
  fick·le·ness
fic·tion (fĭk' shŭn)
  fic·tion·al   -al·ly
fic·ti·tious (fĭk·tĭsh' ŭs)
fid·dle (fĭd' 'l)
  fid·dling   fid·dle-fad·dle
  fid·dle·sticks
fi·del·i·ty (fĭ·dĕl' ĭ·tĭ)
fidg·et (fĭj' ĕt)
  -et·ed   -et·ing
fi·du·ci·ar·y (fĭ·dū' shĭ·ĕr' ĭ)
field (fēld)
fiend (fēnd)
  fiend·ish
fierce (fērs)
fi·er·y (fī' rĭ)
  fi·er·i·er, -i·est, -i·ness

fi·es·ta (fĭ·ĕs′ tȧ)
fif·teen (fĭf′ tēn′)
  fif·teenth
fifth (fĭfth)
  fifth col·um·nist
fif·ty (fĭf′ tĭ)
  -ties fif·ti·eth
  fif·ty·fold
fight·er (fīt′ ẽr)
fig·ment (fĭg′ mĕnt)
fig·ure (fĭg′ ûr)
  -ur·ing
  fig·u·ra·tion (fĭg′ û·rā′ shŭn)
  fig·ur·a·tive (fĭg′ ûr·ȧ·tĭv)
  fig·ure·head
  fig·u·rine (fĭg′ û·rēn′)
fil·a·ment (fĭl′ ȧ·mĕnt)
fil·bert (fĭl′ bẽrt)
fil·i·al (fĭl′ ĭ·ăl)
fil·i·bus·ter (fĭl′ ĭ·bŭs′ tẽr)
fil·i·gree (fĭl′ ĭ·grē)
Fil·i·pi·no (fĭl′ ĭ·pē′ nō)
  -nos
  But: Phil·ip·pine Is·lands
fil·let (fĭl′ ĕt)
fil·ly (fĭl′ ĭ)
  fil·lies
film (fĭlm)
  film·i·er, -i·est, -i·ness
  film·strip film·y
fil·ter (fĭl′ tẽr)
  (porous article; see *philter*)
  fil·ter·a·bil·i·ty
    (fĭl′ tẽr·ȧ·bĭl′ ĭ·tĭ)
  fil·ter·a·ble
  fil·tra·tion (fĭl·trā′ shŭn)
filth·y (fĭl′ thĭ)
  filth·i·er, -i·est, -i·ly, -i·ness
fi·na·gler (fĭ·nā′ glẽr)
fi·nal (fī′ năl)
  fi·nal·i·ty (fī·năl′ ĭ·tĭ)
  fi·nal·ly
fi·na·le (fê·nä′ lȧ)
fi·nance (fĭ·năns′)
  -nanc·ing
  fi·nan·cial (fĭ·năn′ shăl)
  fin·an·cier (fĭn′ ăn·sẽr′)
fine (fīn)
  fine arts fin·er·y
  fine·spun fine-tooth comb
fi·nesse (fĭ·nĕs′)
fin·ger (fĭng′ gẽr)
  fin·ger bowl fin·ger·nail
  fin·ger·print
fin·ick·y (fĭn′ ĭ·kĭ)

fi·nis (fī′ nĭs)
fin·ish (fĭn′ ĭsh)
fi·nite (fī′ nīt)
Fin·land (fĭn′ lănd)
  Finn Finn·ish
fiord (fyôrd)
fire (fīr)
  fir·ing fire·arm
  fire·bug fire·brand
  fire·crack·er fire-eat·er
  fire en·gine fire es·cape
  fire ex·tin·guish·er
  fire·man fire·place
  fire·plug fire·pow·er
  fire·proof fire·side
  fire·trap fire·ward·en
  fire·wood fire·works
fir·ma·ment (fûr′ mȧ·mĕnt)
first (fûrst)
  first aid first base
  first-born first class *n.*
  first-class *adj.* first·hand
  first-rate
fis·cal (fĭs′ kăl)
fish (fĭsh)
  fish·er·man fish·er·y, -er·ies
  fish·hook fish meal
  fish mon·ger
fis·sion (fĭsh′ ŭn)
  fis·sion·a·ble fis·sion bomb
fis·sure (fĭsh′ ẽr)
fist·ic (fĭs′ tĭk)
  fist·i·cuffs
fit·ful (fĭt′ fŏŏl)
  -ful·ly -ful·ness
five·fold (fīv′ fōld′)
fix·a·tion (fĭks·ā′ shŭn)
fix·ture (fĭks′ tûr)
fiz·zle (fĭz′ ′l)
  fiz·zling
flab·ber·gast (flăb′ ẽr·găst)
flab·by (flăb′ ĭ)
  flab·bi·ness
flac·cid (flăk′ sĭd)
flag (flăg)
  flagged flag·ging
  flag·pole flag·ship
  flag stop
flag·el·late (flăj′ ĕ·lāt)
  -el·lat·ing flag·el·lant
flag·on (flăg′ ŭn)
fla·grant (flā′ grănt)
  -gran·cy
flair (flâr)
  (aptitude; see *flare*)

flake (flāk)
  flak·y   flak·i·er
  -i·est, -i·ly, -i·ness
flam·boy·ant (flăm·boi′ ănt)
  -an·cy
flame (flām)
  flam·ing   flame·proof
  flame throw·er
fla·min·go (flȧ·mǐng′ gō)
  -gos
flam·ma·ble (flăm′ ȧ·b′l)
  flam·ma·bil·ity
          (flăm′ ȧ·bǐl′ ǐ·tǐ)
flap·per (flăp′ ĕr)
flare (flâr)
  (blaze; see *flair*)
  flare-up   flar·ing
flash (flăsh)
  flash·back   flash flood
  flash·light   flash·y,
  flash·i·er, -i·est, -i·ly, -i·ness
flat (flăt)
  flat·boat   flat·car
  flat-foot·ed
  Flat·head In·di·an
  flat·i·ron   flat·tened
  flat·top   flat·ware
flat·ter·y (flăt′ ĕr·ǐ)
  flat·ter·ies   flat·ter·er
flaunt (flônt)
fla·vor (flā′ vĕr)
  fla·vor·ful
flax·en (flăk′ s′n)
flea (flē)
  (insect)
  flea·bite
  flea-bit·ten
fledg·ling (flĕj′ lǐng)
flee (flē)
  (escape)
fleece (flēs)
fleet (flēt)
Flem·ish (flĕm′ ǐsh)
flesh·y (flĕsh′ ǐ)
  flesh·i·ness
fleur-de-lis (flûr′ dē·lē′)
flex·i·ble (flĕk′ sǐ·b′l)
  flex·i·bil·i·ty (flĕk′ sǐ·bǐl′ ǐ·tǐ)
flib·ber·ti·gib·bet
      (flǐb′ ĕr·tǐ·jǐb′ ĕt)
flick·er (flǐk′ ĕr)
fli·er (flī′ ĕr)
flight (flīt)
  flight·y   flight·i·er
  -i·est, -i·ly, -i·ness

flim·sy (flǐm′ zǐ)
  flim·si·er, -si·est, -si·ly, -si·ness
flint·lock (flǐnt′ lŏk′)
flip·pant (flǐp′ ănt)
  flip·pan·cy
flir·ta·tion (flûr·tā′ shŭn)
  flir·ta·tious (flûr·tā′ shŭs)
float (flōt)
  flo·ta·tion (flō·tā′ shŭn)
floc·cu·late (flŏk′ û·lāt)
  -lat·ing
  floc·cu·la·tion (flŏk′ û·lā′ shŭn)
flog·ging (flŏg′ ǐng)
flood (flŭd)
  flood·gate   flood·light
  flood tide
floor (flōr)
  floor lead·er   floor show
  floor·walk·er
flop·house (flŏp′ hous′)
flop·py (flŏp′ ǐ)
flo·ral (flō′ rȧl)
flo·ri·cul·ture (flō′ rǐ·kŭl′ tụr)
flor·id (flŏr′ ǐd)
Flor·i·da (flŏr′ ǐ·dȧ)
  abbr. Fla.
  Flo·rid·i·an (flō·rǐd′ ǐ·ăn)
flo·rist (flō′ rǐst)
flo·ta·tion (flō·tā′ shŭn)
flo·til·la (flō·tǐl′ ȧ)
flot·sam (flŏt′ săm)
flounce (flouns)
  flounc·ing
floun·der (floun′ dĕr)
flour·ish (flûr′ ǐsh)
flow·age (flō′ ǐj)
flow·er (flou′ ĕr)
  flow·er·i·ness   flow·er·pot
  flow·er·y
flown (flōn)
flu (flo̅o̅)
  (influenza)
fluc·tu·ate (flŭk′ tụ·āt)
  -at·ing
  fluc·tu·a·tion (flŭk′tụ·ā′ shŭn)
flue (flo̅o̅)
  (chimney)
flu·ent (flo̅o̅′ ĕnt)
  -en·cy
flu·id (flo̅o̅′ ǐd)
  flu·id·i·ty (flo̅o̅·ǐd′ ǐ·tǐ)
fluke (flo̅o̅k)
flum·mox (flŭm′ ŭks)
flunk·y (flŭngk′ ǐ)
  flunk·ies

flu·o·res·cent (flōō′ ô·rĕs′ ĕnt)
  -cence
flu·o·ri·date (flōō′ ô·rĭ·dāt)
  -dat·ing
  flu·o·ri·da·tion
      (flōō′ ô·rĭ·dā′ shŭn)
flu·o·ri·nate (flōō′ ô·rĭ·nāt)
  -nat·ing
  flu·o·ri·na·tion
      (flōō′ ô·rĭ·nā′ shŭn)
flu·o·ro·scope (flōō′ ô·rŏ·skōp)
flur·ry (flûr′ ĭ)
  flur·ries
flute (flōōt)
  flut·ist
flut·ter (flŭt′ ĕr)
flux (flŭks)
fly (flī)
  flew   fly·ing
  flies   fly-by-night
  fly·ing fish fly·ing sau·cer
  fly·leaf   fly·pa·per
  fly·speck   fly·wheel
fo·cal (fō′ kăl)
fo·cus (fō′ kŭs)
  -cused   -cus·ing
fod·der (fŏd′ ĕr)
fog·gy (fŏg′ ĭ)
  fog·gi·ness
fo·gy (fō′ gĭ)
  ("old fogy") -gies
foi·ble (foi′ b'l)
foist (foist)
fo·li·age (fō′ lĭ·ĭj)
fo·li·o (fō′ lĭ·ō)
folk (fōk)
  folk dance folk·lore
  folk mu·sic folk tale
  folk·way
fol·li·cle (fŏl′ ĭ·k'l)
fol·low (fŏl′ ō)
  fol·low-through
  fol·low-up
fol·ly (fŏl′ ĭ)
  fol·lies
fo·ment (fô·mĕnt′)
  fo·men·ta·tion
      (fō′ mĕn·tā′ shŭn)
fon·dant (fŏn′ dănt)
fon·dle (fŏn′ d'l)
  -dling
fon·due (fŏn·dōō′)
fool (fōōl)
  fool·er·y   -er·ies
  fool·har·dy -di·ness

fool·proof   fool's gold
fool's par·a·dise
foot (fŏŏt)
  foot·age   (fŏŏt′ ĭj)
  foot·ball   foot brake
  foot·bridge foot-can·dle
  foot·fall   foot·hill
  foot·hold   foot·lights
  foot·loose   foot·man
  foot·note   foot·print
  foot·rest   foot sol·dier
  foot·step   foot·stool
  foot·work
fop·per·y (fŏp′ ĕr·ĭ)
for·age (fŏr′ ĭj)
  -ag·ing
for·ay (fŏr′ ā)
  -ay·ing
for·bear (fôr·bâr′)
  for·bear·ance for·borne
for·bid (fôr·bĭd′)
  -bid·ding
for·bade (fôr·băd′)
  for·bid·den for·bid·ding·ly
force (fôrs)
  forc·ing   force·ful
  -ful·ly   -ful·ness
  for·ci·ble
for·ceps (fôr′ sĕps)
Ford·ham (univ.) (fôr′ dăm)
fore- (fōr-)
  fore·arm
  fore·bode   -bod·ing
  fore·cast   fore·close
  fore·clo·sure fore·fa·thers
  fore·fin·ger fore·go
  fore·gone con·clu·sion
  fore·hand   fore·man
  fore·most   fore·noon
  fore·or·dain fore·quar·ter
  fore·run·ner fore·see·a·ble
  fore·shad·ow fore·stall
  fore·tell
for·eign (fŏr′ ĭn)
fo·ren·sic (fô·rĕn′ sĭk)
for·est (fŏr′ ĕst)
  for·est·a·tion (fŏr′ ĕs·tā′ shŭn)
for·ev·er (fôr·ĕv′ ĕr)
for·feit (fôr′ fĭt)
  -feit·ed   -feit·ing
  for·feit·a·ble for·fei·ture
forge (fôrj)
  forg·ing
for·ger·y (fôr′ jĕr·ĭ)
  -ger·ies

for·get (fôr·gĕt′)
  -get·ting for·get·ful
  -ful·ly -ful·ness
  for·get-me-not for·get·ta·ble
for·give (fôr·gĭv′)
  -giv·ing for·giv·a·ble
  for·give·ness
for·go (fôr·gō′)
for·got (fôr·gŏt′)
  for·got·ten
for·lorn (fôr·lôrn′)
  for·lorn·ly for·lorn·ness
for·mal (fôr′mal)
  for·mal·ism for·mal·ly
  for·mal·i·ty (fôr·măl′ĭ·tĭ)
form·al·de·hyde
        (fôr·măl′dê·hĭd)
for·mal·ize fôr′mal·ĭz)
  -iz·ing
  for·mal·i·za·tion
      (fôr′măl·ĭ·zā′shŭn)
for·mat (fôr′măt)
for·ma·tion (fôr·mā′shŭn)
form·a·tive (fôr′ma·tĭv)
for·mi·da·ble (fôr′mĭ·da·b′l)
For·mo·sa (fôr·mō′sa)
  (also: Taiwan)
for·mu·la (fôr′mŭ·la)
  pl. -las or -lae (-lē)
for·mu·late (fôr′mŭ·lāt)
  -lat·ing
  for·mu·la·tion
      (fôr′mŭ·lā′shŭn)
  for·mu·la·tor
for·sake (fôr·sāk′)
  -sak·ing for·sak·en
for·syth·i·a (fôr·sĭth′ĭ·a)
forth (fôrth)
  forth·com·ing forth·right
  forth·with
for·ti·eth (fôr′tĭ·ĕth)
for·ti·fy (fôr′tĭ·fĭ)
  -fied -fy·ing
  for·ti·fi·ca·tion
      (fôr′tĭ·fĭ·kā′shŭn)
for·tis·si·mo (fôr·tĭs′ĭ·mō)
for·ti·tude (fôr′tĭ·tūd)
Fort Lau·der·dale,
  Fla. (fôrt lô′dĕr·dāl)
fort·night (fôrt′nĭt)
for·tress (fôr′trĕs)
for·tu·i·tous (fôr·tū′ĭ·tŭs)
  for·tu·i·ty
for·tu·nate (fôr′tû·nĭt)
  -nate·ly

for·tune (fôr′tûn)
  for·tune hunt·er
  for·tune·tell·er
for·ty (fôr′tĭ)
  -ties for·ti·eth
  for·ty·fold for·ty·nin·er
fo·rum (fō′rŭm)
for·ward (fôr′wĕrd)
fos·sil (fŏs′ĭl)
  fos·sil·ized (fŏs′ĭ·lĭzd)
fought (fôt)
foul (foul)
  (dirty; see fowl)
  foul-mouthed foul play
found (found)
foun·da·tion (foun·dā′shŭn)
found·ry (foun′drĭ)
  -ries
foun·tain (foun′tĭn)
  foun·tain·head foun·tain pen
four (fōr)
  four-di·men·sion·al
  four·flush·er four-in-hand
  four-post·er four·score
  four·some four·square
  four-wheeled
four·teen (fôr′tēn′)
fowl (foul)
  (poultry; see foul)
fox (fŏks)
  fox·glove fox·hole
  fox·hound fox·tail
  fox ter·ri·er fox·trot
  fox·y
foy·er (foi′ĕr)
fra·cas (frā′kas)
frac·tion (frăk′shŭn)
  frac·tion·al -al·ly
frac·ture (frăk′tûr)
frag·ile (frăj′ĭl)
  -ile·ly
  fra·gil·i·ty (fra·jĭl′ĭ·tĭ)
frag·ment (frăg′mĕnt)
  frag·men·tar·y
  frag·men·ta·tion
      (frăg′mĕn·tā′shŭn)
fra·grant (frā′grant)
  -grance
frail (frāl)
  frail·ty -ties
frame-up (frām′ŭp′)
frame·work (frām′wûrk′)
fran·chise (frăn′chĭz)
  fran·chise·ment

Fran·co, Fran·cis·co
    (fräng' kŏ,
    frän·thēs' kŏ)
Fran·co·phile (frăng' kŏ·fĭl)
Frank·en·stein (frăngk' ĕn·stīn)
frank·furt·er (frăngk' fẽr·tẽr)
frank·in·cense (frăngk' ĭn·sĕns)
fran·tic (frăn' tĭk)
  fran·ti·cal·ly
frap·pé (frá' pā')
fra·ter·nal (frȧ·tûr' nȧl)
  -nal·ly fra·ter·nal·ism
fra·ter·ni·ty (frȧ·tûr' nĭ·tĭ)
  -ties
frat·er·nize (frăt' ẽr·nīz)
  -niz·ing
  frat·er·ni·za·tion
    (frăt' ẽr·nĭ·zā' shŭn)
fraud (frôd)
  fraud·u·lent -lence
fraught (frôt)
Fräu·lein (froi' līn)
freak·ish (frēk' ĭsh)
freck·le (frĕk' 'l)
  -ling
Fred·er·icks·burg ,Va.
    (frĕd' rĭks·bûrg)
free (frē)
  fre·er
  free on board (f.o.b.)
  free·born free-for-all
  free·hand *adj.*
  free-lance *adj. & v.*
  Free·ma·son free·think·er
  free·way
  free-will of·fer·ing
free·dom (frē' dŭm)
freez·er (frēz' ẽr)
freight (frāt)
  freight·age freight·er
fren·zy (frĕn' zĭ)
  -zied -zy·ing
fre·quent (frē' kwĕnt)
  -quen·cy
fres·co (frĕs' kŏ)
  -coes
fresh (frĕsh)
  fresh·en fresh-water *adj.*
  fresh·man
fret (frĕt)
  fret·ted fret·ting
  fret·ful, -ful·ly, -ful·ness
Freud·i·an (froid' ĭ·ăn)
fri·ar (frī' ẽr)
  (churchman; see *fryer*)

fric·as·see (frĭk' ȧ·sē')
fric·tion (frĭk' shŭn)
Fri·day (frī' dĭ)
fried (frīd)
friend·ly (frĕnd' lĭ)
  friend·li·er, -li·est, -li·ness
frieze (frēz)
  (ornamented band)
frig·ate (frĭg' ĭt)
fright (frīt)
  -ful·ly -ful·ness
  fright·en fright·ful
frig·id (frĭj' ĭd)
  fri·gid·i·ty (frĭ·jĭd' ĭ·tĭ)
fri·jole (frē' hōl)
fringe (frĭnj)
  fring·ing
frip·per·y (frĭp' ẽr·ĭ)
  frip·per·ies
frisk·y (frĭs' kĭ)
  frisk·i·er, -i·est, -i·ly, -i·ness
frit·ter (frĭt' ẽr)
friv·o·lous (frĭv' ŏ·lŭs)
  fri·vol·i·ty (frĭ·vŏl' ĭ·tĭ)
  -ties
frog·man (frŏg' măn)
frol·ic (frŏl' ĭk)
  frol·ick·er frol·ick·y
  frol·ic·some
front·age (frŭn' tĭj)
fron·tal (frŭn' tȧl)
  -tal·ly
fron·tiers·man (frŭn·tẽrz' măn)
fron·tis·piece (frŭn' tĭs·pēs)
frost·bite (frôst' bīt')
  frost·bit·ten (-bĭt' 'n)
froth·y (frôth' ĭ)
  froth·i·ness
frown (froun)
fro·zen (frō' z'n)
fru·gal (frōō' găl)
  fru·gal·i·ty (frōō·găl' ĭ·tĭ)
  fru·gal·ly
fruit (frōōt)
  -ful·ly -ful·ness
  fruit·cake fruit·ful
  fruit·less
fru·i·tion (frōō·ĭsh' ŭn)
frus·trate (frŭs' trȧt)
  -trat·ing
  frus·tra·tion (frŭs·trȧ' shŭn)
fry (frī)
  fried fry·ing
  fry·er (chicken; see *friar*)
fuch·sia (fū' shá)

fu·el (fū′ ĕl)
-eled -el·ing
fu·gi·tive (fū′ jĭ·tĭv)
fugue (fūg)
ful·crum (fŭl′ krŭm)
ful·fill (fŏŏl·fĭl′)
ful·fill·ment
full (fŏŏl)
full-back full-blood·ed
full-blown full-fledged
full-sized ful·ly
ful·some (fŏŏl′ sŭm)
fum·ble (fŭm′ b'l)
-bling
fu·mi·gate (fū′ mĭ·gāt)
-gat·ing
fu·mi·ga·tion (fū′ mĭ·gā′ shŭn)
fu·mi·ga·tor
func·tion (fŭngk′ shŭn)
func·tion·al -al·ly
func·tion·ar·y
fun·da·men·tal
(fŭn′ đá·men′ tăl)
·tal·ly
fu·ner·al (fū′ nēr·ăl)
fu·ne·re·al (fū·nē′ ē·ăl)
fun·gus (fŭng′ gŭs)
pl. fun·gi (fŭn′ jī)
fun·nel (fŭn′ ĕl)
fun·neled fun·nel·ing
fun·ny (fŭn′ ĭ)
fun·ni·est
fur (fûr)
fur·ry
fur·bish (fûr′ bĭsh)
fu·ri·ous (fū′ rĭ·ŭs)
furl (fûrl)
fur·long (fûr′ lŏng)
fur·lough (fûr′ lō)
fur·nace (fûr′ nĭs)
fur·nish·ings (fûr′ nĭsh·ĭngz)
fur·ni·ture (fûr′ nĭ·tûr)
fu·ror (fū′ rôr)
fur·ri·er (fûr′ ĭ·ēr)
fur·row (fûr′ ō)
fur·ther (fûr′ thēr)
(more distant in time, degree, or
quantity; see *farther*)
fur·ther·ance fur·ther·more
fur·ther·most fur·thest
fur·tive (fûr′ tĭv)
fu·ry (fū′ rĭ)
-ries
fuse (fūz)
fus·ing

fu·se·lage (fū′ zĕ·läzh′)
fu·sel oil (fū′ zĕl)
fu·si·ble (fū′ zĭ·b'l)
fu·sil·lade (fū′ zĭ·lād′)
fu·sion bomb (fū′ zhŭn)
fus·sy (fŭs′ ĭ)
fuss·i·ly -i·ness
fu·tile (fū′ tĭl)
fu·tile·ly
fu·til·i·ty (fû·tĭl′ ĭ·tĭ)
fu·ture (fū′ tûr)
fu·tu·ri·ty (fû·tū′ rĭ·tĭ)
fuz·zy (fŭz′ ĭ)

G

gab·ar·dine (găb′ ēr·dēn′)
gad·a·bout (găd′ á·bout′)
gad·fly (găd′ flī′)
-flies
gadg·et (găj′ ĕt)
Gael·ic (gāl′ ĭk)
(Irish; see *Gallic*)
gai·e·ty (gā′ ĕ·tĭ)
-ties
gai·ly (gā′ lĭ)
gain·ful (gān′ fŏŏl)
-ful·ly -ful·ness
gain·say (gān′ sā′)
gait (gāt)
(manner of walking; see *gate*)
gal·ax·y (găl′ ăk·sĭ)
-ax·ies
ga·lac·tic (gá·lăk′ tĭk)
Gal·i·lee (găl′ ĭ·lē)
Gal·i·le·an (găl′ ĭ·lē′ ăn)
gal·lant (găl′ ănt)
gal·lant·ry -ries
gal·le·on (găl′ ĕ·ŭn)
gal·ler·y (găl′ ēr·ĭ)
gal·ler·ies
gal·ley (găl′ ĭ)
Gal·lic (găl′ ĭk)
(French; see *Gaelic*)
gal·lon (găl′ ŭn)
abbr. gal.
gal·lop (găl′ ŭp)
gal·loped gal·lop·ing
gall·stone (gôl′ stōn′)
Gal·lup poll (găl′ ŭp)
ga·lore (gá·lōr′)
ga·losh (gá·lŏsh′)
(overshoe; see *goulash*)

gal·va·nize (găl′ vȧ·nīz)
-niz·ing
  gal·van·ic (găl·văn′ ĭk)
  gal·va·ni·za·tion
    (găl′ vȧ·nĭ·zā′ shŭn)
Gal·ves·ton, Tex.
    (găl′ vĕs·tŭn)
gam·bit (găm′ bĭt)
gam·ble (găm′ b'l)
  (bet) -bling
gam·bol (găm′ bŭl)
  (frolic) -boled, -bol·ing
game (gām)
  game bird   game dog
  game fish   game·keep·er
  game laws   game·ster
  game ward·en gam·y
gam·ma (găm′ ȧ)
  gam·ma glob·u·lin
  gam·ma rays
gam·ut (găm′ ŭt)
Gan·dhi, Mo·han·das
    (găn′ dē,
    mō′ hȧn·däs)
  title: Ma·hat·ma (mȧ·hät′ mȧ)
gan·gling (găng′ glĭng)
gang·plank (găng′ plăngk′)
gan·grene (găng′ grēn)
  gan·gre·nous (-grĕ′ nŭs)
gang·ster (găng′ stēr)
ga·rage (gȧ·räzh′)
gar·bage (gär′ bĭj)
gar·den·er (gär′ d'n·ēr)
gar·de·ni·a (gär·dē′ nĭ·ȧ)
gar·gle (gär′ g'l)
  -gling
gar·goyle (gär′ goil)
gar·ish (gâr′ ĭsh)
gar·land (gär′ lȧnd)
gar·lic (gär′ lĭk)
  gar·lick·y
gar·nish·ee (gär′ nĭsh·ē′)
gar·ri·son (găr′ ĭ·sŭn)
gar·ru·lous (găr′ û·lŭs)
  gar·ru·li·ty (gȧ·rōō′ lĭ·tĭ)
gas (găs)
  gas·e·ous (găs′ ē·ŭs)
  gas·light   gas·o·line
  gas·sing   gas sta·tion
gas·ket (găs′ kĕt)
gas·tric (găs′ trĭk)
gas·tron·o·my (găs·trŏn′ ō·mĭ)
  gas·tro·nom·ic
    (găs′ trŏ·nŏm′ ĭk)

gate (gāt)
  (fence opening; see *gait*)
  gate·house   gate·keep·er
  gate·way
gath·er·ing (găth′ ēr·ĭng)
gauche (gōsh)
  gauche·ly
  gau·che·rie (gō′ shĕ·rē′)
gaud·y (gôd′ ĭ)
  gaud·i·er, -i·est, -i·ly, -i·ness
gauge (gāj)
  gaug·ing
Gau·guin, Paul (gō′ găN′)
gaunt (gônt)
gaunt·let (gônt′ lĕt)
gauze (gôz)
  gauz·y
gav·el (găv′ ĕl)
gawk·y (gôk′ ĭ)
  gawk·i·ness
ga·zelle (gȧ·zĕl′)
ga·zette (gȧ·zĕt′)
  gaz·et·teer (găz′ ĕ·tēr′)
gear·shift (gēr′ shĭft′)
Gei·ger count·er
    (gī′ gēr)
gei·sha (gā′ shȧ)
gel·a·tin (jĕl′ ȧ·tĭn)
  ge·lat·i·nous (jĕ·lăt′ ĭ·nŭs)
gen·darme (zhän·därm′)
gen·e·al·o·gy (jĕn′ ē·ăl′ ō·jĭ)
  gen·e·al·o·gist
gen·er·al (jĕn′ ēr·ȧl)
  gen·er·al·is·si·mo
    (jĕn′ ēr·ȧl·ĭs′ ĭ·mō)
  gen·er·al·i·za·tion
    (jĕn′ ēr·ȧl·ĭ·zā′ shŭn)
  gen·er·al·ly
gen·er·ate (jĕn′ ēr·āt)
  -at·ing
  gen·er·a·tion (jĕn′ ēr·ā′ shŭn)
  gen·er·a·tive (jĕn′ ēr·ā′ tĭv)
  gen·er·a·tor
ge·ner·ic (jĕ·nĕr′ ĭk)
gen·er·ous (jĕn′ ēr·ŭs)
  gen·er·os·i·ty (jĕn′ ēr·ŏs′ ĭ·tĭ)
  -ties
gen·e·sis (jĕn′ ē·sĭs)
ge·net·ics (jĕ·nĕt′ ĭks)
  ge·net·i·cist (jĕ·nĕt′ ĭ·sĭst)
Gen·ghis Khan (jĕng′ gĭs kän′)
gen·ial (jēn′ yȧl)
  -ial·ly
  ge·ni·al·i·ty (jē′ nĭ·ăl′ ĭ·tĭ)
gen·i·tal (jĕn′ ĭ·tȧl)

gen·i·tive   (jĕn′ ĭ·tĭv)
gen·ius   (jĕn′ yŭs)
gen·o·cide   (jĕn′ ō·sīd)
gen·re   (zhäɴ′ r′)
gen·teel   (jĕn·tēl′)
  -teel·ly
gen·tian   (jĕn′ shăn)
gen·tile   (jĕn′ tīl)
gen·til·i·ty   (jĕn·tĭl′ ĭ·tĭ)
gen·tle   (jĕn′ t′l)
  gen·tle·man   gen·tle·ness
  gen·tlest   gen·tly
gen·try   (jĕn′ trĭ)
gen·u·flect   (jĕn′ û·flĕkt)
  gen·u·flec·tion
                      (jĕn′ û·flĕk′ shŭn)
gen·u·ine   (jĕn′ û·ĭn)
ge·nus   (jē′ nŭs)
  pl. gen·er·a   (jĕn′ ĕr·á)
ge·o·det·ic   (jē′ ô·dĕt′ ĭk)
ge·og·ra·phy   (jē·ŏg′ rá·fĭ)
  ge·og·ra·pher
  ge·o·graph·i·cal
                      (jē′ ô·grăf′ ĭ·kăl)
ge·ol·o·gy   (jē·ŏl′ ô·jĭ)
  ge·o·log·ic   (jē′ ô·lŏj′ ĭk)
  ge·ol·o·gist   (jē·ŏl′ ô·jĭst)
ge·om·e·try   (jē·ŏm′ ê·trĭ)
  ge·o·met·ric   (jē′ ô·mĕt′ rĭk)
  ge·o·met·ri·cal
                      (jē′ ô·mĕt′ rĭ·kăl)
ge·o·phys·ics   (jē′ ô·fĭz′ ĭks)
ge·o·po·lit·i·cal
                      (jē′ ô·pô·lĭt′ ĭ·kăl)
Geor·gia   (jôr′ já)
  abbr. Ga.
  Geor·gi·an   (jôr′ jĭ·ăn)
ge·ra·ni·um   (jê·rā′ nĭ·ŭm)
ger·i·at·rics   (jĕr′ ĭ·ăt′ rĭks)
ger·mane   (jûr·mān′)
ger·mi·cide   (jûr′ mĭ·sīd)
ger·mi·nal   (jûr′ mĭ·năl)
ger·mi·na·tion   (jûr′ mĭ·nā′ shŭn)
germ·proof   (jûrm′ prōōf′)
ger·ry·man·der   (gĕr′ ĭ·măn′ dĕr)
ger·und   (jĕr′ ŭnd)
Ge·sta·po   (gĕ·stä′ pō)
ges·ta·tion   (jĕs·tā′ shŭn)
ges·tic·u·late   (jĕs·tĭk′ û·lāt)
  -lat·ing
  ges·tic·u·la·tion
                      (jĕs·tĭk′ û·lā′ shŭn)
ges·ture   (jĕs′ tŭr)
Ge·sund·heit   (gĕ·zōōnt′ hīt)
get·a·way   (gĕt′ á·wā′)

get·ting   (gĕt′ ĭng)
gey·ser   (gī′ zēr)
Gha·na   (gä′ ná)
  Gha·na·ian   (gä′ ná·yăn)
ghast·ly   (gàst′ lĭ)
  ghast·li·er, -li·est, -li·ness
ghet·to   (gĕt′ ō)
  ghet·tos
ghost   (gōst)
  ghost·like   ghost·li·ness
  ghost·ly   ghost writ·er
  ghost·writ·ten
ghoul·ish   (gōōl′ ĭsh)
GI   (jē′ ī′)
  pl. GIs
gi·ant   (jī′ ănt)
gib·ber·ish   (jĭb′ ĕr·ĭsh)
gibe   (jīb)
  (also jibe)
gib·let   (jĭb′ lĕt)
Gi·bral·tar   (jĭ·brôl′ tēr)
gid·dy   (gĭd′ ĭ)
  gid·di·ness
gi·gan·tic   (jĭ·găn′ tĭk)
gig·gle   (gĭg′ ′l)
  gig·gling   gig·gly
gig·o·lo   (jĭg′ ô·lō)
  -los
gild   (gĭld)
  (plate with gold; see guild)
  gilt-edged
gim·mick   (gĭm′ ĭk)
gin·ger   (jĭn′ jĕr)
  gin·ger ale   gin·ger·bread
  gin·ger·snap
ging·ham   (gĭng′ ăm)
gin·gi·vi·tis   (jĭn′ jĭ·vī′ tĭs)
gin rum·my   (jĭn′ rŭm′ ĭ)
gi·raffe   (jĭ·răf′)
gird·er   (gûr′ dĕr)
gir·dle   (gûr′ d′l)
  -dling
girth   (gûrth)
gist   (jĭst)
give   (gĭv)
  giv·ing   give-and-take
  give·a·way
giz·zard   (gĭz′ ĕrd)
gla·cier   (glā′ shēr)
  gla·cial   (glā′ shăl)
  gla·ci·a·tion   (glā′ sĭ·ā′ shŭn)
glad   (glăd)
  glad·den   glad·dest
  glad·ly
glad·i·a·tor   (glăd′ ĭ·ā′ tēr)

glad·i·o·la (glăd′ ĭ·ō′ lá)
glam·our (glăm′ ẽr)
  glam·or·ize -iz·ing
  glam·or·ous
glance (gláns)
  glanc·ing
glan·du·lar (glăn′ dụ·lẽr)
glar·ing (glâr′ ĭng)
Glas·gow, Scot·land
  (glăs′ kō)
glass (glás)
  glass blow·er   glass·ful
  glass·ware
gleam·ing (glēm′ ĭng)
glee club (glē)
glee·ful (glē′ fŏŏl)
glib·ness (glĭb′ nĕs)
glide (glīd)
  glid·ing
glim·mer (glĭm′ ẽr)
glimpse (glĭmps)
  glimps·ing
glis·ten (glĭs′ ′n)
gloat·ing (glōt′ ĭng)
glob·al (glōb′ ăl)
  -al·ly
glob·u·lar (glōb′ û·lẽr)
gloom·y (glŏŏm′ ĭ)
  gloom·i·er, -i·est, -i·ly, -i·ness
glo·ri·fy (glō′ rĭ·fī)
  -fied   -fy·ing
  glo·ri·fi·ca·tion
  (glō′ rĭ·fĭ·kā′ shŭn)
glo·ri·ous (glō′ rĭ·ŭs)
glos·sa·ry (glŏs′ á·rĭ)
  -ries
glos·sy (glŏs′ ĭ)
  gloss·i·ness
Glouces·ter, Mass.
  (glŏs′ tẽr)
glow·worm (glō′ wûrm′)
glu·cose (glŏŏ′ kōs)
glue (glŏŏ)
  glue·y   glu·ing
glum·ly (glŭm′ lĭ)
glut·ton (glŭt′ ′n)
  glut·ton·ous (glŭt′ ′n·ŭs)
  glut·ton·y
glyc·er·in (glĭs′ ẽr·ĭn)
gnarl (närl)
gnash (năsh)
gnat (năt)
gnaw (nô)
gnome (nōm)
goad (gōd)

goal (gōl)
  goal·ee (gōl′ ė)
gob·let (gŏb′ lĕt)
gob·lin (gŏb′ lĭn)
god (gŏd)
  god·child   god·daugh·ter
  god·dess   god·fa·ther
  god·send
Goe·the, Jo·hann von
  (fôn gû′ tĕ, yō′ hän)
go-get·ter (gō′ gĕt′ ẽr)
gog·gles (gŏg′ ′lz)
  gog·gle-eyed
Gogh, Vin·cent van
  (văn kôk′, vĭn·sĕnt′)
gold (gōld)
  gold·brick v.   gold dig·ger
  gold·fish
gold·en·rod (gōl′ dĕn·rŏd′)
golf (gŏlf)
  (game; see gulf)
  golf club
Go·li·ath (gō·lī′ ăth)
Go·mor·rah (gō·mŏr′ á)
gon·do·la (gŏn′ dō·lá)
gon·or·rhe·a (gŏn′ ō·rē′ á)
good (gŏŏd)
  good-bye   good·heart·ed
  good-hu·mored   good will
goose (gŏŏs)
  goose·ber·ry   goose pim·ple
  goose step
go·pher (gō′ fẽr)
gor·geous (gôr′ jŭs)
go·ril·la (gō·rĭl′ á)
  (ape; see guerrilla)
gos·pel (gŏs′ pĕl)
gos·sa·mer (gŏs′ á·mẽr)
gos·sip (gŏs′ ĭp)
  gos·sip·ing   gos·sip·y
Go·tham (gŏth′ ăm)
Goth·ic (gŏth′ ĭk)
got·ten (gŏt′ ′n)
gouge (gouj)
  goug·ing
gou·lash (gŏŏ′ läsh)
  (Hungarian dish; see galosh)
gourd (gōrd)
gour·met (gŏŏr′ mā)
gout (gout)
  gout·y
gov·ern·a·ble (gŭv′ ẽr·ná·b′l)
gov·ern·ess (gŭv′ ẽr·nĕs)

gov·ern·ment   (gŭv′ ẽrn·mĕnt)
  gov·ern·men·tal
          (gŭv′ ẽrn·mĕn′ tᴀl)
  -tal·ly
gov·er·nor   (gŭv′ ẽr·nẽr)
  gov·er·nor gen·er·al
  gov·er·nor·ship
gown   (goun)
grace   (grās)
  grace·ful, -ful·ly, -ful·ness
  grace·less
gra·cious   (grā′ shŭs)
gra·da·tion   (grȧ·dā′ shŭn)
  (series)
gra·di·ent   (grā′ dĭ·ĕnt)
grad·u·al   (grăd′ ū·ᴀl)
  -al·ly   -al·ness
grad·u·ate   (grăd′ ū·āt)
  -at·ing
  grad·u·a·tion (grăd′ ū·ā′ shŭn)
  (commencement)
grain·y   (grān′ ĭ)
  grain·i·ness
gram   (grăm)
gram·mar   (grăm′ ẽr)
  gram·mar·i·an (grᴀ·mâr′ ĭ·ᴀn)
  gram·mat·i·cal
         (grᴀ·măt′ ĭ·kᴀl)
  -cal·ly
gran·a·ry   (grăn′ ȧ·rĭ)
  -ries
grand   (grănd)
  grand·child   grand·dad
  grand·daugh·ter
  grand duke   grand·par·ent
  grand·son   grand·stand
gran·deur   (grăn′ dūr)
gran·dil·o·quence
       (grăn·dĭl′ ᴏ·kwĕns)
gran·di·ose   (grăn′ dĭ·ōs)
  -ose·ly
gran·ite   (grăn′ ĭt)
grant-in-aid   (grȧnt′ ĭn·ād′)
  grants-in-aid
gran·u·late   (grăn′ ū·lāt)
  -lat·ing
  gran·u·lar   (grăn′ ū·lẽr)
grape   (grāp)
  grape·fruit   grape juice
  grape·shot   grape·vine
graph·ic   (grăf′ ĭk)
  graph·i·cal·ly
graph·ite   (grăf′ īt)
grap·ple   (grăp′ 'l)
  grap·pling hook

grass·hop·per   (grȧs′ hŏp′ ẽr)
grate   (grāt)
  grat·ing
grate·ful   (grāt′ fŏŏl)
  grate·ful·ly   -ful·ness
grat·i·fy   (grăt′ ĭ·fī)
  -fied   -fy·ing
  grat·i·fi·ca·tion
       (grăt′ ĭ·fĭ·kā′ shŭn)
grat·i·tude   (grăt′ ĭ·tūd)
gra·tu·i·ty   (grȧ·tū′ ĭ·tĭ)
  -ties
  gra·tu·i·tous (grȧ·tū′ ĭ·tŭs)
grav·el   (grăv′ ĕl)
  -el·ly
grav·en im·age   (grāv′ ĕn)
grave·stone   (grāv′ stōn′)
grav·i·ty   (grăv′ ĭ·tĭ)
gra·vy   (grā′ vĭ)
  -vies
gray   (grā)
  gray·beard   gray·ness
grease   (grēs)
  greas·ing   greas·i·ness
  greas·y
great   (grāt)
  great-grand·fa·ther
  Great Lakes
  Great Smok·y Mts.
Gre·cian   (grē′ shᴀn)
Gre·co, El   (ĕl grā′ kô)
greed·y   (grēd′ ĭ)
  greed·i·er, -i·est, -i·ly, -i·ness
green   (grēn)
  green·er·y   green-eyed
  green·gage   green·horn
  green·house
Green·wich Vil·lage
       (grĕn′ ĭch)
greet·ing   (grēt′ ĭng)
gre·gar·i·ous   (grē·gâr′ ĭ·ŭs)
Gre·go·ri·an cal·en·dar
       (grē·gō′ rĭ·ᴀn)
grem·lin   (grĕm′ lĭn)
gre·nade   (grē·nād′)
gren·a·dier   (grĕn′ ȧ·dēr′)
gren·a·dine   (grĕn′ ȧ·dēn′)
Gresh·am's law   (grĕsh′ ᴀmz)
grey·hound   (grā′ hound′)
grid·dle·cake   (grĭd′ 'l kāk′)
grid·i·ron   (grĭd′ ī·ẽrn)
grief·-strick·en   (grēf′ strĭk′ ĕn)
grieve   (grēv)
  griev·ing
  griev·ance   (grēv′ ᴀns)

griev·ous (grēv′ ŭs)
grill (grĭl)
(to broil)
grille (grĭl)
(a grating)
grim (grĭm)
grim·mest grim·ly
gri·mace (grĭ·mās′)
-mac·ing
grime (grīm)
grim·i·ness grim·y
grin (grĭn)
grinned grin·ning
grind·stone (grīnd′ stōn′)
grip (grĭp)
gripped grip·ping
gripe (grīp)
grip·ing
gris·ly (grĭz′ lĭ)
gris·li·est gris·li·ness
gris·tle (grĭs′ 'l)
grist·mill (grĭst′ mĭl′)
griz·zly bear (grĭz′ 'lĭ)
gro·cer (grō′ sēr)
gro·cer·y -cer·ies
grog·gy (grŏg′ ĭ)
grog·gi·ness
grom·met (grŏm′ ĕt)
gros·beak (grōs′ bēk′)
gros·grain rib·bon
(grō′ grān′)
gro·tesque (grō·tĕsk′)
-tesque·ly
grot·to (grŏt′ ō)
grouch·y (grouch′ ĭ)
grouch·i·ness
ground (ground)
ground floor ground hog
ground·work
grouse (grous)
grov·el (grŏv′ 'l)
-eled -el·ing
grown·up (grōn′ ŭp′) n.
growth (grōth)
grub (grŭb)
grub·bi·ness grub·by
grub·stake
grudge (grŭj)
grudg·ing·ly
gru·el (grōō′ ĕl)
gru·el·ing
grue·some (grōō′ sŭm)
grum·ble (grŭm′ b'l)
-bling

Gua·da·lupe (gwŏd′ 'l·ōōp)
Riv. & Mt., Tex.
Gua·de·loupe Is.,
West In·dies (gwŏd′ 'l·ōōp)
Guan·tá·na·mo
(gwän·tä′ nä·mŏ)
guar·an·tee (găr′ ăn·tē′)
-tee·ing
guar·an·tor (găr′ ăn·tôr)
guar·an·ty (găr′ ăn·tĭ)
-ties
guard (gärd)
guard·i·an (gär′ dĭ·ăn)
Gua·te·ma·la (gwä′ tĕ·mä′ lȧ)
Gua·ya·quil, (gwä′ yä·kēl′)
Ec·ua·dor
gu·ber·na·to·ri·al
(gū′ bĕr·nȧ·tō′ rĭ·ȧl)
Guern·sey (gûrn′ zĭ)
-seys
guer·ril·la (gĕ·rĭl′ ȧ)
(irregular warrior; see gorilla)
guess·work (gĕs′ wûrk′)
guest (gĕst)
guf·faw (gŭ·fô′)
Gui·a·na (gē·ä′ nȧ)
(S. Amer. region)
guide (gīd)
guid·ing guid·a·ble
guid·ance guide·book
guide·post guid·ed mis·sile
guild (gĭld)
(association; see gild)
guile (gīl)
guile·less
guil·lo·tine (gĭl′ ō·tēn)
guilt·y (gĭl′ tĭ)
guilt·i·ly
Guin·ea, Afr. (gĭn′ ĭ)
guin·ea pig (gĭn′ ĭ)
guise (gīz)
gui·tar (gĭ·tär′)
gulf (gŭlf)
(separation; see golf)
gul·li·ble (gŭl′ ĭ·b'l)
gul·ly (gŭl′ ĭ)
gul·lies
gum·bo (gŭm′ bō)
gun (gŭn)
gun·man gun·ner
gun·ner·y gun play
gun pow·der gun·shot
gur·gle (gûr′ g'l)
-gling
gus·to (gŭs′ tō)

gust·y (gŭs′ tĭ)
  gust·i·ness
gut·ter·snipe (gŭt′ ẽr·snĭp′)
gut·tur·al (gŭt′ ẽr·ăl)
  -al·ly
guz·zle (gŭz′ ′l)
  guz·zling
gym·na·si·um (jĭm·nā′ zĭ·ŭm)
gym·nast (jĭm′ năst)
  gym·nas·tic (jĭm·năs′ tĭk)
gyn·e·col·o·gy (jĭn′ ĕ·kŏl′ ŏ·jĭ)
  gyn·e·co·log·i·cal
          (jĭn′ ĕ·kŏ·lŏj′ ĭ·kăl)
gyp (jĭp)
  gypped   gyp·ping
gyp·sum (jĭp′ sŭm)
gyp·sy (jĭp′ sĭ)
  -sies
gy·rate (jī′ rāt)
  -rat·ing
  gy·ra·tion (jī·rā′ shŭn)
  gy·ra·tor
gy·ro·scope (jī′ rŏ·skōp)

H

ha·be·as cor·pus
      (hā′ bĕ·ăs kôr′ pŭs)
hab·er·dash·er·y
      (hăb′ ẽr·dăsh′ ẽr·ĭ)
hab·it (hăb′ ĭt)
  hab·it·a·ble   hab·i·tat
  hab·i·ta·tion (hăb′ ĭ·tā′ shŭn)
  ha·bit·u·al (há·bĭt′ û·ăl)
  -al·ly
  ha·bit·u·a·tion
      (há·bĭt′ û·ā′ shŭn)
  ha·bit·u·é (há·bĭt′ û·ā′)
ha·ci·en·da (häs′ ĭ·ĕn′ dá)
hack·neyed (hăk′ nĭd)
had·dock (hăd′ ŭk)
Ha·des (hā′ dēz)
hag·gard (hăg′ ẽrd)
hag·gle (hăg′ ′l)
  hag·gling
Hague, The, Neth·er·lands
      (hāg)
hail (hāl)
  hail·stone   hail·storm
hair (hâr)
  hair·breadth   hair·dress·er
  hair·split·ter   hair·spring
  hair trig·ger   hair·y

Hai·ti (hā′ tĭ)
  Hai·ti·an (hā′ tĭ·ăn)
hal·cy·on (hăl′ sĭ·ŭn)
hale (hāl)
  (and hearty)
half (häf)
  pl. halves   half-and-half
  half·back   half-baked
  half-breed   half broth·er
  half-caste   half dol·lar
  half·heart·ed   half-hour
  half life   half-mast
  half-moon   half nel·son
  half sis·ter   half-tim·bered
  half·way   half-wit·ted
hal·i·but (hăl′ ĭ·bŭt)
hal·i·to·sis (hăl′ ĭ·tō′ sĭs)
hal·le·lu·jah (hăl′ ĕ·lōō′ yá)
hall·mark (hôl′ märk′)
hal·lowed ground
      (hăl′ ōd)
Hal·low·een (hăl′ ŏ·ēn′)
hal·lu·ci·na·tion
      (há·lū′ sĭ·nā′ shŭn)
ha·lo (hā′ lō)
  -los
hal·ter (hôl′ tẽr)
halt·ing (hôl′ tĭng)
halve (häv)
  halv·ing
hal·yard (hăl′ yẽrd)
ham·burg·er (hăm′ bûr·gẽr)
Ham·let (hăm′ lĕt)
ham·mer and sick·le
      (hăm′ ẽr ănd sĭk′ ′l)
ham·mer·head shark
      (hăm′ ẽr·hĕd′)
ham·mock (hăm′ ŭk)
ham·per (hăm′ pẽr)
ham·ster (hăm′ stẽr)
ham·string (hăm′ strĭng′)
hand (hănd)
  hand·bag   hand·bill
  hand·cuff   hand·ful
  hand gre·nade   hand·made
  hand-me-down   hand·out
  hand·spring   hand-to-mouth
  hand·writ·ing
hand·i·cap (hăn′ dĭ·kăp)
  -capped   -cap·ping
hand·i·craft (hăn′ dĭ·krăft)
hand·i·work (hăn′ dĭ·wûrk′)
han·dle (hăn′ d′l)
  -dling

hand·some (hăn′ sŭm)
  -some·ly
hand·y (hăn′ dĭ)
  hand·i·ly   hand·y man
hang (hăng)
  hang·nail   hang·out
  hang-o·ver
hang·ar (hăng′ ĕr)
  (for aircraft)
hang·er (hăng′ ĕr)
  (for clothes)
han·ker·ing (hăng′ kĕr·ĭng)
han·som cab (hăn′ sŭm)
Ha·nuk·kah (hä′ nŏŏ·kä)
hap·haz·ard (hăp′ hăz′ ĕrd)
hap·pen·ing (hăp′ ĕn·ĭng)
hap·py (hăp′ ĭ)
  hap·pi·er   hap·pi·est
  hap·pi·ly   hap·pi·ness
  hap·py-go-luck·y
har·a·kir·i (hăr′ ȧ·kĭr′ ĭ)
ha·rangue (hȧ·răng′)
  -rangu·ing
har·ass (hăr′ ȧs)
  har·ass·ment
har·bin·ger (här′ bĭn·jĕr)
har·bor (här′ bĕr)
hard (härd)
  hard-bit·ten   hard-boiled
  hard·en   hard·head·ed
  hard·heart·ed   hard·ship
  hard·tack   hard·ware
har·dy (här′ dĭ)
  har·di·ness
hare·brained (hâr′ brānd′)
hare·lip (hâr′ lĭp′)
ha·rem (hā′ rĕm)
hark·en (här′ kĕn)
Har·le·quin (här′ lĕ·kwĭn)
har·lot (här′ lŏt)
harm·ful (härm′ fŏŏl)
  -ful·ly   -ful·ness
har·mon·i·ca (här·mŏn′ ĭ·kȧ)
har·mo·ny (här′ mŏ·nĭ)
  -nies
  har·mon·ic (här·mŏn′ ĭk)
  har·mo·ni·ous (här·mō′ nĭ·ŭs)
  har·mo·niz·ing
      (här′ mŏ·nĭz′ ĭng)
har·ness (här′ nĕs)
har·poon (här·pōōn′)
harp·si·chord (härp′ sĭ·kôrd)
har·row·ing (hăr′ ō·ĭng)
har·ry (hăr′ ĭ)
  har·ried   har·ry·ing

Har·vard (univ.) (här′ vĕrd)
har·vest·er (här′ vĕs·tĕr)
has-been (hăz′ bĭn′)
ha·sen·pfef·fer (hä′ zĕn(p)fĕf′ ĕr)
has·sock (hăs′ ŭk)
haste (hāst)
  has·ten (hās′ ′n)
  hast·y
hatch (hăch)
  hatch·er·y (hăch′ ĕr·ĭ)
hatch·et (hăch′ ĕt)
  hatch·et-faced
hate·ful (hāt′ fŏŏl)
  -ful·ly   -ful·ness
ha·tred (hā′ trĕd)
Hat·ter·as, Cape, (hăt′ ĕr·ȧs)
  N.C.
haugh·ty (hô′ tĭ)
  haugh·ti·er   -ti·est
  -ti·ly   -ti·ness
haul (hôl)
haunch (hônch)
haunt (hônt)
Ha·van·a, Cu·ba
      (hȧ·văn′ ȧ)
ha·ven (hā′ vĕn)
hav·er·sack (hăv′ ĕr·săk)
hav·oc (hăv′ ŭk)
Ha·wai·i (hȧ·wī′ ė)
  Ha·wai·ian (hȧ·wī′ đn)
hawk-eyed (hôk′ īd′)
haw·thorn (hô′ thôrn)
hay (hā)
  hay fe·ver   hay·fork
  hay·loft   hay·seed
  hay·stack   hay·wire
haz·ard·ous (hăz′ ĕr·dŭs)
haze (hāz)
  ha·zy
ha·zel·nut (hā′ z′l·nŭt′)
H-bomb (āch′ bŏm′)
head (hĕd)
  head·ache   head·dress
  head·first   head·gear
  head-hunt·er   head·light
  head·line   head·long
  head·mas·ter
  head-on col·li·sion
  head·phone   head·piece
  head·quar·ters head·strong
  head·wait·er   head wind
heal (hēl)
  (cure)
health·ful (hĕlth′ fŏŏl)
  -ful·ly   -ful·ness

health·y (hĕl′thĭ)
  health·i·ness
hear·say ev·i·dence
  (hĕr′ sā′)
hearse (hûrs)
heart (härt)
  heart·ache   heart·break·ing
  heart·burn   heart dis·ease
  heart·en·ing heart·felt
  heart·less   heart-rend·ing
  heart-to-heart
hearth (härth)
heat·er (hēt′ ēr)
hea·then (hē′ thĕn)
  hea·then·ish
heath·er (hĕth′ ēr)
heave (hēv)
  heav·ing
heav·en (hĕv′ ĕn)
  heav·en·ward
heav·y (hĕv′ ĭ)
  heav·i·er, -i·est, -i·ly, -i·ness
  heav·y-du·ty heav·y·heart·ed
  heav·y·weight
He·bra·ic (hē·brā′ ĭk)
heck·le (hĕk′ 'l)
  -ling
hec·tic (hĕk′ tĭk)
  hec·ti·cal·ly
hec·to·graph (hŏk′ tō·grȧf)
hedge (hĕj)
  hedge·hog   hedge·row
he·don·ism (hē′ dŏn·ĭz′m)
  he·don·ist
heed (hēd)
  heed·ful, -ful·ly, -ful·ness
  heed·less
heel (hēl)
  (foot part)
heft·y (hĕf′ tĭ)
  heft·i·ness
He·ge·li·an (hȧ·gā′ lĭ·ȧn)
he·gem·o·ny (hē·jĕm′ ō·nĭ)
heif·er (hĕf′ ēr)
heigh-ho (hī′ hō′)
height (hīt)
  height·en (hīt′ 'n)
hei·nous (hā′ nŭs)
heir (âr)
  heir ap·par·ent
  heir·ess   heir·loom
hel·i·cal (hĕl′ ĭ·kȧl)
hel·i·cop·ter (hĕl′ ĭ·kŏp′ tēr)
he·li·o·trope (hē′ lĭ·ō·trōp)
he·li·um (hē′ lĭ·ŭm)

hell (hĕl)
  hell·cat   hell-div·er
  hell-fire
Hel·len·ic (hĕ·lĕn′ ĭk)
helm (hĕlm)
hel·met (hĕl′ mĕt)
  -met·ed
help (hĕlp)
  help·ful, -ful·ly, -ful·ness
  help·less   help·mate
hel·ter-skel·ter (hĕl′ tēr·skĕl′ tēr)
hem·i·sphere (hĕm′ ĭ·sfēr)
  hem·i·spher·ic (hĕm′ ĭ·sfēr′ ĭk)
hem·lock (hĕm′ lŏk)
he·mo·glo·bin (hē′ mō·glō′ bĭn)
he·mo·phil·i·a (hē′ mō·fĭl′ ĭ·ȧ)
  he·mo·phil·i·ac (-fĭl′ ĭ·ăk)
hem·or·rhage (hĕm′ ŏ·rĭj)
hem·or·rhoid (hĕm′ ŏ·roid)
hence·forth (hĕns′ fōrth′)
  hence·for·ward
hench·man (hĕnch′ mȧn)
hen·na (hĕn′ ȧ)
  hen·naed   hen·na·ing
hen·pecked (hĕn′ pĕkt′)
hep·a·ti·tis (hĕp′ ȧ·tī′ tĭs)
Hep·ple·white (hĕp′ 'l·hwīt)
her·ald (hĕr′ ȧld)
  he·ral·dic (hĕ·răl′ dĭk)
  her·ald·ry (hĕr′ ȧld·rĭ)
herb (ûrb)
  her·ba·ceous (hûr·bā′ shŭs)
  herb·age (ûr′ bĭj)
  her·biv·o·rous (hûr·bĭv′ ŏ·rŭs)
  her·cu·le·an (hûr·kū′ lė·ȧn)
  herds·man (hûrdz′ mȧn)
here (hēr)
  here·a·bout   here·aft·er
  here·at   here·by
  here·in   here·in·aft·er
  here·to·fore here·unto
  here·up·on   here·with
he·red·i·tar·y (hē·rĕd′ ĭ·tĕr′ ĭ)
he·red·i·ty (hē·rĕd′ ĭ·tĭ)
Her·e·ford cat·tle
  (hĕr′ ĕ·fērd)
her·e·sy (hĕr′ ĕ·sĭ)
  -sies
  her·e·tic (hĕr′ ĕ·tĭk)
  he·ret·i·cal (hĕ·rĕt′ ĭ·kȧl)
her·it·age (hĕr′ ĭ·tĭj)
her·met·ic (hûr·mĕt′ ĭk)
  her·met·i·cal·ly sealed
her·mit (hûr′ mĭt)
  her·mit·age (hûr′ mĭ·tĭj)

her·ni·a (hûr′ nĭ·ȧ)
he·ro (hēr′ ō)
-roes
he·ro·ic (hē·rō′ ĭk)
he·ro·i·cal·ly
her·o·ine (hĕr′ ō·ĭn)
her·o·ism (hĕr′ ō·ĭz′m)
her·o·in (hĕr′ ō·ĭn)
(drug)
her·on (hĕr′ ŭn)
(bird)
her·ring·bone (hĕr′ ĭng·bōn′)
her·self (hûr·sĕlf′)
hes·i·tate (hĕz′ ĭ·tāt)
-tat·ing
hes·i·tan·cy (hĕz′ ĭ·tăn·sĭ)
hes·i·tant (hĕz′ ĭ·tănt)
hes·i·ta·tion (hĕz′ ĭ·tā′ shŭn)
Hes·sian (hĕsh′ ȧn)
het·er·o·dox (hĕt′ ĕr·ō·dŏks)
het·er·o·ge·ne·ous
(hĕt′ ĕr·ō·jē′ nĕ·ŭs)
het·er·o·ge·ne·i·ty
(-jē·nē′ ĭ·tĭ)
het·er·o·sex·u·al (hĕt′ ĕr·ō·sĕk′ shŏō·ȧl)
heu·ris·tic (hū·rĭs′ tĭk)
hew (hū)
(cut; see *hue*)
hewn (hūn)
hex·a·gon (hĕk′ sȧ·gŏn)
hex·ag·o·nal (hĕks·ăg′ ō·nȧl)
hex·am·e·ter (hĕks·ăm′ ĕ·tĕr)
hey·day (hā′ dā′)
hi·a·tus (hī·ā′ tŭs)
Hi·a·wa·tha (hī′ ȧ·wô′ thȧ)
hi·ber·nate (hī′ bĕr·nāt)
-nat·ing
hi·ber·na·tion
(hī′ bĕr·nā′ shŭn)
hi·bis·cus (hī·bĭs′ kŭs)
hic·cup (hĭk′ ŭp)
hick·o·ry (hĭk′ ō·rĭ)
hid·den (hĭd′ ’n)
hide·bound (hīd′ bound′)
hid·e·ous (hĭd′ ĕ·ŭs)
hie (hī)
hied hy·ing
hi·er·arch·y (hī′ ĕr·är′ kĭ)
-arch·ies
hi·er·o·glyph·ic
(hī′ ĕr·ō·glĭf′ ĭk)
hi-fi (hī′ fī′)
high (hī)
high·ball high·born

high·brow high fi·del·i·ty
high-flown high-fre·quen·cy
high jump high·light
high school high-sound·ing
high-spir·it·ed high-strung
high-ten·sion high·way
hi·jack (hī′ jăk′)
hi·lar·i·ous (hĭ·lâr′ ĭ·ŭs)
hi·lar·i·ty (hĭ·lăr′ ĭ·tĭ)
hill·bil·ly (hĭl′ bĭl′ ĭ)
Hi·ma·la·ya (mts.)
(hĭ·mä′ lȧ·yȧ)
him·self (hĭm·sĕlf′)
hind·quar·ter (hīnd′ kwôr′ tēr)
hin·drance (hĭn′ drȧns)
hind·sight (hīnd′ sīt′)
Hin·du (hĭn′ dōō)
Hin·du·ism (hĭn′ dōō·ĭz′m)
Hin·du·sta·ni (hĭn′ dōō·stä′ nē)
hinge (hĭnj)
hing·ing
hin·ter·land (hĭn′ tēr·lănd′)
Hip·po·crat·ic oath
(hĭp′ ō·krăt′ ĭk)
hip·po·drome (hĭp′ ō·drōm)
hip·po·pot·a·mus
(hĭp′ ō·pŏt′ ȧ·mŭs)
-mus·es
hir·a·ble (hīr′ ȧ·b’l)
hire·ling (hīr′ lĭng)
Hi·ro·hi·to (hē′ rō·hē′ tō)
hir·sute (hûr′ sūt)
his·ta·mine (hĭs′ tȧ·mēn)
his·tol·o·gy (hĭs·tŏl′ ō·jĭ)
his·to·ry (hĭs′ tō·rĭ)
-ries
his·to·ri·an (hĭs·tō′ rĭ·ȧn)
his·tor·ic (hĭs·tŏr′ ĭk)
his·tor·i·cal (hĭs·tŏr′ ĭ·kȧl)
-cal·ly
his·to·ri·og·ra·pher
(hĭs·tō′ rĭ·ŏg′ rȧ·fēr)
his·tri·on·ic (hĭs′ trĭ·ŏn′ ĭk)
hit-and-run (hĭt′ ănd rŭn′)
hitch·hike (hĭch′ hīk′)
-hik·ing
hith·er·to (hĭth′ ĕr·tōō′)
hives (hīvz)
hoard (hōrd)
hoar·frost (hōr′ frŏst′)
hoarse (hōrs)
hoarse·ly
hoar·y (hōr′ ĭ)
hoar·i·ness
hoax (hōks)

hob·ble (hŏb′ ′l)
  hob·bling
hob·by (hŏb′ ĭ)
  hob·bies   hob·by·horse
hob·gob·lin (hŏb′ gŏb′ lĭn)
hob·nail (hŏb′ nāl′)
hob·nob (hŏb′ nŏb′)
  -nobbed   -nob·bing
ho·bo (hō′ bō)
  -boes
hock·ey (hŏk′ ĭ)
ho·cus-po·cus (hō′ kŭs·pō′ kŭs)
hod car·ri·er (hod)
hodge·podge (hŏj′ pŏj′)
hoe (hō)
  hoe·ing
hog·wash (hŏg′ wŏsh′)
hoi pol·loi (hoi′ pə·loi′)
hoist (hoist)
ho·kum (hō′ kŭm)
hold·up (hōld′ ŭp′)
hol·i·day (hŏl′ ĭ·dā)
ho·li·ness (hō′ lĭ·nĕs)
hol·lan·daise sauce
      (hŏl′ ăn·dāz′)
hol·low (hŏl′ ō)
hol·ly·hock (hŏl′ ĭ·hŏk)
hol·o·caust (hŏl′ ŏ·kôst)
hol·ster (hōl′ stĕr)
ho·ly (hō′ lĭ)
  ho·li·er   ho·li·est
  ho·li·ness
hom·age (hŏm′ ĭj)
Hom·burg hat (hŏm′ bûrg)
home (hōm)
  home e·co·nom·ics
  home·made   home·mak·er
  home run   home·sick
  home·spun   home·stead
  home·ward   home·work
home·ly (hōm′ lĭ)
  home·li·ness
home·y (hōm′ ĭ)
hom·i·cide (hŏm′ ĭ·sīd)
  hom·i·cid·al (hŏm′ ĭ·sīd′ ăl)
hom·i·let·ic (hŏm′ ĭ·lĕt′ ĭk)
hom·i·ly (hŏm′ ĭ·lĭ)
  -lies
hom·i·ny grits (hŏm′ ĭ·nĭ)
ho·mo·ge·ne·ous
      (hō′ mŏ·jē′ nĕ·ŭs)
  ho·mo·ge·ne·i·ty
      (-jĕ·nē′ ĭ·tĭ)
ho·mog·e·nized milk
      (hŏ·mŏj′ ĕ·nīzd)

ho·mol·o·gous (hŏ·mŏl′ ŏ·gŭs)
hom·o·nym (hŏm′ ŏ·nĭm)
ho·mo·sex·u·al
      (hō′ mŏ·sĕk′ shoō·ăl)
Hon·du·ras, (hŏn·dŏŏr′ ăs)
  Cen. Am.
hon·es·ty (ŏn′ ĕs·tĭ)
hon·ey (hŭn′ ĭ)
  hon·eyed   hon·ey·bee
  hon·ey·comb
  hon·ey·dew mel·on
  hon·ey·moon   hon·ey·suck·le
Hong Kong (hŏng′ kŏng′)
honk·y-tonk (hŏngk′ ĭ·tŏngk′)
hon·or (ŏn′ ĕr)
  hon·or·a·ble
  hon·or·ar·y (ŏn′ ĕr·ĕr′ ĭ)
hon·o·rar·i·um (ŏn′ ŏ·râr′ ĭ·ŭm)
hood·lum (hŏŏd′ lŭm)
hoo·doo (hŏŏ′ dŏŏ)
hood·wink (hŏŏd′ wĭngk)
hoo·ey (hŏŏ′ ĭ)
hoof·er (hŏŏf′ ĕr)
hook·up (hŏŏk′ ŭp′)
hook·y (hŏŏk′ ĭ)
hoo·li·gan (hŏŏ′ lĭ·găn)
Hoo·sier (hŏŏ′ zhēr)
hope·ful (hōp′ fŏŏl)
  -ful·ly   -ful·ness
hop·per (hŏp′ ĕr)
hop·scotch (hŏp′ skŏch′)
horde (hôrd)
ho·ri·zon (hŏ·rī′ z′n)
hor·i·zon·tal (hŏr′ ĭ·zŏn′ tăl)
  -tal·ly
hor·mone (hôr′ mōn)
hor·net (hôr′ nĕt)
hor·o·scope (hŏr′ ŏ·skōp)
hor·ren·dous (hŏ·rĕn′ dŭs)
hor·ri·ble (hŏr′ ĭ·b′l)
hor·rid (hŏr′ ĭd)
hor·ri·fy (hŏr′ ĭ·fī)
  -fied   -fy·ing
  hor·ri·fi·ca·tion
      (hŏr′ ĭ·fī·kā′ shŭn)
hor·ror (hŏr′ ĕr)
hors d'oeuvre (ôr′ dû′ vr′)
horse (hôrs)
  horse·back   horse·fly
  horse·man·ship
  horse·pow·er   horse-rad·ish
  horse sense   horse·shoe
  hors·y
hor·ti·cul·ture (hôr′ tĭ·kŭl′ tûr)
ho·san·na (hŏ·zăn′ à)

ho·sier·y (hō′ zhēr·ĭ)
hos·pi·ta·ble (hŏs′ pĭ·tá·b'l)
  hos·pi·tal·i·ty (hŏs′ pĭ·tăl′ ĭ·tĭ)
hos·pi·tal (hŏs′ pĭt·ál)
  hos·pi·tal·ize -iz·ing
hos·tage (hŏs′ tĭj)
hos·tel (hŏs′ tĕl)
  (inn; see *hostile*)
host·ess (hōs′ tĕs)
hos·tile (hŏs′ tĭl)
  (unfriendly; see *hostel*)
  hos·til·i·ty (hŏs·tĭl′ ĭ·tĭ)
  -ties
hot (hŏt)
  hot·bed   hot-blood·ed
  hot dog   hot·head·ed
  hot·house   hot plate
  hot rod
ho·tel (hō·tĕl′)
hour·glass (our′ glás′)
house (hous) -
  house·boat   house·coat
  house·fly   house·ful
  house·hold   house·keep·er
  house or·gan   house par·ty
  house·top   house·warm·ing
  house·wife   -wives
  house·work
hous·ing (houz′ ĭng)
hov·el (hŏv′ ĕl)
hov·er·ing (hŭv′ ēr·ĭng)
how·be·it (hou·bē′ ĭt)
how·ev·er (hou·ĕv′ ēr)
how·itz·er (hou′ ĭt·sēr)
howl (houl)
how·so·ev·er (hou′ sŏ·ĕv′ ēr)
hub·bub (hŭb′ ŭb)
huck·le·ber·ry (hŭk′ 'l·bĕr′ ĭ)
  -ber·ries
huck·ster (hŭk′ stēr)
hud·dle (hŭd′ 'l)
  hud·dling
hue (hū)
  (color; see *hew*)
  hue and cry
huge (hūj)
  huge·ness
Hu·gue·not (hū′ gē·nŏt)
hu·la (hōō′ lä)
hulk·ing (hŭl′ kĭng)
hul·la·ba·loo (hŭl′ á·bá·lōō′)
hu·man (hū′ mán)
  hu·mane (hū·mān′)
  hu·man·is·tic (hū′ mán·ĭs′ tĭk)

hu·man·i·tar·i·an
    (hū·măn′ ĭ·târ′ ĭ·dn)
hu·man·i·ty (hū·măn′ ĭ·tĭ)
  -ties
hum·ble (hŭm′ b'l)
  -bling
hum·bug (hŭm′ bŭg′)
hum·drum (hŭm′ drŭm′)
hu·mid (hū′ mĭd)
  hu·mid·i·fy (hū·mĭd′ ĭ·fī)
  -fied   -fy·ing
  hu·mid·i·ty (hū·mĭd′ ĭ·tĭ)
hu·mi·dor (hū′ mĭ·dôr)
hu·mil·i·ate (hû·mĭl′ ĭ·āt)
  -at·ing
  hu·mil·i·a·tion
    (hû·mĭl′ ĭ·ā′ shŭn)
hu·mil·i·ty (hû·mĭl′ ĭ·tĭ)
hum·ming·bird (hŭm′ ĭng·bûrd′)
hum·mock (hŭm′ ŭk)
hu·mor (hū′ mēr)
  hu·mor·ist   hu·mor·ous
hu·mor·esque (hū′ mēr·ĕsk′)
hu·mus (hū′ mŭs)
hunch·back (hŭnch′ băk′)
hun·dred (hŭn′ drĕd)
  hun·dred·fold
  hun·dred-per·cent·er
  hun·dredth   hun·dred·weight
Hun·ga·ry (hŭng′ gá·rĭ)
  Hun·gar·i·an (hŭng·gâr′ ĭ·dn)
hun·ger (hŭng′ gēr)
hun·gry (hŭng′ grĭ)
  hun·gri·ly
hunt·ress (hŭn′ trĕs)
hunts·man (hŭnts′ mán)
hur·dle (hûr′ d'l)
  (a barrier; or to leap a barrier; see
  hurtle)   -dling
hur·dy-gur·dy (hûr′ dĭ·gûr′ dĭ)
hurl (hûrl)
hur·rah (hŏō·rô′)
  or: hur·ray (hŏō·rā′)
hur·ri·cane (hûr′ ĭ·kān)
hur·ry (hûr′ ĭ)
  hur·ried   hur·ry·ing
hurt·ful (hûrt′ fŏŏl)
  -ful·ly   -ful·ness
hur·tle (hûr′ t'l)
  (to throw violently; see *hurdle*)
  -tling
hus·band (hŭz′ bánd)
husk·y (hŭs′ kĭ)
  hus·ki·ness
hus·sar (hŏō·zär′)

hus·sy   (hŭz′ ĭ)
  hus·sies
hus·tings   (hŭs′ tĭngz)
hus·tle   (hŭs′ 'l)
  -tling
hy·a·cinth   (hī′ a·sĭnth)
hy·brid   (hī′ brĭd)
  hy·brid·i·za·tion
       (hī′ brĭd·ĭ·zā′ shŭn)
hy·drant   (hī′ drănt)
hy·drate   (hī′ drāt)
  -drat·ing
  hy·dra·tion   (hī·drā′ shŭn)
hy·drau·lic   (hī·drô′ lĭk)
  -li·cal·ly
hy·dro·car·bon
      (hī′ drŏ·kär′ bŏn)
hy·dro·chlo·ric   (hī′ drŏ·klō′ rĭk)
hy·dro·dy·nam·ics
      (hī′ drŏ·dī·năm′ ĭks)
hy·dro·e·lec·tric
      (hī′ drŏ·ê·lĕk′ trĭk)
hy·dro·gen   (hī′ drŏ·jĕn)
  hy·dro·gen per·ox·ide
hy·dro·gen·ate   (hī′ drŏ·jĕn·āt)
  -at·ing
  hy·dro·gen·a·tion
      (hī′ drŏ·jĕn·ā′ shŭn)
hy·drol·y·sis   (hī·drŏl′ ĭ·sĭs)
hy·drom·e·ter   (hī·drŏm′ ê·tēr)
hy·dro·pho·bi·a
      (hī′ drŏ·fō′ bĭ·a)
hy·dro·ther·a·py
      (hī′ drŏ·thĕr′ a·pĭ)
hy·drox·ide   (hī·drŏk′ sīd)
hy·giene   (hī′ jēn)
  hy·gi·en·ic   (hī′ jĭ·ĕn′ ĭk)
hy·men   (hī′ mĕn)
hymn   (hĭm)
  hym·nal   (hĭm′ năl)
  hym·nol·o·gy   (hĭm·nŏl′ ŏ·jĭ)
hy·per·   (hī′ pēr)
  hy·per·a·cid·i·ty
  hy·per·ac·tive hy·per·crit·i·cal
  hy·per·sen·si·tive
  hy·per·son·ic hy·per·ten·sion
hy·per·bo·le   (hī·pûr′ bŏ·lē)
hy·phen   (hī′ fĕn)
  hy·phen·a·tion
      (hī′ fĕn·ā′ shŭn)
hyp·no·sis   (hĭp·nō′ sĭs)
  hyp·not·ic   (hĭp·nŏt′ ĭk)
  hyp·no·tist   (hĭp′ nŏ·tĭst)
  hyp·no·tize   (hĭp′ nŏ·tīz)
  -tiz·ing

hy·po·chon·dri·a
      (hī′ pŏ·kŏn′ drĭ·a)
  hy·po·chon·dri·ac (-ăk)
hy·poc·ri·sy   (hĭ·pŏk′ rĭ·sĭ)
  -sies
hyp·o·crite   (hĭp′ ŏ·krĭt)
hyp·o·crit·i·cal
      (hĭp′ ŏ·krĭt′ ĭ·kăl)
hy·po·der·mic   (hī′ pŏ·dûr′ mĭk)
hy·po·ten·sion   (hī′ pŏ·tĕn′ shŭn)
hy·pot·e·nuse   (hĭ·pŏt′ ê·nūs)
hy·po·thal·a·mus
      (hī′ pŏ·thăl′ a·mŭs)
hy·poth·e·sis   (hĭ·pŏth′ ê·sĭs)
  pl. hy·poth·e·ses
  hy·poth·e·size -siz·ing
  hy·po·thet·i·cal
      (hī′ pŏ·thĕt′ ĭ·kăl)
hys·sop   (hĭs′ ŭp)
hys·ter·ec·to·my
      (hĭs′ tēr·ĕk′ tŏ·mĭ)
hys·te·ri·a   (hĭs·tēr′ ĭ·a)
  hys·ter·i·cal (-tēr′ ĭ·kăl)
  hys·ter·ics   (-tēr′ ĭks)

I

i·am·bic   (ĭ·ăm′ bĭk)
i·bi·dem   (ĭ·bĭ′ dĕm)
  abbr. ibid.
i·bis   (ī′ bĭs)
Ib·sen, Hen·rik
      (ĭb′ s'n, hĕn′ rĭk)
ice   (īs)
  ice bag   ice·berg
  ice·boat   ice·break·er
  ice·cap   ice cream
  ice·house   ice·man
  ice pack
Ice·land   (īs′ lănd)
  Ice·lan·dic   (īs·lăn′ dĭk)
ich·thy·ol·o·gy   (ĭk′ thĭ·ŏl′ ŏ·jĭ)
i·ci·cle   (ī′ sĭk·'l)
ic·ing   (īs′ ĭng)
i·con   (ī′ kŏn)
  i·con·o·clast (ĭ·kŏn′ ŏ·klăst)
  i·co·nog·ra·phy
      (ī′ kŏ·nŏg′ ra·fĭ)
i·cy   (ī′ sĭ)
  i·ci·ly   (ī′ sĭ·lĭ)
I·da·ho   (ī′ da·hō)
  abbr. Ida.
  I·da·ho·an   (-hō′ ăn)
i·de·a   (ī·dē′ a)

i·de·al (ĭ·dē′ ăl)
  i·de·al·ism
  i·de·al·is·tic (ĭ·dē′ ăl·ĭs′ tĭk)
  i·de·al·i·za·tion
    (ĭ·dē′ ăl·ĭ·zā′ shŭn)
  i·de·al·ly
i·de·a·tion (ĭ′ dē·ā′ shŭn)
i·den·ti·cal (ĭ·dĕn′ tĭ·kăl)
i·den·ti·fy (ĭ·dĕn′ tĭ·fī)
  -fied,   -fy·ing
  i·den·ti·fi·ca·tion
    (ĭ·dĕn′ tĭ·fī·kā′ shŭn)
id·e·ol·o·gy (ĭd′ ê·ŏl′ ŏ·jĭ)
  -gies
  id·e·o·log·i·cal
    (ĭd′ ê·ŏ·lŏj′ ĭ·kăl)
ides of March (īdz)
id·i·o·cy (ĭd′ ĭ·ŏ·sĭ)
id·i·om (ĭd′ ĭ·ŭm)
  id·i·o·mat·ic (ĭd′ ĭ·ŏ·măt′ ĭk)
  -i·cal·ly
id·i·o·syn·cra·sy
    (ĭd′ ĭ·ŏ·sĭng′ krá·sĭ)
id·i·ot (ĭd′ ĭ·ŭt)
  id·i·o·cy (ĭd′ ĭ·ŏ·sĭ)
  id·i·ot·ic (ĭd′ ĭ·ŏt′ ĭk)
i·dle (ī′ d′l)
  (inactive; see *idol, idyl*)
  i·dle·ness
  i·dly
i·dol (ī′ dŭl)
  (deity; see *idle, idyl*)
  i·dol·a·ter (ĭ·dŏl′ á·tēr)
  i·dol·a·trous (ĭ·dŏl′ á·trŭs)
  i·dol·a·try (ĭ·dŏl′ á·trĭ)
  -tries
  i·dol·i·za·tion
    (ī′ dŭl·ĭ·zā′ shŭn)
  i·dol·ize (ī′ dŭl·ĭz)
  -iz·ing
i·dyl (ī′ dĭl)
  (literary work; see *idle, idol*)
  i·dyl·lic (ĭ·dĭl′ ĭk)
ig·loo (ĭg′ lōō)
ig·ne·ous (ĭg′ nê·ŭs)
ig·nite (ĭg·nīt′)
  -nit·ing   ig·nit·i·ble
ig·ni·tion (ĭg·nĭsh′ ŭn)
ig·no·ble (ĭg·nō′ b′l)
ig·no·min·i·ous
    (ĭg′ nŏ·mĭn′ ĭ·ŭs)
  ig·no·min·y (ĭg′ nŏ·mĭn·ĭ)
  -min·ies
ig·no·ra·mus (ĭg′ nŏ·rā′ mŭs)

ig·no·rance (ĭg′ nŏ·răns)
  -rant
ig·nore (ĭg·nōr′)
  -nor·ing
i·gua·na (ĭ·gwä′ ná)
Il·i·ad (ĭl′ ĭ·ăd)
ill (ĭl)
  ill-ad·vised   ill-bred
  ill-con·ceived   ill-de·fined
  ill-fat·ed   ill-got·ten
  ill-hu·mored   ill-kept
  ill-man·nered   ill-na·tured
  ill-starred   ill tem·per
  ill-tem·pered   ill-treat·ment
  ill-us·age
il·le·gal (ĭl·lē′ găl)
  -gal·ly
il·le·gal·i·ty (ĭl′ lê·găl′ ĭ·tĭ)
il·leg·i·ble (ĭl·lĕj′ ĭ·b′l)
il·le·git·i·mate (ĭl′ lê·jĭt′ ĭ·mĭt)
  -ma·cy
il·lib·er·al (ĭl·lĭb′ ēr·ăl)
il·lic·it (ĭl·lĭs′ ĭt)
  (unlawful; see *elicit*)
il·lim·i·ta·ble (ĭl·lĭm′ ĭt·á·b′l)
Il·li·nois (ĭl′ ĭ·noi′)
  abbr. Ill
  Il·li·nois·an (-noi′ ăn)
il·lit·er·a·cy (ĭl·lĭt′ ēr·á·sĭ)
  -er·ate
il·log·i·cal (ĭl·lŏj′ ĭ·kăl)
  -cal·ly
il·lume (ĭ·lūm′)
  il·lum·ing
il·lu·mi·nate (ĭ·lū′ mĭ·nāt)
  -nat·ing
  il·lu·mi·nant (ĭ·lū′ mĭ·nănt)
  il·lu·mi·na·tion
    (ĭ·lū′ mĭ·nā′ shŭn)
il·lu·sion (ĭ·lū′ zhŭn)
  (misconception; see *allusion*)
  il·lu·sion·al
il·lu·sive (ĭ·lū′ sĭv)
  (unreal; see *elusive*)
il·lu·so·ry (ĭ·lū′ sŏ·rĭ)
il·lus·trate (ĭl′ ŭs·trāt)
  -trat·ing
  il·lus·tra·tion (ĭl′ ŭs·trā′ shŭn)
  il·lus·tra·tive (ĭ·lŭs′ trá·tĭv)
  il·lus·tra·tor
il·lus·tri·ous (ĭ·lŭs′ trĭ·ŭs)
im·age (ĭm′ ĭj)
  im·age·ry (ĭm′ ĭj·rĭ)
im·ag·ine (ĭ·măj′ ĭn)
  -in·ing   im·ag·i·na·ble

im·ag·i·nar·y
im·ag·i·na·tion
        (ĭ·măj′ ĭ·nā′ shŭn)
im·ag·i·na·tive
        (ĭ·măj′ ĭ·nā′ tĭv)
im·bal·ance   (ĭm·băl′ ăns)
im·be·cile   (ĭm′ bĕ·sĭl)
  im·be·cil·i·ty (ĭm′ bĕ·sĭl′ ĭ·tĭ)
im·bibe   (ĭm·bīb′)
  -bib·ing
im·bro·glio   (ĭm·brōl′ yō)
im·bue   (ĭm·bū′)
  -bu·ing
im·i·tate   (ĭm′ ĭ·tāt)
  -tat·ing
  im·i·ta·ble   (ĭm′ ĭ·tȧ·b'l)
  im·i·ta·tive   (ĭm′ ĭ·tā′ tĭv)
  im·i·ta·tor
im·mac·u·late   (ĭ·măk′ û·lĭt)
  Im·mac·u·late Con·cep·tion
im·ma·nent   (ĭm′ ȧ·nĕnt)
  (indwelling; see *imminent*)
  im·ma·nence
im·ma·te·ri·al   (ĭm′ mȧ·tẽr′ ĭ·ȧl)
im·ma·ture   (ĭm′ ȧ·tūr′)
  im·ma·tu·ri·ty
im·meas·ur·a·ble
        (ĭ·mĕzh′ ẽr·ȧ·b'l)
im·me·di·ate   (ĭ·mē′ dĭ·ĭt)
  im·me·di·a·cy (-dĭ·ȧ·sĭ)
  im·me·di·ate·ly
im·me·mo·ri·al
        (ĭm′ mĕ·mō′ rĭ·ȧl)
im·mense   (ĭ·mĕns′)
  im·men·si·ty
im·merse   (ĭ·mûrs′)
  im·mers·ing
  im·mer·sion   (ĭ·mûr′ shŭn)
im·mi·grate   (ĭm′ ĭ·grāt)
  (to enter a country; see *emigrate*)
  -grat·ing   im·mi·grant
  im·mi·gra·tion
        (ĭm′ ĭ·grā′ shŭn)
im·mi·nent   (ĭm′ ĭ·nĕnt)
  (about to happen; see *immanent*)
  im·mi·nence
im·mo·bile   (ĭm·mō′ bĭl)
  im·mo·bil·i·ty (ĭm′ ō·bĭl′ ĭ·tĭ)
  im·mo·bi·lized (ĭm·mō′ bĭ·līzd)
im·mod·er·ate   (ĭm·mŏd′ ẽr·ĭt)
im·mod·est   (ĭm·mŏd′ ĕst)
im·mo·late   (ĭm′ ō·lāt)
  -lat·ing
  im·mo·la·tion   (ĭm′ ō·lā′ shŭn)

im·mor·al   (ĭm·mŏr′ ăl)
  (not moral)
  im·mo·ral·i·ty
        (ĭm′ mō·răl′ ĭ·tĭ)
im·mor·tal   (ĭ·môr′ tăl)
  (deathless)
  im·mor·tal·i·ty
        (ĭm′ ôr·tăl′ ĭ·tĭ)
  im·mor·tal·ize (ĭ·môr′ tăl·īz)
  -iz·ing
im·mov·a·ble   (ĭm·mōōv′ ȧ·b'l)
im·mune   (ĭ·mūn′)
  im·mu·ni·ty   (ĭ·mū′ nĭ·tĭ)
  -ties
  im·mu·ni·za·tion
        (ĭm′ û·nĭ·zā′ shŭn)
im·mu·ta·ble   (ĭ·mū′ tȧ·b'l)
im·pact·ed   (ĭm·păk′ tĕd)
  im·pac·tion   (ĭm·păk′ shŭn)
im·pair·ment   (ĭm·pâr′ mĕnt)
im·pale   (ĭm·pāl′)
  -pal·ing
im·pal·pa·ble   (ĭm·păl′ pȧ·b'l)
im·part   (ĭm·pärt′)
im·par·tial   (ĭm·pär′ shăl)
  -tial·ly
  im·par·ti·al·i·ty
        (ĭm′ pär·shĭ·ăl′ ĭ·tĭ)
im·pass·a·ble   (ĭm·păs′ ȧ·b'l)
im·passe   (ĭm·pȧs′)
im·pas·sioned   (ĭm·păsh′ ŭnd)
im·pas·sive   (ĭm·păs′ ĭv)
im·pa·tient   (ĭm·pā′ shĕnt)
  -tience
im·peach   (ĭm·pēch′)
im·pec·ca·ble   (ĭm·pĕk′ ȧ·b'l)
im·pe·cu·ni·ous
        (ĭm′ pĕ·kū′ nĭ·ŭs)
im·pede   (ĭm·pēd′)
  -ped·ing
  im·ped·i·ment (ĭm·pĕd′ ĭ·mĕnt)
im·pel   (ĭm·pĕl′)
  -pelled   -pel·ling
im·pend·ing   (ĭm·pĕnd′ ĭng)
im·pen·e·tra·ble
        (ĭm·pĕn′ ĕ·trȧ·b'l)
  im·pen·e·tra·bil·i·ty
        (ĭm·pĕn′ ĕ·trȧ·bĭl′ ĭ·tĭ)
im·pen·i·tence   (ĭm·pĕn′ ĭ·tĕns)
im·per·a·tive   (ĭm·pĕr′ ȧ·tĭv)
im·per·cep·ti·ble
        (ĭm′ pẽr·sĕp′ tĭ·b'l)
im·per·cep·tive   (-tĭv)
im·per·fect   (ĭm·pûr′ fĕkt)

im·pe·ri·al (ĭm·pḗr′ ĭ·ᴅl)
  im·pe·ri·al·is·tic
         (ĭm·pḗr′ ĭ·ᴅl·ĭs′ tĭk)
im·pe·ri·ous (ĭm·pḗr′ ĭ·ŭs)
im·per·ish·a·ble
        (ĭm·pḗr′ ĭsh·à·b′l)
im·per·ma·nent
        (ĭm·pûr′ mà·nĕnt)
  -nence
im·per·me·a·ble
        (ĭm·pûr′ mĕ·à·b′l)
im·per·son·al (ĭm·pûr′ sŭn·ᴅl)
  -al·ly
im·per·son·ate (ĭm·pûr′ sŭn·āt)
  -at·ing
  im·per·son·a·tion
     (ĭm·pûr′ sŭn·ā′ shŭn)
  im·per·son·a·tor
im·per·ti·nence
      (ĭm·pûr′ tĭ·nĕns)
im·per·turb·a·ble
     (ĭm′ pēr·tûr′ bà·b′l)
im·per·vi·ous (ĭm·pûr′ vĭ·ŭs)
im·pe·ti·go (ĭm′ pĕ·tī′ gō)
im·pet·u·ous (ĭm·pĕt′ û·ŭs)
  (impulsive)
  im·pet·u·os·i·ty
     (ĭm·pĕt′ û·ŏs′ ĭ·tĭ)
im·pe·tus (ĭm′ pĕ·tŭs)
  (momentum)
im·pi·e·ty (ĭm·pī′ ĕ·tĭ)
  -ties
im·pi·ous (ĭm·pī′ ŭs)
im·pinge (ĭm·pĭnj)
  -ping·ing
imp·ish (ĭmp′ ĭsh)
im·pla·ca·ble (ĭm·plā′ kà·b′l)
im·plant (ĭm·plánt′)
im·plau·si·ble (ĭm·plô′ zĭ·b′l)
im·ple·ment (ĭm′ plĕ·mĕnt)
  im·ple·men·ta·tion
    (ĭm′ plĕ·mĕn·tā′ shŭn)
im·pli·cate (ĭm′ plĭ·kāt)
  -cat·ing
  im·pli·ca·tion
     (ĭm′ plĭ·kā′ shŭn)
im·plic·it (ĭm·plĭs′ ĭt)
im·plore (ĭm·plōr′)
  -plor·ing
im·ply (ĭm·plī′)
  -plied -ply·ing
im·po·lite (ĭm′ pô·līt′)
  im·po·lite·ness
im·pol·i·tic (ĭm·pŏl′ ĭ·tĭk)

im·pon·der·a·ble
     (ĭm·pŏn′ dēr·à·b′l)
im·port (ĭm·pōrt′) v.
     (ĭm′ pōrt) n.
  im·port·a·ble (ĭm·pōr′ tà·b′l)
  im·por·ta·tion
     (ĭm′ pôr·tā′ shŭn)
im·por·tance (ĭm·pôr′ tᴅns)
  -tant
im·por·tu·nate (ĭm·pôr′ tû·nĭt)
im·por·tune (ĭm′ pôr·tûn′)
im·pos·ing (ĭm·pōz′ ĭng)
im·po·si·tion (ĭm′ pô·zĭsh′ ŭn)
im·pos·si·ble (ĭm·pŏs′ ĭ·b′l)
  -bly
  im·pos·si·bil·i·ty
    (ĭm·pŏs′ ĭ·bĭl′ ĭ·tĭ)
im·pos·tor (ĭm·pŏs′ tēr)
im·pos·ture (ĭm·pŏs′ tûr)
im·po·tent (ĭm′ pô·tĕnt)
  -tence
im·pound (ĭm·pound′)
im·pov·er·ish (ĭm·pŏv′ ēr·ĭsh)
im·prac·ti·ca·ble
    (ĭm·prăk′ tĭ·kà·b′l)
im·prac·ti·cal (ĭm·prăk′ tĭ·kᴅl)
  im·prac·ti·cal·i·ty
    (ĭm·prăk′ tĭ·kăl′ ĭ·tĭ)
im·pre·cate (ĭm′ prĕ·kāt)
  -cat·ing
  im·pre·ca·tion
     (ĭm′ prĕ·kā′ shŭn)
im·preg·na·ble
    (ĭm·prĕg′ nà·b′l)
im·preg·nate (ĭm·prĕg′ nāt)
  -nat·ing
im·pre·sa·ri·o (ĭm′ prå·sä′ rĭ·ō)
im·press (ĭm′ prĕs) n.
im·press (ĭm·prĕs′) v.
  im·press·i·ble
  im·pres·sion (ĭm·prĕsh′ ŭn)
  im·pres·sion·a·ble
  im·pres·sion·is·tic
    (ĭm·prĕsh′ ŭn·ĭs′ tĭk)
  im·pres·sive
im·pri·ma·tur (ĭm′ prĭ·mā′ tēr)
im·print (ĭm·prĭnt′) v.
     (ĭm′ prĭnt) n.
im·pris·on (ĭm·prĭz′′n)
  im·pris·on·ment
im·prob·a·ble (ĭm·prŏb′ à·b′l)
  im·prob·a·bil·i·ty
    (ĭm′ prŏb·à·bĭl′ ĭ·tĭ)
im·promp·tu (ĭm·prŏmp′ tū)
im·prop·er (ĭm·prŏp′ ēr)

im·pro·pri·e·ty
       (ĭm′ prô·prī′ ĕ·tĭ)
 -ties
im·prove   (ĭm·prōōv′)
 -prov·ing   im·prov·a·ble
im·prove·ment
im·prov·i·dent (ĭm·prŏv′ ĭ·děnt)
 -dence
im·pro·vise (ĭm′ prô·vīz)
 -vis·ing
im·pro·vi·sa·tion
    (ĭm′ prô·vī·zā′ shŭn)
im·pru·dent (ĭm·prōō′ děnt)
 -dence
im·pugn (ĭm·pūn′)
im·pulse (ĭm′ pŭls)
 im·pul·sion (ĭm·pŭl′ shŭn)
 im·pul·sive (ĭm·pŭl′ sĭv)
im·pu·ni·ty (ĭm·pū′ nĭ·tĭ)
im·pure (ĭm·pūr′)
 im·pu·ri·ty -ties
im·pute (ĭm·pūt′)
 -put·ing im·put·a·ble
im·pu·ta·tion
    (ĭm′ pû·tā′ shŭn)
in·a·bil·i·ty (ĭn′ à·bĭl′ ĭ·tĭ)
 -ties
in ab·sen·ti·a (ĭn ăb·sĕn′ shĭ·à)
in·ac·ces·si·ble (ĭn′ ăk·sĕs′ ĭ·b'l)
in·ac·cu·ra·cy (ĭn·ăk′ û·rà·sĭ)
 -cies
 in·ac·cu·rate -rate·ly
in·ac·tive (ĭn·ăk′ tĭv)
 in·ac·tiv·i·ty (ĭn′ ăk·tĭv′ ĭ·tĭ)
in·ad·e·quate (ĭn·ăd′ ê·kwĭt)
 -qua·cy
in·ad·mis·si·ble
    (ĭn′ ăd·mĭs′ ĭ·b'l)
in·ad·vert·ence
    (ĭn′ ăd·vûr′ těns)
 -ent
in·ad·vis·a·ble
    (ĭn′ ăd·vīz′ à·b'l)
in·al·ien·a·ble (ĭn·āl′ yěn·à·b'l)
in·al·ter·a·ble (ĭn·ôl′ těr·à·b'l)
in·am·o·ra·ta (ĭn·ăm′ ô·rä′ tà)
in·ane (ĭn·ān′)
 in·an·i·ty (ĭn·ăn′ ĭ·tĭ)
in·an·i·mate (ĭn·ăn′ ĭ·măt)
in·ap·peas·a·ble
    (ĭn′ à·pēz′ à·b'l)
in·ap·pli·ca·ble
    (ĭn·ăp′ lĭ·kà·b'l)
in·ap·pre·ci·a·ble
    (ĭn′ à·prē′ shĭ·à·b'l)

in·ap·pre·ci·a·tive
    (ĭn′ à·prē′ shĭ·ā′ tĭv)
in·ap·proach·a·ble
    (ĭn′ à·prōch′ à·b'l)
in·ar·tic·u·late
    (ĭn′ är·tĭk′ û·lăt)
 -late·ly
in·ar·tis·tic (ĭn′ är·tĭs′ tĭk)
in·as·much as (ĭn′ ăz·mŭch′)
in·at·ten·tion (ĭn′ à·tĕn′ shŭn)
in·at·ten·tive (ĭn′ à·tĕn′ tĭv)
 -tive·ly
in·au·di·ble (ĭn·ô′ dĭ·b'l)
in·au·gu·ral (ĭn·ô′ gû·ràl)
in·au·gu·rate (ĭn·ô′ gû·rāt)
 -rat·ing
in·au·gu·ra·tion
    (ĭn·ô′ gû·rā′ shŭn)
in·aus·pi·cious
    (ĭn′ ôs·pĭsh′ ŭs)
in·born (ĭn′ bôrn′)
in·cal·cu·la·ble
    (ĭn·kăl′ kû·là·b'l)
in·can·des·cent
    (ĭn′ kăn·děs′ ěnt)
 -cence
in·can·ta·tion (ĭn′ kăn·tā′ shŭn)
in·ca·pa·ble (ĭn·kā′ pà·b'l)
in·ca·pa·cious (ĭn·kà·pā′ shŭs)
in·ca·pac·i·tate
    (ĭn′ kà·păs′ ĭ·tāt)
 -tat·ing
in·ca·pac·i·ta·tion
    (ĭn′ kà·păs′ ĭ·tā′ shŭn)
in·car·cer·ate (ĭn·kär′ sěr·āt)
 -at·ing
in·car·cer·a·tion
    (ĭn·kär′ sěr·ā′ shŭn)
in·car·nate (ĭn·kär′ năt)
 in·car·na·tion (ĭn′ kär·nā′ shŭn)
in·cau·tious (ĭn·kô′ shŭs)
in·cen·di·ar·y (ĭn·sĕn′ dĭ·ěr′ ĭ)
in·cense (ĭn·sĕns′) *v.*
 -cens·ing (ĭn′ sĕns) *n.*
in·cen·tive (ĭn·sĕn′ tĭv)
in·cep·tion (ĭn·sĕp′ shŭn)
in·ces·sant·ly (ĭn·sĕs′ ănt·lĭ)
in·cest (ĭn′ sĕst)
 in·ces·tu·ous (ĭn·sĕs′ tû·ŭs)
in·cho·ate (ĭn·kō′ ĭt)
in·ci·dent (ĭn′ sĭ·děnt)
 in·ci·dence
 in·ci·den·tal (ĭn′ sĭ·děn′ tăl)
 -tal·ly

in·cin·er·ate   (ĭn·sĭn′ ĕr·āt)
 -at·ing   in·cin·er·a·tor
in·cip·i·ent   (ĭn·sĭp′ ĭ·ĕnt)
 -ence
in·cise   (ĭn·sīz′)
 -cis·ing
in·ci·sion   (ĭn·sĭzh′ ŭn)
in·ci·sive   (ĭn·sī′ sĭv)
in·ci·sor tooth   (ĭn·sī′ zĕr)
in·cite   (ĭn·sīt′)
 -cit·ing   in·cite·ment
in·clem·ent   (ĭn·klĕm′ ĕnt)
in·cline   (ĭn′ klīn) n.
in·cline   (ĭn·klīn′) v.
 -clin·ing   in·clin·a·ble
 in·cli·na·tion   (ĭn′ klĭ·nā′ shŭn)
in·clude   (ĭn·klōōd′)
 -clud·ing
in·clu·sion   (ĭn·klōō′ zhŭn)
in·clu·sive   -sive·ly
in·cog·ni·to   (ĭn·kŏg′ nĭ·tō)
in·co·her·ent   (ĭn′ kō·hĕr′ ĕnt)
 -ence
in·com·bus·ti·ble
                   (ĭn′ kŏm·bŭs′ tĭ·b'l)
in·come   (ĭn′ kŭm)
 in·com·ing   (ĭn′ kŭm′ ĭng)
in·com·men·su·rate
                   (ĭn′ kŏ·mĕn′ shŏō·rĭt)
 in·com·men·su·ra·ble
in·com·mo·di·ous
                   (ĭn′ kŏ·mō′ dĭ·ŭs)
in·com·mu·ni·ca·ble
                   (ĭn′ kŏ·mū′ nĭ·kȧ·b'l)
 in·com·mu·ni·ca·tive
in·com·mu·ni·ca·do
                   (ĭn′ kŏ·mū′ nĭ·kä′ dō)
in·com·pa·ra·ble
                   (ĭn·kŏm′ pȧ·rȧ·b'l)
in·com·pat·i·ble
                   (ĭn′ kŏm·păt′ ĭ·b'l)
 in·com·pat·i·bil·i·ty
                   (ĭn′ kŏm·păt′ ĭ·bĭl′ ĭ·tĭ)
in·com·pe·tence
                   (ĭn·kŏm′ pĕ·tĕns)
 -tent
in·com·plete   (ĭn′ kŏm·plēt′)
in·com·pli·ant   (ĭn′ kŏm·plī′ ȧnt)
in·com·pre·hen·si·ble
                   (ĭn′ kŏm·prĕ·hĕn′ sĭ·b'l)
in·con·ceiv·a·ble
                   (ĭn′ kŏn·sēv′ ȧ·b'l)
in·con·clu·sive
                   (ĭn′ kŏn·klōō′ sĭv)

in·con·gru·ous
                   (ĭn·kŏng′ grōō·ŭs)
 in·con·gru·i·ty
                   (ĭn′ kŏng·grōō′ ĭ·tĭ)
 -ties
in·con·se·quen·tial
                   (ĭn·kŏn′ sĕ·kwĕn′ shȧl)
in·con·sid·er·ate
                   (ĭn′ kŏn·sĭd′ ĕr·ĭt)
in·con·sist·ent
                   (ĭn′ kŏn·sĭs′ tĕnt)
 -ten·cy
in·con·sol·a·ble
                   (ĭn′ kŏn·sōl′ ȧ·b'l)
in·con·so·nant   (ĭn·kŏn′ sŏ·nȧnt)
 -nance
in·con·spic·u·ous
                   (ĭn′ kŏn·spĭk′ û·ŭs)
in·con·stant   (ĭn·kŏn′ stȧnt)
 -stan·cy
in·con·test·a·ble
                   (ĭn′ kŏn·tĕs′ tȧ·b'l)
in·con·ti·nent   (ĭn·kŏn′ tĭ·nĕnt)
 -nence
in·con·tro·vert·i·ble
                   (ĭn′ kŏn·trŏ·vûr′ tĭ·b'l)
in·con·ven·ient
                   (ĭn′ kŏn·vēn′ yĕnt)
 -ience
in·cor·po·rat·ed
                   (ĭn·kôr′ pŏ·rāt′ ĕd)
in·cor·rect·ly   (ĭn′ kŏ·rĕkt′ lĭ)
in·cor·ri·gi·ble
                   (ĭn·kŏr′ ĭ·jĭ·b'l)
 in·cor·ri·gi·bil·i·ty
                   (ĭn·kŏr′ ĭ·jĭ·bĭl′ ĭ·tĭ)
in·cor·rupt·i·ble
                   (ĭn′ kŏ·rŭp′ tĭ·b'l)
in·crease   (ĭn′ krēs) n.
 -creas·ing   (ĭn·krēs′) v.
in·cred·i·ble   (ĭn·krĕd′ ĭ·b'l)
 in·cred·i·bil·i·ty
                   (ĭn·krĕd′ ĭ·bĭl′ ĭ·tĭ)
in·cred·u·lous   (ĭn·krĕd′ û·lŭs)
 in·cre·du·li·ty   (ĭn′ krĕ·dū′ lĭ·tĭ)
in·cre·ment   (ĭn′ krĕ·mĕnt)
in·crim·i·nat·ing
                   (ĭn·krĭm′ ĭ·nāt′ ĭng)
in·crus·ta·tion   (ĭn′ krŭs·tā′ shŭn)
in·cu·bate   (ĭn′ kŭ·bāt)
 -bat·ing
 in·cu·ba·tion   (ĭn′ kŭ·bā′ shŭn)
 in·cu·ba·tor   (ĭn′ kŭ·bā′ tĕr)
in·cu·bus   (ĭn′ kŭ·bŭs)

in·cul·cate   (ĭn·kŭl′ kāt)
-cat·ing
in·cul·ca·tion
     (ĭn′ kŭl·kā′ shŭn)
in·cul·pate   (ĭn·kŭl′ pāt)
-pat·ing
in·cum·bent   (ĭn·kŭm′ bĕnt)
-ben·cy
in·cur   (ĭn·kûr′)
-curred   -cur·ring
in·cur·a·ble   (ĭn·kûr′ à·b'l)
in·cur·sion   (ĭn·kûr′ zhŭn)
in·debt·ed·ness   (ĭn·dĕt′ ĕd·nĕs)
in·de·cen·cy   (ĭn·dē′ sĕn·sĭ)
in·de·ci·pher·a·ble
     (ĭn′ dē·sī′ fēr·à·b'l)
in·de·ci·sive   (ĭn′ dē·sī′ sĭv)
in·de·ci·sion   (ĭn′ dē·sĭzh′ ŭn)
in·dec·o·rous   (ĭn·dĕk′ ô·rŭs)
in·de·co·rum   (ĭn′ dē·kō′ rŭm)
in·deed   (ĭn·dēd′)
in·de·fat·i·ga·ble
     (ĭn′ dē·făt′ ĭ·gà·b'l)
in·de·fat·i·ga·bil·i·ty
     (ĭn′ dē·făt′ ĭ·gà·bĭl′ ĭ·tĭ)
in·de·fea·si·ble   (ĭn′ dē·fē′ zĭ·b'l)
in·de·fen·si·ble
     (ĭn′ dē·fĕn′ sĭ·b'l)
in·de·fin·a·ble
     (ĭn′ dē·fīn′ a·b'l)
in·def·i·nite   (ĭn·dĕf′ ĭ·nĭt)
-nite·ly
in·del·i·ble   (ĭn·dĕl′ ĭ·b'l)
in·del·i·cate   (ĭn·dĕl′ ĭ·kĭt)
-ca·cy
in·dem·ni·fy   (ĭn·dĕm′ nĭ·fī)
-fied   -fy·ing
in·dem·ni·ty   (ĭn·dĕm′ nĭ·tĭ)
-ties
in·den·ta·tion   (ĭn′ dĕn·tā′ shŭn)
in·den·ture   (ĭn·dĕn′ tûr)
in·de·pend·ence
     (ĭn′ dē·pĕn′ dĕns)
-dent
in·de·scrib·a·ble
     (ĭn′ dē·skrīb′ à·b'l)
in·de·struct·i·ble
     (ĭn′ dē·strŭk′ tĭ·b'l)
in·de·ter·mi·na·ble
     (ĭn′ dē·tûr′ mĭ·nà·b'l)
in·de·ter·mi·nate
     (ĭn′ dē·tûr′ mĭ·nåt)
in·dex   (ĭn′ dĕks)
-dex·es
In·di·a ink   (ĭn′ dĭ·à)

In·di·an·a   (ĭn′ dĭ·ăn′ à)
    abbr. Ind.
In·di·an·i·an   (ăn′ ĭ·ăn)
in·di·cate   (ĭn′ dĭ·kāt)
-cat·ing
in·di·ca·tion   (ĭn′ dĭ·kā′ shŭn)
in·dic·a·tive   (ĭn·dĭk′ à·tĭv)
in·di·ca·tor
in·dict   (ĭn·dīt′)
in·dict·ment
in·dif·fer·ence   (ĭn·dĭf′ ēr·ĕns)
in·di·gence   (ĭn′ dĭ·jĕns)
in·dig·e·nous   (ĭn·dĭj′ ê·nŭs)
in·di·ges·tion   (ĭn′ dĭ·jĕs′ chŭn)
in·di·gest·i·ble
in·dig·nant   (ĭn·dĭg′ nånt)
-nance
in·dig·na·tion
     (ĭn′ dĭg·nā′ shŭn)
in·dig·ni·ty   (ĭn·dĭg′ nĭ·tĭ)
-ties
in·di·go   (ĭn′ dĭ·gō)
in·di·rect   (ĭn′ dĭ·rĕkt′)
in·dis·cern·i·ble
     (ĭn′ dĭ·zûr′ nĭ·b'l)
in·dis·creet   (ĭn′ dĭs·krēt′)
in·dis·cre·tion
     (ĭn′ dĭs·krĕsh′ ŭn)
in·dis·crim·i·nate
     (ĭn′ dĭs·krĭm′ ĭ·nĭt)
in·dis·pen·sa·ble
     (ĭn′ dĭs·pĕn′ sà·b'l)
in·dis·posed   (ĭn′ dĭs·pōzd′)
in·dis·pu·ta·ble
     (ĭn·dĭs′ pû·tà·b'l)
in·dis·sol·u·ble
     (ĭn′ dĭ·sŏl′ û·b'l)
in·dis·tinct   (ĭn′ dĭs·tĭngkt′)
in·dis·tin·guish·a·ble
     (ĭn′ dĭs·tĭng′ gwĭsh·à·b'l)
in·di·vid·u·al   (ĭn′ dĭ·vĭd′ û·ål)
in·di·vid·u·al·ism, -al·ist
in·di·vid·u·al·i·ty
     (ĭn′ dĭ·vĭd′ û·ăl′ ĭ·tĭ)
in·di·vid·u·al·ize, -iz·ing
in·di·vid·u·al·ly
in·di·vis·i·ble   (ĭn′ dĭ·vĭz′ ĭ·b'l)
In·do·chi·na   (ĭn′ dô·chī′ nà)
in·doc·tri·nate   (ĭn·dŏk′ trĭ·nāt)
-nat·ing
in·doc·tri·na·tion
     (ĭn·dŏk′ trĭ·nā′ shŭn)
in·do·lent   (ĭn′ dô·lĕnt)
-lence

in·dom·i·ta·ble
       (ĭn·dŏm′ ĭ·tȧ·b'l)
In·do·ne·sia   (ĭn′ dō·nē′ zhȧ)
in·doors   (ĭn′ dōrz′)
in·du·bi·ta·ble   (ĭn·dū′ bĭ·tȧ·b'l)
in·duce   (ĭn·dūs′)
  -duc·ing   in·duce·ment
in·duct   (ĭn·dŭkt′)
  in·duc·tion   (ĭn·dŭk′ shŭn)
  in·duc·tive   in·duc·tor
in·due   (ĭn·dū′)
  -du·ing
in·dulge   (ĭn·dŭlj′)
  -dulg·ing
  in·dul·gent   -gence
in·dus·try   (ĭn′ dŭs·trĭ)
  -tries
  in·dus·tri·al   (ĭn·dŭs′ trĭ·ȧl)
  -al·ly   -al·ism
  in·dus·tri·al·ist
        (ĭn·dŭs′ trĭ·ȧl·ĭst)
  in·dus·tri·al·i·za·tion
       (ĭn·dŭs′ trĭ·ȧl·ĭ·zā′ shŭn)
  in·dus·tri·ous   (ĭn·dŭs′ trĭ·ŭs)
in·dwell·ing   (ĭn′ dwĕl′ ĭng)
in·e·bri·at·ed   (ĭn·ē′ brĭ·āt′ ĕd)
in·e·bri·a·tion
       (ĭn·ē′ brĭ·ā′ shŭn)
in·ed·i·ble   (ĭn·ĕd′ ĭ·b'l)
in·ef·fa·ble   (ĭn·ĕf′ ȧ·b'l)
in·ef·face·a·ble
       (ĭn′ ĕ·fās′ ȧ·b'l)
in·ef·fec·tive   (ĭn′ ĕ·fĕk′ tĭv)
in·ef·fec·tu·al   (ĭn′ ĕ·fĕk′ tů·ȧl)
  in·ef·fec·tu·al·i·ty
       (ĭn′ ĕ·fĕk′ tů·ȧl′ ĭ·tĭ)
in·ef·fi·ca·cious
       (ĭn·ĕf·ĭ·kā′ shŭs)
  in·ef·fi·ca·cy   (ĭn·ĕf′ ĭ·kȧ·sĭ)
in·ef·fi·cient   (ĭn′ ĕ·fĭsh′ ĕnt)
  -cien·cy
in·e·las·tic   (ĭn′ ē·lăs′ tĭk)
in·el·e·gance   (ĭn·ĕl′ ē·gȧns)
in·el·i·gi·ble   (ĭn·ĕl′ ĭ·jĭ·b'l)
  in·el·i·gi·bil·i·ty
       (ĭn·ĕl′ ĭ·jĭ·bĭl′ ĭ·tĭ)
in·e·luc·ta·ble   (ĭn′ ē·lŭk′ tȧ·b'l)
in·ept   (ĭn·ĕpt′)
  in·ept·i·tude   (ĭn·ĕpt′ ĭ·tūd)
in·e·qual·i·ty   (ĭn′ ē·kwŏl′ ĭ·tĭ)
  -ties
in·eq·ui·ta·ble
       (ĭn·ĕk′ wĭ·tȧ·b'l)
in·eq·ui·ty   (ĭn·ĕk′ wĭ·tĭ)
  -ties

in·e·rad·i·ca·ble
       (ĭn′ ē·răd′ ĭ·kȧ·b'l)
in·e·ras·a·ble   (ĭn′ ē·rās′ ȧ·b'l)
in·ert   (ĭn·ûrt′)
in·er·tia   (ĭn·ûr′ shȧ)
in·es·cap·a·ble
       (ĭn′ ĕs·kāp′ ȧ·b'l)
in·es·sen·tial   (ĭn′ ĕ·sĕn′ shȧl)
in·es·ti·ma·ble   (ĭn·ĕs′ tĭ·mȧ·b'l)
in·ev·i·ta·ble   (ĭn·ĕv′ ĭ·tȧ·b'l)
  in·ev·i·ta·bil·i·ty
       (ĭn·ĕv′ ĭ·tȧ·bĭl′ ĭ·tĭ)
in·ex·cus·a·ble
       (ĭn′ ĕks·kūz′ ȧ·b'l)
in·ex·haust·i·ble
       (ĭn′ ĕg·zôs′ tĭ·b'l)
in·ex·o·ra·ble   (ĭn·ĕk′ sō·rȧ·b'l)
in·ex·pe·di·ent
       (ĭn′ ĕks·pē′ dĭ·ĕnt)
in·ex·pen·sive   (ĭn′ ĕks·pĕn′ sĭv)
in·ex·pe·ri·enced
       (ĭn′ ĕks·pẽr′ ĭ·ĕnst)
in·ex·pert   (ĭn′ ĕks·pûrt′)
in·ex·pli·ca·ble
       (ĭn·ĕks′ plĭ·kȧ·b'l)
in·ex·press·i·ble
       (ĭn′ ĕks·prĕs′ ĭ·b'l)
  in·ex·pres·sive
in·ex·tri·ca·ble
       (ĭn·ĕks′ trĭ·kȧ·b'l)
in·fal·li·ble   (ĭn·făl′ ĭ·b'l)
  in·fal·li·bil·i·ty
       (ĭn·făl′ ĭ·bĭl′ ĭ·tĭ)
in·fa·mous   (ĭn′ fȧ·mŭs)
  in·fa·my   (ĭn′ fȧ·mĭ)
in·fant   (ĭn′ fȧnt)
  in·fan·cy
  in·fan·ti·cide   (ĭn·făn′ tĭ·sīd)
  in·fan·tile   (ĭn′ fȧn·tīl)
in·fan·try   (ĭn′ fȧn·trĭ)
  in·fan·try·man
in·fat·u·ate   (ĭn·făt′ û·āt)
  -at·ing
  in·fat·u·a·tion
       (ĭn·făt′ û·ā′ shŭn)
in·fec·tion   (ĭn·fĕk′ shŭn)
  in·fec·tious   (ĭn·fĕk′ shŭs)
in·fer   (ĭn·fûr′)
  -ferred   -fer·ring
  in·fer·ence   (ĭn′ fẽr·ĕns)
  in·fer·en·tial   (ĭn′ fẽr·ĕn′ shȧl)
in·fe·ri·or   (ĭn·fẽr′ ĭ·ẽr)
  in·fe·ri·or·i·ty com·plex
       (ĭn·fẽr′ ĭ·ŏr′ ĭ·tĭ)
in·fer·nal   (ĭn·fûr′ nȧl)

in·fer·no (ĭn·fûr′ nō)
in·fi·del (ĭn′ fĭ·dĕl)
in·fi·del·i·ty (ĭn′ fĭ·dĕl′ ĭ·tĭ)
in·field·er (ĭn′ fēl′ dēr)
in·fil·trate (ĭn·fĭl′ trāt)
-trat·ing
in·fil·tra·tion (ĭn′ fĭl·trā′ shŭn)
in·fi·nite (ĭn′ fĭ·nĭt)
in·fi·nite·ly
in·fin·i·tes·i·mal
     (ĭn′ fĭn·ĭ·tĕs′ ĭ·măl)
in·fin·i·tive (ĭn·fĭn′ ĭ·tĭv)
in·fin·i·ty (ĭn·fĭn′ ĭ·tĭ)
in·firm (ĭn·fûrm′)
in·fir·ma·ry (ĭn·fûr′ ma·rĭ)
-ries
in·fir·mi·ty (ĭn·fûr′ mĭ·tĭ)
-ties
in·flame (ĭn·flām′)
-flam·ing
in·flam·ma·ble (ĭn·flăm′ a·b'l)
in·flam·ma·to·ry
     (ĭn·flăm′ a·tō′ rĭ)
in·flam·ma·tion (ĭn′ flă·mā′ shŭn)
in·flate (ĭn·flāt′)
-flat·ing in·flat·a·ble
in·fla·tion (ĭn·flā′ shŭn)
in·fla·tion·ar·y
in·flec·tion (ĭn·flĕk′ shŭn)
-tion·al
in·flex·i·ble (ĭn·flĕk′ sĭ·b'l)
in·flex·i·bil·i·ty
     (ĭn·flĕk′ sĭ·bĭl′ ĭ·tĭ)
in·flict (ĭn·flĭkt′)
in·flic·tion (ĭn·flĭk′ shŭn)
in·flu·ence (ĭn′ floo·ĕns)
in·flu·en·tial (ĭn′ floo·ĕn′ shăl)
in·flu·en·za (ĭn′ floo·ĕn′ za)
in·flux (ĭn′ flŭks)
in·form (ĭn·fôrm′)
in·form·ant (ĭn·fôr′ mănt)
in·for·ma·tion
     (ĭn′ fŏr·mā′ shŭn)
in·form·a·tive (ĭn·fôr′ ma·tĭv)
in·form·er
in·for·mal (ĭn·fôr′ măl)
-mal·ly
in·for·mal·i·ty
     (ĭn′ fôr·măl′ ĭ·tĭ)
in·frac·tion (ĭn·frăk′ shŭn)
in·fra·red (ĭn′ frà·rĕd′)
in·fre·quent (ĭn·frē′ kwĕnt)
-quen·cy
in·fringe (ĭn·frĭnj′)
-fring·ing in·fringe·ment

in·fu·ri·ate (ĭn·fū′ rĭ·āt)
-at·ing
in·fuse (ĭn·fūz′)
-fus·ing
in·fu·sion (ĭn·fū′ zhŭn)
in·gen·ious (ĭn·jēn′ yŭs)
(clever; see *ingenuous*)
in·gé·nue (ăN′ zhā′ nū′)
in·ge·nu·i·ty (ĭn′ jĕ·nū′ ĭ·tĭ)
in·gen·u·ous (ĭn·jĕn′ û·ŭs)
(frank; see *ingenious*)
in·gen·u·ous·ness
in·gest (ĭn·jĕst′)
in·ges·tion
in·glo·ri·ous (ĭn·glō′ rĭ·ŭs)
in·got i·ron (ĭng′ gŏt)
in·grained (ĭn′ grānd′)
in·grate (ĭn′ grāt)
in·grat·i·tude (ĭn·grăt′ ĭ·tūd)
in·gra·ti·ate (ĭn·grā′ shĭ·āt)
-at·ing
in·gra·ti·a·tion
     (ĭn·grā′ shĭ·ā′ shŭn)
in·gre·di·ent (ĭn·grē′ dĭ·ĕnt)
in·grown (ĭn′ grōn′)
in·hab·it (ĭn·hăb′ ĭt)
-ited -it·ing
in·hab·it·a·ble
in·hab·it·an·cy
     (ĭn·hăb′ ĭ·tăn·sĭ)
in·hab·it·ant
in·hale (ĭn·hāl′)
-hal·ing
in·hal·ant (ĭn·hāl′ ănt)
in·ha·la·tion (ĭn′ hà·lā′ shŭn)
in·ha·la·tor (ĭn′ hà·lā′ tēr)
in·her·ent (ĭn·hĕr′ ĕnt)
-en·cy
in·her·it (ĭn·hĕr′ ĭt)
-it·ed -it·ing
in·her·it·a·ble in·her·it·ance
in·her·i·tor
in·hib·it (ĭn·hĭb′ ĭt)
-it·ed -it·ing
in·hi·bi·tion (ĭn′ hĭ·bĭsh′ ŭn)
in·hib·i·tor
in·hib·i·to·ry (ĭn·hĭb′ ĭ·tō′ rĭ)
in·hos·pi·ta·ble
     (ĭn·hŏs′ pĭ·tà·b'l)
in·hu·man (ĭn·hū′ măn)
in·hu·man·i·ty
     (ĭn′ hū·măn′ ĭ·tĭ)
in·hu·man·ness
in·hu·mane (ĭn′ hû·mān′)
-mane·ly

in·hume (ĭn·hūm′)
-hum·ing
in·im·i·cal (ĭn·ĭm′ ĭ·kăl)
in·im·i·ta·ble (ĭn·ĭm′ ĭ·tȧ·b'l)
in·iq·ui·tous (ĭ·nĭk′ wĭ·tŭs)
in·iq·ui·ty -ties
in·i·tial (ĭ·nĭsh′ ȧl)
-tialed -tial·ing
in·i·tial·ly
in·i·ti·ate (ĭ·nĭsh′ ĭ·āt)
-at·ing
in·i·ti·a·tion
(ĭ·nĭsh′ ĭ·ā′ shŭn)
in·i·ti·a·tive (ĭ·nĭsh′ ĭ·ā′ tĭv)
in·ject (ĭn·jĕkt′)
in·jec·tion in·jec·tor
in·ju·di·cious (ĭn′ jŏŏ·dĭsh′ ŭs)
in·junc·tion (ĭn·jŭngk′ shŭn)
in·jure (ĭn′ jẽr)
-jur·ing
in·ju·ri·ous (ĭn·jŏŏr′ ĭ·ŭs)
in·ju·ry (ĭn′ jẽr·ĭ)
-ries
in·jus·tice (ĭn·jŭs′ tĭs)
ink·ling (ĭngk′ lĭng)
in·laid (ĭn·lād′)
in·land (ĭn′ lănd)
in-law (ĭn′ lô′)
in·lay (ĭn′ lā′) n.
in·let (ĭn′ lĕt)
in·mate (ĭn′ māt)
in·most (ĭn′ mōst)
in·nards (ĭn′ ẽrdz)
in·nate (ĭn′ nāt)
in·ner·most (ĭn′ ẽr·mōst)
in·ner·vate (ĭ·nûr′ vāt)
(to supply with nerves; see ener-
vate)
-vat·ing
in·ner·va·tion (ĭn′ ẽr·vā′ shŭn)
in·ning (ĭn′ ĭng)
inn·keep·er (ĭn′ kĕp′ ẽr)
in·no·cent (ĭn′ ŏ·sĕnt)
-cence
in·noc·u·ous (ĭ·nŏk′ û·ŭs)
in·no·vate (ĭn′ ŏ·vāt)
-vat·ing
in·no·va·tion (ĭn′ ŏ·vā′ shŭn)
in·no·va·tor (ĭn′ ŏ·vā′ tẽr)
in·nu·en·do (ĭn′ û·ĕn′ dō)
-does
in·nu·mer·a·ble
(ĭ·nū′ mẽr·ȧ·b'l)
in·oc·u·late (ĭn·ŏk′ û·lāt)
-lat·ing

in·oc·u·la·tion
(ĭn·ŏk′ û·lā′ shŭn)
in·of·fen·sive (ĭn′ ŏ·fĕn′ sĭv)
in·op·er·a·ble (ĭn·ŏp′ ẽr·ȧ·b'l)
in·op·er·a·tive (ĭn·ŏp′ ẽr·ā′ tĭv)
in·op·por·tune (ĭn·ŏp′ ŏr·tūn′)
-tune·ly
in·or·di·nate (ĭn·ôr′ dĭ·nĭt)
in·or·gan·ic (ĭn′ ôr·găn′ ĭk)
in·put (ĭn′ pŏŏt′)
in·quest (ĭn′ kwĕst)
in·quire (ĭn·kwīr′)
-quir·ing
in·quir·y (ĭn·kwīr′ ĭ)
-quir·ies
in·qui·si·tion (ĭn′ kwĭ·zĭsh′ ŭn)
in·quis·i·tive (ĭn·kwĭz′ ĭ·tĭv)
in·quis·i·tor (ĭn·kwĭz′ ĭ·tẽr)
in·quis·i·to·ri·al
(ĭn·kwĭz′ ĭ·tō′ rĭ·ȧl)
in·rush·ing (ĭn′ rŭsh′ ĭng)
in·sane (ĭn·sān′)
in·san·i·ty (ĭn·săn′ ĭ·tĭ)
in·sa·ti·a·ble (ĭn·sā′ shĭ·ȧ·b'l)
in·scribe (ĭn·skrīb′)
-scrib·ing
in·scrip·tion (ĭn·skrĭp′ shŭn)
in·scru·ta·ble (ĭn·skrŏŏ′ tȧ·b'l)
in·sect (ĭn′ sĕkt)
in·sec·ti·cide (ĭn·sĕk′ tĭ·sīd)
in·se·cure (ĭn′ sĕ·kūr′)
in·se·cu·ri·ty (ĭn′ sĕ·kū′ rĭ·tĭ)
in·sem·i·na·tion
(ĭn·sĕm′ ĭ·nā′ shŭn)
in·sen·sate (ĭn·sĕn′ săt)
in·sen·si·ble (ĭn·sĕn′ sĭ·b'l)
in·sen·si·tive (ĭn·sĕn′ sĭ·tĭv)
in·sen·si·tiv·i·ty
(ĭn·sĕn′ sĭ·tĭv′ ĭ·tĭ)
in·sep·a·ra·ble (ĭn·sĕp′ ȧ·rȧ·b'l)
in·sert (ĭn·sûrt′) v.
(ĭn′ sûrt) n.
in·ser·tion (ĭn·sûr′ shŭn)
in·sid·i·ous (ĭn·sĭd′ ĭ·ŭs)
in·sight (ĭn′ sīt′)
in·sig·ni·a (ĭn·sĭg′ nĭ·ȧ)
n. pl.
sing. in·sig·ne (-nē)
in·sig·nif·i·cant
(ĭn′ sĭg·nĭf′ ĭ·kănt)
-cance
in·sin·cere (ĭn′ sĭn·sẽr′)
-cere·ly
in·sin·cer·i·ty (ĭn′ sĭn·sẽr′ ĭ·tĭ)

in·sin·u·ate   (ĭn·sĭn′ ū·āt)
  -at·ing
  in·sin·u·a·tion
         (ĭn·sĭn′ ū·ā′ shŭn)
in·sip·id   (ĭn·sĭp′ ĭd)
in·sist   (ĭn·sĭst′)
  in·sist·ence   (ĭn·sĭs′ tĕns)
  -tent
in·so·far   (ĭn′ sō·fär′)
in·sole   (ĭn′ sōl′)
in·so·lent   (ĭn′ sō·lĕnt)
  -lence
in·sol·u·ble   (ĭn·sŏl′ ū·b'l)
in·solv·a·ble   (ĭn·sŏl′ vȧ·b'l)
in·sol·ven·cy   (ĭn·sŏl′ vĕn·sĭ)
in·som·ni·a   (ĭn·sŏm′ nĭ·ȧ)
  in·som·ni·ac   (-ăk)
in·so·much·as   (ĭn′ sō·mŭch′)
in·sou·ci·ance   (ĭn·sōō′ sĭ·ȧns)
in·spect   (ĭn·spĕkt′)
  in·spec·tion   (ĭn·spĕk′ shŭn)
  in·spec·tor
in·spire   (ĭn·spīr′)
  -spir·ing
  in·spi·ra·tion·al
         (ĭn′ spĭ·rā′ shŭn·ȧl)
in·spir·it   (ĭn·spĭr′ ĭt)
in·sta·bil·i·ty   (ĭn′ stȧ·bĭl′ ĭ·tĭ)
in·stall   (ĭn·stôl′)
  in·stal·la·tion   (ĭn·stȧ·lā′ shŭn)
  in·stall·ment
in·stant   (ĭn′ stȧnt)
  -stance
  in·stan·ta·ne·ous
         (ĭn′ stȧn·tā′ nē·ŭs)
in·state   (ĭn·stāt′)
  -stat·ing
in·stead   (ĭn·stĕd′)
in·step   (ĭn′ stĕp)
in·sti·gate   (ĭn′ stĭ·gāt)
  -gat·ing
  in·sti·ga·tion   (ĭn′ stĭ·gā′ shŭn)
  in·sti·ga·tor
in·still   (ĭn·stĭl′)
in·stinct   (ĭn′ stĭngkt)
  in·stinc·tive   (ĭn·stĭngk′ tĭv)
in·sti·tute   (ĭn′ stĭ·tūt)
  -tut·ing
  in·sti·tu·tion   (ĭn′ stĭ·tū′ shŭn)
in·struct   (ĭn·strŭkt′)
  in·struc·tion   (ĭn·strŭk′ shŭn)
  -tion·al   in·struc·tive
  in·struc·tor   in·struc·tress
in·stru·ment   (ĭn′ strōō·mĕnt)

in·stru·men·tal
         (ĭn′ strōō·mĕn′ tȧl)
in·stru·men·tal·i·ty
         (ĭn′ strōō·mĕn·tăl′ ĭ·tĭ)
in·stru·men·ta·tion
         (ĭn′ strōō·mĕn·tā′ shŭn)
in·sub·or·di·nate
         (ĭn′ sŭ·bôr′ dĭ·nĭt)
in·sub·or·di·na·tion
         (ĭn′ sŭ·bôr′ dĭ·nā′ shŭn)
in·sub·stan·tial
         (ĭn′ sŭb·stăn′ shȧl)
  -tial·ly
in·suf·fer·a·ble
         (ĭn·sŭf′ ēr·ȧ·b'l)
in·suf·fi·cient   (ĭn′ sŭ·fĭsh′ ĕnt)
  -cien·cy
in·su·lar   (ĭn′ sû·lēr)
  in·su·lar·i·ty   (ĭn′ sû·lăr′ ĭ·tĭ)
in·su·late   (ĭn′ sû·lāt)
  -lat·ing
  in·su·la·tion   (ĭn′ sû·lā′ shŭn)
  in·su·la·tor
in·su·lin   (ĭn′ sû·lĭn)
in·sult   (ĭn·sŭlt′) *v.*
         (ĭn′ sŭlt) *n.*
in·su·per·a·ble
         (ĭn·sū′ pēr·ȧ·b'l)
in·sup·port·a·ble
         (ĭn′ sŭ·pōr′ tȧ·b'l)
in·sure   (ĭn·shōōr′)
  -sur·ing   in·sur·a·ble
  in·sur·ance   (ĭn·shōōr′ ȧns)
in·sur·gent   (ĭn·sûr′ jĕnt)
  -gen·cy
in·sur·mount·a·ble
         (ĭn′ sûr·moun′ tȧ·b'l)
in·sur·rec·tion   (ĭn′ sŭ·rĕk′ shŭn)
in·sus·cep·ti·ble
         (ĭn′ sŭ·sĕp′ tĭ·b'l)
in·tact   (ĭn·tăkt′)
in·tagl·io   (ĭn·tăl′ yō)
in·take   (ĭn′ tāk′)
in·tan·gi·ble   (ĭn·tăn′ jĭ·b'l)
in·te·ger   (ĭn′ tĕ·jēr)
in·te·gral   (ĭn′ tĕ·grȧl)
  -gral·ly
in·te·grate   (ĭn′ tĕ·grāt)
  -grat·ing
in·te·gra·tion   (ĭn′ tĕ·grā′ shŭn)
in·teg·ri·ty   (ĭn·tĕg′ rĭ·tĭ)
in·tel·lect   (ĭn′ tĕ·lĕkt)
  in·tel·lec·tu·al
         (ĭn′ tĕ·lĕk′ tû·ȧl)
  -al·ly

in·tel·li·gent (ĭn·tĕl′ ĭ·jĕnt)
-gence
in·tel·li·gent·si·a
(ĭn·tĕl′ ĭ·jĕnt′ sĭ·á)
in·tel·li·gi·ble (ĭn·tĕl′ ĭ·jĭ·b'l)
in·tel·li·gi·bil·i·ty
(ĭn·tĕl′ ĭ·jĭ·bĭl′ ĭ·tĭ)
in·tem·per·ate (ĭn·tĕm′ pēr·ĭt)
-ance
in·tend (ĭn·tĕnd′)
in·tense (ĭn·tĕns′)
in·ten·si·fy -fied, -fy·ing
in·ten·si·ty
in·ten·sive -sive·ly
in·tent (ĭn·tĕnt′)
in·ten·tion (ĭn·tĕn′ shŭn)
-tion·al
in·ter (ĭn·tûr′)
-terred -ter·ring
in·ter·ac·tion (ĭn′ tēr·ăk′ shŭn)
in·ter·breed (ĭn′ tēr·brēd′)
in·ter·cede (ĭn′ tēr·sēd′)
-ced·ing
in·ter·cept (ĭn′ tēr·sĕpt′)
in·ter·cep·tion in·ter·cep·tor
in·ter·ces·sion (ĭn′ tēr·sĕsh′ ŭn)
in·ter·change (ĭn′ tēr·chānj′)
-chang·ing
in·ter·change·a·ble
in·ter·com (ĭn′ tēr·kŏm′)
in·ter·con·nec·tion
(ĭn′ tēr·kŏ·nĕk′ shŭn)
in·ter·course (ĭn′ tēr·kōrs′)
in·ter·de·pend·ence
(ĭn′ tēr·dĕ·pĕn′ dĕns)
in·ter·dict (ĭn′ tēr·dĭkt′)
in·ter·est (ĭn′ tēr·ĕst′)
in·ter·est·ed·ly
in·ter·fere (ĭn′ tēr·fēr′)
-fer·ing
in·ter·fer·ence (ĭn′ tēr·fēr′ ĕns)
in·ter·im (ĭn′ tēr·ĭm)
in·te·ri·or (ĭn·tĕr′ ĭ·ēr)
in·ter·ject (ĭn′ tēr·jĕkt′)
in·ter·jec·tion
in·ter·lace (ĭn′ tēr·lās′)
-lac·ing
in·ter·lard (ĭn′ tēr·lärd′)
in·ter·lin·ing (ĭn′ tēr·līn′ ĭng)
in·ter·lock (ĭn′ tēr·lŏk′)
in·ter·loc·u·tor
(ĭn′ tēr·lŏk′ û·tēr)
in·ter·lop·er (ĭn′ tēr·lŏp′ ēr)
in·ter·lude (ĭn′ tēr·lūd)

in·ter·mar·riage
(ĭn′ tēr·măr′ ĭj)
in·ter·me·di·ar·y
(ĭn′ tēr·mē′ dĭ·ĕr′ ĭ)
in·ter·me·di·ate
(ĭn′ tēr·mē′ dĭ·ĭt)
in·ter·mez·zo (ĭn′ tēr·mĕd′ zō)
in·ter·mi·na·ble
(ĭn·tûr′ mĭ·ná·b'l)
in·ter·mis·sion (ĭn′ tēr·mĭsh′ ŭn)
in·ter·mit·tent (ĭn′ tēr·mĭt′ ĕnt)
-mit·ten·cy
in·ter·mix·ture (ĭn′ tēr·mĭks′ tûr)
in·tern (ĭn′ tûrn)
in·tern·ship
in·ter·nal (ĭn·tûr′ nál)
-nal·ly
in·ter·na·tion·al
(ĭn′ tēr·năsh′ ŭn·ál)
in·ter·ne·cine (ĭn′ tēr·nē′ sĭn)
in·tern·ment (ĭn·tûrn′ mĕnt)
in·ter·phone (ĭn′ tēr·fōn′)
in·ter·po·late (ĭn·tûr′ pŏ·lāt)
-lat·ing
in·ter·po·la·tion
(ĭn·tûr′ pŏ·lā′ shŭn)
in·ter·pose (ĭn′ tēr·pōz′)
-pos·ing
in·ter·pret (ĭn·tûr′ prĕt)
in·ter·pre·ta·tion
(ĭn·tûr′ prĕ·tā′ shŭn)
in·ter·pret·er in·ter·pre·tive
in·ter·reg·num
(ĭn′ tēr·rĕg′ nŭm)
in·ter·ro·gate (ĭn·tĕr′ ō·gāt)
-gat·ing in·ter·ro·ga·tor
in·ter·rog·a·tive
(ĭn′ tĕ·rŏg′ á·tĭv)
in·ter·rog·a·to·ry
(ĭn′ tĕ·rŏg′ á·tō′ rĭ)
in·ter·rupt (ĭn′ tĕ·rŭpt′)
in·ter·rup·tion
(ĭn′ tĕ·rŭp′ shŭn)
in·ter·sect (ĭn′ tēr·sĕkt′)
in·ter·sperse (ĭn′ tēr·spûrs′)
-spers·ing
in·ter·sper·sion (-spûr′ shŭn)
in·ter·state (ĭn′ tēr·stāt′)
in·ter·stel·lar (ĭn′ tēr·stĕl′ ēr)
in·ter·stice (ĭn·tûr′ stĭs)
in·ter·sti·tial (ĭn′ tēr·stĭsh′ ál)
in·ter·val (ĭn′ tēr·vál)
in·ter·vene (ĭn′ tēr·vēn′)
-ven·ing
in·ter·ven·tion (-vĕn′ shŭn)

in·ter·view (ĭn′ tẽr·vū)
  in·ter·view·er
in·ter·weave (ĭn′ tẽr·wēv′)
  -weav·ing
  in·ter·wo·ven (ĭn′ tẽr·wō′ vĕn)
in·tes·tate (ĭn·tĕs′ tāt)
in·tes·tine (ĭn·tĕs′ tĭn)
  in·tes·ti·nal (ĭn·tĕs′ tĭ·nǎl)
in·ti·mate (ĭn′ tĭ·māt) v.
  -mat·ing
  in·ti·ma·tion (ĭn′ tĭ·mā′ shŭn)
in·ti·mate (ĭn′ tĭ·mĭt) adj.
  in·ti·ma·cy (ĭn′ tĭ·mȧ·sĭ)
  in·ti·mate·ly (-mĭt·lĭ)
in·tim·i·date (ĭn·tĭm′ ĭ·dāt)
  -dat·ing
in·tol·er·a·ble (ĭn·tŏl′ ẽr·ȧ·b'l)
in·tol·er·ant (ĭn·tŏl′ ẽr·ȧnt)
  -rance
in·to·na·tion (ĭn′ tō·nā′ shŭn)
in·tox·i·cate (ĭn·tŏk′ sĭ·kāt)
  -cat·ing
  in·tox·i·cant (ĭn·tŏk′ sĭ·kȧnt)
  in·tox·i·ca·tion
       (ĭn·tŏk′ sĭ·kā′ shŭn)
in·trac·ta·ble (ĭn·trăk′ tȧ·b'l)
in·tra·mu·ral (ĭn′ trȧ·mū′ rǎl)
in·tran·si·gent (ĭn·trăn′ sĭ·jĕnt)
  -gen·cy
in·tran·si·tive (ĭn·trăn′ sĭ·tĭv)
in·tra·ve·nous (ĭn′ trȧ·vē′ nŭs)
in·trep·id (ĭn·trĕp′ ĭd)
in·tri·cate (ĭn′ trĭ·kĭt)
  -cate·ly
  in·tri·ca·cy (-kȧ·sĭ)
in·trigue (ĭn·trēg′)
  -tri·guing
in·trin·sic (ĭn·trĭn′ sĭk)
  in·trin·si·cal·ly
in·tro·duce (ĭn′ trō·dūs′)
  -duc·ing
in·tro·duc·tion
       (ĭn′ trō·dŭk′ shŭn)
  in·tro·duc·to·ry
       (ĭn′ trō·dŭk′ tō·rĭ)
in·tro·it (ĭn·trō′ ĭt)
in·tro·jec·tion (ĭn′ trō·jĕk′ shŭn)
in·tro·spec·tive (ĭn′ trō·spĕk′ tĭv)
in·tro·ver·sion (ĭn′ trō·vûr′ shŭn)
in·tro·vert (ĭn′ trō·vûrt′) n.
in·trude (ĭn·trōōd′)
  -trud·ing
  in·tru·sion (ĭn·trōō′ zhŭn)
  in·tru·sive (-sĭv)

in·tu·i·tion (ĭn′ tū·ĭsh′ ŭn)
  in·tu·i·tive (ĭn·tū′ ĭ·tĭv)
  in·tu·i·tive·ness
in·un·date (ĭn′ ŭn·dāt)
  -dat·ing
  in·un·da·tion (ĭn′ ŭn·dā′ shŭn)
in·ure (ĭn·ūr′)
  -ur·ing   in·ure·ment
in·vade (ĭn·vād′)
  -vad·ing
in·val·id (ĭn·văl′ ĭd) adj.
  (null)
  in·val·i·date (ĭn·văl′ ĭ·dāt)
  in·val·i·da·tion
       (ĭn·văl′ ĭ·dā′ shŭn)
in·va·lid (ĭn′ vȧ·lĭd)
  adj., n.; (sick)   in·va·lid·ism
in·val·u·a·ble (ĭn·văl′ û·ȧ·b'l)
in·var·i·a·ble (ĭn·vâr′ ĭ·ȧ·b'l)
in·va·sion (ĭn·vā′ zhŭn)
in·vec·tive (ĭn·vĕk′ tĭv)
in·veigh (ĭn·vā′)
in·vei·gle (ĭn·vē′ g'l)
  -gling
in·vent (ĭn·vĕnt′)
  in·ven·tion (ĭn·vĕn′ shŭn)
  in·ven·tive
in·ven·to·ry (ĭn′ vĕn·tō′ rĭ)
  -ries
in·verse (ĭn·vûrs′)
  -verse·ly
in·ver·sion (ĭn·vûr′ shŭn)
in·vert (ĭn·vûrt′) v.
       (ĭn′ vûrt) n.
in·ver·te·brate (ĭn·vûr′ tē·brāt)
in·ves·ti·gate (ĭn·vĕs′ tĭ·gāt)
  -gat·ing
  in·ves·ti·ga·tion
       (ĭn·vĕs′ tĭ·gā′ shŭn)
  in·ves·ti·ga·tive
       (ĭn·vĕs′ tĭ·gā′ tĭv)
  in·ves·ti·ga·tor
       (ĭn·vĕs′ tĭ·gā′ tẽr)
in·ves·ti·ture (ĭn·vĕs′ tĭ·tũr)
in·vest·ment (ĭn·vĕst′ mĕnt)
in·ves·tor (ĭn·vĕs′ tẽr)
in·vet·er·ate (ĭn·vĕt′ ẽr·ĭt)
in·vid·i·ous (ĭn·vĭd′ ĭ·ŭs)
in·vig·or·at·ing
       (ĭn·vĭg′ ẽr·āt′ ĭng)
in·vin·ci·ble (ĭn·vĭn′ sĭ·b'l)
  in·vin·ci·bil·i·ty
       (ĭn·vĭn′ sĭ·bĭl′ ĭ·tĭ)
in·vi·o·la·ble (ĭn·vī′ ō·lȧ·b'l)
in·vi·o·late (ĭn·vī′ ō·lȧt)

in·vis·i·ble (ĭn·vĭz′ ĭ·b′l)
  in·vis·i·bil·i·ty
      (ĭn·vĭz′ ĭ·bĭl′ ĭ·tĭ)
in·vi·ta·tion (ĭn′ vĭ·tā′ shŭn)
in·vite (ĭn·vīt′)
  -vit·ing
in·vo·ca·tion (ĭn′ vŏ·kā′ shŭn)
in·voice (ĭn′ vois)
in·voke (ĭn·vōk′)
  -vok·ing
  in·vo·ca·tion (ĭn′ vŏ·kā′ shŭn)
in·vol·un·tar·y (ĭn·vŏl′ ŭn·tĕr′ ĭ)
  in·vol·un·tar·i·ly
in·vo·lu·tion (ĭn′ vŏ·lū′ shŭn)
in·volve·ment (ĭn·vŏlv′ mĕnt)
in·vul·ner·a·ble
      (ĭn·vŭl′ nĕr·a·b′l)
  in·vul·ner·a·bil·i·ty
      (ĭn·vŭl′ nĕr·a·bĭl′ ĭ·tĭ)
in·ward (ĭn′ wĕrd)
i·o·dide (ī′ ô·dīd)
  i·o·dine (ī′ ô·dīn)
i·on (ī′ ŏn)
  i·on·ic (ī·ŏn′ ĭk)
  i·on·ize (ī′ ŏn·īz)
  i·on·o·sphere (ī·ŏn′ ô·sfĕr)
i·o·ta (ī·ō′ tȧ)
I·O·U (ī′ ō′ ū′)
I·o·wa (ī′ ô·wȧ)
  abbr. Ia.
  I·o·wan
I·Q (ī′ kū′)
  I·Qs
I·ra·ni·an (ī·rā′ nĭ·ɑ̆n)
I·ra·qi (ê·rä′ kê)
i·ras·ci·ble (ī·răs′ ĭ·b′l)
i·rate (ī′ rāt)
ire·ful (īr′ fŏŏl)
ir·i·des·cent (ĭr′ ĭ·dĕs′ ĕnt)
  -cence
i·ris (ī′ rĭs)
I·rish·man (ī′ rĭsh·mɑ̆n)
irk·some (ûrk′ sŭm)
i·ron (ī′ ĕrn)
  i·ron·clad i·ron cur·tain
  i·ron lung i·ron·work
i·ro·ny (ī′ rô·nĭ)
  i·ron·i·cal (ī·rŏn′ ĭ·kɑ̆l)
  -cal·ly
Ir·o·quois (ĭr′ ô·kwoi)
ir·ra·di·ate (ĭ·rā′ dĭ·āt)
  -at·ing
  ir·ra·di·a·tion (ĭ·rā′ dĭ·ā′ shŭn)
ir·ra·tion·al (ĭr·răsh′ ŭn·ɑ̆l)

ir·ra·tion·al·i·ty
      (ĭr·răsh′ ŭn·ăl′ ĭ·tĭ)
ir·re·claim·a·ble
      (ĭr′ rê·klām·′ ȧ·b′l)
ir·rec·on·cil·a·ble
      (ĭr′ rĕk′ ŏn·sīl′ ȧ·b′l)
ir·re·cov·er·a·ble
      (ĭr′ rê·kŭv′ ĕr·ȧ·b′l)
ir·re·deem·a·ble
      (ĭr′ rê·dēm′ ȧ·b′l)
ir·re·duc·i·ble (ĭr′ rê·dūs′ ĭ·b′l)
ir·ref·u·ta·ble (ĭr·rĕf′ ū·tȧ·b′l)
ir·reg·u·lar (ĭr·rĕg′ û·lēr)
  ir·reg·u·lar·i·ty
      (ĭr·rĕg′ û·lăr′ ĭ·tĭ)
ir·rel·e·vant (ĭr·rĕl′ ê·vȧnt)
  -van·cy
ir·re·li·gious (ĭr′ rê·lĭj′ ŭs)
ir·re·me·di·a·ble
      (ĭr′ rê·mē′ dĭ·ȧ·b′l)
ir·rep·a·ra·ble (ĭ·rĕp′ ȧ·rȧ·b′l)
ir·re·place·a·ble
      (ĭr′ rê·plās′ ȧ·b′l)
ir·re·press·i·ble
      (ĭr′ rê·prĕs′ ĭ·b′l)
ir·re·proach·a·ble
      (ĭr′ rê·prōch′ ȧ·b′l)
ir·re·sist·i·ble (ĭr′ rê·zĭs′ tĭ·b′l)
ir·res·o·lute (ĭ·rĕz′ ô·lūt)
ir·re·spec·tive (ĭr′ rê·spĕk′ tĭv)
ir·re·spon·si·ble
      (ĭr′ rê·spŏn′ sĭ·b′l)
  ir·re·spon·si·bil·i·ty
      (ĭr′ rê·spŏn′ sĭ·bĭl′ ĭ·tĭ)
ir·re·triev·a·ble
      (ĭr′ rê·trēv′ ȧ·b′l)
ir·rev·er·ence (ĭ·rĕv′ ĕr·ĕns)
ir·re·vers·i·ble (ĭr′ rê·vûr′ sĭ·b′l)
ir·rev·o·ca·ble (ĭ·rĕv′ ô·kȧ·b′l)
ir·ri·gate (ĭr′ ĭ·gāt)
  -gat·ing
ir·ri·ga·ble (ĭr′ ĭ·gȧ·b′l)
ir·ri·ga·tion (ĭr′ ĭ·gā′ shŭn)
ir·ri·ta·ble (ĭr′ ĭ·tȧ·b′l)
  ir·ri·ta·bil·i·ty
      (ĭr′ ĭ·tȧ·bĭl′ ĭ·tĭ)
ir·ri·tant (ĭr′ ĭ·tɑ̆nt)
  -tan·cy
ir·ri·tate (ĭr′ ĭ·tāt)
  -tat·ing
ir·ri·ta·tion (ĭr′ ĭ·tā′ shŭn)
ir·rup·tion (ĭ·rŭp′ shŭn)
ir·rup·tive
i·sin·glass (ī′ zĭng·glás′)

Is·lam (ĭs′ lȧm)
  Is·lam·ic (ĭs·lăm′ ĭk)
is·land (ī′ lănd)
  is·land·er
isle (īl)
  (small island; see *aisle*)
  is·let (ī′ lĕt)
i·so·bar (ī′ sō·bär)
i·so·late (ī′ sō·lāt)
  -lat·ing
  i·so·la·tion (ī′ sō·lā′ shŭn)
i·sos·ce·les (ī·sŏs′ ĕ·lēz)
i·so·tope (ī′ sō·tōp)
Is·ra·el (ĭz′ rĭ·ĕl)
  Is·rae·li (ĭz·rā′ lĭ)
  Is·ra·el·ite (ĭz′ rĭ·ĕl·ĭt)
is·sue (ĭsh′ ū)
  is·su·ing
  is·su·ance (ĭsh′ ū·ȧns)
  is·su·ant
Is·tan·bul, Turk. (ĭs′ tăm·bōōl′)
isth·mus (ĭs′ mŭs)
I·tal·ian (ĭ·tăl′ yȧn)
i·tal·ic (ĭ·tăl′ ĭk)
  i·tal·i·cize (ĭ·tăl′ ĭ·sīz)
  -ciz·ing
i·tem·ize (ī′ tĕm·īz)
  -iz·ing
i·tin·er·ant (ĭ·tĭn′ ẽr·ȧnt)
i·tin·er·ar·y (ĭ·tĭn′ ẽr·ĕr′ ĭ)
  -ar·ies
its (ĭts)
  (belonging to it)
it's (ĭts)
  (it is, it has)
it·self (ĭt·sĕlf′)
i·vor·y (ī′ vō·rĭ)
i·vy (ī′ vĭ)
  i·vies

J

ja·bot (zhȧ′ bō′)
jack (jăk)
  jack-in-the-pul·pit
  jack·knife
  jack-of-all-trades
  jack-o′-lan·tern
  jack·pot   jack rab·bit
jack·al (jăk′ ôl)
jack·et (jăk′ ĕt)
jag·ged (jăg′ ĕd)
jag·uar (jăg′ wär)
jail·bird (jāl′ bûrd′)

Ja·mai·ca (jȧ·mā′ kȧ)
jam·bo·ree (jăm′ bō·rē′)
jan·i·tor (jăn′ ĭ·tẽr)
  jan·i·to·ri·al (jăn′ ĭ·tō′ rĭ·ȧl)
Jan·u·ar·y (jăn′ ū·ĕr′ ĭ)
Jap·a·nese (jăp′ ȧ·nēz′)
jar·gon (jär′ gŏn)
jas·mine (jăz′ mĭn)
jaun·dice (jôn′ dĭs)
jaun·ty (jôn′ tĭ)
  jaun·ti·ly
jave·lin (jăv′ lĭn)
jaw·bone (jô′ bōn′)
jay·walk·er (jā′ wôk′ ẽr)
jazz·y (jăz′ ĭ)
jeal·ous·y (jĕl′ ŭs·ĭ)
  -ous·ies
jeans (jēnz)
jeep (jēp)
Jef·fer·so·ni·an
  (jĕf′ ẽr·sō′ nĭ·ȧn)
Je·ho·vah (jē·hō′ vȧ)
je·june (jē·jōōn′)
jel·ly (jĕl′ ĭ)
  jel·lied   jel·ly·ing
  jel·ly·fish
jeop·ard·y (jĕp′ ẽr·dĭ)
  jeop·ard·ize   -iz·ing
jer·kin (jûr′ kĭn)
jerk·y (jûr′ kĭ)
  jerk·i·ness
jer·ry-built (jĕr′ ĭ·bĭlt′)
jer·sey (jûr′ zĭ)
  -seys
Je·ru·sa·lem (jē·rōō′ sȧ·lĕm)
jest·er (jĕs′ tẽr)
Jes·u·it (jĕz′ ū·ĭt)
jet pro·pul·sion (jĕt)
jet·sam (jĕt′ săm)
jet·ti·son (jĕt′ ĭ·sŭn)
jet·ty (jĕt′ ĭ)
  jet·ties
jew·el (jōō′ ĕl)
  -eled   -el·ing
  jew·el·er   jew·el·ry
Jew·ry (jōō′ rĭ)
jew's-harp (jōōz′ härp′)
Jez·e·bel (jĕz′ ĕ·bĕl)
jibe (jīb)
  jib·ing
jif·fy (jĭf′ ĭ)
jig·ger (jĭg′ ẽr)
jig·saw puz·zle (jĭg′ sô′)
jin·gle (jĭng′ g'l)
  -gling

jin·go (jĭng′ gō)
  -goes jin·go·ism
jin·rik·i·sha (jĭn·rĭk′ shä)
jit·ney (jĭt′ nĭ)
jock·ey (jŏk′ ĭ)
jo·cose (jō·kōs′)
  jo·cos·i·ty (jō·kŏs′ ĭ·tĭ)
joc·u·lar (jŏk′ ū·lẽr)
  joc·u·lar·i·ty (jŏk′ ū·lăr′ ĭ·tĭ)
joc·und (jŏk′ ŭnd)
  jo·cun·di·ty (jō·kŭn′ dĭ·tĭ)
jodh·purs (jŏd′ pẽrz)
jog·gle (jŏg′ 'l)
  jog·gling
Jo·han·nes·burg, S. Afr.
  (jō·hăn′ ĭs·bûrg)
John·son City, (jŏn′ s'n)
  N.Y., Tenn.
Johns·town, Pa. (jŏnz′ toun)
joie de vi·vre (zhwá′ dē·vē′ vr′)
joint (joint)
  join·ture (join′ tûr)
jok·ing·ly (jōk′ ĭng·lĭ)
jol·li·ty (jŏl′ ĭ·tĭ)
  jol·li·ness
jon·quil (jŏng′ kwĭl)
jos·tle (jŏs′ 'l)
  -tling
jour·nal (jûr′ năl)
  jour·nal·ese (jûr′ năl·ēz′)
  jour·nal·ism
  jour·nal·is·tic (jûr′ năl·ĭs′ tĭk)
jour·ney (jûr′ nĭ)
  -neys
joust (jŭst)
jo·vi·al (jō′ vĭ·ăl)
  -al·ly
jowl (joul)
joy·ful (joi′ fŏŏl)
  joy·ous (joi′ ŭs)
ju·bi·lant (jōō′ bĭ·lănt)
  -lance
ju·bi·la·tion (jōō′ bĭ·lā′ shŭn)
ju·bi·lee (jōō′ bĭ·lē)
judge (jŭj)
  judg·ing
  judg·ment
ju·di·ca·ture (jōō′ dĭ·ká·tûr)
ju·di·cial (jōō·dĭsh′ ăl)
  -cial·ly
  ju·di·ci·ar·y (jōō·dĭsh′ ĭ·ẽr′ ĭ)
  ju·di·cious (jōō·dĭsh′ ŭs)
jug·ger·naut (jŭg′ ẽr·nôt)
Jug·gler (jŭg′ lẽr)
jug·u·lar vein (jŭg′ ŭ·lẽr)

juice (jōōs)
  juic·i·ness juic·y
ju·jit·su (jōō·jĭt′ sōō)
juke·box (jōōk′ bŏks′)
ju·lep (jōō′ lĕp)
ju·li·enne (jōō′ lĭ·ĕn′)
jum·bled (jŭm′ b'ld)
jum·bo (jŭm′ bō)
junc·tion (jŭngk′ shŭn)
junc·ture (jŭngk′ tûr)
jun·gle (jŭng′ g'l)
jun·ior (jōōn′ yẽr)
ju·ni·per (jōō′ nĭ·pẽr)
jun·ket (jŭng′ kĕt)
jun·ta (jŭn′ tá)
ju·rid·i·cal (jōō·rĭd′ ĭ·kăl)
ju·ris·dic·tion (jōōr′ ĭs·dĭk′ shŭn)
ju·ris·pru·dence
  (jōōr′ ĭs·prōō′ dĕns)
ju·ry (jōōr′ ĭ)
  ju·ries ju·rist
  ju·ror
jus·tice (jŭs′ tĭs)
jus·ti·fy (jŭs′ tĭ·fī)
  -fied, -fy·ing
  jus·ti·fi·a·ble (jŭs′ tĭ·fī′ á·b'l)
  jus·ti·fi·ca·tion
    (jŭs′ tĭ·fĭ·kā′ shŭn)
ju·ve·nile (jōō′ vē·nĭl)
jux·ta·pose (jŭks′ tá·pōz′)
  jux·ta·po·si·tion
    (jŭks′ tá·pô·zĭsh′ ŭn)

K

kai·ser (kī′ zẽr)
kale (kāl)
ka·lei·do·scope (ká·lī′ dô·skōp)
kan·ga·roo (kăng′ gá·rōō′)
Kan·sas (kăn′ zás)
  abbr. Kans. or Kan.
  Kan·san
ka·pok (kā′ pŏk)
ka·put (kä·pŏŏt′)
kar·a·kul (kăr′ á·kŭl)
ka·ty·did (kā′ tĭ dĭd′)
Kau·ai (is.) (kou′ ī)
kay·ak (kī′ ăk)
keel·boat (kēl′ bōt′)
keen·ness (kēn′ nĕs)
keep·sake (kēp′ sāk′)
kelp (kĕlp)
Ken·ne·dy, John F. and
  Jac·que·line (kĕn′ ĕ·dĭ)

ken·nel (kĕn′ ĕl)
Ken·tuck·y (kĕn·tŭk′ ĭ)
  abbr. Ky.
  Ken·tuck·i·an
Ken·ya (kĕn′ yȧ)
ker·chief (kûr′ chĭf)
ker·nel (kûr′ nĕl)
ker·o·sene (kĕr′ ȯ·sēn′)
ketch (kĕch)
ket·tle·drum (kĕt′ 'l·drŭm′)
key (kē)
  key·board   key·hole
  key·note   key·sig·na·ture
  key·stone
khak·i (kăk′ ĭ)
khe·dive (kĕ·dēv′)
Khru·shchev, Ni·ki·ta
    (krōōsh·chôf′, nyĭ·kĕ′ tȧ)
kib·itz·er (kĭb′ ĭt·sēr)
kick·back (kĭk′ băk′)
kid·nap (kĭd′ năp)
  -naped   -nap·ing
  kid·nap·er
kid·ney (kĭd′ nĭ)
kill·deer (kĭl′ dēr′)
kill·joy (kĭl′ joi′)
kiln (kĭl)
ki·lo- (kĭl′ ȯ-)
  kil·o·cy·cle   kil·o·gram
  kil·o·me·ter   kil·o·watt
  kil·o·watt-hour
ki·mo·no (kĭ·mō′ nŭ)
  -nos
kin·der·gar·ten
    (kĭn′ dĕr·gär′ t'n)
  kin·der·gart·ner
kind·heart·ed (kīnd′ här′ tĕd)
kin·dle (kĭn′ d'l)
  -dling
kind·ly (kīnd′ lĭ)
  kind·li·er   -li·est, -li·ness
kin·dred (kĭn′ drĕd)
kin·e·scope (kĭn′ ĕ·skōp)
kin·es·thet·ic (kĭn′ ĕs·thĕt′ ĭk)
ki·net·ic (kĭ·nĕt′ ĭk)
king·dom (kĭng′ dŭm)
king·fish·er (kĭng′ fĭsh′ ēr)
kins·man (kĭnz′ măn)
ki·osk (kē·ŏsk′)
kirsch (kĭrsh)
kis·met (kĭz′ mĕt)
kitch·en (kĭch′ ĕn)
  kitch·en·ette   (kĭch′ ĕ·nĕt′)
  kitch·en·ware
kit·ten (kĭt′ 'n)

klep·to·ma·ni·a
    (klĕp′ tȯ·mā′ nĭ·ȧ)
  klep·to·ma·ni·ac
    (-ăk)
klieg light (klēg)
klis·ter (klĭs′ tēr)
knack (năk)
knap·sack (năp′ săk′)
knave (nāv)
  knav·er·y (nāv′ ēr·ĭ)
  knav·ish
knead (nēd)
knee·cap (nē′ kăp′)
kneel (nēl)
  knelt (nĕlt)
knell (nĕl)
knick·ers (nĭk′ ērz)
knick·knack (nĭk′ năk′)
knife (nīf)
  pl. knives (nīvz)
knight (nīt)
  knight-er·rant   knight·hood
knit (nĭt)
  knit·ting   knit·wear
knob (nŏb)
  knob·by
knock (nŏk)
  knock·down   knock·kneed
  knock·out
knoll (nōl)
knot (nŏt)
  knot·ted   knot·ting
  knot·hole   knot·ty
know (nō)
  know·a·ble   know·how
  know·ing·ly   known
knowl·edge (nŏl′ ĕj)
  knowl·edge·a·ble
    (nŏl′ ĕj·ȧ·b'l)
knuck·le (nŭk′ 'l)
ko·a·la (kȯ·ä′ lȧ)
Ko·dak (kō′ dăk)
  Ko·da·chrome
Ko·di·ak bear (kō′ dĭ·ăk)
kohl·ra·bi (kōl′ rä′ bĭ)
ko·sher (kō′ shēr)
kow·tow (kō′ tou′)
kraft pa·per (krăft)
krem·lin (krĕm′ lĭn)
Ku·blai Khan (kū′ blī kän′)
ku·dos (kū′ dŏs)
Ku Klux Klan (kū klŭks klăn)
kum·quat (kŭm′ kwŏt)

L

la·bel (lā′ bĕl)
  -beled   -bel·ing
la·bor (lā′ bĕr)
  la·bor·er
  la·bo·ri·ous (lá·bō′ rĭ·ŭs)
  la·bor·sav·ing   la·bor un·ion
lab·o·ra·to·ry (lăb′ ŏ·rá·tō′ rĭ)
  -ries
lab·y·rinth (lăb′ ĭ·rĭnth)
lac·er·ate (lăs′ ĕr·āt)
  -at·ing
  lac·er·a·tion (lăs′ ĕr·ā′ shŭn)
lach·ry·mal (lăk′ rĭ·mál)
  lach·ry·mose (lăk′ rĭ·mōs)
lack·a·dai·si·cal
    (lăk′ á·dā′ zĭ·kál)
lack·ey (lăk′ ĭ)
  -eys
lack·lus·ter (lăk′ lŭs′ tĕr)
la·con·ic (lá·kŏn′ ĭk)
  la·con·i·cal·ly
lac·quer (lăk′ ĕr)
la·crosse (lá·krôs′)
lac·ta·tion (lăk·tā′ shŭn)
lac·tic ac·id (lăk′ tĭk)
lac·tose (lăk′ tōs)
lac·y (lās′ ĭ)
  lac·i·ness
lad·der-back chair
    (lăd′ ĕr·băk′)
lad·en (lād′ ′n)
lad·ing (lād′ ĭng)
  (bill of)
la·dle (lā′ d′l)
  -dling
la·dy (lā′ dĭ)
  -dies   la·dy·fin·ger
  la·dy-kill·er   la·dy·like
  la·dy's-slip·per
la·ger beer (lä′ gĕr)
lag·gard (lăg′ ĕrd)
la·goon (lá·gōōn′)
lais·sez faire (lĕ′ sā′ fâr′)
la·i·ty (lā′ ĭ·tĭ)
lama (lä·má′)
  (priest; see *llama*)
La·ma·ism (lä′ má·ĭz′m)
lam·baste (lăm′ bāst′)
  -bast·ing
lamb·skin (lăm′ skĭn′)
la·mé (lá′ mā′)

la·ment (lá·mĕnt′)
lam·en·ta·ble (lăm′ ĕn·tá·b′l)
lam·en·ta·tion
    (lăm′ ĕn·tā′ shŭn)
la·ment·ed (lá·mĕn′ tĕd)
lam·i·nate (lăm′ ĭ·nāt)
  -nat·ing
lam·i·nar (lăm′ ĭ·nĕr)
lam·i·na·tion (lăm′ ĭ·nā′ shŭn)
lamp·black (lămp′ blăk′)
lam·poon (lăm·pōōn′)
  lam·poon·er·y
lam·prey eel (lăm′ prĭ)
lance (láns)
  lanc·ing
lan·cet (lán′ sĕt)
land (lănd)
  land-grant col·lege
  land·hold·er   land·lord
  land·lub·ber   land·own·er
  land·scape   land·slide
lan·guage (lăng′ gwĭj)
lan·guid (lăng′ gwĭd)
lan·guish·ing (lăng′ gwĭsh·ĭng)
lan·guor (lăng′ gĕr)
  lan·guor·ous (lăng′ gĕr·ŭs)
lank·y (lăngk′ ĭ)
  lank·i·ness
lan·o·lin (lăn′ ŏ·lĭn)
lan·tern (lăn′ tĕrn)
lan·yard (lăn′ yĕrd)
Laos (louz)
  La·o·tian (lâ·ō′ shăn)
la·pel (lá· pĕl′)
lap·i·dar·y (lăp′ ĭ·dĕr′ ĭ)
lap·is laz·u·li (lăp′ ĭs lăz′ û·lĭ)
Lap·land·er (lăp′ lăn·dĕr)
  Lapp
lapse (lăps)
  laps·ing
lar·ce·ny (lär′ sĕ·nĭ)
  -nies   lar·ce·nist
  lar·ce·nous
lard·er (lär′ dĕr)
large·ly (lärj′ lĭ)
large-scale (lärj′ skāl′)
lar·gess (lär′ jĕs)
lar·ghet·to (lär·gĕt′ ŏ)
lar·go (lär′ gō)
lar·i·at (lär′ ĭ·át)
lark·spur (lärk′ spûr′)
lar·va (lär′ vá)
  pl. lar·vae (-vē)
  lar·vi·cide (lär′ vĭ·sīd)
lar·yn·gi·tis (lăr′ ĭn·jī′ tĭs)

lar·ynx   (lăr′ ĭngks)
  pl. la·ryn·ges   (lȧ·rĭn′ jēz)
las·civ·i·ous   (lȧ·sĭv′ ĭ·ŭs)
las·si·tude   (lăs′ ĭ·tūd)
las·so   (lăs′ ō)
  las·soed   las·so·ing
  las·sos
last·ing·ly   (lȧst′ ĭng·lĭ)
latch·key   (lăch′ kē′)
la·teen sail   (lȧ·tēn′)
late·ly   (lāt′ lĭ)
la·tent   (lā′ tĕnt)
  la·ten·cy
lat·er·al   (lăt′ ẽr·ȧl)
  -al·ly
la·tex   (lā′ tĕks)
lath·work   (lăth′ wûrk′)
lat·i·tude   (lăt′ ĭ·tūd)
  lat·i·tu·di·nal   (lăt′ ĭ·tū′ dĭ·nȧl)
la·trine   (lȧ·trēn′)
lat·ter·most   (lăt′ ẽr·mōst)
lat·tice   (lăt′ ĭs)
  lat·tice·work   lat·tic·ing
laud   (lôd)
  laud·a·ble
  laud·a·to·ry   (lôd′ ȧ·tō′ rĭ)
lau·da·num   (lô′ dȧ·nŭm)
laugh   (lăf)
  laugh·a·ble   laugh·ing·stock
  laugh·ter
launch   (lônch)
laun·der   (lôn′ dẽr)
  laun·dress   (lôn′ drĕs)
  laun·dry   -dries
  laun·dry·man
lau·re·ate   (lô′ rė·ȧt)
lau·rel   (lô′ rĕl)
lav·a·liere   (lăv′ ȧ·lēr′)
lav·a·to·ry   (lăv′ ȧ·tō′ rĭ)
  -ries
lav·en·der   (lăv′ ĕn·dẽr)
lav·ish   (lăv′ ĭsh)
law   (lô)
  law-a·bid·ing   law break·er
  law·ful   -ful·ly
  -ful·ness   law·giv·er
  law·less·ness   law·mak·er
  law·suit
lawn mow·er   (lôn)
law·yer   (lô′ yẽr)
lax·a·tive   (lăk′ sȧ·tĭv)
lax·i·ty   (lăk′ sĭ·tĭ)
lay·er   (lā′ ẽr)
lay·man   (lā′ mȧn)
lay·off   (lā′ ôf′)

lay·o·ver   (lā′ ō′ vẽr)
la·zy   (lā′ zĭ)
  la·zi·er   -zi·est
  -zi·ly   -zi·ness
  la·zy·bones   La·zy Su·san
leach   (lēch)
  (dissolve; see *leech*)
lead   (lēd) *v.*
lead   (lĕd) *n.*
  lead·en
  lead poi·son·ing
lead·er·ship   (lēd′ ẽr·shĭp)
leaf   (lēf)
  leaves
  leaf·age   (lēf′ ĭj)
  leaf·hop·per   leaf·let
  leaf·y
league   (lēg)
leak   (lēk)
  (crack or hole; see *leek*)
  leak·age   (lēk′ ĭj)
  leak·y
lean-to   (lēn′ tōō′)
leap·frog   (lēp′ frŏg′)
leap year   (lēp yẽr)
learn·ed·ly   (lûr′ nĕd·lĭ)
lease·hold·er   (lēs′ hōl′ dẽr)
leash   (lēsh)
least   (lēst)
leath·er   (lĕth′ ẽr)
  Leath·er·ette   (lĕth′ ẽr·ĕt′)
  leath·er·y
leav·en·ing
Leb·a·non   (lĕb′ ȧ·nŭn)
  Leb·a·nese   (lĕb′ ȧ·nēz′)
lech·er   (lĕch′ ẽr)
  lech·er·ous   (lĕch′ ẽr·ŭs)
  lech·er·y
lec·tern   (lĕk′ tẽrn)
lec·ture   (lĕk′ tûr)
  lec·tur·er
ledge   (lĕj)
ledg·er   (lĕj′ ẽr)
leech   (lēch)
  (worm; see *leach*)
leek   (lēk)
  (plant; see *leak*)
leer·ing   (lẽr′ ĭng)
leer·y   (lẽr′ ĭ)
lee·ward   (lē′ wẽrd)
lee·way   (lē′ wā′)
left-hand·ed   (lĕft′ hăn′ dĕd)
left·ist   (lĕf′ tĭst)
leg·a·cy   (lĕg′ ȧ·sĭ)

le·gal (lē′ găl)
  le·gal·i·ty (lē· găl′ ĭ · tĭ)
  le·gal·ize -iz·ing
  le·gal·i·za·tion
      (lē′ găl· ĭ · zā′ shŭn)
  le·gal·ly le·gal ten·der
leg·ate (lĕg′ ĭt)
  le·ga·tion (lē· gā′ shŭn)
leg·end (lĕj′ ĕnd)
  leg·end·ar·y (lĕj′ ĕn·dĕr′ ĭ)
leg·er·de·main (lĕj′ ĕr·dē·mān′)
le·ger·i·ty (lē· jĕr′ ĭ · tĭ)
leg·gings (lĕg′ ĭngz)
leg·horn (lĕg′ hôrn)
leg·i·ble (lĕj′ ĭ · b′l)
  leg·i·bil·i·ty (lĕj′ ĭ · bĭl′ ĭ · tĭ)
le·gion (lē′ jŭn)
  le·gion·naire (lē′ jŭn·âr′)
leg·is·late (lĕj′ ĭs·lāt)
  -lat·ing
  leg·is·la·tion (lĕj′ ĭs·lā′ shŭn)
  leg·is·la·tive (lĕj′ ĭs·lā′ tĭv)
  leg·is·la·tor (lĕj′ ĭs·lā′ tēr)
  leg·is·la·ture (lĕj′ ĭs·lā′ tụ̄r)
le·git·i·mate (lē· jĭt′ ĭ · mĭt)
  le·git·i·ma·cy
  le·git·i·ma·tion
      (lē· jĭt′ ĭ · mā′ shŭn)
  le·git·i·mize (lē· jĭt′ ĭ · mīz)
  -miz·ing
leg·ume (lĕg′ ūm)
lei·sure (lē′ zhēr)
  lei·sure·li·ness lei·sure·ly
leit·mo·tiv (līt′ mō·tēf′)
lem·ming (lĕm′ ĭng)
lem·on (lĕm′ ŭn)
  lem·on·ade (lĕm′ ŭn·ād′)
le·mur (lē′ mēr)
lend-lease (lĕnd′ lēs′)
length (lĕngth)
  length·en length·i·ness
  length·wise length·y
le·ni·ent (lē′ nĭ · ĕnt)
  -en·cy
len·i·ty (lĕn′ ĭ · tĭ)
lens (lĕnz)
  lens·es
Lent·en (lĕn′ tĕn)
len·til (lĕn′ tĭl)
leop·ard (lĕp′ ērd)
le·o·tard (lē′ ô·tärd)
lep·er (lĕp′ ēr)
  lep·ro·sy (lĕp′ rô·sĭ)
  lep·rous
Les·bi·an (lĕz′ bĭ · ăn)

le·sion (lē′ zhŭn)
less (lĕs)
  less·en·ing less·er
les·see (lĕs·ē′)
  les·sor
les·son (lĕs′ ′n)
lest (lĕst)
let·down (lĕt′ doun′)
le·thal (lē′ thăl)
  -thal·ly
le·thar·gic (lē· thär′ jĭk)
  le·thar·gi·cal·ly
  leth·ar·gy (lĕth′ ēr·jĭ)
let·ter·head (lĕt′ ēr·hĕd′)
let·tuce (lĕt′ ĭs)
let·up (lĕt′ ŭp′)
leu·ke·mi·a (lū·kē′ mĭ · ȧ)
lev·ee (lĕv′ ē)
  (dike; see *levy*)
lev·el (lĕv′ ĕl)
  -eled -eling
  lev·el·er lev·el·head·ed
  lev·el·ly
le·ver (lē′ vēr)
le·ver·age (lē′ vēr·ĭj)
le·vi·a·than (lē· vī′ ȧ · thăn)
Le·vi′s (lē′ vīz)
lev·i·ty (lĕv′ ĭ · tĭ)
lev·y (lĕv′ ĭ)
  (to collect; see *levee*)
  lev·ied lev·y·ing
lewd·ness (lūd′ nĕs)
lex·i·cog·ra·phy
      (lĕk′ sĭ · kŏg′ rȧ · fĭ)
lex·i·con (lĕk′ sĭ · kŏn)
li·a·ble (lī′ ȧ · b′l)
  li·a·bil·i·ty (lī′ ȧ · bĭl′ ĭ · tĭ)
li·ai·son (lē′ ā·zŏn′)
li·ar (lī′ ēr)
li·ba·tion (lī·bā′ shŭn)
li·bel (lī′ bĕl)
  -beled -bel·ing
  li·bel·er li·bel·ous
lib·er·al (lĭb′ ēr·ăl)
  -al·ly lib·er·al·ism
  lib·er·al·i·ty (lĭb′ ēr·ăl′ ĭ · tĭ)
  lib·er·al·ize -iz·ing
lib·er·ate (lĭb′ ēr·āt)
  -at·ing lib·er·a·tor
lib·er·tar·i·an (lĭb′ ēr·târ′ ĭ · ăn)
lib·er·tine (lĭb′ ēr·tēn)
lib·er·ty (lĭb′ ēr·tĭ)
  -ties
li·bi·do (lĭ · bī′ dō)
  li·bid·i·nal (lĭ · bĭd′ ĭ · năl)

li·bid·i·nous (lĭ·bĭd′ ĭ·nŭs)
li·brar·y (lī′ brĕr′ ĭ)
  -brar·ies
  li·brar·i·an (lī·brâr′ ĭ·ăn)
Lib·y·a (lĭb′ ĭ·ȧ)
lice (līs)
li·cense (lī′ sĕns)
  -cens·ing
  li·cen·see (lī′ sĕn·sē′)
li·cen·tious (lĭ·sĕn′ shŭs)
li·chen (lī′ kĕn)
lic·it (lĭs′ ĭt)
lic·o·rice (lĭk′ ō·rĭs)
lie (lī)
  lied   ly·ing
  li·ar
Lie·der·kranz (lē′ dēr·kränts′)
liege (lēj)
lien (lē·ĕn)
lieu (lū)
lieu·ten·ant (lū·tĕn′ ȧnt)
  -an·cy
life (līf)
  pl. lives   life belt
  life·blood   life·boat
  life·guard   life·line
  life·long   life·sav·er
  life·sized   life·time
  life·work
lig·a·ment (lĭg′ ȧ·mĕnt)
lig·a·ture (lĭg′ ȧ·tụr)
light (līt)
  light-fin·gered light·head·ed
  light·heart·ed light·house
  light-year
light·ning (līt′ nĭng)
like (līk)
  lik·ing   lik·a·ble
  like·ly   -li·hood
  like·ness   like·wise
li·lac (lī′ lăk)
lil·y (lĭl′ ĭ)
  lil·ies
  lil·y of the val·ley
limb (lĭm)
lim·ber (lĭm′ bĕr)
lim·bo (lĭm′ bō)
  -boes
Lim·burg·er (lĭm′ bûrg·ĕr)
lime·light (lĭm′ līt′)
Lim·er·ick (lĭm′ ĕr·ĭk)
lime·stone (līm′ stōn′)
lime·wa·ter (lĭm′ wô′ tĕr)

lim·it (lĭm′ ĭt)
  -it·ed   -it·ing
  lim·i·ta·tion (lĭm′ ĭ·tā′ shŭn)
  lim·it·less
limn (lĭm)
lim·ou·sine (lĭm′ ŏŏ·zēn′)
lim·pid (lĭm′ pĭd)
lin·age (līn′ ĭj)
  (alignment; see *lineage*)
linch·pin (lĭnch′ pĭn′)
lin·den tree (lĭn′ dĕn)
lin·e·age (lĭn′ ē·ĭj)
  (ancestry; see *linage*)
lin·e·al (lĭn′ ē·ăl)
lin·e·a·ment (lĭn′ ē·ȧ·mĕnt)
lin·e·ar meas·ure
           (lĭn′ ē·ēr)
line·man (līn′ măn)
lin·en (lĭn′ ĕn)
lin·ge·rie (län′ zhĕ·rē)
lin·guist (lĭng′ gwĭst)
  lin·guis·tics (lĭng·gwĭs′ tĭks)
lin·i·ment (lĭn′ ĭ·mĕnt)
lin·ing (līn′ ĭng)
link·age (lĭngk′ ĭj)
li·no·le·um (lĭ·nō′ lē·ŭm)
Lin·o·type (līn′ ō·tīp)
lin·seed oil (lĭn′ sēd′)
li·on·ess (lī′ ŭn·ĕs)
li·on·ize (lī′ ŭn·īz)
  -iz·ing
liq·ue·fac·tion (lĭk′ wē·făk′ shŭn)
liq·ue·fy (lĭk′ wē·fī)
  -fied,   -fy·ing
  liq·ue·fi·a·ble (lĭk′ wē·fī′ ȧ·b'l)
li·queur (lē·kûr′)
liq·uid (lĭk′ wĭd)
liq·ui·date (lĭk′ wĭ·dāt)
  -dat·ing
  liq·ui·da·tion
           (lĭk′ wĭ·dā′ shŭn)
liq·uor (lĭk′ ēr)
lisle (līl)
lis·some (lĭs′ ŭm)
lis·ten (lĭs′ 'n)
list·less (lĭst′ lĕs)
lit·a·ny (lĭt′ ȧ·nĭ)
  -nies
li·ter (lē′ tēr)
lit·er·a·cy (lĭt′ ēr·ȧ·sĭ)
lit·er·al (lĭt′ ēr·ăl)
  -al·ly
lit·er·ar·y (lĭt′ ēr·ĕr′ ĭ)
lit·er·ate (lĭt′ ēr·ĭt)
  lit·er·a·ture (lĭt′ ēr·ȧ·tụr)

lithe (lĭth)
  lithe·ness
lith·o·graph (lĭth′ ŏ·grȧf)
lit·i·gate (lĭt′ ĭ·gāt)
  -gat·ing
  lit·i·gant (lĭt′ ĭ·gȧnt)
  lit·i·ga·tion (lĭt′ ĭ·gā′ shŭn)
  li·ti·gious (lĭ·tĭj′ ŭs)
lit·mus pa·per (lĭt′ mŭs)
lit·ter (lĭt′ ẽr)
lit·tle·ness (lĭt′ ′l·nĕs)
lit·ur·gy (lĭt′ ẽr·jĭ)
  -gies
  li·tur·gi·cal (lĭ·tûr′ jĭ·kȧl)
live (lĭv) v.
  liv·ing (lĭv) adj.
  liv·a·ble (lĭv′ ȧ·b′l)
live·li·hood (līv′ lĭ·hŏŏd)
live·ly (līv′ lĭ)
  live·li·er -li·est
  -li·ness
liv·en (lĭv′ ĕn)
liv·er (lĭv′ ẽr)
liv·er·wurst (lĭv′ ẽr·wûrst′)
liv·er·y sta·ble (lĭv′ ẽr·ĭ)
live·stock (līv′ stŏk′)
liv·id (lĭv′ ĭd)
liv·ing room (lĭv′ ĭng)
liz·ard (lĭz′ ẽrd)
lla·ma (lä′ mȧ)
  (animal; see *lama*)
loaf (lōf)
  pl. loaves (lōvz)
loaf·er (lōf′ ẽr)
loam (lōm)
loathe (lōth)
  loath·ing loath·some
lob·by (lŏb′ ĭ)
  lob·bies lob·by·ist
lobe (lōb)
  lo·bar (lō′ bẽr)
lob·lol·ly pine (lŏb′ lŏl′ ĭ)
lo·bot·o·my (lō·bŏt′ ŏ·mĭ)
lob·ster (lŏb′ stẽr)
lob·ule (lŏb′ ūl)
lo·cal (lō′ kȧl)
  lo·cal·ism
  lo·cal·i·ty (lō·kăl′ ĭ·tĭ)
  -ties lo·cal·ize
  -iz·ing
lo·cate (lō′ kāt)
  -cat·ing
  lo·ca·tion (lō·kā′ shŭn)
lock·et (lŏk′ ĕt)
lock·jaw (lŏk′ jô′)

lo·co·mo·tion (lō′ kŏ·mō′ shŭn)
  lo·co·mo·tive (lō′ kŏ·mō′ tĭv)
lo·co·weed (lō′ kŏ·wēd′)
lo·cust (lō′ kŭst)
lo·cu·tion (lō·kū′ shŭn)
lode·star (lōd′ stär′)
lode·stone (lōd′ stōn′)
lodge (lŏj)
  lodg·ing
loft·y (lôf′ tĭ)
  loft·i·ly -i·ness
lo·gan·ber·ry (lō′ găn·bĕr′ ĭ)
  -ber·ries
log·a·rithm (lŏg′ ȧ·rĭth′m)
log·ger·head (lŏg′ ẽr·hĕd′)
log·ging (lŏg′ ĭng)
log·ic (lŏj′ ĭk)
  log·i·cal -cal·ly
  lo·gi·cian (lō·jĭsh′ ăn)
lo·gis·tics (lō·jĭs′ tĭks)
lo·gy (lō′ gĭ)
  log·i·ness
Lo·hen·grin (lō′ ĕn·grĭn)
loin·cloth (loin′ klôth′)
loi·ter·er (loi′ tẽr·ẽr)
lol·li·pop (lŏl′ ĭ·pŏp)
lone·ly (lōn′ lĭ)
  lone·li·ness
lone·some (lōn′ sŭm)
  -some·ness
long (lŏng)
  long·bow long-dis·tance
  long·hand long-lived
  long-play·ing long·shore·man
  long-suf·fer·ing
  long-term bond
  long-wind·ed
lon·gev·i·ty (lŏn·jĕv′ ĭ·tĭ)
lon·gi·tude (lŏn′ jĭ·tūd)
  lon·gi·tu·di·nal
    (lŏn′ jĭ·tū′ dĭ·nȧl)
look·ing glass (lŏŏk′ ĭng glăs)
look·out (lŏŏk′ out′)
loom·ing (lōōm′ ĭng)
loon·y (lōōn′ ĭ)
  loon·i·ness
loop·hole (lōōp′ hōl′)
loose (lōōs)
  loose-joint·ed loose·ly
  loos·en loose·ness
loot·er (lōōt′ ẽr)
lop-eared (lŏp′ ẽrd′)
lop·sid·ed (lŏp′ sīd′ ĕd)
lo·qua·cious (lō·kwā′ shŭs)
  lo·quac·i·ty (lō·kwăs′ ĭ·tĭ)

lor·do·sis (lôr·dō′ sĭs)
lord·ship (lôrd′ shĭp)
lore (lōr)
Lor·e·lei (lôr′ ĕ·lī)
lor·gnette (lôr′ nyĕt′)
lose (lōōz) v.
  los·ing
loss (lôs) n.
  loss lead·er
lo·tion (lō′ shŭn)
lot·ter·y (lŏt′ ēr·ĭ)
  lot·ter·ies
lo·tus (lō′ tŭs)
loud (loud)
  loud·mouthed   loud-speak·er
Lou·i·si·an·a (lōō′ ĭ·zĭ·ăn′ à)
  abbr. La.
  Lou·i·si·an·i·an
  or Lou·i·si·an·an
lounge (lounj)
  loung·ing
louse (lous)
  pl. lice (līs)
  lous·y (louz′ ĭ)
lout·ish (lout′ ĭsh)
lou·ver (lōō′ vēr)
  lou·vered
love (lŭv)
  lov·ing   lov·a·ble
  love·bird   love·less
  love·lorn   love-mak·ing
  love·sick
love·ly (lŭv′ lĭ)
  love·li·er   -li·est, -li·ness
low (lō)
  low·born   low·brow
  low-pres·sure   low tide
low·er·class·man
        (lō′ ēr·klàs′ mǎn)
low·ly (lō′ lĭ)
  low·li·er   -li·est, -li·ness
loy·al (loi′ ǎl)
  loy·al·ty
Loy·o·la, St. Ig·na·ti·us
    (loi·ō′ là, ĭg·nā′ shĭ·ŭs)
loz·enge (lŏz′ ĕnj)
lub·ber·ly (lŭb′ ēr·lĭ)
lu·bri·cate (lū′ brĭ·kāt)
  -cat·ing
  lu·bri·cant (-brĭ·kǎnt)
  lu·bri·ca·tion (lū′ brĭ·kā′ shŭn)
  lu·bri·ca·tor
lu·cid (lū′ sĭd)
  lu·cid·i·ty (lū·sĭd′ ĭ·tĭ)
luck·less (lŭk′ lĕs)

luck·y (lŭk′ ĭ)
  luck·i·er   -i·est
  -i·ly   -i·ness
lu·cra·tive (lū′ krà·tĭv)
lu·cre (lū′ kēr)
lu·di·crous (lū′ dĭ·krŭs)
lug·gage (lŭg′ ĭj)
lu·gu·bri·ous (lù·gū′ brĭ·ŭs)
luke·warm (lūk′ wôrm′)
lull (lŭl)
lull·a·by (lŭl′ à·bī′)
  -bied   -by·ing
lum·ba·go (lŭm·bā′ gō)
lum·bar (lŭm′ bēr)
  (vertebra; see lumber)
lum·ber (lŭm′ bēr)
  (timber; see lumbar)
  lum·ber·jack   lum·ber·yard
lu·mi·nar·y (lū′ mĭ·nĕr′ ĭ)
  -nar·ies
lu·mi·nes·cent (lū′ mĭ·nĕs′ ĕnt)
  -cence
lu·mi·nous (lū′ mĭ·nŭs)
  lu·mi·nos·i·ty (lū′ mĭ·nŏs′ ĭ·tĭ)
lum·mox (lŭm′ ŭks)
lump·y (lŭmp′ ĭ)
  lump·i·ness
lu·na·cy (lū′ nà·sĭ)
lu·nar (lū′ nēr)
lu·na·tic (lū′ nà·tĭk)
lunch·eon (lŭn′ chŭn)
  lunch·eon·ette (lŭn′ chŭn·ĕt′)
lunge (lŭnj)
  lung·ing
lung·fish (lŭng′ fĭsh′)
lu·pine (lū′ pĭn) n.
  (flower)
lu·pine (lŭ′ pĭn) adj.
  (wolffish)
lurch (lûrch)
lu·rid (lū′ rĭd)
lurk (lûrk)
lus·cious (lŭsh′ ŭs)
lus·ter·ware (lŭs′ tēr·wâr′)
lust·ful (lŭst′ fōōl)
  -ful·ly   -ful·ness
lus·trous (lŭs′ trŭs)
lust·y (lŭs′ tĭ)
  lust·i·er   -i·est
  -i·ly   -i·ness
Lu·ther·an (lū′ thēr·ǎn)
Lux·em·bourg (lŭk′ sĕm·bûrg)
lux·u·ri·ant (lŭks·ū′ rĭ·ǎnt)
  lux·u·ri·ance

lux·u·ri·ate (lŭks·ū′ rĭ·āt)
  -at·ing
lux·u·ry (lŭk′ shoͦo·rĭ)
  -ries
  lux·u·ri·ous (lŭks·ū′ rĭ·ŭs)
ly·ce·um (lī·sē′ ŭm)
lye (lī)
ly·ing-in (lī′ ĭng·ĭn′)
lymph (lĭmf)
  lym·phat·ic (lĭm·făt′ ĭk)
lynch law (lĭnch)
lynx (lĭngks)
ly·on·naise (lī′ ŭ·nāz′)
lyr·ic (lĭr′ ĭk)
  lyr·i·cal (lĭr′ ĭ·kăl)
  lyr·i·cism (lĭr′ ĭ·sĭz′m)

M

ma'am (măm)
ma·ca·bre (má·kä′ b'r)
mac·ad·am (măk·ăd′ ăm)
  mac·ad·am·ize
    (măk·ăd′ ăm·īz)
mac·a·ro·ni (măk′ á·rō′ nĭ)
mac·a·roon (măk′ á·roͦon′)
ma·caw (má·kô′)
Mc·Coy, the (má·koi′)
ma·che·te (mä·chā′ tá)
Mach·i·a·vel·li·an
  (măk′ ĭ·á·vĕl′ ĭ·ăn)
mach·i·na·tion (măk′ ĭ·nā′ shŭn)
ma·chine (má·shēn′)
  ma·chin·er·y ma·chine shop
  ma·chin·ist
mack·er·el (măk′ ĕr·ĕl)
Mack·i·naw coat
  (măk′ ĭ·nô)
Mac·mil·lan, Har·old
  (măk·mĭl′ ăn)
mac·ro·cosm (măk′ rŏ·kŏz′m)
mad·am (măd′ ăm)
mad·ame (mă′ dăm′)
  pl. mes·dames (mā′ dăm′)
mad·den·ing (măd′ 'n·ĭng)
Ma·dei·ra wine (má·dĕr′ á)
ma·de·moi·selle
  (măd′ mwä′ zĕl′)
ma·don·na (má·dŏn′ á)
ma·dras (má·drăs′)
mad·ri·gal (măd′ rĭ·găl)
mael·strom (māl′ strŏm)
ma·e·stro (mä·ĕ′ strŏ)
maf·fi·a (măf′ fĕ·ä)

mag·a·zine (măg′ á·zēn′)
ma·gen·ta (má·jĕn′ tá)
mag·got (măg′ ŭt)
mag·ic (măj′ ĭk)
  mag·i·cal -cal·ly
  ma·gi·cian (má·jĭsh′ ăn)
mag·is·trate (măj′ ĭs·trāt)
  mag·is·te·ri·al
    (măj′ ĭs·tḛr′ ĭ·ăl)
  mag·is·tra·cy (măj′ ĭs·trá·sĭ)
Mag·na Char·ta
  (măg′ ná kär′ tá)
mag·na cum lau·de
  (măg′ ná kŭm lô′ dē)
mag·nan·i·mous
  (măg·năn′ ĭ·mŭs)
  mag·na·nim·i·ty
    (măg′ ná·nĭm′ ĭ·tĭ)
mag·nate (măg′ nāt)
mag·ne·sia (măg·nē′ shá)
  mag·ne·si·um
    (măg·nē′ shĭ·ŭm)
mag·net (măg′ nĕt)
  mag·net·ic (măg·nĕt′ ĭk)
  mag·net·ism mag·net·ize
Mag·nif·i·cat (măg·nĭf′ ĭ·kăt)
mag·ni·fi·ca·tion
  (măg′ nĭ·fĭ·kā′ shŭn)
mag·nif·i·cent (măg·nĭf′ ĭ·sĕnt)
  -cence
mag·nif·i·co (măg·nĭf′ ĭ·kō)
  -coes
mag·ni·fy (măg′ nĭ·fī)
  -fied -fy·ing
  mag·ni·fi·er
mag·ni·tude (măg′ nĭ·tūd)
mag·no·li·a (măg·nō′ lĭ·á)
mag·num o·pus
  (măg′ nŭm ō′ pŭs)
mag·pie (măg′ pī)
mag·uey (măg′ wā)
Mag·yar (măg′ yär)
ma·ha·ra·ja (má·hä′ rä′ já)
  n. masc.
ma·ha·ra·ni (má·hä′ rä′ nē)
  n. fem.
ma·hat·ma (má·hät′ má)
mah-jongg (mä′ jŏng′)
ma·hog·a·ny (má·hŏg′ á·nĭ)
maid·en (mād′ 'n)
mail (māl)
  mail·a·ble mail·box
  mail·man
  mail-or·der house
mail·lot (má′ yō′)

maim (măm)
Maine (mān)
  abbr. Me.
main·land (mān′ lănd′)
main·stay (mān′ stā′)
main·tain (mān·tān′)
  main·tain·a·ble
  main·te·nance (mān′ t′n·ᴐns)
maî·tre d′hô·tel (mâ′ trē dô′ tĕl′)
maize (māz)
  (corn; see *maze*)
maj·es·ty (măj′ ĕs·tĭ)
  -ties
  ma·jes·tic (mᴐ·jĕs′ tĭk)
  -ti·cal·ly
ma·jor (mā′ jēr)
  ma·jor-do·mo (mā′ jēr·dō′ mō)
  ma·jor·ette (mā′ jēr·ĕt′)
  ma·jor league
ma·jor·i·ty (mᴐ·jŏr′ ĭ·tĭ)
  -ties
make (māk)
  mak·ing make-be·lieve
  make·shift make-up
mal·a·chite (măl′ ᴐ·kīt)
mal·ad·justed (măl′ ᴐ·jŭs′ tĕd)
mal·a·dy (măl′ ᴐ·dĭ)
  -dies
ma·laise (mă·lāz′)
ma·lar·i·a (mᴐ·lâr′ ĭ·ᴐ)
Ma·lay·a (mᴐ·lā′ ᴐ)
mal·con·tent (măl′ kŏn·tĕnt′)
mal de mer (mál′ dē mâr′)
mal·e·fac·tor (măl′ ê·făk′ tēr)
ma·lev·o·lent (mᴐ·lĕv′ ô·lĕnt)
mal·fea·sance (măl·fē′ zᴐns)
mal·for·ma·tion
        (măl′ fôr·mā′ shŭn)
mal·ice (măl′ ĭs)
ma·li·cious (mᴐ·lĭsh′ ŭs)
ma·lign (mᴐ·līn′)
  ma·lig·nan·cy (mᴐ·lĭg′ nᴐn·sĭ)
  ma·lig·nant
ma·lin·ger (mᴐ·lĭng′ gēr)
  ma·lin·ger·er
mal·lard (măl′ ērd)
mal·le·a·ble (măl′ ê·ᴐ·b′l)
  mal·le·a·bil·i·ty
        (măl′ ê·ᴐ·bĭl′ ĭ·tĭ)
mal·let (măl′ ĕt)
malm·sey wine (mäm′ zĭ)
mal·nu·tri·tion
        (măl′ nŭ·trĭsh′ ŭn)
mal·prac·tice (măl′ prăk′ tĭs)
malt (môlt)

Mal·thu·sian (măl·thū′ zhᴐn)
malt·ose (môl′ tōs)
mam·ba snake (măm′ bä)
mam·mal (măm′ ᴐl)
  mam·ma·li·an (mă·mā′ lĭ·ᴐn)
  mam·ma·ry (măm′ ᴐ·rĭ)
mam·mon (măm′ ŭn)
mam·moth (măm′ ŭth)
man (măn)
  manned man·ning
  man-at-arms man-eat·er
  man·ful -ful·ly
  -ful·ness man·hole
  man·hood man·kind
  man·ly -li·ness
  man·nish man-of-war
  man·pow·er
man·a·cle (măn′ ᴐ·k′l)
  -cling
man·age (măn′ ĭj)
  -ag·ing
  man·age·a·bil·i·ty
        (măn′ ĭj·ᴐ·bĭl′ ĭ·tĭ)
  man·age·a·ble man·age·ment
  man·ag·er man·ag·er·ess
  man·a·ge·ri·al
        (măn′ ᴐ·jēr′ ĭ·ᴐl)
  -al·ly
ma·ña·na (mä·nyä′ nä)
man·a·tee (măn′ ᴐ·tē′)
man·da·mus, writ of
        (măn·dā′ mŭs)
man·da·rin (măn′ dᴐ·rĭn)
man·date (măn′ dāt)
man·da·to·ry (măn′ dᴐ·tō′ rĭ)
man·di·ble (măn′ dĭ·b′l)
man·do·lin (măn′ dô·lĭn)
ma·neu·ver (mᴐ·nōō′ vēr)
  ma·neu·ver·a·bil·i·ty
        (mᴐ·nōō′ vēr·ᴐ·bĭl′ ĭ·tĭ)
  ma·neu·ver·a·ble
man·ga·nate (măng′ gᴐ·nāt)
man·ga·nese (măng′ gᴐ·nēs)
man·gle (măng′ g′l)
  -gling
man·go (măng′ gō)
  -goes
man·gy (mān′ jĭ)
  man·gi·ness
ma·ni·a (mā′ nĭ·ᴐ)
ma·ni·ac (mā′ nĭ·ăk)
  ma·ni·a·cal (mᴐ·nī′ ᴐ·kᴐl)
ma·nic (mā′ nĭk)
  ma·nic-de·pres·sive

man·i·cure (măn′ ĭ·kūr)
man·i·cur·ist
man·i·fest (măn′ ĭ·fĕst)
man·i·fes·ta·tion
(măn′ ĭ·fĕs·tā′ shŭn)
man·i·fest·ly
man·i·fes·to (măn′ ĭ·fĕs′ tō)
man·i·fold (măn′ ĭ·fōld)
Ma·nil·a paper (må·nĭl′ å)
ma·nip·u·late (må·nĭp′ û·lāt)
-lat·ing
ma·nip·u·la·tion
(må·nĭp′ û·lā′ shŭn)
ma·nip·u·la·tive
(må·nĭp′ û·lā′ tĭv)
ma·nip·u·la·tor
(-lā′ tẽr)
man·na (măn′ å)
man·ne·quin (măn′ ĕ·kĭn)
man·ner (măn′ ẽr)
(way of acting; see manor)
man·ner·ism
man·ner·ly -li·ness
man·or (măn′ ẽr)
(house of an estate; see manner)
ma·no·ri·al (må·nō′ rĭ·ål)
man·sard roof (măn′ särd)
manse (măns)
man·sion (măn′ shŭn)
man·tel (măn′ t′l)
(fireplace framework; see mantle)
man·tel·piece
man·til·la (măn·tĭl′ å)
man·tle (măn′ t′l)
(cloak; see mantel)
man·u·al (măn′ û·ål)
man·u·al·ly
man·u·fac·ture (măn′ û·făk′ tûr)
-tur·ing
man·u·fac·tur·er
ma·nure (må·nūr′)
man·u·script (măn′ û·skrĭpt)
Manx cat (măngks)
man·y-sid·ed (mĕn′ ĭ·sīd′ ĕd)
Ma·o·ri (mä′ ô·rĭ)
Mao Tse-tung (mä′ ô·dzŭ′ dŏŏng′)
map (măp)
mapped map·ping
ma·ple sir·up (mā′ p′l)
ma·ra·ca (må·rä′ kä)
mar·a·schi·no cher·ry
(măr′ å·skē′ nō)
mar·a·thon (măr′ å·thŏn)
ma·raud·er (må·rôd′ ẽr)

mar·ble (mär′ b′l)
-bling mar·ble·ize
mar·chion·ess (mär′ shŭn·ĕs)
Mar·di gras (mär′ dĕ grä′)
mar·ga·rine (mär′ jå·rĭn)
mar·gin (mär′ jĭn)
mar·gin·al
mar·i·gold (măr′ ĭ·gōld)
mar·i·jua·na (măr′ ĭ·wä′ nå)
ma·rim·ba (må·rĭm′ bå)
mar·i·nade (măr′ ĭ·nād′)
mar·i·nate (măr′ ĭ·nāt)
-nat·ing
ma·rine (må·rēn′)
mar·i·ner (măr′ ĭ·nẽr)
mar·i·o·nette (măr′ ĭ·ô·nĕt′)
mar·i·tal (măr′ ĭ·tål)
(matrimonial; see martial)
mar·i·tal·ly
mar·i·time (măr′ ĭ·tīm)
mar·jo·ram (măr′ jô·rắm)
mark·ed·ly (mär′ kĕd·lĭ)
mar·ket (mär′ kĕt)
-ket·ed -ket·ing
mar·ket·a·ble mar·ket place
mar·ket val·ue
marks·man·ship
(märks′ mån·shĭp)
mark·up (märk′ ŭp′)
marl (märl)
mar·lin (mär′ lĭn)
mar·ma·lade (mär′ må·lād)
mar·mo·set (mär′ mô·zĕt)
mar·mot (mär′ mŭt)
ma·roon (må·rōōn′)
mar·quee (mär·kē′)
mar·quis (mär′ kwĭs)
mar·qui·sette (mär′ kĭ·zĕt′)
mar·riage (măr′ ĭj)
mar·riage·a·bil·i·ty
(măr′ ĭj·å·bĭl′ ĭ·tĭ)
mar·riage·a·ble
(măr′ ĭj·å·b′l)
mar·row (măr′ ō)
mar·ry (măr′ ĭ)
mar·ried mar·ry·ing
mar·shal (mär′ shål)
-shaled -shal·ing
marsh·mal·low (märsh′ măl′ ō)
mar·su·pi·al (mär·sū′ pĭ·ål)
mar·ten (mär′ tĕn)
(mammal; see martin)
mar·tial (mär′ shål)
(warlike; see marital)

Mar·ti·an   (mär′ shǐ·ǎn)
  (of Mars)
mar·tin   (mär′ tǐn)
  (bird; see *marten*)
mar·ti·net   (mär′ tǐ·nět′)
mar·tyr   (mär′ tẽr)
  mar·tyr·dom
mar·vel   (mär′ věl)
  -veled   -vel·ing
  mar·vel·ous   (mär′ věl·ŭs)
Marx·ist   (märk′ sǐst)
Mar·y·land   (měr′ ǐ·lǎnd)
  abbr. Md.   Mar·y·land·er
mas·car·a   (măs·kăr′ à)
mas·cot   (măs′ kŏt)
mas·cu·line   (măs′ kŭ·lǐn)
  mas·cu·lin·i·ty
                   (măs′ kŭ·lǐn′ ǐ·tǐ)
mas·och·ism   (măz′ ŏk·ǐz′m)
  mas·och·ist   (-ǐst)
ma·son   (mā′ s′n)
  ma·son·ic   (mà·sŏn′ ǐk)
  ma·son·ry
Ma·son-Dix·on line
                   (mā′ s′n·dǐk′ s′n)
mas·quer·ade   (măs′ kẽr·ād′)
Mas·sa·chu·setts
                   (măs′ à·chōō′ sěts)
  abbr. Mass.
mas·sa·cre   (măs′ à·kẽr)
  mas·sa·cred   (-kẽrd)
  mas·sa·cring   (-krǐng)
mas·sage   (mà·säzh′)
  mas·sag·ing
mas·seur   (mă·sûr′)
  mas·seuse   (mă·sûz′) *fem.*
mas·sive   (măs′ ǐv)
  mas·sive·ly
mas·ter   (măs′ tẽr)
  mas·ter·dom   mas·ter-at-arms
  mas·ter·ful, -ful·ly, -ful·ness
  mas·ter·ly   mas·ter·piece
  mas·ter stroke   mas·ter·work
  mas·ter·y
mast·head   (măst′ hěd′)
mas·ti·cate   (măs′ tǐ·kāt)
  -cat·ing
  mas·ti·ca·tion
                   (măs′ tǐ·kā′ shŭn)
mas·tiff   (măs′ tǐf)
mas·to·don   (măs′ tô·dŏn)
mas·toid   (măs′ toid)
mat·a·dor   (măt′ à·dôr)
match·less   (măch′ lěs)
match·mak·er   (măch′ māk′ ẽr)

ma·te·ri·al   (mà·tẽr′ ǐ·ǎl)
  (substance; see *matériel*)
  ma·te·ri·al·ism
  ma·te·ri·al·ist   ma·te·ri·al·ize
  ma·te·ri·al·ly
ma·té·ri·el   (mà·tẽr′ ǐ·ěl′)
  (equipment; see *material*)
ma·ter·nal   (mà·tûr′ nǎl)
  ma·ter·nal·ly
  ma·ter·ni·ty   (mà·tûr′ nǐ·tǐ)
math·e·mat·ics
                   (măth′ ê·măt′ ǐks)
  math·e·mat·i·cal, -cal·ly
  math·e·ma·ti·cian
                   (măth′ ê·mà·tǐsh′ ǎn)
mat·in   (măt′ ǐn)
  mat·in·al   (măt′ ǐ·nǎl)
mat·i·nee   (măt′ ǐ·nā′)
ma·tri·arch   (mā′ trǐ·ärk)
  ma·tri·arch·y   (mā′ trǐ·är′ kǐ)
ma·tric·u·late   (mà·trǐk′ ū·lāt)
  -lat·ing
  ma·tric·u·la·tion
                   (mà·trǐk′ ū·lā′ shŭn)
mat·ri·mo·ny   (măt′ rǐ·mō′ nǐ)
  mat·ri·mo·ni·al
                   (măt′ rǐ·mō′ nǐ·ǎl)
  -al·ly
ma·trix   (mā′ trǐks)
  pl. ma·tri·ces   (mā′ trǐ·sēz)
ma·tron   (mā′ trŭn)
  ma·tron·ly   -li·ness
mat·ter   (măt′ ẽr)
  mat·ter-of-fact *adj.*
mat·ting   (măt′ ǐng)
mat·tress   (măt′ rěs)
ma·ture   (mà·tūr′)
  -tur·ing
  mat·u·ra·tion   (măt′ û·rā′ shŭn)
  ma·ture·ly
  ma·tu·ri·ty   (mà·tū′ rǐ·tǐ)
maud·lin   (môd′ lǐn)
Mau·i is., Ha·wai·i
                   (mou′ ê)
maul·er   (môl′ ẽr)
Maun·dy Thurs·day
                   (môn′ dǐ)
Mau·re·ta·ni·a, Afr.
                   (mô′ rě·tā′ nǐ·à)
mau·so·le·um   (mô′ sò·lē′ ŭm)
mauve   (mōv)
mav·er·ick   (măv′ ẽr·ǐk)
mawk·ish   (môk′ ǐsh)
max·im   (măk′ sǐm)
max·i·mal   (măk′ sǐ·mǎl)

max·i·mum (măk′ sĭ·mŭm)
  pl. max·i·ma
  max·i·mize -miz·ing
may·hem (mā′ hĕm)
may·on·naise (mā′ ŏ·nāz′)
may·or (mā′ ēr)
  may·or·al·ty (mā′ ēr·ăl·tĭ)
maze (māz)
  (labyrinth; see *maize*)
ma·zur·ka (má·zûr′ ká)
mead (mēd)
  (fermented drink; see *meed*)
mead·ow (mĕd′ ō)
mea·ger (mē′ gēr)
meal·time (mēl′ tīm′)
meal·y (mēl′ ĭ)
  meal·i·ness meal·y·mouthed
mean (mēn)
  (intend; see *mien*)
  mean·ing·less mean·ness
  mean·time mean·while
me·an·der·ing (mē·ăn′ dēr·ĭng)
mea·sles (mē′ z′lz)
meas·ure (mĕzh′ ēr)
  -ur·ing
  meas·ur·a·bil·i·ty
    (mĕzh′ ēr·á·bĭl′ ĭ·tĭ)
  meas·ur·a·ble meas·ure·less
  meas·ure·ment
meat (mēt)
  (food; see *meet*, *mete*)
meat·y (mēt′ ĭ)
  meat·i·er, -i·est, -i·ness
me·chan·ic (mē·kăn′ ĭk)
  me·chan·i·cal
  mech·a·nism (mĕk′ á·nĭz′m)
  mech·a·nis·tic (mĕk′ á·nĭs′ tĭk)
  mech·a·nize (mĕk′ á·nīz)
med·al (mĕd′ ′l)
  med·al·ist
  me·dal·lion (mē·dăl′ yŭn)
med·dle (mĕd′ ′l)
  med·dling med·dler
  med·dle·some
me·di·a (mē′ dĭ·á)
  pl. of me·di·um
me·di·an (mē′ dĭ·ăn)
me·di·ate (mē′ dĭ·āt)
  -at·ing
  me·di·a·tion (mē′ dĭ·ā′ shŭn)
  me·di·a·tor
med·i·cal (mĕd′ ĭ·kăl)
med·i·cate (mĕd′ ĭ·kāt)
  -cat·ing

med·i·ca·tion
    (mĕd′ ĭ·kā′ shŭn)
med·i·ca·tive (mĕd′ ĭ·kā′ tĭv)
med·i·cine (mĕd′ ĭ·sĭn)
  me·dic·i·nal (mē·dĭs′ ĭ·năl)
  -nal·ly
me·di·e·val (mē′ dĭ·ē′ văl)
me·di·o·cre (mē′ dĭ·ō′ kēr)
  me·di·oc·ri·ty (mē′ dĭ·ŏk′ rĭ·tĭ)
med·i·tate (mĕd′ ĭ·tāt)
  -tat·ing
  med·i·ta·tion (mĕd′ ĭ·tā′ shŭn)
  med·i·ta·tive (mĕd′ ĭ·tā′ tĭv)
  med·i·ta·tor
Med·i·ter·ra·ne·an (sea)
    (mĕd′ ĭ·tĕ·rā′ nē·ăn)
me·di·um (mē′ dĭ·ŭm)
  pl. me·di·ums (in general sense)
  pl. me·di·a (as in "communica-
  tions media" and in scientific
  sense)
med·ley (mĕd′ lĭ)
  -leys
Me·du·sa (mē·dū′ sá)
meed (mēd)
  (reward; see *mead*)
meek (mēk)
meer·schaum (mēr′ shŭm)
meet (mēt)
  (come upon; see *meat*, *mete*)
meet·ing·house (mēt′ ĭng·hous′)
meg·a·cy·cle (mĕg′ á·sī′ k′l)
meg·a·lo·ma·ni·a
    (mĕg′ á·lō·mā′ nĭ·á)
meg·a·phone (mĕg′ á·fōn)
meg·a·ton (mĕg′ á·tŭn′)
Meis·ter·sing·er
    (mīs′ tēr·sĭng′ ēr)
mel·an·cho·li·a
    (mĕl′ ăn·kō′ lĭ·á)
  mel·an·chol·ic (-kŏl′ ĭk)
  mel·an·chol·y (-kŏl′ ĭ)
Mel·a·ne·sia (mĕl′ á·nē′ zhá)
mé·lange (mā′ länzh′)
me·lee (má·lā′)
mel·lif·lu·ent (mē·lĭf′ lōō·ĕnt)
  -ence mel·lif·lu·ous
mel·low (mĕl′ ō)
mel·o·dra·ma (mĕl′ ō·drä′ má)
  mel·o·dra·mat·ic
    (mĕl′ ō·drá·măt′ ĭk)
mel·o·dy (mĕl′ ō·dĭ)
  -dies
  me·lo·dic (mē·lŏd′ ĭk)
  me·lo·di·ous (mē·lō′ dĭ·ŭs)

mel·on　　　　　(měl′ ŭn)
melt　　　　　　(mělt)
　melt·a·ble　　melt·ing pot
mem·brane　　　(měm′ brān)
　mem·bra·nous　(měm′ brȧ·nŭs)
me·men·to　　　(mě·měn′ tō)
　-tos
mem·o　　　　　(měm′ ō)
　-os
mem·oir　　　　(měm′ wär)
mem·o·ra·ble　　(měm′ ŏ·rȧ·b'l)
　mem·o·ra·bil·i·a
　　　　　　　　(měm′ ŏ·rȧ·bĭl′ ĭ·ȧ)
　mem·o·ra·bil·i·ty
　　　　　　　　(měm′ ŏ·rȧ·bĭl′ ĭ·tĭ)
mem·o·ran·dum
　　　　　　　　(měm′ ŏ·răn′ dŭm)
　pl. -dums or -da
me·mo·ri·al　　(mě·mō′ rĭ·ȧl)
　me·mo·ri·al·ize
mem·o·ry　　　　(měm′ ŏ·rĭ)
　-ries
　mem·o·ri·za·tion
　　　　　　　　(měm′ ŏ·rĭ·zā′ shŭn)
　mem·o·rize　　-iz·ing
men·ace　　　　(měn′ ĭs)
　men·ac·ing·ly
mé·nage　　　　(mȧ·näzh′)
me·nag·er·ie　　(mě·năj′ ĕr·ĭ)
men·da·cious　　(měn·dā′ shŭs)
　men·dac·i·ty　(měn·dăs′ ĭ·tĭ)
Men·del's law　　(měn′ dělz)
　Men·de·li·an　(měn·dē′ lĭ·ȧn)
men·di·cant　　(měn′ dĭ·kȧnt)
　-can·cy
me·ni·al　　　　(mē′ nĭ·ȧl)
　-al·ly
men·in·gi·tis　　(měn′ ĭn·jī′ tĭs)
men·o·pause　　(měn′ ŏ·pôz)
men·stru·ate　　(měn′ strŏŏ·āt)
　-at·ing　　　men·stru·al
　men·stru·a·tion
　　　　　　　　(měn′ strŏŏ·ā′ shŭn)
men·su·ra·tion
　　　　　　　　(měn′ shŏŏ·rā′ shŭn)
men·tal　　　　(měn′ tȧl)
　men·tal·i·ty　(měn·tăl′ ĭ·tĭ)
　men·tal·ly
men·thol　　　　(měn′ thōl)
　men·tho·lat·ed
　　　　　　　　(měn′ thŏ·lāt′ ĕd)
men·tion　　　　(měn′ shŭn)
　men·tiŏn·a·ble
men·tor　　　　(měn′ tēr)

men·u　　　　　(měn′ ū)
　-us
Meph·i·stoph·e·les
　　　　　　　　(měf′ ĭ·stŏf′ ě·lēz)
mer·can·tile　　(mûr′ kȧn·tĭl)
　mer·can·til·ism
　　　　　　　　(mûr′ kȧn·tĭl·ĭz'm)
mer·ce·nar·y　　(mûr′ sě·něr′ ĭ)
　nari·es
mer·cer·ized thread
　　　　　　　　(mûr′ sěr·ĭzd)
mer·chan·dise　(mûr′ chȧn·dīz)
mer·chant　　　(mûr′ chȧnt)
Mer·cu·ro·chrome
　　　　　　　　(mûr·kū′ rŏ·krōm′)
mer·cu·ry　　　(mûr′ kŭ·rĭ)
　mer·cu·ri·al　(mûr·kū′ rĭ·ȧl)
　mer·cu·ric　　(mûr·kū′ rĭk)
　mer·cu·ry-va·por lamp
mer·cy　　　　　(mûr′ sĭ)
　-cies
　mer·ci·ful, -ful·ly, -ful·ness
　mer·ci·less　　-less·ness
mere　　　　　(mēr)
　mere·ly
mer·e·tri·cious　(měr′ ě·trĭsh′ ŭs)
mer·gan·ser duck
　　　　　　　　(měr·găn′ sēr)
merge　　　　　(mûrj)
　merg·ing　　　mer·gence
　merg·er
me·rid·i·an　　(mě·rĭd′ ĭ·ȧn)
me·ringue　　　(mě·răng′)
mer·it　　　　　(měr′ ĭt)
　-it·ed　　　　-it·ing
　mer·i·to·ri·ous
　　　　　　　　(měr′ ĭ·tō′ rĭ·ŭs)
mer·maid　　　(mûr′ mād′)
mer·ry　　　　　(měr′ ĭ)
　mer·ri·ment　mer·ri·ly
　mer·ry-go-round
　mer·ry·mak·er
me·sa　　　　　(mā′ sȧ)
Me·sa·bi (iron range)
　　　　　　　　(mě·sä′ bĭ)
mes·cal　　　　(měs·kăl′)
mes·mer·ize　　(měz′ mēr·īz)
　-iz·ing
　mes·mer·ism　(měz′ mēr·ĭz'm)
mes·quite　　　(měs·kēt′)
mes·sage　　　　(měs′ ĭj)
　mes·sen·ger　(měs′ ěn·jēr)
Mes·si·ah　　　(mě·sī′ ȧ)
　Mes·si·an·ic　(měs′ ĭ·ăn′ ĭk)
mess kit　　　　(měs)

mess·mate (mĕs′ māt′)
mess·y (mĕs′ ĭ)
  mess·i·ness
mes·ti·zo (mĕs·tē′ zō)
  -zos
me·tab·o·lism (mĕ·tăb′ ô·lĭz′m)
  met·a·bol·ic (mĕt′ ȧ·bŏl′ ĭk)
met·al (mĕt′ ′l)
  (substance; see *mettle*)
  me·tal·lic (mĕ·tăl′ ĭk)
  met·al·lur·gist (mĕt′ ′l·ûr′ jĭst)
  met·al·lur·gy (mĕt′ ′l·ûr′ jĭ)
  met·al·ware met·al·work·er
met·a·mor·pho·sis
        (mĕt′ ȧ·môr′ fô·sĭs)
  pl. met·a·mor·pho·ses
  met·a·mor·phic
        (mĕt′ ȧ·môr′ fĭk)
met·a·phor (mĕt′ ȧ·fêr)
  met·a·phor·i·cal
        (mĕt′ ȧ·fŏr′ ĭ·kȧl)
met·a·phys·ics (mĕt′ ȧ·fĭz′ ĭks)
  met·a·phys·i·cal (-fĭz′ ĭ·kȧl)
  met·a·phy·si·cian (-fĭ·zĭsh′ ȧn)
met·a·tar·sal (mĕt′ ȧ·tär′ sȧl)
mete (mēt)
  (allot; see *meat, meet*)
  met·ing
me·te·or (mē′ tê·ẽr)
  me·te·or·ic (mē′ tê·ŏr′ ĭk)
  me·te·or·ite (mē′ tê·ẽr·īt)
me·te·or·ol·o·gy
        (mē′ tê·ẽr·ŏl′ ô·jĭ)
  me·te·or·o·log·i·cal
        (mē′ tê·ẽr·ô·lŏj′ ĭ·kȧl)
  me·te·or·ol·o·gist
        (mē′ tê·ẽr·ŏl′ ô·jĭst)
me·ter (mē′ tẽr)
meth·ane (mĕth′ ān)
meth·od (mĕth′ ŭd)
  me·thod·i·cal (mĕ·thŏd′ ĭ·kȧl)
  meth·od·o·log·i·cal
        (mĕth′ ŭd·ô·lŏj′ ĭ·kȧl)
  meth·od·ol·o·gy
        (mĕth′ ŭd·ŏl′ ô·jĭ)
Meth·od·ist (mĕth′ ŭd·ĭst)
Me·thu·se·lah (mē·thū′ zĕ·lȧ)
meth·yl (mĕth′ ĭl)
  meth·yl·ene
me·tic·u·lous (mē·tĭk′ û·lŭs)
met·ric (mĕt′ rĭk)
  met·ri·cal
met·ro·nome (mĕt′ rô·nōm)
me·trop·o·lis (mē·trŏp′ ô·lĭs)

met·ro·pol·i·tan
        (mĕt′ rô·pŏl′ ĭ·tăn)
met·tle (mĕt′ ′l)
  (spirit; see *metal*)
mez·za·nine (mĕz′ ȧ·nēn)
mez·zo-so·pra·no
        (mĕd′ zô·sô·prä′ nō)
mi·as·ma (mī·ăz′ mȧ)
mi·ca (mī′ kȧ)
Mich·i·gan (mĭsh′ ĭ·gȧn)
  abbr. Mich.
  Mich·i·gan·ite *or*
  Mich·i·gan·der
        (mĭsh′ ĭ·găn′ dẽr)
micro- (mī′ krô-)
  mi·cro·a·nal·y·sis
  mi·cro·cosm (mī′ krô·kŏz′m)
  mi·cro·cos·mic
        (mī′ krô·kŏz′ mĭk)
  mi·cro·film mi·cro·groove
  mi·crom·e·ter (mī·krŏm′ ê·tẽr)
  mi·cro·or·gan·ism
        (mī′ krô·ôr′ găn·ĭz′m)
  mi·cro·phone mi·cro·print
  mi·cro·scope (mī′ krô·skōp)
  mi·cro·scop·ic (-skŏp′ ĭk)
  mi·cro·wave
mi·crobe (mī′ krōb)
mi·cron (mī′ krŏn)
mid- (mĭd-)
  mid-chan·nel mid-con·ti·nent
  mid·day mid·land
  mid-o·cean mid·night
  mid-point mid·riff
  mid·ship·man mid·sum·mer
  mid·way mid·week
  Mid·west Mid·west·ern·er
  mid·wife mid·win·ter
  mid·year
Mi·das (mī′ dȧs)
mid·dle (mĭd′ ′l)
  mid·dle age mid·dle-aged
  mid·dle class *n.*
  mid·dle-class *adj.*
  mid·dle ear Mid·dle East
  mid·dle·man mid·dle·weight
  Mid·dle West
  Mid·dle West·ern·er
mid·dling (mĭd′ lĭng)
mid·dy blouse (mĭd′ ĭ)
midg·et (mĭj′ ĕt)
mid·riff (mĭd′ rĭf)
midst (mĭdst)
mien (mēn)
  (demeanor; see *mean*)

might (mīt)
(strength; see *mite*)
might·y (mīt′ ĭ)
 might·i·er, -i·est, -i·ly, -i·ness
mi·gnon·ette (mĭn′ yŭn·ĕt′)
mi·graine head·ache
 (mī′ grān)
mi·grate (mī′ grāt)
 -grat·ing
mi·grant (mī′ grănt)
mi·gra·tion (mī·grā′ shŭn)
mi·gra·to·ry (mī′ grȧ·tō′ rĭ)
mi·ka·do (mĭ·kä′ dō)
mi·la·dy (mĭ·lā′ dĭ)
mil·dew (mĭl′ dū)
mile·age (mīl′ ĭj)
mile·stone (mīl′ stōn′)
mi·lieu (mē′ lyû′)
mil·i·tar·y (mĭl′ ĭ·tĕr′ ĭ)
 mil·i·tan·cy (-tăn′ sĭ)
 mil·i·tant (-tănt)
 mil·i·ta·rist (mĭl′ ĭ·tȧ·rĭst)
 mil·i·ta·ris·tic
 (mĭl′ ĭ·tȧ·rĭs′ tĭk)
 mil·i·ta·rize -riz·ing
 mil·i·tate -tat·ing
mi·li·tia (mĭ·lĭsh′ ȧ)
milk (mĭlk)
 milk·man
 milk of mag·ne·sia
 milk shake milk·sop
 milk·weed milk·y
mil·len·ni·um (mĭ·lĕn′ ĭ·ŭm)
 pl. mil·len·nia mil·len·ni·al
mil·le·pede (mĭl′ ĕ·pēd′)
mil·let (mĭl′ ĕt)
mil·li·me·ter (mĭl′ ĭ·mē′ tĕr)
mil·li·ner (mĭl′ ĭ·nĕr)
 mil·li·ner·y (-nĕr′ ĭ)
mil·lion (mĭl′ yŭn)
 mil·lion·aire (mĭl′ yŭn·âr′)
 mil·lionth
mill·stone (mĭl′ stōn′)
mill·wright (mĭl′ rīt′)
mi·lord (mĭ·lôrd′)
Mil·wau·kee, Wis.
 (mĭl′ wô′ kĕ)
mime (mīm)
 mi·met·ic (mĭ·mĕt′ ĭk)
mim·e·o·graph (mĭm′ ĕ·ō·grȧf′)
mim·ic (mĭm′ ĭk)
 mim·ick·er mim·ic·ry
mi·mo·sa (mĭ·mō′ sȧ)
min·a·ret (mĭn′ ȧ·rĕt′)
mince·meat (mĭns′ mēt′)

minc·ing·ly (mĭn′ sĭng·lĭ)
mind (mīnd)
 mind·ful, -ful·ly, -ful·ness
 mind·less mind read·er
 mind's eye
min·er (mīn′ ĕr)
 (one who mines; see *minor*)
min·er·al (mĭn′ ĕr·ăl)
 min·er·al·ize -iz·ing
 min·er·al·og·i·cal
 (mĭn′ ĕr·ăl·ŏj′ ĭ·kăl)
 min·er·al·o·gy
 (mĭn′ ĕr·ăl′ ō·jĭ)
mi·ne·stro·ne soup
 (mĕ·nȧ·strō′ nȧ)
min·gle (mĭng′ g'l)
 -gling
min·i·a·ture (mĭn′ ĭ·ȧ·tụr)
min·i·mum (mĭn′ ĭ·mŭm)
 min·i·mal (-măl)
 min·i·mize -miz·ing
min·ing (mĭn′ ĭng)
min·ion (mĭn′ yŭn)
min·is·ter (mĭn′ ĭs·tĕr)
 min·is·te·ri·al (mĭn′ ĭs·tẽr′ ĭ·ăl)
 min·is·tra·tion (mĭn′ ĭs·trā′ shŭn)
 min·is·try (mĭn′ ĭs·trĭ)
 -tries
Min·ne·ap·o·lis, (mĭn′ ĕ·ăp′ ō·lĭs)
 Minn.
Min·ne·so·ta (mĭn′ ĕ·sō′ tȧ)
 abbr. Minn. Min·ne·so·tan
min·now (mĭn′ ō)
mi·nor (mī′ nĕr)
 (under age; see *miner*)
mi·nor·i·ty (mĭ·nŏr′ ĭ·tĭ)
 -ties
min·strel (mĭn′ strĕl)
mint·age (mĭn′ tĭj)
mint ju·lep (mĭnt)
min·u·et (mĭn′ û·ĕt′)
mi·nus (mī′ nŭs)
mi·nus·cule (mĭ·nŭs′ kūl)
min·ute (mĭn′ ĭt)
 (time unit) min·ute·man
mi·nute (mĭ·nūt′)
 (little) mi·nute·ly
mi·nu·ti·a (mĭ·nū′ shĭ·ȧ)
 pl. mi·nu·tiae (-ē)
minx (mĭngks)
 minx·es
mir·a·cle (mĭr′ ȧ·k'l)
 mi·rac·u·lous (mĭ·răk′ û·lŭs)
mi·rage (mĭ·räzh′)
mire (mīr)

mir·ror   (mǐr′ ĕr)
  mir·rored   mir·ror·ing
mirth   (mûrth)
  mirth·ful, -ful·ly, -ful·ness
mis·al·li·ance   (mǐs′ ȧ·lī′ ȧns)
mis·an·thrope   (mǐs′ ăn·thrōp)
  mis·an·throp·ic
       (mǐs′ ăn·thrŏp′ ǐk)
mis·be·got·ten   (mǐs′ bê·gŏt′ 'n)
mis·cal·cu·la·tion
    (mǐs′ kăl·kû·lā′ shŭn)
mis·car·riage   (mǐs·kăr′ ǐj)
mis·ce·ge·na·tion
    (mǐs′ ê·jê·nā′ shŭn)
mis·cel·la·ne·ous
    (mǐs′ ê·lā′ nê·ŭs)
  mis·cel·la·ny   (mǐs′ ê·lā′ nǐ)
mis·chief   (mǐs′ chǐf)
  mis·chie·vous   (mǐs′ chǐ·vŭs)
mis·con·cep·tion
    (mǐs′ kŏn·sĕp′ shŭn)
mis·con·strue   (mǐs′ kŏn·strōō′)
  -stru·ing
mis·de·mean·or
    (mǐs′ dê·mēn′ ĕr)
mi·ser   (mī′ zĕr)
mis·er·a·ble   (mǐz′ ĕr·ȧ·b'l)
mis·fea·sance   (mǐs·fē′ zȧns)
mis·hap   (mǐs·hăp′)
mis·in·ter·pre·ta·tion
    (mǐs′ ǐn·tûr′ prê·tā′ shŭn)
mis·judgment   (mǐs·jǔj′ mĕnt)
mis·man·age·ment
    (mǐs′ măn′ ǐj·mĕnt)
mis·no·mer   (mǐs·nō′ mĕr)
mi·sog·y·ny   (mǐ·sŏj′ ǐ·nǐ)
mis·rep·re·sen·ta·tion
    (mǐs′ rĕp·rê·zĕn·tā′ shŭn)
mis·sal   (mǐs′ ȧl)
  (devotional book; see *missile*)
mis·shap·en   (mǐs·shāp′ ĕn)
mis·sile   (mǐs′ ǐl)
  (self-propelling weapon; see *missal*)
mis·sion   (mǐsh′ ŭn)
mis·sion·ar·y   (mǐsh′ ŭn·ĕr′ ǐ)
  -aries
Mis·sis·sip·pi   (mǐs′ ǐ·sǐp′ ǐ)
  abbr. Miss.
  Mis·sis·sip·pi·an
mis·sive   (mǐs′ ǐv)
Mis·sou·ri   (mǐ·zōōr′ ǐ)
  abbr. Mo.   Mis·sou·ri·an
mis·spell   (mǐs·spĕl′)

mis·state   (mǐs·stāt′)
  mis·stat·ing
mis·step   (mǐs·stĕp′)
  mis·stepped   mis·step·ping
mis·take   (mǐs·tāk′)
  -tak·ing   mis·tak·a·ble
  mis·tak·en
mis·tle·toe   (mǐs′ 'l·tō)
mis·tress   (mǐs′ trĕs)
mis·un·der·stand·ing
    (mǐs′ ŭn·dĕr·stănd′ ǐng)
mite   (mīt)
  (a bit; see *might*)
mi·ter   (mī′ tĕr)
mit·i·gate   (mǐt′ ǐ·gāt)
  -gat·ing   mit·i·gant
  mit·i·ga·tion (mǐt′ ǐ·gā′ shŭn)
  mit·i·ga·tor
mitt   (mǐt)
mit·ten   (mǐt′ 'n)
mix   (mǐks)
  mix·ture   (mǐks′ tûr)
  mix-up
mne·mon·ics   (nê·mŏn′ ǐks)
moat   (mōt)
  (ditch; see *mote*)
mo·bile   (mō′ bǐl) *adj.*
  mo·bil·i·ty   (mô·bǐl′ ǐ·tǐ)
mo·bile   (mō′ bēl) *n.*
mo·bi·lize   (mō′ bǐ·līz)
  -liz·ing
  mo·bi·li·za·tion
    (mō′ bǐ·lǐ·zā′ zhŭn)
mob·oc·ra·cy   (mŏb·ŏk′ rȧ·sǐ)
moc·ca·sin   (mŏk′ ȧ·sǐn)
mock   (mŏk)
  mock·er·y   mock-he·ro·ic
  mock·ing·bird
mod·al   (mōd′ ȧl)
  (pertaining to mode; see *model*)
mod·el   (mŏd′ 'l)
  (design; see *modal*)
  -eled   -el·ing
mod·er·ate   (mŏd′ ĕr·ǐt)
  mod·er·ate·ly
  mod·er·a·tion (mŏd′ĕr·ā′shŭn)
  mod·er·a·tor   (mŏd′ ĕr·ā′ tĕr)
mod·ern   (mŏd′ ĕrn)
  mod·ern·is·tic (mŏd′ ĕr·nǐs′ tǐk)
  mo·der·ni·ty   (mŏ·dûr′ nǐ·tǐ)
  mod·ern·i·za·tion
    (mŏd′ ĕr·nǐ·zā′ shŭn)
mod·ern·ize   (mŏd′ ĕr·nīz)
  -iz·ing   mod·ern·ness

mod·est   (mŏd′ ĕst)
  mod·est·ly   mod·es·ty
mod·i·cum   (mŏd′ ĭ·kŭm)
mod·i·fy   (mŏd′ ĭ·fī)
  -fied,   -fy·ing
  mod·i·fi·a·ble   (mŏd′ ĭ·fī′ ȧ·b'l)
  mod·i·fi·ca·tion
                    (mŏd′ ĭ·fĭ·kā′ shŭn)
  mod·i·fi·er
mod·ish   (mŏd′ ĭsh)
mo·diste   (mō·dēst′)
mod·u·late   (mŏd′ ū·lāt)
  -lat·ing
  mod·u·la·tion   (mŏd·û·lā′shŭn)
  mod·u·la·tor
mo·dus o·pe·ran·di
              (mō′ dŭs ŏp′ ĕ·răn′ dī)
mo·gul   (mō′ gŭl)
mo·hair   (mō′ hâr′)
Mo·ham·med·an
                    (mō·hăm′ ĕ·dȧn)
Mo·hawk   (mō′ hôk)
moi·ré   (mwȧ′ rā′)
moist   (moist)
  mois·ten   (mois′ 'n)
  mois·ture   (mois′ tŭr)
  mois·ture·proof
  mois·tur·ize   -iz·ing
mo·lar   (mō′ lĕr)
mo·las·ses   mȯ·lăs′ ĕz)
mold   (mōld)
  mold·a·ble   mold·ing
  mold·y
mol·e·cule   (mŏl′ ĕ·kūl)
  mo·lec·u·lar   (mō·lĕk′ û·lēr)
mole·hill   (mōl′ hĭl′)
mo·lest   (mō·lĕst′)
  mo·les·ta·tion
                    (mō′ lĕs·tā′ shŭn)
  mo·lest·er
mol·li·fy   (mŏl′ ĭ·fī)
  -fied,   -fy·ing
  mol·li·fi·ca·tion
                    (mŏl′ ĭ·fĭ·kā′ shŭn)
mol·lusk   (mŏl′ ŭsk)
mol·ly·cod·dle   (mŏl′ ĭ·kŏd′ 'l)
  -cod·dling
mol·ten   (mōl′ tĕn)
mo·lyb·de·num
                    (mō·lĭb′ dĕ·nŭm)
mo·ment   (mō′ mĕnt)
mo·men·tar·y   (mō′ mĕn·tĕr′ ĭ)
  mo·men·tar·i·ly
mo·men·tous   (mō·mĕn′ tŭs)

mo·men·tum   (mō·mĕn′ tŭm)
  pl. mo·men·ta
Mo·na Li·sa   (mō′ nȧ lē′ zȧ)
mon arch   (mŏn′ ĕrk)
  mo·nar·chic   (mō·när′ kĭk)
  mon·arch·y   (mŏn′ ĕr·kĭ)
  -arch·ies
mon·as·ter·y   (mŏn′ ȧs·tĕr′ ĭ)
  -ter·ies
mo·nas·tic   (mō·năs′ tĭk)
  mo·nas·ti·cism
                    (mō·năs′ tĭ·sĭz'm)
mon·e·tar·y   (mŏn′ ĕ·tĕr′ ĭ)
  mon·e·tar·i·ly
mon·e·tize   (mŏn′ ĕ·tīz)
  -tiz·ing
mon·ey   (mŭn′ ĭ)
  mon·eyed
  mon·ey-chang·er
  mon·ey-lend·er
  mon·ey-mak·ing
  mon·ey or·der
mon·ger   (mŭng′ gĕr)
Mon·gol   (mŏng′ gŏl)
  Mon·go·lian   (mŏng·gō′ yȧn)
  Mon·gol·oid   (mŏng′ gŏl·oid)
mon·goose   (mŏng′ gōōs)
mon·grel   (mŭng′ grĕl)
mon·i·ker   (mŏn′ ĭ·kĕr)
mon·i·tor   (mŏn′ ĭ·tĕr)
monk   (mŭngk)
  monk·er·y   monk·ish
mon·key   (mŭng′ kĭ)
  -keys   mon·key·shine
  mon·key wrench
mon·o·chro·ma·tic
                    (mŏn′ ō·krō·măt′ ĭk)
mon·o·cle   (mŏn′ ō·k'l)
mo·nog·a·my   (mō·nŏg′ ȧ·mĭ)
  mo·nog·a·mist (-mĭst)
  mo·nog·a·mous   (-mŭs)
mon·o·gram   (mŏn′ ō·grăm)
  mon·o·gram·mat·ic
                    (mŏn′ ō·grȧ·măt′ ĭk)
mon·o·graph   (mŏn′ ō·grȧf)
mo·nog·y·ny   (mō·nŏj′ ĭ·nĭ)
mon·o·lith·ic   (mŏn′ ō·lĭth′ ĭk)
mon·o·logue   (mŏn′ ō·lŏg)
mon·o·man·ia   (mŏn′ ō·mā′ nĭ·ȧ)
mo·nop·o·ly   (mō·nŏp′ ō·lĭ)
  -lies
  mo·nop·o·lis·tic
                    (mō·nŏp′ ō·lĭs′ tĭk)
mo·nop·o·lize, -liz·ing

mon·o·syl·la·ble
    (mŏn′ ô·sĭl′ ȧ·b'l)
  mon·o·syl·lab·ic
    (mŏn′ ô·sĭ·lăb′ ĭk)
mon·o·the·ism
    (mŏn′ ô·thē·ĭz'm)
  mon·o·the·is·tic
    (mŏn′ ô·thē·ĭs′ tĭk)
mon·o·tone   (mŏn′ ô·tōn)
mo·not·o·nous (mô·nŏt′ ô·nŭs)
  mo·not·o·ny (mô·nŏt′ ô·nĭ)
mon·ox·ide   (mŏn·ŏk′ sīd)
mon·sieur   (mẽ·syûʹ)
mon·si·gnor (mŏn·sē′ nyôr)
mon·soon   (mŏn·sōōn′)
mon·ster   (mŏn′ stẽr)
  mon·stros·i·ty (mŏn·strŏs′ ĭ·tĭ)
  -ties
  mon·strous (mŏn′ strŭs)
mon·tage   (mŏn·täzh′)
Mon·tan·a   (mŏn·tăn′ ȧ)
  abbr. Mont. Mon·tan·an
Mon·te Car·lo (mŏn′ tĕ kär′ lō)
Mon·te·rey, Calif.
    (mŏn′ tĕ·rā′)
Mon·ter·rey, Mex.
    (mŏn′ tĕ·rā′)
month·ly   (mŭnth′ lĭ)
  -lies
mon·u·ment (mŏn′ û·mĕnt)
  mon·u·men·tal
    (mŏn′ û·mĕn′ tăl)
mood·y   (mōōd′ ĭ)
  mood·i·er, -i·est, -i·ly, -i·ness
moon   (mōōn)
  moon·beam moon·light
  moon·shine moon·stone
  moon-struck
moor·age   (mŏŏr′ ĭj)
Moor·ish   (mŏŏr′ ĭsh)
moose   (mōōs)
  n. sing. & pl.
moot court   (mōōt)
mope   (mōp)
  mop·ing mop·ish
mop·pet   (mŏp′ ĕt)
mo·raine   (mô·rān′)
mor·al   (mŏr′ ăl)
  (ethical)
  mor·al·ist
  mor·al·is·tic (mŏr′ ăl·ĭs′ tĭk)
  mor·al·i·ty (mô·răl′ ĭ·tĭ)
  mor·al·i·za·tion
    (mŏr′ ăl·ĭ·zā′ shŭn)
  mor·al·i·zer mor·al·ly

mo·rale   (mô·rál′)
  (zeal)
mo·rass   (mô·răs′)
mor·a·to·ri·um
    (mŏr′ ȧ·tō′ rĭ·ŭm)
  pl. mor·a·to·ri·a
mo·ray eel   (mô·rā′)
mor·bid   (môr′ bĭd)
  mor·bid·i·ty (môr·bĭd′ ĭ·tĭ)
mor·dant   (môr′ dănt)
  -dan·cy
more·o·ver (môr·ō′ vẽr)
mo·res   (mō′ rēz)
  (customs)
mor·ga·nat·ic (môr′ gȧ·năt′ ĭk)
morgue   (môrg)
mor·i·bund (môr′ ĭ·bŭnd)
Mor·mon   (môr′ mŭn)
morn·ing   (môr′ nĭng)
  (early day; see *mourning*)
  morn·ing-glo·ry
  morn·ing star
Mo·roc·can (mô·rŏk′ ăn)
mo·roc·co leath·er
    (mô·rŏk′ ō)
mo·ron   (mō′ rŏn)
  mo·ron·ic (mô·rŏn′ ĭk)
mo·rose   (mô·rōs′)
  mo·rose·ly
mor·phine (môr′ fēn)
mor·phol·o·gy (môr·fŏl′ ô·jĭ)
  mor·pho·log·i·cal
    (môr′ fô·lŏj′ ĭ·kăl)
Mor·ris chair (môr′ ĭs)
mor·row   (môr′ ō)
Morse code (môrs)
mor·sel   (môr′ sĕl)
mor·tal   (môr′ tăl)
  mor·tal·i·ty (môr·tăl′ ĭ·tĭ)
  mor·tal·ly
mor·tar   (môr′ tẽr)
  mor·tar·board
mort·gage (môr′ gĭj)
  -gag·ing
  mort·ga·gee (môr′ gĭ·jē′)
  mort·ga·gor
mor·ti·cian (môr·tĭsh′ ăn)
mor·ti·fy   (môr′ tĭ·fī)
  -fied -fy·ing
  mor·ti·fi·ca·tion
    (môr′ tĭ·fĭ·kā′ shŭn)
mor·tise   (môr′ tĭs)
mor·tu·ar·y (môr′ tû·ĕr′ ĭ)
  -ar·ies
mo·sa·ic   (mô·zā′ ĭk)

Mo·selle wine   (mô·zĕl′)
Mo·ses   (mō′ zĭz)
    Mo·sa·ic law   (mō·zā′ ĭk)
mo·sey   (mō′ zĭ)
    -sey·ing
Mos·lem   (mŏz′ lĕm)
mosque   (mŏsk)
mos·qui·to   (mŭs·kē′ tō)
    -toes
moss   (môs)
most·ly   (mōst′ lĭ)
mote   (mōt)
    (particle; see *moat*)
mo·tel   (mō·tĕl′)
mo·tet   (mō·tĕt′)
moth ball   (môth bôl)
moth-eat·en   (môth′ ēt′ 'n)
moth·er   (mŭth′ ĕr)
    Mother Goose   moth·er·hood
    moth·er-in-law   moth·ers-in-law
    moth·er·land
    moth·er·ly   -li·ness
    moth·er-of-pearl
    Moth·er's Day
    moth·er tongue
mo·tif   (mō·tēf′)
mo·tile   (mō′ tĭl)
    mo·til·i·ty   (mō·tĭl′ ĭ·tĭ)
mo·tion   (mō′ shŭn)
    mo·tion·less   mo·tion pic·ture
    mo·tion-pic·ture pro·jec·tor
mo·ti·vate   (mō′ tĭ·vāt)
    -vat·ing
    mo·ti·va·tion   (mō′ tĭ·vā′ shŭn)
mo·tive   (mō′ tĭv)
mot·ley   (mŏt′ lĭ)
mo·tor   (mō′ tĕr)
    mo·tor·boat   mo·tor·cade
    mo·tor·cy·cle   -cy·clist
    mo·tor-driv·en   mo·tor·drome
    mo·tor·ist   mo·tor·ized
    mo·tor·man
mot·tled   (mŏt′ 'ld)
mot·to   (mŏt′ ō)
    mot·toes
mound   (mound)
mount   (mount)
    mount·a·ble
moun·tain   (moun′ tĭn)
    moun·tain·eer   (moun′ tĭ·nēr′)
    moun·tain lau·rel
    moun·tain·ous   (moun′ tĭ·nŭs)
    moun·tain·side
moun·te·bank   (moun′ tĕ·băngk)

mourn·ful   (mōrn′ fŏŏl)
    -ful·ly   -ful·ness
mourn·ing   (mōrn′ ĭng)
    (lamentation; see *morning*)
    mourn·ing dove
mouse   (mous)
    pl. mice   (mīs)
mousse   (mōōs)
mousse·line de soie
          (mōōs′ lēn′ dĕ swá′)
mous·y   (mous′ ĭ)
    mous·i·ness
mouth   (mouth)
    mouth·ful   -fuls
    mouth or·gan   mouth·piece
mou·ton coat   (mōō′ tŏn)
move   (mōōv)
    mov·ing
    mov·a·bil·i·ty
          (mōōv·a·bĭl′ ĭ·tĭ)
    mov·a·ble   (mōōv′ a·b'l)
    move·ment
mov·ie   (mōōv′ ĭ)
    mov·ing pic·ture
mow·er   (mō′ ĕr)
Mo·zam·bique,   (mō′ zăm·bēk′)
Afr.
mu·ci·lage   (mū′ sĭ·lĭj)
    mu·ci·lag·i·nous
          (mū′ sĭ·lăj′ ĭ·nŭs)
muck·rak·er   (mŭk′ rāk′ ĕr)
mu·cous mem·brane
          (mū′ kŭs)
mud·dle   (mŭd′ 'l)
    mud·dling
    mud·dle·head·ed
mud·dy   (mŭd′ ĭ)
    mud·di·ness
mud·guard   (mŭd′ gärd′)
mud·sling·er   (mŭd′ slĭng′ ĕr)
muff   (mŭf)
muf·fin   (mŭf′ ĭn)
muf·fle   (mŭf′ 'l)
    muf·fling   muf·fler
muf·ti   (mŭf′ tĭ)
mug·gy   (mŭg′ ĭ)
    mug·gi·ness
mug·wump   (mŭg′ wŭmp′)
muk·luk   (mŭk′ lŭk)
mu·lat·to   (mù·lăt′ ō)
    -lat·toes
mul·ber·ry   (mŭl′ bĕr′ ĭ)
    -ber·ries
mulch   (mŭlch)
mulct   (mŭlkt)

mule   (mūl)
  mule skin·ner
  mu·le·teer   (mū′ lĕ·tẽr′)
  mul·ish
mulled ci·der   (mŭld)
mul·let   (mŭl′ ĕt)
mul·ti·far·i·ous   (mŭl′ tĭ·fâr′ ĭ·ŭs)
mul·ti·fold   (mŭl′ tĭ·fōld)
Mul·ti·graph   (mŭl′ tĭ·gráf)
mul·ti·lat·er·al
               (mŭl′ tĭ·lăt′ ẽr·ál)
  -al·ly
mul·ti·lin·e·ar   (mŭl′ tĭ·lĭn′ ĕ·ẽr)
mul·ti·mil·lion·aire
         (mŭl′ tĭ·mĭl′ yŭn·âr′)
mul·ti·par·tite   (mŭl′ tĭ·pär′ tīt)
mul·ti·ple   (mŭl′ tĭ·p'l)
  mul·ti·ple scle·ro·sis
  mul·ti·plic·i·ty
         (mŭl′ tĭ·plĭs′ ĭ·tĭ)
mul·ti·ply   (mŭl′ tĭ·plĭ)
  -plied   -ply·ing
mul·ti·pli·cand
         (mŭl′ tĭ·plĭ·kănd′)
mul·ti·pli·ca·tion
         (mŭl′ tĭ·plĭ·kā′ shŭn)
mul·ti·pli·er
mul·ti·tude   (mŭl′ tĭ·tūd)
  mul·ti·tu·di·nous
         (mŭl′ tĭ·tū′ dĭ·nŭs)
mum·ble   (mŭm′ b'l)
  -bling
mum·bo jum·bo
         (mŭm′ bō jŭm′ bō)
mum·mer   (mŭm′ ẽr)
mum·mi·fy   (mŭm′ ĭ·fĭ)
  -fied   -fy·ing
  mum·mi·fi·ca·tion
         (mŭm′ ĭ·fĭ·kā′ shŭn)
mum·my   (mŭm′ ĭ)
  mum·mies
mumps   (mŭmps)
mun·dane   (mŭn′ dān)
  mun·dane·ly
mu·nic·i·pal   (mū·nĭs′ ĭ·pál)
  mu·nic·i·pal·i·ty
         (mū·nĭs′ ĭ·păl′ ĭ·tĭ)
mu·nif·i·cent   (mū·nĭf′ ĭ·sĕnt)
  -cence
mu·ni·tions   (mū·nĭsh′ ŭnz)
mu·ral   (mū′ rál)
mur·der   (mûr′ dẽr)
  mur·der·er   mur·der·ess
  mur·der·ous   (-ŭs)

murk·y   (mûr′ kĭ)
  murk·i·ness
mur·mur   (mûr′ mẽr)
  -mured   -mur·ing
mus·ca·tel   (mŭs′ ká·tĕl′)
mus·cle   (mŭs′ 'l)
  (body tissue; see mussel)
  -cling   mus·cle-bound
mus·cu·lar   (mŭs′ kû·lẽr)
  mus·cu·lar dys·tro·phy
  mus·cu·lar·i·ty
         (mŭs′ kû·lăr′ ĭ·tĭ)
  mus·cu·la·ture
         (mŭs′ kû·lá·tûr)
muse   (mūz)
  mus·ing
mu·sette bag   (mū·zĕt′)
mu·se·um   (mū·zē′ ŭm)
mush·room   (mŭsh′ rōōm)
mu·sic   (mū′ zĭk)
  mu·si·cal   (mū′ zĭ·kál)
  -cal·ly
  mu·si·cale   (mū′ zĭ·kál′)
  mu·si·cian   (mū·zĭsh′ án)
musk deer   (mŭsk)
mus·keg   (mŭs′ kĕg)
mus·kel·lunge   (mŭs′ kĕ·lŭnj)
mus·ket   (mŭs′ kĕt)
  mus·ket·eer   (mŭs′ kĕ·tẽr′)
  mus·ket·ry
musk·mel·on   (mŭsk′ mĕl′ ŭn)
musk ox   (mŭsk)
musk·rat   (mŭsk′ răt′)
mus·lin   (mŭz′ lĭn)
mus·sel   (mŭs′ 'l)
  (shellfish; see muscle)
mus·tache   (mŭs·tásh′)
  mus·ta·chio   (mŭs·tä′ shō)
  -chioed
mus·tard   (mŭs′ tẽrd)
mus·ter   (mŭs′ tẽr)
mus·ty   (mŭs′ tĭ)
  mus·ti·ness
mu·ta·ble   (mū′ tá·b'l)
  mu·ta·bil·i·ty   (mū′ tá·bĭl′ ĭ·tĭ)
mu·ti·late   (mū′ tĭ·lāt)
  -lat·ing
  mu·ti·la·tion   (mū′ tĭ·lā′ shŭn)
  mu·ti·la·tor
mu·ti·ny   (mū′ tĭ·nĭ)
  -nies, -nied, -ny·ing
  mu·ti·neer   (mū′ tĭ·nẽr′)
  mu·ti·nous
mutt   (mŭt)
mut·ter   (mŭt′ ẽr)

mut·ton   (mŭt′ 'n)
mu·tu·al   (mū′ tu̵ · ăl)
  -al·ly
  mu·tu·al·i·ty   (mū′ tu̵ · ăl′ ĭ · tĭ)
muz·zle   (mŭz′ 'l)
  muz·zling   muz · zle-load · er
my·o·pi·a   (mī · ō′ pĭ · ȧ)
  my·op·ic   (mī · ŏp′ ĭk)
myr·i·ad   (mĭr′ ĭ · ȧd)
myrrh   (mûr)
myr·tle   (mûr′ t'l)
my·self   (mī · sĕlf′)
mys·te·ri·ous   (mĭs · tẽr′ ĭ · ŭs)
  mys·ter·y   (mĭs′ tẽr · ĭ)
  -ter·ies
mys·tic   (mĭs′ tĭk)
  mys·ti·cal   mys · ti · cism
mys·ti·fy   (mĭs′ tĭ · fī)
  -fied   -fy · ing
  mys·ti·fi·ca·tion
                        (mĭs′ tĭ · fĭ · kā′ shŭn)
myth   (mĭth)
  myth·i·cal   myth · i · cal · ly
  myth·o·log·i·cal
                        (mĭth′ ō · lŏj′ ĭ · kȧl)
  my·thol·o·gy   (mĭ · thŏl′ ō · jĭ)
  -gies

                    N

na·dir   (nā′ dẽr)
nag·ging   (năg′ ĭng)
na·ïve   (nä · ēv′)
  na·ïve·ly
  na·ïve·té   (nä · ēv′ tā′)
na·ked   (nā′ kĕd)
  na·ked·ness
nam·by-pam·by
                        (năm′ bĭ · păm′ bĭ)
name   (nām)
  nam·ing   nam · a · ble
  name·less   name · ly
  name·sake
na·palm bomb   (nā′ päm)
naph·tha   (năf′ thȧ)
  naph·tha·lene   (năf′ thȧ · lēn)
  naph·thol   (năf′ thŏl)
nap·kin   (năp′ kĭn)
Na·po·le·on Bo·na·parte
                        (nȧ · pō′ lē · ŭn bō′ nȧ · pärt)
  Na·po·le·on·ic wars
                        (nȧ · pō′ lē · ŏn′ ĭk)
nar·cis·sus   (när · sĭs′ ŭs)
  nar·cis·sis·tic   (när′ sĭ · sĭs′ tĭk)

nar·co·sis   (när · kō′ sĭs)
nar·co·syn·the·sis
                        (när · kō · sĭn′ thē · sĭs)
nar·cot·ic   (när · kŏt′ ĭk)
  nar·co·tize   (när · kō · tīz)
  tiz·ing
Nar·ra·gan·sett (bay)
                        (năr′ ȧ · găn′ sĕt)
nar·rate   (nă · rāt′)
  nar·rat·ing
  nar·ra·tion   (nă · rā′ shŭn)
  nar·ra·tive   (năr′ ȧ · tĭv)
  -tive·ly
  nar·ra·tor   (nă · rā′ tẽr)
nar·row   (năr′ ō)
  nar·row-gauge
  nar·row-mind·ed
  nar·row·ness
na·sal   (nā′ zȧl)
  na·sal·i·ty   (nā · zăl′ ĭ · tĭ)
  na·sal·ize   -iz · ing
  na·sal·ly
nas·cent   (năs′ ĕnt)
Nas·sau   (năs′ ô)
nas·tur·tium   (năs · tûr′ shŭm)
nas·ty   (năs′ tĭ)
  nas·ti·er, -ti·est, -ti·ly, -ti·ness
na·tal   (nā′ tȧl)
na·ta·to·ri·um   (nā′ tȧ · tō′ rĭ · ŭm)
na·tion   (nā′ shŭn)
na·tion·al   (năsh′ ŭn · ȧl)
  na·tion·al·ism
  na·tion·al·is·tic
                        (năsh′ ŭn · ȧl · ĭs′ tĭk)
  na·tion·al·i·ty
                        (năsh′ ŭn · ăl′ ĭ · tĭ)
  -ties
  na·tion·al·i·za·tion
                        (năsh′ ŭn · ȧl · ĭ · zā′ shŭn)
  na·tion·al·ize   (năsh′ ŭn · ȧl · īz)
  -iz·ing   na · tion · al · ly
na·tive   (nā′ tĭv)
  na·tive·ly
  na·tiv·is·tic   (nā′ tĭv · ĭs′ tĭk)
na·tiv·i·ty   (nă · tĭv′ ĭ · tĭ)
nat·ty   (năt′ ĭ)
  nat·ti·ly
nat·u·ral   (năt′ û · rȧl)
  nat·u·ral·ism   nat · u · ral · ist
  nat·u·ral·is·tic
                        (năt′ û · rȧl · ĭs′ tĭk)
  nat·u·ral·i·za·tion
                        (năt′ û · rȧl · ĭ · zā′ shŭn)
  nat·u·ral·ize   -iz · ing
  nat·u·ral·ly   nat · u · ral · ness

na·ture (nā′ tŭr)
na·tur·o·path (nā′ tŭr·ō·păth′)
naugh·ty (nô′ tĭ)
  naugh·ti·er -ti·est
  -ti·ly -ti·ness
nau·se·a (nô′ shē·à)
  nau·se·ate (nô′ shē·āt)
  -at·ing
  nau·se·a·tion (nô′ shē·ā′ shŭn)
  nau·seous (nô′ shŭs)
nau·ti·cal (nô′ tĭ·kăl)
nau·ti·lus (nô′ tĭ·lŭs)
na·val (nā′ văl)
  (of ships; see *navel*)
nave (nāv)
na·vel (nā′ věl)
  (umbilicus; see *naval*)
  na·vel or·ange
nav·i·gate (năv′ ĭ·gāt)
  -gat·ing
  nav·i·ga·bil·i·ty
    (năv′ ĭ·gà·bĭl′ ĭ·tĭ)
  nav·i·ga·ble (năv′ ĭ·gà·b′l)
  nav·i·ga·tion (năv′ ĭ·gā′ shŭn)
  -tion·al nav·i·ga·tor
na·vy (nā′ vĭ)
  -vies
Naz·a·rene (năz′ à·rēn′)
Na·zi (nä′ tsē)
  Na·zism (nä′ tsĭz′m)
Ne·an·der·thal man
  (nē·ăn′·děr·täl′)
Ne·a·pol·i·tan (nē′ à·pŏl′ ĭ·tăn)
neap tide (nēp)
near (nēr)
  near·by Near East
  near·est near·ly
  near·ness
  near·sight·ed·ness
neat·ness (nēt′ něs)
neat's-foot oil (nēts′ fŏŏt′)
Ne·bras·ka (ně·brăs′ kà)
  abbr. Nebr., Neb.
  Ne·bras·kan
neb·u·la (něb′ ù·là)
  pl. neb·u·lae (-lē)
  neb·u·lar (-lēr)
neb·u·lous (něb′ ù·lŭs)
nec·es·sar·y (něs′ ě·sěr′ ĭ)
  nec·es·sar·i·ly (něs′ ě·sěr′ ĭ·lĭ)
  ne·ces·si·tate (ně·sěs′ ĭ·tāt)
  -tat·ing
  ne·ces·si·tous (ně·sěs′ ĭ·tŭs)
  ne·ces·si·ty (ně·sěs′ ĭ·tĭ)
  -ties

neck·er·chief (něk′ ēr·chĭf)
neck·lace (něk′ lĭs)
neck·tie (něk′ tĭ′)
ne·crol·o·gy (ně·krŏl′ ō·jĭ)
nec·ro·man·cy (něk′ rŏ·măn′ sĭ)
nec·tar (něk′ tēr)
nec·tar·ine (něk′ tēr·ēn′)
need (nēd)
  need·ful need·i·est
  need·less -less·ly
  need·y
nee·dle (nē′ d′l)
  nee·dle-point lace
  nee·dle·work
ne′er-do-well (nâr′ dŏŏ·wěl′)
ne·far·i·ous (ně·fâr′ ĭ·ŭs)
ne·gate (ně·gāt′)
  -gat·ing
  ne·ga·tion (ně·gā′ shŭn)
neg·a·tive (něg′ à·tĭv)
  neg·a·tive·ly neg·a·tiv·ism
neg·lect (ně·glěkt′)
  neg·lect·ful, -ful·ly, -ful·ness
neg·li·gee (něg′ lĭ·zhā′)
neg·li·gent (něg′ lĭ·jěnt)
  -gence
neg·li·gi·ble (něg′ lĭ·jĭ·b′l)
  neg·li·gi·bil·i·ty
    (něg′ lĭ·jĭ·bĭl′ ĭ·tĭ)
ne·go·ti·ate (ně·gō′ shĭ·āt)
  -at·ing
  ne·go·ti·a·bil·i·ty
    (ně·gō′ shĭ·à·bĭl′ ĭ·tĭ)
  ne·go·ti·a·ble
    (ně·gō′ shĭ·à·b′l)
  ne·go·ti·a·tion
    (ně·gō′ shĭ·ā′ shŭn)
  ne·go·ti·a·tor
Ne·gro (nē′ grō)
  -groes Ne·groid
Neh·ru, Ja·wa·har·lal
  (nā′ rŏŏ, jà·wä′ hàr·läl)
neigh (nā)
neigh·bor (nā′ bēr)
  neigh·bor·hood
  neigh·bor·ly -li·ness
nei·ther (nē′ thēr)
nem·a·tode (něm′ à·tōd)
nem·e·sis (něm′ ě·sĭs)
  pl. nem·e·ses
ne·o- (nē′ ō)
  ne·o-Cath·o·lic
  ne·o·clas·sic ne·o-Goth·ic
  ne·o-Hel·len·ic
  ne·o·im·pres·sion·ism

ne·o·lith·ic　　ne·o·phyte
ne·o·plasm　　Ne·o·pla·ton·ic
ne·o·prene
Ne·o·Scho·las·tic
Ne·o·zo·ic
neph·ew　　　　(něf′ ū)
ne·phri·tis　　　(ně·frī′ tĭs)
　ne·phrit·ic　　(ně·frĭt′ ĭk)
nep·o·tism　　　(něp′ ŏ·tĭz′m)
Nep·tune　　　　(něp′ tūn)
nerve　　　　　　(nûrv)
　nerve·less　　　nerve-rack·ing
　nerv·ous　　　　nerv·ous·ness
　nerv·y
nes·tle　　　　　(něs′ ′l)
　-tling
neth·er·most　　(něth′ ĕr·mōst)
net·ting　　　　(nět′ ĭng)
net·tle　　　　　(nět′ ′l)
net·work　　　　(nět′ wûrk′)
neu·ral·gia　　　(nū·răl′ já)
neu·ras·the·ni·a
　　　　　　　(nū′ răs·thē′ nĭ·á)
neu·ri·tic　　　　(nū·rĭt′ ĭk)
　neu·ri·tis　　　(nū·rī′ tĭs)
neu·rol·o·gy　　(nū·rŏl′ ŏ·jĭ)
　neu·ro·log·i·cal
　　　　　　　(nū′ rŏ·lŏj′ ĭ·kăl)
neu·ro·psy·cho·sis
　　　　　　　(nū′ rŏ·sī·kō′ sĭs)
neu·ro·sis　　　(nū·rō′ sĭs)
　pl. neu·ro·ses　(-sēz)
neu·rot·ic　　　　(nū·rŏt′ ĭk)
neu·ter　　　　　(nū′ tēr)
neu·tral　　　　(nū′ trăl)
　neu·tral·i·ty　　(nū·trăl′ ĭ·tĭ)
　neu·tral·i·za·tion
　　　　　　　(nū′ trăl·ĭ·zā′ shŭn)
　neu·tral·ize　　-iz·ing
　neu·tral·iz·er
neu·tron　　　　(nū′ trŏn)
Ne·va·da　　　　(ně·văd′ á)
　abbr. Nev.　　Ne·va·dan
nev·er·the·less　(něv′ ĕr·thě·lěs′)
new　　　　　　(nū)
　new·born　　　new·com·er
　new·fan·gled　　new-fash·ioned
　new·ly-wed　　new·ness
new·el　　　　　(nū′ ĕl)
New·found·land
　　　　　　　(nū′ fŭnd·lănd′)
New Guin·ea　　(nū gĭn′ ĭ)
New Hamp·shire
　　　　　　　(nū hăm(p)′ shēr)
　abbr. N.H.

New Heb·ri·des　(nū hěb′ rĭ·dēz)
New Jer·sey　　　(nū jûr′ zĭ)
　abbr. N.J.　　New Jer·sey·ite
New Mex·i·co　　(nū měk′ sĭ·kō)
　abbr. N. Mex.　New Mex·i·can
news　　　　　　(nūz)
　news·cast·er　　news·let·ter
　news·man
　news·pa·per·man
　news·print　　news·reel
　news·stand　　news·y
New York　　　　(nū yôrk′)
　abbr. N.Y.
New Zea·land　　(nū zē′ lǎnd)
　abbr. N.Z.
nex·us　　　　　(něk′ sŭs)
ni·a·cin　　　　(nī′ á·sĭn)
Ni·ag·a·ra　　　(nī·ǎg′ á·rá)
nib·ble　　　　　(nĭb′ ′l)
　nib·bling
Nic·a·ra·gua　　(nĭk′ á·rä′ gwá)
Ni·cene (creed)　(nī·sēn′)
ni·ce·ty　　　　(nī′ sě·tĭ)
　-ties
niche　　　　　(nĭch)
nick·el　　　　　(nĭk′ ĕl)
nick·el·o·de·on　(nĭk′ ĕl·ŏ′ dě·ŭn)
nick·name　　　(nĭk′ nām′)
nic·o·tine　　　(nĭk′ ŏ·tēn)
nic·o·tin·ic ac·id
　　　　　　　(nĭk′ ŏ·tĭn′ ĭk)
niece　　　　　(nēs)
Ni·ge·ri·a, Afr.　(nī·jēr′ ĭ·á)
nig·gard·ly　　　(nĭg′ ērd·lĭ)
nig·gling　　　　(nĭg′ ′lĭng)
nigh　　　　　　(nī)
night　　　　　(nĭt)
　night blind·ness
　night·cap　　　night club
　night crawl·er　night·fall
　night·gown　　night·hawk
　night·in·gale　　night·latch
　night·long　　　night·mare
　night owl　　　night·shade
　night·shirt　　night·time
　night·wear
night·in·gale　　(nĭt′ ĭn·gāl)
ni·hil·ism　　　(nī′ ĭ·lĭz′m)
　ni·hil·ist　　　(nī′ ĭ·lĭst)
Ni·ke mis·sile　(nī′ kē)
nil　　　　　　(nĭl)
nim·ble　　　　(nĭm′ b′l)
　nim·ble·ness　　nim·bly
nim·bus　　　　(nĭm′ bŭs)

nine (nīn)
  nine·fold   nine·pins
  ninth
nine·teen (nīn′ tēn′)
nine·ty (nīn′ tĭ)
  -ties   nine·ti·eth
  nine·ty·fold
nip·ple (nĭp′ 'l)
Nip·pon·ese (nĭp′ ŏ·nēz′)
nip·py (nĭp′ ĭ)
  nip·pi·ness
nir·va·na (nĭr·vä′ nȧ)
ni·sei (nē′ sā′)
  n. sing. & pl.
ni·trate (nī′ trāt)
ni·tric ac·id (nī′ trĭk)
ni·tride (nī′ trīd)
ni·tri·fy (nī′ trĭ·fī)
  -fied   -fy·ing
ni·trite (nī′ trīt)
ni·tro·gen (nī′ trŏ·jĕn)
  ni·tro·gen·ize (nī′ trŏ·jĕn·īz)
  ni·trog·e·nous (nī·trŏj′ ĕ·nŭs)
ni·tro·glyc·er·in
      (nī′ trŏ·glĭs′ ĕr·ĭn)
ni·trous ox·ide (nī′ trŭs)
nit·wit (nĭt′ wĭt′)
No·bel prize (nŏ·bĕl′)
no·ble (nō′ b'l)
  no·bil·i·ty (nŏ·bĭl′ ĭ·tĭ)
  no·ble·man   no·ble·ness
  no·bly
no·blesse o·blige
      (nō′ blĕs′ ō′ blēzh′)
no·bod·y (nō′ bŏd·ĭ)
noc·tur·nal (nŏk·tûr′ nȧl)
  -nal·ly
noc·turne (nŏk′ tûrn)
noc·u·ous (nŏk′ ū·ŭs)
node (nōd)
nod·ule (nŏd′ ūl)
no·el (nŏ·ĕl′)
nog·gin (nŏg′ ĭn)
noise (noiz)
  noise·less   noise·mak·er
  nois·y   nois·i·er
  -i·est, -i·ly, -i·ness
noi·some (noi′ sŭm)
no·mad (nō′ măd)
  no·mad·ic (nŏ·măd′ ĭk)
nom de plume (nŏm′ dĕ plōōm′)
no·men·cla·ture
      (nō′ mĕn·klā′ tụ̂r)
nom·i·nal (nŏm′ ĭ·nȧl)
  -nal·ly

nom·i·nate (nŏm′ ĭ·nāt)
  -nat·ing
  nom·i·na·tion
      (nŏm′ ĭ·nā′ shŭn)
  nom·i·na·tor
  nom·i·nee (nŏm′ ĭ·nē′)
nom·i·na·tive (nŏm′ ĭ·nȧ·tĭv)
non- (nŏn)
  non·ab·sorb·ent
  non·ac·cept·ance
  non·ag·gres·sive
  non·al·co·ho·lic
  non-Ar·y·an
  non·be·liev·er
  non·bel·lig·er·ent
  non·bloom·ing
  non·cha·lance
  non-Chris·tian
  non·co·er·cive
  non·com·bat·ant
  non·com·bus·ti·ble
  non·com·mis·sioned
  non·com·mit·tal
  non·com·mu·nist
  non·com·pet·i·tive
  non·com·pli·ance
  non·con·duc·tor
  non·con·form·ist
  non·con·tro·ver·sial
  non·cor·ro·sive
  non·de·script
  non·e·lec·tive
  non·en·ti·ty
  non·es·sen·tial
  non·ex·ist·ence
  non·fea·sance
  non·fic·tion
  non·in·ter·ven·tion
  non·ir·ri·tant
  non·mem·ber
  non·me·tal·lic
  non·ob·jec·tive
  non·par·ti·san
  non·pay·ment
  non·pro·duc·tive
  non·prof·it
  non·rec·og·ni·tion
  non·re·cur·ring
  non·re·new·a·ble
  non·res·i·dent, -den·tial
  non·re·stric·tive
  non·sec·tar·i·an
  non·stra·te·gic
  non·tech·ni·cal
  non·tox·ic

non·trans·fer·a·ble
non·typ·i·cal
non·vi·o·lence
non·cha·lant   (nŏn′ shá·lănt)
 -lance
non·pa·reil   (nŏn′ pá·rĕl′)
non·plus   (nŏn′ plŭs)
 -plused   -plus·ing
non·sense   (nŏn′ sĕns)
 -sen·si·cal
non se·qui·tur   (nŏn sĕk′ wĭ·tĕr)
noo·dle   (nōō′ d′l)
no one   (nō′ wŭn′)
noose   (nōōs)
norm   (nôrm)
nor·mal   (nôr′ măl)
 nor·mal·cy
 nor·mal·i·ty   (nôr·măl′ ĭ·tĭ)
 nor·mal·ly
nor·ma·tive   (nôr′ má·tĭv)
Norse·man   (nôrs′ măn)
north   (nôrth)
 north·east   north·east·er·ly
 north·er·ly   north·ern·er
 north·ern lights
 north·ern·most
 north·land   North Pole
 north·ward
 north·west·er·ly
North Car·o·li·na
                      (nôrth kăr′ ŏ·lī′ ná)
 abbr. N.C.,   N. Car.
 North Car·o·lin·i·an
                      (-kăr′ ŏ·lĭn′ ĭ·ǎn)
North Da·ko·ta   (nôrth dá·kō′ tá)
 abbr. N. Dak.
 North Da·ko·tan
Nor·we·gian   (nôr·wē′ jǎn)
nose   (nōz)
 nose·bleed   nose dive
 nose-dive v.   nose·gay
 nose·piece   nos·y
nos·tal·gi·a   (nŏs·tăl′ jĭ·á)
 nos·tal·gic
nos·tril   (nŏs′ trĭl)
nos·trum   (nŏs′ trŭm)
no·ta·ble   (nō′ tá·b′l)
 no·ta·bil·i·ty   (nō′ tá·bĭl′ ĭ·tĭ)
no·ta·ry   (nō′ tá·rĭ)
 -ries   no·ta·ry pub·lic
 no·ta·rize   (nō′ tá·rīz)
 -riz·ing
no·ta·tion   (nŏ·tā′ shŭn)
 no·ta·tion·al
notch   (nŏch)

note·book   (nōt′ bŏŏk′)
note·wor·thy   (nōt′ wûr′ thĭ)
no·tice   (nō′ tĭs)
 -tic·ing   no·tice·a·ble
no·ti·fy   (nō′ tĭ·fī)
 -fied   -fy·ing
 no·ti·fi·ca·tion
                      (nō′ tĭ·fĭ·kā′ shŭn)
 no·ti·fi·er
no·tion   (nō′ shŭn)
no·to·ri·e·ty   (nō′ tô·rī′ ĕ·tĭ)
no·to·ri·ous   (nŏ·tō′ rĭ·ŭs)
No·tre Dame, U. of
                      (nō′ tĕr dām′)
no-trump   (nō′ trŭmp′)
not·with·stand·ing
                      (nŏt′ wĭth·stăn′ dĭng)
nou·gat   (nōō′ găt)
nought   (nôt)
noun   (noun)
nour·ish   (nûr′ ĭsh)
 nour·ish·ment
No·va Sco·tia   (nō′ vá skō′ shá)
nov·el   (nŏv′ ĕl)
 nov·el·ette   (nŏv′ ĕl·ĕt′)
 nov·el·ist
 no·vel·la   (nŏ·vĕl′ lä)
 nov·el·ty   -ties
No·vem·ber   (nŏ·vĕm′ bĕr)
no·ve·na   (nŏ·vē′ ná)
 pl. no·ve·nae   (-nē)
nov·ice   (nŏv′ ĭs)
 no·vi·ti·ate   (nŏ·vĭsh′ ĭ·ǎt)
No·vo·cain   (nō′ vō·kān)
now·a·days   (nou′ á·dāz′)
no·where   (nō′ hwâr)
nox·ious   (nŏk′ shŭs)
noz·zle   (nŏz′ ′l)
nth de·gree   (ĕnth)
nu·ance   (nŭ·äns′)
nub·bin   (nŭb′ ĭn)
nu·bile   (nū′ bĭl)
 nu·bil·i·ty   (nū·bĭl′ ĭ·tĭ)
nu·cle·ar   (nū′ klĕ·ĕr)
 nu·cle·ar en·er·gy
 nu·cle·ar fis·sion
 nu·cle·ar phys·ics
 nu·cle·on   (nū′ klĕ·ŏn)
nu·cle·us   (nū′ klĕ·ŭs)
 pl. nu·cle·i   (-ī)
nude   (nūd)
 nud·ism   nud·ist
 nu·di·ty
nug·get   (nŭg′ ĕt)
nui·sance   (nū′ sǎns)

null (nŭl)
 (and void)

nul·li·fi·ca·tion
　　　　　　(nŭl′ ĭ·fĭ·kā′ shŭn)
nul·li·fy (nŭl′ ĭ·fī)
 -fied　　　　　-fy·ing
nul·li·ty (nŭl′ ĭ·tĭ)
numb (nŭm)
 numb·ly　　　numb·ness
num·ber (nŭm′ bẽr)
 num·ber·less
nu·mer·a·ble (nū′ mẽr·ȧ·b′l)
nu·mer·al (nū′ mẽr·ȧl)
nu·mer·ate (nū′ mẽr·āt)
 -at·ing
 nu·mer·a·tion
　　　　　　(nū·mẽr·ā′ shŭn)
nu·mer·i·cal (nū·mẽr′ ĭ·kȧl)
 -cal·ly
nu·mer·ol·o·gy (nū′ mẽr·ŏl′ ȯ·jĭ)
nu·mer·ous (nū′ mẽr·ŭs)
nu·mis·mat·ics (nū′ mĭz·măt′ ĭks)
num·skull (nŭm′ skŭl′)
nun (nŭn)
 nun·nery
nun·ci·o (nŭn′ shĭ·ō)
nup·tial (nŭp′ shȧl)
nurse (nûrs)
 nurs·ing　　　nurse·maid
 nurs·er·y (nûr′ sẽr·ĭ)
 -er·ies
 nurs·er·y rhyme
nur·ture (nûr′ tŭr)
 -tur·ing
nut·crack·er (nŭt′ krăk′ ẽr)
nut·hatch (nŭt′ hăch′)
nut·meg (nŭt′ mĕg)
nu·tri·a (nū′ trĭ·ȧ)
nu·tri·ent (nū′ trĭ·ĕnt)
 nu·tri·ment (nū′ trĭ·mĕnt)
 nu·tri·tion (nū·trĭsh′ ŭn)
 nu·tri·tion·al (nū·trĭsh′ ŭn·ȧl)
 -al·ly
 nu·tri·tious (nū·trĭsh′ ŭs)
 nu·tri·tive (nū′ trĭ·tĭv)
nut·shell (nŭt′ shĕl′)
nuz·zle (nŭz′ ′l)
 nuz·zling
Ny·as·a·land, Afr.
　　　　　　(nĭ·ăs′ ȧ·lănd′)
ny·lon (nī′ lŏn)
nymph (nĭmf)
nym·pho·ma·ni·ac
　　　　　　(nĭm′ fȯ·mā′ nĭ·ăk)

O

oaf·ish (ōf′ ĭsh)
O·a·hu is., Ha·wai·i
　　　　　　(ȯ·ä′ hōō)
oak·en (ōk′ ĕn)
oars·man (ōrz′ mȧn)
o·a·sis (ȯ·ā′ sĭs)
 pl. o·a·ses (-sēz)
oath (ōth)
oat·meal (ōt′ mēl′)
ob·bli·ga·to (ŏb′ lĭ·gä′ tō)
ob·du·rate (ŏb′ dū·rȧt)
 ob·du·ra·cy
o·be·di·ent (ȯ·bē′ dĭ·ĕnt)
 -ence
o·bei·sance (ȯ·bā′ sȧns)
ob·e·lisk (ŏb′ ĕ·lĭsk)
o·bese (ȯ·bēs′)
 o·bes·i·ty (ȯ·bēs′ ĭ·tĭ)
o·bey (ȯ·bā′)
 -beyed　　　-bey·ing
ob·fus·cate (ŏb·fŭs′ kāt)
 -cat·ing
 ob·fus·ca·tion
　　　　　　(ŏb′ fŭs·kā′ shŭn)
o·bit·u·ar·y (ȯ·bĭt′ û·ẽr′ ĭ)
 -ar·ies
ob·ject (ŏb′ jĕkt) n.
ob·ject (ŏb·jĕkt′) v.
 ob·jec·ti·fy (ŏb·jĕk′ tĭ·fī)
 -fied
 ob·jec·tion (ŏb·jĕk′ shŭn)
 ob·jec·tion·a·ble
 ob·jec·tive　　　-tive·ly
 ob·jec·tiv·ism
 ob·jec·tiv·i·ty (ŏb′ jĕk·tĭv′ ĭ·tĭ)
 ob·jec·tor
ob·jet d′art (ŏb′ zhĕ′ dár′)
 ob·jets d′art (ŏb′ zhĕ′ dár′)
ob·late (ŏb′ lāt)
 ob·la·tion (ŏb·lā′ shŭn)
ob·li·gate (ŏb′ lĭ·gāt)
 -gat·ing
 ob·li·ga·tion (ŏb′ lĭ·gā′ shŭn)
 ob·lig·a·to·ry (ŏb·lĭg′ ȧ·tō′ rĭ)
o·blige (ȯ·blīj′)
 -blig·ing
o·blique (ŏb·lēk′)
 -blique·ly
ob·lit·er·ate (ŏb·lĭt′ ẽr·āt)
 -at·ing
 ob·lit·er·a·tion
　　　　　　(ŏb·lĭt′ ẽr·ā′ shŭn)

ob·liv·i·on (ŏb·lĭv′ ĭ·ŭn)
 ob·liv·i·ous (ŏb·lĭv′ ĭ·ŭs)
ob·long (ŏb′ lŏng)
ob·lo·quy (ŏb′ lŏ·kwĭ)
 -quies
ob·nox·ious (ŏb·nŏk′ shŭs)
o·boe (ō′ bō)
 o·bo·ist
ob·scene (ŏb·sēn′)
 -scene·ly
 ob·scen·i·ty (ŏb·sĕn′ ĭ·tĭ)
 -ties
ob·scur·ant·ism
 (ŏb·skŭr′ ăn·tĭz′m)
ob·scure (ŏb·skūr′)
 ob·scu·ri·ty (ŏb·skū′ rĭ·tĭ)
ob·se·qui·ous (ŏb·sē′ kwĭ·ŭs)
ob·se·quies (ŏb′ sĕ·kwĭz)
ob·serve (ŏb·zûrv′)
 -serv·ing ob·serv·a·ble
 ob·serv·ant -ance
 ob·ser·va·tion
 (ŏb′ zĕr·vā′ shŭn)
 -tion·al
 ob·serv·a·to·ry
 (ŏb·zûr′ va·tō′ rĭ)
 -ries ob·serv·er
ob·sess (ŏb·sĕs′)
 ob·ses·sion ob·ses·sive
ob·sid·i·an (ŏb·sĭd′ ĭ·ăn)
ob·so·lete (ŏb′ sŏ·lēt)
 ob·so·les·cent (ŏb′ sŏ·lĕs′ ĕnt)
 -cence
ob·sta·cle (ŏb′ stà·k′l)
ob·stet·rics (ŏb·stĕt′ rĭks)
 ob·stet·ri·cal (ŏb·stĕt′ rĭ·kăl)
 ob·ste·tri·cian
 (ŏb′ stĕ·trĭsh′ ăn)
ob·sti·nate (ŏb′ stĭ·nĭt)
 ob·sti·na·cy (-nà·sĭ)
 ob·sti·nate·ly
ob·strep·er·ous
 (ŏb·strĕp′ ĕr·ŭs)
ob·struct (ŏb·strŭkt′)
 ob·struct·er ob·struc·tion
 ob·struc·tion·ist
ob·tain (ŏb·tān′)
 ob·tain·a·ble
ob·trude (ŏb·trōōd′)
 -trud·ing
 ob·tru·sion (ŏb·trōō′ zhŭn)
 ob·tru·sive (ŏb·trōō′ sĭv)
 -sive·ness
ob·tuse (ŏb·tūs′)
 -tuse·ness

ob·verse (ŏb·vûrs′)
 ob·verse·ly ob·ver·sion
ob·vi·ate (ŏb′ vĭ·āt)
 -at·ing
ob·vi·ous (ŏb′ vĭ·ŭs)
oc·a·ri·na (ŏk′ à·rē′ nà)
oc·ca·sion (ŏ·kā′ zhŭn)
 oc·ca·sion·al -al·ly
oc·ci·dent (ŏk′ sĭ·dĕnt)
 oc·ci·den·tal (ŏk′ sĭ·dĕn′ tăl)
oc·cip·i·tal (ŏk·sĭp′ ĭ·tăl)
oc·clude (ŏ·klōōd′)
 oc·clud·ing
 oc·clu·sion (ŏ·klōō′ zhŭn)
oc·cult (ŏ·kŭlt′)
 oc·cult·ism
oc·cu·pant (ŏk′ û·pănt)
 -pan·cy
oc·cu·pa·tion (ŏk′ û·pā′ shŭn)
 oc·cu·pa·tion·al, -al·ly
oc·cu·py (ŏk′ û·pī)
 -pied -py·ing
oc·cur (ŏ·kûr′)
 oc·curred oc·cur·ring
 oc·cur·rence
o·cean (ō′ shăn)
 o·ce·an·ic (ō′ shē·ăn′ ĭk)
 o·ce·a·nog·ra·phy
 (ō′ shē·à·nŏg′ rà·fĭ)
o·ce·lot (ō′ sĕ·lŏt)
o·cher (ō′ kĕr)
o'clock (ŏ·klŏk′)
oc·ta·gon (ŏk′ tà·gŏn)
 oc·tag·o·nal (ŏk·tăg′ ŏ·năl)
 -nal·ly
oc·ta·he·dron (ŏk′ tà·hē′ drŭn)
oc·tane (ŏk′ tān)
oc·tave (ŏk′ tāv)
oc·tet (ŏk·tĕt′)
Oc·to·ber (ŏk·tō′ bĕr)
oc·to·ge·nar·i·an
 (ŏk′ tŏ·jĕ·nâr′ ĭ·ăn)
oc·to·pus (ŏk′ tŏ·pŭs)
 -pus·es
oc·to·roon (ŏk′ tŏ·rōōn′)
oc·u·lar (ŏk′ û·lĕr)
oc·u·list (ŏk′ û·lĭst)
odd (ŏd)
 odd·i·ty (ŏd′ ĭ·tĭ)
 odd·ly odd·ment
 odds and ends
ode (ōd)
o·di·ous (ō′ dĭ·ŭs)
 o·di·um (ō′ dĭ·ŭm)
o·dom·e·ter (ŏ·dŏm′ ĕ·tĕr)

o·dor (ō′ dĕr)
  o·dor·if·er·ous
    (ō′ dĕr·ĭf′ ĕr·ŭs)
  o·dor·less
  o·dor·ous (ō′ dĕr·ŭs)
od·ys·sey (ŏd′ ĭ·sĭ)
Oed·i·pus com·plex
    (ĕd′ ĭ·pŭs)
oes·trus (ĕs′ trŭs)
off (ŏf)
  off and on   off·cast
  off-chance   off-col·or
  off·hand   off·ing
  off·set   off·set·ting
  off·shoot   off·shore
  off side   off·spring
of·fal (ŏf′ ăl)
of·fend (ŏ·fĕnd′)
  of·fend·er
of·fense (ŏ·fĕns′)
  of·fen·sive   -sive·ly
of·fer (ŏf′ ĕr)
  of·fer·ing
of·fer·to·ry (ŏf′ ĕr·tō′ rĭ)
of·fice (ŏf′ ĭs)
  of·fice boy
  of·fice·hold·er (ŏf′ ĭs·hōl′ dĕr)
  of·fi·cer (ŏf′ ĭ·sĕr)
of·fi·cial (ŏ·fĭsh′ ăl)
  of·fi·cial·dom of·fi·cial·ly
of·fi·ci·ate (ŏ·fĭsh′ ĭ·āt)
  -at·ing
  of·fi·ci·a·tion
    (ŏ·fĭsh′ ĭ·ā′ shŭn)
  of·fi·ci·a·tor
of·fi·cious (ŏ·fĭsh′ ŭs)
of·ten (ŏf′ ĕn)
  of·ten·er   of·ten·est
  of·ten·times
o·gre (ō′ gĕr)
  o·gre·ish (ō′ gĕr·ĭsh)
O·hi·o (ŏ·hī′ ō)
  abbr. O.   O·hi·o·an
ohm (ōm)
oil·skin (oil′ skĭn′)
oil·y (oil′ ĭ)
  oil·i·ness
oint·ment (oint′ mĕnt)
O.K. (ō′ kā′)
  (also okay) O.K.′ d
  O·K.′ ing
O·ki·na·wa Is. (ō′ kĭ·nä′ wȧ)
O·kla·ho·ma (ō′ klȧ·hō′ mȧ)
  abbr. Okla. O·kla·ho·man
o·kra (ō′ krȧ)

old (ōld)
  old coun·try old-fash·ioned
  old-fo·gy·ish Old Glo·ry
  old maid·ish
  Old Tes·ta·ment
  old-tim·er old wives′ tale
  old-world adj.
old·ster (ōld′ stĕr)
o·le·ag·i·nous (ō′ lĕ·ăj′ ĭ·nŭs)
o·le·an·der (ō′ lĕ·ăn′ dĕr)
o·le·o·mar·ga·rine
    (ō′ lĕ·ō·mär′ jȧ·rĭn)
ol·fac·to·ry (ŏl·făk′ tō·rĭ)
ol·i·garch (ŏl′ ĭ·gärk)
  ol·i·gar·chic (ŏl′ ĭ·gär′ kĭk)
  -chi·cal
  ol·i·garch·y (ŏl′ ĭ·gär′ kĭ)
  -chies
O·lym·pic (ō·lĭm′ pĭk)
  O·lym·pi·an
o·me·ga (ō·mē′ gȧ)
om·e·let (ŏm′ ĕ·lĕt)
o·men (ō′ mĕn)
om·i·nous (ŏm′ ĭ·nŭs)
o·mis·sion (ō·mĭsh′ ŭn)
o·mit (ō·mĭt′)
  -mit·ted   -mit·ting
om·ni·bus (ŏm′ nĭ·bŭs)
om·nip·o·tent (ŏm·nĭp′ ŏ·tĕnt)
  -tence
om·ni·pres·ent (ŏm′ nĭ·prĕz′ ĕnt)
om·nis·cient (ŏm·nĭsh′ ĕnt)
  -cience
om·niv·o·rous (ŏm·nĭv′ ŏ·rŭs)
once (wŭns)
on·com·ing (ŏn′ kŭm′ ĭng)
one (wŭn)
  one-horse town one·self
  one-sid·ed one·time
  one-track mind one-way street
on·er·ous (ŏn′ ĕr·ŭs)
on·ion·skin (ŭn′ yŭn·skĭn′)
on·look·er (ŏn′ lŏŏk′ ĕr)
on·ly (ŏn′ lĭ)
on·o·mat·o·poe·ia
    (ŏn′ ŏ·măt′ ŏ·pē′ yȧ)
on·set (ŏn′ sĕt′)
on·slaught (ŏn′ slŏt′)
on·to (ŏn′ tōō)
on·tol·o·gy (ŏn·tŏl′ ŏ·jĭ)
  on·to·log·i·cal (ŏn′ tŏ·lŏj′ ĭ·kăl)
o·nus (ō′ nŭs)
on·ward (ŏn′ wĕrd)
on·yx (ŏn′ ĭks)

ooze (ōōz)
  ooz·ing
o·pac·i·ty (ō·păs′ ĭ·tĭ)
o·pal (ō′ păl)
o·pal·es·cent (ō′ păl·ĕs′ ĕnt)
  -cence
o·paque (ō·pāk′)
  o·paque·ness
o·pen (ō′ pĕn)
  o·pen-air *adj.*
  o·pen-and-shut case
  o·pen·er   o·pen-eyed
  o·pen·hand·ed
  o·pen house   o·pen let·ter
  o·pen-mind·ed o·pen·work
op·er·a (ŏp′ ĕr·à)
  op·er·a·tic (ŏp′ ĕr·ăt′ ĭk)
op·er·a·ble (ŏp′ ĕr·à·b′l)
op·er·ate (ŏp′ ĕr·āt)
  -at·ing
  op·er·a·tion (ŏp′ ĕr·ā′ shŭn)
  -tion·al
  op·er·a·tive (ŏp′ ĕr·ā′ tĭv)
  op·er·a·tor
op·er·et·ta (ŏp′ ĕr·ĕt′ à)
oph·thal·mol·o·gist
    (ŏf′ thăl·mŏl′ ō·jĭst)
o·pi·ate (ō′ pĭ·āt)
o·pine (ō·pīn′)
  -pin·ing
o·pin·ion (ō·pĭn′ yŭn)
  o·pin·ion·at·ed
    (ō·pĭn′ yŭn·āt′ ĕd)
  o·pin·ion·a·tive
    (ō·pĭn′ yŭn·ā′ tĭv)
o·pi·um (ō′ pĭ·ŭm)
o·pos·sum (ō·pŏs′ ŭm)
op·po·nent (ō·pō′ nĕnt)
op·por·tune (ŏp′ ŏr·tūn′)
  op·por·tune·ly
op·por·tun·ism (ŏp′ ŏr·tūn′ ĭz'm)
  op·por·tun·ist
  op·por·tun·is·tic
    (ŏp′ ŏr·tūn′ ĭs′ tĭk)
op·por·tu·ni·ty (ŏp′ ŏr·tū′ nĭ·tĭ)
  -ties
op·pose (ō·pōz′)
  op·pos·ing   op·pos·a·ble
op·po·site (ŏp′ ō·zĭt)
  op·po·site·ly
  op·po·si·tion (ŏp′ ō·zĭsh′ ŭn)
op·press (ō·prĕs′)
  op·pres·sion (ō·prĕsh′ ŭn)
  op·pres·sive   op·pres·sor

op·pro·bri·ous (ō·prō′ brĭ·ŭs)
  op·pro·bri·um
op·tic (ŏp′ tĭk)
  op·ti·cal
  op·ti·cian (ŏp·tĭsh′ ăn)
op·ti·mism (ŏp′ tĭ·mĭz'm)
  op·ti·mist
  op·ti·mis·tic (ŏp′ tĭ·mĭs′ tĭk)
  -ti·cal·ly
op·ti·mum (ŏp′ tĭ·mŭm)
op·tion (ŏp′ shŭn)
  op·tion·al   -al·ly
op·tom·e·try (ŏp·tŏm′ ĕ·trĭ)
  op·tom·e·trist (ŏp·tŏm′ ĕ·trĭst)
op·u·lence (ŏp′ û·lĕns)
  -lent
o·pus (ō′ pŭs)
  pl. op·e·ra (ŏp′ ĕ·rà)
or·a·cle (ŏr′ à·k′l)
  o·rac·u·lar (ō·răk′ û·lĕr)
o·ral (ō′ răl)
  (spoken; see *aural*)
  o·ral·ly
or·ange (ŏr′ ĕnj)
  or·ange·ade (ŏr′ ĕnj·ād′)
  or·ange pe·koe
o·rang·u·tan (ō·răng′ ōō·tăn′)
o·rate (ō·rāt′)
  -rat·ing
  o·ra·tion (ō·rā′ shŭn)
  or·a·tor (ŏr′ à·tĕr)
  or·a·tor·i·cal (ŏr′ à·tŏr′ ĭ·kăl)
  or·a·to·ry (ŏr′ à·tō′ rĭ)
or·a·to·ri·o (ŏr′ à·tō′ rĭ·ō)
or·bit (ŏr′ bĭt)
  -bit·ed   -bit·ing
  or·bit·al
or·chard (ŏr′ chĕrd)
or·ches·tra (ŏr′ kĕs·trà)
  or·ches·tral (ŏr·kĕs′ trăl)
  or·ches·trate (ŏr′ kĕs·trāt)
  or·ches·tra·tion
    (ŏr′ kĕs·trā′ shŭn)
or·chid (ŏr′ kĭd)
or·dain (ŏr·dān′)
or·deal (ŏr·dēl′)
or·der (ŏr′ dĕr)
  or·der·ly   -li·ness
or·di·nal (ŏr′ dĭ·năl)
or·di·nance (ŏr′ dĭ·năns)
  (law; see *ordnance*)
or·di·nar·y (ŏr′ dĭ·nĕr′ ĭ)
  or·di·nar·i·ly -i·ness
or·di·nate (ŏr′ dĭ·nāt)
  -nat·ing

or·di·na·tion (ôr′ dĭ·nā′ shŭn)
ord·nance (ôrd′ năns)
　(military supplies: see *ordinance*)
or·dure (ôr′ dūr)
Or·e·gon (ôr′ ê·gŏn)
　abbr. Oreg. *or* Ore.
　Or·e·go·ni·an (ôr′ ê·gō′ nĭ·ăn)
or·gan (ôr′ găn)
　or·gan·ic (ôr·găn′ ĭk)
　or·gan·ism (ôr′ găn·ĭz′m)
　or·gan·ist
or·gan·dy (ôr′ găn·dĭ)
　-dies
or·gan·ize (ôr′ găn·īz)
　-iz·ing　　or·gan·iz·able
　or·gan·i·za·tion
　　　　(ôr′ găn·ĭ·zā′ shŭn)
　or·gan·iz·er
or·gan·za (ôr·găn′ ză)
or·gasm (ôr′ găz′m)
or·gy (ôr′ jĭ)
　-gies
　or·gi·as·tic (ôr′ jĭ·ăs′ tĭk)
o·ri·ent (ō′ rĭ·ĕnt)
　o·ri·en·tal (ō′ rĭ·ĕn′ tăl)
o·ri·en·ta·tion (ō′ rĭ·ĕn·tā′ shŭn)
or·i·fice (ôr′ ĭ·fĭs)
or·i·gin (ôr′ ĭ·jĭn)
o·rig·i·nal (ō·rĭj′ ĭ·năl)
　o·rig·i·nal·i·ty
　　　　(ō·rĭj′ ĭ·năl′ ĭ·tĭ)
　o·rig·i·nal·ly
o·rig·i·nate (ō·rĭj′ ĭ·nāt)
　-nat·ing
　o·rig·i·na·tion
　　　　(ō·rĭj′ ĭ·nā′ shŭn)
　o·rig·i·na·tor
o·ri·ole (ō′ rĭ·ōl)
or·i·son (ôr′ ĭ·zŭn)
or·lon (ôr′ lŏn)
or·na·ment (ôr′ nă·mĕnt)
　or·na·men·tal (ôr′ nă·mĕn′ tăl)
　-tal·ly
　or·na·men·ta·tion
　　　　(ôr′ nă·mĕn·tā′ shŭn)
or·nate (ôr·nāt′)
　or·nate·ly　　-nate·ness
or·ner·y (ôr′ nĕr·ĭ)
　or·ner·i·ness
or·ni·thol·o·gy (ôr′ nĭ·thŏl′ ô·jĭ)
or·phan (ôr′ făn)
　or·phan·age
or·tho·don·tist (ôr′ thô·dŏn′ tĭst)
or·tho·dox·y (ôr′ thô·dŏk′ sĭ)
　-dox·ies

or·tho·gen·ic (ôr′ thô·jĕn′ ĭk)
or·thog·ra·phy (ôr·thŏg′ ră·fĭ)
or·tho·pe·dics (ôr′ thô·pē′ dĭks)
os·cil·late (ŏs′ ĭ·lāt)
　(vibrate; see *osculate*)
　-cil·lat·ing
　os·cil·la·tion (ŏs′ ĭ·lā′ shŭn)
　os·cil·la·tor (ŏs′ ĭ·lā′ tĕr)
os·cu·late (ŏs′ kû·lāt)
　(to kiss; see *oscillate*)
　-lat·ing
　os·cu·la·tion (ŏs′ kû·lā′ shŭn)
os·mo·sis (ŏs·mō′ sĭs)
　os·mot·ic (ŏs·mŏt′ ĭk)
os·prey (ŏs′ prĭ)
　-preys
os·si·cle (ŏs′ ĭ·k′l)
os·si·fy (ŏs′ ĭ·fī)
　-fied　　-fy·ing
　os·si·fi·ca·tion
　　　　(ŏs′ ĭ·fĭ·kā′ shŭn)
os·ten·si·ble (ŏs·tĕn′ sĭ·b′l)
os·ten·ta·tion (ŏs′ tĕn·tā′ shŭn)
　os·ten·ta·tious (-shŭs)
os·te·o·path (ŏs′ tê·ô·păth)
os·tra·cize (ŏs′ tră·sīz)
　-ciz·ing
　os·tra·cism (ŏs′ tră·sĭz′m)
os·trich (ŏs′ trĭch)
oth·er·wise (ŭth′ ĕr·wīz′)
oth·er·world·ly
　　　　(ŭth′ ĕr·wûrld′ lĭ)
o·ti·ose (ō′ shĭ·ōs)
Ot·ta·wa, Can. (ŏt′ à·wà)
ot·ter (ŏt′ ĕr)
Ot·to·man (ŏt′ ô·măn)
ought (ôt)
　(bound by duty; see *aught*)
Oui·ja board (wē′ jà)
ounce (ouns)
our·selves (our·sĕlvz′)
oust (oust)
　oust·er
out (out)
　out-and-out　　out·bal·ance
　out·board　　out·break
　out·burst　　out·cast
　out·class　　out·come
　out·crop　　out·cry
　out·dis·tance　　out·do
　out·doors　　out·er·most
　out·field　　out·fit·ter
　out·go·ing　　out·growth
　out·land·ish　　out·last
　out·law　　out·let

out·line   out·look
out·ly·ing   out·ma·neu·ver
out·mod·ed   out-of-date
out-of-door   out-of-the-way
out·pa·tient   out·post
out·pour·ing   out·put
out·rage   out·ra·geous
out·reach   out·rig·ger
out·right   out·sell
out·set   out·sid·er
out·size   out·skirts
out·smart   out·spo·ken
out·spo·ken·ness
out·spread   out·stand·ing
out·strip   out·ward
out·weigh   out·wit

o·va·ry (ō′ vȧ·rĭ)
   -ries
o·va·tion (ō·vā′ shŭn)
ov·en (ŭv′ ĕn)
o·ver (ō′ vẽr)
   o·ver·act   o·ver-all
   o·ver·alls   o·ver·awed
   o·ver·bear·ing   o·ver·board
   o·ver·cast
   o·ver·de·vel·op·ment
   o·ver·dose   o·ver·draft
   o·ver·ex·po·sure
   o·ver·haul   o·ver·head
   o·ver·lap·ping   o·ver·lay
   o·ver·look   o·ver·night
   o·ver·pass
   o·ver·pow·er·ing
   o·ver·pro·duc·tion
   o·ver·rate   o·ver·reach
   o·ver·ride   o·ver·rul·ing
   o·ver·run   o·ver·seas
   o·ver·seer   o·ver·shoe
   o·ver·sight   o·ver·sup·ply
   o·ver-the-count·er
   o·ver·throw   o·ver·time
   o·ver·tone   o·ver·ween·ing
   o·ver·weight   o·ver·whelm·ing
   o·ver·work   o·ver·wrought
o·vert (ō′ vûrt)
o·ver·ture (ō′ vẽr·tụ̂r)
o·vip·a·rous (ō·vĭp′ ȧ·rŭs)
o·vum (ō′ vŭm)
   pl. o·va
owe (ō)
   ow·ing
owl·ish (oul′ ĭsh)
own·er·ship (ōn′ ẽr·shĭp)
ox (ŏks)
   pl. ox·en

ox·al·ic (ŏks·ăl′ ĭk)
ox·eye dai·sy (ŏks′ ī′)
ox·i·da·tion (ŏk′ sĭ·dā′ shŭn)
ox·ide (ŏk′ sīd)
ox·i·dize (ŏk′ sĭ·dīz)
   -diz·ing
ox·tail (ŏks′ tāl′)
ox·y·gen (ŏk′ sĭ·jĕn)
oys·ter (ois′ tẽr)
o·zone (ō′ zōn)

P

pab·u·lum (păb′ û·lŭm)
pace·mak·er (pās′ māk′ ẽr)
pach·y·derm (păk′ ĭ·dûrm)
pac·i·fy (păs′ ĭ·fī)
   -fied   -fy·ing
   pa·cif·ic (pȧ·sĭf′ ĭk)
   pac·i·fi·ca·tion
       (păs′ ĭ·fĭ·kā′ shŭn)
   pac·i·fi·er   pac·i·fist
pack·age (păk′ ĭj)
   -ag·ing
pack·et (păk′ ĕt)
pack·ing house (păk′ ĭng)
pack·sack (păk′ săk′)
pack·sad·dle (păk′ săd′ ′l)
pact (păkt)
pad·ding (păd′ ĭng)
pad·dle wheel (păd′ ′l)
pad·dock (păd′ ŭk)
pad·lock (pad′ lok′)
pa·dre (pä′ drĭ)
pae·an (pē′ ȧn)
pa·gan (pā′ găn)
   pa·gan·ism
pag·eant (păj′ ĕnt)
   pag·eant·ry
pag·i·na·tion (păj′ ĭ·nā′ shŭn)
pa·go·da (pȧ·gō′ dȧ)
paid (pād)
pail·ful (pāl′ fŏŏl)
pain (pān)
   (punishment; see *pane*)
   pain·ful   -ful·ly
   -ful·ness   pain·less
   pains·tak·ing
paint·brush (pānt′ brŭsh′)
paint·ing (pānt′ ĭng)
pair (pâr)
   (two; see *pear*)
Pais·ley print (pāz′ lĭ)
pa·ja·ma (pȧ·jä′ mȧ)

Pak·i·stan   (păk′ ĭ·stăn′)
  Pak·i·stan·i   (-ĭ)
pal·ace   (păl′ ĭs)
  pa·la·tial   (pȧ·lā′ shᵈl)
pal·a·din   (păl′ ȧ·dĭn)
pal·at·a·ble   (păl′ ĭt·ȧ·b′l)
  pal·at·a·bil·i·ty
                  (păl′ ĭt·ȧ·bĭl′ ĭ·tĭ)
pal·ate   (păl′ ĭt)
  (roof of mouth; see *palette, pallet*)
  pal·a·tal   (păl′ ȧ·tᵈl)
pa·la·tial   (pȧ·lā′ shᵈl)
  -tial·ly
pal·a·tine   (păl′ ȧ·tīn)
pa·lav·er   (pȧ·lăv′ ēr)
pale   (pāl)
  pale·face   pale·ness
pa·le·o-   (pā′ lĕ·ŏ-)
  pa·le·o·bot·a·ny
                  (-bŏt′ ȧ·nĭ)
  pa·le·o·lith·ic (-lĭth′ ĭk)
  pa·le·on·tol·o·gy
                  (pā′ lĕ·ŏn·tŏl′ ŏ·jĭ)
  Pa·le·o·zo·ic era
                  (-zō′ ĭk)
  pa·le·o·zo·ol·o·gy
                  (-zō·ŏl′ ŏ·jĭ)
pal·ette   (păl′ ĕt)
  (painter's board; see *palate,*
  pallet)
  pal·ette knife
pal·frey   (pôl′ frĭ)
pal·i·sade   (păl′ ĭ·sād′)
pal·la·di·um   (pȧ·lā′ dĭ·ŭm)
Pal·las Ath·e·na
                  (păl′ ȧs ȧ·thē′ nȧ)
pall·bear·er   (pôl′ bâr′ ēr)
pal·let   (păl′ ĕt)
  (bed; see *palate, palette*)
pal·li·ate   (păl′ ĭ·āt)
  -at·ing
  pal·li·a·tion   (păl′ ĭ·ā′ shŭn)
  pal·li·a·tive   (păl′ ĭ·ā′ tĭv)
pal·lid   (păl′ ĭd)
  pal·lor   (păl′ ēr)
pal·met·to   (păl·mĕt′ ō)
palm·is·try   (päm′ ĭs·trĭ)
pal·my·ra   (păl·mī′ rȧ)
pal·o·mi·no   (păl′ ŏ·mē′ nō)
pal·pa·ble   (păl′ pȧ·b′l)
pal·pi·tate   (păl′ pĭ·tāt)
  -tat·ing
  pal·pi·ta·tion   (păl′ pĭ·tā′ shŭn)
pal·sy   (pôl′ zĭ)
  -sied

pal·try   (pôl′ trĭ)
  pal·tri·ness
pam·pas   (păm′ pȧz)
pam·per   (păm′ pēr)
pam·phlet   (păm′ flĕt)
  pam·phlet·eer   (păm′ flĕt·ēr′)
pan·a·ce·a   (păn′ ȧ·sē′ ȧ)
Pan·a·ma   (păn′ ȧ·mô)
  Pan·a·ma hat
  Pan·a·ma·ni·an
                  (păn′ ȧ·mä′ nĭ·ᵈn)
Pan-A·mer·i·can
                  (păn′ ȧ·mĕr′ ĭ·kᵈn)
pan·a·tel·la   (păn′ ȧ·tĕl′ ȧ)
pan·cake   (păn′ kāk′)
pan·chro·mat·ic
                  (păn′ krŏ·măt′ ĭk)
pan·cra·ti·um   (păn·krā′ shĭ·ŭm)
pan·cre·as   (păn′ krĕ·ᵈs)
  pan·cre·at·ic juice
                  (păng′ krĕ·ăt′ ĭk)
pan·da   (păn′ dȧ)
pan·dem·ic   (păn·dĕm′ ĭk)
pan·de·mo·ni·um
                  (păn′ dĕ·mō′ nĭ·ŭm)
pan·der   (păn′ dēr)
  pan·der·er
Pan·do·ra's box   (păn·dō′ rȧz)
pan·dow·dy   (păn·dou′ dĭ)
pane   (pān)
  (a panel; glass; see *pain*)
pan·e·gyr·ic   (păn′ ē·jĭr′ ĭk)
pan·el   (păn′ ĕl)
  -eled   -el·ing
  pan·el·ist
pan·han·dle   (păn′ hăn′ d′l)
  -dling
Pan·hel·len·ic   (păn′ hĕ·lĕn′ ĭk)
pan·ic   (păn′ ĭk)
  -icked   -ick·ing
  pan·ick·y   pan·ic-strick·en
pan·nier   (păn′ yēr)
pan·o·ply   (păn′ ŏ·plĭ)
  -plies   pan·o·plied
pan·o·ra·ma   (păn′ ŏ·rä′ mȧ)
  pan·o·ram·ic   (-răm′ ĭk)
pan·sy   (păn′ zĭ)
  -sies
pan·ta·loon   (păn′ tȧ·lōōn′)
pan·the·ism   (păn′ thē·ĭz′m)
  pan·the·is·tic (păn′ thē·ĭs′ tĭk)
pan·the·on   (păn′ thē·ŏn)
pan·ther   (păn′ thēr)
  pan·ther·ess
pant·ing   (pănt′ ĭng)

pan·to·mime   (păn′ tȯ·mīm)
  pan·to·mim·ic
             (păn′ tȯ·mĭm′ ĭk)
  pan·to·mim·ist
pan·to·then·ic ac·id
           (păn′ tȯ·thŏn′ ĭk)
pan·try   (păn′ trĭ)
 -tries
pant·y   (păn′ tĭ)
  pant·ies   pant·y gir·dle
  pant·y·waist
Pan·zer di·vi·sion
           (păn′ tsĕr)
pa·pa·cy   (pā′ pȧ·sĭ)
  pa·pal   (pā′ pȧl)
pa·paw   (pȧ·pô′)
pa·pay·a   (pȧ·pī′ ȧ)
pa·per   (pā′ pĕr)
  pa·per·back   pa·per·board
  pa·per cut·ter pa·per knife
  pa·per-thin   pa·per·weight
  pa·per work
pa·pier-mâ·ché
          (pā′ pĕr·mȧ·shā′)
pa·pil·la   (pȧ·pĭl′ ȧ)
  pl. pa·pil·lae   (-ē)
  pap·il·lar·y   (păp′ ĭ·lĕr′ ĭ)
pa·poose   (pă·pōōs′)
pa·pri·ka   (pȧ·prē′ kȧ)
pa·py·rus   (pȧ·pī′ rŭs)
  pl. pa·py·ri   (-rī)
par·a·ble   (păr′ ȧ·b′l)
pa·rab·o·la   (pȧ·răb′ ȯ·lȧ)
  par·a·bol·ic   (păr′ ȧ·bŏl′ ĭk)
  -i·cal·ly
  pa·rab·o·loid   (pȧ·răb′ ȯ·loid)
par·a·chute   (păr′ ȧ·shōōt)
 -chut·ist
pa·rade   (pȧ·rād′)
 -rad·ing
par·a·digm   (păr′ ȧ·dĭm)
par·a·dise   (păr′ ȧ·dīs)
par·a·dox   (păr′ ȧ·dŏks)
  par·a·dox·i·cal
        (păr′ ȧ·dŏk′ sĭ·kȧl)
  -cal·ly
par·af·fin   (păr′ ă·fĭn)
par·a·gon   (păr′ ȧ·gŏn)
par·a·graph   (păr′ ȧ·grȧf)
Par·a·guay   (păr′ ȧ·gwī)
par·a·keet   (păr′ ȧ·kēt)
par·al·lax   (păr′ ȧ·lăks)
  par·al·lac·tic (păr′ ȧ·lăk′ tĭk)
par·al·lel   (păr′ ȧ·lĕl)
 -al·leled   -al·lel·ing

par·al·lel·o·gram
        (păr′ ă·lĕl′ ȯ·grăm)
pa·ral·y·sis   (pȧ·răl′ ĭ·sĭs)
par·a·lyt·ic   (păr′ ȧ·lĭt′ ĭk)
par·a·lyze   (păr′ ȧ·līz)
 -lyz·ing
par·a·me·ci·um
        (păr′ ȧ·mē′ shĭ·ŭm)
  pl. par·a·me·ci·a
pa·ram·e·ter   (pȧ·răm′ ĕ·tĕr)
par·a·mount   (păr′ ȧ·mount)
par·a·mour   (păr′ ȧ·mŏŏr)
par·a·noi·a   (păr′ ȧ·noi′ ȧ)
  par·a·noi·ac   (-ăk)
par·a·pet   (păr′ ȧ·pĕt)
 -pet·ed
par·a·pher·na·li·a
       (păr′ ȧ·fĕr·nā′ lĭ·ȧ)
par·a·phrase   (păr′ ȧ·frāz)
  phras·ing
  par·a·phras·tic
       (păr′ ȧ·frăs′ tĭk)
par·a·ple·gi·a   (păr′ ȧ·plē′ jĭ·ȧ)
  par·a·pleg·ic   (-plĕj′ ĭk)
par·a·psy·chol·o·gy
      (păr′ ȧ·sī·kŏl′ ȯ·jĭ)
par·a·site   (păr′ ȧ·sīt)
  par·a·sit·ic   (păr′ ȧ·sĭt′ ĭk)
 -i·cal
  par·a·sit·ism   (păr′ ȧ·sīt·ĭz′m)
  par·a·si·tol·o·gy
      (păr′ ȧ·sī·tŏl′ ȯ·jĭ)
par·a·sym·pa·thet·ic
     (păr′ ȧ·sĭm′ pȧ·thĕt′ ĭk)
par·a·troop·er   (păr′ ȧ·trōōp′ ĕr)
par·boil   (pär′ boil′)
par·cel   (pär′ sĕl)
 -celed   -cel·ing
  par·cel post
par·chee·si   (pär·chē′ zĭ)
parch·ment   (pärch′ mĕnt)
par·don   (pär′ d′n)
  par·don·a·ble   par·don·er
pare   (pâr)
  par·ing
par·ent   (pâr′ ĕnt)
  par·ent·age   (pâr′ ĕn·tĭj)
  pa·ren·tal   (pȧ·rĕn′ tȧl)
  par·ent·hood
pa·ren·the·sis   (pȧ·rĕn′ thĕ·sĭs)
  pl. pa·ren·the·ses (-sēz)
  par·en·thet·ic (păr′ ĕn·thĕt′ ĭk)
 -i·cal·ly
pa·re·sis   (pȧ·rē′ sĭs)
pa·ret·ic   (pȧ·rĕt′ ĭk)

par ex·cel·lence
    (pär ĕk′ sĕ·läns)
par·fait (pär fā′)
pa·ri·ah (pȧ·rī′ ȧ)
pa·ri·e·tal (pȧ·rī′ ě·tȧl)
par·i·mu·tu·el (pär′ ĭ·mū′ tů·ĕl)
par·ish (pär′ ĭsh)
  par·ish·ion·er (pȧ·rĭsh′ ŭn·ēr)
par·i·ty (pär′ ĭ·tĭ)
par·ka (pär′ kȧ)
park·way (pärk′ wā′)
par·lance (pär′ lȧns)
par·lay (pär′ lā)
  (bet; see *parley*)
par·ley (pär′ lĭ)
  (conversation; see *parlay*)
par·lia·ment (pär′ lĭ·měnt)
  par·lia·men·tar·i·an
    (pär′ lĭ·měn·târ′ ĭ·ȧn)
  par·lia·men·ta·ry
    (pär′ lĭ·měn′ tȧ·rĭ)
par·lor (pär′ lēr)
  par·lor·car par·lor·maiđ
Par·me·san cheese
    (pär′ mě·zăn′)
Par·nas·sus (pär·năs′ ŭs)
pa·ro·chi·al (pȧ·rō′ kĭ·ȧl)
par·o·dy (pär′ ô·dĭ)
 -dies
  par·o·dieđ -đy·ing
  par·o·dist
pa·role (pȧ·rōl′)
  pa·rol·ee (pȧ·rōl′ ē′)
par·ox·ysm (pär′ ŏk·sĭz'm)
par·quet (pär·kā′)
par·ri·cide (pär′ ĭ·sīd)
 -cid·al
Par·ris Is., S.C. (pär′ ĭs)
par·rot (pär′ ŭt)
  par·rot·eđ par·rot·ing
par·ry (pär′ ĭ)
  par·rieđ par·ry·ing
parse (pärs)
  pars·ing
par·si·mo·ni·ous
    (pär′ sĭ·mō′ nĭ·ŭs)
  par·si·mo·ny (pär′ sĭ·mō′ nĭ)
pars·ley (pärs′ lĭ)
pars·nip (pärs′ nĭp)
par·son (pär′ s'n)
  par·son·age (-ĭj)
par·take (pär·tāk′)
 tak·ing
par·the·no·gen·e·sis
    (pär′ thě·nô·jěn′ ě·sĭs)

Par·the·non (pär′ thě·nŏn)
par·tial (pär′ shȧl)
  par·ti·al·i·ty (pär′ shĭ·ăl′ ĭ·tĭ)
  par·tial·ly
par·tic·i·pate (pär·tĭs′ ĭ·pāt)
 -pat·ing
  par·tic·i·pant (-pȧnt)
  par·tic·i·pa·tion
    (pär·tĭs′ ĭ·pā′ shŭn)
  par·tic·i·pa·tor
par·ti·ci·ple (pär′ tĭ·sĭ·p'l)
  par·ti·cip·i·al (pär′ tĭ·sĭp′ ĭ·ȧl)
par·ti·cle (pär′ tĭ·k'l)
par·tic·u·lar (pēr·tĭk′ û·lēr)
  par·tic·u·lar·i·ty
    (pēr·tĭk′ û·lăr′ ĭ·tĭ)
  par·tic·u·lar·ize
 -iz·ing par·tic·u·lar·ly
par·ti·san (pär′ tĭ·zȧn)
  par·ti·san·ship
par·ti·tion (pär·tĭsh′ ŭn)
  par·ti·tion·ment
par·ti·tive (pär′ tĭ·tĭv)
part·ner (pärt′ nēr)
  part·ner·ship
par·tridge (pär′ trĭj)
par·tu·ri·tion (pär·tů·rĭsh′ ŭn)
par·ty (pär′ tĭ)
 -ties
par·ve·nu (pär′ vě·nū)
pas·chal lamb (pȧs′ kȧl)
pa·sha (pȧ·shä′)
pasque·flow·er (pȧsk′ flou′ ēr)
pass·a·ble (pȧs′ ȧ·b'l)
pas·sage (pȧs′ ĭj)
  pas·sage·way
Pas·sa·ic, N.J. (pȧ·sā′ ĭk)
pass·book (pȧs′ bŏŏk′)
pas·sé (pȧ·sā′)
pas·sen·ger pi·geon
    (pȧs′ ěn·jēr)
pass·er-by (pȧs′ ēr·bĭ′)
pas·sion (pȧsh′ ŭn)
  pas·sion·ate (-ĭt)
  -ate·ly pas·sion·flow·er
  pas·sion·less Pas·sion play
pas·sive (pȧs′ ĭv)
  pas·sive·ly
  pas·siv·i·ty (pȧ·sĭv′ ĭ·tĭ)
pass·key (pȧs′ kē′)
pass·port (pȧs′ pȯrt)
paste (pāst)
  past·ing paste·board
  past·y
pas·tel (pȧs·těl′)

pas·teur·ize (păs′ tẽr· īz)
  -iz·ing
  pas·teur·i·za·tion
    (păs′ tẽr·ĭ·zā′ shŭn)
pas·tiche (păs·tēsh′)
pas·time (pás′ tīm′)
pas·tor (pás′ tẽr)
  pas·tor·ate (-ĭt)
pas·to·ral (pás′ tŏ·răl)
  (rural; see *pastorale*)
pas·to·ra·le (pás′ tŏ·rä′ lá)
  (music; see *pastoral*)
  pl. -ra·li (-rä′ lĕ)
pas·tra·mi (pás·trä′ mĭ)
pas·try (pās′ trĭ)
  -tries
pas·ture (pás′ tûr)
  -tur·ing
  pas·tur·age (-ĭj)
patch·work (păch′ wûrk′)
pâ·té de foie gras
    (pä′ tā′ dĕ fwä′ grä′)
pa·tel·la (pá·tĕl′ á)
  pl. pa·tel·lae (-ē)
pat·en (păt′ ĕn)
pat·ent (păt′ ĕnt)
  pat·ent·a·ble
  pat·ent·ee (păt′ ĕn·tē′)
  pa·tent·ly pat·en·tor
pa·ter·fa·mil·i·as
    (pä′ tẽr·fá·mĭl′ ĭ·ás)
pa·ter·nal (pá·tûr′ năl)
  pa·ter·nal·is·tic
    (pá·tûr′ năl·ĭs′ tĭk)
  pa·ter·ni·ty (pá·tûr′ nĭ·tĭ)
pa·ter·nos·ter (pä′ tẽr·nŏs′ tẽr)
Pat·er·son, N. J. (păt′ ẽr·s′n)
pa·thet·ic (pá·thĕt′ ĭk)
  -i·cal·ly
  pa·thet·ic fal·la·cy
path·find·er (păth′ fīn′ dẽr)
pa·thol·o·gy (pá·thŏl′ ŏ·jĭ)
  -gies
  path·o·log·i·cal
    (păth′ ŏ·lŏj′ ĭ·kăl)
  pa·thol·o·gist (pá·thŏl′ ŏ·jĭst)
pa·thos (pā′ thŏs)
pa·tient (pā′ shĕnt)
  pa·tience
pat·i·na (păt′ ĭ·ná)
pat·i·o (păt′ ĭ·ō)
pat·ois (păt′ wä)
pa·tri·arch (pā′ trĭ·ärk)
  pa·tri·ar·chal (pā′ trĭ·är′ kăl)
  pa·tri·arch·y -arch·ies

pa·tri·cian (pá·trĭsh′ ăn)
pat·ri·mo·ny (păt′ rĭ·mō′ nĭ)
pa·tri·ot (pā′ trĭ·ŭt)
  pa·tri·ot·ic (pā′ trĭ·ŏt′ ĭk)
  -i·cal·ly
  pa·tri·ot·ism (pā′ trĭ·ŭt·ĭz′m)
pa·trol (pá·trōl′)
  -trolled, -trol·ling
  pa·trol·man pa·trol wag·on
pa·tron (pā′ trŭn)
  pa·tron·age (pā′ trŭn·ĭj)
  pa·tron·ess (pā′ trŭn·ĕs)
  pa·tron·ize
  pa·tron·iz·ing·ly
pat·ro·nym·ic (păt′ rŏ·nĭm′ ĭk)
pa·troon (pá·trōōn′)
pat·ter (păt′ ẽr)
pat·tern (păt′ ẽrn)
pat·ty shell (păt′ ĭ)
pau·ci·ty (pô′ sĭ·tĭ)
Paul·ist (pôl′ ĭst)
paunch·y (pôn′ chĭ)
pau·per (pô′ pẽr)
  pau·per·ize -iz·ing
pause (pôz)
  paus·ing
pav·an (păv′ ăn)
pave·ment (pāv′ mĕnt)
pa·vil·ion (pá·vĭl′ yŭn)
pav·ing (pāv′ ĭng)
pawn·bro·ker (pôn′ brō′ kẽr)
Paw·nee· In·di·ans
    (pô·nē′)
pay (pā)
  pay·a·ble
  pay·ee (pā′ ē′)
  pay·er pay·mas·ter
  pay·ment pay·off
  pay·roll
peace (pēs)
  peace·a·ble
  peace·ful, -ful·ly, -ful·ness
  peace·mak·er peace of·fer·ing
  peace of·fi·cer
peach (pēch)
pea·cock (pē′ kŏk′)
pea·hen (pē′ hĕn′)
pea jack·et (pē)
peaked (pēk′ ĕd)
  (thin; see *peeked*)
peal·ing (pēl′ ĭng)
  (of a bell; see *peeling*)
pea·nut (pē′ nŭt′)
pearl (pûrl)
  (gem; see *purl*)

pearl·y   (pûr′ lĭ)
peas·ant   (pĕz′ ᵈnt)
  peas·ant·ry
peb·ble   (pĕb′ ′l)
  peb·bly
pe·can   (pē· kăn′)
pec·ca·dil·lo   (pĕk′ ȧ· dĭl′ ō)
  -dil·loes
pec·ca·ry   (pĕk′ ȧ· rĭ)
pec·tin   (pĕk′ tĭn)
  pec·tic ac·id
pec·to·ral   (pĕk′ tō· rᵈl)
pe·cul·iar   (pē· kūl′ yēr)
  pe·cu·li·ar·i·ty
                   (pē· kū′ lĭ· ăr′ ĭ· tĭ)
  -ties
pe·cu·ni·ar·y   (pē· kū′ nĭ· ĕr′ ĭ)
ped·a·gogue   (pĕd′ ȧ· gŏg)
  ped·a·gog·ic   (pĕd′ ȧ· gŏj′ ĭk)
  -i·cal
  ped·a·go·gy   (pĕd′ ȧ· gō′ jĭ)
ped·al   (pĕd′ ᵈl)
  (on a bike; see peddle)
  -aled   -al· ing
ped·ant   (pĕd′ ᵈnt)
  pe·dan·tic   (pē· dăn′ tĭk)
  -ti·cal·ly
  ped·ant·ry   (pĕd′ ᵈnt· rĭ)
ped·dle   (pĕd′ ′l)
  (sell; see pedal)
  ped·dling   ped·dler
ped·es·tal   (pĕd′ ĕs· tᵈl)
pe·des·tri·an   (pē· dĕs′ trĭ· ᵈn)
pe·di·at·rics   (pē′ dĭ· ăt′ rĭks)
  pe·di·a·tri·cian
                   (pē′ dĭ· ȧ· trĭsh′ ᵈn)
ped·i·cure   (pĕd′ ĭ· kūr)
ped·i·gree   (pĕd′ ĭ· grē)
peeked   (pēkt)
  (looked; see peaked)
peel·ing   (pēl′ ĭng)
  (of an apple; see pealing)
Peep·ing Tom   (pēp′ ĭng)
peer   (pēr)
  (an equal; see pier)
  peer·age   (pēr′ ĭj)
  peer·less
peeve   (pēv)
  peev·ing   pee·vish
pee·wee   (pē′ wē)
Peg·a·sus   (pĕg′ ȧ· sŭs)
peign·oir   (pān· wär′)
pe·jo·ra·tive   (pē′ jŏ· rā′ tĭv)
  -tive·ly
Pe·king·ese   (pē′ kĭng· ēz′)

pe·koe   (pē′ kō)
pelf   (pĕlf)
pel·i·can   (pĕl′ ĭ· kᵈn)
pel·la·gra   (pĕ· lă′ grȧ)
pel·let   (pĕl′ ĕt)
pell-mell   (pĕl′ mĕl′)
pel·lu·cid   (pĕ· lū′ sĭd)
pel·vic   (pĕl′ vĭk)
  pel·vis
pem·mi·can   (pĕm′ ĭ· kᵈn)
pe·nal   (pē′ nᵈl)
  pe·nal code
  pe·nal·ize   -iz· ing
pen·al·ty   (pĕn′ ᵈl· tĭ)
  -ties
pen·ance   (pĕn′ ᵈns)
pence   (pĕns)
pen·chant   (pĕn′ chᵈnt)
pen·cil   (pĕn′ sĭl)
  -ciled   -cil· ing
pend·ant   (pĕn′ dᵈnt)
  (ornament; see pendent)
pend·ent   (pĕn′ dĕnt)
  (suspended; see pendant)
  pend·en·cy
pend·ing   (pĕnd′ ĭng)
pen·du·lous   (pĕn′ dụ· lŭs)
pen·du·lum   (pĕn′ dụ· lŭm)
pen·e·trate   (pĕn′ ĕ· trāt)
  -trat· ing
  pen·e·tra·ble   (pĕn′ ĕ· trȧ· b′l)
  pen·e·trant   (pĕn′ ĕ· trᵈnt)
  pen·e·tra·tion
                   (pĕn′ ĕ· trā′ shŭn)
  pen·e·tra·tive   (pĕn′ ĕ· trā′ tĭv)
pen·guin   (pĕn′ gwĭn)
pen·hold·er   (pĕn′ hōl′ dēr)
pen·i·cil·lin   (pĕn′ ĭ· sĭl′ ĭn)
pen·in·su·la   (pĕn· ĭn′ sụ· lȧ)
  pen·in·su·lar   (-lēr)
pen·i·tent   (pĕn′ ĭ· tĕnt)
  -tence
  pen·i·ten·tial   (pĕn′ ĭ· tĕn′ shᵈl)
pen·i·ten·tia·ry
                   (pĕn′ ĭ· tĕn′ shȧ· rĭ)
  -ries
pen·knife   (pĕn′ nīf′)
pen·man·ship   (pĕn′ mᵈn· shĭp)
pen·nant   (pĕn′ ᵈnt)
pen·ni·less   (pĕn′ ĭ· lĕs)
Penn·syl·va·nia
                   (pĕn′ sĭl· văn′ yȧ)
  abbr. Pa. or Penna.
  Penn·syl·va·nian

pen·ny (pĕn′ ĭ)
  pen·nies
  pen·ni·less (pĕn′ ĭ·lĕs)
  pen·ny an·te   pen·ny·weight
  pen·ny-wise
pe·nol·o·gy (pē·nŏl′ ō·jĭ)
pen·sion (pĕn′ shŭn)
  pen·sion·er
pen·ta· (pĕn′ tà-)
  pen·ta·gon (pĕn′ tà·gŏn)
  pen·tag·o·nal (pĕn·tăg′ ō·nǎl)
  pen·ta·he·dron
            (pĕn′ tà·hē′ drŭn)
  pen·tam·e·ter (pĕn·tăm′ ĕ·tēr)
  Pen·ta·teuch (pĕn′ tà·tūk)
  pen·tath·lon (pĕn·tăth′ lŏn)
Pen·te·cos·tal (pĕn′ tĕ·kŏs′ tǎl)
pent·house (pĕnt′ hous′)
pe·nu·che (pē·nōō′ chĕ)
pe·nul·ti·mate (pē·nŭl′ tĭ·mĭt)
pe·nu·ri·ous (pē·nū′ rĭ·ŭs)
  pen·u·ry (pĕn′ û·rĭ)
pe·on (pē′ ŏn)
  pe·on·age (pē′ ŏn·ĭj)
pe·o·ny (pē′ ō·nĭ)
  -nies
peo·ple (pē′ p'l)
  -pling
pep·lum (pĕp′ lŭm)
pep·per (pĕp′ ēr)
  pep·per·corn   pep·per·mint
  pep·per·y
pep·sin (pĕp′ sĭn)
pep·tic (pĕp′ tĭk)
pep·tone (pĕp′ tōn)
per·ad·ven·ture
            (pûr′ ǎd·vĕn′ tûr)
per·am·bu·late
            (pēr·ăm′ bû·lāt)
  -lat·ing
  per·am·bu·la·tion
         (pēr·ăm′ bû·lā′ shŭn)
  per·am·bu·la·tor
         (pēr·ăm′ bû·lā′ tēr)
per an·num (pēr ăn′ ŭm)
per·bo·rate (pûr·bō′ rāt)
per·cale (pēr·kāl′)
per cap·i·ta (pēr·kăp′ ĭ·tà)
per·ceive (pēr·sēv′)
  -ceiv·ing   per·ceiv·a·ble
per cent (pēr sĕnt′)
  per·cent·age (pēr·sĕn′ tĭj)
  per·cen·tile (pēr·sĕn′ tĭl)
per·cept (pûr′ sĕpt)
per·cep·ti·ble (pēr·sĕp′ tĭ·b'l)

per·cep·tion (pēr·sĕp′ shŭn)
per·cep·tive (pēr·sĕp′ tĭv)
perch (pûrch)
per·chance (pēr·chăns′)
per·cip·i·ent (pēr·sĭp′ ĭ·ĕnt)
  -ence
per·co·late (pûr′ kō·lāt)
  -lat·ing   per·co·la·tor
per·cus·sion (pēr·kŭsh′ ŭn)
per·di·tion (pēr·dĭsh′ ŭn)
per·dur·a·ble (pûr·dūr′ à·b'l)
per·e·gri·nate (pēr′ ē·grĭ·nāt)
  -nat·ing
  per·e·gri·na·tion
         (pēr′ ē·grĭ·nā′ shŭn)
per·emp·to·ry (pēr·ĕmp′ tō·rĭ)
  per·emp·to·ri·ly
per·en·ni·al (pēr·ĕn′ ĭ·ǎl)
  per·en·ni·al·ly
per·fect (pûr′ fĕkt) *adj.*
  per·fect par·ti·ci·ple
per·fect (pēr·fĕkt′) *v.*
  per·fect·i·bil·i·ty
       (pēr·fĕk′ tĭ·bĭl′ ĭ·tĭ)
  per·fect·i·ble
  per·fec·tion (pēr·fĕk′ shŭn)
  per·fec·tion·ist
per·fec·to (pēr·fĕk′ tō)
per·fi·dy (pûr′ fĭ·dĭ)
  -dies
  per·fid·i·ous (pēr·fĭd′ ĭ·ŭs)
per·fo·rate (pûr′ fō·rāt)
  -rat·ing
  per·fo·ra·tion
         (pûr′ fō·rā′ shŭn)
per·force (pēr·fōrs′)
per·form (pēr·fôrm′)
  per·form·a·ble   per·form·ance
per·fume (pēr·fūm′)
  -fum·ing
per·func·to·ry (pēr·fŭngk′ tō·rĭ)
  per·func·to·ri·ly
  per·func·to·ri·ness
per·haps (pēr·hăps′)
Per·i·cles (pēr′ ĭ·klēz)
  Per·i·cle·an (pēr′ ĭ·klē′ ǎn)
per·i·gee (pēr′ ĭ·jē)
per·i·he·li·on (pēr′ ĭ·hē′ lĭ·ŏn)
per·il (pēr′ ĭl)
  -iled   -il·ing
  per·il·ous (pēr′ ĭ·lŭs)
per·im·e·ter (pē·rĭm′ ĕ·tēr)
per·i·ne·um (pēr′ ĭ·nē′ ŭm)
pe·ri·od (pēr′ ĭ·ŭd)
  pe·ri·od·ic (pēr′ ĭ·ŏd′ ĭk)

pe·ri·od·i·cal   (pēr′ Ĭ·ŏd′ Ĭ·kᵃl)
 -cal·ly
pe·ri·o·dic·i·ty
                (pēr′ Ĭ·ŏ·dĬs′ Ĭ·tĬ)
per·i·os·te·um   (pēr′ Ĭ·ŏs′ tē·ŭm)
per·i·pa·tet·ic   (pēr′ Ĭ·pა·tĕt′ Ĭk)
pe·riph·er·y   (pĕ·rĬf′ ēr·Ĭ)
 -er·ies
pe·riph·er·al   (pĕ·rĬf′ ēr·ᵃl)
per·i·scope   (pēr′ Ĭ·skōp)
 per·i·scop·ic   (pēr′ Ĭ·skŏp′ Ĭk)
per·ish   (pēr′ Ĭsh)
 per·ish·a·ble
per·i·stal·sis   (pēr′ Ĭ·stăl′ sĬs)
 per·i·stal·tic   (-tĬk)
per·i·to·ni·tis   (pēr′ Ĭ·tŏ·nī′ tĬs)
per·i·wig   (pēr′ Ĭ·wĬg)
per·i·win·kle   (pēr′ Ĭ·wĬng′ k'l)
per·jure   (pûr′ jēr)
 -jur·ing   per·jur·er
 per·ju·ry
perk·y   (pûrk′ Ĭ)
per·ma·nent   (pûr′ mა·nĕnt)
 -nence
per·man·ga·nate
                (pēr·măng′ gა·nāt)
per·me·ate   (pûr′ mē·āt)
 -at·ing
 per·me·a·bil·i·ty
                (pûr′ mē·ა·bĬl′ Ĭ·tĬ)
 per·me·a·ble   (pûr′ mē·ა·b'l)
per·mis·si·ble   (pēr·mĬs′ Ĭ·b'l)
 per·mis·si·bil·i·ty
                (pēr·mĬs′ Ĭ·bĬl′ Ĭ·tĬ)
per·mis·sion   (pēr·mĬsh′ ŭn)
per·mis·sive   (pēr·mĬs′ Ĭv)
 -mis·sive·ly
per·mit   (pēr·mĬt′) v
 -mit·ted   -mit·ting
per·mit   (pûr′ mĬt) n
per·mute   (pēr·mūt′)
 -mut·ing
 per·mu·ta·tion
                (pûr′ mū·tā′ shŭn)
per·ni·cious a·ne·mi·a
                (pēr·nĬsh′ ŭs)
per·nick·et·y   (pēr·nĬk′ ĕ·tĬ)
per·o·rate   (pēr′ ŏ·rāt)
 -rat·ing
 per·o·ra·tion   (pēr′ ŏ·rā′ shŭn)
per·ox·ide   (pēr·ŏk′ sĬd)
per·pen·dic·u·lar
                (pûr′ pĕn·dĬk′ ū·lēr)
per·pe·trate   (pûr′ pē·trāt)
 -trat·ing

per·pe·tra·tion
                (pûr′ pē·trā′ shŭn)
 per·pe·tra·tor
per·pet·u·al   (pēr·pĕt′ ū·ᵃl)
 -al·ly
 per·pet·u·ate   (pēr·pĕt′ ū·āt)
 -at·ing
 per·pet·u·a·tion
                (pēr·pĕt′ ū·ā′ shŭn)
 per·pe·tu·i·ty   (pûr′ pē·tū′ Ĭ·tĬ)
per·plex   (pēr·plĕks′)
per·se·cute   (pûr′ sē·kūt)
 -cut·ing
 per·se·cu·tion
                (pûr′ sē·kū′ shŭn)
 per·se·cu·tor
per·se·vere   (pûr′ sē·vēr′)
 -ver·ing   per·se·ver·ance
Per·sian lamb   (pûr′ zhᵃn)
per·si·flage   (pûr′ sĬ·fläzh)
per·sim·mon   (pēr·sĬm′ ŭn)
per·sist   (pēr·sĬst′)
 per·sis·tence   -tent
per·son   (pûr′ s'n)
 per·son·a·ble   (pûr′ sŭn·ა·b'l)
 per·son·age   (-Ĭj)
 per·son·al·i·ty
                (pûr′ sŭ·năl′ Ĭ·tĬ)
 -ties
 per·son·al·ize, -iz·ing
 per·son·al·ly
per·so·na non gra·ta
                (pēr·sō′ nა nŏn grä′ tა)
per·son·al   (pûr′ sŭn·ᵃl)
 (private; see *personnel*)
per·son·i·fy   (pēr·sŏn′ Ĭ·fī)
 -fied   -fy·ing
 per·son·i·fi·ca·tion
                (pēr·sŏn′ Ĭ·fĬ·kā′ shŭn)
per·son·nel   (pûr′ sŏ·nĕl′)
 (employees; see *personal*)
per·spec·tive   (pēr·spĕk′ tĬv)
 (n.; appearance; see *prospective*)
per·spi·ca·cious
                (pûr′ spĬ·kā′ shŭs)
 per·spi·cac·i·ty
                (pûr′ spĬ·kăs′ Ĭ·tĬ)
per·spi·cu·i·ty   (pûr′ spĬ·kū′ Ĭ·tĬ)
per·spire   (pēr·spīr′)
 -spir·ing
 per·spi·ra·tion
                (pûr′ spĬ·rā′ shŭn)
per·suade   (pēr·swād′)
 -suad·ing   per·suad·a·ble
 per·suad·er

per·sua·sion (-swā′ zhŭn)
per·sua·sive
per·sua·sive·ness
per·tain (pĕr·tān′)
per·ti·na·cious (pûr′ tĭ·nā′ shŭs)
per·ti·nac·i·ty (-năs′ ĭ·tĭ)
per·ti·nent (pûr′ tĭ·nĕnt)
-nence
per·turb (pĕr·tûrb′)
per·turb·a·ble
per·tur·ba·tion
(pûr′ tĕr·bā′ shŭn)
pe·ruke (pĕ·rōōk′)
pe·ruse (pĕ·rōōz′)
-rus·ing
pe·rus·al (pĕ·rōōz′ ăl)
per·vade (pĕr·vād′)
-vad·ing per·va·sion
per·va·sive
per·verse (pĕr·vûrs′)
per·verse·ly
per·ver·sion (pĕr·vûr′ zhŭn)
per·vert (pĕr·vûrt′) v.
per·vert (pûr′ vûrt) n.
pe·so (pā′ sō)
-sos
pes·si·mism (pĕs′ ĭ·mĭz′m)
pes·si·mist
pes·si·mis·ti·cal·ly
(pĕs′ ĭ·mĭs′ tĭ·kăl·ĭ)
pes·ti·cide (pĕs′ tĭ·sīd)
pes·tif·er·ous (pĕs·tĭf′ ĕr·ŭs)
pes·ti·lent (pĕs′ tĭ·lĕnt)
-lence
pes·ti·len·tial (pĕs′ tĭ·lĕn′ shăl)
pes·tle (pĕs′ ′l)
pet·al (pĕt′ ′l)
pe·tard (pĕ·tärd′)
pet·cock (pĕt′ kŏk′)
pe·tite (pĕ·tēt′)
pe·ti·tion (pĕ·tĭsh′ ŭn)
pe·ti·tion·ar·y
pe·ti·tion·er
pet·it ju·ry (pĕt′ ĭ)
pe·tits fours (pē·tē′ fōōr′)
pet·ri·fy (pĕt′ rĭ·fī)
-fied -fy·ing
pe·tro·le·um (pĕ·trō′ lĕ·ŭm)
pe·trol·o·gy (pĕ·trŏl′ ŏ·jĭ)
pet·ti·coat (pĕt′ ĭ·kōt)
pet·ti·fog (pĕt′ ĭ·fŏg)
-fogged -fog·ging
pet·ti·fog·ger
pet·ty (pĕt′ ĭ)
pet·ti·ness pet·ty cash

pet·ty lar·ce·ny
pet·u·lant (pĕt′ û·lănt)
-lance -lan·cy
pe·tu·ni·a (pĕ·tū′ nĭ·á)
pew (pū)
pew·ter (pū′ tĕr)
pha·lanx (fā′ lăngks)
-lanx·es
phal·lus (făl′ ŭs)
phal·lic (făl′ ĭk)
phan·tom (făn′ tŭm)
Phar·aoh (fâr′ ō)
Phar·i·see (făr′ ĭ·sē)
phar·i·sa·i·cal (făr′ ĭ·sā′ ĭ·kăl)
phar·ma·cy (fär′ má·sĭ)
-cies
phar·ma·ceu·ti·cal
(fär′ má·sū′ tĭ·kăl)
phar·ma·cist (fär′ má·sĭst)
phar·ma·col·o·gy
(fär′ má·kŏl′ ŏ·jĭ)
phar·ynx (fär′ ĭngks)
pl. pha·ryn·ges
(fá·rĭn′ jēz)
phase (fāz)
(aspect; see *faze*)
pheas·ant (fĕz′ ănt)
phe·no·bar·bi·tal
(fē′ nŏ·bär′ bĭ·tôl)
phe·nom·e·non (fĕ·nŏm′ ĕ·nŏn)
pl. phe·nom·e·na
phe·nom·e·nal
Phil·a·del·phi·a,
Pa. (fĭl′ á·dĕl′ fĭ·á)
phi·lan·der·er (fĭ·lăn′ dĕr·ĕr)
phi·lan·thro·py
(fĭ·lăn′ thrŏ·pĭ)
phil·an·throp·ic
(fĭl′ ăn·thrŏp′ ĭk)
phil·an·throp·ist
phi·lat·e·ly (fĭ·lăt′ ĕ·lĭ)
phi·lat·e·list (fĭ·lăt′ ĕ·lĭst)
phil·har·mon·ic
(fĭl′ ĕr·mŏn′ ĭk)
Phil·ip, Prince, Duke of
Ed·in·burgh
(fĭl′ ĭp;
ĕd′ ′n·bûr′ ō)
phi·lip·pic (fĭ·lĭp′ ĭk)
Phil·ip·pine (is.) (fĭl′ ĭ·pēn)
But: Fil·i·pi·no
Phi·lis·tine (fĭ·lĭs′ tĭn)
phil·o·den·dron
(fĭl′ ō·dĕn′ drŏn)

phi·lol·o·gy   (fĭ·lŏl′ ō·jĭ)
   phi·lol·o·gist
phi·los·o·phy   (fĭ·lŏs′ ō·fĭ)
   -phies   phi·los·o·pher
   phil·o·soph·i·cal
       (fĭl′ ō·sŏf′ ĭ·kǎl)
   phi·los·o·phize
phil·ter   (fĭl′ tẽr)
   (as in *love philter;* see *filter*)
phlegm   (flĕm)
   phleg·mat·ic   (flĕg·mǎt′ ĭk)
phlo·gis·tic   (flō·jĭs′ tĭk)
phlo·gis·ton   (flō·jĭs′ tŏn)
phlox   (flŏks)
pho·bi·a   (fō′ bĭ·à)
   pho·bic   (fō′ bĭk)
phoe·be   (fē′ bĕ)
Phoe·ni·cian   (fē·nĭsh′ ǎn)
Phoe·nix, Ariz.   (fē′ nĭks)
pho·net·ic   (fō·nĕt′ ĭk)
   pho·net·i·cal·ly
phon·ics   (fŏn′ ĭks)
pho·no·graph   (fō′ nō·gráf)
phos·gene   (fŏz′ jēn)
phos·phate   (fŏs′ fāt)
phos·pho·res·cence
       (fŏs′ fō·rĕs′ ĕns)
   -cent
phos·pho·rus   (fŏs′ fō·rŭs)
   phos·phor·ic   (fŏs·fŏr′ ĭk)
pho·to   (fō′ tō)
   -toed, -to·ing, -tos
pho·to·e·lec·tric   (fō′ tō·ē·lĕk′ trĭk)
pho·to·en·grav·ing
       (fō′ tō·ĕn·grāv′ ĭng)
pho·to·flood lamp
       (fō′ tō·flŭd′)
pho·to·gen·ic   (fō′ tō·jĕn′ ĭk)
pho·to·graph   (fō′ tō·gráf)
   pho·tog·ra·pher
       (fō·tŏg′ rà·fẽr)
   pho·to·graph·ic
       (fō′ tō·gráf′ ĭk)
   pho·tog·ra·phy
       (fō·tŏg′ rà·fĭ)
pho·to·gra·vure   (fō′ tō·grà·vūr′)
pho·to·mu·ral   (fō′ tō·mū′ rǎl)
pho·to-off·set   (fō′ tō·ôf′ sĕt′)
pho·to·sen·si·tive
       (fō′ tō·sĕn′ sĭ·tĭv)
pho·to·sphere   (fō′ tō·sfẽr)
Pho·to·stat   (fō′ tō·stăt)
pho·to·syn·the·sis
       (fō′ tō·sĭn′ thĕ·sĭs)

phrase   (frāz)
   phras·ing   phras·al
   phra·se·o·log·i·cal
       (frā′ zĕ·ō·lŏj′ ĭ·kǎl)
   phra·se·ol·o·gy
       (frā′ zĕ·ŏl′ ō·jĭ)
phre·net·ic   (frĕ·nĕt′ ĭk)
phre·nol·o·gy   (frĕ·nŏl′ ō·jĭ)
phy·log·e·ny   (fī·lŏj′ ê·nĭ)
phy·lum   (fī′ lŭm)
   pl. phy·la
phys·ic   (fĭz′ ĭk)
phys·i·cal   (fĭz′ ĭ·kǎl)
   phys·i·cal ther·a·py
phy·si·cian   (fĭ·zĭsh′ ǎn)
phys·ics   (fĭz′ ĭks)
   phys·i·cist   (fĭz′ ĭ·sĭst)
phys·i·og·no·my
       (fĭz′ ĭ·ŏg′ nō·mĭ)
   -mies
phys·i·ol·o·gy   (fĭz′ ĭ·ŏl′ ō·jĭ)
   phys·i·o·log·i·cal
       (fĭz′ ĭ·ō·lŏj′ ĭ·kǎl)
phys·i·o·ther·a·py
       (fĭz′ ĭ·ō·thĕr′ à·pĭ)
phy·sique   (fĭ·zēk′)
pi·a·nis·si·mo   (pē′ à·nĭs′ ĭ·mō)
pi·an·o   (pĭ·ǎn′ ō)
   -os
   pi·an·ist   (pĭ·ǎn′ ĭst)
pi·az·za   (pĭ·ǎz′ à)
pi·ca   (pī′ kà)
pic·a·resque   (pĭk′ à·rĕsk′)
pic·a·yune   (pĭk′ à·yōōn′)
   pic·a·yun·ish
Pic·ca·dil·ly   (pĭk′ à·dĭl′ ĭ)
pic·ca·lil·li   (pĭk′ à·lĭl′ ĭ)
pic·co·lo   (pĭk′ ō·lō)
   -los
pick·a·back   (pĭk′ à·băk′)
pick·a·nin·ny   (pĭk′ à·nĭn′ ĭ)
   -nin·nies
pick·ax   (pĭk′ ăks′)
   -ax·es
pick·er·el   (pĭk′ ẽr·ĕl)
   pick·er·el·weed
pick·et   (pĭk′ ĕt)
   -et·ed   -et·ing
   pick·et·er
pick·le   (pĭk′ 'l)
   -ling
pick·pock·et   (pĭk′ pŏk′ ĕt)
pick·up   (pĭk′ ŭp′)
pic·nic   (pĭk′ nĭk)
   -nicked   -nick·ing

pic·nick·er
pic·to·graph (pĭk′ tŏ·gráf)
pic·to·ri·al (pĭk·tō′ rĭ·ăl)
  -al·ly
pic·ture (pĭk′ tu̲r)
  -tur·ing
pic·tur·esque (pĭk′ tu̲r·ĕsk′)
pid·dling (pĭd′ lĭng)
pidg·in Eng·lish
        (pĭj′ ĭn)
pie·bald (pī′ bôld′)
piece (pēs)
  piec·ing   piece·meal
  piece·work
pièce de ré·sis·tance
    (pyĕs′ dĕ rā′ zēs′ täns′)
pied (pīd)
pied·mont (pēd′ mŏnt)
pier (pẽr)
  (breakwater; see peer)
pierce (pẽrs)
  pierc·ing
pi·e·ty (pī′ ĕ·tĭ)
  -ties
pig (pĭg)
  pig·head·ed   pig i·ron
  pig·pen   pig·skin
  pig·sty   -sties
  pig·tail
pi·geon (pĭj′ ŭn)
  pi·geon-breast·ed
  pi·geon·hole   pi·geon-toed
pig·gy bank (pĭg′ ĭ)
pig·ment (pĭg′ mĕnt)
  pig·men·tar·y (pĭg′ mĕn·tĕr′ ĭ)
  pig·men·ta·tion
    (pĭg′ mĕn·tā′ shŭn)
pi·las·ter (pĭ·lăs′ tẽr)
pi·lau (pĭ·lō′)
pil·chard (pĭl′ chẽrd)
pile driv·er (pīl)
pil·fer (pĭl′ fẽr)
  pil·fer·age   pil·fer·er
pil·grim (pĭl′ grĭm)
  pil·grim·age (pĭl′ grĭ·mĭj)
  Pil·grim Fa·thers
pil·ing (pīl′ ĭng)
pil·lage (pĭl′ ĭj)
pil·lar (pĭl′ ẽr)
pill·box (pĭl′ bŏks′)
pil·lo·ry (pĭl′ ŏ·rĭ)
  -ries
pil·low (pĭl′ ō)
  pil·low·case   pil·low slip

pi·lot (pī′ lŭt)
  -lot·ed   -lot·ing
Pilt·down man (pĭlt′ doun′)
pi·men·to (pĭ·mĕn′ tō)
  -tos
pim·per·nel (pĭm′ pẽr·nĕl)
pim·ple (pĭm′ p'l)
  -ply
pin·a·fore (pĭn′ à·fōr′)
pin·ball ma·chine
        (pĭn′ bôl′)
pince-nez (păns′ nā′)
pin·cers (pĭn′ sẽrz)
pinch hit·ter (pĭnch)
pin·cush·ion (pĭn′ kŏŏsh′ ŭn)
pin·e·al gland (pĭn′ ĕ·ăl)
pine·ap·ple (pīn′ ăp′ 'l)
pin·feath·er (pĭn′ fĕth′ ẽr)
Ping-pong (pĭng′ pŏng′)
pin·hole (pĭn′ hōl′)
pin·ion (pĭn′ yŭn)
pink·eye (pĭngk′ ī′)
pin·nace (pĭn′ ĭs)
pin·na·cle (pĭn′ à·k'l)
pin·nate (pĭn′ āt)
pi·noch·le (pē′ nŭk′ 'l)
pin·point (pĭn′ point′)
pin·tail duck (pĭn′ tāl′)
pin·to (pĭn′ tō)
pin-up (pĭn′ ŭp′)
pi·o·neer (pī′ ŏ·nẽr′)
pi·ous (pī′ ŭs)
  pi·e·ty (pī′ ĕ·tĭ)
pipe (pīp)
  pip·ing   pipe dream
  pipe·line   pipe or·gan
pi·pette (pĭ·pĕt′)
pi·quant (pē′ kănt)
  pi·quan·cy (pē′ kăn·sĭ)
pique (pēk)
pi·qué (pĕ·kā′)
pi·ra·nha fish (pĭ·rän′ yà)
pi·rate (pī′ rĭt)
  pi·ra·cy (pī′ rà·sĭ)
pir·ou·ette (pĭr′ ŏŏ·ĕt′)
  -ett·ing
pis·ca·to·ri·al (pĭs′ kà·tō′ rĭ·ăl)
pis·tach·i·o (pĭs·tăsh′ ĭ·ō)
pis·til (pĭs′ tĭl)
  (plant part; see pistol)
pis·tol (pĭs′ t'l)
  (firearm; see pistil)
pis·ton ring (pĭs′ tŭn)
pitch (pĭch)
  pitch-black

pitch·blende (pĭch' blĕnd')
pitch·er pitch·fork
pitch pipe
pit·e·ous (pĭt' ĕ·ŭs)
pit·fall (pĭt' fôl')
pith·y (pĭth' ĭ)
pit·i·a·ble (pĭt' ĭ·à·b'l)
pit·i·ful (pĭt' ĭ·fŏŏl)
  -ful·ly -ful·ness
pit·i·less (pĭt' ĭ·lĕs)
pi·ton (pē' tôN')
pit·tance (pĭt' ăns)
Pitts·burg, Kans. (pĭts' bûrg)
Pitts·burgh, Pa. (pĭts' bûrg)
pi·tu·i·tar·y gland
                (pĭ·tū' ĭ·tĕr' ĭ)
pit·y (pĭt' ĭ)
  pit·ied pit·y·ing
  pit·e·ous (pĭt' ĕ·ŭs)
  pit·i·a·ble
  pit·i·ful, -ful·ly, -ful·ness
  pit·i·less
piv·ot (pĭv' ŭt)
  -ot·ed -ot·ing
  piv·ot·al
pix·y (pĭk' sĭ)
  pix·ies
piz·za (pēt' sà)
  piz·ze·ri·a (pēt' sĕ·rē' à)
plac·ard (plăk' ärd)
pla·cate (plā' kāt)
  -cat·ing
pla·ce·bo (plà·sē' bō)
place·ment (plās' mĕnt)
pla·cen·ta (plà·sĕn' tà)
  pla·cen·tal
plac·er min·ing (plăs' ẽr)
plac·id (plăs' ĭd)
  pla·cid·i·ty (plà·sĭd' ĭ·tĭ)
plack·et (plăk' ĕt)
pla·gia·rism (plā' jĭ·à·rĭz'm)
  pla·gia·rist pla·gia·rize
  pla·gia·ry
plague (plāg)
plaid (plăd)
plain (plān)
  plain-clothes man
  plains·man
plaint (plānt)
plain·tiff (plān' tĭf)
plain·tive (plān' tĭv)
  plain·tive·ly
plait·ing (plăt' ĭng)
plane (plān)
  plane an·gle

plane ge·om·e·try
plan·et (plăn' ĕt)
  plan·e·tar·y (plăn' ĕ·tĕr' ĭ)
plan·e·tar·i·um
                (plăn' ĕ·târ' ĭ·ŭm)
  pl. plan·e·tar·i·a
plank (plăngk)
plank·ton (plăngk' tŏn)
  plank·ton·ic (plăngk·tŏn' ĭk)
pla·no·graph (plā' nŏ·gráf)
plan·tain (plăn' tĭn)
plan·ta·tion (plăn·tā' shŭn)
plaque (plăk)
plas·ma (plăz' mà)
plas·ter (plăs' tẽr)
  plas·ter·board plas·ter cast
  plas·ter of Par·is
plas·tic (plăs' tĭk)
  plas·tic·i·ty (plăs·tĭs' ĭ·tĭ)
  plas·tic sur·ger·y
plate (plāt)
  plat·ing plate·ful
  plate glass plate·let
pla·teau (plà·tō')
plat·en (plăt' 'n)
plat·form (plăt' fôrm')
plat·i·num (plăt' ĭ·nŭm)
plat·i·tude (plăt' ĭ·tūd)
  plat·i·tu·di·nous
                (plăt' ĭ·tū' dĭ·nŭs)
Pla·ton·ic (plà·tŏn' ĭk)
pla·toon (plà·tōōn')
plat·ter (plăt' ẽr)
plat·y·pus (plăt' ĭ·pŭs)
  -pus·es
plau·dit (plô' dĭt)
plau·si·ble (plô' zĭ·b'l)
  plau·si·bil·i·ty
                (plô' zĭ·bĭl' ĭ·tĭ)
play (plā)
  play·bill play·boy
  play·ful, -ful·ly, -ful·ness
  play·go·er play·ground
  play-off play·wright
  play·writ·ing
pla·za (plä' zà)
plea (plē)
plead (plēd)
  plead·a·ble
pleas·ant (plĕz' ǎnt)
  pleas·ance pleas·ant·ry
  -ries
please (plēz)
  pleas·ing

pleas·ure   (plĕzh′ ẽr)
  pleas·ur·a·ble
pleat   (plēt)
ple·be·ian   (plē·bē′ yắn)
pleb·i·scite   (plĕb′ ĭ·sĭt)
pledge   (plĕj)
  pledg·ing
  pledg·ee   (plĕj′ ē′)
Pleis·to·cene   (plīs′ tŏ·sēn)
ple·na·ry   (plē′ nȧ·rĭ)
plen·i·po·ten·ti·ar·y
             (plĕn′ ĭ·pŏ·tĕn′ shĭ·ĕr′ ĭ)
plen·te·ous   (plĕn′ tê·ŭs)
plen·ti·ful   (plĕn′ tĭ·fŏŏl)
  -ful·ly   -ful·ness
pleth·o·ra   (plĕth′ ŏ·rȧ)
pleu·ri·sy   (plŏŏr′ ĭ·sĭ)
plex·us   (plĕk′ sŭs)
pli·a·ble   (plī′ ȧ·b′l)
  pli·a·bil·i·ty   (plī′ ȧ·bĭl′ ĭ·tĭ)
  pli·a·ble·ness
pli·ant   (plī′ ȧnt)
  pli·an·cy
pli·ers   (plī′ ẽrz)
plight   (plīt)
plinth   (plĭnth)
Pli·o·cene   (plī′ ŏ·sēn)
plod   (plŏd)
  plod·ded   plod·ding
plot·ter   (plŏt′ ẽr)
plov·er   (plŭv′ ẽr)
plow·share   (plou′ shâr′)
pluck·y   (plŭk′ ĭ)
  pluck·i·ness
plum·age   (plŏŏm′ ĭj)
plumb   (plŭm)
  plumb·er   plumb·ing
  plumb line
plume   (plŏŏm)
  plum·age
plum·met   (plŭm′ ĕt)
  plum·met·ed   plum·met·ing
plun·der   (plŭn′ dẽr)
plunge   (plŭnj)
  plung·ing
plu·per·fect   (plŏŏ′ pûr′ fĕkt)
plu·ral   (plŏŏr′ ȧl)
  plu·ral·is·tic   (plŏŏr′ ȧl·ĭs′ tĭk)
  plu·ral·i·ty   (plŏŏ·răl′ ĭ·tĭ)
plus   (plŭs)
plu·toc·ra·cy   (plŏŏ·tŏk′ rȧ·sĭ)
  plu·to·crat   (plŏŏ′ tŏ·krăt)
plu·to·ni·um   (plŏŏ·tŏ′ nĭ·ŭm)
ply   (plī)
  plied   ply·ing

ply·wood
Ply·mouth rock   (plĭm′ ŭth)
pneu·mat·ic   (nû·măt′ ĭk)
pneu·mo·ni·a   (nû·mŏ′ nĭ·ȧ)
poach·er   (pōch′ ẽr)
pock·et   (pŏk′ ĕt)
  -et·ed   -et·ing
  pock·et·book   pock·et·knife
  pock·et mon·ey
  pock·et ve·to
pock·mark   (pŏk′ märk′)
  pock-marked
po·di·um   (pō′ dĭ·ŭm)
  pl. po·di·a
po·et   (pō′ ĕt)
  po·em
  po·et·ic   (pō·ĕt′ ĭk)
  po·et·i·cal   (pō·ĕt′ ĭ·kȧl)
  -cal·ly   po·et·ic li·cense
  po·et lau·re·ate
  po·et·ry
po·grom   (pŏ·grŏm′)
poign·ant   (poin′ yȧnt)
  poign·an·cy
poin·set·ti·a   (poin·sĕt′ ĭ·ȧ)
point·less   (point′ lĕs)
poi·son   (poi′ z'n)
  poi·son i·vy   poi·son·ous
  poi·son su·mac
poke bon·net   (pōk)
po·ker face   (pŏ′ kẽr)
po·lar   (pŏ′ lẽr)
  po·lar bear
  po·lar·i·ty   (pŏ·lăr′ ĭ·tĭ)
Po·la·ris   (pŏ·lā′ rĭs)
po·lar·ize   (pŏ′ lẽr·īz)
  -iz·ing
  po·lar·i·za·tion
                     (pŏ′ lẽr·ĭ·zā′ shŭn)
Po·lar·oid   (pŏ′ lẽr·oid)
pole   (pōl)
  (long piece of wood; see *poll*)
po·lem·ic   (pŏ·lĕm′ ĭk)
  po·lem·i·cist   (pŏ·lĕm′ ĭ·sĭst)
pole·star   (pōl′ stär′)
pole vault·er   (pōl)
  pole-vault *v.*
po·lice·man   (pŏ·lēs′ mȧn)
pol·i·cy   (pŏl′ ĭ·sĭ)
  -cies   pol·i·cy·hold·er
po·li·o   (pŏ′ lĭ·ō)
  po·li·o·my·e·li·tis
                     (pŏ′ lĭ·ŏ·mī′ ĕ·lī′ tĭs)
pol·ish   (pŏl′ ĭsh)

po·lite (pŏ·līt′)
  po·lite·ly
pol·i·tics (pŏl′ ĭ·tĭks)
  po·lit·i·cal (pŏ·lĭt′ ĭ·kăl)
  pol·i·ti·cian (pŏl′ ĭ·tĭsh′ ăn)
  po·lit·i·co (pŏ·lĭt′ ĭ·kō)
  -cos
pol·i·ty (pŏl′ ĭ·tĭ)
pol·ka (pō(l)′ kă)
  pol·ka dot
poll (pōl)
  (survey; see *pole*)
  poll·ee   poll·ster
  poll tax
pol·len (pŏl′ ĕn)
pol·li·nate (pŏl′ ĭ·nāt)
  -nat·ing
  pol·li·na·tion (pŏl′ ĭ·nā′ shŭn)
pol·li·wog (pŏl′ ĭ·wŏg)
pol·lute (pŏ·lūt′)
  pol·lut·ing
  pol·lu·tion (pŏ·lū′ shŭn)
Pol·ly·an·na (pŏl′ ĭ·ăn′ ă)
po·lo (pō′ lō)
  po·lo coat   po·lo shirt
pol·o·naise (pŏl′ ô·nāz′)
pol·ter·geist (pŏl′ tĕr·gīst′)
pol·troon (pŏl·trōōn′)
pol·y·an·dry (pŏl′ ĭ·ăn′ drĭ)
pol·y·chro·mat·ic
    (pŏl′ ĭ·krô·măt′ ĭk)
pol·y·eth·yl·ene
    (pŏl′ ĭ·ĕth′ ĭ·lēn)
po·lyg·a·my (pŏ·lĭg′ ă·mĭ)
  po·lyg·a·mist po·lyg·a·mous
pol·y·glot (pŏl′ ĭ·glŏt)
pol·y·gon (pŏl′ ĭ·gŏn)
  po·lyg·o·nal (pŏ·lĭg′ ô·năl)
pol·y·g·y·ny (pŏ·lĭj′ ĭ·nĭ)
Pol·y·ne·sian (pŏl′ ĭ·nē′ shăn)
pol·yp (pŏl′ ĭp)
pol·y·phon·ic (pŏl′ ĭ·fŏn′ ĭk)
pol·y·tech·nic (pŏl′ ĭ·tĕk′ nĭk)
po·made (pŏ·mād′)
pome·gran·ate (pŏm′ grăn′ ĭt)
pom·pa·dour (pŏm′ pă·dōr)
pom·pa·no (pŏm′ pă·nō)
pom·pon (pŏm′ pŏn)
pomp·ous (pŏmp′ ŭs)
  pom·pos·i·ty (pŏm·pŏs′ ĭ·tĭ)
pon·cho (pŏn′ chō)
  -chos
pon·der (pŏn′ dĕr)
  pon·der·a·ble pon·der·ous
pon·gee (pŏn·jē′)

pon·tiff (pŏn′ tĭf)
  pon·tif·i·cal (pŏn·tĭf′ ĭ·kăl)
  pon·tif·i·cate (pŏn·tĭf′ ĭ·kāt)
  -cat·ing
pon·toon (pŏn·tōōn′)
po·ny (pō′ nĭ)
  -nies
poo·dle (pōō′ d'l)
pooh-pooh (pōō′ pōō′)
pope (pōp)
  pop·er·y pop·ish
pop·lar (pŏp′ lēr)
pop·lin (pŏp′ lĭn)
pop·py (pŏp′ ĭ)
  pop·pies
pop·u·lace (pŏp′ ŭ·lĭs)
pop·u·lar (pŏp′ ŭ·lēr)
  pop·u·lar·i·ty (pŏp′ ŭ·lăr′ ĭ·tĭ)
  pop·u·lar·i·za·tion
    (pŏp′ ŭ·lēr·ĭ·zā′ shŭn)
  pop·u·lar·ize -izing
pop·u·late (pŏp′ ŭ·lāt)
  -lat·ing
  pop·u·la·tion (pŏp′ ŭ·lā′ shŭn)
Pop·u·list (pŏp′ ŭ·lĭst)
pop·u·lous (pŏp′ ŭ·lŭs)
por·ce·lain (pōr′ sĕ·lĭn)
por·cu·pine (pôr′ kŭ·pīn)
pore (pōr)
  por·ing (*n.*: a tiny opening;
    v.: to study; see *pour*)
  po·ros·i·ty (pŏ·rŏs′ ĭ·tĭ)
  po·rous (pō′ rŭs)
por·no·graph·ic
    (pôr′ nô·grăf′ ĭk)
por·poise (pôr′ pŭs)
por·ridge (pôr′ ĭj)
port·a·ble (pōr′ tă·b'l)
  port·a·bil·i·ty (pōr′ tă·bĭl′ ĭ·tĭ)
por·tage (pōr′ tĭj)
por·tal (pōr′ tăl)
por·tend (pōr·tĕnd′)
  por·tent (pōr′ tĕnt)
  por·ten·tous (pōr·tĕn′ tŭs)
por·ter·house steak
    (pōr′ tĕr·hous′)
port·fo·li·o (pōrt·fō′ lĭ·ō)
  -os
por·ti·co (pōr′ tĭ·kō)
  -coes
por·tion (pōr′ shŭn)
port·land ce·ment
    (pōrt′ lănd)
port·ly (pōrt′ lĭ)
  port·li·ness

port·man·teau (pōrt·măn′ tō)
por·trait (pōr′ trāt)
  por·trai·ture (pōr′ trȧ·tŭr)
por·tray (pōr·trā′)
  por·tray·a·ble por·tray·al
Por·tu·guese (pōr′ tṳ·gēz)
pos·it (pŏz′ ĭt)
  -it·ed -it·ing
po·si·tion (pȯ·zĭsh′ ŭn)
pos·i·tive (pŏz′ ĭ·tĭv)
  pos·i·tive·ly -tive·ness
  pos·i·tiv·ism
pos·se (pŏs′ ė)
pos·sess (pȯ·zĕs′)
  pos·ses·sion pos·ses·sive
  pos·ses·sive·ness
  pos·ses·sor
pos·si·ble (pŏs′ ĭ·b'l)
  pos·si·bil·i·ty (pŏs′ ĭ·bĭl′ ĭ·tĭ)
pos·sum (pŏs′ ŭm)
post- (pōst-)
  post card post·date
  post ex·change
  post·grad·u·ate
  post·haste
  post·hu·mous (pŏs′ tṳ·mŭs)
  post·im·pres·sion·ism
  post·lude post·man
  post·mark post·mas·ter
  post me·rid·i·em
    (-mȯ·rĭd′ ĭ·ĕm)
  post·mis·tress post-mor·tem
  post·na·tal post of·fice
  post·or·bit·al post·paid
  post·pon·a·ble (pōst·pŏn′ ȧ·b'l)
  post·pone·ment
  post-Rev·o·lu·tion·ar·y
  post·script post·war
post·age (pōs′ tĭj)
post·al (pōs′ tȧl)
post·er (pōs′ tēr)
pos·te·ri·or (pŏs·tēr′ ĭ·ēr)
pos·ter·i·ty (pŏs·tĕr′ ĭ·tĭ)
pos·tu·late (pŏs′ tṳ·lāt)
  -lat·ing
pos·ture (pŏs′ tṳr)
  pos·tur·al
po·sy (pō′ zĭ)
  -sies
pot- (pŏt-)
  pot·bel·ly -bel·lied
  pot·boil·er pot·hole
  pot·latch pot liq·uor
  pot·luck pot·pie
  pot shot

po·ta·ble (pō′ tȧ·b'l)
pot·ash (pŏt′ ăsh′)
po·tas·si·um (pȯ·tăs′ ĭ·ŭm)
  po·tas·si·um bro·mide
  car·bon·ate chlo·rate
  chlo·ride hy·drox·ide
  per·man·ga·nate
po·ta·tion (pō·tā′ shŭn)
po·ta·to (pȯ·tā′ tō)
  -toes po·ta·to bee·tle
  po·ta·to chips
po·tent (pō′ tĕnt)
po·ten·cy (pō′ tĕn·sĭ)
po·ten·tate (pō′ tĕn·tāt)
po·ten·tial (pȯ·tĕn′ shȧl)
  -tial·ly
  po·ten·ti·al·i·ty
    (pȯ·tĕn′ shĭ·ăl′ ĭ·tĭ)
pot·pour·ri (pō′ pōō′ rē′)
pot·sherd (pŏt′ shûrd′)
pot·tage (pŏt′ ĭj)
pot·ter·y (pŏt′ ēr·ĭ)
pouch (pouch)
Pough·keep·sie, (pȯ·kĭp′ sĭ)
  N. Y.
poul·tice (pōl′ tĭs)
poul·try (pōl′ trĭ)
pounce (pouns)
  pounc·ing
pound (pound)
  pound·age pound·cake
  pound-fool·ish
pour (pōr)
  (to flow; see *pore*)
pousse-ca·fé (pōōs′ kȧ′ fā′)
pout (pout)
pout·er pi·geon (pout′ ēr)
pov·er·ty (pŏv′ ēr·tĭ)
  pov·er·ty-strick·en
pow·der (pou′ dēr)
  pow·der horn pow·der room
pow·er (pou′ ēr)
  pow·er am·pli·fi·er
  pow·er·boat pow·er-driv·en
  pow·er·ful, -ful·ly, -ful·ness
  pow·er·less
pow·wow (pou′ wou′)
pox (pŏks)
prac·ti·ca·ble (prăk′ tĭ·kȧ·b'l)
  prac·ti·ca·bil·i·ty
    (prăk′ tĭ·kȧ·bĭl′ ĭ·tĭ)
prac·ti·cal (prăk′ tĭ·kȧl)
  prac·ti·cal·i·ty
    (prăk′ tĭ·kăl′ ĭ·tĭ)
  prac·ti·cal·ly

prac·tice (prăk′ tĭs)
-tic·ing
prac·ti·tion·er (prăk·tĭsh′ ŭn·ēr)
Prae·to·ri·an guard
(prē·tō′ rĭ·ʠn)
prag·mat·ic (prăg·măt′ ĭk)
prag·mat·i·cal·ly
prag·ma·tism (prăg′ mʠ·tĭz′m)
prai·rie (prâr′ ĭ)
prai·rie schoon·er
praise (prāz)
prais·ing
praise·wor·thy, -wor·thi·ness
pra·line (prä′ lēn)
prance (prăns)
pranc·ing
prank·ish (prăngk′ ĭsh)
prate (prāt)
prat·ing
prat·tle (prăt′ ′l)
prat·tling
prawn (prôn)
pray (prā)
(entreat; see prey)
prayer (prâr)
pray·ing man·tis
(prā′ ĭng măn′ tĭs)
preach (prēch)
preach·er preach·ment
pre·am·ble (prē′ ăm′ b′l)
Pre-Cam·bri·an
(prē′ kăm′ brĭ·ʠn)
pre·can·cel (prē·kăn′ sĕl)
-celed -cel·ing
pre·car·i·ous (prē·kâr′ ĭ·ŭs)
pre·cau·tion (prē·kô′ shŭn)
-tion·ar·y
pre·cede (prē·sēd′)
-ced·ing
pre·ced·ence (prē·sēd′ ĕns)
pre·ced·ent (prē·sēd′ ĕnt)
(going before)
prec·e·dent (prĕs′ ē·dĕnt)
(setting an example)
pre·cept (prē′ sĕpt)
pre·cinct (prē′ sĭngkt)
pre·cious (prĕsh′ ŭs)
prec·i·pice (prĕs′ ĭ·pĭs)
pre·cip·i·tant (prē·sĭp′ ĭ·tʠnt)
pre·cip·i·tate (prē·sĭp′ ĭ·tāt)
-tat·ing
pre·cip·i·ta·tion
(prē·sĭp′ ĭ·tā′ shŭn)
pre·cip·i·tous (prē·sĭp′ ĭ·tŭs)

pré·cis (prā·sē′)
(summary; see precise)
pre·cise (prē·sīs′)
(sharply defined; se précis)
pre·cise·ly
pre·ci·sion (prē·sĭzh′ ŭn)
pre·clude (prē·klōōd′)
-clud·ing
pre·clu·sion (-klōō′ zhŭn)
pre·co·cious (prē·kō′ shŭs)
pre·con·cep·tion
(prē′ kŏn·sĕp′ shŭn)
pre·con·di·tion
(prē′ kŏn·dĭsh′ ŭn)
-tion·ing
pre·cur·sor (prē·kûr′ sēr)
pred·a·tor (prĕd′ ʠ·tēr)
pred·a·to·ry (prĕd′ ʠ·tō′ rĭ)
pred·e·ces·sor (prĕd′ ē·sĕs′ ēr)
pre·des·ti·na·tion
(prē·dĕs′ tĭ·nā′ shŭn)
pre·des·tine (prē·dĕs′ tĭn)
-tin·ing
pre·de·ter·mine
(prē′ dē·tûr′ mĭn)
-min·ing
pred·i·ca·ment
(prē·dĭk′ ʠ·mĕnt)
pred·i·cate (prĕd′ ĭ·kāt) v.
-cat·ing (-kĭt) adj., n.
pred·i·ca·tion
(prĕd′ ĭ·kā′ shŭn)
pre·dict (prē·dĭkt′)
pre·dict·a·ble
pre·dic·tion (prē·dĭk′ shŭn)
pre·dic·tive pre·dic·tor
pre·di·lec·tion (prē′ dĭ·lĕk′ shŭn)
pre·dom·i·nant
(prē·dŏm′ ĭ·nʠnt)
-nance
pre·dom·i·nate (-nāt)
-nat·ing
pre·dom·i·na·tion
(prē·dŏm′ ĭ·nā′ shŭn)
pre-em·i·nent (prē·ĕm′ ĭ·nĕnt)
pre-em·i·nence
pre-empt (prē·ĕmpt′)
pre-emp·tion pre-emp·tive
pre-emp·to·ry
preen (prēn)
pre-ex·ist·ence (prē′ ĕg·zĭs′ tĕns)
pre·fab·ri·cate (prē·făb′ rĭ·kāt)
-cat·ing
pre·fab·ri·ca·tion
(prē′ făb·rĭ·kā′ shŭn)

pref·ace (prĕf′ ĭs)
-ac·ing
pre·fect (prē′ fĕkt)
pre·fec·ture
pre·fer (prē·fûr′)
-ferred -fer·ring
pref·er·a·ble (prĕf′ ĕr·a·b′l)
pref·er·ence (prĕf′ ĕr·ĕns)
pref·er·en·tial
(prĕf′ ĕr·ĕn′ shăl)
pre·fer·ment (prē·fûr′ mĕnt)
pre·ferred stock (prē·fûrd′)
preg·nant (prĕg′ nănt)
preg·nan·cy
pre·hen·sile (prē·hĕn′ sĭl)
pre·his·tor·ic (prē′ hĭs·tŏr′ ĭk)
prej·u·dice (prĕj′ ŏŏ·dĭs)
prej·u·di·cial
(prĕj′ ŏŏ·dĭsh′ ăl)
prel·ate (prĕl′ ĭt)
prel·a·cy (-a·sĭ)
prel·a·ture (-a·tûr)
pre·lim·i·nar·y
(prē·lĭm′ ĭ·nĕr′ ĭ)
-nar·ies
pre·lim·i·nar·i·ly
(prē·lĭm′ ĭ·nĕr′ ĭ·lĭ)
prel·ude (prĕl′ ūd)
pre·ma·ture (prē′ ma·tūr′)
pre·ma·ture·ly
pre·med·i·cal (prē·mĕd′ ĭ·kăl)
pre·med·i·tate (prē·mĕd′ ĭ·tāt)
-tat·ing
pre·med·i·ta·tion
(prē′ mĕd·ĭ·tā′ shŭn)
pre·mi·er (prē′ mĭ·ēr)
(chief officer; see première)
pre·mière (prē·mêr′)
(first showing; see premier)
prem·ise (prĕm′ ĭs)
pre·mi·um (prē′ mĭ·ŭm)
pre·mo·lar (prē·mō′ lēr)
pre·mo·ni·tion (prē′ mō·nĭsh′ ŭn)
pre·mon·i·to·ry
(prē·mŏn′ ĭ·tō′ rĭ)
pre·na·tal (prē·nā′ tăl)
pre·oc·cu·pa·tion
(prē·ŏk′ û·pā′ shŭn)
pre·oc·cu·py (prē·ŏk′ û·pĭ)
-pied, -py·ing
pre·or·dain (prē′ ôr·dān′)
pre·or·di·na·tion
(prē′ ôr·dĭ·nā′ shŭn)
prep school (prĕp)

pre·pare (prē·pâr′)
-par·ing
prep·a·ra·tion
(prĕp′ a·rā′ shŭn)
pre·par·a·tive (prē·păr′ a·tĭv)
pre·par·a·to·ry
(prē·păr′ a·tō′ rĭ)
pre·par·ed·ness
(prē·păr′ ĕd·nĕs)
pre·pay (prē·pā′)
-paid -pay·ing
pre·pay·ment
pre·pon·der·ance
(prē·pŏn′ dēr·ăns)
-ant
prep·o·si·tion
(prĕp′ ŏ·zĭsh′ ŭn)
-tion·al
pre·pos·ses·sing
(prē′ pŏ·zĕs′ ĭng)
pre·pos·ter·ous
(prē·pŏs′ tēr·ŭs)
pre·req·ui·site (prē·rĕk′ wĭ·zĭt)
pre·rog·a·tive (prē·rŏg′ a·tĭv)
pres·age (prĕs′ ĭj) n.
pre·sage (prē·sāj′) v.
-sag·ing
Pres·by·te·ri·an
(prĕz′ bĭ·tēr′ ĭ·ăn)
pres·by·ter·y (prĕz′ bĭ·tēr′ ĭ)
-ter·ies
pre·school (prē·skōōl′)
pre·sci·ence (prē′ shĭ·ĕns)
pre·scind (prē·sĭnd′)
pre·scribe (prē·skrīb′)
(dictate; see proscribe)
-scrib·ing
pre·scrip·tion (prē·skrĭp′ shŭn)
pres·ence (prĕz′ ĕns)
pre·sent (prē·zĕnt′) v.
pre·sent·a·ble
pres·ent·a·tion
(prĕz′ ĕn·tā′ shŭn)
pres·ent (prĕz′ ĕnt) n., adj.
pre·sen·ti·ment
(prē·zĕn′ tĭ·mĕnt)
pre·sent·ment (prē·zĕnt′ mĕnt)
pre·serv·a·tive (prē·zûr′ va·tĭv)
pre·serve (prē·zûrv′)
-serv·ing pre·serv·a·ble
pres·er·va·tion
(prĕz′ ēr·vā′ shŭn)
pre·side (prē·zīd′)
-sid·ing

pres·i·dent (prĕz′ ĭ·dĕnt)
 pres·i·den·cy
 pres·i·den·tial
 (prĕz′ ĭ·dĕn′ shǎl)
pre·si·di·o (prē·sē′ dĭ·ō)
pre·sid·i·um (prē·sĭd′ ĭ·ŭm)
press a·gent (prĕs)
pres·sure (prĕsh′ ẽr)
 pres·sur·ize -iz·ing
pres·ti·dig·i·ta·tion
 (prĕs′ tĭ·dĭj′ ĭ·tā′ shŭn)
 -ta·tor
pres·tige (prĕs·tēzh′)
pres·to (prĕs′tō)
pre·sume (prē·zūm′)
 -sum·ing pre·sum·a·ble
 pre·sum·ed·ly
 pre·sump·tion
 (prē·zŭmp′ shŭn)
 pre·sump·tive (-zŭmp′ tĭv)
 pre·sump·tu·ous
 (-zŭmp′ tū·ŭs)
pre·sup·pose (prē′ sŭ·pōz′)
 -sup·pos·ing
 pre·sup·po·si·tion
 (prē′ sŭp·ō·zĭsh′ ŭn)
pre·tend (prē·tĕnd′)
 pre·tend·er
 pre·tense (prē·tĕns′)
 pre·ten·sion (prē·tĕn′ shŭn)
 pre·ten·tious (prē·tĕn′ shŭs)
pre·ter·nat·u·ral
 (prē′ tēr·nǎt′ û·rǎl)
pre·text (prē′ tĕkst)
pret·ti·fy (prĭt′ ĭ·fī)
 -fied -fy·ing
pret·ty (prĭt′ ĭ)
 pret·ti·er pret·ti·est
 pret·ti·ly pret·ti·ness
pre·vail (prē·vāl′)
 -vailed -vail·ing
 prev·a·lent (prĕv′ ȧ·lĕnt)
pre·var·i·cate (prē·vǎr′ ĭ·kāt)
 -cat·ing pre·var·i·ca·tor
pre·vent (prē·vĕnt′)
 pre·vent·a·tive
 (prē·vĕn′ tȧ·tĭv)
 pre·ven·tive (prē·vĕn′ tĭv)
pre·view (prē′ vū′)
pre·vi·ous (prē′ vĭ·ŭs)
prey (prā)
 (victim; see pray)
price·less (prīs′ lĕs)
prick·le (prĭk′ ′l)
 -ling prick·ly heat

pride·ful (prīd′ fŏŏl)
 -ful·ly -ful·ness
priest (prēst)
 priest·ess priest·hood
 priest·ly -li·ness
prig (prĭg)
 prig·gish
pri·ma·cy (prī′ mȧ·sĭ)
pri·ma don·na (prē′ mȧ dŏn′ ȧ)
pri·ma-fa·ci·e ev·i·dence
 (prī′ mȧ fā′ shĭ·ē)
pri·mal (prī′ mǎl)
pri·ma·ry (prī′ mĕr·ĭ)
 -ries
 pri·ma·ri·ly (prī′ mĕr·ĭ·lĭ)
pri·mate (prī′ mĭt)
prim·er (prĭm′ ẽr)
 (book)
pri·me·val (prī·mē′ vǎl)
prim·i·tive (prĭm′ ĭ·tĭv)
pri·mo·gen·i·ture
 (prī′ mŏ·jĕn′ ĭ·tûr)
pri·mor·di·al (prī·môr′ dĭ·ǎl)
prim·rose (prĭm′ rōz′)
prince·ly (prĭns′ lĭ)
prin·cess (prĭn′ sĕs)
prin·ci·pal (prĭn′ sĭ·pǎl)
 (adj., highest-ranking;
 n., school official; see principle)
 prin·ci·pal·i·ty
 (prĭn′ sĭ·pǎl′ ĭ·tĭ)
 prin·ci·pal·ly
prin·ci·ple (prĭn′ sĭ·p′l) n.
 (rule; see principal)
 prin·ci·pled
print·a·ble (prĭnt′ ȧ·b′l)
pri·or (prī′ ẽr)
 pri·or·ess
 pri·or·i·ty (prī·ŏr′ ĭ·tĭ)
 -ties
prism (prĭz′m)
 pris·mat·ic (prĭz·mǎt′ ĭk)
pris·on (prĭz′ ′n)
 pris·on·er
pris·sy (prĭs′ ĭ)
pris·tine (prĭs′ tēn)
prith·ee (prĭth′ ē)
pri·vate (prī′ vĭt)
 pri·va·cy (-vȧ·sĭ)
pri·va·tion (prī·vā′ shŭn)
priv·i·lege (prĭv′ ĭ·lĭj)
priv·y coun·cil (prĭv′ ĭ)
prize (prīz)
 priz·ing prize fight·er

prob·a·ble   (prŏb′ a·b'l)
  prob·a·bil·i·ty
         (prŏb′ a·bĭl′ ĭ·tĭ)
  prob·a·bly
pro·bate   (prō′ bāt)
  pro·ba·tion   (prō·bā′ shŭn)
  pro·ba·tion·er
       (prō·bā′ shŭn·ēr)
probe   (prōb)
  prob·ing
prob·i·ty   (prŏb′ ĭ·tĭ)
prob·lem   (prŏb′ lĕm)
  prob·lem·at·i·cal
    (prŏb′ lĕm·ăt′ ĭ·kăl)
pro·bos·cis   (prō·bŏs′ ĭs)
pro·caine   (prō·kān′)
pro·ce·dure (prō·sē′ dūr)
  pro·ce·dur·al
pro·ceed   (prō·sēd′) v.
pro·ceeds   (prō′ sēdz) n.
proc·ess   (prŏs′ ĕs)
pro·ces·sion (prō·sĕsh′ ŭn)
  -ces·sion·al
pro·claim   (prō·klām′)
  proc·la·ma·tion
    (prŏk′ la·mā′ shŭn)
pro·cliv·i·ty (prō·klĭv′ ĭ·tĭ)
  -ties
pro·con·sul (prō·kŏn′ sŭl)
pro·cras·ti·nate
    (prō·krăs′ tĭ·nāt)
  -nat·ing
  pro·cras·ti·na·tion
    (prō·krăs′ tĭ·nā′ shŭn)
  pro·cras·ti·na·tor
pro·cre·ate (prō′ krē·āt)
  -at·ing
  pro·cre·a·tion
    (prō′ krē·ā′ shŭn)
  pro·cre·a·tor
proc·tor   (prŏk′ tēr)
proc·u·ra·tor (prŏk′ û·rā′ tēr)
  proc·u·ra·cy (prŏk′ û·ra·sĭ)
pro·cure   (prō·kūr′)
  -cur·ing   pro·cure·ment
  pro·cur·er
prod·i·gal   (prŏd′ ĭ·găl)
  prod·i·gal·i·ty
    (prŏd′ ĭ·găl′ ĭ·tĭ)
pro·di·gious (prō·dĭj′ ŭs)
prod·i·gy   (prŏd′ ĭ·jĭ)
  -gies
pro·duce   (prō·dūs′) v.
  -duc·ing   pro·duc·er
  pro·duc·i·ble

prod·uce   (prŏd′ ūs) n.
prod·uct   (prŏd′ ŭkt)
  pro·duc·tion (prō·dŭk′ shŭn)
  pro·duc·tive (prō·dŭk′ tĭv)
  pro·duc·tiv·i·ty
    (prō′ dŭk·tĭv′ ĭ·tĭ)
pro·fane   (prō·fān′)
  -fan·ing
  prof·a·na·tion
    (prŏf′ a·nā′ shŭn)
  pro·fan·i·ty (prō·făn′ ĭ·tĭ)
pro·fess   (prō·fĕs′)
  pro·fess·ed·ly
pro·fes·sion (prō·fĕsh′ ŭn)
  pro·fes·sion·al
pro·fes·sor (prō·fĕs′ ēr)
  pro·fes·sor·ate (prō·fĕs′ ēr·ĭt)
  pro·fes·so·ri·al
    (prō′ fĕ·sō′ rĭ·ăl)
prof·fer   (prŏf′ ēr)
  prof·fered   prof·fer·ing
pro·fi·cient (prō·fĭsh′ ĕnt)
  pro·fi·cien·cy
pro·file   (prō′ fīl)
prof·it   (prŏf′ ĭt)
  (gain; see *prophet*)
  -it·ed   -it·ing
  prof·it·a·ble
  prof·it-and-loss state·ment
  prof·it·eer (prŏf′ ĭ·tēr′)
  prof·it·less
prof·li·gate (prŏf′ lĭ·găt)
  prof·li·ga·cy (-ga·sĭ)
pro·found   (prō·found′)
  pro·fun·di·ty (prō·fŭn′ dĭ·tĭ)
  -ties
pro·fuse   (prō·fūs′)
  pro·fuse·ly
  pro·fu·sion (-fū′ zhŭn)
pro·gen·i·tor (prō·jĕn′ ĭ·tēr)
prog·e·ny   (prŏj′ ĕ·nĭ)
prog·no·sis (prŏg·nō′ sĭs)
  pl. prog·no·ses (-sēz)
  prog·nos·tic (prŏg·nŏs′ tĭk)
  prog·nos·ti·cate
    (prŏg·nŏs′ tĭ·kāt)
  -cat·ing
pro·gram   (prō′ grăm)
  pro·gram·mat·ic
    (prō′ grá·măt′ ĭk)
prog·ress   (prŏg′ rĕs) n.
pro·gress   (prō·grĕs′) v.
  pro·gres·sion (prō·grĕsh′ ŭn)
  pro·gres·sive -sive·ly

pro·hib·it (prȯ·hĭb′ ĭt)
  -it·ed -it·ing
  pro·hi·bi·tion (prō′ ĭ·bĭsh′ ŭn)
  pro·hib·i·tive (prȯ·hĭb′ ĭ·tĭv)
  pro·hib·i·to·ry
            (prȯ·hĭb′ ĭ·tō′ rĭ)
pro·ject (prȯ·jĕkt′) v.
  pro·jec·tile (prȯ·jĕk′ tĭl)
  pro·jec·tion (prȯ·jĕk′ shŭn)
  pro·jec·tive (prȯ·jĕk′ tĭv)
  pro·jec·tor (prȯ·jĕk′ tēr)
proj·ect (prŏj′ ĕkt) n.
pro·lac·tin (prȯ·lăk′ tĭn)
pro·le·tar·i·an (prō′ lĕ·târ′ ĭ·∂n)
  pro·le·tar·i·at
pro·lif·er·ate (prȯ·lĭf′ ēr·āt)
  -at·ing
  pro·lif·er·a·tion
            (prȯ·lĭf′ ēr·ā′ shŭn)
pro·lif·ic (prȯ·lĭf′ ĭk)
  pro·lif·i·cal·ly
pro·lix (prȯ·lĭks′)
  pro·lix·i·ty (prȯ·lĭk′ sĭ·tĭ)
pro·logue (prō′ lôg)
pro·long (prȯ·lông′)
prom·e·nade (prŏm′ ĕ·näd′)
prom·i·nence (prŏm′ ĭ·nĕns)
  -nent
pro·mis·cu·ous (prȯ·mĭs′ kū·ŭs)
  prom·is·cu·i·ty
       (prŏm′ ĭs·kū′ ĭ·tĭ)
prom·ise (prŏm′ ĭs)
  -is·ing
  prom·is·so·ry (prŏm′ ĭ·sō′ rĭ)
prom·on·to·ry (prŏm′ ŭn·tō′ rĭ)
  -ries
pro·mote (prȯ·mōt′)
  -mot·ing pro·mot·er
  pro·mo·tion
prompt (prŏmpt)
  prompt·ness
pro·mul·gate (prȯ·mŭl′ gāt)
  -gat·ing
  pro·mul·ga·tion
       (prō′ mŭl·gā′ shŭn)
  pro·mul·ga·tor
prone (prōn)
  prone·ness
prong·horn (prông′ hôrn′)
pro·noun (prō′ noun)
pro·nounce (prȯ·nouns′)
  -nounc·ing
  pro·nounce·a·ble
  pro·nounc·ed·ly
  pro·nounce·ment

pro·nun·ci·a·tion
      (prȯ·nŭn′ sĭ·ā′ shŭn)
proof (prōōf)
  proof·read·er
prop·a·gan·da (prŏp′ ȧ·găn′ dȧ)
  prop·a·gan·dist
  prop·a·gan·dize
  -diz·ing
prop·a·gate (prŏp′ ȧ·gāt)
  -gat·ing
  prop·a·ga·tion
      (prŏp′ ȧ·gā′ shŭn)
  prop·a·ga·tor
pro·pane (prō′ pān)
pro·pel (prȯ·pĕl′)
  -pelled -pel·ling
  pro·pel·lant (prȯ·pĕl′ ∂nt)
  pro·pel·ler
pro·pen·si·ty (prȯ·pĕn′ sĭ·tĭ)
  -ties
prop·er (prŏp′ ēr)
prop·er·ty (prŏp′ ēr·tĭ)
  -ties prop·er·tied
proph·e·cy (prŏf′ ĕ·sĭ) n.
  -cies
proph·e·sy (prŏf′ ĕ·sī) v.
  -sied -sy·ing
  proph·e·si·er
proph·et (prŏf′ ĕt)
  (seer; see profit)
  proph·et·ess
  pro·phet·ic (prȯ·fĕt′ ĭk)
pro·phy·lac·tic
      (prō′ fĭ·lăk′ tĭk)
  pro·phy·lax·is (-lăk′ sĭs)
pro·pin·qui·ty (prȯ·pĭng′ kwĭ·tĭ)
pro·pi·ti·ate (prȯ·pĭsh′ ĭ·āt)
  -at·ing
  pro·pi·ti·a·tion
      (prȯ·pĭsh′ ĭ·ā′ shŭn)
pro·pi·tious (prȯ·pĭsh′ ŭs)
  pro·pi·tious·ness
pro·po·nent (prȯ·pō′ nĕnt)
pro·por·tion (prȯ·pōr′ shŭn)
  pro·por·tion·al
  pro·por·tion·ate
      (-ĭt)
pro·pose (prȯ·pōz′)
  -pos·ing pro·pos·al
prop·o·si·tion (prŏp′ ȯ·zĭsh′ ŭn)
  -tion·al
pro·pound (prȯ·pound′)
pro·pri·e·tor (prȯ·prī′ ĕ·tēr)
  pro·pri·e·tar·y
      (prȯ·prī′ ĕ·tēr′ ĭ)

pro·pri·e·ty   (prō·prī′ ĕ·tĭ)
 -ties
pro·pul·sion   (prō·pŭl′ shŭn)
 pro·pul·sive
pro·rate   (prō′ rāt′)
 -rat·ing
pro·ra·tion   (prō·rā′ shŭn)
pro·sa·ic   (prō·zā′ ĭk)
 pro·sa·i·cal·ly
pro·sce·ni·um   (prō·sē′ nĭ·ŭm)
pro·scribe   (prō·skrīb′)
 (condemn; see *prescribe*)
 pro·scrip·tion   (-skrĭp′ shŭn)
pros·e·cute   (prŏs′ ē·kūt)
 -cut·ing
 pros·e·cu·tion
         (prŏs′ ē·kū′ shŭn)
 pros·e·cu·tor
pros·e·lyte   (prŏs′ ē·līt)
pro·slav·er·y   (prō·slāv′ ēr·ĭ)
pros·o·dy   (prŏs′ ō·dĭ)
pros·pect   (prŏs′ pĕkt)
pro·spec·tive   (prō·spĕk′ tĭv)
 adj. (confidently expected; see
 perspective)
pro·spec·tus   (prō·spĕk′ tŭs)
pros·per   (prŏs′ pēr)
 pros·per·i·ty   (prŏs·pĕr′ ĭ·tĭ)
 pros·per·ous
pros·tate gland   (prŏs′ tāt)
pros·ti·tute   (prŏs′ tĭ·tūt)
 pros·ti·tu·tion
         (prŏs′ tĭ·tū′ shŭn)
pros·trate   (prŏs′ trāt)
 pros·tra·tion   (prŏs·trā′ shŭn)
pros·y   (prōz′ ĭ)
pro·tag·o·nist   (prō·tăg′ ō·nĭst)
pro·tect   (prō·tĕkt′)
 pro·tec·tion   (prō·tĕk′ shŭn)
 pro·tec·tion·ism
 pro·tec·tive tar·iff
 pro·tec·tor   pro·tec·tress
 pro·tec·tor·ate
         (prō·tĕk′ tēr·ĭt)
pro·té·gé   (prō′ tĕ·zhā)
pro·te·in   (prō′ tē·ĭn)
pro tem·po·re   (prō tĕm′ pō·rē)
pro·test   (prō·tĕst′) *v.*
         (prō′ tĕst) *n.*
 prot·es·ta·tion
         (prŏt′ ĕs·tā′ shŭn)
Prot·es·tant   (prŏt′ ĕs·tănt)
pro·to·col   (prō′ tō·kŏl)
pro·ton   (prō′ tŏn)
pro·to·plasm   (prō′ tō·plăz′m)

pro·to·type   (prō′ tō·tīp)
pro·to·zo·an   (prō′ tō·zō′ ăn)
 pre·to·zo·ic   (-ĭk)
pro·trude   (prō·trōōd′)
 -trud·ing
 pro·tru·sion   (prō·trōō′ zhŭn)
pro·tu·ber·ance
         (prō·tū′ bĕr·ăns)
 -ant
proud   (proud)
prove   (prōōv)
 prov·ing   prov·a·ble
 prov·en
prov·en·der   (prŏv′ ĕn·dēr)
prov·erb   (prŏv′ ûrb)
 pro·ver·bi·al   (prō·vûr′ bĭ·ăl)
pro·vide   (prō·vīd′)
 -vid·ing   pro·vid·er
prov·i·dence   (prŏv′ ĭ·dĕns)
 -dent
 prov·i·den·tial
         (prŏv′ ĭ·dĕn′ shăl)
prov·ince   (prŏv′ ĭns)
 pro·vin·cial   (prō·vĭn′ shăl)
 -cial·ism
pro·vi·sion   (prō·vĭzh′ ŭn)
 pro·vi·sion·al, -al·ly
 pro·vi·sion·er
pro·vi·so   (prō·vī′ zō)
 -sos
pro·voke   (prō·vōk′)
 -vok·ing
 prov·o·ca·tion
         (prŏv′ ō·kā′ shŭn)
 pro·voc·a·tive   (prō·vŏk′ ă·tĭv)
 -tive·ly   pro·vok·er
pro·vost mar·shal
         (prō′ vō)
prow·ess   (prou′ ĕs)
prowl·er   (proul′ ēr)
prox·im·i·ty   (prŏks·ĭm′ ĭ·tĭ)
prox·y   (prŏk′ sĭ)
 prox·ies
prude   (prōōd)
 prud·er·y   prud·ish
pru·dent   (prōō′ dĕnt)
 -dence
prun·ing hook   (prōōn′ ĭng)
pru·ri·ent   (prōōr′ ĭ·ĕnt)
 -ence
Prus·sian blue   (prŭsh′ ăn)
prus·sic ac·id   (prŭs′ ĭk)
pry   (prī)
 pried   pry·ing
 pry·er

psalm   (säm)
  psalm·ist
  psal·mo·dy   (săl′ mō·dĭ)
Psal·ter   (sôl′ tẽr)
pseu·do·nym   (sū′ dō·nĭm)
pso·ri·a·sis   (sō·rī′ ả·sĭs)
psy·chi·a·try   (sī·kī′ ả·trĭ)
  psy·chi·at·ric   (sī′ kĭ·ăt′ rĭk)
  psy·chi·a·trist   (sī·kī′ ả·trĭst)
psy·chic   (sī′ kĭk)
psy·cho-   (sī′ kō-)
  psy·cho·a·nal·y·sis
  psy·cho·an·a·lyt·i·cal
  psy·cho·an·a·lyze, -lyz·ing
  psy·cho·dra·ma
  psy·cho·mo·tor
  psy·cho·neu·ro·sis
  psy·cho·neu·rot·ic
  psy·cho·path·ic
  psy·cho·so·mat·ic
  psy·cho·sur·ger·y
  psy·cho·ther·a·peu·tics
  psy·cho·ther·a·py
psy·chol·o·gy   (sī·kŏl′ ō·jĭ)
  psy·cho·log·i·cal
       (sī′ kō·lŏj′ ĭ·kắl)
psy·chom·e·try   (sī·kŏm′ ě·trĭ)
psy·cho·sis   (sī·kō′ sĭs)
  pl. -ses
ptar·mi·gan   (tär′ mĭ·gắn)
pter·o·dac·tyl   (tẽr′ ō·dăk′ tĭl)
Ptol·e·my   (tŏl′ ě·mĭ)
  Ptol·e·ma·ic   (tŏl′ ě·mā′ ĭk)
pto·maine   (tō′ mān)
pu·ber·ty   (pū′ bẽr·tĭ)
pu·bic   (pū′ bĭk)
pub·lic   (pŭb′ lĭk)
  pub·lic-ad·dress sys·tem
  pub·lic·ly
pub·li·ca·tion   (pŭb′ lĭ·kā′ shŭn)
pub·li·cize   (pŭb′ lĭ·sīz)
  -ciz·ing
  pub·li·cist   (pŭb′ lĭ·sĭst)
  pub·lic·i·ty   (pŭb·lĭs′ ĭ·tĭ)
pub·lish   (pŭb′ lĭsh)
  pub·lish·a·ble   pub·lish·er
puck·er   (pŭk′ ẽr)
puck·ish   (pŭk′ ĭsh)
pud·ding   (pŏŏd′ ĭng)
pud·dle   (pŭd′ ′l)
pudg·y   (pŭj′ ĭ)
pueb·lo   (pwĕb′ lō)
  -los
pu·er·ile   (pū′ ẽr·ĭl)
  pu·er·il·i·ty   (pū′ ẽr·ĭl′ ĭ·tĭ)

Puer·to Ri·co   (pwĕr′ tŭ rē′ kō)
  Puer·to Ri·can
puf·fin   (pŭf′ ĭn)
puff·y   (pŭf′ ĭ)
  puff·i·ness
Pu·get (sound)   (pū′ jĕt)
pu·gil·ist   (pū′ jĭ·lĭst)
pug·na·cious   (pŭg·nā′ shŭs)
  pug·nac·i·ty   (pŭg·năs′ ĭ·tĭ)
pu·is·sance   (pū′ ĭ·sảns)
  pu·is·sant
pul·chri·tude   (pŭl′ krĭ·tūd)
  pul·chri·tu·di·nous
       (pŭl′ krĭ·tū′ dĭ·nŭs)
pul·let   (pŏŏl′ ĕt)
pul·ley   (pŏŏl′ ĭ)
Pull·man car   (pŏŏl′ mắn)
pull-o·ver   (pŏŏl′ ō′ vẽr)
pul·mo·nar·y   (pŭl′ mō·nĕr′ ĭ)
Pul·mo·tor   (pŭl′ mō′ tēr)
pul·pit   (pŏŏl′ pĭt)
pulp·wood   (pŭlp′ wŏŏd′)
pul·que   (pŏŏl′ kả)
pul·sate   (pŭl′ sāt)
  -sat·ing
  pul·sa·tion   (pŭl·sā′ shŭn)
pul·ver·ize   (pŭl′ vẽr·īz)
  -iz·ing
pu·ma   (pū′ mả)
pum·ice   (pŭm′ ĭs)
pum·per·nick·el
       (pŭm′ pẽr·nĭk′ ′l)
pump·kin   (pŭmp′ kĭn)
punch·ing bag   (pŭnch′ ĭng)
punc·til·i·ous   (pŭngk·tĭl′ ĭ·ŭs)
punc·tu·al   (pŭngk′ tụ·ắl)
  -al·ly
  punc·tu·al·i·ty
       (pŭngk′ tụ·ăl′ ĭ·tĭ)
punc·tu·ate   (pŭngk′ tụ·āt)
  -at·ing
  punc·tu·a·tion
       (pŭngk′ tụ·ā′ shŭn)
punc·ture   (pŭngk′ tụr)
  -tur·ing   punc·tur·a·ble
pun·dit   (pŭn′ dĭt)
pun·gent   (pŭn′ jĕnt)
  pun·gen·cy
pun·ish   (pŭn′ ĭsh)
  pun·ish·a·ble   pun·ish·ment
pu·ni·tive   (pū′ nĭ·tĭv)
pun·ster   (pŭn′ stēr)
pu·pa   (pū′ pả)
  pl. pu·pae   (-pē)
pu·pil   (pū′ p′l)

pup·pet (pŭp′ ĕt)
  pup·pet·ry
pup·py (pŭp′ ĭ)
  pup·pies
pur·blind (pûr′ blīnd′)
pur·chase (pûr′ chĭs)
  -chas·ing   pur·chas·a·ble
Pur·due (univ.) (pēr·dū′)
pure (pūr)
  pure·bred   pure·ly
  pu·ri·fi·ca·tion
     (pū′ rĭ·fī·kā′ shŭn)
  pu·ri·fi·er   pu·ri·fy
  -fied, -fy·ing   pu·ri·ty
pu·rée (pú·rā′)
pur·ga·tive (pûr′ gȧ·tĭv)
pur·ga·to·ry (pûr′ gȧ·tō′ rĭ)
  pur·ga·to·ri·al
     (pûr′ gȧ·tō′ rĭ·ăl)
purge (pûrj)
  purg·ing
Pu·ri·tan (pū′ rĭ·tăn)
  pu·ri·tan·i·cal
     (pū′ rĭ·tăn′ ĭ·kăl)
purl (pûrl)
  (knitting stitch; see *pearl*)
pur·lieu (pûr′ lū)
pur·loin (pûr·loin′)
pur·ple (pûr′ p′l)
pur·port (pûr·pōrt′) *v.*
     (pûr′ pōrt) *n.*
pur·pose (pûr′ pŭs)
  pur·pose·ful, -ful·ly, -ful·ness
  pur·pose·less   pur·pose·ly
  pur·pos·ive
purr (pûr)
purse (pûrs)
purs·lane (pûrs′ lān)
pur·sue (pēr·sū′)
  -su·ing
  pur·su·ance (pēr·sū′ ăns)
  pur·su·ant   pur·su·er
  pur·suit (pēr·sūt′)
pur·vey (pûr·vā′)
  pur·vey·ance   pur·vey·or
pur·view (pûr′ vū)
pus (pŭs)
  pus·sy
push (po͝osh)
  push-but·ton *adj.*
  push·cart   push·o·ver
pu·sil·lan·i·mous
     (pū′ sĭ·lăn′ ĭ·mŭs)
  pu·sil·la·nim·i·ty
     (pū′ sĭ·lȧ·nĭm′ ĭ·tĭ)

puss·y·foot (po͝os′ ĭ·fo͝ot′)
pus·tule (pŭs′ tu̱l)
pu·tre·fy (pū′ trĕ·fī)
  -fied   -fy·ing
  pu·tre·fac·tion
     (pū′ trĕ·făk′ shŭn)
pu·tres·cent (pû·trĕs′ ĕnt)
pu·trid (pū′ trĭd)
putt (pŭt)
put·tee (pŭt′ ĭ)
  (legging; see *putty*)
put·ty (pŭt′ ĭ)
  (cement; see *puttee*)
puz·zle (pŭz′ ′l)
  puz·zling   puz·zle·ment
Pyg·my (pĭg′ mĭ)
py·lon (pī′ lŏn)
py·lo·rus (pī·lō′ rŭs)
  py·lor·ic (pī·lŏr′ ĭk)
py·or·rhe·a (pī′ ŏ·rē′ ȧ)
pyr·a·mid (pĭr′ ȧ·mĭd)
pyre (pīr)
Py·rex (pī′ rĕks)
py·ri·tes (pī·rī′ tēz)
py·ro·ma·ni·ac
     (pī′ rŏ·mā′ nĭ·ăk)
py·ro·tech·nics
     (pī′ rŏ·tĕk′ nĭks)
Pyr·rhic vic·to·ry
     (pĭr′ ĭk)
py·thon (pī′ thŏn)

Q

quack (kwăk)
  quack·er·y   quack grass
quad·ran·gle (kwŏd′ răng′ g′l)
quad·rant (kwŏd′ rănt)
quad·ri·lat·er·al
     (kwŏd′ rĭ·lăt′ ĕr·ăl)
quad·roon (kwŏd·ro͞on′)
quad·ru·ped (kwŏd′ ro͝o·pĕd)
quad·ru·ple (kwŏd′ ro͝o·p′l)
quad·ru·plet (kwŏd′ ro͝o·plĕt)
quad·ru·pli·cate
     (kwŏd·ro͞o′ plĭ·kāt)
quaff (kwáf)
quag·mire (kwăg′ mīr)
quail (kwāl)
quaint (kwānt)
Quak·er (kwāk′ ĕr)
qual·i·fy (kwŏl′ ĭ·fī)
  -fied   -fy·ing

qual·i·fi·ca·tion
    (kwŏl′ ĭ·fĭ·kā′ shŭn)
qual·i·fi·er
qual·i·ty   (kwŏl′ ĭ·tĭ)
  -ties
qual·i·ta·tive   (kwŏl′ ĭ·tā′ tĭv)
qualm   (kwäm)
quan·da·ry   (kwŏn′ dȧ·rĭ)
  -ries
quan·ti·fy   (kwŏn′ tĭ·fī)
  -fied   -fy·ing
quan·ti·ty   (kwŏn′ tĭ·tĭ)
  -ties
  quan·ti·ta·tive
    (kwŏn′ tĭ·tā′ tĭv)
quan·tum theory
    (kwŏn′ tŭm)
quar·an·tine   (kwŏr′ ȧn·tēn)
quar·rel   (kwŏr′ ĕl)
  quar·reled   quar·rel·ing
  quar·rel·some
quar·ry   (kwŏr′ ĭ)
  quar·ried   quar·ry·ing
quar·ter   (kwôr′ tẽr)
  quar·ter·back   quar·ter-deck
  quar·ter·mas·ter
quar·ter·ly   (kwôr′ tẽr·lĭ)
  -lies
quar·tet   (kwôr·tĕt′)
quar·to   (kwôr′ tō)
  -tos
quartz   (kwôrts)
quartz·ite   (kwôrts′ īt)
qua·si-ju·di·cial
    (kwā′ sī·jōō·dĭsh′ ȧl)
quat·rain   (kwŏt′ rān)
quat·re·foil   (kăt′ ẽr·foil′)
qua·ver   (kwā′ vẽr)
quay   (kwā)
quea·sy   (kwē′ zĭ)
  quea·si·ness
queen   (kwēn)
  queen·ly   -li·ness
queer   (kwẹr)
quell   (kwĕl)
quench   (kwĕnch)
quer·u·lous   (kwẽr′ ů·lŭs)
que·ry   (kwẹr′ ĭ)
  -ries
quest   (kwĕst)
ques·tion   (kwĕs′ chŭn)
  ques·tion·a·ble
  ques·tion·er   ques·tion·ing·ly
  ques·tion·naire   (kwĕs′ chŭn·âr′)
quet·zal   (kĕt·säl′)

queue   (kū)
  (waiting line; see *cue*)
  queu·ing
quib·ble   (kwĭb′ ′l)
  quib·bling
quick   (kwĭk)
  quick·en   quick-fir·ing
  quick-freeze   quick·sand
  quick·sil·ver   quick-wit·ted
quid·di·ty   (kwĭd′ ĭ·tĭ)
quid pro quo   (kwĭd prō kwō)
quies·cent   (kwī·ĕs′ ĕnt)
  quies·cence
qui·et   (kwī′ ĕt)
  qui·et·er   qui·et·ly
  qui·e·tude   (kwī′ ĕ·tūd)
qui·e·tus   (kwī·ē′ tŭs)
quill   (kwĭl)
quilt   (kwĭlt)
quince   (kwĭns)
qui·nine   (kwī′ nīn)
quin·sy   (kwĭn′ zĭ)
quint·es·sence   (kwĭnt·ĕs′ ĕns)
quin·tet   (kwĭn·tĕt′)
quin·til·lion   (kwĭn·tĭl′ yŭn)
quin·tu·ple   (kwĭn′ tů·p′l)
quin·tu·plet   (kwĭn′ tů·plĕt)
quin·tu·pli·cate
    (kwĭn·tū′ plĭ·kāt)
quip   (kwĭp)
  quipped   quip·ping
  quip·ster
quire   (kwīr)
quirk   (kwûrk)
quirt   (kwûrt)
quis·ling   (kwĭz′ lĭng)
quit   (kwĭt)
  quit·ting   quit·tance
  quit·ter
quite   (kwīt)
quiv·er   (kwĭv′ ẽr)
Quix·ote, Don   (kē·hō′ tȧ, dŏn)
  quix·ot·ic   (kwĭks·ŏt′ ĭk)
quiz   (kwĭz)
  quizzed   quiz·zing
  quiz·zes
quiz·zi·cal   (kwĭz′ ĭ·kȧl)
  quiz·zi·cal·ly
quoits   (kwoits)
quon·dam   (kwŏn′ dăm)
quo·rum   (kwō′ rŭm)
quo·ta   (kwō′ tȧ)
quote   (kwōt)
  quot·ing   quot·a·ble
  quo·ta·tion   (kwō·tā′ shŭn)

quoth   (kwōth)
quo·tid·i·an   (kwō·tĭd′ ĭ·ắn)
quo·tient   (kwō′ shĕnt)

R

rab·bet joint   (răb′ ĕt)
rab·bi   (răb′ ī)
   rab·bin·i·cal   (rắ·bĭn′ ĭ·kắl)
rab·bit   (răb′ ĭt)
   rab·bit fe·ver rab·bit punch
rab·ble   (răb′ 'l)
Rab·e·lai·si·an
             (răb′ ĕ·lā′ zĭ·ắn)
rab·id   (răb′ ĭd)
ra·bies   (rā′ bēz)
rac·coon   (ră·kōōn′)
ra·cial   (rā′ shắl)
rac·ism   (rās′ ĭz′m)
   rac·ist
rack·et   (răk′ ĕt)
   rack·et·eer   (răk′ ĕ·têr′)
rac·on·teur   (răk′ ŏn·tûr′)
rac·y   (rās′ ĭ)
   rac·i·ness
ra·dar   (rā′ dăr)
   ra·dar·scope
Rad·cliffe (coll.)   (răd′ klĭf)
ra·di·ant   (rā′ dĭ·ắnt)
   ra·di·ance
ra·di·ate   (rā′ dĭ·āt)
   -at·ing
   ra·di·a·tion   (rā′ dĭ·ā′ shŭn)
   ra·di·a·tor   (rā′ dĭ·ā′ têr)
rad·i·cal   (răd′ ĭ·kắl)
   rad·i·cal·ism rad·i·cal·ly
ra·di·o·ac·tive   (rā′ dĭ·ō·ăk′ tĭv)
   ra·di·o·ac·tiv·i·ty
            (-ăk·tĭv′ ĭ·tĭ)
ra·di·ol·o·gy   (rā′ dĭ·ŏl′ ŏ·jĭ)
   ra·di·o·log·i·cal
       (rā′ dĭ·ō·lŏj′ ĭ·kắl)
ra·di·o·sen·si·tive
       (rā′ dĭ·ō·sĕn′ sĭ·tĭv)
ra·di·o·sonde   (rā′ dĭ·ō·sŏnd′)
ra·di·o·tel·e·gram
       (rā′ lĭ·ō·tĕl′ ĕ·grăm)
ra·di·o·ther·a·py
       (rā′ dĭ·ō·thĕr′ ắ·pĭ)
rad·ish   (răd′ ĭsh)
ra·di·um   (rā′ dĭ·ŭm)
ra·di·us   (rā′ dĭ·ŭs)
   pl. ra·di·i   (-ī)
raf·fi·a   (răf′ ĭ·ắ)

raff·ish   (răf′ ĭsh)
raf·fle   (răf′ 'l)
   raf·fling
raft·er   (răf′ têr)
rag·a·muf·fin   (răg′ ắ·mŭf′ ĭn)
rag·ged   (răg′ ĕd)
rag·lan   (răg′ lắn)
ra·gout   (ră·gōō′)
rag·weed   (răg′ wēd′)
raid·er   (rād′ ēr)
rail·ing   (rāl′ ĭng)
rail·ler·y   (rāl′ ĕr·ĭ)
rail·road   (rāl′ rōd′)
rail·way   (rāl′ wā′)
rai·ment   (rā′ mĕnt)
rain   (rān)
   (falling drops of water; see *reign,*
   rein)
   rain·bow   rain·coat
   rain·drop   rain·fall
   rain gauge   rain·proof
   rain·storm   rain wa·ter
   rain·y
Rai·nier, Mt.   (rắ·nēr′)
raise   (rāz)
   (awaken; see *raze*)
   rais·ing
rai·sin   (rā′ z'n)
ra·ja   (rä′ jắ)
rak·ish   (rāk′ ĭsh)
ral·ly   (răl′ ĭ)
   ral·lied   ral·ly·ing
ram·bler   (răm′ blêr)
ram·e·kin   (răm′ ĕ·kĭn)
ram·i·fi·ca·tion
       (răm′ ĭ·fĭ·kā′ shŭn)
ram·jet en·gine   (răm′ jĕt′)
ram·page   (răm·pāj′)
   -pag·ing
ramp·ant   (răm′ pắnt)
ram·part   (răm′ pärt)
ram·rod   (răm′ rŏd′)
ram·shack·le   (răm′ shăk′ 'l)
ranch house   (rănch)
ran·cid   (răn′ sĭd)
ran·cor
   ran·cor·ous   (răng′ kĕr·ŭs)
ran·dom   (răn′ dŭm)
range   (rānj)
   rang·ing   rang·er
   rang·y, rang·i·er, -i·est, -i·ness
ran·kle   (răng′ k'l)
   -kling
ran·sack   (răn′ săk)
ran·som   (răn′ sŭm)

rant (rănt)
ra·pa·cious (rà·pā′ shŭs)
  ra·pac·i·ty (rà·păs′ ĭ·tĭ)
rap·id (răp′ ĭd)
  rap·id-fire
  ra·pid·i·ty (rà·pĭd′ ĭ·tĭ)
ra·pi·er (rā′ pĭ·ēr)
rap·ine (răp′ ĭn)
Rap·pa·han·nock (riv.)
       (răp′ à·hăn′ ŭk)
rap·port (rà′ pôr′)
rapt (răpt)
rap·ture (răp′ tụr)
  rap·tur·ous (răp′ tụr·ŭs)
rar·e·fy (râr′ ĕ·fĭ)
  -fied   -fy·ing
rare·ly (râr′ lĭ)
rar·i·ty (răr′ ĭ·tĭ)
  -ties
ras·cal (răs′ kăl)
  ras·cal·i·ty (răs·kăl′ ĭ·tĭ)
  ras·cal·ly
rash·er (răsh′ ēr)
rasp·ber·ry (răz′ bĕr′ ĭ)
  -ber·ries
rasp·ing (rás′ pĭng)
ratch·et (răch′ ĕt)
rate (rāt)
  rat·ing   rat·a·ble
rath·skel·ler (răts′ kĕl′ ēr)
rat·i·fy (răt′ ĭ·fĭ)
  -fied   -fy·ing
  rat·i·fi·ca·tion
       (răt′ ĭ·fĭ·kā′ shŭn)
  rat·i·fi·er
ra·tio (rā′ shō)
ra·ti·oc·i·na·tion
    (răsh′ ĭ·ŏs′ ĭ·nā′ shŭn)
ra·tion·al (răsh′ ŭn·ăl)
  ra·tion·al·is·tic
    (răsh′ ŭn·ăl·ĭs′ tĭk)
  ra·tion·al·i·ty
    (răsh′ ŭn·ăl′ ĭ·tĭ)
ra·tion·ale (răsh′ ŭn·ăl′)
ra·tion·al·ize (răsh′ ŭn·ăl·ĭz)
  -iz·ing
  ra·tion·al·i·za·tion
    (răsh′ ŭn·ăl·ĭ·zā′ shŭn)
rat·tan (ră·tăn′)
rat·tle (răt′ ′l)
  rat·tling   rat·tle·brained
  rat·tle·snake
rat·trap (răt′ trăp′)
rau·cous (rô′ kŭs)

rav·age (răv′ ĭj)
  -ag·ing
rav·el (răv′ ĕl)
  -eled   -el·ing
rav·en·ing (răv′ ĕn·ĭng)
rav·en·ous (răv′ ĕn·ŭs)
ra·vi·o·li (rä·vyô·lē)
rav·ish·ing (răv′ ĭsh·ĭng)
raw (rô)
  raw·boned   raw·hide
  raw ma·te·ri·al
ray·on (rā′ ŏn)
raze (rāz)
  (demolish; see raise)
  raz·ing
ra·zor (rā′ zēr)
re·ab·sorb (rē′ ăb·sôrb′)
reach (rēch)
re·act (rē·ăkt′)
  re·ac·tion (rē·ăk′ shŭn)
  re·ac·tion·ar·y
    (rē·ăk′ shŭn·ĕr′ ĭ)
  re·ac·tor (rē·ăk′ tēr)
read (rēd)
  (peruse; see reed)
read·a·ble (rēd′ à·b′l)
  read·a·bil·i·ty (rēd′ à·bĭl′ ĭ·tĭ)
read·er·ship (rēd′ ēr·shĭp)
read·i·ly (rĕd′ ĭ·lĭ)
read·i·ness (rĕd′ ĭ·nĕs)
re·ad·just·ment (rē′ ă·jŭst′ mĕnt)
re·ad·mis·sion (rē′ ăd·mĭsh′ ŭn)
re·ad·mit (rē′ ăd·mĭt′)
  -mit·ted   -mit·ting
  re·ad·mit·tance
    (rē′ ăd·mĭt′ ăns)
read·y (rĕd′ ĭ)
  read·ied   read·y·ing
  read·i·er, -i·est, -i·ly, -i·ness
  read·y-made   read·y-to-wear
re·af·firm (rē′ ă·fûrm′)
  re·af·fir·ma·tion
    (rē′ ăf·ēr·mā′ shŭn)
re·a·gent (rē·ā′ jĕnt)
re·al (rē′ ăl)
  (actual; see reel)
  re·al es·tate
  re·al·is·tic (rē′ ăl·ĭs′ tĭk)
  re·al·i·ty (rē·ăl′ ĭ·tĭ)
re·al·ize (rē′ ăl·ĭz)
  -iz·ing   re·al·iz·a·ble
  re·al·i·za·tion
    (rē′ ăl·ĭ·zā′ shŭn)
re·al·lo·ca·tion
    (rē′ ăl·ŏ·kā′ shŭn)

re·al·ly   (rē′ ăl·ĭ)
realm   (rĕlm)
re·al·ty   (rē′ ăl·tĭ)
  re·al·tor   (rē′ ăl·tĕr)
ream   (rēm)
reap·er   (rēp′ ĕr)
re·ap·pear·ance
                    (rē′ ă·pēr′ ăns)
re·ap·point   (rē′ ă·point′)
re·ar·ma·ment   (rē·är′ mă·mĕnt)
re·ar·range·ment
                    (rē′ ă·rānj′ mĕnt)
rea·son   (rē′ z'n)
  -soned   -son·ing
  rea·son·a·ble
re·as·sem·ble   (rē′ ă·sĕm′ b'l)
  -bling
re·as·sign   (rē′ ă·sīn′)
re·as·sure   (rē′ ă·shoõr′)
  -as·sur·ing
re·a·wak·en   (rē′ ȧ·wāk′ ĕn)
re·bate   (rē′ bāt)
  -bat·ing
re·bel   (rē·bĕl′) v.
  -belled   -bel·ling
reb·el   (rĕb′ ĕl) n., adj.
re·bel·lion   (rē·bĕl′ yŭn)
re·bel·lious   (rē·bĕl′ yŭs)
re·birth   (rē·bûrth′)
re·bound   (rē·bound′)
re·buff   (rē·bŭf′)
re·buke   (rē·būk′)
re·bus   (rē′ bŭs)
re·but   (rē·bŭt′)
  -but·ted   -but·ting
  re·but·tal   (rē·bŭt′ ăl)
re·cal·ci·trant   (rē·kăl′ sĭ·trănt)
  -trance
re·call·a·ble   (rē·kôl′ ȧ·b'l)
re·cant   (rē·kănt′)
re·cap   (rē·kăp′)
  -capped   -cap·ping
  re·cap·pa·ble
re·ca·pit·u·late
                    (rē′ kȧ·pĭt′ ū·lāt)
  -lat·ing
  re·ca·pit·u·la·tion
                    (rē′ kȧ·pĭt′ ū·lā′ shŭn)
re·cede   (rē·sēd′)
  -ced·ing
re·ceipt   (rē·sēt′)
re·ceive   (rē·sēv′)
  -ceiv·ing   re·ceiv·a·ble
  re·ceiv·er·ship

re·cent   (rē′ sĕnt)
  re·cen·cy   re·cent·ly
re·cep·ta·cle   (rē·sĕp′ tȧ·k'l)
re·cep·tion   (rē·sĕp′ shŭn)
  re·cep·tion·ist
re·cep·tive   (rē·sĕp′ tĭv)
  re·cep·tive·ness
  re·cep·tiv·i·ty   (rē′ sĕp·tĭv′ ĭ·tĭ)
re·cep·tor   (rē·sĕp′ tĕr)
re·ces·sion   (rē·sĕsh′ ŭn)
  re·ces·sion·al   re·ces·sive
rec·i·pe   (rĕs′ ĭ·pē)
re·cip·i·ent   (rē·sĭp′ ĭ·ĕnt)
  -ence
re·cip·ro·cal   (rē·sĭp′ rō·kăl)
  re·cip·ro·cate,   -cat·ing
  re·cip·ro·ca·tion
                    (rē·sĭp′ rō·kā′ shŭn)
  rec·i·proc·i·ty   (rĕs′ ĭ·prŏs′ ĭ·tĭ)
re·cite   (rē·sīt′)
  -cit·ing   re·cit·al
  rec·i·ta·tion   (rĕs′ ĭ·tā′ shŭn)
reck·less   (rĕk′ lĕs)
reck·on   (rĕk′ ŭn)
  reck·on·ing
re·claim   (rē·klām′)
  re·claim·a·ble
  rec·la·ma·tion
                    (rĕk′ lȧ·mā′ shŭn)
re·clin·er   (rē·klīn′ ĕr)
re·cluse   (rē·kloōs′)
rec·og·ni·tion   (rĕk′ ŏg·nĭsh′ ŭn)
rec·og·nize   (rĕk′ ŏg·nīz)
  -niz·ing   rec·og·niz·a·ble
re·coil   (rē·koil′)
  -coiled   -coil·ing
re·col·lect   (rĕk′ ŏ·lĕkt′)
rec·om·mend   (rĕk′ ŏ·mĕnd′)
  rec·om·men·da·tion
                    (rĕk′ ŏ·mĕn·dā′ shŭn)
re·com·mit   (rē′ kŏ·mĭt′)
  -com·mit·ted   -com·mit·ting
  re·com·mit·ment
rec·om·pense   (rĕk′ ŏm·pĕns)
rec·on·cile   (rĕk′ ŏn·sīl)
  -cil·ing   rec·on·cil·a·ble
  rec·on·cil·i·a·tion
                    (rĕk′ ŏn·sĭl′ ĭ·ā′ shŭn)
rec·on·dite   (rĕk′ ŭn·dĭt)
re·con·di·tioned
                    (rē′ kŏn·dĭsh′ ŭnd)
re·con·nais·sance
                    (rē·kŏn′ ĭ·sȧns)
rec·on·noi·ter   (rĕk′ ŏ·noi′ tĕr)
re·con·sid·er   (rē′ kŏn·sĭd′ ĕr)

re·con·sti·tute   (rē·kŏn′ stĭ·tūt)
  -tut·ing
re·con·struc·tion
        (rē′ kŏn·strŭk′ shŭn)
re·con·vene   (rē′ kŏn·vēn′)
  -ven·ing
re·con·vert   (rē′ kŏn·vûrt′)
re·con·ver·sion
        (rē′ kŏn·vûr′ shŭn)
re·cord   (rē·kôrd′) v.
rec·ord   (rĕk′ ẽrd) n.
re·coup   (rē·kōōp′)
re·course   (rē·kōrs′)
re·cov·er   (rē·kŭv′ ẽr)
  re·cov·er·a·ble
  re·cov·er·y
rec·re·ant   (rĕk′ rē·ănt)
rec·re·a·tion   (rĕk′ rē·ā′ shŭn)
re·crim·i·na·tion
        (rē·krĭm′ ĭ·nā′ shŭn)
re·cru·des·cence
        (rē′ krōō·dĕs′ ĕns)
re·cruit   (rē·krōōt′)
  re·cruit·er   re·cruit·ment
rec·tal   (rĕk′ tăl)
rec·tan·gle   (rĕk′ tăng′ g′l)
  rec·tan·gu·lar
        (rĕk·tăng′ gû·lẽr)
rec·ti·fy   (rĕk′ tĭ·fī)
  -fied   -fy·ing
  rec·ti·fi·a·ble
rec·ti·lin·e·ar   (rĕk′ tĭ·lĭn′ ē·ẽr)
rec·ti·tude   (rĕk′ tĭ·tūd)
rec·tor   (rĕk′ tẽr)
  rec·tor·y   -tor·ies
rec·tum   (rĕk′ tŭm)
re·cum·bent   (rē·kŭm′ bĕnt)
  -ben·cy
re·cu·per·ate   (rē·kū′ pẽr·āt)
  -at·ing
re·cu·per·a·tion
        (rē·kū′ pẽr·ā′ shŭn)
re·cu·per·a·tive
        (rē·kū′ pẽr·ā′ tĭv)
re·cur   (rē·kûr′)
  -curred   -cur·ring
  re·cur·rence   re·cur·rent
red   (rĕd)
  red-blood·ed   red·coat
  red·den   red·dish
  red-hand·ed   red·head
  red-hot   red-let·ter day
  red o·cher   red·skin
  red tape

re·deem   (rē·dēm′)
  re·deem·a·ble   re·deem·er
re·demp·tion   (rē·dĕmp′ shŭn)
re·demp·tive   (rē·dĕmp′ tĭv)
re·de·vel·op·ment
        (rē′ dē·vĕl′ ŭp·mĕnt)
red·in·gote   (rĕd′ ĭng·gōt)
re·dis·cov·er·y
        (rē′ dĭs·kŭv′ ẽr·ĭ)
red·o·lent   (rĕd′ ô·lĕnt)
  -lence
re·dou·ble   (rē·dŭb′ ′l)
  -bling
re·doubt·a·ble   (rē·dout′ à·b′l)
re·dound   (rē·dound′)
re·dress   (rē·drĕs′)
re·duce   (rē·dūs′)
  -duc·ing   re·duc·i·ble
  re·duc·tion   (rē·dŭk′ shŭn)
re·dun·dant   (rē·dŭn′ dănt)
  -dan·cy
re·du·pli·ca·tion
        (rē·dū′ plĭ·kā′ shŭn)
re·ech·o   (rē·ĕk′ ō)
reed   (rēd)
  (grass; see *read*)
re·ed·u·ca·tion
        (rē·ĕd′ û·kā′ shŭn)
reef   (rēf)
reek   (rēk)
reel   (rēl)
  (dance; see *real*)
re·e·lect   (rē′ ē·lĕkt′)
re·e·mer·gence   (rē′ ē·mûr′ jĕns)
re·em·ploy   (rē′ ĕm·ploi′)
re·en·act   (rē′ ĕn·ăkt′)
re·en·gage   (rē′ ĕn·gāj′)
  -gag·ing
re·en·list·ment   (rē′ ĕn·lĭst′ mĕnt)
re·en·ter   (rē·ĕn′ tẽr)
  re·en·try   -tries
re·es·tab·lish   (rē′ ĕs·tăb′ lĭsh)
re·ex·am·ine   (rē′ ĕg·zăm′ ĭn)
  -in·ing
re·fer   (rē·fûr′)
  -ferred   -fer·ring
  ref·er·a·ble   (rĕf′ ẽr·à·b′l)
  re·fer·ral
ref·er·ee   (rĕf′ ẽr·ē′)
ref·er·ence   (rĕf′ ẽr·ĕns)
ref·er·en·dum   (rĕf′ ẽr·ĕn′ dŭm)
re·fill·a·ble   (rē·fĭl′ à·b′l)
re·fine   (rē·fīn′)
  -fin·ing   re·fine·ment
  re·fin·er·y   -er·ies

re·flect (rĕ·flĕkt′)
  re·flec·tion   re·flec·tive
  re·flec·tive·ness
  re·flec·tor
re·flex (rē′ flĕks)
re·for·est·a·tion
        (rē′ fŏr·ĕs·tā′ shŭn)
re·form (rĕ·fôrm′)
  re·form·a·ble
  ref·or·ma·tion
        (rĕf′ ŏr·mā′ shŭn)
re·form·a·to·ry
        (rĕ·fôr′ ma·tō′ rĭ)
  -ries
re·fract (rĕ·frăkt′)
  re·frac·tion   re·frac·tive
re·frac·to·ry (rĕ·frăk′ tō·rĭ)
re·frain (rĕ·frān′)
re·fresh·ment (rĕ·frĕsh′ mĕnt)
re·frig·er·ate (rĕ·frĭj′ ĕr·āt)
  -at·ing   re·frig·er·a·tor
  re·frig·er·a·tion
        (rĕ·frĭj′ ĕr·ā′ shŭn)
ref·uge (rĕf′ ūj)
ref·u·gee (rĕf′ ŭ·jē′)
re·fund (rē·fŭnd′)
re·fur·bish (rē·fûr′ bĭsh)
re·fuse (rĕ·fūz′) v.
  -fus·ing
  re·fus·al (rĕ·fūz′ ăl)
ref·use (rĕf′ ŭs) adj., n.
re·fute (rĕ·fūt′)
  -fut·ing
  ref·u·ta·ble (rĕf′ ŭ·ta·b'l)
  ref·u·ta·tion (rĕf′ ŭ·tā′ shŭn)
re·gal (rē′ găl)
  -gal·ly
re·gale (rĕ·gāl′)
  -gal·ing   re·gale·ment
re·ga·li·a (rĕ·gā′ lĭ·a)
re·gard·ing (rĕ·gärd′ ĭng)
re·gat·ta (rĕ·găt′ a)
re·gen·er·a·tion
        (rĕ·jĕn′ ĕr·ā′ shŭn)
re·gent (rē′ jĕnt)
  -gen·cy
re·gime (rå·zhēm′)
reg·i·men (rĕj′ ĭ·mĕn)
reg·i·ment (rĕj′ ĭ·mĕnt)
  reg·i·men·tal (rĕj′ ĭ·mĕn′ tăl)
  reg·i·men·ta·tion
        (rĕj′ ĭ·mĕn·tā′ shŭn)
re·gion (rē′ jŭn)
  re·gion·al

reg·is·ter (rĕj′ ĭs·tẽr)
  reg·is·trant   (-trănt)
  reg·is·trar   (-trär)
  reg·is·tra·tion (rĕj′ ĭs·trā′ shŭn)
  reg·is·try
re·gress (rĕ·grĕs′)
  re·gres·sive   re·gres·sion
re·gret (rĕ·grĕt′)
  -gret·ted   -gret·ting
  re·gret·ful, -ful·ly, -ful·ness
  re·gret·ta·ble
reg·u·lar (rĕg′ û·lẽr)
  reg·u·lar·i·ty (rĕg′ û·lăr′ ĭ·tĭ)
  reg·u·lar·ize   -iz·ing
reg·u·late (rĕg′ û·lāt)
  -lat·ing
  reg·u·la·tion (rĕg′ û·lā′ shŭn)
  reg·u·la·tive (rĕg′ û·lā′ tĭv)
  reg·u·la·tor (rĕg′ û·lā′ tẽr)
  reg·u·la·to·ry (rĕg′ û·la·tō′ rĭ)
re·gur·gi·tate (rĕ·gûr′ jĭ·tāt)
  -tat·ing
re·ha·bil·i·tate
        (rē′ ha·bĭl′ ĭ·tāt)
  -tat·ing
  re·ha·bil·i·ta·tion
        (rē′ ha·bĭl′ ĭ·tā′ shŭn)
re·hearse (rĕ·hûrs′)
  -hears·ing   re·hears·al
Reich (rīк)
reign (rān)
  (royal authority; see *rain, rein*)
re·im·burse·ment
        (rē′ ĭm·bûrs′ mĕnt)
rein (rān)
  (bridle strap; see *rain, reign*)
re·in·car·na·tion
        (rē′ ĭn·kär·nā′ shŭn)
rein·deer (rān′ dẽr′)
re·in·force·ment
        (rē′ ĭn·fôrs′ mĕnt)
re·in·sert (rē′ ĭn·sûrt′)
re·in·state·ment
        (rē′ ĭn·stāt′ mĕnt)
re·in·te·grate (rĕ·ĭn′ tĕ·grāt)
  -grat·ing
re·in·tro·duce (rē′ ĭn·trō·dūs′)
  -duc·ing
re·in·vest (rē′ ĭn·vĕst′)
re·is·sue (rĕ·ĭsh′ ū)
  -is·su·ing
re·it·er·ate (rĕ·ĭt′ ĕr·āt)
  -at·ing
  re·it·er·a·tion
        (rĕ·ĭt′ ĕr·ā′ shŭn)

re·ject (rē·jĕkt′)
  re·jec·tion (rē·jĕk′ shŭn)
re·joice (rē·jois′)
  -joic·ing
re·join·der (rē·join′ dēr)
re·ju·ve·nate (rē·joō′ vē·nāt)
  -nat·ing
  re·ju·ve·na·tion
         (rē·joō′ vē·nā′ shŭn)
re·kin·dle (rē·kĭn′ d′l)
  -dling
re·lapse (rē·lăps′)
  -laps·ing
re·late (rē·lāt′)
  -lat·ing
re·la·tion (rē·lā′ shŭn)
  re·la·tion·ship
rel·a·tive (rĕl′ ȧ·tĭv)
  rel·a·tiv·i·ty (rĕl′ ȧ·tĭv′ ĭ·tĭ)
re·lax (rē·lăks′)
  re·lax·a·tion (rē′ lăk·sā′ shŭn)
  re·lax·er
re·lay (rē·lā′)
  -layed -lay·ing
re·lease (rē·lēs′)
  -leas·ing
rel·e·gate (rĕl′ ē·gāt)
  -gat·ing
  rel·e·ga·tion (rĕl′ ē·gā′ shŭn)
re·lent (rē·lĕnt′)
  re·lent·less
rel·e·vant (rĕl′ ē·vănt)
  -vance, -van·cy
re·li·a·ble (rē·lī′ ȧ·b′l)
re·li·a·bil·i·ty (rē·lī′ ȧ·bĭl′ ĭ·tĭ)
re·li·ant (rē·lī′ ănt)
  re·li·ance
rel·ic (rĕl′ ĭk)
re·lief (rē·lēf′)
re·lieve (rē·lēv′)
  -liev·ing re·liev·a·ble
re·li·gion (rē·lĭj′ ŭn)
  re·li·gious
re·lin·quish (rē·lĭng′ kwĭsh)
rel·ish (rĕl′ ĭsh)
re·lo·ca·tion (rē′ lō·kā′ shŭn)
re·luc·tant (rē·lŭk′ tănt)
  -tance
re·ly (rē·lī′)
  -lied -ly·ing
Rem·brandt van Rijn
      (rĕm′ brănt văn rīn′)
re·main (rē·mān′)
  re·main·der
re·mand (rē·mánd′)

re·mark·a·ble (rē·mär′ kȧ·b′l)
re·mar·riage (rē·măr′ ĭj)
rem·e·dy (rĕm′ ē·dĭ)
  -died, -dies, -dy·ing
  re·me·di·a·ble (rē·mē′ dĭ·ȧ·b′l)
  re·me·di·al (rē·mē′ dĭ·ăl)
  rem·e·di·less
re·mem·ber (rē·mĕm′ bēr)
  re·mem·brance (-brăns)
re·mind·er (rē·mīn′ dēr)
rem·i·nisce (rĕm′ ĭ·nĭs′)
  -nis·cing rem·i·nis·cence
  rem·i·nis·cent
re·miss (rē·mĭs′)
re·mis·sion (rē·mĭsh′ ŭn)
re·mit (rē·mĭt′)
  -mit·ted -mit·ting
  re·mit·ta·ble re·mit·tal
  re·mit·tance re·mit·tent
  re·mit·tor
rem·nant (rĕm′ nănt)
re·mod·el (rē·mŏd′ ′l)
  -eled -el·ing
re·mon·strate (rē·mŏn′ strāt)
  -strat·ing
  re·mon·strance
      (rē·mŏn′ străns)
re·morse (rē·môrs′)
  re·morse·ful, -ful·ly, -ful·ness
  re·morse·less
re·mote (rē·mōt′)
  re·mote·ly -mote·ness
re·move (rē·moōv′)
  -mov·ing re·mov·a·ble
  re·mov·al
re·mu·ner·a·tion
      (rē·mū′ nēr·ā′ shŭn)
  re·mu·ner·a·tive
      (rē·mū′ nēr·ā′ tĭv)
ren·ais·sance (rĕn′ ē·zäns′)
  Ren·ais·sance art
ren·der (rĕn′ dēr)
ren·dez·vous (rän′ dē·voō)
ren·di·tion (rĕn·dĭsh′ ŭn)
ren·e·gade (rĕn′ ē·gād)
re·nege (rē·nĕg′)
  -neg·ing
re·ne·go·ti·ate
      (rē′ nē·gō′ shĭ·āt)
  -at·ing
  re·ne·go·ti·a·ble
      (rē′ nē·gō′ shĭ·ȧ·b′l)
re·new·al (rē·nū′ ăl)
ren·net (rĕn′ ĕt)

re·nom·i·nate   (rē·nŏm′ ĭ·nāt)
  -nat·ing
re·nounce   (rě·nouns′)
  -nounc·ing   re·nounce·ment
ren·o·vate   (rĕn′ ŏ·vāt)
  -vat·ing
ren·o·va·tion   (rĕn′ ŏ·vā′ shŭn)
re·nown   (rě·noun′)
  re·nowned   (-nound)
rent·al   (rĕn′ tăl)
re·nun·ci·a·tion
                 (rē·nŭn′ sĭ·ā′ shŭn)
re·oc·cu·py   (rē·ŏk′ û·pī)
  pied   -py·ing
re·oc·cu·pa·tion
                 (rē′ ŏk·û·pā′ shŭn)
re·o·pen   (rē·ō′ pĕn)
re·or·der   (rē·ôr′ dēr)
re·or·gan·i·za·tion
                 (rē′ ôr·găn·ĭ·zā′ shŭn)
re·pair   (rě·pâr′)
rep·a·ra·tion   (rĕp′ à·rā′ shŭn)
rep·ar·tee   (rĕp′ ēr·tē′)
re·past   (rě·pást′)
re·pay   (rě·pā′)
  -paid   -pay·ing
  re·pay·a·ble   re·pay·ment
re·peal   (rě·pēl′)
  -pealed   -peal·ing
  re·peal·a·ble
re·peat   (rě·pēt′)
  re·peat·ed·ly re·peat·er
re·pel   (rě·pĕl′)
  -pelled   -pel·ling
  re·pel·lent
re·pent   (rě·pĕnt′)
  re·pent·ance
re·per·cus·sion
                 (rē′ pēr·kŭsh′ ŭn)
rep·er·toire   (rĕp′ ēr·twär)
rep·er·to·ry   (rĕp′ ēr·tō′ rĭ)
rep·e·ti·tion   (rĕp′ ê·tĭsh′ ŭn)
  rep·e·ti·tious
  re·pet·i·tive (rě·pĕt′ ĭ·tĭv)
re·place   (rě·plās′)
  -plac·ing   re·place·a·ble
  re·place·ment
re·plen·ish   (rě·plĕn′ ĭsh)
re·plete   (rě·plēt′)
  re·ple·tion   (rě·plē′ shŭn)
rep·li·ca   (rĕp′ lĭ·kà)
rep·li·ca·tion   (rĕp′ lĭ·kā′ shŭn)
re·ply   (rě·plī′)
  -plied   -ply·ing

re·port   (rě·pōrt′)
  re·port·a·ble re·port·er
  rep·or·to·ri·al (rĕp′ ôr·tō′ rĭ·ăl)
re·pose   (rě·pōz′)
  -pos·ing   re·pose·ful
re·pos·i·to·ry   (rě·pŏz′ ĭ·tō′ rĭ)
  -ries
re·pos·sess   (rē′ pŏ·zĕs′)
  re·pos·ses·sion
rep·re·hend   (rĕp′ rě·hĕnd′)
rep·re·hen·si·ble
                 (rĕp′ rě·hĕn′ sĭ·b′l)
rep·re·sent   (rĕp′ rě·zĕnt′)
  rep·re·sent·a·ble
  rep·re·sen·ta·tion
                 (rĕp′ ɾě·zĕn·tā′ shŭn)
  rep·re·sent·a·tive
                 (rĕp′ rě·zĕn′ tà·tĭv)
re·press   (rě·prĕs′)
  re·pres·sion   (rě·prĕsh′ ŭn)
  re·pres·sive
re·prieve   (rě·prēv′)
  -priev·ing
rep·ri·mand   (rĕp′ rĭ·mánd′)
re·pris·al   (rě·prīz′ ăl)
re·proach·ful   (rě·prōch′ fŏŏl)
  -ful·ly   -ful·ness
rep·ro·bate   (rĕp′ rŏ·bāt)
  rep·ro·ba·tion
                 (rĕp′ rŏ·bā′ shŭn)
re·pro·duce   (rē′ prŏ·dūs′)
  -duc·ing   re·pro·duc·i·ble
  re·pro·duc·tion
                 (rē′ prŏ·dŭk′ shŭn)
  re·pro·duc·tive
                 (rē′ prŏ·dŭk′ tĭv)
re·proof   (rě·prōōf′) n.
re·prove   (rě·prōōv′) v.
  -prov·ing
rep·tile   (rĕp′ tĭl)
  rep·til·i·an   (rĕp·tĭl′ ĭ·ăn)
re·pub·lic   (rě·pŭb′ lĭk)
  re·pub·li·can
re·pu·di·ate   (rě·pū′ dĭ·āt)
  -at·ing
  re·pu·di·a·tion
                 (rě·pū′ dĭ·ā′ shŭn)
re·pug·nant   (rě·pŭg′ nănt)
  -nance
re·pulse   (rě·pŭls′)
  -puls·ing
  re·pul·sion   (rě·pŭl′ shŭn)
  re·pul·sive   -sive·ness
rep·u·ta·ble   (rĕp′ û·tà·b′l)

rep·u·ta·bil·i·ty
   (rĕp' ū·tá·bĭl' ĭ·tĭ)
rep·u·ta·tion (rĕp' ū·tā' shŭn)
re·put·ed·ly (rē·pūt' ĕd·lĭ)
re·quest (rē·kwĕst')
re·qui·em (rē' wĭ·ĕm)
re·quire·ment (rē·kwīr' mĕnt)
req·ui·site (rĕk' wĭ·zĭt)
req·ui·si·tion (rĕk' wĭ·zĭsh' ŭn)
re·quite (rē·kwīt')
  re·quit·al
re·sale   (rē·sāl')
  re·sal·a·ble
re·scind (rē·sĭnd')
  re·scis·sion (rē·sĭzh' ŭn)
res·cue (rĕs' kū)
  -cu·ing
re·search (rē·sûrch')
re·sem·ble (rē·zĕm' b'l)
  -bling
  re·sem·blance (rē·zĕm' blǎns)
re·sent (rē·zĕnt')
  re·sent·ful, -ful·ly, -ful·ness
  re·sent·ment
res·er·va·tion (rĕz' ĕr·vā' shŭn)
re·serve (rē·zûrv')
  -serv·ing re·serv·ed·ly
  re·serv·ist
res·er·voir (rĕz' ĕr·vwôr)
re·set·tle·ment (rē·sĕt' 'l·mĕnt)
re·side (rē·zīd')
  -sid·ing
res·i·dent (rĕz' ĭ·dĕnt)
  res·i·dence
  res·i·den·tial (rĕz' ĭ·dĕn' shǎl)
res·i·due (rĕz' ĭ·dū)
  re·sid·u·al (rē·zĭd' ū·ǎl)
re·sign (rē·zīn')
  res·ig·na·tion (rĕz' ĭg·nā' shŭn)
  re·sign·ed·ly (rē·zīn' ĕd·lĭ)
re·sil·i·ent (rē·zĭl' ĭ·ĕnt)
  re·sil·i·ence
res·in (rĕz' ĭn)
  res·in·ous (rĕz' ĭ·nŭs)
re·sist (rē·zĭst')
  re·sis·tance (rē·zĭs' tǎns)
  re·sis·tant re·sist·i·ble
  re·sis·tive re·sis·tor
res·o·jet en·gine
    (rĕz' ō·jĕt')
res·o·lute (rĕz' ō·lūt)
  -lute·ly
res·o·lu·tion (rĕz' ō·lū' shŭn)
re·solve (rē·zŏlv')
  -solv·ing re·solv·a·ble

res·o·nant (rĕz' ō·nǎnt)
  -nance res·o·na·tor
re·sort (rē·zôrt')
re·sound (rē·zound')
re·source (rē·sōrs')
  re·source·ful, -ful·ly, -ful·ness
re·spect (rē·spĕkt')
  re·spect·a·bil·i·ty
    (rē·spĕk' tá·bĭl' ĭ·tĭ)
  re·spect·a·ble (rē·spĕk' tá·b'l)
  re·spect·er
  re·spect·ful, -ful·ly, -ful·ness
  re·spect·ing
  re·spec·tive -tive·ly
res·pi·ra·tion (rĕs' pĭ·rā' shŭn)
  res·pi·ra·tor (rĕs' pĭ·rā' tēr)
  re·spir·a·to·ry (rē·spīr' á·tō' rĭ)
res·pite (rĕs' pĭt)
re·splend·ent (rē·splĕn' dĕnt)
  -ence
re·spond·ent (rē·spŏn' dĕnt)
re·sponse (rē·spŏns')
re·spon·si·ble (rē·spŏn' sĭ·b'l)
  re·spon·si·bil·i·ty
    (rē·spŏn' sĭ·bĭl' ĭ·tĭ)
re·spon·sive (rē·spŏn' sĭv)
  -sive·ness
res·tau·rant (rĕs' tō·rǎnt)
  res·tau·ra·teur (rĕs' tō·rá·tûr')
  (NOTE: no n)
rest·ful (rĕst' fŏŏl)
  -ful·ly -ful·ness
res·ti·tu·tion (rĕs' tĭ·tū' shŭn)
res·tive (rĕs' tĭv)
rest·less (rĕst' lĕs)
res·to·ra·tion (rĕs' tō·rā' shŭn)
re·stor·a·tive (rē·stōr' á·tĭv)
re·strain (rē·strān')
  re·strain·a·ble re·straint
re·strict (rē·strĭkt')
  re·stric·tion (rē·strĭk' shŭn)
  re·stric·tive (rē·strĭk' tĭv)
re·sult (rē·zŭlt')
  re·sult·ant
re·sume (rē·zūm') v.
  -sum·ing
ré·su·mé (rā' zŭ·mā') n.
re·sump·tion (rē·zŭmp' shŭn)
re·sur·gent (rē·sûr' jĕnt)
  -gence
res·ur·rect (rĕz' ŭ·rĕkt')
  res·ur·rec·tion
    (rĕz' ŭ·rĕk' shŭn)
re·sus·ci·tate (rē·sŭs' ĭ·tāt)
  -tat·ing

re·sus·ci·ta·tion
    (rḗ·sŭs′ ĭ·tā′ shŭn)
re·sus·ci·ta·tor
    (rḗ·sŭs′ ĭ·tā′ tēr)
re·tail   (rḗ′ tāl)
  re·tail·er
re·tain   (rḗ·tān′)
  re·tain·a·ble   re·tain·er
re·tal·i·ate   (rḗ·tăl′ ĭ·āt)
 -at·ing
  re·tal·i·a·tion
    (rḗ·tăl′ ĭ·ā′ shŭn)
  re·tal·i·a·tive   (rḗ·tăl′ ĭ·ā′ tĭv)
  re·tal·i·a·to·ry
    (rḗ·tăl′ ĭ·à·tō′ rĭ)
re·tard   (rḗ·tärd′)
  re·tar·da·tion   (rē′ tär·dā′ shŭn)
retch   (rěch)
  (vomit; see *wretch*)
re·ten·tion   (rḗ·těn′ shŭn)
  re·ten·tive
ret·i·cent   (rět′ ĭ·sĕnt)
 -cence
ret·i·na   (rět′ ĭ·nà)
ret·i·nue   (rět′ ĭ·nū)
re·tire   (rḗ·tīr′)
 -tir·ing   re·tire·ment
re·tort   (rḗ·tôrt′)
re·touch   (rḗ·tŭch′)
re·tract   (rḗ·trăkt′)
  re·tract·a·ble   re·trac·tion
re·tread   (rē·trĕd′)
re·treat   (rḗ·trēt′)
re·trench·ment   (rḗ·trĕnch′ mĕnt)
re·tri·al   (rḗ·trī′ ǎl)
ret·ri·bu·tion   (rět′ rĭ·bū′ shŭn)
re·trieve   (rḗ·trēv′)
 -triev·ing   re·triev·a·ble
  re·triev·er
ret·ro·ac·tive   (rět′ rŏ·ăk′ tĭv)
ret·ro·ces·sion   (rět′ rŏ·sĕsh′ ŭn)
ret·ro·gres·sion
    (rět′ rŏ·grĕsh′ ŭn)
ret·ro·spect   (rět′ rŏ·spĕkt)
ret·ro·ver·sion   (rět′ rŏ·vûr′ shŭn)
re·turn   (rḗ·tûrn′)
  re·turn·a·ble
re·un·ion   (rḗ·ūn′ yŭn)
re·u·nite   (rē′ ŭ·nīt′)
 -nit·ing
rev   (rěv)
  revved   rev·ving
re·vamp   (rē·vămp′)
re·veal   (rḗ·vēl′)
 -vealed   -veal·ing

re·veal·a·ble   re·veal·ment
rev·eil·le   (rĕv′ ĕ·lĭ)
rev·el   (rĕv′ ĕl)
 -eled   -el·ing
  rev·el·ry
rev·e·la·tion   (rĕv′ ĕ·lā′ shŭn)
re·venge   (rḗ·vĕnj′)
 -veng·ing   re·venge·ful
rev·e·nue   (rĕv′ ĕ·nū)
re·ver·ber·ate   (rḗ·vûr′ bēr·āt)
 -at·ing
  re·ver·ber·a·tion
    (rḗ·vûr′ bēr·ā′ shŭn)
re·vere   (rḗ·vēr′)
 -ver·ing
rev·er·end   (rĕv′ ēr·ĕnd)
rev·er·ent   (rĕv′ ēr·ĕnt)
  rev·er·ence
rev·er·ie   (rĕv′ ēr·ĭ)
re·verse   (rḗ·vûrs′)
 -vers·ing   re·ver·sal
  re·vers·i·ble
re·ver·sion   (rḗ·vûr′ shŭn)
re·vert   (rḗ·vûrt′)
  re·vert·i·ble
re·view   (rḗ·vū′)
  (survey; see *revue*)
re·vile   (rḗ·vīl′)
 -vil·ing   re·vile·ment
re·vise   (rḗ·vīz′)
 -vis·ing
  re·vi·sion   (rḗ·vĭzh′ ŭn)
re·vi·tal·ize   (rḗ·vī′ tǎl·īz)
 -iz·ing
  re·vi·tal·i·za·tion
    (rē′ vī·tǎl·ĭ·zā′ shŭn)
re·viv·al   (rḗ·vīv′ ǎl)
  re·viv·al·ist
re·vive   (rḗ·vīv′)
 -viv·ing
re·viv·i·fy   (rḗ·vīv′ ĭ·fī)
 -fied,   -fy·ing
re·voke   (rḗ·vōk′)
 -vok·ing
  rev·o·ca·ble   (rĕv′ ŏ·kà·b'l)
re·volt·ing   (rḗ·vōl′ tĭng)
rev·o·lu·tion   (rĕv′ ŏ·lū′ shŭn)
  rev·o·lu·tion·ar·y
  rev·o·lu·tion·ize, -iz·ing
re·volv·er   (rḗ·vōl′ vēr)
re·vue   (rḗ·vū′)
  (burlesque; see *review*)
re·vul·sion   (rḗ·vŭl′ shŭn)
re·ward   (rḗ·wôrd′)

rhap·so·dy (răp′ sŏ·dĭ)
-dies
rhap·so·dize -diz·ing
Rhen·ish (rĕn′ ĭsh)
rhe·o·stat (rē′ ŏ·stăt)
rhet·o·ric (rĕt′ ŏ·rĭk)
rhe·tor·i·cal (rĕ·tŏr′ ĭ·kăl)
rhet·o·ri·cian (rĕt′ ŏ·rĭsh′ ăn)
rheu·ma·tism (rōō′ mȧ·tĭz′m)
rheu·mat·ic (rōō·mă t′ ĭk)
rheu·ma·toid ar·thri·tis
(rōō′ mȧ·toid)
Rh fac·tor (är′ ăch′)
Rh-neg·a·tive Rh-pos·i·tive
rhine·stone (rīn′ stōn′)
Rhine wine (rīn)
rhi·ni·tis (rī·nī′ tĭs)
rhi·noc·er·os (rī·nŏs′ ĕr·ŏs)
Rhode Is·land (rōd ī′ lănd)
abbr. R. I.
Rhode Is·land·er
Rho·de·sia (rŏ·dē′ zhȧ)
Rhodes schol·ar·ship
(rōdz)
rhom·bus (rŏm′ bŭs)
rhu·barb (rōō′ bärb)
rhyme (rīm)
rhym·ing
rhythm (rĭth′m)
rhyth·mic (rĭth′ mĭk)
-mi·cal
Ri·al·to (rĭ·ăl′ tō)
rib·ald (rĭb′ ăld)
rib·ald·ry (-rĭ)
rib·bing (rĭb′ĭng)
rib·bon (rĭb′ŭn)
ri·bo·fla·vin (rī′ bŏ·flā′ vĭn)
rich·es (rĭch′ ĕz)
rick·ets (rĭk′ ĕts)
rick·et·y (rĭk′ ĕ·tĭ)
rick·ey (rĭk′ ĭ)
rick·rack (rĭk′ răk′)
rick·sha (rĭk′ shä)
ric·o·chet (rĭk′ ŏ·shā′)
-cheted -chet·ing
rid·dance (rĭd′ ăns)
rid·dle (rĭd′ ′l)
rid·dling
ride (rīd)
rid·ing
rid·den (rĭd′ ′n)
ridge (rĭj)
rid·i·cule (rĭd′ ĭ·kūl)
-cul·ing
ri·dic·u·lous (rĭ·dĭk′ û·lŭs)

rife (rīf)
rif·fle (rĭf′ ′l)
(shuffle; see rifle)
rif·fling
riff·raff (rĭf′ răf′)
ri·fle (rī′ f′l)
(gun; see riffle)
-fling ri·fle·man
rift (rĭft)
rig·ging (rĭg′ ĭng)
right (rīt)
(correct; see rite, wright, write)
right an·gle right-an·gled
right·eous (rī′ chŭs)
right·ful, -ful·ly, -ful·ness
right-hand·ed
right of way (pl. rights of way)
rig·id (rĭj′ ĭd)
ri·gid·i·ty (rĭ·jĭd′ ĭ·tĭ)
rig·ma·role (rĭg′ mȧ·rōl)
rig·or (rĭg′ ĕr)
ri·gor mor·tis (rĭg′ ĕr môr′ tĭs)
rig·or·ous (rĭg′ ĕr·ŭs)
ring (rĭng)
ring·lead·er ring·mas·ter
ring·side ring·worm
rinse (rĭns)
rins·ing
Rio de Ja·nei·ro,
Bra·zil (rē′ ŏ dĕ jȧ·nā′ rō)
Ri·o Grande (riv.)
(rē′ ŏ grănd′)
ri·ot (rī′ ŭt)
-ot·ed -ot·ing
ri·o·ter ri·ot·ous
rip·cord (rĭp′ kôrd′)
rip·en (rĭp′ ĕn)
rip·ple (rĭp′ ′l)
rip·pling
rip-roar·ing (rĭp′ rôr′ ĭng)
Rip van Win·kle
(rĭp′ văn wĭng′ k′l)
rise (rīz)
ris·ing
ris·en (rĭz′ ′n)
risk·y (rĭs′ kĭ)
risk·i·ness
ri·sot·to (rē·sôt′ tŏ)
ris·qué (rĭs·kā′)
rite (rīt)
(liturgy; see right, wright, write)
rit·u·al (rĭt′ û·ăl)
rit·u·al·is·tic (rĭt′ û·ăl·ĭs′ tĭk)
rit·u·al·ly

ri·val (rī′ văl)
  -valed -val·ing
  ri·val·ry
Ri·vie·ra (rĕ·vyâ′ră)
riv·u·let (rĭv′ û·lĕt)
roach (rōch)
road (rōd)
  road·bed road·block
  road·house road run·ner
  road·way
roam (rōm)
roan (rōn)
Ro·a·noke, Va. (rō′ à·nōk)
roar·ing (rōr′ ĭng)
roast (rōst)
rob·ber·y (rŏb′ ĕr·ĭ)
  rob·ber·ies
rob·in (rŏb′ ĭn)
Rob·in·son Cru·soe
      (rŏb′ ĭn·s'n krōō′ sō)
ro·bot (rō′ bŏt)
ro·bust (rō·bŭst′)
rock (rŏk)
  rock bot·tom n.
  rock-bot·tom adj.
  rock gar·den rock-ribbed
  rock salt
Rock·e·fel·ler, John
      (rŏk′ ĕ·fĕl′ ĕr)
rock·er (rŏk′ ĕr)
rock·et (rŏk′ ĕt)
  rock·et launch·er
  rock·et·ry
rock·y (rŏk′ ĭ)
  rock·i·er, -i·est, -i·ly, -i·ness
  Rock·ies (mts.)
ro·co·co (rō·kō′ kō)
ro·dent (rō′ dĕnt)
ro·de·o (rō′ dĕ·ō)
roe (rō)
  (doe; eggs; see row)
roent·gen (rŭnt′ gĕn)
rogue (rōg)
  ro·guer·y (rō′ gĕr·ĭ)
  rogues' gal·ler·y
  ro·guish
roil (roil)
  roil·ing
roist·er (rois′ tĕr)
role (rōl)
  (actor's part; see roll)
roll (rōl)
  (revolve; see role)
  roll·back roll call

roll·er (rōl′ ĕr)
  roll·er bear·ing
  roll·er coast·er
  roll·er skate
rol·lick·ing (rŏl′ ĭk·ĭng)
rol·y-pol·y (rō′ lĭ·pō′ lĭ)
ro·maine let·tuce
      (rō·mān′)
Ro·man Cath·o·lic (church)
      (rō′ măn kăth′ ŏ·lĭk)
ro·mance (rō·măns′)
Ro·man·esque (rō′ măn·ĕsk′)
Ro·ma·nia (rō·mān′ yà)
ro·man·tic (rō·măn′ tĭk)
  ro·man·ti·cal·ly
  ro·man·ti·cize (-tĭ·sīz)
Ro·me·o (rō′ mĕ·ō)
romp·er (rŏmp′ ĕr)
ron·do (rŏn′ dō)
  -dos
roof·ing (rōōf′ ĭng)
rook·er·y (rōōk′ ĕr·ĭ)
  -er·ies
rook·ie (rōōk′ ĭ)
room (rōōm)
  room·ette (rōōm·ĕt′)
  room·ful room·i·ness
  room·mate room·y
Roo·se·velt, Frank·lin D.
      (rō′ zĕ·vĕlt)
roost·er (rōōs′ tĕr)
root (rōōt)
  (stem; see rout, route)
  root beer root·er
  root·less
rop·y (rōp′ ĭ)
  rop·i·ness
Roque·fort cheese
      (rōk′ fĕrt)
Ror·schach test (rōr′ shäк)
ro·sa·ry (rō′ zà·rĭ)
  -ries
rose (rōz)
  rose·bud rose-col·ored
  rose·mar·y rose wa·ter
  rose·wood
ro·se·ate (rō′ zĕ·ăt)
Ro·set·ta stone (rō·zĕt′ à)
ro·sette (rō·zĕt′)
Rosh Ha·sha·na
      (rōsh hä·shä′ nä)
ros·in (rŏz′ ĭn)
ros·ter (rŏs′ tĕr)
ros·trum (rŏs′ trŭm)
  pl. ros·tra

ros·y (rōz′ ĭ)
  ros·i·er, -i·est, -i·ly, -i·ness
ro·ta·ry (rō′ tà·rĭ)
ro·tate (rō′ tāt)
  -tat·ing
  ro·ta·tion (rô·tā′ shŭn)
  ro·ta·tor
ro·te·none (rō′ t′n·ōn)
ro·tis·se·rie (rô′ tĕs′ rē′)
ro·to·gra·vure (rō′ tô·grà·vūr′)
ro·to sec·tion (rō′ tô)
rot·ten (rŏt′ ′n)
  rot·ten·ness
ro·tund (rô·tŭnd′)
  ro·tun·di·ty (rô·tŭn′ dĭ·tĭ)
ro·tun·da (rô·tŭn′ dà)
rou·é (rōō·ā′)
rouge (rōōzh)
rough (rŭf)
  rough·age
  rough-and-read·y
  rough·hew rough·house
  rough·neck rough·rid·er
  rough·shod
rou·lette (rōō·lĕt′)
round (round)
  round·a·bout round rob·in
  round-shoul·dered
  round steak Round Ta·ble
  round trip round·up
roun·de·lay (roun′ dĕ·lā)
rouse (rouz)
  rous·ing
Rous·seau, Jean Jacques
                (rōō′ sō′)
roust·a·bout (roust′ à·bout′)
rout (rout)
  (conquer; see *route*)
route (rōōt)
  (path; see *root*, *rout*)
  rout·ing
rou·tine (rōō·tēn′)
rov·er (rōv′ ēr)
row (rō)
  (propel with oars; see *roe*)
row·boat (rō′ bōt′)
row·dy (rou′ dĭ)
  row·dy·ish
roy·al (roi′ ăl)
  roy·al·ist roy·al·ty
rub·ber (rŭb′ ēr)
  rub·ber·neck rub·ber-stamp
rub·bish (rŭb′ ĭsh)
rub·ble (rŭb′ ′l)
rub·down (rŭb′ doun′)

ru·bel·la (rōō·bĕl′ à)
Ru·bi·con (rōō′ bĭ·kŏn)
ru·bric (rōō′ brĭk)
ruche (rōōsh)
  ruch·ing
ruck·sack (rŭk′ săk′)
ruc·tion (rŭk′ shŭn)
rud·der (rŭd′ ēr)
rud·dy (rŭd′ ĭ)
  rud·di·ness
rude (rōōd)
  rude·ly rude·ness
ru·di·ment (rōō′ dĭ·mĕnt)
ru·di·men·ta·ry
        (rōō′ dĭ·mĕn′ tà·rĭ)
rue (rōō)
  ru·ing
  rue·ful, -ful·ly, -ful·ness
ruffed grouse (rŭft)
ruf·fi·an (rŭf′ ĭ·ăn)
ruf·fle (rŭf′ ′l)
  ruf·fling ruf·fly
Rug·by foot·ball
             (rŭg′ bĭ)
rug·ged (rŭg′ ĕd)
ru·in (rōō′ ĭn)
  ru·in·a·tion (rōō′ ĭ·nā′ shŭn)
  ru·in·ous (rōō′ ĭ·nŭs)
rul·er (rōōl′ ēr)
rul·ing (rōōl′ ĭng)
rum·ba (rōōm′ bä)
rum·ble (rŭm′ b′l)
  -bling
ru·mi·nant (rōō′ mĭ·nănt)
ru·mi·nate (rōō′ mĭ·nāt)
  -nat·ing
  ru·mi·na·tion
        (rōō′ mĭ·nā′ shŭn)
rum·mage (rŭm′ ĭj)
rum·my (rŭm′ ĭ)
ru·mor (rōō′ mēr)
rum·ple (rŭm′ p′l)
  -pling
rum·pus room (rŭm′ pŭs)
rum·run·ner (rŭm′ rŭn′ ēr)
run (rŭn)
  ran run·ning
  run·a·way run-down
  run-on run·way
run·ci·ble spoon
        (rŭn′ sĭ·b′l)
rune (rōōn)
  ru·nic
run·ner-up (rŭn′ ēr·ŭp′)
rup·ture (rŭp′ tụr)

ru·ral   (roor' dl)
ruse   (rooz)
rus·set   (rŭs' ĕt)
Rus·sian   (rŭsh' dn)
rus·tic   (rŭs' tĭk)
rus·tle   (rŭs' 'l)
  -tling   rus·tler
rust·y   (rŭs' tĭ)
  rust·i·ness
ru·ta·ba·ga   (roo' tà·bā' gà)
ruth·less   (rooth' lĕs)
rye   (rī)
Ryu·kyu (is.)   (rĭ·oo' kū)

S

Sab·bath   (săb' dth)
sab·bat·i·cal   (sd·băt' ĭ·kdl)
sa·ber   (sā' bĕr)
sa·ble   (sā' b'l)
sab·o·tage   (săb' ŏ·täzh')
  sab·o·teur   (săb' ŏ·tûr')
sac·cha·rine   (săk' à·rĭn)
sac·er·do·tal   (săs' ĕr·dō' tdl)
sa·chem   (sā' chĕm)
sa·chet   (să·shā')
sack·cloth   (săk' klŏth')
sa·cral   (sā' krdl)
sac·ra·ment   (săk' rà·mĕnt)
  sac·ra·men·tal
                      (săk' rà·mĕn' tdl)
sa·cred   (sā' krĕd)
sac·ri·fice   (săk' rĭ·fīs)
  -fic·ing
  sac·ri·fi·cial   (săk' rĭ·fĭsh' dl)
  sac·ri·fi·cial·ly
sac·ri·lege   (săk' rĭ·lĕj)
  sac·ri·le·gious   (săk' rĭ·lē' jŭs)
sa·cro·il·i·ac   (sā' krŏ·ĭl' ĭ·ăk)
sac·ro·sanct   (săk' rŏ·săngkt)
sad·den   (săd' 'n)
sad·dle   (săd' 'l)
  sad·dling   sad·dle·bag
  sad·dle soap
sad·ism   (săd' ĭz'm)
  sad·ist
  sa·dis·tic   (sà·dĭs' tĭk)
  -ti·cal·ly
sa·fa·ri   (sà·fä' rĭ)
safe   (sāf)
  safe·break·er   safe-con·duct
  safe-de·pos·it box
  safe·guard   safe·keep·ing

safe·ty   (sāf' tĭ)
  safe·ty belt   safe·ty ra·zor
  safe·ty valve   safe·ty zone
saf·fron   (săf' rŭn)
sa·ga   (sä' gà)
sa·ga·cious   (sà·gā' shŭs)
  sa·gac·i·ty   (sà·găs' ĭ·tĭ)
sage·brush   (sāj' brŭsh')
sa·hib   (sä' ĭb)
sail   (sāl)
  sailed   sail·ing
  sail·boat   sail·or
saint·ed   (sān' tĕd)
St. John (riv., Me.)
                      (sānt jŏn')
St. Johns (riv., Fla.)
                      (sānt jŏnz')
St. Law·rence   (sànt lô' rĕns)
Saint Pat·rick's   (sànt păt' rĭks)
St. Vi·tus's dance
                      (sànt vī' tŭs·ĭz)
sa·laam   (sà·läm')
sa·la·cious   (sà·lā' shŭs)
sal·ad   (săl' dd)
sal·a·man·der   (săl' à·măn' dĕr)
sa·la·mi   (sà·lä' mē)
sal·a·ry   (săl' à·rĭ)
  -ried   -ries
sale   (sāl)
  sal·a·ble   sales·man
  sales tax
sa·li·ent   (sā' lĭ·ĕnt)
  sa·li·ence
sa·line   (sā' līn)
  sa·lin·i·ty   (sà·lĭn' ĭ·tĭ)
sa·li·va   (sà·lī' và)
  sal·i·var·y   (săl' ĭ·vĕr' ĭ)
  sal·i·vate   (săl' ĭ·vāt)
  -vat·ing
  sal·i·va·tion   (săl' ĭ·vā' shŭn)
sal·low   (săl' ō)
sal·ma·gun·di   (săl' mà·gŭn' dĭ)
salm·on   (săm' ŭn)
sa·lon   (sá' lòn')
  (drawing room; see saloon)
sa·loon   (sà·loon')
  (alehouse; see salon)
sal so·da   (săl' sō' dà)
salt·cel·lar   (sôlt' sĕl' ĕr)
salt·pe·ter   (sôlt' pē' tĕr)
salt·y   (sôl' tĭ)
  salt·i·ness
sa·lu·bri·ous   (sà·lū' brĭ·ŭs)
sal·u·tar·y   (săl' û·tĕr' ĭ)

sa·lu·ta·to·ri·an
      (sȧ·lū′ tȧ·tō′ rĭ·ản)
sa·lute   (sȧ·lūt′)
  -lut·ing
  sal·u·ta·tion   (săl′ ů·tā′ shŭn)
sal·vage   (săl′ vĭj)
  (save; see *selvage*)
  -vag·ing
sal·va·tion   (săl·vā′ shŭn)
salve   (săv)
sal·vo   (săl′ vŏ)
  -vos
Sa·mar·i·tan   (sȧ·măr′ ĭ·tản)
same·ness   (sām′ nĕs)
Sa·mo·a   (sȧ·mō′ ȧ)
sam·o·var   (săm′ ŏ·vär)
sam·pan   (săm′ păn)
sam·ple   (săm′ p'l)
  -pling   sam·pler
sam·u·rai   (săm′ ŏŏ·rī)
san·a·to·ri·um (săn′ ȧ·tō′ rĭ·ŭm)
  pl. san·a·to·ri·a
sanc·ti·fy   (săngk′ tĭ·fī)
  -fied,   -fy·ing
sanc·ti·mo·ni·ous
      (săngk′ tĭ·mō′ nĭ·ŭs)
sanc·tion   (săngk′ shŭn)
sanc·ti·ty   (săngk′ tĭ·tĭ)
  -ties
sanc·tu·ar·y (săngk′ tů·ĕr′ ĭ)
  -ar·ies
sanc·tum sanc·to·rum
   (săngk′ tŭm săngk·tō′ rŭm)
sand   (sănd)
  sand·bag   sand bar
  sand·blast sand·bur
  sand-lot base·ball
  sand·pa·per sand·stone
  sand·storm
san·dal   (săn′ dǎl)
  san·dal·wood
sand·wich   (sănd′ wĭch)
sane   (sān)
  sane·ly
San·for·ized (săn′ fēr·ĭzd)
San Fran·cis·co,
  Calif.   (săn′ frản·sĭs′ kō)
sang-froid (säN′ frwä′)
san·guine   (săng′ gwĭn)
  san·gui·nar·y (săng′ gwĭ·nĕr′ ĭ)
  san·guin·e·ous
      (săng·gwĭn′ ê·ŭs)
san·i·tar·i·um (săn′ ĭ·târ′ ĭ·ŭm)
san·i·tar·y (săn′ ĭ·tĕr′ ĭ)
san·i·ta·tion (săn′ ĭ·tā′ shŭn)

san·i·ty   (săn′ ĭ·tĭ)
San·skrit   (săn′ skrĭt)
sans-ser·if (sănz′ sĕr′ ĭf)
San·ta Claus (săn′ tȧ klôz)
San·ti·a·go, Chile
      (săn′ tĭ·ä′ gō)
São Pau·lo, Bra·zil
      (souN pou′ lōō)
sa·pi·ent   (sā′ pĭ·ĕnt)
  -ence
sap·o·dil·la (săp′ ŏ·dĭl′ ȧ)
sap·phire   (săf′ īr)
sap·sa·go   (săp′ sȧ·gō)
Sar·a·cen   (săr′ ȧ·sĕn)
sar·casm   (săr′ kăz′m)
  sar·cas·tic (sär·kăs′ tĭk)
sar·coph·a·gus
      (sär·kŏf′ ȧ·gŭs)
  pl. sar·coph·a·gi (-jī)
sar·dine   (sär·dēn′)
sar·don·ic (sär·dŏn′ ĭk)
  sar·don·i·cal·ly
sar·gas·so (sär·găs′ ō)
sa·ri   (sä′ rē)
sa·rong   (sȧ·rông′)
sar·sa·pa·ril·la
      (săs′ pȧ·rĭl′ ȧ)
sar·to·ri·al (sär·tō′ rĭ·ǎl)
Sas·katch·e·wan,
  Can.   (săs·kăch′ ĕ·wŏn)
sas·sa·fras (săs′ ȧ·frăs)
Sa·tan   (sā′ tản)
  sa·tan·ic (sȧ·tăn′ ĭk)
satch·el   (săch′ ĕl)
sate   (sāt)
  sat·ing
sa·teen   (sȧ·tēn′)
sat·el·lite (săt′ ĕ·līt)
sa·ti·ate   (sā′ shĭ·āt)
  -at·ing
  sa·ti·a·ble (sā′ shĭ·ȧ·b'l)
  sa·ti·e·ty (sȧ·tī′ ĕ·tĭ)
sat·in   (săt′ ĭn)
sat·ire   (săt′ īr)
  sa·tir·ic (sȧ·tĭr′ ĭk)
sat·i·rist (săt′ ĭ·rĭst)
sat·i·rize (săt′ ĭ·rīz)
  -riz·ing
sat·is·fac·tion (săt′ ĭs·făk′ shŭn)
sat·is·fac·to·ry
      (săt′ ĭs·făk′ tŏ·rĭ)
  sat·is·fac·to·ri·ly, -i·ness
sat·is·fy   (săt′ ĭs·fī)
  -fied   -fy·ing

sat·u·rate   (săt′ ū·rāt)
  -rat·ing
sat·u·ra·tion   (săt′ ū·rā′ shŭn)
sat·ur·nine   (săt′ ēr·nīn)
sat·yr   (săt′ ēr)
sauce   (sôs)
  sauce·pan   sau·cer
  sau·cy
Sa·u·di A·ra·bi·a
       (sả·ōō′ dĭ ả·rā′ bĭ·ả)
sauer·kraut   (sour′ krout′)
Sault Sainte Ma·rie,
  Mich.   (sōō′ sănt mả·rē′)
saun·ter   (sôn′ tēr)
sau·sage   (sô·sĭj)
sau·té   (sō·tā′)
  sau·téed   sau·té·ing
sau·terne   (sō·tûrn′)
sav·age   (săv′ ĭj)
  sav·age·ly
  sav·age·ry   (săv′ ĭj·rĭ)
sa·van·na   (sả·văn′ ả)
Sa·van·nah, Ga.
       (sả·văn′ ả)
sa·vant   (sả·vănt′)
sav·ior   (săv′ yēr)
sa·voir-faire   (sả′ vwàr′ fâr′)
sa·vor   (sā′ vēr)
  -vored   -vor·ing
  sa·vor·less   sa·vor·y
sa·voy cab·bage
       (sả·voi′)
saw·mill   (sô′ mĭl′)
saw-toothed   (sô′ tōōtht′)
saw·yer   (sô′ yēr)
sax·o·phone   (săk′ sồ·fōn)
scab·bard   (skăb′ ērd)
sca·brous   (skā′ brŭs)
scaf·fold·ing   (skăf′ ŭld·ĭng)
scal·a·wag   (skăl′ ả·wăg)
scald   (skôld)
scale   (skāl)
  scal·ing   scal·a·ble
scal·lion   (skăl′ yŭn)
scal·lop   (skŏl′ ŭp)
  scal·loped
scalp   (skălp)
scal·pel   (skăl′ pĕl)
scal·y   (skāl′ ĭ)
  scal·i·ness
scam·per   (skăm′ pēr)
scan   (skăn)
  scanned   scan·ning
scan·dal   (skăn′ dắl)
  scan·dal·ize   -iz·ing

scan·dal·mon·ger   (-mŭng′ gēr)
scan·dal·ous   (-ŭs)
Scan·di·na·vi·an
       (skăn′ dĭ·nā′ vĭ·ẩn)
scant·y   (skăn′ tĭ)
  scant·i·ly   -i·ness
scape·goat   (skāp′ gōt′)
scar   (skär)
  scarred   scar·ring
scarce   (skârs)
  scarce·ly
  scar·ci·ty   (skâr′ sĭ·tĭ)
scare   (skâr)
  scar·ing   scare·crow
  scar·y
scarf   (skärf)
  pl. scarves
scar·let   (skär′ lĕt)
scathe   (skāth)
  scath·ing·ly
scat·ter·brain   (skăt′ ēr·brān′)
scav·enge   (skăv′ ĕnj)
  -eng·ing   scav·en·ger
sce·nar·i·o   (sē·nâr′ ĭ·ō)
  sce·nar·ist   (sē·nâr′ ĭst)
scene   (sēn)
  scen·er·y   (sēn′ ēr·ĭ)
  sce·nic   (sē′ nĭk)
scent   (sĕnt)
scep·ter   (sĕp′ tēr)
sched·ule   (skĕd′ ūl)
  -ul·ing
scheme   (skēm)
  schem·ing
  sche·mat·ic   (skē·măt′ ĭk)
  schem·er
Sche·nec·ta·dy,   (skē·nĕk′ tả·dĭ)
  N. Y.
scher·zo   (skĕr′ tsō)
schism   (sĭz′m)
  schis·mat·ic   (sĭz·măt′ ĭk)
schist   (shĭst)
schiz·oid   (skĭz′ oid)
schiz·o·phre·ni·a
       (skĭz′ ồ·frē′ nĭ·ả)
  schiz·o·phren·ic   (-frĕn′ ĭk)
schmaltz   (shmôlts)
schnapps   (shnäps)
schnau·zer   (shnou′ zēr)
schol·ar   (skŏl′ ēr)
  schol·ar·ship
scho·las·tic   (skồ·lăs′ tĭk)
  scho·las·ti·cism
       (skồ·lăs′ tĭ·sĭz′m)

school (skōōl)
  school·boy   school·house
  school·mas·ter   school·room
  school·teach·er
  school·work
schoon·er (skōōn′ ẽr)
schot·tische (shŏt′ ĭsh)
schuss (shōōs)
Schwei·tzer, Al·bert
      (shvī′ tsẽr)
sci·at·i·ca (sī·ăt′ ĭ·ká)
  sci·at·ic nerve
sci·ence (sī′ ĕns)
  sci·en·tif·ic (sī′ ĕn·tĭf′ ĭk)
  -i·cal·ly   sci·en·tist
scim·i·tar (sĭm′ ĭ·tẽr)
scin·til·late (sĭn′ tĭ·lāt)
  -til·lat·ing
  scin·til·la·tion (sĭn′ tĭ·lā′ shŭn)
sci·on (sī′ ŭn)
scis·sors (sĭz′ ẽrz)
scle·ro·sis (sklĕ·rō′ sĭs)
scoff (skŏf)
scone (skōn)
scoot·er (skōōt′ ẽr)
scope (skōp)
scorch (skôrch)
scorn·ful (skôrn′ fōōl)
  -ful·ly   -ful·ness
Scor·pi·o (skôr′ pĭ·ō)
scor·pi·on (skôr′ pĭ·ŭn)
Scotch (skŏch)
scot-free (skŏt′ frē′)
Scots·man (skŏts′ mán)
Scot·tish (skŏt′ ĭsh)
scoun·drel (skoun′ drĕl)
  scoun·drel·ly
scour (skour)
scourge (skûrj)
scout·mas·ter (skout′ más′ tẽr)
scowl (skoul)
  scowled   scowl·ing
scrab·ble (skrăb′ 'l)
scrag·gy (skrăg′ ĭ)
scram·ble (skrăm′ b'l)
  -bling
scrap·book (skrăp′ bōōk′)
scrap·py (skrăp′ ĭ)
scratch (skrăch)
scrawl (skrôl)
  scrawl·y
scraw·ny (skrô′ nĭ)
scream (skrēm)
screech (skrēch)
screen·play (skrēn′ plā′)

screw (skrōō)
scrib·ble (skrĭb′ 'l)
  scrib·bling
scribe (skrīb)
scrim·mage (skrĭm′ ĭj)
  scrim·mag·ing
scrimp (skrĭmp)
scrip (skrĭp)
  (money; see *script*)
script (skrĭpt)
  (manuscript; see *scrip*)
  script-writ·er
scrip·ture (skrĭp′ tụr)
  scrip·tur·al
scroll (skrōl)
scrounge (skrounj)
  scroung·ing
scrub·by (skrŭb′ ĭ)
scruff (skrŭf)
scru·ple (skrōō′ p'l)
  scru·pu·lous (skrōō′ pụ·lŭs)
scru·ti·ny (skrōō′ tĭ·nĭ)
  -nies
  scru·ti·nize   -niz·ing
scuff (skŭf)
scuf·fle (skŭf′ 'l)
  scuf·fling
scul·ler·y (skŭl′ ẽr·ĭ)
scul·lion (skŭl′ yŭn)
sculp·tor (skŭlp′ tẽr)
  sculp·tress   sculp·ture
  sculp·tur·al
scum (skŭm)
  scum·my
scup·per·nong (skŭp′ ẽr·nŏng)
scur·ril·ous (skŭr′ ĭ·lŭs)
scur·ry (skûr′ ĭ)
  scur·ried   scur·ry·ing
scur·vy (skûr′ vĭ)
scut·tle (skŭt′ 'l)
  scut·tling
  scut·tle·butt (skŭt′ 'l·bŭt′)
scythe (sīth)
sea (sē)
  sea·board   sea·coast
  sea·far·ing   sea·go·ing
  sea gull   sea·man
  sea·plane   sea·scape
  sea·shore   sea·sick·ness
  sea·side   sea ur·chin
  sea wall   sea·ward
  sea·wor·thy
seal·skin (sēl′ skĭn′)
seam (sēm)
  seam·less   seam·y

seam·stress (sēm′ strĕs)
sé·ance (sā′ äns′)
sear (sẽr)
search (sûrch)
  search·light   search war·rant
sea·son (sē′ z′n)
  sea·son·a·ble
  sea·son·al   -al·ly
  sea·son·ing   sea·son tick·et
Se·at·tle, Wash. (sē·ăt′ ′l)
se·cede (sē·sēd′)
  -ced·ing
se·ces·sion (sē·sĕsh′ ŭn)
  se·ces·sion·ist
se·clude (sē·klo͞od′)
  -clud·ing
  se·clu·sion (-klo͞o′ zhŭn)
sec·ond (sĕk′ ŭnd)
  sec·ond·ar·y   sec·ond-class
  sec·ond fid·dle sec·ond·hand
  sec·ond na·ture
  sec·ond-rate   sec·ond sight
se·cret (sē′ krĕt)
  se·cre·cy (sē′ krĕ·sĭ)
  se·cre·tive (sē·krē′ tĭv)
sec·re·tar·i·at (sĕk′ rĕ·târ′ ĭ·ăt)
sec·re·tar·y (sĕk′ rĕ·tĕr′ ĭ)
  -tar·ies
  sec·re·tar·i·al (sĕk′ rĕ·târ′ ĭ·ăl)
  sec·re·tar·y·ship
se·crete (sē·krēt′)
  -cret·ing
  se·cre·tion (sē·krē′ shŭn)
se·cre·tive (sē·krē′ tĭv)
sect (sĕkt)
sec·tar·i·an (sĕk·târ′ ĭ·ăn)
sec·tion (sĕk′ shŭn)
  sec·tion·al
sec·tor (sĕk′ tĕr)
sec·u·lar (sĕk′ û·lĕr)
  sec·u·lar·ize   -iz·ing
se·cure (sē·kūr′)
  -cur·ing
  se·cure·ly   -cure·ness
  se·cu·ri·ty   -ties
se·dan (sē·dăn′)
se·date (sē·dāt′)
  se·date·ly
se·da·tion (sē·dā′ shŭn)
sed·a·tive (sĕd′ à·tĭv)
sed·en·tar·y (sĕd′ ĕn·tĕr′ ĭ)
sedge (sĕj)
sed·i·ment (sĕd′ ĭ·mĕnt)
  sed·i·men·ta·ry
        (sĕd′ ĭ·mĕn′ tá·rĭ)

sed·i·men·ta·tion
        (sĕd′ ĭ·mĕn·tā′ shŭn)
se·di·tion (sē·dĭsh′ ŭn)
se·di·tious (-ŭs)
se·duce (sē·dūs′)
  -duc·ing   se·duce·ment
  se·duc·i·ble
se·duc·tion (sē·dŭk′ shŭn)
  se·duc·tive   -tive·ly
  se·duc·tress
sed·u·lous (sĕd′ û·lŭs)
seed·ling (sēd′ lĭng)
seed·y (sēd′ ĭ)
  seed·i·ness
see·ing (sē′ ĭng)
seem·ing·ly (sēm′ ĭng·lĭ)
seem·ly (sēm′ lĭ)
  seem·li·ness
seep·age (sēp′ ĭj)
se·er (sē′ ĕr)
seer·suck·er (sẽr′ sŭk′ ŏr)
see·saw (sē′ sô′)
seethe (sēth)
  seeth·ing
seg·ment (sĕg′ mĕnt)
  seg·men·tar·y
  seg·men·ta·tion
        (sĕg′ mĕn·tā′ shŭn)
seg·re·gate (sĕg′ rĕ·gāt)
  -gat·ing
  seg·re·ga·tion (sĕg′ rĕ·gā′ shŭn)
seine (sān)
  sein·ing
seis·mo·graph (sīz′ mŏ·gráf)
seize (sēz)
  seiz·ing   seiz·a·ble
  sei·zure (sē″ zhĕr)
sel·dom (sĕl′ dŭm)
se·lect (sē·lĕkt′)
  se·lec·tee (sē·lĕk′ tē′)
  se·lec·tion   se·lec·tive
  se·lec·tiv·i·ty (sē·lĕk′ tĭv′ ĭ·tĭ)
se·le·ni·um (sē·lē′ nĭ·ŭm)
self (sĕlf)
  self-a·base·ment
  self-ad·dressed
  self-cen·tered
  self-con·fi·dence
  self-con·scious
  self-con·trol
  self-de·ni·al
  self-dis·ci·pline
  self-ev·i·dent
  self-ex·plan·a·to·ry
  self-ex·pres·sion

self-ful·fill·ment
self-in·dul·gence
self-made
self-pit·y
self-pres·er·va·tion
self-pro·tec·tion
self-re·li·ance
self-re·spect·ing
self-right·eous
self-sac·ri·fice
self·same
self-sat·is·fied
self-styled
self-sup·port·ing
sell·out   (sĕl′ out′)
Selt·zer wa·ter   (sĕlt′ sĕr)
sel·vage   (sĕl′ vĭj)
  (fabric edge; see *salvage*)
se·man·tics   (sĕ·măn′ tĭks)
sem·a·phore   (sĕm′ à·fōr)
sem·blance   (sĕm′ blăns)
se·men   (sē′ mĕn)
se·mes·ter   (sĕ·mĕs′ tĕr)
sem·i-   (sĕm′ ĭ-)
  sem·i·au·to·mat·ic
  sem·i·cir·cle   sem·i·co·lon
  sem·i·fi·nal·ist
  sem·i·month·ly
  sem·i·pre·cious
  sem·i·week·ly
sem·i·nal   (sĕm′ ĭ·nàl)
sem·i·nar   (sĕm′ ĭ·när′)
sem·i·nar·y   (sĕm′ ĭ·nĕr′ ĭ)
  -nar·ies
Sem·i·nole   (sĕm′ ĭ·nōl)
Se·mit·ic   (sĕ·mĭt′ ĭk)
sem·o·li·na   (sĕm′ ō·lē′ nà)
sen·ate   (sĕn′ ĭt)
  sen·a·tor   (sĕn′ à·tĕr)
  sen·a·to·ri·al   (sĕn′ à·tō′ rĭ·àl)
send-off   (sĕnd′ ôf′)
Sen·e·gal,   (sĕn′ ĕ·gôl′)
  Repub. of
se·nile   (sē′ nīl)
  se·nil·i·ty   (sĕ·nĭl′ ĭ·tĭ)
sen·ior   (sēn′ yĕr)
  sen·ior·i·ty   (sēn·yŏr′ ĭ·tĭ)
sen·na   (sĕn′ à)
se·ñor   (sā·nyôr′)
sen·sa·tion   (sĕn·sā′ shŭn)
  sen·sa·tion·al
sense   (sĕns)
  sens·ing   sense·less
sen·si·ble   (sĕn′ sĭ·b′l)
  sen·si·bil·i·ty   (sĕn′ sĭ·bĭl′ ĭ·tĭ)

sen·si·tive   (sĕn′ sĭ·tĭv)
  sen·si·tive·ness
  sen·si·tiv·i·ty   (sĕn′ sĭ·tĭv′ ĭ·tĭ)
sen·si·tize   (sĕn′ sĭ·tīz)
  -tiz·ing
sen·so·ry   (sĕn′ sŏ·rĭ)
sen·su·al   (sĕn′ shŏŏ·àl)
  -al·ly
  sen·su·al·i·ty
        (sĕn′ shŏŏ·ăl′ ĭ·tĭ)
  sen·su·ous
sen·tence   (sĕn′ tĕns)
sen·ten·tious   (sĕn·tĕn′ shŭs)
sen·tient   (sĕn′ shĕnt)
  sen·ti·ence   (sĕn′ shĭ·ĕns)
sen·ti·ment   (sĕn′ tĭ·mĕnt)
  sen·ti·men·tal   (sĕn′ tĭ·mĕn′ tàl)
  sen·ti·men·tal·i·ty
        (sĕn′ tĭ·mĕn·tăl′ ĭ·tĭ)
sen·ti·nel   (sĕn′ tĭ·nĕl)
sen·try   (sĕn′ trĭ)
  -tries
sep·a·ra·ble   (sĕp′ à·rà·b′l)
  sep·a·ra·bil·i·ty
        (sĕp′ à·rà·bĭl′ ĭ·tĭ)
sep·a·rate   (sĕp′ à·rāt)
  -rat·ing   sep·a·rate·ly
  sep·a·ra·tion   (sĕp′ à·rā′ shŭn)
  sep·a·ra·tist   (sĕp′ à·rā′ tĭst)
  sep·a·ra·tor   (sĕp′ à·rā′ tĕr)
se·pi·a   (sē′ pĭ·à)
Sep·tem·ber   (sĕp·tĕm′ bĕr)
sep·tet   (sĕp·tĕt′)
sep·tic   (sĕp′ tĭk)
sep·tu·a·ge·nar·i·an
      (sĕp′ tū·à·jĕ·nâr′ ĭ·àn)
sep·tum   (sĕp′ tŭm)
  pl. sep·ta
sep·ul·cher   (sĕp′ ŭl·kĕr)
  se·pul·chral   (sĕ·pŭl′ krà l)
se·quel   (sē′ kwĕl)
se·quence   (sē′ kwĕns)
  se·quen·tial   (sĕ·kwĕn′ shàl)
se·ques·ter   (sĕ·kwĕs′ tĕr)
  se·ques·tra·tion
      (sē′ kwĕs·trā′ shŭn)
se·quin   (sē′ kwĭn)
se·quoi·a   (sĕ·kwoi′ à)
se·ragl·io   (sĕ·răl′ yō)
se·ra·pe   (sĕ·rä′ pā)
ser·a·phim   (sĕr′ à·fĭm)
ser·e·nade   (sĕr′ ĕ·nād′)
  -nad·ing
ser·en·dip·i·ty   (sĕr′ ĕn·dĭp′ ĭ·tĭ)

se·rene (sĕ·rēn′)
  se·rene·ly
  se·ren·i·ty (sĕ·rĕn′ ĭ·tĭ)
serf·dom (sûrf′ dŭm)
serge (sûrj)
  (fabric; see *surge*)
ser·geant (sär′ jĕnt)
  ser·geant at arms
se·ri·al (sēr′ ĭ·ăl)
  (in a series; see *cereal*)
se·ri·al·i·za·tion
          (sēr′ ĭ·ăl·ĭ·zā′ shŭn)
  se·ri·al·ize -iz·ing
se·ries (sēr′ ēz)
  n. sing. & pl.
ser·if (sĕr′ ĭf)
se·ri·ous (sēr′ ĭ·ŭs)
ser·mon (sûr′ mŭn)
  ser·mon·ize -iz·ing
ser·pent (sûr′ pĕnt)
  ser·pen·tine (sûr′ pĕn·tēn)
ser·rat·ed (sĕr′ āt·ĕd)
se·rum (sēr′ ŭm)
serv·ant (sûr′ vănt)
serv·ice (sûr′ vĭs)
  -ic·ing
  serv·ice·a·bil·i·ty
          (sûr′ vĭs·à·bĭl′ ĭ·tĭ)
  serv·ice·a·ble (sûr′ vĭs·à·b′l)
  serv·ice·man serv·ice sta·tion
ser·vile (sûr′ vĭl)
  ser·vil·i·ty (sĕr·vĭl′ ĭ·tĭ)
ser·vi·tude (sûr′ vĭ·tūd)
ses·a·me seed (sĕs′ à·mē)
ses·qui·cen·ten·nial
     (sĕs′ kwĭ·sĕn·tĕn′ ĭ·ăl)
ses·sion (sĕsh′ ŭn)
  (meeting; see *cession*)
set (sĕt)
  set·back set·ter
  set·ting set-to
  set·up
set·tee (sĕ·tē′)
set·tle (sĕt′ ′l)
  set·tling set·tle·ment
  set·tler
sev·en·fold (sĕv′ ĕn·fōld′)
sev·en·teen (sĕv′ ĕn·tēn′)
sev·en·ty (sĕv′ ĕn·tĭ)
  -ties sev·en·ti·eth
sev·er (sĕv′ ēr)
  -ered -er·ing
sev·er·al (sĕv′ ēr·ăl)
  sev·er·al·ly
sev·er·ance (sĕv′ ēr·ăns)

se·vere (sĕ·vēr′)
  se·vere·ly
  se·ver·i·ty (sĕ·vĕr′ ĭ·tĭ)
sew·age (sū′ ĭj)
sew·er (sū′ ēr)
sewn (sōn)
sex·tet (sĕks·tĕt′)
sex·ton (sĕks′ tŭn)
sex·u·al (sĕk′ shōō·ăl)
  -al·ly
  sex·u·al·i·ty
      (sĕk′ shōō·ăl′ ĭ·tĭ)
shab·by (shăb′ ĭ)
  shab·bi·ly shab·bi·ness
shack·le (shăk′ ′l)
  shack·ling
shad·dock (shăd′ ŭk)
shad·ow (shăd′ ō)
  shad·ow·box shad·ow·y
shad·y (shād′ ĭ)
  shad·i·ness
shaft (shàft)
shag (shăg)
  shag·gy shag rug
shah (shä)
shake (shāk)
  shak·ing shak·a·ble
  shake·down shake-up
Shake·speare, Wil·liam
       (shāk′ spēr)
  Shake·spear·e·an
      (shāk·spēr′ ē·ăn)
shak·y (shāk′ ĭ)
  shak·i·ness
shale (shāl)
shal·lot (shà·lŏt′)
shal·low (shăl′ ō)
sha·man (shä′ măn)
sham·bles (shăm′ b′lz)
shame (shām)
  sham·ing shame·faced
  shame·fac·ed·ly
  shame·ful, -ful·ly, -ful·ness
  shame·less
sham·poo (shăm·pōō′)
  -pooed -poo·ing
sham·rock (shăm′ rŏk)
shang·hai (shăng·hī′)
  -haied -hai·ing
Shan·gri-La (shăng′ grē·lä′)
Shan·tung (shăn·tŭng′)
shan·ty (shăn′ tĭ)
  -ties
shape·less (shāp′ lĕs)

shape·ly (shāp'lĭ)
  shape·li·ness
share·crop·per (shâr' krŏp' ẽr)
share·hold·er (shâr' hōl' dẽr)
shark·skin (shärk' skĭn')
sharp (shärp)
  sharp·en·er sharp-eyed
  sharp·shoot·er sharp-sight·ed
  sharp-wit·ted
Shas·ta dai·sy (shăs' tȧ)
shat·ter (shăt' ẽr)
Sha·vi·an (shā' vĭ·ȧn)
shawl (shôl)
Shaw·nee (shô·nē')
sheaf (shēf)
  pl. sheaves (shēvz)
shear (shẽr)
  (to cut; see *sheer*)
  shorn
sheath (shēth) *n.*
sheathe (shēth) *v.*
  sheath·ing
shed (shĕd)
  shed·ding
sheen (shēn)
sheep (shēp)
  sheep·herd·er sheep·ish
  sheep·shank sheeps·head
  sheep·shear·ing
  sheep·skin
sheer (shẽr)
  (transparent; see *shear*)
sheet (shēt)
sheik (shēk)
  sheik·dom
shelf (shĕlf)
  pl. shelves
shell (shĕl)
  shell·fire shell·fish
  shell shock
shel·lac (shĕ·lăk')
  shel·lacked shel·lack·ing
shel·ter (shĕl' tẽr)
shelve (shĕlv)
  shelv·ing
Shen·an·do·ah riv.
  (shĕn' ȧn·dō' ȧ)
she·nan·i·gans
  (shė·năn' ĭ·gȧnz)
shep·herd (shĕp' ẽrd)
sher·bet (shûr' bĕt)
sher·iff (shĕr' ĭf)
sher·ry (shĕr' ĭ)
  sher·ries

Shet·land po·ny
  (shĕt' lȧnd)
shib·bo·leth (shĭb' ō·lĕth)
shield (shēld)
shift·less (shĭft' lĕs)
shift·y (shĭf' tĭ)
  shift·i·ness
shil·le·lagh (shĭ·lā' lĕ)
shil·ling (shĭl' ĭng)
shil·ly-shal·ly (shĭl' ĭ·shăl' ĭ)
shim·mer (shĭm' ẽr)
shim·my (shĭm' ĭ)
shine (shīn)
  shin·ing shin·y
  shone
shin·gle (shĭng' g'l)
  -gling
Shin·to (shĭn' tō')
  Shin·to·ist
ship (shĭp)
  shipped ship·ping
  ship·board ship·load
  ship·mate ship·pa·ble
  ship·shape ship·wreck
shirk (shûrk)
  shirk·er
shirr (shûr)
shirt·waist (shûrt' wăst')
shiv·er (shĭv' ẽr)
  -ered, -er·ing shiv·er·y
shoal (shōl)
shock (shŏk)
  shock ab·sorb·er
  shock ther·a·py
shod·dy (shŏd' ĭ)
  shod·di·ness
shoe (shōō)
  shoe·ing shoe·horn
  shoe·lace shoe·mak·er
  shoe·shop shoe·string
  shoe tree
shop (shŏp)
  shopped shop·ping
  shop·keep·er shop·lift·er
  shop·walk·er shop·win·dow
  shop·worn
shorn (shōrn)
short (shôrt)
  short·cake short·change
  short cir·cuit short·com·ing
  short cut short·hand
  short·hand·ed short·horn
  short-lived (shôrt' līvd')
  short shrift short·sight·ed
  short·stop short sto·ry

short·tem·pered	
short-term	short-wave *adj.*
short-wind·ed	
short·age	(shôrt′ ĭj)
short·en·ing	(shôr′ t'n·ĭng)
shot·gun	(shŏt′ gŭn′)
shot-put	(shŏt′ pŏŏt′)
should	(shŏŏd)
should·n't	
shoul·der	(shōl′ dẽr)
shout	(shout)
shove	(shŭv)
shov·ing	
shov·el	(shŭv′ 'l)
-eled	-el·ing
show	(shō)
show bill	show·boat
show·case	show·down
show·man·ship	
show-off	show·room
show·er	(shou′ ẽr)
show·er·y	
show·y	(shō′ ĭ)
show·i·ly	-i·ness
shrank	(shrăngk)
shrap·nel	(shrăp′ něl)
shred	(shrĕd)
shred·ded	shred·ding
shred·der	
shrew	(shrōō)
shrew·ish	
shrewd	(shrōōd)
shriek	(shrēk)
shrift	(shrĭft)
shrike	(shrīk)
shrill	(shrĭl)
shrimp	(shrĭmp)
shrine	(shrīn)
Shrin·er	
shrink	(shrĭngk)
shrink·age	(shrĭngk′ ĭj)
shrunk·en	
shriv·el	(shrĭv′ 'l)
-eled	-el·ing
shroud	(shroud)
shrub	(shrŭb)
shrub·ber·y	
shrunk·en	(shrŭngk′ ĕn)
shuck	(shŭk)
shud·der	(shŭd′ ẽr)
shuf·fle	(shŭf′ 'l)
shuf·fling	shuf·fle·board
shun	(shŭn)
shunned	shun·ning
shunt	(shŭnt)

shut·down	(shŭt′ doun′)
shut-in	(shŭt′ ĭn′)
shut·out	(shŭt′ out′)
shut·ter	(shŭt′ ẽr)
shut·tle·cock	(shŭt′ 'l·kŏk′)
shy	(shī)
shied	shy·ing
shi·er	shy·ly
shy·ness	
shy·ster	(shī′ stẽr)
Si·a·mese cat	(sī′ ȧ·mēz′)
sib·i·lant	(sĭb′ ɩ·lȧnt)
-lance	
sib·ling	(sĭb′ lĭng)
sick	(sĭk)
sick·bed	sick·en·ing
sick·ly	-li·ness
sick·ness	
side	(sīd)
sid·ing	side·board
side·burns	side·car
side is·sue	side·light
side·long	side·split·ting
side-step	side stroke
side·swipe	side·track
side·walk	side·ways
side·wind·er	
si·de·re·al	(sī·dẽr′ ĕ·ȧl)
si·dle	(sī′ d'l)
-dling	
siege	(sēj)
si·er·ra	(sī·ĕr′ ȧ)
si·es·ta	(sī·ĕs′ tȧ)
sieve	(sĭv)
sift	(sĭft)
sigh	(sī)
sight	(sīt)
(view; see *cite, site*)	
sight bill	sight·less
sight·ly	-li·ness
sign	(sīn)
sign·board	sign·post
sig·nal	(sĭg′ nȧl)
sig·nal·ize	-iz·ing
sig·nal·man	
sig·na·to·ry	(sĭg′ nȧ·tō′ rĭ)
sig·na·ture	(sĭg′ nȧ·tụr)
sig·net ring	(sĭg′ nĕt)
sig·nif·i·cant	(sĭg·nĭf′ ɩ·kȧnt)
-cance	
sig·ni·fi·ca·tion	
	(sĭg′ nĭ·fĭ·kā′ shŭn)
sig·ni·fy	(sĭg′ nĭ·fī)
-fied	-fy·ing
si·lage	(sī′ lĭj)

si·lence (sī′ lĕns)
  si·lenc·er   si·lent
sil·hou·ette (sĭl′ ŏŏ·ĕt′)
sil·i·ca gel (sĭl′ ĭ·kȧ)
sil·i·cate (sĭl′ ĭ·kȧt)
sil·i·con (sĭl′ ĭ·kŏn)
silk·en (sĭl′ kĕn)
silk·y (sĭl′ kĭ)
  silk·i·ly   -i·ness
sil·ly (sĭl′ ĭ)
  sil·li·ness
si·lo (sī′ lō)
  -los
sil·ver·ware (sĭl′ vĕr·wâr′)
sim·i·an (sĭm′ ĭ·ăn)
sim·i·lar (sĭm′ ĭ·lẽr)
  sim·i·lar·i·ty (sĭm′ ĭ·lăr′ ĭ·tĭ)
sim·i·le (sĭm′ ĭ·lē)
si·mil·i·tude (sĭ·mĭl′ ĭ·tūd)
sim·mer (sĭm′ ẽr)
sim·o·ny (sĭm′ ō·nĭ)
sim·ple (sĭm′ p′l)
  sim·plic·i·ty (sĭm·plĭs′ ĭ·tĭ)
  sim·pli·fi·ca·tion
    (sĭm′ plĭ·fĭ·kā′ shŭn)
  sim·pli·fy, -fied, -fy·ing
  sim·ply
sim·u·late (sĭm′ û·lāt)
  -lat·ing
  sim·u·la·tion (sĭm′ û·lā′ shŭn)
si·mul·ta·ne·ous
    (sī′ mŭl·tā′ nė·ŭs)
since (sĭns)
sin·cere (sĭn·sẽr′)
  sin·cere·ly
  sin·cer·i·ty (sĭn·sĕr′ ĭ·tĭ)
si·ne·cure (sī′ nė·kūr)
sin·ew (sĭn′ ū)
  sin·ew·y
sin·ful (sĭn′ fŏŏl)
  -ful·ly   -ful·ness
sing (sĭng)
  sing·a·ble
singe (sĭnj)
  singe·ing
sin·gle (sĭng′ g′l)
  sin·gle-breast·ed
  sin·gle file   sin·gle·hand·ed
  sin·gle-mind·ed
  sin·gle·ness   sin·gly
sin·gle·ton (sĭng′ g′l·tŭn)
sing·song (sĭng′ sŏng′)
sin·gu·lar (sĭng′ gû·lẽr)
  sin·gu·lar·i·ty
    (sĭng′ gû·lăr′ ĭ·tĭ)

sin·is·ter (sĭn′ ĭs·tẽr)
sink·age (sĭngk′ ĭj)
sin·ner (sĭn′ ẽr)
sin·u·ous (sĭn′ û·ŭs)
si·nus (sī′ nŭs)
  si·nus·i·tis (sī′ nŭs·ī′ tĭs)
Sioux Cit·y, Ia. (sŏŏ)
si·phon (sī′ fŏn)
si·ren (sī′ rĕn)
sir·loin (sûr′ loin′)
si·roc·co (sĭ·rŏk′ ō)
sir·up (sĭr′ ŭp)
  sir·up·y
si·sal (sī′ sȧl)
sis·ter-in-law (sĭs′ tẽr·ĭn·lô′)
  pl. sis·ters-in-law
site (sīt)
  (location; see *sight, cite*)
sit·ter (sĭt′ ẽr)
sit·u·ate (sĭt′ û·āt)
  -at·ing
  sit·u·a·tion (sĭt′ û·ā′ shŭn)
sitz bath (sĭts)
six·pence (sĭks′ pĕns)
six·teenth (sĭks′ tēnth′)
sixth (sĭksth)
six·ty (sĭks′ tĭ)
  -ties   six·ti·eth
size (sīz)
  siz·ing   siz·a·ble
siz·zle (sĭz′ ′l)
  siz·zling
skate (skāt)
  skat·ing
skeet (skēt)
skein (skān)
skel·e·ton (skĕl′ ĕ·tŭn)
  skel·e·tal
sketch (skĕch)
  sketch·book   sketch·y
skew·er (skū′ ẽr)
ski (skē)
  skied   ski·ing
  ski·er
skill (skĭl)
  skill·ful, -ful·ly, -ful·ness
skim milk (skĭm)
skimp·y (skĭmp′ ĭ)
  skimp·i·ness
skin (skĭn)
  skinned,   skin·ning
  skin-deep   skin div·ing
  skin·flint   skin·tight
skin·ny (skĭn′ ĭ)
  skin·ni·ness

skip·per (skĭp' ẽr)
skir·mish (skûr' mĭsh)
skirt (skûrt)
skit·tish (skĭt' ĭsh)
skit·tles (skĭt' 'lz)
skul·dug·ger·y (skŭl·dŭg' ẽr·ĭ)
skulk (skŭlk)
skull (skŭl)
  skull·cap
skunk (skŭngk)
sky (skī)
  skies sky·lark
  sky·light sky line
  sky·scrap·er sky·ward
  sky·writ·ing
slack (slăk)
  slack·en
slake (slāk)
  slak·ing
sla·lom (slä' lŭm)
slan·der (slăn' dẽr)
  slan·der·er slan·der·ous
slant·wise (slănt' wīz')
slap·dash (slăp' dăsh')
slap·stick (slăp' stĭk')
slat·tern·ly (slăt' ẽrn·lĭ)
slaugh·ter (slô' tẽr)
  slaugh·ter·house
Slav (släv)
slave (slāv)
  slav·ing slave·hold·er
  slav·er·y slav·ey
  slav·ish
slay·er (slā' ẽr)
slea·zy (slā' zĭ)
sled·ding (slĕd' ĭng)
sledge ham·mer
  (slĕj)
sleek (slēk)
sleep (slēp)
  sleep·walk·er sleep·i·ly
  sleep·i·ness sleep·y
sleet (slēt)
sleeve (slēv)
  sleeve·less
sleigh (slā)
sleight of hand (slīt)
slen·der·ize (slĕn' dẽr·ĭz)
  -iz·ing
sleuth (slōōth)
slew (slōō)
  (killed; see *slough*)
slice (slīs)
  slic·ing
slick·er (slĭk' ẽr)

slight (slīt)
slime (slīm)
  slim·y
sling·shot (slĭng' shŏt')
slink·y (slĭngk' ĭ)
slip·knot (slĭp' nŏt')
slip·page (slĭp' ĭj)
slip·per·y (slĭp' ẽr·ĭ)
  slip·per·i·ness
slip·shod (slĭp' shŏd')
sliv·er (slĭv' ẽr)
sloe-eyed (slō' ĭd')
sloe gin (slō)
slo·gan (slō' găn)
sloop (slōōp)
slope (slōp)
  slop·ing
slop·py (slŏp' ĭ)
  slop·pi·ly slop·pi·ness
sloth·ful (slŏth' fōōl)
slouch (slouch)
slough
  (when pron. slŭf, means to cast
  off; when pron. slōō, means
  swamp or inlet; see *slew*)
Slo·vak (slō' văk)
slov·en·ly (slŭv' ĕn·lĭ)
  slov·en·li·ness
slow·down (slō' doun')
sludge (slŭj)
slug·gard (slŭg' ẽrd)
slug·gish (slŭg' ĭsh)
sluice (slōōs)
  sluic·ing
slum·ber (slŭm' bẽr)
  slum·ber·ous
slur (slûr)
  slurred slur·ring
sly (slī)
  sli·est sly·ness
smack (smăk)
small (smôl)
  small change small-mind·ed
  small·pox small talk
smart (smärt)
smash·up (smăsh' ŭp')
smat·ter·ing (smăt' ẽr·ĭng)
smear (smẽr)
smel·ling salts (smĕl' ĭng)
smelt (smĕlt)
smelt·er (smĕl' tẽr)
smile (smīl)
  smil·ing
smirch (smûrch)
smirk (smûrk)

smite   (smīt)
  smit·ing
  smit·ten   (smĭt' 'n)
smith·er·eens   (smĭth' ĕr·ēnz')
smock   (smŏk)
smog   (smŏg)
smoke   (smōk)
  smok·ing
  smoke screen   smoke·stack
  smok·y
smol·der   (smōl' dĕr)
smooth   (smōōth)
smor·gas·bord   (smôr' gäs·bôrd')
smoth·er   (smŭth' ĕr)
smudge   (smŭj)
  smudg·ing   smudg·y
smug   (smŭg)
  snug·gest   smug·ly
smug·gle   (smŭg' 'l)
  smug·gling   smug·gler
smut   (smŭt)
  smut·ty
snack   (snăk)
sna·fu   (snă·fōō')
 -fued   -fu·ing
snail   (snāl)
  snail-paced
snap·drag·on   (snăp' drăg' ŭn)
snap·per   (snăp' ĕr)
snap·shot   (snăp' shŏt')
snare drum   (snâr)
snarl·ing   (snärl' ĭng)
sneak·ers   (snēk' ĕrz)
sneak·y   (snēk' ĭ)
  sneak·i·ly
sneer·ing   (snēr' ĭng)
sneeze   (snēz)
  sneez·ing
snick·er   (snĭk' ĕr)
snif·fle   (snĭf' 'l)
  snif·fling
snip·pet   (snĭp' ĕt)
snitch   (snĭch)
sniv·el   (snĭv' 'l)
 -eled   -el·ing
snob   (snŏb)
  snob·ber·y   snob·bish
snoop·y   (snōōp' ĭ)
snooze   (snōōz)
  snooz·ing
snore   (snōr)
  snor·ing
snor·kel   (snôr' kĕl)
snout   (snout)

snow   (snō)
  snow·ball   snow·bound
  snow-blind   snow-capped
  snow·drift   snow·flake
  snow·plow   snow·shoe
  snow·storm   snow·y
snug·gle   (snŭg' 'l)
  snug·gling
so-and-so   (sō' ănd·sō')
soap   (sōp)
  soap·box   soap op·e·ra
  soap·suds
soar·ing   (sōr' ĭng)
so·be·it   (sō·bē' ĭt)
so·ber   (sō' bĕr)
so·bri·e·ty   (sō·brī' ĕ·tĭ)
so·bri·quet   (sō' brĭ·kā)
so-called   (sō' kôld')
soc·cer   (sŏk' ĕr)
so·cia·ble   (sō' shả·b'l)
  so·cia·bil·i·ty   (sō' shả·bĭl' ĭ·tĭ)
so·cial   (sō' shảl)
  so·cial·ism
  so·cial·is·tic   (sō' shảl·ĭs' tĭk)
  so·cial·ite   (sō' shảl·īt)
  so·cial·ized
so·ci·e·ty   (sō·sī' ĕ·tĭ)
 -ties
  so·ci·e·tal   (sō·sī' ĕ·tảl)
so·ci·ol·o·gy   (sō' sĭ·ŏl' ŏ·jĭ)
  so·ci·o·log·i·cal
              (sō' sĭ·ô·lŏj' ĭ·kảl)
  so·ci·ol·o·gist   (sō' sĭ·ŏl' ŏ·jĭst)
sock·et   (sŏk' ĕt)
Soc·ra·tes   (sŏk' rả·tēz)
  So·crat·ic   (sō·krăt' ĭk)
so·dal·i·ty   (sō·dăl' ĭ·tĭ)
 -ties
sod·den   (sŏd' 'n)
  sod·den·ness
so·di·um   (sō' dĭ·ŭm)
  so·di·um bi·car·bon·ate
  so·di·um car·bon·ate
  so·di·um chlo·ride
  so·di·um hy·drox·ide
  so·di·um ni·trate
Sod·om   (sŏd' ŭm)
  (and Gomorrah)
sod·om·y   (sŏd' ŭm·ĭ)
soft   (sŏft)
  soft·ball   soft·heart·ed
  soft-ped·al   soft-shell
  soft-soap   soft-spo·ken
sog·gy   (sŏg' ĭ)
  sog·gi·ness

soil·age (soil′ ĭj)
soi·ree (swä·rā′)
so·journ (sō·jûrn′)
sol·ace (sŏl′ ĭs)
so·lar (sō′ lẽr)
  so·lar·i·um (sō·lâr′ ĭ·ŭm)
  so·lar plex·us
sol·der·ing i·ron
          (sŏd′ ẽr·ĭng)
sol·dier (sōl′ jẽr)
sole (sōl)
  sole·ly
sol·e·cism (sŏl′ ĕ·sĭz′m)
sol·emn (sŏl′ ĕm)
  so·lem·ni·ty (sō·lĕm′ nĭ·tĭ)
  -ties
  sol·em·nize (sŏl′ ĕm·nīz)
  -niz·ing
so·lic·it (sō·lĭs′ ĭt)
  -it·ed   -it·ing
  so·lic·i·ta·tion
       (sō·lĭs′ ĭ·tā′ shŭn)
  so·lic·i·tor
so·lic·it·ous (sō·lĭs′ ĭ·tŭs)
  so·lic·i·tude (sō·lĭs′ ĭ·tūd)
sol·id (sŏl′ ĭd)
  sol·i·dar·i·ty (sŏl′ ĭ·dăr′ ĭ·tĭ)
  so·lid·i·fy (sō·lĭd′ ĭ·fī)
  -fied   -fy·ing
  so·lid·i·ty (sō·lĭd′ ĭ·tĭ)
so·lil·o·quy (sō·lĭl′ ō·kwĭ)
  pl. -quies
  so·lil·o·quize (sō·lĭl′ ō·kwīz)
  -quiz·ing
sol·i·taire (sŏl′ ĭ·târ)
sol·i·tar·y (sŏl′ ĭ·tẽr′ ĭ)
  sol·i·tar·i·ness
sol·i·tude (sŏl′ ĭ·tūd)
so·lo (sō′ lō)
  -los   so·lo·ist
Sol·o·mon (sŏl′ ō·mŭn)
sol·stice (sŏl′ stĭs)
sol·u·ble (sŏl′ û·b′l)
  sol·u·bil·i·ty (sŏl′ û·bĭl′ ĭ·tĭ)
so·lu·tion (sō·lū′ shŭn)
solve (sŏlv)
  solv·ing
  solv·a·bil·i·ty (sŏl′ và·bĭl′ ĭ·tĭ)
  solv·a·ble
sol·vent (sŏl′ vĕnt)
  sol·ven·cy
So·ma·li·land, Afr.
      (sō·mä′ lē·lănd′)
so·mat·ic (sō·măt′ ĭk)
som·ber (sŏm′ bẽr)

som·bre·ro (sŏm·brâr′ ō)
some (sŭm)
  some·bod·y   some·one
  some·thing   some·times
  some·where
som·er·sault (sŭm′ ẽr·sôlt)
som·nam·bu·list
     (sŏm·năm′ bû·lĭst)
so·nar (sō′ när)
so·na·ta (sō·nä′ tà)
song·ster (sŏng′ stẽr)
  song·stress
son·ic (sŏn′ ĭk)
son-in-law (sŭn′ ĭn·lô′)
  pl. sons-in-law
son·net (sŏn′ ĕt)
  son·net·eer (sŏn′ ĕ·tẽr′)
so·no·rous (sō·nō′ rŭs)
  so·nor·i·ty (sō·nŏr′ ĭ·tĭ)
soothe (sōōth)
  sooth·ing
sooth·say·er (sōōth′ sā′ ẽr)
soot·y (sōōt′ ĭ)
  soot·i·ness
soph·ism (sŏf′ ĭz′m)
so·phis·ti·cat·ed
     (sō·fĭs′ tĭ·kāt′ ĕd)
  so·phis·ti·ca·tion
     (sō·fĭs′ tĭ·kā′ shŭn)
soph·ist·ry (sŏf′ ĭs·trĭ)
  -ries
soph·o·more (sŏf′ ō·mōr)
  soph·o·mor·ic (sŏf′ ō·mŏr′ ĭk)
so·po·rif·ic (sō′ pō·rĭf′ ĭk)
so·pran·o (sō·prăn′ ō)
  -os
Sor·bonne (sôr·bŏn′)
sor·cer·y (sôr′ sẽr·ĭ)
  sor·cer·er   sor·cer·ess
sor·did (sôr′ dĭd)
sore·ly (sōr′ lĭ)
sor·ghum (sôr′ gŭm)
so·ror·i·ty (sō·rŏr′ ĭ·tĭ)
  -ties
sor·rel (sôr′ ĕl)
sor·row (sŏr′ ō)
  sor·row·ful, -ful·ly, -ful·ness
sor·ry (sŏr′ ĭ)
  sor·ri·er   sor·ri·est
sor·tie (sôr′ tē)
sot·tish (sŏt′ ĭsh)
sou·brette (sōō·brĕt′)
souf·flé (sōō′ flā′)
sought (sôt)

soul (sōl)
  soul·ful, -ful·ly, -ful·ness
  soul·less
sound (sound)
  sound·proof
soup (sōōp)
soup·çon (sōōp' soN')
sour (sour)
  sour·dough
source (sōrs)
souse (sous)
south (south)
  south·east
  south·er·ly (sŭth' ēr·lĭ)
  south·ern·er (sŭth' ēr·nēr)
  south·ern·most
    (sŭth' ērn·mōst)
  south·paw   South Pole
  south·ward   south·west·ern
South Car·o·li·na
    (south kăr' ō·lĭ' nả)
  abbr. S. C.
  South Car·o·lin·i·an
    (-kăr' ō·lĭn'ĭ' ản)
South Da·ko·ta (south dả·kō' tả)
  abbr. S. Dak.
  South Da·ko·tan
sou·ve·nir (sōō' vē·nēr')
sou'west·er (sou' wĕs' tēr)
sov·er·eign (sŏv' ēr·ĭn)
  sov·er·eign·ty
so·vi·et (sō' vĭ·ĕt)
soy·bean (soi' bĕn')
space·ship (spās' shĭp')
spa·cious (spā' shŭs)
spa·ghet·ti (spả·gĕt' ĭ)
span·gle (spăng' g'l)
Span·iard (spăn' yērd)
span·iel (spăn' yĕl)
Span·ish (spăn' ĭsh)
span·ner (spăn' ēr)
spare (spâr)
  spar·ing   spare·ness
  spare·ribs
spar·kle (spär' k'l)
  -kling
spar·row (spăr' ō)
sparse (spärs)
  sparse·ly
Spar·tan (spär' t'n)
spasm (spăz'm)
  spas·mod·ic (spăz·mŏd' ĭk)
spas·tic (spăs' tĭk)
spa·tial (spā' shảl)
  spa·tial·ly

spat·ter (spăt' ēr)
spat·u·la (spăt' ū·lả)
spawn (spôn)
speak·eas·y (spēk' ēz' ĭ)
spear·mint (spēr' mĭnt')
spe·cial (spĕsh' ảl)
  spe·cial·ist
  spe·cial·i·za·tion
    (spĕsh' ảl·ĭ·zā' shŭn)
  spe·cial·ize   -iz·ing
  spe·cial·ty
spe·cie (spē' shĭ)
  (coin; see species)
spe·cies (spē' shĭz)
  (kind, variety; see specie)
spe·cif·ic (spĕ·sĭf' ĭk)
  spe·cif·i·cal·ly
spec·i·fy (spĕs' ĭ·fī)
  -fied   -fy·ing
  spec·i·fi·a·ble (spĕs' ĭ·fī' ả·b'l)
  spec·i·fi·ca·tion
    (spĕs' ĭ·fĭ·kā' shŭn)
spec·i·men (spĕs' ĭ·mĕn)
spe·cious (spē' shŭs)
speck·led (spĕk' 'ld)
spec·ta·cle (spĕk' tả·k'l)
spec·tac·u·lar (spĕk·tăk' ū·lēr)
spec·ta·tor (spĕk·tā' tēr)
spec·ter (spĕk' tēr)
  spec·tral (spĕk' trảl)
spec·tro·scope (spĕk' trō·skōp)
spec·trum (spĕk' trŭm)
  pl. spec·tra
spec·u·late (spĕk' ū·lāt)
  -lat·ing
  spec·u·la·tion
    (spĕk' ū·lā' shŭn)
  spec·u·la·tive (spĕk' ū·lā' tĭv)
  spec·u·la·tor
speech (spēch)
speed (spēd)
  speed·boat   speed·i·ly
  speed in·di·ca·tor
  speed lim·it
  speed·om·e·ter
    (spēd·ŏm' ĕ·tēr)
  speed·way   speed·y
spell·bound (spĕl' bound')
spell·ing (spĕl' ĭng)
spend·thrift (spĕnd' thrĭft')
sperm (spûrm)
sper·ma·ce·ti (spûr' mả·sē' tĭ)
spew (spū)
sphag·num (sfăg' nŭm)

sphere	(sfĕr)	spoof	(spōof)
spher·al	spher·i·cal	spoon·ful	(spōon′ fŏŏl)
sphinc·ter	(sfĭngk′ tĕr)	spoon·fuls	
sphinx	(sfĭngks)	spoor	(spŏŏr)
spick-and-span	(spĭk′ ănd·spăn′)	(animal track; see *spore*)	
spic·y	(spīs′ ĭ)	spo·rad·ic	(spŏ·răd′ ĭk)
spic·i·er, -i·est, -i·ly, -i·ness		spore	(spōr)
spi·der	(spī′ dĕr)	(germ; see *spoor*)	
spiel	(spēl)	sport	(spōrt)
spig·ot	(spĭg′ ŭt)	spor·tive	sports·man·like
spike·let	(spīk′ lĕt)	sports·wear	sport·y
spill·age	(spĭl′ ĭj)	spot·light	(spŏt′ līt′)
spin·ach	(spĭn′ ĭch)	spot·ty	(spŏt′ ĭ)
spi·nal	(spī′ năl)	spouse	(spous)
spin·dle	(spĭn′ d’l)	spout	(spout)
spin·dly		sprain	(sprān)
spine·less	(spīn′ lĕs)	sprawl·ing	(sprôl′ ĭng)
spin·et	(spĭn′ ĕt)	spread	(sprĕd)
spin·ner·et	(spĭn′ ĕr·ĕt)	spright·ly	(sprīt′ lĭ)
spin·ning wheel		spright·li·ness	
	(spĭn′ ĭng)	spring	(sprĭng)
spin·ster	(spĭn′ stĕr)	spring·board	spring·time
spin·y	(spĭn′ ĭ)	sprin·kle	(sprĭng′ k’l)
spi·ral	(spī′ răl)	-kling	
-raled	-ral·ing	sprint	(sprĭnt)
spi·ral·ly		sprite	(sprīt)
spir·it	(spĭr′ ĭt)	sprock·et wheel	(sprŏk′ ĕt)
spir·it·ed	spir·it·less	sprout	(sprout)
spir·it·u·al	(spĭr′ ĭt·û·ăl)	spruce	(sprŏŏs)
spir·it·u·al·i·ty		spry	(sprī)
	(spĭr′ ĭt·û·ăl′ ĭ·tĭ)	spri·est	spry·ness
spite·ful	(spīt′ fŏŏl)	spu·ri·ous	(spū′ rĭ·ŭs)
-ful·ly	-ful·ness	spurn	(spûrn)
spit·fire	(spĭt′ fīr′)	spurt	(spûrt)
spit·tle	(spĭt′ ’l)	sput·nik	(spŏŏt′ nĭk)
spit·toon	(spĭ·tōon′)	sput·ter	(spŭt′ ĕr)
spleen	(splēn)	spu·tum	(spū′ tŭm)
splen·did	(splĕn′ dĭd)	spy·glass	(spī′ glăs′)
splen·dor	(splĕn′ dĕr)	squab	(skwŏb)
splice	(splīs)	squab·ble	(skwŏb′ ’l)
splic·ing		squab·bling	
splin·ter	(splĭn′ tĕr)	squad	(skwŏd)
split-lev·el	(splĭt′ lĕv′ ĕl)	squad·ron	(skwŏd′ rŭn)
spoil	(spoil)	squal·id	(skwŏl′ ĭd)
spoiled	spoil·ing	squall	(skwôl)
spoil·age	(spoil′ ĭj)	squal·or	(skwŏl′ ĕr)
spo·ken	(spō′ kĕn)	squan·der	(skwŏn′ dĕr)
spokes·man	(spōks′ măn)	square	(skwâr)
sponge	(spunj)	squar·ing	square dance
spong·ing	sponge·cake	square·ly	square-rig·ger
spon·gy		squash	(skwŏsh)
spon·sor	(spŏn′ sĕr)	squat	(skwŏt)
spon·ta·ne·ous	(spŏn·tā′ nĕ·ŭs)	squatted	squat·ting
spon·ta·ne·i·ty		squat·ter	
	(spŏn′ tå·nē′ ĭ·tĭ)	squaw	(skwô)

squawk (skwôk)
squeak (skwēk)
squeal (skwēl)
  squeal·er
squeam·ish (skwēm' ĭsh)
squee·gee (skwē' jē)
squeeze (skwēz)
  squeez·ing
squelch (skwĕlch)
squib (skwĭb)
squid (skwĭd)
squint (skwĭnt)
squire (skwīr)
  squir·ing
squirm (skwûrm)
squir·rel (skwûr' ĕl)
squirt (skwûrt)
sta·ble (stā' b'l)
  sta·bil·i·ty (stà·bĭl' ĭ·tĭ)
  sta·bil·ize -iz·ing
  sta·bly
stac·ca·to (stà·kä' tō)
sta·di·um (stā' dĭ·ŭm)
staff (stăf)
stage (stāj)
  stag·ing stage·coach
  stage fright stage·hand
  stage man·ag·er
  stage-struck stag·y
stag·ger (stăg' ĕr)
stag·nant (stăg' nànt)
stag·nate (stăg' nāt)
  -nat·ing
  stag·na·tion (stăg·nā' shŭn)
staid (stād)
stain·less (stān' lĕs)
stair·way (stâr' wā')
stake (stāk)
  (post; see *steak*)
sta·lac·tite (stà·lăk' tīt)
sta·lag·mite (stà·lăg' mīt)
stale·mate (stāl' māt')
Sta·lin·ist (stä' lĭn·ĭst)
stalk (stôk)
stall (stôl)
stal·lion (stăl' yŭn)
stal·wart (stôl' wĕrt)
sta·men (stā' mĕn)
stam·i·na (stăm' ĭ·nà)
stam·mer (stăm' ĕr)
stam·pede (stăm·pēd')
  -ped·ing
stance (stăns)
stan·chion (stăn' shŭn)

stand (stănd)
  stand·ee (stăn·dē')
  stand-in stand·out
  stand·still
stand·ard (stăn' dĕrd)
  stand·ard-bear·er
  stand·ard·i·za·tion
    (stăn' dĕr·dĭ·zā' shŭn)
  stand·ard·ize -iz·ing
stan·za (stăn' zà)
sta·ple (stā' p'l)
star (stär)
  star·board star·fish
  star·let star·light
  star·lit star·ry
  star sap·phire
starch (stärch)
star·ling (stär' lĭng)
star·tle (stär' t'l)
  -tling
starve (stärv)
  starv·ing
  star·va·tion (stär·vā' shŭn)
state (stāt)
  stat·ing state·hood
  state·house state·less
  state·ly -li·ness
  state·ment states' rights
  state·room
  state's at·torn·ey
  state's ev·i·dence
  states·man·like
stat·ic (stăt' ĭk)
sta·tion (stā' shŭn)
  sta·tion·mas·ter
  sta·tion wag·on
sta·tion·ar·y (stā' shŭn·ĕr' ĭ)
  (unmoving; see *stationery*)
sta·tion·er·y (stā' shŭn·ĕr' ĭ)
  (paper; see *stationary*)
sta·tis·tics (stà·tĭs' tĭks)
stat·u·ar·y (stăt' ū·ĕr' ĭ)
stat·ue (stăt' ū)
stat·u·esque (stăt' ū·ĕsk')
stat·u·ette (stăt' ū·ĕt')
stat·ure (stăt' ûr)
sta·tus (stā' tŭs)
stat·ute (stăt' ūt)
stat·u·to·ry (stăt' ū·tō' rĭ)
stead·fast (stĕd' fást)
stead·y (stĕd' ĭ)
  stead·i·ness
steak (stāk)
  (meat; see *stake*)

steal (stēl)
  (take feloniously; see *steel*)
  stole   steal·ing
stealth·y (stĕl′ thĭ)
  stealth·i·ness
steam (stēm)
  steam·boat   steam en·gine
  steam-roll·er   steam·ship
steel (stēl)
  (metal; see *steal*)
  steel·head   steel wool
  steel·y
steep (stēp)
stee·ple (stē′ p'l)
  stee·ple·chase   stee·ple jack
steer (stēr)
steer·age (stēr′ ĭj)
stein (stīn)
stel·lar (stĕl′ ēr)
stench (stĕnch)
sten·cil (stĕn′ sĭl)
  -ciled   -cil·ing
ste·nog·ra·pher
        (stĕ·nŏg′ rå·fēr)
  sten·o·graph·ic
        (stĕn′ ŏ·grăf′ ĭk)
  sten·o·type (stĕn′ ŏ·tīp)
sten·to·ri·an (stĕn·tō′ rĭ·ăn)
step (stĕp)
  (pace; see *steppe*)
  stepped,   step·ping
  step·child   step·fa·ther
  step·par·ent   step·ping·stone
steppe (stĕp)
  (Russian plains; see *step*)
ster·e·o·phon·ic
        (stĕr′ ĕ·ŏ·fŏn′ ĭk)
ster·e·op·ti·con
        (stĕr′ ĕ·ŏp′ tĭ·kŏn)
ster·e·o·scope (stĕr′ ĕ·ŏ·skōp′)
ster·e·o·type (stĕr′ ĕ·ŏ·tīp′)
ster·ile (stĕr′ ĭl)
  ste·ril·i·ty (stĕ·rĭl′ ĭ·tĭ)
  ster·i·li·za·tion
        (stĕr′ ĭ·lĭ·zā′ shŭn)
  ster·i·lize   -iz·ing
ster·ling (stûr′ lĭng)
stern (stûrn)
  stern·ness
ster·num (stûr′ nŭm)
steth·o·scope (stĕth′ ŏ·skōp)
  steth·o·scop·ic
        (stĕth′ ŏ·skŏp′ ĭk)
ste·ve·dore (stē′ vĕ·dōr′)

Ste·ven·son, Ad·lai E.
     (stē′ vĕn·s'n, ăd′ lā)
stew·ard (stū′ ērd)
  stew·ard·ess
stick·ler (stĭk′ lēr)
stick·pin (stĭk′ pĭn′)
stick-to-it·ive·ness
     (stĭk′ tōō′ ĭt·ĭv·nĕs)
stiff·en (stĭf′ ĕn)
sti·fle (stī′ f'l)
  -fling
stig·ma (stĭg′ må)
  stig·ma·tize   -tiz·ing
stig·ma·tism (stĭg′ må·tĭz'm)
stilt·ed (stĭl′ tĕd)
stim·u·late (stĭm′ û·lāt)
  -lat·ing
  stim·u·lant (-lănt)
  stim·u·la·tion
        (stĭm′ û·lā′ shŭn)
  stim·u·la·tive (stĭm′ û·lā′ tĭv)
  stim·u·la·tor
stim·u·lus (stĭm′ û·lŭs)
  pl. stim·u·li (-lī)
sting·y (stĭn′ jĭ)
  sting·i·ness
sti·pend (stī′ pĕnd)
stip·ple (stĭp′ 'l)
  stip·pling
stip·u·late (stĭp′ û·lāt)
  -lat·ing
  stip·u·la·tion (stĭp′ û·lā′ shŭn)
stir·rup (stĭr′ ŭp)
stitch (stĭch)
stock (stŏk)
  stock·bro·ker   stock ex·change
  stock·hold·er   stock mar·ket
  stock·pile
stock·ade (stŏk·ād′)
stock·i·net (stŏk′ ĭ·nĕt′)
stock·ing (stŏk′ ĭng)
stodg·y (stŏj′ ĭ)
  stodg·i·ness
sto·gie (stō′ gĭ)
sto·ic (stō′ ĭk)
  sto·i·cal·ly
stok·er (stōk′ ēr)
sto·len (stō′ lĕn)
stol·id (stŏl′ ĭd)
  sto·lid·i·ty (stŏ·lĭd′ ĭ·tĭ)
stom·ach (stŭm′ ăk)
stone (stōn)
  stone·cut·ter   stone-deaf
  stone·mas·on·ry
  stone·ware   ston·y

stooge	(stōōj)
stool pi·geon	(stōōl)
stop	(stŏp)
stopped	stop·ping
stop·cock	stop·gap
stop light	stop·o·ver
stop·page	stop·per
stor·age	(stōr′ ĭj)
store·keep·er	(stōr′ kēp′ ẽr)
sto·ry	(stō′ rĭ)
-ries	
(story of a building sometimes	
spelled *storey*)	
sto·ried	sto·ry·tell·er
stout·heart·ed	(stout′ här′ tĕd)
stove·pipe	(stōv′ pīp′)
stow·a·way	(stō′ ȧ·wā′)
strad·dle	(străd′ 'l)
strad·dling	
strag·gly	(străg′ lĭ)
straight	(strāt)
(without curves; see *strait*)	
straight·a·way straight·en	
straight·for·ward	
strain·er	(strān′ ẽr)
strait	(strāt)
(tight, narrow; see *straight*)	
strait·jack·et strait-laced	
strange	(strānj)
strange·ly strange·ness	
stran·gle	(străng′ g'l)
-gling stran·gle hold	
stran·gu·la·tion	
(străng′ gů·lā′ shŭn)	
strap·ping	(străp′ ĭng)
strat·e·gy	(străt′ ĕ·jĭ)
-gies	
strat·a·gem	(străt′ ȧ·jĕm)
stra·te·gic	(strȧ·tē′ jĭk)
strat·e·gist	(străt′ ĕ·jĭst)
strat·i·fy	(străt′ ĭ·fī)
-fied	-fy·ing
strat·i·fi·ca·tion	
(străt′ ĭ·fĭ·kā′ shŭn)	
strat·o·sphere	(străt′ ō·sfẽr)
stra·tum	(strā′ tŭm)
pl. -ta	
stra·tus	(strā′ tŭs)
pl. -ti	(-tī)
straw·ber·ry	(strô′ bĕr′ ĭ)
-ber·ries	
streak·y	(strēk′ ĭ)
streak·i·ness	
stream·lined	(strēm′ līnd′)
street·car	(strēt′ kär′)

strength	(strĕngth)
strength·ened	
stren·u·ous	(strĕn′ ů·ŭs)
strep·to·coc·cus	
(strĕp′ tō·kŏk′ ŭs)	
pl. strep·to·coc·ci (-kŏk′ sī)	
strep·to·my·cin	
(strĕp′ tō·mī′ sĭn)	
stress	(strĕs)
stretch	(strĕch)
stretch·a·ble	
strewn	(strōōn)
stri·at·ed	(strī′ āt·ĕd)
stri·a·tion	(strī·ā′ shŭn)
strick·en	(strĭk′ ĕn)
strict	(strĭkt)
stric·ture	(strĭk′ tůr)
stri·dent	(strī′ dĕnt)
-dence	-den·cy
strife	(strīf)
strike	(strīk)
strik·ing	strike·break·er
strin·gent	(strĭn′ jĕnt)
-gen·cy	
string·y	(strĭng′ ĭ)
striped	(strīpt)
strip·ling	(strĭp′ lĭng)
stroke	(strōk)
strok·ing	
stroll·er	(strōl′ ẽr)
strong	(strŏng)
strong-arm	strong·box
strong-willed	
stron·ti·um	(strŏn′ shĭ·ŭm)
struc·ture	(strŭk′ tůr)
struc·tur·al	
stru·del	(shtrōō′ dĕl)
strug·gle	(strŭg′ 'l)
strug·gling	
strum	(strŭm)
strummed	strum·ming
strum·pet	(strŭm′ pĕt)
strych·nine	(strĭk′ nĭn)
stub·ble	(stŭb′ 'l)
stub·bly	
stub·born	(stŭb′ ẽrn)
stub·born·ly	stub·born·ness
stuc·co	(stŭk′ ō)
stu·dent	(stū′ dĕnt)
stu·di·o	(stū′ dĭ·ō)
-os	
stu·di·ous	(stū′ dĭ·ŭs)
stud·y	(stŭd′ ĭ)
stud·ied	stud·ies
stud·y·ing	

stuff·ing   (stŭf′ ĭng)
stuff·y   (stŭf′ ĭ)
  stuff·i·ly   -i·ness
stul·ti·fy   (stŭl′ tĭ·fī)
 -fied   -fy·ing
  stul·ti·fi·ca·tion
        (stŭl′ tĭ·fī·kā′ shŭn)
stum·ble   (stŭm′ b′l)
 -bling
stun·ning   (stŭn′ ĭng)
stu·pe·fy   (stū′ pĕ·fī)
 -fied   -fy·ing
  stu·pe·fac·tion
        (stū′ pĕ·făk′ shŭn)
stu·pen·dous   (stū·pĕn′ dŭs)
stu·pid   (stū′ pĭd)
  stu·pid·i·ty   (stū·pĭd′ ĭ·tĭ)
stu·por   (stū′ pĕr)
  stu·por·ous
stur·dy   (stûr′ dĭ)
  stur·di·ly   -di·ness
stur·geon   (stûr′ jŭn)
stut·ter   (stŭt′ ĕr)
sty   (stī)
  sties
style   (stīl)
  styl·ing   styl·ish
  styl·ist
  sty·lis·tic   (stĭ·lĭs′ tĭk)
  styl·ize   -iz·ing
sty·lus   (stī′ lŭs)
sty·mie   (stī′ mĭ)
 -mied   -my·ing
styp·tic   (stĭp′ tĭk)
suave   (swäv)
  suave·ly   suave·ness
  suav·i·ty   (swăv′ ĭ·tĭ)
sub·al·tern   (sŭ·bôl′ tĕrn)
sub·com·mit·tee
        (sŭb′ kǒ·mĭt′ ĕ)
sub·con·scious (sŭb·kǒn′ shŭs)
sub·con·trac·tor
        (sŭb·kǒn′ trăk·tĕr)
sub·due   (sŭb·dū′)
 -du·ing
sub·ject   (sŭb·jĕkt′) *v.*
        (sŭb′ jĕkt) *adj.,n.*
  sub·jec·tive   (sŭb·jĕk′ tĭv)
 -tive·ly
  sub·jec·tiv·i·ty
        (sŭb′ jĕk·tĭv′ ĭ·tĭ)
sub·ju·gate   (sŭb′ jŏŏ·gāt)
 -gat·ing
sub·junc·tive   (sŭb·jŭngk′ tĭv)

sub·lease   (sŭb′ lēs′)
 -leas·ing
sub·li·mate   (sŭb′ lĭ·māt)
 -mat·ing
  sub·li·ma·tion
        (sŭb′ lĭ·mā′ shŭn)
sub·lime   (sŭb·līm′)
  sub·lime·ly
  sub·lim·i·ty   (sŭb·lĭm′ ĭ·tĭ)
sub·lim·i·nal   (sŭb·lĭm′ ĭ·nǎl)
 -nal·ly
sub·mar·gin·al (sŭb·mär′ jĭ·nǎl)
 -al·ly
sub·ma·rine   (sŭb′ mȧ·rēn′)
sub·merge   (sŭb·mûrj′)
 -merg·ing
  sub·mer·gence (sŭb·mûr′ jĕns)
sub·merse   (sŭb·mûrs′)
 -mers·ing   sub·mers·i·ble
sub·mis·sion   (sŭb·mĭsh′ ŭn)
sub·mis·sive   (sŭb·mĭs′ ĭv)
  sub·mis·sive·ness
sub·mit   (sŭb·mĭt′)
 -mitted   -mit·ting
sub·nor·mal   (sŭb·nôr′ mǎl)
  sub·nor·mal·i·ty
        (sŭb′ nôr·mǎl′ ĭ·tĭ)
sub·or·di·nate (sŭ·bôr′ dĭ·nĭt)
        adj., n
        (-nāt) *v.*
 -nat·ing
  sub·or·di·na·tion
        (sŭ·bôr′ dĭ·nā′ shŭn)
sub·orn   (sŭb·ôrn′)
sub·poe·na   (sŭb·pē′ nȧ)
sub·scribe   (sŭb·skrīb′)
 -scrib·ing
  sub·scrip·tion
        (sŭb·skrĭp′ shŭn)
sub·se·quent   (sŭb′ sĕ·kwĕnt)
 -quence
sub·ser·vi·ent (sŭb·sûr′ vĭ·ĕnt)
 -ence
sub·side   (sŭb·sīd′)
 -sid·ing
sub·sid·i·ar·y (sŭb·sĭd′ ĭ·ĕr′ ĭ)
 -ar·ies
sub·si·dy   (sŭb′ sĭ·dĭ)
 -dies
  sub·si·di·za·tion
        (sŭb′ sĭ·dĭ·zā′ shŭn)
  sub·si·dize   -diz·ing
sub·sist·ence   (sŭb·sĭs′ tĕns)
sub·soil   (sŭb′ soil′)
sub·spe·cies   (sŭb·spē′ shĭz)

sub·stance (sŭb′ stăns)
sub·stand·ard (sŭb·stăn′ dĕrd)
sub·stan·tial (sŭb·stăn′ shăl)
  -tial·ly
sub·stan·ti·ate (sŭb·stăn′ shĭ·āt)
  -at·ing
  sub·stan·ti·a·tion
       (sŭb·stăn′ shĭ·ā′ shŭn)
sub·stan·tive (sŭb′ stăn·tĭv)
sub·sti·tute (sŭb′ stĭ·tūt)
  -tut·ing
sub·stra·tum (sŭb·strā′ tŭm)
sub·struc·ture (sŭb·strŭk′ tŭr)
sub·ter·fuge (sŭb′ tĕr·fūj)
sub·ter·ra·ne·an
    (sŭb′ tĕ·rā′ nĕ·ăn)
sub·tle (sŭt′ ′l)
  sub·tle·ness
  sub·tle·ty, -ties (sŭt′ ′l·tĭ)
  sub·tly (sŭt′ lĭ)
sub·tract (sŭb·trăkt′)
  sub·trac·tion
sub·trop·i·cal (sŭb·trŏp′ ĭ·kăl)
sub·urb (sŭb′ ŭrb)
  sub·ur·ban (sŭb·ûr′ băn)
  sub·ur·ban·ite (sŭb·ûr′ băn·ĭt)
  sub·ur·bi·a (sŭb·ûr′ bĭ·à)
sub·ver·sive (sŭb·vûr′ sĭv)
  sub·ver·sion
sub·vert (sŭb·vûrt′)
  sub·vert·er
suc·ceed (sŭk·sēd′)
suc·cess (sŭk·sĕs′)
  suc·cess·ful, -ful·ly, -ful·ness
suc·ces·sion (sŭk·sĕsh′ ŭn)
suc·ces·sive (sŭk·sĕs′ ĭv)
  suc·ces·sive·ly suc·ces·sor
suc·cinct (sŭk·sĭngkt′)
suc·cor (sŭk′ ĕr)
suc·co·tash (sŭk′ ŏ·tăsh)
suc·cu·lent (sŭk′ ŭ·lĕnt)
  -lence
suc·cumb (sŭ·kŭm′)
suck·ling (sŭk′ lĭng)
suc·tion (sŭk′ shŭn)
sud·den -(sŭd′ ′n)
  sud·den·ly sud·den·ness
suds·y (sŭd′ zĭ)
sue (sū)
  su·ing
suède (swād)
su·et (sū′ ĕt)
suf·fer (sŭf′ ĕr)
  suf·fer·ance (sŭf′ ĕr·ăns)

suf·fice (sŭ·fīs′)
  suf·fic·ing
suf·fi·cient (sŭ·fĭsh′ ĕnt)
  -cien·cy
suf·fix (sŭf′ ĭks)
suf·fo·cate (sŭf′ ŏ·kāt)
  -cat·ing
  suf·fo·ca·tion (sŭf′ ŏ·kā′ shŭn)
suf·frage (sŭf′ rĭj)
  suf·fra·gette (sŭf′ rà·jĕt′)
suf·fuse (sŭ·fūz′)
  suf·fus·ing
  suf·fu·sion (sŭ·fū′ zhŭn)
sug·ar (shŏŏg′ ĕr)
  sug·ar-coat sug·ar·plum
  sug·ar·y
sug·gest (sŭg·jĕst′)
  sug·gest·i·ble
  sug·ges·tion (sŭg·jĕs′ chŭn)
  sug·ges·tive -tive·ness
su·i·cide (sū′ ĭ·sīd)
  su·i·cid·al (sū′ ĭ·sīd′ ăl)
suit·a·ble (sūt′ à·b′l)
  suit·a·bil·i·ty (sūt′ à·bĭl′ ĭ·tĭ)
suit·case (sūt′ kās′)
suite (swēt)
  (retinue; see *sweet*)
suit·or (sūt′ ĕr)
sul·fa (sŭl′ fà)
sul·fa·nil·a·mide
    (sŭl′ fà·nĭl′ à·mīd)
sul·fate (sŭl′ fāt)
sul·fide (sŭl′ fīd)
sul·fite (sŭl′ fīt)
sul·fur (sŭl′ fĕr)
  sul·fur di·ox·ide
  sul·fu·ric ac·id (sŭl·fū′ rĭk)
  sul·fu·rous
sulk·y (sŭl′ kĭ)
  sulk·i·ness
sul·len (sŭl′ ĕn)
  sul·len·ly sul·len·ness
sul·tan (sŭl′ tăn)
  sul·tan·a (sŭl·tăn′ à)
sul·try (sŭl′ trĭ)
  sul·tri·ness
su·mac (shōō′ măk)
sum·ma·ry (sŭm′ à·rĭ)
  -ries
  sum·ma·ri·ly (sŭm′ à·rĭ·lĭ)
  sum·ma·ri·za·tion
    (sŭm′ à·rĭ·zā′ shŭn)
  sum·ma·rize -riz·ing
sum·mer (sŭm′ ĕr)
  sum·mer·house

sum·mer·time   sum·mer·y
sum·mit   (sŭm′ ĭt)
sum·mon   (sŭm′ ŭn)
   sum·mon·er
sump·tu·ous   (sŭmp′ tū̇ ·ŭs)
sun   (sŭn)
   sunned   sun·ning
   sun bath   sun·burn
   sun·di·al   sun-dried
   sun·fast   sun·flow·er
   sun·glass·es   sun lamp
   sun·light   sun·ny
   sun·rise   sun·set
   sun·shade   sun·shine
   sun·stroke   sun·up
sun·dae   (sŭn′ dī)
sun·der   (sŭn′ dẽr)
sunk·en   (sŭngk′ ĕn)
su·per   (sū′ pẽr)
su·per·a·bun·dance
     (sū′ pẽr·ȧ·bŭn′ dăns)
su·per·an·nu·ate
     (sū′ pẽr·ăn′ ū·āt)
su·perb   (su̇·pûrb′)
su·per·car·go   (sū′ pẽr·kär′ gō)
su·per·cil·i·ous
     (sū′ pẽr·sĭl′ ĭ·ŭs)
su·per·e·go   (sū′ pẽr·ē′ gō)
su·per·fi·cial   (sū′ pẽr·fĭsh′ ăl)
   -cial·ly
   su·per·fi·ci·al·i·ty
     (sū′ pẽr·fĭsh′ ĭ·ăl′ ĭ·tĭ)
   -ties
su·per·flu·ous   (su̇·pûr′ flōō·ŭs)
   su·per·flu·i·ty
     (sū′ pẽr·flōō′ ĭ·tĭ)
   -ties
su·per·high·way
     (sū′ pẽr·hī′ wā′)
su·per·hu·man
     (sū′ pẽr·hū′ măn)
su·per·im·pose   (sū′ pẽr·ĭm·pōz′)
   -pos·ing
su·per·in·tend   (sū′ pẽr·ĭn·tĕnd′)
   su·per·in·tend·ent
su·pe·ri·or   (su̇·pẽr′ ĭ·ẽr)
   su·pe·ri·or·i·ty
     (su̇·pẽr′ ĭ·ŏr′ ĭ·tĭ)
su·per·la·tive   (su̇·pûr′ lȧ·tĭv)
   -tive·ly
su·per·mar·ket
     (sū′ pẽr·mär′ kĕt)
su·per·nu·mer·ar·y
     (sū′ pẽr·nū′ mẽr·ĕr′ ĭ)
   -ar·ies

su·per·sat·u·rate
     (sū′ pẽr·săt′ û·rāt)
   -rat·ing
su·per·sede   (sū′ pẽr·sēd′)
   -sed·ing
   su·per·ses·sion (-sĕsh′ ŭn)
su·per·son·ic   (sū′ pẽr·sŏn′ ĭk)
su·per·sti·tion   (sū′ pẽr·stĭsh′ ŭn)
   su·per·sti·tious
su·per·struc·ture
     (sū′ pẽr·strŭk′ tū̇r)
su·per·vise   (sū′ pẽr·vīz′)
   -vis·ing   su·per·vi·sor
   su·per·vi·so·ry
     (sū′ pẽr·vī′ zȯ·rĭ)
su·pine   (su̇·pīn′)
sup·per   (sŭp′ ẽr)
sup·plant   (su̇·plant′)
sup·ple   (sŭp′ 'l)
   sup·ple·ness
sup·ple·ment   (sŭp′ lĕ·mĕnt)
   sup·ple·men·tal
     (sŭp′ lĕ·mĕn′ tăl)
   sup·ple·men·ta·ry
     (sŭp′ lĕ·mĕn′ tȧ·rĭ)
sup·pli·ant   (sŭp′ lĭ·ănt)
   -ance
sup·pli·cant   (sŭp′ lĭ·kănt)
sup·pli·cate   (sŭp′ lĭ·kāt)
   -cat·ing
sup·ply   (su̇·plī′)
   sup·plied   sup·ply·ing
   sup·pli·er   sup·plies
sup·port   (su̇·pōrt′)
   sup·port·a·ble   sup·port·er
sup·pose   (su̇·pōz′)
   sup·pos·ing   sup·pos·a·ble
   sup·pos·ed·ly
sup·po·si·tion   (sŭp′ ȯ·zĭsh′ ŭn)
   sup·po·si·tion·al
sup·pos·i·to·ry   (su̇·pŏz′ ĭ·tō′ rĭ)
   -ries
sup·press   (su̇·prĕs′)
   sup·press·i·ble
   sup·pres·sion   (-prĕsh′ ŭn)
   sup·pres·sive
su·preme   (su̇·prēm′)
   su·prem·a·cy   (su̇·prĕm′ ȧ·sĭ)
   su·preme·ly
sur·cease   (sûr·sēs′)
sur·charge   (sûr′ chärj′) *n.*
sure·ly   (shŏŏr′ lĭ)
sure·ty   (shŏŏr′ tĭ)
   -ties

sur·face (sûr′ fĭs)
  -fac·ing
surf·board (sûrf′ bōrd′)
sur·feit (sûr′ fĭt)
  -feit·ed
surge (sûrj)
  (to swell; see *serge*)
  surg·ing
sur·geon (sûr′ jŭn)
sur·ger·y (sûr′ jĕr·ĭ)
  sur·gi·cal (sûr′ jĭ·kăl)
  -cal·ly
sur·ly (sûr′ lĭ)
  sur·li·ness
sur·mise (sûr·mīz′)
  -mis·ing
sur·mount (sûr·mount′)
  sur·mount·a·ble
sur·name (sûr′ nām′)
sur·pass (sẽr·pås′)
  sur·pass·a·ble
sur·plice (sûr′ plĭs)
  (vestment; see *surplus*)
sur·plus (sûr′ plŭs)
  (excess; see *surplice*)
sur·prise (sẽr·prīz′)
  -pris·ing
sur·re·al·ism (sŭ·rē′ ăl·ĭz′m)
sur·ren·der (sŭ·rĕn′ dẽr)
sur·rep·ti·tious (sûr′ ĕp·tĭsh′ ŭs)
sur·rey (sûr′ ĭ)
sur·ro·gate (sûr′ ŏ·gāt)
sur·round (sŭ·round′)
sur·tax (sûr′ tăks′)
sur·veil·lance (sûr·vāl′ ăns)
sur·vey (sẽr·vā′) *v.*
  (sûr′ vā) *n.*
  sur·vey·or (sẽr·vā′ ẽr)
sur·vive (sẽr·vīv′)
  -viv·ing   sur·viv·al
  sur·vi·vor
sus·cep·ti·ble (sŭ·sĕp′ tĭ·b′l)
  sus·cep·ti·bil·i·ty
  (sŭ·sĕp′ tĭ·bĭl′ ĭ·tĭ)
sus·pect (sŭs′ pĕkt) *n.*
  (sŭs·pĕkt′)
  adj., v.
sus·pend (sŭs·pĕnd′)
sus·pend·er (sŭs·pĕn′ dẽr)
sus·pen·sion (sŭs·pĕn′ shŭn)
sus·pi·cious (sŭs·pĭsl′ ŭs)
  sus·pi·cion (sŭs·pĭsl′ ŭn)
sus·tain·ing (sŭs·tāɪ′ ĭng)
sus·te·nance (sŭs′ tĕ·năns)
su·ture (sū′ tụr)

su·ze·rain·ty (sū′ zĕ·rân·tĭ)
svelte (svĕlt)
swab·ber (swŏb′ ẽr)
swad·dling clothes
  (swŏd′ lĭng)
swag·ger (swăg′ ẽr)
Swa·hi·li (swä·hē′ lē)
swain (swān)
swal·low (swŏl′ ō)
swa·mi (swä′ mĭ)
swank·y (swăngk′ ĭ)
swan's-down (swŏnz′ doun′)
swarth·y (swôr′ thĭ)
  swarth·i·ness
swash·buck·ler (swŏsh′ bŭk′ lẽr)
swas·ti·ka (swŏs′ tĭ·kå)
swatch (swŏch)
swat·ter (swŏt′ ẽr)
sway-backed (swā′ băkt′)
Swa·zi·land (swä′ zĕ·lănd′)
swear (swâr)
sweat (swĕt)
  sweat·i·ness   sweat shirt
  sweat·shop
sweat·er (swĕt′ ẽr)
Swede (swēd)
  Swed·ish
sweep·stake (swēp′ stāk′)
sweet (swēt)
  (agreeable; see *suite*)
  sweet·bread   sweet·bri·er
  sweet·en·ing   sweet·meats
  sweet po·ta·to sweet Wil·liam
swel·ter·ing (swĕl′ tẽr·ĭng)
swept (swĕpt)
swerve (swûrv)
  swerv·ing
swill (swĭl)
swim (swĭm)
  swam   swim·ming
  swim·mer
swin·dler (swĭn′ dlẽr)
swine (swīn)
  swin·ish
swirl (swûrl)
switch (swĭch)
  switch·back   switch·board
  switch·man
swiv·el (swĭv′ 'l)
  -eled,   -el·ing
swol·len (swōl′ ĕn)
sword (sōrd)
  sword·fish   swords·man
syc·a·more (sĭk′ å·mōr)

syc·o·phant   (sĭk′ ŏ·fănt)
  -phan·cy
syl·la·ble   (sĭl′ à·b'l)
  syl·lab·ic   (sĭ·lăb′ ĭk)
  syl·lab·i·ca·tion
                      (sĭ·lăb′ ĭ·kā′ shŭn)
  syl·lab·i·fy   (sĭ·lăb′ ĭ·fī)
  -fied   -fy·ing
syl·la·bus   (sĭl′ à·bŭs)
  -bus·es
syl·lo·gism   (sĭl′ ŏ·jĭz'm)
  syl·lo·gis·tic   (sĭl′ ŏ·jĭs′ tĭk)
sylph   (sĭlf)
  sylph·like
syl·van   (sĭl′ văn)
sym·bi·o·sis   (sĭm′ bĭ·ō′ sĭs)
  sym·bi·ot·ic   (-ŏt′ ĭk)
sym·bol   (sĭm′ bŭl)
  (emblem; see cymbal)
  sym·bol·ic   (sĭm·bŏl′ ĭk)
  sym·bol·i·cal   (sĭm·bŏl′ ĭ·kàl)
  -cal·ly   sym·bol·ism
  sym·bol·ize   -iz·ing
sym·met·ri·cal   (sĭ·mĕt′ rĭ·kàl)
  -cal·ly
sym·me·try   (sĭm′ ĕ·trĭ)
sym·pa·thy   (sĭm′ pà·thĭ)
  -thies
  sym·pa·thet·ic
                      (sĭm′ pà·thĕt′ ĭk)
  sym·pa·thize   -thiz·ing
sym·pho·ny   (sĭm′ fŏ·nĭ)
  -nies
  sym·phon·ic   (sĭm·fŏn′ ĭk)
sym·po·si·um   (sĭm·pō′ zĭ·ŭm)
  pl. sym·po·si·a
symp·tom   (sĭmp′ tŭm)
  symp·to·mat·ic
                      (sĭmp′ tŏ·măt′ ĭk)
syn·a·gogue   (sĭn′ à·gŏg)
syn·chro·mesh   (sĭng′krŏ·mĕsh′)
syn·chro·nize   (sĭng′ krŏ·nīz)
  -niz·ing
  syn·chro·ni·za·tion
            (sĭng′ krŏ·nĭ·zā′ shŭn)
syn·co·pa·tion
            (sĭng′ kŏ·pā′ shŭn)
syn·di·cate   (sĭn′ dĭ·kàt) n.
  -cat·ing   (-kāt) v.
syn·drome   (sĭn′ drōm)
syn·od   (sĭn′ ŭd)
syn·o·nym   (sĭn′ ŏ·nĭm)
  syn·on·y·mous
                      (sĭ·nŏn′ ĭ·mŭs)

syn·op·sis   (sĭ·nŏp′ sĭs)
  pl. -ses
  syn·op·tic   (sĭ·nŏp′ tĭk)
syn·tax   (sĭn′ tăks)
syn·the·sis   (sĭn′ thĕ·sĭs)
  pl. -ses
  syn·the·size   (sĭn′ thĕ·sīz)
  -siz·ing
  syn·thet·ic   (sĭn·thĕt′ ĭk)
  syn·thet·i·cal·ly
syph·i·lis   (sĭf′ ĭ·lŭs)
sy·rin·ga   (sĭ·rĭng′ gà)
syr·inge   (sĭr′ ĭnj)
  sy·rin·ge·al   (sĭ·rĭn′ jĕ·àl)
syr·inx   (sĭr′ ĭngks)
  pl. syr·in·ges   (sĭ·rĭn′ jĕz)
sys·tem   (sĭs′ tĕm)
  sys·tem·at·ic   (sĭs′ tĕm·ăt′ ĭk)
  -i·cal·ly
  sys·tem·a·tize   (sĭs′ tĕm·à·tīz)
  -tiz·ing

T

Ta·bas·co   (tà·băs′ kō)
tab·er·nac·le   (tăb′ ẽr·năk'l)
tab·leau   (tăb′ lō)
  pl. tab·leaux   (-lōz)
ta·ble·cloth   (tā′ b'l·klôth′)
ta·ble d'hôte   (tá′ blĕ dōt′)
ta·ble·spoon   (tā′ b'l·spōōn′)
  ta·ble·spoon·ful, -fuls
tab·let   (tăb′ lĕt)
tab·loid   (tăb′ loid)
ta·boo   (tà·bōō′)
  -booed   -boo·ing
ta·bor   (tā′ bẽr)
tab·u·late   (tăb′ û·làt)
  -lat·ing
  tab·u·lar   (tăb′ û·lẽr)
  tab·u·la·tion   (tăb′ û·lā′ shŭn)
  tab·u·la·tor
tac·it   (tăs′ ĭt)
tac·i·turn   (tăs′ ĭ·tûrn)
  tac·i·tur·ni·ty   (tăs′ ĭ·tûr′ nĭ·tĭ)
tack·le   (tăk′l)
  -ling
tact   (tăkt)
  tact·ful, -ful·ly, -ful·ness
  tact·less   -less·ness
tac·tics   (tăk′ tĭks)
  tac·ti·cal   (tăk′ tĭ·kàl)
  -cal·ly
  tac·ti·cian   (tăk·tĭsh′ ăn)

tac·tile (tăk′ tĭl)
tad·pole (tăd′ pōl′)
taf·fe·ta (tăf′ ĕ·tȧ)
Ta·hi·ti·an (tȧ·hē′ tĭ·ȧn)
tail (tāl)
  tailed, tail·ing
  tail·first tail·less
  tail·piece tail spin
  tail wind
tai·lor (tā′ lēr)
  tai·lor·ing tai·lor-made
taint (tānt)
Tai·wan (tī·wän′)
  (*also* Formosa)
Taj Mahal (täj mȧ·häl′)
talc (tălk)
tal·cum pow·der
  (tăl′ kŭm)
tal·ent (tăl′ ĕnt)
tale·tell·er (tăl′ tĕl′ ēr)
tal·is·man (tăl′ ĭs·mȧn)
talk·a·tive (tôk′ ȧ·tĭv)
  -tive·ness
Tal·la·has·see, Fla.
  (tăl′ ȧ·hăs′ ē)
tal·low (tăl′ ō)
tal·ly·ho (tăl′ ĭ·hō′)
Tal·mud (tăl′ mŭd)
tal·on (tăl′ ŭn)
tam·a·rack (tăm′ ȧ·răk)
tam·bou·rine (tăm′ bŏŏ·rēn′)
tame (tām)
  tam·ing tam·a·ble
  tame·ly
Tam·ma·ny Hall (tăm′ ȧ·nĭ)
tamp·er (tăm′ pēr)
tam·pon (tăm′ pŏn)
tan·a·ger (tăn′ ȧ·jēr)
tan·dem (tăn′ dĕm)
Tan·gan·yi·ka (tăn′ găn·yē′ kȧ)
tan·gent (tăn′ jĕnt)
  tan·gen·tial (tăn·jĕn′ shȧl)
tan·ge·rine (tăn′ jĕ·rēn′)
tan·gi·ble (tăn′ jĭ·b′l)
tan·gle (tăng′ g′l)
  -gling
tang·y (tăng′ ĭ)
  tang·i·ness
tank·ard (tăngk′ ērd)
tan·ner·y (tăn′ ēr·ĭ)
  tan·ner·ies
tan·nic ac·id (tăn′ ĭk)
tan·ta·lize (tăn′ tȧ·līz)
  -liz·ing
tan·ta·mount (tăn′ tȧ·mount′)

tan·trum (tăn′ trŭm)
Tao·ism (tou′ ĭz′m)
ta·pa cloth (tä′ pä)
ta·per (tä′ pēr)
  (candle; see *tapir*)
tap·es·try (tăp′ ĕs·trĭ)
  -tries
tape·worm (tāp′ wûrm′)
tap·i·o·ca (tăp′ ĭ·ō′ kȧ)
ta·pir (tä′ pēr)
  (animal; see *taper*)
tap·ster (tăp′ stēr)
tar·an·tel·la (tăr′ ȧn·tĕl′ ȧ)
  (dance)
ta·ran·tu·la (tȧ·răn′ tṳ·lȧ)
  (spider)
tar·dy (tär′ dĭ)
  tar·di·ly -i·ness
tar·get (tär′ gĕt)
tar·iff (tär′ ĭf)
tar·nish (tär′ nĭsh)
  tar·nish·a·ble
ta·ro root (tä′ rō)
tar·pau·lin (tär·pô′ lĭn)
tar·pon (tär′ pŏn)
tar·ra·gon (tär′ ȧ·gŏn)
tar·ry (tär′ ĭ)
  tar·ried tar·ry·ing
tar·tan (tär′ tȧn)
tar·tar (tär′ tēr)
  (cream of tartar)
tar·tare sauce (tär′ tēr)
task·mas·ter (tȧsk′ măs′ tēr)
tas·sel (tăs′ ′l)
  tas·seled tas·sel·ing
taste (tāst)
  tast·ing
  taste·ful, -ful·ly, -ful·ness
  taste·less
  tast·i·ly -i·ness
  tast·y
tat·tered (tăt′ ērd)
tat·tle (tăt′ ′l)
  tat·tling tat·tle·tale
tat·too (tă·tōō′)
  tat·tooed tat·too·ing
taught (tôt)
  (instructed; see *taut*)
taunt (tônt)
taupe (tōp)
taut (tôt)
  (tight; see *taught*)
tau·tol·o·gy (tô·tŏl′ ō·jĭ)
  -gies

tau·to·log·i·cal

    (tô′ tô·lŏj′ ĭ·kăl)

tav·ern   (tăv′ ẽrn)

taw·dry   (tô′ drĭ)

    taw·dri·ness

taw·ny   (tô′ nĭ)

    taw·ni·ness

tax   (tăks)

    tax·a·ble

    tax·a·tion   (tăks·ā′ shŭn)

    tax-ex·empt   tax·gath·er·er

    tax·pay·er

tax·i   (tăk′ sĭ)

    tax·is   tax·i·cab

tax·i·der·mist   (tăk′ sĭ·dûr′ mĭst)

Tchai·kov·sky, Pe·ter Il·ich

    (chī·kôf′ skĭ)

teach   (tēch)

    teach·a·bil·i·ty

    (tēch′ a·bĭl′ ĭ·tĭ)

    teach·a·ble   teach·er

tea·cup·ful   (tē′ kŭp·foŏl′)

    -fuls

teak·wood   (tēk′ woŏd′)

team   (tēm)

    team·mate   team·ster

    team·work

tea·pot   (tē′ pŏt′)

tear·ful   (tẽr′ foŏl)

    -ful·ly   -ful·ness

tease   (tēz)

    teas·ing

tea·spoon·ful   (tē′ spoŏn·foŏl′)

    -fuls

teat   (tēt)

tech·ni·cal   (tĕk′ nĭ·kăl)

    -cal·ly

    tech·ni·cal·i·ty

    (tĕk′ nĭ·kăl′ ĭ·tĭ)

    tech·ni·cian   (tĕk·nĭsh′ ăn)

Tech·ni·col·or   (tĕk′ nĭ·kŭl′ ẽr)

tech·nique   (tĕk·nēk′)

tech·nol·o·gy   (tĕk·nŏl′ ô·jĭ)

    -gies

    tech·no·log·i·cal

    (tĕk′ nô·lŏj′ ĭ·kăl)

    -cal·ly

    tech·nol·o·gist   (tĕk·nŏl′ ô·jĭst)

te·di·ous   (tē′ dĭ·ŭs)

    te·di·um   (tē′ dĭ·ŭm)

teem·ing   (tēm′ ĭng)

    (crowded)

teen-ag·er   (tēn′ āj′ ẽr)

tee shirt   (tē)

teeth   (tēth) n. pl.

teethe   (tēth) v.

    teeth·ing

tee·to·tal·er   (tē·tō′ t'lẽr)

Te·hran, I·ran   (tĕ·hrän′)

Tel A·viv, Is·ra·el

    (tĕl′ a·vēv′)

tel·e·cast   (tĕl′ ê·kăst′)

    tel·e·cast·er

tel·e·graph   (tĕl′ ê·gráf)

tel·e·ol·o·gy   (tĕl′ ê·ŏl′ ô·jĭ)

te·lep·a·thy   (tê·lĕp′ a·thĭ)

tel·e·phone   (tĕl′ ê·fōn)

tel·e·scope   (tĕl′ ê·skōp)

    tel·e·scop·ic   (tĕl′ ê·skōp′ ĭk)

tel·e·type   (tĕl′ ê·tĭp)

tel·e·vi·sion   (tĕl′ ê·vĭzh′ ŭn)

    tel·e·view·er

    tel·e·vise   -vis·ing

tell·tale   (tĕl′ tāl′)

te·mer·i·ty   (tê·mĕr′ ĭ·tĭ)

tem·per   (tĕm′ pĕr)

tem·per·a   (tĕm′ pĕr·a)

tem·per·a·ment

    (tĕm′ pĕr·a·mĕnt)

    tem·per·a·men·tal

    (tĕm′ pĕr·a·mĕn′ tăl)

    -tal·ly

tem·per·ance   (tĕm′ pĕr·ảns)

tem·per·ate   (tĕm′ pĕr·ĭt)

    -ate·ly

tem·per·a·ture   (tĕm′ pĕr·a·tûr′)

tem·pest   (tĕm′ pĕst)

    tem·pes·tu·ous

    (tĕm·pĕs′ tû·ŭs)

tem·plate   (tĕm′ plĭt)

tem·ple   (tĕm′ p'l)

tem·po·ral   (tĕm′ pô·răl)

    tem·po·ral·ly

tem·po·rar·y   (tĕm′ pô·rĕr′ ĭ)

    tem·po·rar·i·ly

    (tĕm′ pô·rĕr′ ĭ·lĭ)

tem·po·rize   (tĕm′ pô·rĭz)

    -riz·ing

tempt   (tĕmpt)

    tempt·a·ble

    temp·ta·tion   (tĕmp·tā′ shŭn)

    tempt·er   tempt·ress

ten·a·ble   (tĕn′ a·b'l)

te·na·cious   (tê·nā′ shŭs)

te·nac·i·ty   (tê·năs′ ĭ·tĭ)

ten·ant   (tĕn′ ảnt)

    -an·cy

tend·en·cy   (tĕn′ dĕn·sĭ)

    -cies

ten·den·tious   (tĕn·dĕn′ shŭs)

tend·er (těn′ dẽr)
  ten·der·foot   ten·der·heart·ed
  ten·der·loin
ten·don (těn′ dŭn)
ten·dril (těn′ drĭl)
Ten·e·brae (těn′ ė·brē)
ten·e·ment (těn′ ė·měnt)
ten·et (těn′ ět)
ten·fold (těn′ fōld′)
Ten·nes·see (těn′ ĕ·sē′)
  abbr. Tenn.
  Ten·nes·see·an (-sē′ ăn)
ten·nis (těn′ ĭs)
ten·or (těn′ ẽr)
ten·pins (těn′ pĭnz′)
tense (těns)
  tense·ly   tense·ness
  ten·si·ty (těn′ sĭ·tĭ)
ten·sile strength (těn′ sĭl)
ten·sion (těn′ shŭn)
ten·sor (těn′ sẽr)
ten·ta·cle (těn′ tȧ·k'l)
ten·ta·tive (těn′ tȧ·tĭv)
  ten·ta·tive·ly, -tive·ness
ten·ter·hooks (těn′ tẽr·hŏŏks′)
ten·u·ous (těn′ û·ŭs)
ten·ure (těn′ ûr)
te·pee (tē′ pē)
tep·id (těp′ ĭd)
te·qui·la (tȧ·kē′ lä)
ter·ma·gant (tûr′ mȧ·gȧnt)
ter·mi·na·ble (tûr′ mĭ·nȧ·b'l)
ter·mi·nal (tûr′ mĭ·năl)
ter·mi·nate (tûr′ mĭ·nāt)
  -nat·ing
  ter·mi·na·tion
      (tûr′ mĭ·nā′ shŭn)
ter·mi·nol·o·gy
      (tûr′ mĭ·nŏl′ ŏ·jĭ)
  ter·mi·no·log·i·cal
      (tûr′ mĭ·nŏ·lŏj′ ĭ·kăl)
ter·mi·nus (tûr′ mĭ·nŭs)
  pl. ter·mi·ni (-nī)
ter·mite (tûr′ mīt)
tern (tûrn)
  (bird; see *turn*)
ter·race (těr′ ĭs)
ter·ra cot·ta (těr′ ȧ·kŏt′ ȧ) n.
  ter·ra-cot·ta *adj.*
ter·rain (tě·rān′)
ter·ra·pin (těr′ ȧ·pĭn)
ter·raz·zo (těr·rät′ tsŏ)
ter·res·tri·al (tě·rěs′ trĭ·ăl)
ter·ri·ble (těr′ ĭ·b'l)
  ter·ri·ble·ness ter·ri·bly

ter·ri·er (těr′ ĭ·ẽr)
ter·rif·ic (tě·rĭf′ ĭk)
  ter·rif·i·cal·ly
ter·ri·fy (těr′ ĭ·fī)
  -fied, -fy·ing
ter·ri·to·ri·al (těr′ ĭ·tō′ rĭ·ăl)
ter·ri·to·ry (těr′ ĭ·tō′ rĭ)
ter·ror (těr′ ẽr)
  ter·ror·ize -iz·ing
ter·ry cloth (těr′ ĭ)
terse (tûrs)
  terse·ness
ter·ti·ar·y (tûr′ shĭ·ěr′ ĭ)
tes·ta·ment (těs′ tȧ·měnt)
tes·ti·cle (těs′ tĭ·k'l)
tes·ti·fy (těs′ tĭ·fī)
  -fied, -fy·ing
  tes·ti·fi·er
tes·ti·mo·ny (těs′ tĭ·mō′ nĭ)
  -nies
  tes·ti·mo·ni·al
      (těs′ tĭ·mō′ nĭ·ăl)
tet·a·nus (tět′ ȧ·nŭs)
tête-à-tête (tāt′ ȧ·tāt′)
teth·er (těth′ ẽr)
tet·ra·chlo·ride (tět′ rȧ·klō′ rīd)
tet·ra·he·dron (tět′ rȧ·hē′ drŭn)
tet·ral·o·gy (tě·trăl′ ŏ·jĭ)
  -gies
te·tram·e·ter (tě·trăm′ ė·tẽr)
te·trarch (tē′ trärk)
Teu·ton·ic (tû·tŏn′ ĭk)
Tex·as (těk′ sȧs)
  abbr. Tex.
  Tex·an (těk′ săn)
text·book (těkst′ bŏŏk′)
tex·tile (těks′ tĭl)
tex·tu·al (těks′ tụ·ăl)
tex·ture (těks′ tụr)
  tex·tur·al
Thai·land (tī′ lănd)
than (thăn)
  (other, else; "none other *than*
  yourself"; see *then*)
thank (thăngk)
  thank·ful, -ful·ly, -ful·ness
  thank·less
Thanks·giv·ing (thănks·gĭv′ ĭng)
thatched (thăcht)
the·a·ter (thē′ ȧ·tẽr)
  the·a·ter-in-the-round
  the·at·ri·cal (thě·ăt′ rĭ·kăl)
  -cal·ly
theft (thěft)

their   (thâr)
  (of them; see *there*)
  theirs
the·ism   (thē' ĭz'm)
  the·is·tic   (thē·ĭs' tĭk)
theme   (thēm)
  the·mat·ic   (thē·măt' ĭk)
them·selves   (thĕm·sĕlvz')
then   (thĕn)
  (at that time; see *than*)
thence   (thĕns)
  thence·forth   thence·for·ward
the·oc·ra·cy   (thē·ŏk' rá·sĭ)
the·ol·o·gy   (thē·ŏl' ô·jĭ)
  the·o·lo·gi·an   (thē' ô·lō' jĭ·ăn)
  the·o·log·i·cal   (thē' ô·lŏj' ĭ·kăl)
  -cal·ly
the·o·rem   (thē' ô·rĕm)
the·o·ry   (thē' ô·rĭ)
  -ries
  the·o·ret·i·cal   (thē' ô·rĕt' ĭ·kăl)
  -cal·ly
  the·o·re·ti·cian
            (thē' ô·rĕ·tĭsh' ăn)
  the·o·rist   (thē' ô·rĭst)
  the·o·rize   -riz·ing
the·os·o·phy   (thē·ŏs' ô·fĭ)
ther·a·peu·tic   (thĕr' á·pū' tĭk)
  ther·a·peu·ti·cal·ly
ther·a·py   (thĕr' á·pĭ)
there   (thâr)
  (in that place; see *their*)
  there·a·bouts   there·aft·er
  there·by   there·fore
  there·in   there·in·aft·er
  there·in·to   there·of
  there·on   there·un·der
  there·un·to   there·up·on
  there·with
ther·mal   (thûr' măl)
ther·mo·dy·nam·ics
         (thûr' mô·dĭ·năm' ĭks)
ther·mom·e·ter
         (thēr·mŏm' ê·tēr)
ther·mo·nu·cle·ar
         (thûr' mô·nū' klê·ēr)
Ther·mos bot·tle
         (thûr' mŏs)
ther·mo·stat   (thûr' mô·stăt)
  ther·mo·stat·i·cal·ly
         (thûr' mô·stăt' ĭ·kăl·ĭ)
the·sau·rus   (thē·sô' rŭs)
these   (thēz)
the·sis   (thē' sĭs)
  pl. the·ses   (-sēz)

Thes·pi·an   (thĕs' pĭ·ăn)
thi·a·mine   (thī' á·mēn)
thick·ened   (thĭk' ĕnd)
thick·et   (thĭk' ĕt)
thick-skinned   (thĭk' skĭnd')
thief   (thēf) *n.*
  pl. thieves   (thēvz)
thieve   (thēv) *v.*
  thiev·ing   thiev·er·y
  thiev·ish
thigh·bone   (thī' bōn')
thim·ble·ful   (thĭm' b'l·fŏol)
thin   (thĭn)
  thin·ly   thin·ness
  thin·ner   thin·ning
  thin-skinned
think·a·ble   (thĭngk' á·b'l)
third   (thûrd)
  third class
  third-class *adj. & adv.*
  third de·gree   third-rate
thirst·y   (thûrs' tĭ)
  thirst·i·er, -i·est, -i·ly, -i·ness
thir·teen   (thûr' tēn')
thir·ty   (thûr' tĭ)
  -ties   thir·ti·eth
this·tle   (thĭs' 'l)
thith·er   (thĭth' ēr)
thong   (thŏng)
tho·rax   (thō' răks)
  tho·rac·ic   (thō·răs' ĭk)
tho·ri·um   (thō' rĭ·ŭm)
thor·ough   (thûr' ô)
  thor·ough·bred
  thor·ough·go·ing
  thor·ough·ness
though   (thō)
thought   (thôt)
  thought·ful, -ful·ly, -ful·ness
  thought·less, -less·ly, -less·ness
thou·sand   (thou' zănd)
  thou·sand·fold thou·sandth
thrall·dom   (thrôl' dŭm)
thread·bare   (thrĕd' bâr')
threat·en   (thrĕt' 'n)
three   (thrē)
  three-di·men·sion·al
  three·pen·ny
  three-point land·ing
  three·some
thresh·er   (thrĕsh' ēr)
thresh·old   (thrĕsh' ōld)
thrice   (thrīs)
thrift·y   (thrĭf' tĭ)
  thrift·i·er, -i·est, -i·ly, -i·ness

thrill·ing (thrĭl′ ĭng)
thriv·ing (thrīv′ ĭng)
throat (thrōt)
throes (thrōz)
throm·bo·sis (thrŏm·bō′ sĭs)
throt·tle (thrŏt′ ʼl)
through (thrōō)
  through·out
throw (thrō)
  throw·a·way throw·back
thug (thŭg)
  thug·gish
thumb (thŭm)
  thumb·nail thumb·tack
thun·der (thŭn′ dĕr)
  thun·der·bird thun·der·bolt
  thun·der·clap thun·der·cloud
  thun·der·head thun·der·ous
  thun·der·show·er
  thun·der·struck
thwart (thwôrt)
thyme (tīm)
  (seasoning; see *time*)
thy·mus gland (thī′ mŭs)
thy·roid gland (thī′ roid)
thy·self (thĭ·sĕlf′)
ti·ar·a (tĭ·âr′ à)
Ti·bet·an (tĭ·bĕt′ ăn)
tic (tĭk)
  (twitching; see *tick*)
tick (tĭk)
  (parasite; see *tic*)
tick·et (tĭk′ ĕt)
tick·le (tĭk′ ʼl)
  -ling
  tick·lish (tĭk′ lĭsh)
tick·tack·toe (tĭk′ tăk·tō′)
tid·bit (tĭd′ bĭt′)
tid·dly·winks (tĭd′ ʼl·ĭ·wĭngks′)
tide (tīd)
  tid·al (tīd′ ăl)
  tide·wa·ter
ti·dy (tī′ dĭ)
  -died -dy·ing
  ti·di·er, -i·est, -i·ly, -i·ness
tie (tī)
  tied ty·ing
  tie-up
tier (tēr)
  (row)
tiff (tĭf)
tight (tīt)
  tight·en tight·fist·ed
  tight-lipped tight·rope
ti·gress (tī′ grĕs)

Ti·jua·na, Mex. (tē·hwä′ nä)
tile (tīl)
  til·ing
till (tĭl)
  till·a·ble
  till·age (tĭl′ ĭj)
tim·bale (tĭm′ băl)
tim·ber (tĭm′ bĕr)
  (wood; see *timbre*)
tim·bre (tĭm′ bĕr)
  (tone; see *timber*)
Tim·buk·tu (tĭm·bŭk′ tōō)
time (tīm)
  (period, occasion; see *thyme*)
  tim·ing time-hon·ored
  time·keep·er time·less
  time·li·ness time·ly
  time·piece time·sav·ing
  time·ta·ble time·worn
  time zone
tim·id (tĭm′ ĭd)
  ti·mid·i·ty (tĭ·mĭd′ ĭ·tĭ)
tim·or·ous (tĭm′ ĕr·ŭs)
tim·pa·ni (tĭm′ pá·nē)
tinc·ture (tĭngk′ tûr)
tin·der·box (tĭn′ dĕr·bŏks′)
tine (tīn)
tin (tĭn)
  tin foil tin·ny
  tin-pan al·ley tin type
tinge (tĭnj)
  tinge·ing
tin·gle (tĭng′ g′l)
  -gling
tin·sel (tĭn′ sĕl)
  -seled
ti·ny (tī′ nĭ)
  ti·ni·er, -i·est, -i·ness
tip-off (tĭp′ ôf′)
Tip·pe·rar·y (tĭp′ ĕ·râr′ ĭ)
tip·pler (tĭp′ lĕr)
tip·ster (tĭp′ stĕr)
tip·toe (tĭp′ tō′)
  -toe·ing
ti·rade (tī′ răd)
tire (tīr)
  tir·ing tired·ness
  tire·less
  tire·some -some·ly
tis·sue (tĭsh′ ū)
Ti·tan·ic (tĭ·tăn′ ĭk)
tithe (tĭth)
  tith·ing
ti·tian (tĭsh′ ăn)

tit·il·late (tĭt′ ĭ·lāt)
 -il·lat·ing
tit·il·la·tion (tĭt′ ĭ·lā′ shŭn)
ti·tle (tī′ t'l)
 -tling
 ti·tle·hold·er
ti·tlist (tī′ tlĭst)
tit·mouse (tĭt′ mous′)
ti·trate (tī′ trāt)
 -trat·ing
 ti·tra·tion (tī·trā′ shŭn)
tit·u·lar (tĭt′ û·lẽr)
to (tōō)
 (toward; see *too, two*)
toad·stool (tōd′ stōōl′)
toad·y (tōd′ ĭ)
 toad·ied
 toad·y·ing
to-and-fro (tōō′ ănd·frō′)
toast·mas·ter (tōst′ măs′ tẽr)
to·bac·co (tŏ·băk′ ō)
 -bac·cos
to·bog·gan (tŏ·bŏg′ ăn)
to·day (tōō·dā′)
tod·dy (tŏd′ dĭ)
 (hot toddy)
 tod·dies
to-do (tōō·dōō′)
toe (tō)
 toe·ing
 toe dance *n.*
 toe hold
 toe·nail
to·ga (tō′ gá)
to·geth·er (tōō·gĕth′ ẽr)
togged (tŏgd)
tog·gle switch (tŏg′ 'l)
toil (toil)
 toil·er
 toil·worn
toi·let (toi′ lĕt)
toi·lette (toi·lĕt′)
To·kay wine (tŏ·kā′)
to·ken (tō′ kĕn)
tol·er·a·ble (tŏl′ ẽr·á·b'l)
tol·er·ant (tŏl′ ẽr·ănt)
 -ance
tol·er·ate (tŏl′ ẽr·āt)
 -at·ing
 tol·er·a·tion (tŏl′ ẽr·ā′ shŭn)
toll (tōl)
 toll booth
 toll·gate
 toll·keep·er
 toll road
Tol·stoy, Le·o (tŏl·stoi′)
tom·a·hawk (tŏm′ á·hôk)
to·ma·to (tŏ·mā′ tō)
 -toes
tomb·stone (tōōm′ stōn′)
tom·boy·ish (tŏm′ boi′ ĭsh)
tome (tōm)
tom·fool·er·y (tŏm′ fōōl′ ẽr·ĭ)

to·mor·row (tōō·mŏr′ ō)
tom-tom (tŏm′ tŏm′)
ton·al (tōn′ ắl)
 to·nal·i·ty (tŏ·năl′ ĭ·tĭ)
tone·less (tōn′ lĕs)
tongue (tŭng)
 tongue-tied
ton·ic (tŏn′ ĭk)
 to·nic·i·ty (tŏ·nĭs′ ĭ·tĭ)
to·night (tōō·nīt′)
ton·nage (tŭn′ ĭj)
ton·sil (tŏn′ sĭl)
 ton·sil·lec·to·my
 (tŏn′ sĭ·lĕk′ tŏ·mĭ)
 ton·sil·li·tis (tŏn′ sĭ·lī′ tĭs)
ton·sure (tŏn′ shẽr)
 ton·so·ri·al (tŏn·sō′ rĭ·ắl)
too (tōō)
 (also; see *to, two*)
tool·mak·er (tōōl′ māk′ ẽr)
tooth (tōōth)
 tooth·ache
 tooth·brush
 tooth·less
 tooth·pick
top (tŏp)
 top·coat
 top·flight
 top hat
 top-heav·y
 top·most
 top·notch
 top·per
 top·sail
 top se·cret
 top ser·geant
 top·soil
to·paz (tō′ păz)
top·ic (tŏp′ ĭk)
 top·i·cal (tŏp′ ĭ·kắl)
to·pog·ra·phy (tŏ·pŏg′ rá·fĭ)
to·pol·o·gy (tŏ·pŏl′ ŏ·jĭ)
top·ple (tŏp′ 'l)
 top·pling
top·sy-tur·vy (tŏp′ sĭ·tûr′ vĭ)
toque (tōk)
to·rah (tō′ rä)
torch·bear·er (tôrch′ bâr′ ẽr)
tor·e·a·dor (tŏr′ ĕ·á·dôr′)
tor·ment (tôr·mĕnt′) *v.*
 (tôr′ mĕnt) *n.*
 tor·men·tor (tôr·mĕn′ tẽr)
tor·na·do (tôr·nā′ dō)
 -does
tor·pe·do (tôr·pē′ dō)
 -does
tor·por (tôr′ pẽr)
tor·pid (tôr′ pĭd)
torque (tôrk)
tor·rent (tôr′ ĕnt)
 tor·ren·tial (tŏ·rĕn′ shắl)
tor·rid (tôr′ ĭd)

tor·sion (tôr′ shŭn)
tor·so (tôr′ sō)
  -sos
tor·til·la (tôr·tē′ yä)
tor·toise (tôr′ tŭs)
tor·tu·ous (tôr′ tŭ·ŭs)
tor·ture (tôr′ tŭr)
  -tur·ing tor·tur·er
To·ry (tō′ rǐ)
  -ries
toss·up (tŏs′ ŭp′)
to·tal (tō′ tăl)
  to·tal·i·ty (tō·tăl′ ǐ·tǐ)
  -ties
  to·tal·ize -iz·ing
  to·tal·ly
to·tal·i·tar·i·an
    (tō·tăl′ ǐ·târ′ ǐ·ăn)
to·tem (tō′ tĕm)
  to·tem·ic (tō·tĕm′ ǐk)
tou·can (tōō·kän′)
touch (tŭch)
  touch·a·ble touch·down
  touch·y
tou·ché (tōō′ shā′)
tough (tŭf)
  tough·ened
tou·pee (tōō·pā′)
tour de force (tōōr′ dĕ fôrs′)
tour·ist (tōōr′ ǐst)
  tour·ism
tour·na·ment (tōōr′ nȧ·mĕnt)
tour·ney (tōōr′ nǐ′)
  -neys
tour·ni·quet (tōōr′ nǐ·kĕt)
tou·sled (tou′ z'ld)
to·ward (tō′ ĕrd)
tow·el (tou′ ĕl)
  -eled -el·ing
tow·er (tou′ ĕr)
  -ered -er·ing
tow·head (tō′ hĕd′)
tow·line (tō′ līn′)
town (toun)
  town cri·er town hall
  town·ship towns·peo·ple
tox·ic (tŏk′ sǐk)
  tox·ic·i·ty (tŏks·ǐs′ ǐ·tǐ)
tox·in (tŏk′ sǐn)
trace (trās)
  trac·ing trace·a·ble
  trac·er·y
tra·che·a (trā′ kĕ·ȧ)
trac·ta·ble (trăk′ tȧ·b'l)

trac·ta·bil·i·ty
    (trăk′ tȧ·bǐl′ ǐ·tǐ)
trac·tion (trăk′ shŭn)
trac·tor (trăk′ tēr)
trade (trād)
  trad·ing trade-in
  trade·mark trade name
  trade school trades·man
  trade wind
tra·di·tion (trȧ·dǐsh′ ŭn)
  tra·di·tion·al, -al·ly
  tra·di·tion·al·ist
traf·fic (trăf′ ǐk)
  traf·ficked traf·fick·ing
trag·e·dy (trăj′ ĕ·dǐ)
  -dies
  tra·ge·di·an (trȧ·jē′ dǐ·ăn)
trag·ic (trăj′ ǐk)
  trag·i·cal·ly
  trag·i·com·ic (trăj′ ǐ·kŏm′ ǐk)
trail·er (trāl′ ēr)
train (trān)
  train·a·ble
  train·ee (trān·ē′)
trait (trāt)
trai·tor (trā′ tēr)
  trai·tor·ous
tra·jec·to·ry (trȧ·jĕk′ tō·rǐ)
tram·meled (trăm′ ĕld)
tram·ple (trăm′ p'l)
  -pling
tram·po·line (trăm′ pō·lǐn)
tram·way (trăm′ wā′)
trance (trȧns)
tran·quil (trăng′ kwǐl)
  tran·quil·iz·er
  tran·quil·li·ty (trăn·kwǐl′ ǐ·tǐ)
  tran·quil·ly
trans·act (trăns·ăkt′)
  trans·ac·tion
trans·at·lan·tic
    (trăns′ ăt·lăn′ tǐk)
tran·scend (trăn·sĕnd′)
  tran·scend·ent (trăn·sĕn′ dĕnt)
  -ence
  tran·scen·den·tal
    (trăn′ sĕn·dĕn′ tăl)
tran·scribe (trăn·skrīb′)
  -scrib·ing
  tran·scrip·tion
    (trăn·skrǐp′ shŭn)
tran·sept (trăn′ sĕpt)
trans·fer (trăns·fûr′)
  -ferred -fer·ring
  trans·fer·a·ble

trans·fer·ence (trăns·fûr′ ĕns)

trans·fig·u·ra·tion
        (trăns·fĭg′ û·rā′ shŭn)

trans·fixed (trăns·fĭkst′)

trans·for·ma·tion
        (trăns′ fôr·mā′ shŭn)

trans·form·er (trăns·fôr′ mĕr)

trans·fu·sion (trăns·fū′ zhŭn)

trans·gress (trăns·grĕs′)
  trans·gres·sion (-grĕsh′ ŭn)
  trans·gres·sor (-grĕs′ ĕr)

tran·sience (trăn′ shĕns)
 -sient

tran·sis·tor (trăn·zĭs′ tĕr)

trans·it (trăn′ sĭt)

tran·si·tion (trăn·zĭsh′ ŭn)
  tran·si·tion·al

tran·si·tive (trăn′ sĭ·tĭv)

tran·si·to·ry (trăn′ sĭ·tō′ rĭ)

trans·late (trăns·lāt′)
 -lat·ing trans·lat·a·ble
  trans·la·tion trans·la·tor

trans·lit·er·a·tion
     (trăns·lĭt′ ĕr·ā′ shŭn)

trans·lu·cent (trăns·lū′ sĕnt)
 -cence

trans·mi·gra·tion
    (trăns′ mĭ·grā′ shŭn)

trans·mit (trăns·mĭt′)
 -mit·ted -mit·ting
  trans·mit·tal (trăns·mĭt′ ᴅl)
  trans·mit·ter

trans·mute (trăns·mūt′)
 -mut·ing

tran·som (trăn′ sŭm)

trans·par·ent (trăns·pâr′ ĕnt)
 -en·cy

tran·spire (trăn·spīr′)
 -spir·ing

trans·plant (trăns·plănt′)

trans·port (trăns·pōrt′)
  trans·port·a·ble
  trans·por·ta·tion
     (trăns′ pôr·tā′ shŭn)

trans·pose (trăns·pōz′)
 -pos·ing
  trans·po·si·tion
    (trăns′ pŏ·zĭsh′ ŭn)

Trans·vaal, S. Afr.
     (trăns·väl′)

trans·verse (trăns·vûrs′)

tra·peze (trȧ·pēz′)

trap·per (trăp′ ĕr)

Trap·pist (trăp′ ĭst)

trau·ma (trô′ mȧ)
 trau·mat·ic (trô·măt′ ĭk)

trav·ail (trăv′ āl)

trav·el (trăv′ ĕl)
 -eled -el·ing
 trav·el·er
 trav·e·logue (trăv′ ĕ·lŏg)

trav·erse (trăv′ ĕrs)
 -vers·ing trav·ers·a·ble

trav·es·ty (trăv′ ĕs·tĭ)
 -ties

trawl·er (trôl′ ĕr)

treach·er·y (trĕch′ ĕr·ĭ)
 -er·ies treach·er·ous

trea·cle (trē′ k'l)
 trea·cly

trea·dle (trĕd′ 'l)

tread·mill (trĕd′ mĭl′)

trea·son (trē′ z'n)
 trea·son·a·ble trea·son·ous

treas·ure (trĕzh′ ĕr)
 treas·ur·er treas·ur·y

treat (trēt)
 treat·a·ble treat·ment

trea·tise (trē′ tĭs)

trea·ty (trē′ tĭ)
 -ties

tre·ble (trĕb′ 'l)
 tre·ble clef

tree·top (trē′ tŏp′)

tre·foil (trē′ foil)

trek (trĕk)
 trekked trek·king

trel·lis (trĕl′ ĭs)

trem·ble (trĕm′ b'l)
 -bling

tre·men·dous (trĕ·mĕn′ dŭs)

trem·o·lo (trĕm′ ồ·lō)

trem·or (trĕm′ ĕr)

trem·u·lous (trĕm′ û·lŭs)

trench·ant (trĕn′ chȧnt)

trep·i·da·tion (trĕp′ ĭ·dā′ shŭn)

tres·pass·er (trĕs′ pȧs·ĕr)

tres·tle (trĕs′ 'l)

tri·ad (trī′ ăd)

tri·al (trī′ ȧl)

tri·an·gle (trī′ ăng′ g'l)
 tri·an·gu·lar (trī·ăng′ gû·lĕr)

Tri·as·sic (trī·ăs′ ĭk)

tribe (trīb)
 trib·al tribes·man

trib·u·la·tion (trĭb′ û·lā′ shŭn)

trib·une (trĭb′ ūn)
 tri·bu·nal (trī·bū′ nȧl)

trib·u·tar·y	(trĭb′ ū·tĕr′ ĭ)	troop	(trōōp)
-tar·ies		(boy scouts, soldiers; see *troupe*)	
trib·ute	(trĭb′ ūt)	tro·phy	(trō′ fĭ)
trice	(trīs)	-phies	
tri·ceps	(trī′ sĕps)	trop·ic	(trŏp′ ĭk)
tri·chi·na	(trĭ·kī′ nå)	trŏp·i·cal	
trich·i·no·sis	(trĭk′ ĭ·nō′ sĭs)	tro·pism	(trō′ pĭz′m)
trick·er·y	(trĭk′ ĕr·ĭ)	trop·o·sphere	(trŏp′ ŏ·sfĕr)
trick·le	(trĭk′ ′l)	trot·ter	(trŏt′ ĕr)
-ling		trou·ba·dour	(trōō′ bå·dōōr)
tri·col·or	(trī′ kŭl′ ēr)	trou·ble	(trŭb′ ′l)
tri·cot	(trē′ kō)	-bling	trou·ble·some
tri·cy·cle	(trī′ sĭk·′l)	trou·blous	
tri·dent	(trī′ dĕnt)	trough	(trŏf)
tri·en·ni·al	(trī·ĕn′ ĭ·ål)	troupe	(trōōp)
tri·fling	(trī′ flĭng)	(actors; see *troop*)	
trig·ger	(trĭg′ ĕr)	trou·sers	(trou′ zĕrz)
tri·lin·gual	(trī·lĭng′ gwål)	trous·seau	(trōō′ sō′)
tril·lion	(trĭl′ yŭn)	*pl.* trous·seaux	(-sō′)
(number)		trout	(trout)
tril·li·um	(trĭl′ ĭ·ŭm)	trow·el	(trou′ ĕl)
(flower)		-eled	-el·ing
tril·o·gy	(trĭl′ ŏ·jĭ)	tru·ant	(trōō′ ånt)
-gies		-an·cy	
trim·ming	(trĭm′ ĭng)	truce	(trōōs)
trin·i·ty	(trĭn′ ĭ·tĭ)	truck·age	(trŭk′ ĭj)
trin·ket	(trĭng′ kĕt)	truck·le	(trŭk′ ′l)
tri·o	(trē′ ō)	-ling	
-os		truc·u·lence	(trŭk′ ū·lĕns)
tri·par·tite	(trī·pär′ tīt)	trudge	(trŭj)
tri·ple	(trĭp′ ′l)	trudg·ing	
-pling		trudg·en stroke	(trŭj′ ĕn)
tri·plet	(trĭp′ lĕt)	true	(trōō)
tri·ply		true·love	true·ness
trip·li·cate	(trĭp′ lĭ·kåt)	tru·ism	tru·ly
tri·pod	(trī′ pŏd)	truf·fle	(trŭf′ ′l)
trip·tych	(trĭp′ tĭk)	trum·pet·er	(trŭm′ pĕt·ēr)
trite	(trīt)	trun·cate	(trŭng′ kāt)
trite·ness		-cat·ing	
tri·umph	(trī′ ŭmf)	trun·dle bed	(trŭn′ d′l)
tri·um·phal	(trī·ŭm′ fål)	trun·nion	(trŭn′ yŭn)
tri·um·phant	(trī·ŭm′ fånt)	truss	(trŭs)
tri·um·vi·rate	(trī·ŭm′ vĭ·råt)	trus·tee	(trŭs·tē′)
triv·et	(trĭv′ ĕt)	(one holding property in trust;	
triv·i·a	(trĭv′ ĭ·å)	see *trusty*)	
triv·i·al	(trĭv′ ĭ·ål)	trus·tee·ship	
triv·i·al·i·ty	(trĭv′ ĭ·ăl′ ĭ·tĭ)	trust·ful	(trŭst′ fōōl)
triv·i·al·ly		-ful·ly	-ful·ness
trod·den	(trŏd′ ′n)	trust·wor·thy	(trŭst′ wûr′ thĭ)
troi·ka	(troi′ kå)	-wor·thi·ness	
trol·ley	(trŏl′ ĭ)	trust·y	(trŭs′ tĭ)
trol·leys		(convict allowed special privi-	
trol·lop	(trŏl′ ŭp)	leges; see *trustee*)	
trom·bone	(trŏm′ bōn)	trust·ies	

truth·ful (trōōth′ fŏŏl)
-ful·ly -ful·ness
try (trī)
tried try·ing
try·out
tryst·ing place (trĭs′ tĭng)
tsar (zär)
(or czar)
tset·se fly (tsĕt′ sĕ)
tu·ba (tū′ bȧ)
pl. tu·bae (-bē)
tub·ba·ble (tŭb′ ȧ·b′l)
tu·ber·cu·lar (tû·bûr′ kŭ·lẽr)
tu·ber·cu·lo·sis
(tû·bûr′ kŭ·lō′ sĭs)
tu·ber·ous (tū′ bẽr·ŭs)
tub·ing (tūb′ ĭng)
tu·bu·lar (tū′ bû·lẽr)
Tuc·son, Ariz. (tōō·sŏn′)
Tu·dor (tū′ dẽr)
Tues·day (tūz′ dĭ)
tuft·ed (tŭf′ tĕd)
tu·i·tion (tû·ĭsh′ ŭn)
tu·la·re·mi·a (tōō′ lȧ·rē′ mĭ·ȧ)
tu·lip (tū′ lĭp)
tum·ble-down (tŭm′ b′l·doun′)
tum·ble·weed (tŭm′ b′l·wēd′)
tu·mor (tū′ mẽr)
tu·mult (tū′ mŭlt)
tu·mul·tu·ous (tû·mŭl′ tụ·ŭs)
tu·na fish (tōō′ nȧ)
tun·dra (tŏŏn′ drȧ)
tune·ful (tūn′ fŏŏl)
-ful·ly -ful·ness
tune·less
tung·sten (tŭng′ stĕn)
tu·nic (tū′ nĭk)
tun·ing fork (tūn′ ĭng)
Tu·ni·si·a (tû·nĭzh′ ĭ·ȧ)
tun·nel (tŭn′ ĕl)
tun·neled tun·nel·ing
tur·ban (tûr′ bȧn)
(headdress)
tur·bine (tûr′ bĭn)
(rotary engine)
tur·bo·jet en·gine
(tûr′ bŏ·jĕt′)
tur·bu·lent (tûr′ bû·lĕnt)
-lence
tu·reen (tû·rēn′)
turf (tûrf)
tur·gid (tûr′ jĭd)
tur·gid·i·ty (tûr·jĭd′ ĭ·tĭ)
tur·key (tûr′ kĭ)
-keys

Turk·ish (tûr′ kĭsh)
tur·mer·ic (tûr′ mẽr·ĭk)
tur·moil (tûr′ moil)
turn (tûrn)
(revolve; see tern)
turn·a·bout turn·coat
turn·key turn·out
turn·o·ver turn·pike
turn·plate turn·stile
turn·ta·ble
tur·nip (tûr′ nĭp)
tur·pen·tine (tûr′ pĕn·tĭn)
tur·pi·tude (tûr′ pĭ·tūd)
tur·quoise (tûr′ koiz)
tur·ret (tûr′ ĕt)
tur·ret·ed
tur·tle (tûr′ t′l)
tur·tle·back tur·tle-neck adj.
tus·sle (tŭs′ ′l)
tus·sling
tu·te·lage (tū′ tĕ·lĭj)
tu·te·lar·y (tū′ tĕ·lẽr′ ĭ)
tu·tor (tū′ tẽr)
tu·tor·age (tū′ tẽr·ĭj)
tu·to·ri·al (tû·tō′ rĭ·ȧl)
tux·e·do (tŭk·sē′ dō)
-dos
twad·dle (twŏd′ ′l)
twain (twān)
twang (twăng)
tweak (twēk)
tweed (twēd)
tweet·er (twēt′ ẽr)
tweez·ers (twēz′ ẽrz)
twelfth (twĕlfth)
twen·ty (twĕn′ tĭ)
-ties twen·ti·eth
twen·ty-twen·ty
twice (twīs)
twi·light (twī′ līt′)
twinge (twĭnj)
twing·ing
twin·kle (twĭng′ k′l)
-kling
twirl (twûrl)
twist·er (twĭs′ tẽr)
twitch (twĭch)
two (tōō)
(pair; see to, too)
two-by-four two-faced
two-fist·ed two-fold
two·some two-way
ty·coon (tī·kōōn′)
ty·ing (tī′ ĭng)
tyke (tīk)

tym·pan·ic   (tĭm·păn′ ĭk)
type   (tīp)
　typ·ing   type·script
　type·set·ter   type·writ·er
ty·phoid   (tī′ foid)
ty·phoon   (tī·fōōn′)
ty·phus   (tī′ fŭs)
typ·i·cal   (tĭp′ ĭ·k/l)
　typ·i·cal·ly   -cal·ness
typ·i·fy   (tĭp′ ĭ·fī)
　-fied   -fy·ing
typ·ist   (tĭp′ ĭst)
ty·pog·ra·phy   (tī·pŏg′ rá·fī)
　ty·po·graph·i·cal
                    (tī′ pô·grăf′ ĭ·k/l)
tyr·an·ny   (tĭr′ á·nĭ)
　-an·nies
　ty·ran·ni·cal   (tĭ·răn′ ĭ·k/l)
　tyr·an·nize   -an·niz·ing
　tyr·an·nous
ty·rant   (tī′ rá̆nt)
ty·ro   (tī′ rō)
　-ros

U

u·biq·ui·tous   (ū·bĭk′ wĭ·tŭs)
　u·biq·ui·ty   (-tĭ)
U-boat   (ū′ bōt′)
ud·der   (ŭd′ ēr)
ugh   (ŭ)
ug·ly   (ŭg′ lĭ)
　ug·li·er, -li·est, -li·ness
u·ku·le·le   (ū′ kŭ·lā′ lĕ)
ul·cer   (ŭl′ sēr)
　ul·ce·ra·tion   (ŭl′ sēr·ā′ shŭn)
　ul·cer·ous
ul·te·ri·or   (ŭl·tēr′ ĭ·ēr)
ul·ti·mate   (ŭl′ tĭ·mĭt)
　-mate·ly
ul·ti·ma·tum   (ŭl′ tĭ·mā′ tŭm)
ul·tra-   (ŭl′ trá-)
　ul·tra·con·serv·a·tive
　ul·tra·lib·er·al ul·tra·ma·rine
　ul·tra·mod·ern
　ul·tra·vi·o·let
U·lys·ses   (û·lĭs′ ēz)
um·ber   (ŭm′ bēr)
um·bil·i·cal cord
                    (ŭm·bĭl′ ĭ·k/l)
um·brage   (ŭm′ brĭj)
um·brel·la   (ŭm·brĕl′ á)
um·laut   (ŏŏm′ lout)
um·pire   (ŭm′ pīr)

un·a·ble   (ŭn·ā′ b′l)
un·a·bridged   (ŭn′ á·brĭjd′)
un·ac·count·a·ble
                    (ŭn′ á·koun′ tá·b′l)
un·ac·cus·tomed
                    (ŭn′ á·kŭs′ tŭmd)
un·af·fect·ed   (ŭn′ á·fĕk′ tĕd)
un-A·mer·i·can
                    (ŭn′ á·mĕr′ ĭ·kán)
u·na·nim·i·ty   (ū′ ná·nĭm′ ĭ·tĭ)
　u·nan·i·mous   (û·năn′ ĭ·mŭs)
un·as·sum·ing   (ŭn′ á·sūm′ ĭng)
un·a·void·a·ble
                    (ŭn′ á·void′ á·b′l)
un·be·com·ing
                    (ŭn′ bĕ·kŭm′ ĭng)
un·be·knownst   (ŭn′ bĕ·nōnst′)
un·bi·ased   (ŭn·bī′ á̆st)
un·bid·den   (ŭn·bĭd′ 'n)
un·bri·dled   (ŭn·brī′ d′lĕ̆d)
un·can·ny   (ŭn·kăn′ ĭ)
un·cer·e·mo·ni·ous
                    (ŭn′ sĕr·ĕ·mō′ nĭ·ŭs)
un·cer·tain·ty   (ŭn·sûr′ tĭn·tĭ)
　-ties
un·chris·tian   (ŭn·krĭs′ chán)
un·civ·i·lized   (ŭn·sĭv′ ĭ·līzd)
un·clas·si·fi·a·ble
                    (ŭn·klăs′ ĭ·fī′ á·b′l)
un·cle   (ŭng′ k′l)
un·com·fort·a·ble
                    (ŭn·kŭm′ fērt·á·b′l)
un·com·mit·ted   (ŭn′ kó·mĭt′ ĕd)
un·com·mon   (ŭn·kŏm′ ŭn)
　un·com·mon·ly
　un·com·mon·ness
un·com·mu·ni·ca·tive
                    (ŭn′ kó·mū′ nĭ·kā′ tĭv)
un·com·pro·mis·ing
                    (ŭn·kŏm′ prô·mīz′ ĭng)
un·con·cern·ed·ly
                    (ŭn′ kŏn·sûr′ nĕd·lĭ)
un·con·di·tion·al
                    (ŭn′ kŏn·dĭsh′ ŭn·ál)
un·con·scion·a·ble
                    (ŭn·kŏn′ shŭn·á·b′l)
un·con·scious   (ŭn·kŏn′ shŭs)
un·con·sti·tu·tion·al
                    (ŭn′ kŏn·stĭ·tū′ shŭn·ál)
un·couth   (ŭn·kōōth′)
unc·tion   (ŭngk′ shŭn)
unc·tu·ous   (ŭngk′ tṵ·ŭs)
un·daunt·ed   (ŭn·dôn′ tĕd)
un·de·mon·stra·tive
                    (ŭn′ dĕ·mŏn′ strá·tĭv)

un·de·ni·a·ble   (ŭn′ dĕ·nī′ ȧ·b′l)
un·der   (ŭn′ dĕr)
  un·der·brush   un·der·clothes
  un·der·cur·rent
  un·der·es·ti·mate
  un·der·ex·po·sure
  un·der·grad·u·ate
  un·der·hand·ed
  un·der·lie   -ly·ing
  un·der·neath
  un·der·nour·ished
  un·der·pin·ning
  un·der·priv·i·leged
  un·der·rate   un·der·signed
  un·der·stand·a·ble
  un·der·stood   un·der·tow
  un·der·weight   un·der·writ·er
un·de·sir·a·ble
        (ŭn′ dĕ·zīr′ ȧ·b′l)
un·do·ing   (ŭn·dōō′ ĭng)
un·doubt·ed·ly
        (ŭn·dout′ ĕd·lĭ)
un·du·la·tion   (ŭn′ dụ·lā′ shŭn)
un·du·ly   (ŭn·dū′ lĭ)
un·dy·ing   (ŭn·dī′ ĭng)
un·eas·i·ness   (ŭn·ēz′ ĭ·nĕs)
un·em·ploy·a·ble
        (ŭn′ ĕm·ploi′ ȧ·b′l)
un·e·qual   (ŭn·ē′ kwȧl)
  -qualed   un·e·qual·ly
un·e·quiv·o·cal
        (ŭn′ ĕ·kwĭv′ ô·kȧl)
  -cal·ly
un·err·ing   (ŭn·ûr′ ĭng)
un·e·ven·ness   (ŭn·ē′ vĕn·nĕs)
un·ex·pur·gat·ed
        (ŭn·ĕks′ pēr·gāt′ ĕd)
un·faith·ful   (ŭn·fāth′ fōōl)
  -ful·ly,   -ful·ness
un·fa·mil·i·ar·i·ty
        (ŭn′ fȧ·mĭl′ ĭ·ăr′ ĭ·tĭ)
un·fas·ten   (ŭn·fás′ 'n)
un·fa·vor·a·ble
        (ŭn·fā′ vēr·ȧ·b′l)
un·feigned   (ŭn·fānd′)
un·fet·tered   (ŭn·fĕt′ ērd)
un·flinch·ing   (ŭn·flĭn′ chĭng)
un·for·get·ta·ble
        (ŭn′ fŏr·gĕt′ ȧ·b′l)
un·for·tu·nate·ly
        (ŭn·fôr′ tụ·nĭt·lĭ)
un·friend·li·ness
        (ŭn·frĕnd′ lĭ·nĕs)
un·furled   (ŭn·fûrld′)

un·gain·li·ness
        (ŭn·gān′ lĭ·nĕs)
un·grace·ful   (ŭn·grās′ fōōl)
un·grate·ful   (ŭn·grāt′ fōōl)
un·hap·pi·ness   (ŭn·hăp′ ĭ·nĕs)
un·har·nessed   (ŭn·här′ nĕst)
un·hinged   (ŭn·hĭnjd′)
un·hur·ried   (ŭn·hûr′ ĭd)
u·ni·cam·er·al
        (ū′ nĭ·kăm′ ēr·ȧl)
u·ni·corn   (ū′ nĭ·kôrn)
u·ni·fi·ca·tion   (ū′ nĭ·fĭ·kā′ shŭn)
u·ni·form·i·ty   (ū′ nĭ·fôr′ mĭ·tĭ)
u·ni·fy   (ū′ nĭ·fī)
  -fied,   -fy·ing
u·ni·lat·er·al   (ū′ nĭ·lăt′ ēr·ȧl)
un·im·peach·a·ble
        (ŭn′ ĭm·pēch′ ȧ·b′l)
un·ion·ize   (ūn′ yŭn·īz)
  -iz·ing
u·nique   (ū·nēk′)
  -nique·ly
u·ni·son   (ū′ nĭ·sŭn)
u·nit   (ū′ nĭt)
  u·ni·tar·y   (ū′ nĭ·tĕr′ ĭ)
u·nite   (ū·nīt′)
  -nit·ing
u·ni·ty   (ū′ nĭ·tĭ)
  -ties
u·ni·ver·sal   (ū′ nĭ·vûr′ sȧl)
  -sal·ly
  u·ni·ver·sal·i·ty
        (ū′ nĭ·vûr·săl′ ĭ·tĭ)
u·ni·verse   (ū′ nĭ·vûrs)
u·ni·ver·si·ty   (ū′ nĭ·vûr′ sĭ·tĭ)
  -ties
un·kempt   (ŭn·kĕmpt′)
un·know·a·ble   (ŭn·nō′ ȧ·b′l)
un·leash   (ŭn·lēsh′)
un·less   (ŭn·lĕs′)
un·like·ly   (ŭn·līk′ lĭ)
  un·like·li·hood
un·lim·it·ed   (ŭn·lĭm′ ĭ·tĕd)
un·men·tion·a·ble
        (ŭn·mĕn′ shŭn·ȧ·b′l)
un·mer·ci·ful   (ŭn·mûr′ sĭ·fōōl)
un·mis·tak·a·ble
        (ŭn′ mĭs·tāk′ ȧ·b′l)
un·mit·i·gat·ed
        (ŭn·mĭt′ ĭ·gāt′ ĕd)
un·named   (ŭn·nāmd′)
un·nat·u·ral   (ŭn·năt′ ū·rȧl)
un·nec·es·sar·y
        (ŭn·nĕs′ ĕ·sĕr′ ĭ)
un·nerv·ing   (ŭn·nûrv′ ĭng)

un·num·bered (ŭn·nŭm′ bẽrd)
un·oc·cu·pied (ŭn·ŏk′ ū·pīd)
un·par·al·leled (ŭn·păr′ ă·lĕld)
un·plumbed (ŭn·plŭmd′)
un·prec·e·dent·ed
             (ŭn·prĕs′ ê·dĕn′ tĕd)
un·prej·u·diced
             (ŭn·prĕj′ ŏo·dĭst)
un·prin·ci·pled
             (ŭn·prĭn′ sĭ·p'ld)
un·pro·nounce·a·ble
             (ŭn′ prŏ·nouns′ à·b'l)
un·qual·i·fied (ŭn·kwŏl′ ĭ·fīd)
un·ques·tion·a·ble
             (ŭn·kwĕs′ chŭn·à·b'l)
un·rav·eled (ŭn·răv′ ĕld)
un·re·al·i·ty (ŭn′ rê·ăl′ ĭ·tĭ)
un·rea·son·a·ble
             (ŭn·rê′ z'n·à·b'l)
un·re·con·struct·ed
             (ŭn′ rê·kŏn·strŭk′ tĕd)
un·re·lent·ing (ŭn·rê·lĕn′ tĭng)
un·re·mit·ting (ŭn′ rê·mĭt′ ĭng)
un·right·eous (ŭn·rī′ chŭs)
un·ri·valed (ŭn·rī′ vălᵈ)
un·ruf·fled (ŭn·rŭf′ 'ld)
un·rul·y (ŭn·rōōl′ ĭ)
 un·rul·i·ness
un·sat·u·rat·ed
             (ŭn·săt′ û·rāt′ ĕd)
un·sa·vor·y (ŭn·sā′ vẽr·ĭ)
 un·sa·vor·i·ness
un·sea·son·a·ble
             (ŭn·sê′ z'n·à·b'l)
un·seem·ly (ŭn·sēm′ lĭ)
un·shack·led (ŭn·shăk′ 'ld)
un·sheathe (ŭn·shēth′)
 -sheath·ing
un·skill·ful (ŭn·skĭl′ fŏol)
un·so·cia·ble (ŭn·sō′ shà·b'l)
un·so·phis·ti·cat·ed
             (ŭn′ sŏ·fĭs′ tĭ·kāt′ ĕd)
un·spar·ing (ŭn·spâr′ ĭng)
un·speak·a·ble (ŭn·spēk′ à·b'l)
un·spot·ted (ŭn·spŏt′ ĕd)
un·sub·stan·tial
             (ŭn′ sŭb·stăn′ shăl)
un·suit·a·ble (ŭn·sūt′ à·b'l)
un·tan·gled (ŭn·tăng′ g'ld)
un·tie (ŭn·tī′)
 -tied   -ty·ing
un·til (ŭn·tĭl′)
un·time·ly (ŭn·tīm′ lĭ)
un·ti·tled (ŭn·tī′ t'ld)
un·touch·a·ble (ŭn′ tŭch′ à·b'l)

un·to·ward (ŭn·tō′ ẽrd)
un·tram·meled (ŭn·trăm′ ĕld)
un·truth·ful (ŭn·trōōth′ fŏol)
un·tu·tored (ŭn·tū′ tẽrd)
un·u·su·al (ŭn·ū′ zhŏo·ăl)
 un·u·su·al·ly
un·ut·ter·a·ble (ŭn·ŭt′ ẽr·à·b'l)
un·want·ed (ŭn·wŏnt′ ĕd)
 (not desired; see *unwonted*)
un·war·rant·a·ble
             (ŭn·wŏr′ ăn·tà·b'l)
un·war·y (ŭn·wâr′ ĭ)
 -war·i·ness
un·whole·some
             (ŭn·hōl′ sŭm)
un·wield·y (ŭn·wēl′ dĭ)
un·wit·ting (ŭn·wĭt′ ĭng)
un·wont·ed (ŭn·wŭn′ tĕd)
 (unaccustomed; see *unwanted*)
un·world·li·ness
             (ŭn·wûrld′ lĭ·nĕs)
up (ŭp)
 up·braid·ing   up·date
 up·grade   up·heav·al
 up·hol·ster·y   up·lift·ing
 up·right   up·roar·i·ous
 up·stairs   up-to-date *adj.*
 up·town   up·ward
up·per (ŭp′ ẽr)
 up·per-class   up·per·most
u·ra·ni·um (û·rā′ nĭ·ŭm)
ur·ban (ûr′ băn)
 ur·ban·i·za·tion
             (ûr′ băn·ĭ·zā′ shŭn)
 ur·ban·ize   -iz·ing
ur·bane (ûr·bān′)
 ur·bane·ly
ur·chin (ûr′ chĭn)
urge (ûrj)
 urg·ing
ur·gent (ûr′ jĕnt)
 -gen·cy
u·ri·nal (ū′ rĭ·năl)
u·ri·nar·y (ū′ rĭ·nẽr′ ĭ)
urn (ûrn)
Ur·sa Ma·jor (ûr′ sà mā′ jẽr)
U·ru·guay (ū′ rŭ·gwī)
 U·ru·guay·an
use (ūs) *n.*
     (ūz) *v.*
 us·ing
 us·a·ble (ūz′ à·b'l)
 us·age (ūs′ ĭj)
 use·ful (ūs′ fŏol)
 -ful·ly   -ful·ness

use·less (ūs′ lĕs)
ush·er (ŭsh′ ēr)
u·surp (ů·zûrp′)
  u·surp·a·tion (ū′ zēr·pā′ shŭn)
u·su·ry (ū′ zhŏŏ·rĭ)
  u·su·rer (ū′ zhŏŏ·rēr)
  u·su·ri·ous (ů·zhŏŏr′ ĭ·ůs)
U·tah (ū′ tô)
  U·tah·an
u·ten·sil (ů·tĕn′ sĭl)
u·ter·ine (ū′ tēr·ĭn)
u·til·i·tar·i·an (ů·tĭl′ ĭ·târ′ ĭ·ăn)
u·til·i·ty (ů·tĭl′ ĭ·tĭ)
  -ties
u·ti·lize (ū′ tĭ·līz)
  -liz·ing   u·ti·liz·a·ble
  u·ti·li·za·tion
        (ū′ tĭ·lĭ·zā′ shŭn)
ut·most (ŭt′ mōst)
U·to·pi·an (ů·tō′ pĭ·ăn)
ut·ter (ŭt′ ēr)
  ut·ter·a·ble   ut·ter·ance
  ut·ter·ly   ut·ter·most
u·vu·la (ū′ vů·lå)

V

va·cant (vā′ kånt)
  va·can·cy
  va·cate (vā′ kāt)
  -cat·ing
va·ca·tion (vå·kā′ shŭn)
vac·ci·nate (văk′ sĭ·nāt)
  -nat·ing
  vac·ci·na·tion
        (văk′ sĭ·nā′ shŭn)
vac·cine (văk′ sēn)
vac·il·late (văs′ ĭ·lāt)
  -il·lat·ing
  vac·il·la·tion (văs′ ĭ·lā′ shŭn)
vac·u·ous (văk′ ů·ůs)
  va·cu·i·ty (vå·kū′ ĭ·tĭ)
vac·u·um clean·er
        (văk′ ů·ŭm)
vag·a·bond (văg′ å·bŏnd)
va·gar·y (vå·gâr′ ĭ)
  gar·ies
va·gi·na (vå·jī′ nå)
va·gran·cy (vā′ grån·sĭ)
vague (văg)
  vague·ly
vain (văn)
  (empty; conceited; see *vane, vein*)
vain·glo·ri·ous (văn′ glō′ rĭ·ůs)

val·ance (văl′ åns)
  (drapery; see *valence*)
val·e·dic·to·ry (văl′ ė·dĭk′ tô·rĭ)
  val·e·dic·to·ri·an
        (văl′ ė·dĭk·tō′ rĭ·ăn)
va·lence (vā′ lĕns)
  (of chemical elements; see *valance*)
val·en·tine (văl′ ĕn·tīn)
val·et (văl′ ĕt)
val·iant (văl′ yǎnt)
  -iance
val·id (văl′ ĭd)
  val·i·date   -dat·ing
  va·lid·i·ty (vå·lĭd′ ĭ·tĭ)
va·lise (vå·lēs′)
Val·kyr·ie (văl·kĭr′ ĭ)
val·ley (văl′ ĭ)
val·or (văl′ ēr)
  val·or·ous
Val·pa·rai·so, (văl′ på·rā′ zō)
  Chile
val·ue (văl′ ū)
  -u·ing
  val·u·a·ble (văl′ ů·å·b′l)
  val·u·a·tion (văl′ ů·ā′ shŭn)
  val·ue·less
vam·pire (văm′ pīr)
van·dal (văn′ dǎl)
Van·der·bilt (univ.)
        (văn′ dēr·bĭlt)
Van·dyke (beard)
        (văn·dīk′)
vane (văn)
  (weathercock; see *vain, vein*)
van·guard (văn′ gärd′)
va·nil·la (vå·nĭl′ å)
van·ish (văn′ ĭsh)
van·i·ty (văn′ ĭ·tĭ)
  -ties
van·quish (văng′ kwĭsh)
van·tage (văn′ tĭj)
vap·id (văp′ ĭd)
va·por (vā′ pēr)
  va·por·ize   -iz·ing
  va·por·ous
var·i·a·ble (vâr′ ĭ·å·b′l)
  var·i·a·bil·i·ty
        (vâr′ ĭ·å·bĭl′ ĭ·tĭ)
var·i·ant (vâr′ ĭ·ănt)
  -ance
var·i·a·tion (vâr′ ĭ·ā′ shŭn)
var·i·cose vein (văr′ ĭ·kōs)
var·ied (vâr′ ĭd)
var·i·e·gat·ed (vâr′ ĭ·ĕ·gāt′ ĕd)

va·ri·e·ty (và·rī′ ĕ·tĭ)
-ties
var·i·ous (vâr′ ĭ·ŭs)
var·let (vär′ lĕt)
var·si·ty (vär′ sĭ·tĭ)
var·y (vâr′ ĭ)
var·ied, var·ies, var·y·ing
vas·cu·lar (văs′ kû·lēr)
vas·o·mo·tor (văs′ ŏ·mō′ tēr)
vas·sal (văs′ ăl)
vas·sal·age
Vas·sar (coll.) (văs′ ēr)
Vat·i·can (văt′ ĭ·kăn)
vau·de·ville (vô′ dē·vĭl)
vault·ed (vôl′ tĕd)
veal (vēl)
vec·tor (vĕk′ tēr)
veer·ing (vēr′ ĭng)
veg·e·ta·ble (vĕj′ ĕ·tà·b′l)
veg·e·tar·i·an (vĕj′ ĕ·târ′ ĭ·ăn)
veg·e·tate (vĕj′ ĕ·tāt)
-tat·ing
veg·e·ta·tion (vĕj′ ĕ·tā′ shŭn)
veg·e·ta·tive (vĕj′ ĕ·tā′ tĭv)
ve·he·ment (vē′ ĕ·mĕnt)
-mence
ve·hi·cle (vē′ ĭ·k′l)
ve·hic·u·lar (vē·hĭk′ û·lēr)
veil·ing (vāl′ ĭng)
vein (vān)
(fissure; see vain, vane)
vel·lum (vĕl′ ŭm)
ve·loc·i·pede (vē·lŏs′ ĭ·pēd)
ve·loc·i·ty (vē·lŏs′ ĭ·tĭ)
-ties
ve·lours (vē·lōōr′)
vel·vet (vĕl′ vĕt)
vel·vet·een (vĕl′ vē·tēn′)
ve·nal (vē′ năl)
(mercenary, see venial)
ve·nal·i·ty (vē·năl′ ĭ·tĭ)
ven·det·ta (vĕn·dĕt′ à)
ven·dor (vĕn′ dēr)
ven·due (vĕn′ dū)
ve·neer (vē·nēr′)
ven·er·ate (vĕn′ ēr·āt)
-at·ing
ven·er·a·ble (vĕn′ ēr·à·b′l)
ven·er·a·tion (vĕn′ ēr·ā′ shŭn)
ve·ne·re·al (vē·nēr′ ē·ăl)
ven·er·y (vĕn′ ēr·ĭ)
Ve·ne·tian (vē·nē′ shăn)
venge·ance (vĕn′ ẓăns)
venge·ful (vĕn′ fŏŏl)
-ful·ly -ful·ness

ve·ni·al (vē′ nĭ·ăl)
(excusable; see venal)
ven·i·son (vĕn′ ĭ·z′n)
ven·om (vĕn′ ŭm)
ven·om·ous (vĕn′ ŭm·ŭs)
ve·nous (vē′ nŭs)
(of veins; see Venus)
ven·ti·late (vĕn′ tĭ·lāt)
-lat·ing
ven·ti·la·tion (vĕn′ tĭ·lā′ shŭn)
ven·ti·la·tor
ven·tral (vĕn′ trăl)
ven·tril·o·quist
(vĕn·trĭl′ ŏ·kwĭst)
ven·ture (vĕn′ tụ̆r)
-tur·ing ven·ture·some
ven·tur·ous
ven·ue (vĕn′ ū)
Ve·nus (vē′ nŭs)
(goddess of beauty; planet; see
venous)
ve·ra·cious (vē·rā′ shŭs)
ve·rac·i·ty (vē·răs′ ĭ·tĭ)
ve·ran·da (vē·răn′ dà)
ver·bal (vûr′ băl)
-bal·ly
ver·bal·i·za·tion
(vûr′ băl·ĭ·zā′ shŭn)
ver·bal·ize -iz·ing
ver·ba·tim (vûr·bā′ tĭm)
ver·be·na (vēr·bē′ nà)
ver·bi·age (vûr′ bĭ·ĭj)
ver·bose (vûr·bōs′)
ver·bos·i·ty (vûr·bŏs′ ĭ·tĭ)
ver·bo·ten (fēr·bō′ tĕn)
ver·dant (vûr′ dănt)
-dan·cy
ver·dict (vûr′ dĭkt)
ver·dure (vûr′ dụr)
verge (vûrj)
verg·ing
ver·i·fy (vĕr′ ĭ·fī)
-fied -fy·ing
ver·i·fi·a·ble (vĕr′ ĭ·fī′ à·b′l)
ver·i·ly (vĕr′ ĭ·lĭ)
ver·i·si·mil·i·tude
(vĕr′ ĭ·sĭ·mĭl′ ĭ·tūd)
ver·i·ta·ble (vĕr′ ĭ·tà·b′l)
ver·i·ty (vĕr′ ĭ·tĭ)
-ties
ver·mi·cel·li (vûr′ mĭ·sĕl′ ĭ)
ver·mil·ion (vēr·mĭl′ yŭn)
ver·min (vûr′ mĭn)
Ver·mont (vēr·mŏnt′)
abbr. Vt. Ver·mont·er

ver·mouth (ver·mooth′)
ver·nac·u·lar (ver·nak′ ū·ler)
ver·nal e·qui·nox
    (vûr′ nəl)
Ver·sailles (ver·sālz)
ver·sa·tile (vûr′ sà·tĭl)
  ver·sa·til·i·ty (vûr′ sà·tĭl′ ĭ·tĭ)
verse (vûrs)
  vers·ing
  ver·si·fi·ca·tion
    (vûr′ sĭ·fĭ·kā′ shŭn)
  ver·si·fy (vûr′ sĭ·fī)
   -fied -fy·ing
ver·sion (vûr′ shŭn)
ver·sus (vûr′ sŭs)
ver·te·bra (vûr′ tê·brá)
  pl. ver·te·brae (-brē)
  ver·te·bral (vûr′ tê·brəl)
ver·te·brate (vûr′ tê·brāt)
ver·tex (vûr′ teks)
ver·ti·cal (vûr′ tĭ·kəl)
ver·ti·go (vûr′ tĭ·gō)
ves·pers (ves′ pērz)
ves·sel (ves′ ’l)
ves·tal (ves′ təl)
vest·ee (ves′ tē′)
ves·ti·bule (ves′ tĭ·būl)
ves·tige (ves′ tĭj)
  ves·tig·i·al (ves·tĭj′ ĭ·əl)
vest·ment (vest′ ment)
ves·try (ves′ trĭ)
  -tries
ves·ture (ves′ tŭr)
vetch (vech)
vet·er·an (vet′ ēr·ẑn)
vet·er·i·nar·i·an
    (vet′ ēr·ĭ·nâr′ ĭ·ẑn)
  vet·er·i·nar·y (vet′ ēr·ĭ·nẽr′ ĭ)
ve·to (vē′ tō)
  -toes
vex·a·tion (veks·ā′ shŭn)
  vex·a·tious (veks·ā′ shŭs)
vi·a (vī′ à)
vi·a·ble (vī′ à·b’l)
vi·a·duct (vī′ à·dŭkt)
vi·al (vī′ əl)
vi·and (vī′ ənd)
vi·brant (vī′ brənt)
  -bran·cy
vi·brate (vī′ brāt)
  -brat·ing
  vi·bra·tion (vī·brā′ shŭn)
  vi·bra·tor (vī′ brā·tēr)
vi·bra·to (vê·brä′ tổ)

vic·ar (vĭk′ ēr)
  vic·ar·age (-ĭj)
  vic·ar·ate (vĭk′ ēr·ât)
vi·car·i·ous (vī·kâr′ ĭ·ŭs)
vice (vīs)
  (in the place of; evil; see *vise*)
vice- (vīs)
  vice-ad·mi·ral vice-chan·cel·lor
  vice·ge·rent (vīs′ jẽr′ ent)
  vice-pres·i·dent
  vice·roy
vice ver·sa (vī′ sê vûr′ sà)
vi·cin·i·ty (vĭ·sĭn′ ĭ·tĭ)
  -ties
vi·cious (vĭsh′ ŭs)
vi·cis·si·tude (vĭ·sĭs′ ĭ·tūd)
vic·tim (vĭk′ tĭm)
  vic·tim·i·za·tion
    (vĭk′ tĭm·ĭ·zā′ shŭn)
  vic·tim·ize -iz·ing
vic·tor (vĭk′ tēr)
  vic·to·ri·ous (vĭk·tō′ rĭ·ŭs)
  vic·to·ry -ries
Vic·tro·la (vĭk·trō′ là)
vict·ual (vĭt′ ’l)
vi·cu·ña (vĭ·kōōn′ yà)
vid·e·o (vĭd′ ê·ō)
vie (vī)
  vied vy·ing
Vi·et·nam·ese (vê·et′ nä·mēz′)
view·point (vū′ point′)
vig·il (vĭj′ ĭl)
  vig·i·lance (vĭj′ ĭ·ləns)
  -lant
vig·i·lan·te (vĭj′ ĭ·lăn′ tê)
vi·gnette (vĭn·yet′)
vig·or (vĭg′ ēr)
  vig·or·ous (vĭg′ ēr·ŭs)
vi·king (vī′ kĭng)
vile (vīl)
  vile·ness
vil·i·fy (vĭl′ ĭ·fī)
  -fied -fy·ing
  vil·i·fier
vil·la (vĭl′ à)
vil·lage (vĭl′ ĭj)
vil·lain (vĭl′ ĭn)
  (scoundrel; see *villein*)
  vil·lain·ous
vil·lein (vĭl′ ĭn)
  (serf; see *villain*)
  vil·len·age
vin·ai·grette sauce
    (vĭn′ å·gret′)

Vin·ci, da, Le·o·nar·do
  (dä vên′ chĕ, lä·ô·när′ dô)
vin·ci·ble   (vĭn′ sĭ·b'l)
vin·di·cate   (vĭn′ dĭ·kāt)
  -cat·ing
  vin·di·ca·tion
                    (vĭn′ dĭ·kā′ shŭn)
vin·dic·tive   (vĭn·dĭk′ tĭv)
vin·e·gar   (vĭn′ ê·gĕr)
vine·yard   (vĭn′ yĕrd)
vin·tage   (vĭn′ tĭj)
vi·nyl   (vī′ nĭl)
vi·o·la   (vê·ō′ lȧ)
vi·o·la·ble   (vī′ ô·lȧ·b'l)
vi·o·late   (vī′ ô·lāt)
  -lat·ing
  vi·o·la·tion   (vī′ ô·lā′ shŭn)
vi·o·lence   (vī′ ô·lĕns)
  -lent
vi·o·let   (vī′ ô·lĕt)
vi·o·lin   (vī′ ô·lĭn′)
  vi·o·lin·ist
vi·o·lon·cel·lo
                    (vê′ ô·lŏn·chĕl′ ō)
vi·per   (vī′ pêr)
vi·ra·go   (vĭ·rā′ gō)
  -goes
vir·e·o   (vĭr′ ê·ô)
  -os
vir·gin   (vûr′ jĭn)
  vir·gin·al   (vûr′ jĭ·nȧl)
  vir·gin·i·ty   (vêr·jĭn′ ĭ·tĭ)
Vir·gin·ia   (vêr·jĭn′ yȧ)
  abbr. Va.
  Vir·gin·ian   (vêr·jĭn′ yȧn)
  Vir·gin·ia reel
vir·ile   (vĭr′ ĭl)
  vi·ril·i·ty   (vĭ·rĭl′ ĭ·tĭ)
vir·tu·al   (vûr′ tụ̇·ȧl)
  -al·ly
vir·tue   (vûr′ tụ̄)
  vir·tu·ous   (vûr′ tụ̇·ŭs)
vir·tu·os·i·ty   (vûr′ tụ̇·ŏs′ ĭ·tĭ)
  vir·tu·o·so   (vûr′ tụ̇·ō′ sō)
vir·u·lence   (vĭr′ ụ̇·lĕns)
  -lent
vi·rus   (vī′ rŭs)
vi·sa   (vê′ zȧ)
vis·age   (vĭz′ ĭj)
vis-à-vis   (vê′ zȧ·vê′)
vis·cer·al   (vĭs′ ĕr·ȧl)
vis·cose   (vĭs′ kōs)
  vis·cos·i·ty   (vĭs·kŏs′ ĭ·tĭ)
  vis·cous   (vĭs′ kŭs)
vis·count   (vī′ kount′)

vise   (vīs)
  (device for holding work; see vice)
vis·i·ble   (vĭz′ ĭ·b'l)
  vis·i·bil·i·ty   (vĭz′ ĭ·bĭl′ ĭ·tĭ)
vi·sion   (vĭzh′ ŭn)
  vi·sion·al   vi·sion·ar·y
vis·it   (vĭz′ ĭt)
  -it·ed   vis·it·a·ble
  vis·it·ant   (vĭz′ ĭ·tȧnt)
  vis·it·a·tion   (vĭz′ ĭ·tā′ shŭn)
  vis·i·tor
vi·sor   (vī′ zĕr)
  (front of a cap; see vizier)
vis·ta   (vĭs′ tȧ)
vis·u·al   (vĭzh′ û·ȧl)
  vis·u·al·ize   -iz·ing
vi·tal   (vī′ tȧl)
  vi·tal·i·ty   (vī·tăl′ ĭ·tĭ)
  vi·tal·ize   -iz·ing
  vi·tal·ly
vi·ta·min   (vī′ tȧ·mĭn)
vi·ti·ate   (vĭsh′ ĭ·āt)
  -at·ing
vit·re·ous   (vĭt′ rê·ŭs)
vit·ri·fy   (vĭt′ rĭ·fī)
  -fied   -fy·ing
vit·ri·ol   (vĭt′ rĭ·ŭl)
vi·tu·per·ate   (vī·tū′ pêr·āt)
  -at·ing
  vi·tu·per·a·tion
                    (vī·tū′ pêr·ā′ shŭn)
  vi·tu·per·a·tive
                    (vī·tū′ pêr·ā′ tĭv)
vi·va·cious   (vī·vā′ shŭs)
  vi·vac·i·ty   (vī·văs′ ĭ·tĭ)
viv·id   (vĭv′ ĭd)
viv·i·sec·tion   (vĭv′ ĭ·sĕk′ shŭn)
vix·en·ish   (vĭk′ s'n·ĭsh)
vi·zier   (vĭ·zĕr′)
  (high official; see visor)
vo·cab·u·lar·y   (vô·kăb′ û·lĕr′ ĭ)
  -lar·ies
vo·cal   (vō′ kȧl)
  vo·cal·ist
  vo·cal·ize   -iz·ing
  vo·cal·ly
vo·ca·tion   (vô·kā′ shŭn)
  vo·ca·tion·al
vo·cif·er·ous   (vô·sĭf′ ĕr·ŭs)
vod·ka   (vŏd′ kȧ)
vogue   (vōg)
voice   (vois)
  voic·ing   voice·less
void   (void)
  void·a·ble

voile (voil)
vol·a·tile (vŏl′ a·tĭl)
  vol·a·til·i·ty (vŏl′ a·tĭl′ ĭ·tĭ)
  vol·a·til·ize -iz·ing
vol·ca·no (vŏl·kā′ nō)
  -noes
  vol·can·ic (vŏl·kăn′ ĭk)
vo·li·tion (vŏ·lĭsh′ ŭn)
Volks·wa·gen (fōlks′ vä′ gĕn)
vol·ley (vŏl′ ĭ)
  vol·leys vol·ley·ball
volt·age (vōl′ tĭj)
vol·u·ble (vŏl′ ủ·b′l)
  vol·u·bil·i·ty (vŏl′ ủ·bĭl′ ĭ·tĭ)
vol·ume (vŏl′ yŭm)
vo·lu·mi·nous (vŏ·lū′ mĭ·nŭs)
vol·un·tar·y (vŏl′ ŭn·tĕr′ ĭ)
  vol·un·tar·i·ly
vol·un·teer (vŏl′ ŭn·tēr′)
vo·lup·tu·ous (vŏ·lŭp′ tủ·ŭs)
  vo·lup·tu·ar·y (vŏ·lŭp′ tủ·ĕr′ ĭ)
vom·it (vŏm′ ĭt)
  -it·ed -it·ing
voo·doo (vōō′ dōō)
vo·ra·cious (vŏ·rā′ shŭs)
  vo·rac·i·ty (vŏ·răs′ ĭ·tĭ)
vor·tex (vôr′ tĕks)
  -tex·es
vor·ti·cal (vôr′ tĭ·kắl)
vo·ta·ry (vō′ tà·rĭ)
  -ries
vot·ing ma·chine
    (vōt′ ĭng)
vo·tive (vō′ tĭv)
vouch·er (vouch′ ēr)
vouch·safe (vouch·sāf′)
vow·el (vou′ ĕl)
voy·age (voi′ ĭj)
  voy·a·ger
vul·can·ize (vŭl′ kăn·īz)
  -iz·ing
vul·gar (vŭl′ gēr)
  vul·gar·i·an (vŭl·gâr′ ĭ·ắn)
  vul·gar·i·ty (vŭl·găr′ ĭ·tĭ)
  -ties
  vul·gar·ize -iz·ing
Vul·gate (vŭl′ gāt)
vul·ner·a·ble (vŭl′ nēr·à·b′l)
  vul·ner·a·bil·i·ty
    (vŭl′ nēr·à·bĭl′ ĭ·tĭ)
vul·ture (vŭl′ tủr)
vy·ing (vī′ ĭng)

W

wad·dle (wŏd′ ′l)
  wad·dling
wa·fer (wā′ fēr)
waf·fle (wŏf′ ′l)
waft (wăft)
wa·ger (wā′ jēr)
  -gered -ger·ing
wag·gish (wăg′ ĭsh)
Wag·ne·ri·an (väg·nēr′ ĭ·ắn)
wag·on (wăg′ ŭn)
waif (wāf)
Wai·ki·ki beach
    (wī′ kĭ·kē′)
wail (wāl)
  (to lament; see *wale*, *whale*)
  wail·ing
wain·scot (wān′ skŭt)
  -scot·ing
waist·line (wāst′ līn′)
wait·ress (wāt′ rĕs)
waive (wāv)
  (to forgo) waiv·ing
  waiv·er
wake·ful (wāk′ fŏŏl)
  -ful·ly -ful·ness
wak·en (wāk′ ĕn)
wale (wāl)
  (rib in fabric; see *wail*, *whale*)
walk·ie-talk·ie (wôk′ ĭ·tôk′ ĭ)
walk·out (wôk′ out′)
wal·la·by (wŏl′ à·bĭ)
  -bies
wal·let (wŏl′ ĕt)
wall·eyed pike (wôl′ īd′)
wall·flow·er (wŏl′ flou′ ēr)
wal·lop·ing (wŏl′ ŭp·ĭng)
wal·low (wŏl′ ō)
wall·pa·per (wŏl′ pā′ pēr)
wal·nut (wŏl′ nŭt)
wal·rus (wŏl′ rŭs)
waltz (wôlts)
wam·pum (wŏm′ pŭm)
wan·der·er (wŏn′ dēr·ēr)
wan·der·lust (wŏn′ dēr·lŭst′)
wane (wān)
  wan·ing
wan·gle (wăng′ g′l)
  -gling
wan·ton (wŏn′ tŭn)
  wan·ton·ly wan·ton·ness
war (wôr)
  war·fare war·head

war·mon·ger war·time
war·bler (wôr′ blĕr)
war·den (wôr′ d'n)
ward·robe (wôrd′ rōb′)
ware·house (wâr′ hous′)
war·i·ness (wâr′ ĭ·nĕs)
warm (wôrm)
  warm-blood·ed warm·heart·ed
  warmth
warn·ing (wôrn′ ĭng)
war·rant (wŏr′ ∂nt)
  war·rant·a·ble war·rant·ed
  war·rant·y (wŏr′ ∂n·tĭ)
  war·rant·ies
war·ri·or (wŏr′ ĭ·ēr)
war·y (wâr′ ĭ)
  war·i·er, -i·est, -i·ly, -i·ness
wash (wŏsh)
  wash·board wash·cloth
  washed-up
  wash·er·wom·an
  wash·out wash·room
wasp·ish (wŏsp′ ĭsh)
was·sail (wŏs′ 'l)
Was·ser·mann test
  (wŏs′ ēr·m∂n)
waste (wāst)
  wast·ing wast·age
  waste·bas·ket
  waste·ful, -ful·ly, -ful·ness
  waste·pa·per
wast·rel (wās′ trĕl)
watch (wŏch)
  watch·dog
  watch·ful, -ful·ly, -ful·ness
  watch·mak·er watch·man
  watch·word
wa·ter (wô′ tēr)
  wa·ter-cooled wa·ter·course
  wa·ter·fall wa·ter·fowl
  wa·ter·front wa·ter lil·y
  wa·ter·line
  wa·ter·log -logged
  wa·ter main wa·ter·mel·on
  wa·ter me·ter wa·ter·proof
  wa·ter·side wa·ter-sol·u·ble
  wa·ter·spout wa·ter sup·ply
  wa·ter·tight wa·ter tow·er
  wa·ter va·por wa·ter·way
  wa·ter·y
watt (wŏt)
  watt·age (wŏt′ ĭj)
  watt-hour
wat·tle (wŏt′ 'l)
wa·ver·ing (wā′ vēr·ĭng)

wav·y (wāv′ ĭ)
  wav·i·ness
wax·en (wăk′ sĕn)
wax·wing (wăks′ wĭng′)
wax·work (wăks′ wûrk′)
wax·y (wăk′ sĭ)
  wax·i·ness
way (wā)
  way·far·er (wā′ fâr′ ēr)
  way·far·ing
  way·lay way·laid
  way·ward·ness way·side
weak (wēk)
  weak·ened weak-kneed
  weak·ling
wealth (wĕlth)
  wealth·i·ly -i·ness
wean (wēn)
weap·on (wĕp′ ŭn)
wea·ri·some (wēr′ ĭ·sŭm)
  -some·ly
wea·ry (wēr′ ĭ)
  -ried, -ry·ing
  wea·ri·ly wea·ri·ness
wea·sel (wē′ z'l)
weath·er (wĕth′ ēr)
  weath·er-beat·en
  weath·er·cock weath·er gauge
  weath·er·man weath·er·proof
  weath·er vane weath·er-wise
weave (wēv)
  weav·ing
web·bing (wĕb′ ĭng)
wed·ding (wĕd′ ĭng)
wedge (wĕj)
  wedg·ing
Wedg·ie (wĕj′ ĭ)
Wedg·wood ware
  (wĕj′ wŏŏd)
wed·lock (wĕd′ lŏk)
Wednes·day (wĕnz′ dĭ)
week (wēk)
  week·day week end
  week-end adj. week·ly, -lies
wee·vil (wē′ v'l)
weigh (wā)
  weight·y
weird (wērd)
wel·come (wĕl′ kŭm)
weld (wĕld)
wel·fare (wĕl′ fâr′)
well (wĕl)
(NOTE: When "well" combinations come before a noun, they
are usually hyphenated, as in

"*well-acted* play.") When "well" combinations come after a verb, the hyphen is usually dropped, as in "The play was *well acted*."

well-be·ing — well·born
well-bred — well-fa·vored
well-found·ed — well-groomed
well-known — well-mean·ing
well-nigh — well off
well-read — well·spring
well-thought-of — well-to-do
well-wish·er

Welsh rab·bit (wĕlsh răb′ ĭt)
(*often incorrectly written* Welsh rarebit)
wel·ter·weight (wĕl′ tĕr·wāt′)
wench (wĕnch)
wept (wĕpt)
weren't (wûr′ 'nt)
were·wolf (wĕr′ wŏŏlf′)
Wes·ley·an (wĕs′ lĭ·ďn)
west·er·ly (wĕs′ tĕr·lĭ)
-lies
west·ern·er (wĕs′ tĕr·nĕr)
west·ern·most (wĕs′ tĕrn·mōst)
West·min·ste Ab·bey
(wĕst′ mĭn′ stĕr)
West Vir·gin·ia
(wĕst vēr·jĭn′ yà)
abbr. W. Va.
West Vir·gin·ian
west·ward (wĕst′ wĕrd)
whale (hwāl)
(cetacean; see *wail, wale*)
whale·bone (hwāl′ bōn′)
wharf (hwôrf)
pl. wharves
what (hwŏt)
what·ev·er — what·not
what·so·ev·er
wheat (hwēt)
whee·dle (hwē′ d'l)
-dling
wheel (hwēl)
wheel·bar·row — wheel base
wheel chair — wheel·wright
wheeze (hwēz)
wheez·ing — wheez·i·ness
wheez·y
whelp (hwĕlp)
when (hwĕn)
when·ev·er — when·so·ev·er
whence (hwĕns)
where (hwâr)
where·a·bouts — where·as

where·at — where·by
where·fore — where·from
where·in — where·in·to
where·of — where·on
where·so·ev·er — where·to
where·un·to — where·up·on
wher·ev·er — where·with
where·with·al
wher·ry (hwĕr′ ĭ)
wher·ries
wheth·er (hwĕth′ ēr)
(either, if; see *whither*)
whet·stone (hwĕt′ stōn′)
which (hwĭch)
which·ev·er
whiff (hwĭf)
Whig (hwĭg)
Whig·gish
while (hwīl)
whilst (hwīlst)
whim·per (hwĭm′ pēr)
whim·sey (hwĭm′ zĭ)
whim·si·cal (hwĭm′ zĭ·kăl)
whine (hwīn)
whin·ing — whin·y
whin·ny (hwĭn′ ĭ)
whin·nied — whin·ny·ing
whip (hwĭp)
whipped — whip·ping
whip·cord — whip·stitch
whip·per·snap·per
(hwĭp′ ēr·snăp′ ēr)
whip·pet (hwĭp′ ĕt)
whip·poor·will (hwĭp′ pŏŏr·wĭl′)
whirl (hwûrl)
whirl·a·bout
whirl·i·gig (hwûr′ lĭ·gĭg′)
whirl·pool — whirl·wind
whisk broom (hwĭsk)
whis·ky (hwĭs′ kĭ)
-kies
whis·per·ing (hwĭs′ pēr·ĭng)
whist (hwĭst)
whis·tle (hwĭs′ 'l)
-tling
white (hwīt)
white·cap — white-col·lar *adj.*
whit·ed sep·ul·cher
white·fish — white-head·ed
white lie — whit·en·er
white·ness — white oak
white sauce — white·wash
whith·er (hwĭth′ ēr)
(to what place; see *whether*)

whit·tle   (hwĭt′ 'l)
  whit·tling

whiz   (hwĭz)
  whizzed   whiz·zing

whoa   (hwō)

who·dun·it   (hōō′ dŭn′ ĭt)

who·ev·er   (hōō·ĕv′ ēr)

whole   (hōl)
  whole·heart·ed   whole·ness
  whole·sale   whole·some
  whole-wheat *adj.*
  whol·ly

whom   (hōōm)

whoop·ee   (hwōōp′·ē)

whoop·ing cough
           (hōōp′ ĭng)

whop·per   (hwŏp′ ēr)

whore   (hōr)
  whore·mon·ger   whor·ish

whorl   (hwûrl)

who's   (hōōz)
  (contraction of *who is:* "Look
  who's here!")

whose   (hōōz)
  (possessive of *who:* "*Whose* coat
  is this?")

who·so   (hōō′ sō)

who·so·ev·er   (hōō′ sō·ĕv′ ēr)

Wich·i·ta, Kan.   (wĭch′ ĭ·tô)

wick·ed   (wĭk′ ĕd)
  wick·ed·ness

wick·er   (wĭk′ ēr)

wick·et   (wĭk′ ĕt)

wide   (wīd)
  wide-an·gle lens
  wide-a·wake   wide·ly
  wid·en·ing   wide-o·pen
  wide·spread

wid·ow   (wĭd′ ō)
  wid·ow·er

width   (wĭdth)

wield·y   (wēl′ dĭ)

wife   (wīf)
  pl. wives   wife·ly

wig·gle   (wĭg′ 'l)
  wig·gling   wig·gly

wig·wam   (wĭg′ wŏm)

wild·cat   (wīld′ kăt′)
  wild·cat·ter

wil·der·ness   (wĭl′ dēr·nĕs)

wild·fire   (wīld′ fīr′)

wile   (wīl)
  wil·i·ness   wil·y

Wilkes-Bar·re, Pa.
           (wĭlks′ băr′ ĕ)

Wil·lam·ette   (wĭ·lăm′ ĕt)
  (riv., Ore.)

will·ful   (wĭl′ fŏŏl)
  -ful·ly   -ful·ness

will-o′-the-wisp   (wĭl′ ŏ·thē·wĭsp′)

wil·low·y   (wĭl′ ō·ĭ)

wil·ly-nil·ly   (wĭl′ ĭ·nĭl′ ĭ)

Wil·mette, Ill.   (wĭl·mĕt′)

wim·ple   (wĭm′ p'l)

wince   (wĭns)
  winc·ing

winch   (wĭnch)

Win·ches·ter   (wĭn′ chĕs′ tēr)

wind   (wĭnd)
  wind-blown   wind·fall
  wind·jam·mer   wind·lass
  wind·pipe   wind·shield
  wind-swept   wind tun·nel

win·dow   (wĭn′ dō)
  win·dow·pane   win·dow sill

Wind·sor tie   (wĭn′ zēr)

wine   (wĭn)
  wine·bib·ber   (wĭn′ bĭb′ ēr)
  wine cel·lar   wine·glass
  win·er·y   -er·ies
  wine·skin   win·y

wing·spread   (wĭng′ sprĕd′)

Win·ni·peg, Can.
           (wĭn′ ĭ·pĕg)

win·now   (wĭn′ ō)

win·some   (wĭn′ sŭm)

win·ter   (wĭn′ tēr)
  win·ter·green
  win·ter·ize   -iz·ing
  win·ter·time   win·ter wheat
  win·try

wip·er   (wīp′ ēr)

wire   (wīr)
  wir·ing   wire-haired
  wire·less   Wire·pho·to
  wire tap·per   wir·y

Wis·con·sin   (wĭs·kŏn′ s'n)
  abbr. Wis.   Wis·con·sin·ite

wis·dom   (wĭz′ dŭm)

wise·a·cre   (wīz′ ā′ kēr)

wise·crack   (wīz′ krăk′)

wish·ful   (wĭsh′ fŏŏl)
  -ful·ly   -ful·ness

wis·ta·ri·a   (wĭs·tā′ rĭ·à)

wist·ful   (wĭst′ fŏŏl)
  -ful·ly   -ful·ness

witch   (wĭch)
  witch·craft   witch doc·tor
  witch·er·y   witch ha·zel

with	(wĭth)
with·al	(wĭth·ôl′)
with·draw	with·hold·ing
with·in	with·out
with·stand	
with·er	(wĭth′ ẽr)
wit·ness	(wĭt′ nĕs)
wit·ti·cism	(wĭt′ ĭ·sĭz′m)
wiz·ard	(wĭz′ ẽrd)
wiz·ened	(wĭz′ 'nd)
wob·ble	(wŏb′ 'l)
wob·bling	wob·bly
woe·be·gone	(wō′ bĕ·gŏn′)
woe·ful	(wō′ fŏŏl)
-ful·ly	-ful·ness
wol·ver·ine	(wŏŏl′ vẽr·ēn′)
wom·an	(wŏŏm′ ăn)
pl. wom·en	
wom·an·hood	wom·an·ish
wom·an·kind	wom·an·li·ness
wom·an·ly	wom·en·folk
womb	(wŏŏm)
wom·bat	(wŏm′ băt)
won·der	(wŭn′ dẽr)
won·der·ful, -ful·ly, -ful·ness	
won·der·land	won·der·ment
won·der-strick·en	
won·drous	(wŭn′ drŭs)
wont	(wŭnt)
won't	(wōnt)
woo	(wŏŏ)
wooed	woo·ing
wood·bine	(wŏŏd′ bĭn′)
wood·craft	(wŏŏd′ krăft′)
wood·en	(wŏŏd′ 'n)
wood·en·ness	
wood·peck·er	(wŏŏd′ pĕk′ ẽr)
woods·man	(wŏŏdz′ măn)
woof·er	(wŏŏf′ ẽr)
wool·en	(wŏŏl′ ĕn)
wool·ly	(wŏŏl′ ĭ)
wool·li·ness	
wooz·y	(wŏŏz′ ĭ)
Worces·ter, Mass.	
	(wŏŏs′ tẽr)
Worces·ter·shire sauce	
	(wŏŏs′ tẽr·shĭr)
word·y	(wûr′ dĭ)
word·i·ness	
work	(wûrk)
work·a·ble	work·a·day
work·bench	work·day
work·house	work·man·ship
work·out	work·shop
work·week	

world	(wûrld)
world·ling	world-wea·ry
world-wide	
world·ly	(wûrld′ lĭ)
world·li·ness	world·ly-wise
worm·wood	(wûrm′ wŏŏd′)
worn-out	(wōrn′ out′)
wor·ry	(wûr′ ĭ)
wor·ried	wor·ry·ing
wor·ri·er	wor·ri·ment
wor·ri·some	
worse	(wûrs)
wors·en	
wor·ship	(wûr′ shĭp)
-shiped	-ship·ing
wor·ship·er	wor·ship·ful
worst	(wûrst)
wor·sted	(wŏŏs′ tĕd)
worth·while	(wûrth′ hwĭl′)
wor·thy	(wûr′ thĭ)
wor·thi·er, -i·est, -i·ly, -i·ness	
would	(wŏŏd)
would-be	would·n't
wound	(wŏŏnd)
(injury; pron. wound when past of	
wind)	
wo·ven	(wō′ vĕn)
wraith	(rāth)
wran·gler	(răng′ glẽr)
wrap·per	(răp′ ẽr)
wrath·ful	(răth′ fŏŏl)
-ful·ly	-ful·ness
wreak	(rēk)
(give free play to)	
wreath	(rēth) n.
wreathe	(rēth) v.
wreath·ing	
wreck	(rĕk)
(ruin)	wreck·age
wren	(rĕn)
wrench	(rĕnch)
wrest	(rĕst)
wres·tler	(rĕs′ lẽr)
wretch	(rĕch)
(miserable person; see retch)	
wretch·ed	(rĕch′ ĕd)
wretch·ed·ness	
wrig·gle	(rĭg′ 'l)
wrig·gling	wrig·gly
wright	(rīt)
(workman; see right, rite, write)	
wrin·kle	(rĭng′ k'l)
-kling	
wrist	(rĭst)
wrist·band	wrist watch

writ (rĭt)
write (rīt)
  (inscribe; see *right, rite, wright*)
  writ·ing
  writ·er's cramp
  write-up
  writ·ten (rĭt′ 'n)
writhe (rīth)
  with·ing
wrong (rông)
  wrong·do·er wrong·ful
wrought (rôt)
wry (rī)
  wry·ly wry·ness
Wy·o·ming (wī·ō′ mĭng)
  abbr. Wyo. Wy·o·ming·ite

yolk (yōk)
  (yellow of an egg; see *yoke*)
yon·der (yŏn′ dẽr)
York·shire pud·ding
    (yôrk′ shĭr)
young (yŭng)
yours (yōōrz)
your·self (yōōr·sĕlf′)
  your·selves
youth·ful (yōōth′ fōōl)
  -ful·ly -ful·ness
yowl (youl)
yuc·ca plant (yŭk′ ȧ)
Yu·go·sla·vi·a (yōō′ gō·slä′ vĭ·ȧ)
  Yu·go·slav
yule·tide (yōōl′ tīd′)

X

xen·o·pho·bi·a (zĕn′ ō·fō′ bĭ·ȧ)
X ray (ĕks′ rā′)
  X-ray ther·a·py
xy·lo·phone (zī′ lō·fōn)

Y

yachts·man (yŏts′ mǎn)
Yan·kee (yăng′ kē)
yard·age (yär′ dĭj)
yard·stick (yärd′ stĭk′)
yarn-dyed (yärn′ dīd′)
yawn (yôn)
year (yẽr)
  year·book year·ling
  year·long year·ly
yearn·ing (yûr′ nĭng)
yeast (yēst)
yel·low (yĕl′ ō)
yelp (yĕlp)
yen (yĕn)
yeo·man (yō′ mǎn)
yes·ter·day (yĕs′ tẽr·dĭ)
yew tree (yōō)
Yid·dish (yĭd′ ĭsh)
yield (yēld)
yo·del (yō′ d'l)
  -deled -del·ing
yo·ga (yō′ gȧ)
yo·ghurt (yō′ gōōrt)
yo·gi (yō′ gē)
yoke (yōk)
  (frame; see *yolk*)
yo·kel (yō′ kĕl)

Z

za·ny (zā′ nĭ)
  za·ni·ness
Zan·zi·bar (zăn′ zĭ·bär)
zeal (zēl)
  zeal·ot (zĕl′ ŭt)
  zeal·ous (zĕl′ ŭs)
ze·bra (zē′ brȧ)
ze·nith (zē′ nĭth)
zep·pe·lin (zĕp′ ĕ·lĭn)
ze·ro (zēr′ ō)
  -ros
zest·ful (zĕst′ fōōl)
  -ful·ly -ful·ness
Zeus (zūs)
zig·gu·rat (zĭg′ ōō·răt)
zig·zag (zĭg′ zăg′)
  -zagged -zag·ging
zinc ox·ide (zĭngk)
zin·ni·a (zĭn′ ĭ·ȧ)
Zi·on·ism (zī′ ŭn·ĭz′m)
zip·per (zĭp′ ẽr)
zir·con (zûr′ kŏn)
zith·er (zĭth′ ẽr)
zo·di·ac (zō′ dĭ·ăk)
zom·bi (zŏm′ bĭ)
  -bis
zone (zōn)
  zon·ing zon·al
zo·ol·o·gy (zō·ŏl′ ō·jĭ)
  zo·o·log·i·cal (zō′ ō·lŏj′ ĭ·kȧl)
Zo·ro·as·tri·an (zō′ rō·ăs′ trĭ·ȧn)
zuc·chi·ni (zōō·kē′ nē)
Zu·lu (zōō′ lōō)
zwie·back (tsvē′ bäk′)